Exploring C++20

The Programmer's Introduction to C++

Third Edition

Ray Lischner

Apress®

Exploring C++20: The Programmer's Introduction to C++

Ray Lischner
Ellicott City, MD, USA

ISBN-13 (pbk): 978-1-4842-5960-3   ISBN-13 (electronic): 978-1-4842-5961-0
https://doi.org/10.1007/978-1-4842-5961-0

Managing Director, Apress Media LLC: Welmoed Spahr
Acquisitions Editor: Steve Anglin
Development Editor: Matthew Moodie
Coordinating Editor: Mark Powers

Cover designed by eStudioCalamar

Cover image by Barby Dalbosco on Unsplash (www.unsplash.com)

Distributed to the book trade worldwide by Apress Media, LLC, 1 New York Plaza, New York, NY 10004, U.S.A. Phone 1-800-SPRINGER, fax (201) 348-4505, e-mail orders-ny@springer-sbm.com, or visit www.springeronline.com. Apress Media, LLC is a California LLC and the sole member (owner) is Springer Science + Business Media Finance Inc (SSBM Finance Inc). SSBM Finance Inc is a **Delaware** corporation.

For information on translations, please e-mail booktranslations@springernature.com; for reprint, paperback, or audio rights, please e-mail bookpermissions@springernature.com.

Apress titles may be purchased in bulk for academic, corporate, or promotional use. eBook versions and licenses are also available for most titles. For more information, reference our Print and eBook Bulk Sales web page at http://www.apress.com/bulk-sales.

Any source code or other supplementary material referenced by the author in this book is available to readers on GitHub via the book's product page, located at www.apress.com/9781484259603. For more detailed information, please visit http://www.apress.com/source-code.

Printed on acid-free paper

Table of Contents

About the Author

All the world is paged,
And all the men and women merely programs:
They have their exits and their segfaults;
And one man in his time plays many games,
His acts being seven ages. At first, the newbie,
Mewling and puking in BASIC terms.
And then the whining school-boy, with his packages,
And JavaServer Faces, creeping like snail
Downloading from the web. And then the l0v3r,
Sighing like heat sink fan, with an unmerged commit
Made to his github project. Then a hacker,
Full of strange oaths and bearded like a guru,
Jealous in honor, sudden and quick in quarrel,
Seeking the flamebait reputation
Even on lkml. And then the team lead,
In fair round belly with cappuccino drowned,
With eyes severe and beard of two days' cut,
Full of wise saws and modern design patterns;
And so he plays his part. The sixth age shifts
Into the lean and sandal'd manager,
With bifocals on nose and balding pate,
His COBOL code, well saved, a world too wide
For his shrunk shank; and his big noisy voice,
Turning again toward childish errors, buffer
Overruns in his code. Last scene of all,
That ends this strange eventful history,
Is second childishness and mere oblivion,
Sans mouse, sans keyboard, sans debugger, sans everything.

—By William Shakespeare, edited by Ray Lischner

Ray started writing programs before he had access to a computer, and over the subsequent four decades, he progressed steadily through the ages of programming. He currently lives with his family, where he does his best to retard the inexorable descent into the seventh age.

About the Technical Reviewer

Michael Thomas has worked in software development for more than 20 years as an individual contributor, team lead, program manager, and vice president of engineering. Michael has more than 10 years of experience working with mobile devices. His current focus is in the medical sector, using mobile devices to accelerate information transfer between patients and health-care providers.

Acknowledgments

Writing a book suits life during a pandemic. I sit at home, isolated from the world, crafting prose today and code tomorrow. Meanwhile, editors and reviewers fix the prose and critique the code. I never meet them in person. I trust that they, too, work in safety and isolation during this time of global pandemic. But before I issue the common thanks and acknowledgments to those who worked specifically on this book, I must first thank the unsung heroes of the pandemic who are keeping us alive, who are keeping us fed, and who help maintain our safety and isolation. And so I thank the many people who are unable to work in blissful solitude as they grow, pick, pack, truck, stock, prepare, and deliver our food and the supplies of everyday life. I thank the health-care workers who risk their lives daily in care of our loved ones. And I thank Michael Thomas for his technical review, my editor Mark Powers, and the staff at Apress for turning my humble bits and bytes into a finished product.

> *We therefore have great cause of thankfulness,*
>
> *And shall forget the office of our hand*
>
> *Sooner than quittance of desert and merit,*
>
> *According to the weight and worthiness.*
>
> —William Shakespeare, *The Life of Henry the Fifth*, I.i

Introduction

Hi, there. Thank you for reading my book, *Exploring C++ 20*. My name is Ray, and I'll be your author today. And tomorrow. And the day after that. We'll be together for quite a while, so why don't you pull up a chair and get comfortable. My job is to help you learn C++. To do that, I have written a series of lessons, called *Explorations*. Each Exploration is an interactive exercise that helps you learn C++ one step at a time. Your job is to complete the Explorations and, in so doing, learn C++.

No doubt you have already leafed through the book a little bit. If not, do so now. Notice that this book is different from most books. Most programming books are little more than written lectures. The author tells you stuff and expects you to read the stuff, learn it, and understand it.

This book is different. I don't see much point in lecturing at you. That's not how people learn best. You learn programming by reading, modifying, and writing programs. To that end, I've organized this book so that you spend as much time as possible reading, modifying, and writing programs.

How to Use This Book

Each Exploration in this book is a mixture of text and interactive exercises. The exercises are unlike anything you've seen in other books. Instead of multiple choice, fill-in-the-blank, or simple Q&A exercises, my lessons are interactive explorations of key C++ features. Early in the book, I will give you complete programs to work with. As you learn more C++, you will modify and extend programs. Pretty soon, you will write entire programs on your own.

By "interactive," I mean that I ask questions and you answer them. I do my best to respond to your answers throughout the lesson text. It sounds crazy, but by answering the questions, you will be learning C++. To help ensure you answer the questions, I leave space in this book for you to write your answers. I'm giving you permission to write in this book (unless you are borrowing the book from a library or friend). In fact, I encourage you to write all your answers in the book. Only by answering the questions will you learn the material properly.

Sometimes, the questions have no right answer. I pose the question to make you ponder it, perhaps to look at a familiar topic from a new perspective. Other times, the question has an unambiguous, correct answer. I always give the answer in the subsequent text, so don't skip ahead! Write your answer before you continue reading. Then and only then can you check your answer. Some questions are tricky or require information that I have not yet presented. In such cases, I expect your answer to be wrong, but that's okay. Don't worry. I won't be grading you. (If you are using this book as part of a formal class, your teacher should grade this book's exercises solely on whether you complete them, and never on whether your answer was correct. The teacher will have other exercises, quizzes, and tests to assess your progress in the class.) And no fair looking ahead and writing down the "correct" answer. You don't learn anything that way.

Ready? Let's practice.

What is your most important task when reading this book?

_____

_____

_____

This question does not have a single correct answer, but it does have a number of demonstrably wrong answers. I hope you wrote something similar to "Completing every exercise" or "Understanding all the material." Another good answer is "Having fun."

The Book's Organization

C++ is a complicated language. To write even the most trivial program requires an understanding of many disparate aspects of the language. The language does not lend itself to neat compartmentalization into broad topics, such as functions, classes, statements, or expressions. This book, therefore, does not attempt such an organization. Instead, you learn C++ in small increments: a little bit of this, a little bit of that, some more of this, and pretty soon you will have accumulated enough knowledge to start writing nontrivial programs.

Roughly speaking, the book starts with basic expressions, declarations, and statements that are sufficient to work with simple programs. You learn how to use the standard library early in the book. Next, you learn to write your own functions, to write your own classes, to write your own templates, and then to write fairly sophisticated programs.

You won't be an expert, however, when you finish this book. You will need much more practice, more exposure to the breadth and depth of the language and library, and more practice. You will also need more practice. And some more. You get the idea.

Who Should Read This Book

Read this book if you want to learn C++ and you already know at least one other programming language. You don't need to know a specific language or technology, however. In particular, you don't need to know C, nor do you need to know anything about object-oriented programming.

The C programming language influenced the design of many other languages, from PHP to Perl to AWK to C#, not to mention C++. As a result, many programmers who do not know C or C++ nonetheless find many language constructs hauntingly familiar. You might even feel confident enough to skip sections of this book that seem to cover old ground. Don't do that! From the start, the lessons present language features that are unique to C++. In a few, isolated cases, I will tell you when it is safe to skip a section, and only that section. Even when a language feature is familiar, it might have subtle issues that are unique to C++.

The trap is most perilous for C programmers because C++ bears the greatest superficial similarity with C. C programmers, therefore, have the most to overcome. By design, many C programs are also valid C++ programs, leading the unwary C programmer into the trap of thinking that good C programs are also good C++ programs. In fact, C and C++ are distinct languages, each with their own idioms and idiosyncrasies. To become an effective C++ programmer, you must learn the C++ way of programming. C programmers need to break some of their established habits and learn to avoid certain C features (such as arrays) in favor of better C++ idioms. The structure of this book helps you get started thinking in terms of C++, not C.

Projects

This book also contains four projects. The projects are opportunities to apply what you have learned. Each project is a realistic endeavor, based on the amount of C++ covered up to that point. I encourage you to try every project. Design your project using your favorite software design techniques. Remember to write test cases in addition to the source code. Do your best to make the code clean and readable, in addition to correct. After you are confident that your solution is finished, download the files from the book's website and compare your solution with mine.

Work Together

You can use this book alone, teaching yourself C++, or a teacher might adopt this book as a textbook for a formal course. You can also work with a partner. It's more fun to work with friends, and you'll learn more and faster by working together. Each of you needs your own copy of the book. Read the lessons and do the work on your own. If you have questions, discuss them with your partner, but answer the exercises on your own. Then compare answers with your partner. If your answers are different, discuss your reasoning. See if you can agree on a single answer before proceeding.

Work on the projects together. Maybe you can divide the work into two (or more) modules. Maybe one person codes and the other person checks. Maybe you'll practice some form of pair programming. Do whatever works best for you, but make sure you understand every line of code in the project. If you have asymmetric roles, be sure to swap roles for each project. Give everyone a chance to do everything.

For More Information

This book cannot teach you everything you need to know about C++. No single book can. After you finish this book, I encourage you to continue to read and write C++ programs and to seek out other sources of information. To help guide you, this book has a dedicated website, https://cpphelp.com/exploring/. The website has links to other books, other websites, mailing lists, newsgroups, FAQs, compilers, other tools, and more. You can also download all the source code for this book, so you can save yourself some typing.

Why Explorations?

In case you were wondering about the unusual nature of this book, rest assured that "though this be madness, yet there is method in't."

The method is an approach to teaching and writing that I developed while I was teaching computer science at Oregon State University. I wanted to improve the quality of my teaching, so I investigated research into learning and knowledge, especially scientific knowledge, and in particular, computer programming.

To summarize several decades of research: everyone constructs mental models of the world. We acquire knowledge by adding information to our models. The new information must always be in concert with the model. Sometimes, however, new information contradicts the model. In that case, we must adjust our models to accommodate the new information. Our brains are always at work, always taking in new information, always adjusting our mental models to fit.

As a result of this research, the emphasis in the classroom has shifted from teachers to students. In the past, teachers considered students to be empty vessels, waiting to be filled from the fount of the teacher's knowledge and wisdom. Students were passive recipients of information. Now we know better. Students are not passive, but active. Even when their outward appearance suggests otherwise, their brains are always at work, always absorbing new information and fitting that information into their mental models. The teacher's responsibility has changed from being the source of all wisdom to being an indirect manager of mental models. The teacher cannot manage those models directly, but can only create classroom situations in which students have the opportunity to adjust their own models.

Although the research has focused on teachers, the same applies to authors.

In other words, I cannot teach you C++, but I can create Explorations that enable you to learn C++. Explorations are not the only way to apply research to learning and writing, but they are a technique that I have refined over several years of teaching and have found successful. Explorations work because

- They force you to participate actively in the learning process. It's too easy to read a book passively. The questions force you to confront new ideas and to fit them into your mental model. If you skip the questions, you might also skip a crucial addition to your model.

- They are small, so your model grows in easy steps. If you try to grasp too much new information at once, you are likely to incorporate incorrect information into your model. The longer that misinformation festers, the harder it will be to correct. I want to make sure your model is as accurate as possible at all times.

- They build on what you know. I don't toss out new concepts with the vain hope that you will automatically grasp them. Instead, I tie new concepts to old ones. I do my best to ensure that every concept has a strong anchor in your existing mental model.

- They help you learn by doing. Instead of spending the better part of a chapter reading how someone else solves a problem, you spend as much time as possible working hands-on with a program: modifying existing programs and writing new programs.

C++ is a complicated language, and learning C++ is not easy. In any group of C++ programmers, even simple questions can often provoke varied responses. Most C++ programmers' mental models of the language are not merely incomplete, but are flawed, sometimes in fundamental ways. My hope is that I can provide you with a solid foundation in C++, so that you can write interesting and correct programs and, most importantly, so that you can continue to learn and enjoy C++ for many years to come.

The C++ Standard

This book covers the current standard, namely, ISO/IEC 14882:2020 (E), *Programming languages — C++*. The 2020 edition of the standard is the all-new, improved, standard, typically referred to as C++ 20. This book reflects new idioms, new language patterns, and new code. All the exercises have been tested on modern compilers, but not always successfully. Most modern compilers do a decent job of conforming to the standard, but it takes time. The standardization committee approved the final draft in February of 2020. I am writing this in May while we all wait for the International Organization for Standardization (ISO) to accept that final draft as standard 14882:2020. Meanwhile, compiler writers implement different features at different rates, and each provider makes different choices as to which features to implement first. As I write this introduction, no compiler fully implements C++ 20. The book's website will have up-to-date details as vendors release updates to their compilers.

PART I

The Basics

EXPLORATION 1

Honing Your Tools

Before you begin your exploration of the C++ landscape, you must gather some basic supplies: a text editor, a C++ compiler, a linker, and a debugger. You can acquire these tools separately or bundled, possibly as a package deal with an integrated development environment (IDE). Options abound, regardless of your platform, operating system, and budget.

If you are taking a class, the teacher will provide the tools or dictate which tools to use. If you are working at an organization that already uses C++, you probably want to use its tools, so you can become familiar with them and their proper use. If you have to acquire your own tools, check out this book's website, https://cpphelp.com/exploring/. Tool versions and quality change too rapidly to provide details in print form, so you can find up-to-date suggestions on the website. The following section gives some general advice.

C++ Versions

This book covers C++ 20, which is a major update to the C++ standard that the standardization committee approved in 2020. C++ 20 introduces several major features, and it takes time for all compilers to implement these features. Most of the code listings in this book will compile only with an up-to-date C++ 20 compiler, so make sure you are using the latest update of all of your tools. Even then, you may not be able to compile all of the examples. In fact, you may not be able to compile any of them.

One of the major features, modules, affects every program. And if your environment does not fully support this feature, you may not be able to compile any of the code listings. To help you, the book's website hosts a converted copy of all of the code examples to avoid using modules, but with all other C++ 20 features intact.

Ray's Recommendations

C++ is one of the most widely used programming languages in the world (depending on how you measure "widely used"). Therefore, C++ tools abound for many hardware and software environments and at a wide variety of price points.

You can choose command-line tools, which are especially popular in UNIX and UNIX-like environments, or you can opt for an IDE, which bundles all the tools into a single graphical user interface (GUI). Choose whichever style you find most comfortable. Your programs won't care what tools you use to edit, compile, and link them.

© Ray Lischner 2020
R. Lischner, *Exploring C++20*, https://doi.org/10.1007/978-1-4842-5961-0_1

Clang and LLVM

Clang is a C++ compiler (among other languages) that uses LLVM behind the scenes for compiling and optimizing programs. (No, LLVM does not stand for anything.) macOS uses clang as its default compiler, and many Linux developers also like to use clang. You can even download clang and LLVM for Microsoft Windows.

Some Linux distributions come with clang and LLVM already included. For other distributions, you can usually download it from the distribution's central repository or directly from the LLVM website. See the links at cpphelp.com/exploring.

GNU Compiler Collection

The most widely used C++ compiler is part of the GNU Compiler Collection (GCC). The GNU C++ compiler is often called g++. It is typically the default C++ compiler for Linux distributions, and it is also available for macOS and Microsoft Windows.

Microsoft Windows

Most C++ developers who use Microsoft Windows use Microsoft's own compiler, which they include with their Visual Studio product, which is available as a no-cost download. Visual Studio accumulates many tools under a single umbrella, and can be quite complex, so be sure to download the C++ compiler, and use it only in standard C++ mode, not C++/CLI, which is a different language.

When using clang on Microsoft Windows, you will also need GnuWin32 for some related utilities. The Cygwin and MinGW projects include GCC.

Other Tools

Microsoft offers Visual Studio Code, which is an IDE that runs on all popular platforms. It can integrate with your preferred compiler on your platform. Other popular IDEs include Eclipse and NetBeans.

C++ requires a compiler and a standard library. Most C++ products include both, but sometimes, niche compilers expect you to use the library from a different product. For example, you can download Intel's compiler for their hardware. The compiler's optimizer is top-notch, but you will also require a library, such as the libstdc++ that accompanies g++.

The author's website (cpphelp.com/exploring) has links with helpful hints for installing and using these tools.

Most code listings and snippets from the book have an associated test. You need Python 3 to run the tests. Included with the code are CMakeLists.txt files so you can build and test every code sample using cmake, which is a cross-platform tool for building software.

Read the Documentation

Now that you have your tools, take some time to read the product documentation—especially the Getting Started section. Really, I mean it. Look for tutorials and other quick introductions that will help you get up to speed with your tools. If you are using an IDE, you especially need to know how to create simple command-line projects.

IDEs typically require you to create a project, workspace, or some other envelope, or wrapper, before you can actually write a C++ program. You must know how to do this, and I can't help you, because every IDE is different. If you have a choice of project templates, choose "console," "command-line," "terminal," "C++ Tool," or some project with a similar name.

How long did it take you to read the documentation for your compiler and other tools? _____

Was that too much time, too little time, or just right? _____

The C++ language is subject to an international standard. Every compiler (more or less) adheres to that standard but also throws in some nonstandard extras. These extras can be useful—even necessary—for certain projects, but for this book, you have to make sure you use only standard C++. Most compilers can turn off their extensions. Even if you hadn't read the documentation before, do so now, to find out which options you need to enable you to compile standard C++ and only standard C++.

Write down the options, for future reference.

_____

_____

_____

You may have missed some of the options; they can be obscure. To help you, Table 1-1 lists the command-line compiler options you need for Microsoft Visual C++, g++, and clang. This book's website has suggestions for some other popular compilers. If you are using an IDE, look through the project options or properties to find the equivalents.

Table 1-1. *Compiler Options for Standard C++*

Compiler	Options
Visual Studio command line	`/EHsc /Za`
Visual Studio IDE	Enable C++ exceptions, disable language extensions
g++	`-pedantic -std=c++20`
clang/llvm	`-pedantic -std=c++20`

Your First Program

Now that you have your tools, it's time to begin. Fire up your favorite text editor or your C++ IDE and start your first project or create a new file. Name this file list0101.cpp, which is short for Listing 1-1. Several different file-name extensions are popular for C++ programs. I like to use .cpp, where the *p* means "plus." Other common extensions are .cxx and .cc. Some compilers recognize .C (uppercase *C*) as a C++ file extension, but I don't recommend using it, because it is too easy to confuse with .c (lowercase *c*), the default extension for C programs. Many desktop environments do not distinguish between uppercase and lowercase file names, further compounding the problem. Pick your favorite and stick with it. Type in the text contained within Listing 1-1. (With one exception, you can download all the code listings from this book's website. Listing 1-1 is the exception. I want you to get used to typing C++ code in your text editor.)

Listing 1-1. Your First C++ Program

```
/// This program examines features of the C++ library
/// to deduce and print the C++ version.

#include <algorithm>
#include <iomanip>
#include <iostream>
```

```cpp
#include <iterator>
#include <ostream>
#include <string>
#include <vector>

template<std::size_t N>
struct array
{
    char array[N];
    enum { size = N };
};

template<int I>
struct value_of
{};

template<>
struct value_of<1>
{
    enum { value = true };
};

template<>
struct value_of<2>
{
    enum { value = false };
};

void* erase(...);

struct is_cpp20
{
    static array<1> deduce_type(std::vector<int>::size_type);
    static array<2> deduce_type(...);
    static std::vector<int> v;
    static int i;
    enum { value = value_of<sizeof(deduce_type(erase(v, i)))>::value };
};

struct is_cpp17
{
    static array<1> deduce_type(char*);
    static array<2> deduce_type(const char*);
    static std::string s;
    enum { value = value_of<sizeof(deduce_type(s.data()))>::value };
};

int cbegin(...);
```

```cpp
struct is_cpp14
{
    static array<1> deduce_type(std::string::const_iterator);
    static array<2> deduce_type(int);
    enum { value = value_of<sizeof(deduce_type(cbegin(std::string())))>::value };
};

int move(...);

struct is_cpp11
{
    template<class T>
    static array<1> deduce_type(T);
    static array<2> deduce_type(int);
    static std::string s;
    enum { value = value_of<sizeof(deduce_type(move(s)))>::value };
};

enum { cpp_year =
        is_cpp20::value ? 2020 :
        is_cpp17::value ? 2017 :
        is_cpp14::value ? 2014 :
        is_cpp11::value ? 2011 :
        2003
    };

int main()
{
    std::cout << "C++ " << std::setfill('0') << std::setw(2) << cpp_year%100 << '\n';
    std::cout << "C++ " << std::setw(2) << (__cplusplus / 100) % 100 << '\n';
}
```

No doubt, some or all of this code is gibberish to you. That's okay. The point of this exercise is not to understand C++ but to make sure you can use your tools properly. I could have started with a trivial, "Hello, world" type of program, but that touches only a tiny fraction of the language and library. This program looks for features of the standard library that were introduced in different versions of the C++ standard in order to determine which version you are using.

Now go back and double-check your source code. Make sure you entered everything correctly.

Did you actually double-check the program? _____

Did you find any typos that needed correcting? _____

To err is human, and there is no shame in typographical errors. We all make them. Go back and recheck your program.

Now compile your program. If you are using an IDE, find the Compile or Build button or menu item. If you are using command-line tools, be sure to link the program too. For historical (or hysterical) reasons, UNIX tools such as g++ typically produce an executable program named a.out. You should rename it to something more useful or use the -o option to name an output file. Table 1-2 shows sample command lines to use for Visual C++, g++, and clang.

Table 1-2. *Sample Command Lines to Compiler list0101.cpp*

Compiler	Command Line
Visual C++	`cl /EHsc /Za list0101.cpp`
g++	`g++ -o list0101 -pedantic -std=c++20 list0101.cpp`
Clang	`clang++ -o list0101 -pedantic -std=c++20 list0101.cpp`

If you receive any errors from the compiler, it means you made a mistake entering the source code; the compiler, linker, or C++ library has not been installed correctly; or the compiler, linker, or library does not conform to the C++ standard and so are unsuitable for use with this book. Triple-check that you entered the text correctly. If you are confident that the error lies with the tools and not with you, check the date of publication. If the tools predate 2020, they predate the standard. Therefore, by definition, they cannot conform to the standard. Compiler vendors have worked hard at ensuring their tools conform to the latest standard, but this takes time. Caught in a global pandemic, we may have a long wait before we see compilers that truly implement enough of the C++ 20 standard to be useful.

If all else fails, try a different set of tools. Download the current release of GCC or Visual Studio. You may have to use these tools for this book, even if you must revert to some crusty, rusty, old tools for your job.

Successful compilation is one thing, but successful execution is another. How you invoke the program depends on the operating system. In a GUI environment, you will need a console or terminal window where you can type a command line. You may have to type the complete path to the executable file or only the program name—again, this depends on your operating system. When you run the program, it reads text from the standard input stream, which means whatever you type, the program reads. You then have to notify the program you are done, by pressing the magic keystrokes that signal end-of-file. On most UNIX-like operating systems, press Ctrl+D. On Windows, press Ctrl+Z.

Running a console application from an IDE is sometimes tricky. If you aren't careful, the IDE might close the program's window before you have a chance to see any of its output. You have to ensure that the window remains visible. Some IDEs (such as Visual Studio and KDevelop) do this for you automatically, asking you to press a final Enter key before it closes the window.

If the IDE doesn't keep the window open automatically, and you can't find any option or setting to keep the window open, you can force the issue by setting a break point on the program's closing curly brace or the nearest statement where the debugger will let you set a break point.

How would you test list0101 to ensure it is running correctly?

_____

_____

_____

_____

Okay, do it. **Does the program run correctly?** _____

The program prints two lines. The first is what the program deduces from your environment. The second is what the compiler and library claim that they implement. I hope they are the same.

There, that was easy, wasn't it? Read your compiler's documentation to learn how to set the desired C++ version, and rebuild and rerun the program. Make sure the result matches the version you specify.

Before you finish this Exploration, I have one more exercise. This time, the source file is more complicated. It was written by a professional stunt programmer. Do not attempt to read this program, even with adult supervision. Don't try to make any sense of the program. Above all, don't emulate the programming style used in this program. This exercise is not for you, but for your tools. Its purpose is to see whether your compiler can correctly compile this program and that your library implementation has the necessary parts of the standard library. It's not a severe torture test for a compiler, but it does touch on a few advanced C++ features.

So don't even bother trying to read the code. Just download the file list0102.cpp from the book's website and try to compile and link it with your tools. (I include the full text of the program only for readers who lack convenient Internet access.) If your compiler cannot compile and run Listing 1-2 correctly, you must replace it (your compiler, not the program). You may be able to squeak by in the early lessons, but by the end of the book, you will be writing some fairly complicated programs, and you need a compiler that is up to the task.

Listing 1-2. Testing Your Compiler

```cpp
/// Sort the standard input alphabetically.
/// Read lines of text, sort them, and print the results to the standard output.
/// If the command line names a file, read from that file. Otherwise, read from
/// the standard input. The entire input is stored in memory, so don't try
/// this with input files that exceed available RAM.
///
/// Comparison uses a locale named on the command line, or the default, unnamed
/// locale if no locale is named on the command line.

#include <cerrno>
#include <cstdlib>
import <algorithm>;
import <fstream>;
import <initializer_list>;
import <iostream>;
import <iterator>;
import <locale>;
import <string>;
import <system_error>;
import <vector>;

template<class C>
struct text : std::basic_string<C>
{
  using super = std::basic_string<C>;
  constexpr text() noexcept : super{} {}
  text(text&&) = default;
  text(text const&) = default;
  text& operator=(text const&) = default;
  text& operator=(text&&) = default;
  constexpr explicit operator bool() const noexcept {
    return not this->empty();
  }
};
```

```cpp
/// Read lines of text from @p in to @p iter. Lines are appended to @p iter.
/// @param in the input stream
/// @param iter an output iterator
template<class Ch>
auto read(std::basic_istream<Ch>& in) -> std::vector<text<Ch>>
{
    std::vector<text<Ch>> result;

    text<Ch> line;
    while (std::getline(in, line))
        result.emplace_back(std::move(line));

    return result;
}

/// Main program.
int main(int argc, char* argv[])
try
{
    // Throw an exception if an unrecoverable input error occurs, e.g.,
    // disk failure.
    std::cin.exceptions(std::ios_base::badbit);

    // Part 1. Read the entire input into text. If the command line names a file,
    // read that file. Otherwise, read the standard input.
    std::vector<text<char>> text; ///< Store the lines of text here
    if (argc < 2)
        text = read(std::cin);
    else
    {
        std::ifstream in{argv[1]};
        if (not in)
        {
            std::cout << argv[1] << ": " << std::system_category().message(errno) << '\n';
            return EXIT_FAILURE;
        }
        text = read(in);
    }

    // Part 2. Sort the text. The second command line argument, if present,
    // names a locale, to control the sort order. Without a command line
    // argument, use the default locale (which is obtained from the OS).
    std::locale const& loc{ std::locale(argc >= 3 ? argv[2] : "") };
    std::collate<char> const& collate{ std::use_facet<std::collate<char>>(loc) };
    std::ranges::sort(text,
        [&collate](auto const& a, auto const& b)
        {
            return collate.compare(to_address(cbegin(a)), to_address(cend(a)),
                to_address(cbegin(b)), to_address(cend(b))) < 0;
        }
    );
```

```
    // Part 3. Print the sorted text.
    for (auto const& line :  text)
       std::cout << line << '\n';
}
catch (std::exception& ex)
{
    std::cerr << "Caught exception: " << ex.what() << '\n';
    std::cerr << "Terminating program.\n";
    std::exit(EXIT_FAILURE);
}
catch (...)
{
    std::cerr << "Caught unknown exception type.\nTerminating program.\n";
    std::exit(EXIT_FAILURE);
}
```

I caught you peeking. In spite of my warning, you tried to read the source code, didn't you? Just remember that I deliberately wrote this program in a complicated fashion to test your tools. By the time you finish this book, you will be able to read and understand this program. Even more important, you will be able to write it more simply and more cleanly. Before you can run, however, you must learn to walk. Once you are comfortable working with your tools, it's time to start learning C++. The next Exploration begins your journey with a reading lesson.

EXPLORATION 2

■ ■ ■

Reading C++ Code

I suspect you already have some knowledge of C++. Maybe you already know C, Java, Perl, or other C-like languages. Maybe you know so many languages that you can readily identify common elements. Let's test my hypothesis. Take a few minutes to read Listing 2-1, then answer the questions that follow it.

Listing 2-1. Reading Test

```
1 /// Read the program and determine what the program does.
2
3 import <iostream>;
4 import <limits>;
5
6 int main()
7 {
8     int min{std::numeric_limits<int>::max()};
9     int max{std::numeric_limits<int>::min()};
10    bool any{false};
11    int x;
12    while (std::cin >> x)
13    {
14        any = true;
15        if (x < min)
16            min = x;
17        if (x > max)
18            max = x;
19    }
20
21    if (any)
22        std::cout << "min = " << min << "\nmax = " << max << '\n';
23 }
```

What does Listing 2-1 do?

_____

_____

_____

_____

© Ray Lischner 2020
R. Lischner, *Exploring C++20*, https://doi.org/10.1007/978-1-4842-5961-0_2

Listing 2-1 reads integers from the standard input and keeps track of the largest and smallest values entered. After exhausting the input, it then prints those values. If the input contains no numbers, the program prints nothing.

Let's take a closer look at the various parts of the program.

Comments

Line 1 begins with three consecutive slashes to start a comment. The comment ends at the end of the line. Actually, you need only two slashes to signal the start of a comment (//), but as you will learn later in the book, the extra slash has a special meaning.

Note that you cannot put a space between the slashes. That's true in general for all the multicharacter symbols in C++. It's an important rule and one you must internalize early. A corollary to the "no spaces in a symbol" rule is that when C++ sees adjacent characters, it usually constructs the longest possible symbol, even if you can see that doing so would produce meaningless results.

The other method you can use to write a comment in C++ is to begin the comment with /* and end it with */. The difference between this style and the style demonstrated in Listing 2-1 is, with this method, your comment can span multiple lines. You may notice that some programs in this book use /** to start a comment. Much like the third slash in Listing 2-1, this second asterisk (*) is magic, but unimportant at this time. A comment cannot nest within a comment of the same style, but you can nest one style of comment in comments of the other style, as illustrated in Listing 2-2.

Listing 2-2. Demonstrating Comment Styles and Nesting

```
/* Start of a comment /* start of comment characters are not special in a comment
 // still in a comment
 Still in a comment
*/
no_longer_in_a_comment();
// Start of a comment /* start of comment characters are not special in a comment
no_longer_in_a_comment();
```

The C++ community uses both styles widely. Get used to seeing and using both styles.

Modify Listing 2-1 to change the /// comment to use the /** ... */ style, then try to recompile the program. **What happens?**

_____

If you made the change correctly, the program should still compile and run normally. The compiler eliminates comments entirely, so nothing about the final program should be different. (With one exception being that some binary formats include a timestamp, which would necessarily differ from one compilation run to another.)

Modules

Lines 3 and 4 of Listing 2-1 import declarations and definitions from parts of the standard library. C++, like C and many other languages, distinguishes between the core language and the standard library. Both are part of the standard language, and a tool suite is incomplete without both parts. The difference is that the core language is self-contained. For example, certain types are built-in, and the compiler inherently knows about them. Other types are defined in terms of the built-in types, so they are declared in the standard library, and you must instruct the compiler that you want to use them. That's what lines 3 and 4 are all about.

IMPORTING *VS.* INCLUDING

As I write this, no compiler (even the latest prerelease) can compile Listing 2-1 because of its `import` declarations. Understanding what `import` does and how it works is sufficiently complicated that I don't cover it until Exploration 42. But here it is, interfering in Exploration 2.

Any time you see an `import` declaration, you can change it to an `#include` directive. Just substitute `#include` for `import` and delete the semicolon at the end of the line. The code listings on the book's website (`https://cpphelp.com/exploring/`) provide both styles of files. Download the files that work for your development environment without concerning yourself with what `import` or `#include` actually means.

Implementing the `import` keyword is only one part of a much larger task, so it will take some time for the compilers and libraries to catch up. Until then, we have a workaround.

In particular, line 3 informs the compiler about the names of the standard I/O streams (`std::cin` for the standard input and `std::cout` for the standard output), the input operator (`>>`), and the output operator (`<<`). Line 4 brings in the name `std::numeric_limits`. Note that names from the standard library generally begin with `std::` (short for "standard").

In C++ parlance, the `import` keyword is also a verb, as in "line 3 *imports* the `iostream` module," "line 4 imports the `limits` module," and so on. A *module* contains a series of declarations and definitions. (A declaration is a kind of definition. A definition tells the compiler more about a name than a declaration. Don't worry about the difference yet, but notice when I use *declaration* and when I use *definition*.) The compiler needs these declarations and definitions, so it knows what to do with names such as `std::cin`. Somewhere in the documentation for your C++ compiler and standard library is information about its standard modules. If you are curious, you can probably visit a folder or directory that contains the source code for the standard modules and see what you can find there, but don't be disappointed if you can't understand them. The C++ standard library makes full use of the entire range of C++ language features. It's likely you won't be able to decipher most of the library until after you've made it through a large part of this book.

Another important C++ rule: the compiler has to know what every name means. A human can often infer meaning or at least a part of speech from context. For example, if I were to say, "I furbled my drink all over my shirt," you may not know exactly what *furbled* means, but you can deduce that it is the past tense of a verb and that it probably implies something undesirable and somewhat messy.

C++ compilers are a lot dumber than you. When the compiler reads a symbol or identifier, it must know exactly what the symbol or identifier means and what part of "speech" it is. Is the symbol a punctuator (such as the statement-ending semicolon) or an operator (such as a plus sign for addition)? Is the identifier a type? A function? A variable? The compiler also has to know everything you can do with that symbol or name, so it can correctly compile the code. The only way it can know is for you to tell it, and the way you tell it is by writing a declaration or by importing a declaration from a module. And that's what `import` declarations are all about.

Later in the book, you'll even learn to write your own modules.

Modify line 4 to misspell `limits` as `stimil`. Try to compile the program. **What happens?**

_____

_____

_____

The compiler cannot find any module named `stimil`, so it issues a message. Then it may try to compile the program, but it doesn't know what `std::numeric_limits` is, so it issues one or more messages. Some compilers cascade messages, which means every use of `std::numeric_limits` produces additional messages. The actual error becomes lost in the noise. Focus on the first one or few messages the compiler issues. Fix them, then try again. As you gain experience with C++, you will learn which messages are mere noise and which are important. Unfortunately, most compilers will not tell you, for example, that you can't use `std::numeric_limits` until you include the `<limits>` module. Instead, you need a good C++ language reference, so you can look up the correct header on your own. The first place to check is the documentation that accompanies your compiler and library. Authors have been slower than compiler writers to catch up to the C++ 20 standard, so keep checking the website and bookstores for updated references.

Most programmers don't use `<limits>` much; Listing 2-1 included it only to obtain the definition of `std::numeric_limits`. On the other hand, almost every program in this book uses `<iostream>`, because it declares the names and types of the I/O stream objects, `std::cin` and `std::cout`. There are other I/O modules, but for basic console interactions, you need only `<iostream>`. You will meet more modules in coming Explorations.

Main Program

Every C++ program must have `int main()`, as shown on line 6. You are permitted a few variations on a theme, but the name `main` is crucial. A program can have only one `main`, and the name must be spelled using all lowercase characters. The definition must start with `int`.

▇ **Note** A few books instruct you to use `void`. Those books are wrong. If you have to convince someone that `void` is wrong and `int` is right, refer the skeptic to section [basic.start.main] of the C++ standard.

For now, use empty parentheses after the name `main`.

The next line starts the main program. Notice how the statements are grouped inside curly braces (`{` and `}`). That's how C++ groups statements. A common error of novices is to omit a curly brace or miss seeing them when reading a program. If you are used to more verbose languages, such as Pascal, Ada, or Visual Basic, you might need some time acquainting yourself with the more terse C++ syntax. This book will give you plenty of opportunities to practice.

Modify line 6 to spell `main` in capital letters (`MAIN`). Try to compile the program. **What happens?**

_____

_____

_____

The compiler probably accepts the program, but the linker complains. Whether you can see the difference between the compiler and the linker depends on your particular tools. Nonetheless, you failed to create a valid program, because you must have a `main`. Only the name `main` is special. As far as the compiler is concerned, `MAIN` is just another name, like `min` or `max`. Thus, you don't get an error message saying that you misspelled `main`, only that `main` is missing. There's nothing wrong with having a program that has a function named `MAIN`, but to be a complete program, you must be sure to include the definition `main`.

Variable Definitions

Lines 8 through 11 define some variables. The first word on each line is the variable's type. The next word is the variable name. The name is followed optionally by an initial value in curly braces. The type int is short for *integer*, and bool is short for *Boolean*.

■ **Note** Boolean is named after George Boole, the inventor of mathematical logic. As such, some languages use the name logical for this type. It is unclear why languages such as C++ use bool instead of boole for the type named after Boole.

The name std::numeric_limits is part of the C++ standard library and lets you query the attributes of the built-in arithmetic types. You can determine the number of bits a type requires, the number of decimal digits, the minimum and maximum values, and more. Put the type that you are curious about in angle brackets. (You'll see this approach to using types quite often in C++.) Thus, you could also query std::numeric_limits<bool>::min() and get false as the result.

If you were to query the number of bits in bool, what would you expect as a result? _____

Try compiling and running Listing 2-3, and find out if you are correct.

Listing 2-3. Determining the Number of Bits in a bool

```
import <iostream>;
import <limits>;

int main()
{
  // Note that "digits" means binary digits, i.e., bits.
  std::cout << "bits per bool: " << std::numeric_limits<bool>::digits << '\n';
}
```

Did you get the value you expected? If not, do you understand why you got 1 as a result?

Statements

Line 12 of Listing 2-1 contains a while statement. Lines 15, 17, and 21 begin if statements. They have similar syntax: both statements begin with a keyword, followed by a Boolean condition in parentheses, followed by a statement. The statement can be a simple statement, such as the assignment on line 16, or it can be a list of statements within curly braces. Notice that a simple statement ends with a semicolon.

Assignment (lines 14, 16, and 18) uses a single equal sign. For clarity, when I read a program out loud or to myself, I like to read the equal sign as "gets." For example, "x gets min."

A while loop performs its associated statement while the condition is true. The condition is tested prior to executing the statement, so if the condition is false the first time around, the statement never executes.

On line 12, the condition is an input operation. It reads an integer from the standard input (std::cin) and stores that integer in the variable x. The condition is true as long as a value is successfully stored in x. If the input is malformed, or if the program reaches the end of the input stream, the logical condition becomes false, and the loop terminates.

The if statement can be followed by an else branch; you'll see examples in future Explorations.

Line 21's condition consists of a single name: any. Because it has type bool, you can use it directly as a condition.

Modify line 15 to change the statement to just "if (x)". This kind of mistake sometimes occurs when you get careless (and we all get careless from time to time). **What do you expect to happen when you compile the program?**

_____

_____

Were you surprised that the compiler did not complain? **What do you expect to happen when you run the program?**

_____

_____

_____

If you supply the following input to the program, what do you expect as output?

0   1   2   3

_____

_____

If you supply the following input to the program, what do you expect as output?

3   2   1   0

_____

_____

Explain what is happening.

_____

_____

_____

_____

_____

C++ is permissive about what it allows as a condition. Any numerical type can be a condition, and the compiler treats nonzero values as true and zero as false. In other words, it supplies an implicit ≠ 0 to test the numeric value.

Many C and C++ programmers take advantage of the brevity these languages offer, but I find it a sloppy programming practice. Always make sure your conditions are logical in nature, even if that means using an explicit comparison to zero. The C++ syntax for comparing ≠ is !=, as in x != 0.

Output

The output operator is <<, which your program gets by importing <iostream>. You can print a variable's value, a character string, a single character, or a computed expression.

Enclose a single character in single quotes, such as 'X'. Of course, there may be times when you have to include a single quote in your output. To print a single quote, you will have to escape the quote character with a backslash (\'). Escaping a character instructs the compiler to process it as a standard character, not as a part of the program syntax. Other escape characters can follow a backslash, such as \n for a newline (i.e., a magic character sequence to start a new line of text; the actual characters in the output depend on the host operating system). To print a backslash character, escape it: '\\'. Some examples of characters include these: 'x', '#', '7', '\\', '\n'.

If you want to print more than one character at a time, use a character string, which is enclosed in double quotes. To include a double quote in a string, use a backslash escape:

```cpp
std::cout << "not quoted; \"in quotes\", not quoted";
```

A single output statement can use multiple occurrences of <<, as shown in line 22, or you can use multiple output statements. The only difference is readability.

Modify Listing 2-3 to experiment with different styles of output. Try using multiple output statements. Remember to use curly braces when the body of an if statement contains more than one statement.

See! I told you that you could read a C++ program. Now all you have to do is fill in some of your knowledge gaps about the details. The next Exploration starts doing that with the basic arithmetic operators.

EXPLORATION 3

■ ■ ■

Integer Expressions

In Exploration 2, you examined a program that defined a few variables and performed some simple operations on them. This Exploration introduces the basic arithmetic operators. Read Listing 3-1, then answer the questions that follow it.

Listing 3-1. Integer Arithmetic

```
1 /// Read the program and determine what the program does.
2
3 import <iostream>;
4
5 int main()
6 {
7     int sum{0};
8     int count{};
9
10    int x;
11    while (std::cin >> x)
12    {
13        sum = sum + x;
14        count = count + 1;
15    }
16
17    std::cout << "average = " << sum / count << '\n';
18 }
```

What does the program in Listing 3-1 do?

_____

_____

Test the program with the following input:

    10   50   20   40   30

Lines 7 and 8 initialize the variables sum and count to zero. You can enter any integer value in the curly braces to initialize a variable (line 7); the value does not have to be constant. You can even leave the curly braces empty to initialize the variable to a suitable default value (e.g., false for bool, 0 for int), as shown on line 8. Without any curly braces, the variable is not initialized, so the only action the program can do is to assign a new value to the variable, as shown on line 10. Ordinarily, it's a bad idea not to initialize your

© Ray Lischner 2020
R. Lischner, *Exploring C++20*, https://doi.org/10.1007/978-1-4842-5961-0_3

variables, but in this case, x is safe, because line 11 immediately stuffs a value into it by reading from the standard input.

Lines 13 and 14 show examples of addition (+) and assignment (=). Addition follows the normal rules of computer arithmetic (we'll worry about overflow later). Assignment works the way it does in any procedural language.

Thus, you can see that Listing 3-1 reads integers from the standard input, adds them up, and prints the average (mean) value, as computed by the division (/) operator. Or does it?

What is wrong with Listing 3-1?

_____

_____

_____

Try running the program with no input—that is, press the end-of-file keystroke immediately after starting the program. Some operating systems have a "null" file that you can supply as the input stream. When a program reads from the null file, the input stream always sees an end-of-file condition. On UNIX-like operating systems, run the following command line:

```
list0301 < /dev/null
```

On Windows, the null file is called NUL, so type

```
list0301 < NUL
```

What happens?

_____

C++ doesn't like division by zero, does it? Each platform reacts differently. Most systems indicate an error condition one way or another. A few quietly give you garbage results. Either way, you don't get anything meaningful.

Fix the program by introducing an if statement. Don't worry that the book hasn't covered if statements yet. I'm confident you can figure out how to ensure this program avoids dividing by zero. **Write the corrected program here:**

_____

_____

_____

_____

_____

_____

_____

_____

_____

_____

_____

_____

_____

_____

_____

_____

_____

_____

_____

_____

_____

Now try your new program. **Was your fix successful?**

_____

Compare your solution with Listing 3-2.

Listing 3-2. Print Average, Testing for a Zero Count

```
1 /// Read integers and print their average.
2 /// Print nothing if the input is empty.
3
4 import <iostream>;
5
6 int main()
7 {
8     int sum{0};
9     int count{};
10
11    int x;
12    while (std::cin >> x)
13    {
14        sum = sum + x;
15        count = count + 1;
16    }
17
18    if (count != 0)
19        std::cout << "average = " << sum / count << '\n';
20 }
```

Remember that != is the C++ syntax for the ≠ operator. Thus, count != 0 is true when count is not zero, which means the program has read at least one number from its input.

Suppose you were to run the program with the following input:

2   5   3

What do you expect as the output?

_____

Try it. **What is the actual output?**

_____

Did you get what you expected? Some languages use different operators for integer division and floating-point division. C++ (like C) uses the same operator symbol and depends on the context to decide what kind of division to perform. If both operands are integers, the result is an integer.

What do you expect if the input is

2   5   4

_____

Try it. **What is the actual output?**

_____

Integer division truncates the result toward zero, so the C++ expression 5 / 3 equals 4 / 3 equals 1.

The other arithmetic operators are - for subtraction, * for multiplication, and % for remainder. C++ does not have an operator for exponentiation.

Listing 3-3 asks for integers from the user and tells the user whether the number is even or odd. (Don't worry about how input works in detail; Exploration 5 will cover that.) **Complete line 11.**

Listing 3-3. Testing for Even or Odd Integers

```
1 /// Read integers and print a message that tells the user
2 /// whether the number is even or odd.
3
4 import <iostream>;
5
6 int main()
7 {
8
9     int x;
10    while (std::cin >> x)
11        if (                    )              // Fill in the condition.
12            std::cout << x << " is odd.\n";
13        else
14            std::cout << x << " is even.\n";
15 }
```

Test your program. **Did you get it right?**

_____

I hope you used a line that looks something like this:

```
if (x % 2 != 0)
```

In other words, a number is odd if it has a nonzero remainder after dividing it by 2.

You know that != compares for inequality. How do you think you should write an equality comparison? Try reversing the order of the odd and even messages, as shown in Listing 3-4. **Complete the condition on line 11.**

Listing 3-4. Testing for Even or Odd Integers

```
1 /// Read integers and print a message that tells the user
2 /// whether the number is even or odd.
3
4 import <iostream>;
5
6 int main()
7 {
8
9     int x;
10    while (std::cin >> x)
11        if (                    )           // Fill in the condition.
12            std::cout << x << " is even.\n";
13        else
14            std::cout << x << " is odd.\n";
15 }
```

To test for equality, use two equal signs (==). In this case:

```
if (x % 2 == 0)
```

A common mistake that new C++ programmers make, especially those who are accustomed to SQL and similar languages, is to use a single equal sign for comparison. In this case, the compiler usually alerts you to the mistake. Go ahead and try it, to see what the compiler does. **What message does the compiler issue when you use a single equal sign in line 11?**

_____

_____

_____

_____

A single equal sign is the assignment operator. Thus, the C++ compiler thinks you are trying to assign the value 0 to the expression x % 2, which is nonsense, and the compiler rightly tells you so.

What if you want to test whether x is zero? **Modify Listing 3-1 to print a message when count is zero.** Once you get the program right, it should look something like Listing 3-5.

Listing 3-5. Print Average, Testing for a Zero Count

```
1 /// Read integers and print their average.
2 /// Print nothing if the input is empty.
3
4 import <iostream>;
5
6 int main()
7 {
8     int sum{0};
9     int count{};
10
```

25

```
11    int x;
12    while (std::cin >> x)
13    {
14        sum = sum + x;
15        count = count + 1;
16    }
17
18    if (count == 0)
19        std::cout << "No data.\n";
20    else
21        std::cout << "average = " << sum / count << '\n';
22 }
```

Now modify Listing 3-5 to use a single equal sign on line 18. **What message does your compiler issue?**

_____

_____

_____

_____

Most modern compilers recognize this common error and issue a warning. Strictly speaking, the code is correct: the condition assigns zero to count. Recall that a condition of zero means false, so the program always prints No data., regardless of how much data it actually reads.

If your compiler does not issue a warning, read the compiler's documentation. You might have to enable a switch to turn on extra warnings, such as "possible use of assignment instead of comparison" or "condition is always false."

As you can see, working with integers is easy and unsurprising. Text, however, is a little trickier, as you will see in the next Exploration.

Strings

In earlier Explorations, you used quoted character strings as part of each output operation. In this Exploration, you will begin to learn how to make your output a little fancier by doing more with strings. Start by reading Listing 4-1.

Listing 4-1. Different Styles of String Output

```cpp
import <iostream>;

int main()
{
   std::cout << "Shape\tSides\n" << "-----\t-----\n";
   std::cout << "Square\t" << 4 << '\n' <<
               "Circle\t?\n";
}
```

Predict the output from the program in Listing 4-1. You may already know what \t means. If so, this prediction is easy to make. If you don't know, take a guess.

_____

Now check your answer. Were you correct? **So what does \t mean?**

_____

Inside a string, the backslash (\) is a special, even magical, character. It changes the meaning of the character that follows it. You have already seen how \n starts a new line. Now you know that \t is a horizontal tab: that is, it aligns the subsequent output at a tab position. In a typical console, tab stops are set every eight character positions.

How should you print a double-quote character in a string?

_____

Write a program to test your hypothesis, then run the program. **Were you correct?**

_____

Compare your program with Listing 4-2.

© Ray Lischner 2020
R. Lischner, *Exploring C++20*, https://doi.org/10.1007/978-1-4842-5961-0_4

Listing 4-2. Printing a Double-Quote Character

```
import <iostream>;

int main()
{
    std::cout << "\"\n";
}
```

In this case, the backslash turns a special character into a normal character. C++ recognizes a few other backslash character sequences, but these three are the most commonly used. (You'll learn a few more when you read about characters in Exploration 17.)

Now modify Listing 4-1 to add Triangle to the list of shapes.

What does the output look like? A tab character does not automatically align a column but merely positions the output at the next tab position. To align columns, you have to take control of the output. One easy way to do this is to use multiple tab characters, as shown in Listing 4-3.

Listing 4-3. Adding a Triangle and Keeping the Columns Aligned

```
 1  import <iostream>;
 2
 3  int main()
 4  {
 5      std::cout << "Shape\t\tSides\n" <<
 6                   "-----\t\t-----\n";
 7      std::cout << "Square\t\t" << 4 << '\n' <<
 8                   "Circle\t\t?\n"
 9                   "Triangle\t" << 3 << '\n';
10  }
```

I played a trick on you in Listing 4-3. Look closely at the end of line 8 and the start of line 9. Notice that the program lacks an output operator (<<) that ordinarily separates all output items. Any time you have two (or more) adjacent character strings, the compiler automatically combines them into a single string. This trick applies only to strings, not to characters. Thus, you can write lines 8 and 9 in many different ways, all meaning exactly the same thing.

```
std::cout << "\nCircle\t\t?\n" "Triangle\t" << 3 << '\n';
std::cout << "\nCircle\t\t?\nTriangle\t" << 3 << '\n';
std::cout << "\n" "Circle" "\t\t?\n" "Triangle" "\t" << 3 << '\n';
```

Choose the style you like best and stick with it. I like to make a clear break after each newline, so the human who reads my programs can clearly distinguish where each line ends and a new line begins.

You may be asking yourself why I bothered to print the numbers separately, instead of printing one big string. That's a good question. In a real program, printing a single string would be best, but in this book, I want to keep reminding you about the various ways you can write an output statement. Imagine, for example, what you would do if you didn't know beforehand the name of a shape and its number of sides. Perhaps that information is stored in variables, as shown in Listing 4-4.

Listing 4-4. Printing Information That Is Stored in Variables

```
1 import <iostream>;
2 import <string>;
3
4 int main()
5 {
6    std::string shape{"Triangle"};
7    int sides{3};
8
9    std::cout << "Shape\t\tSides\n" <<
10                "-----\t\t-----\n";
11   std::cout << "Square\t\t" << 4 << '\n' <<
12                "Circle\t\t?\n";
13   std::cout << shape << '\t' << sides << '\n';
14 }
```

The type of the string is `std::string`. You must have `import <string>` near the top of your program to inform the compiler that you are using the `std::string` type. Line 6 shows how to give an initial value to a string variable. Sometimes, you want the variable to start out empty. **How do you think you would define an empty string variable?**

_____

_____

Write a program to test your hypothesis.

If you have trouble verifying that the string is truly empty, try printing the string between two other, nonempty strings. Listing 4-5 shows an example.

Listing 4-5. Defining and Printing an Empty String

```
1 import <iostream>;
2 import <string>;
3
4 int main()
5 {
6    std::string empty;
7    std::cout << "|" << empty << "|\n";
8 }
```

Compare your program with Listing 4-5. **Which do you prefer?** _____

Why?

_____

_____

Line 6 does not provide an initial value for the variable `empty`. You learned in Exploration 3 that omitting the initial value leaves the variable uninitialized, which would be an error, because no other value is assigned to `empty`. You are not allowed to print or otherwise access the value of an uninitialized variable. But `std::string` is different. The lack of an initializer in this case is the same as empty braces; namely, the variable is initialized to an empty string.

When you define a string variable with no initial value, C++ guarantees that the string is initially empty. **Modify Listing 4-4 so the shape and sides variables are uninitialized. Predict the output of the program.**

_____

_____

_____

What happened? Explain.

_____

_____

_____

Your program should look like Listing 4-6.

Listing 4-6. Demonstrating Uninitialized Variables

```
1 import <iostream>;
2 import <string>;
3
4 int main()
5 {
6    std::string shape;
7    int sides;
8
9    std::cout << "Shape\t\tSides\n" <<
10               "-----\t\t-----\n";
11   std::cout << "Square\t\t" << 4 << '\n' <<
12               "Circle\t\t?\n";
13   std::cout << shape << '\t' << sides << '\n';
14 }
```

When I run Listing 4-6, I get different answers, depending on which compilers and platforms I use. Most compilers issue warnings, but will still compile the program, so you can run it. One of the answers I get is this:

Shape	Sides
-----	-----
Square	4
Circle	?
4226851	

With another compiler on another platform, the final number is 0. Yet another compiler's program prints -858993460 as the final number. Some systems might even crash instead of printing the value of shape or sides.

Isn't that curious? If you do not supply an initial value for a variable of type std::string, C++ makes sure the variable starts out with an initial value—namely, an empty string. On the other hand, if the variable has type int, you cannot tell what the initial value will actually be, and in fact, you cannot even tell whether the program will run. This is known as _undefined behavior_. The standard permits the C++ compiler and runtime environment to do anything, absolutely anything, when confronted with certain erroneous situations, such as accessing an uninitialized variable.

A design goal of C++ is that the compiler and library should not do any extra work if they can avoid it. Only the programmer knows what value makes sense as a variable's initial value, so assigning that initial value must be the programmer's responsibility. After all, when you are putting the finishing touches on your weather simulator (the one that will finally explain why it always rains when I go to the beach), you don't want the inner loop burdened by even one wasteful instruction. The flip side of that performance guarantee is an added burden on the programmer to avoid situations that give rise to undefined behavior. Some languages help the programmer avoid problem situations, but that help invariably comes with a performance cost.

So what's the deal with `std::string`? The short answer is that complicated types, such as strings, are different from the simple, built-in types. For types such as `std::string`, it is actually simpler for the C++ library to provide a well-defined initial value. Most of the interesting types in the standard library behave the same way.

If you have trouble remembering when it is safe to define a variable without an initial value, play it safe and use empty braces:

```
std::string empty{};
int zero{};
```

I recommend initializing every variable, even if you know the program will overwrite it soon, such as the input loops we used earlier. Omitting initialization in the name of "performance" rarely improves performance and always impairs readability. The next Exploration demonstrates the importance of initializing every variable.

OLD-FASHIONED INITIALIZATION

The brace style of initializing all variables was introduced in C++ 11, so code that predates C++ 11 (or new code that was written by programmers who learned C++ prior to C++ 11 and still haven't come to grips with the new style of initialization) uses different ways to initialize variables.

A common way to initialize integers, for example, uses an equal sign. It looks like an assignment statement, but it isn't. It defines and initializes a variable.

```
int x = 42;
```

You can also use parentheses:

```
int x(42);
```

The same is true for many standard library types:

```
std::string str1 = "sample";
std::string str2("sample");
```

Some types require parentheses and don't work with an equal sign. Other types used curly braces before C++ 11. Equal signs, parentheses, and curly braces all had different rules, and it was hard for beginners to understand the subtle difference between the equal sign and parentheses for initialization.

So the standardization committee made an effort to define a single, uniform initialization style in C++ 11, which they had to tweak in C++ 14. You are not out of the confusion zone entirely, though, because you will see some contexts that require the equal sign for initialization or where braces don't quite work the way you expect. But ordinary variables should always use curly braces, which is what I presented in this Exploration.

EXPLORATION 5

Simple Input

So far, the Explorations have focused on output. Now it's time to turn your attention to input. Given that the output operator is <<, **what do you expect the input operator to be?** _____

That didn't take a rocket scientist to deduce, did it? The input operator is >>, the opposite direction of the output operator. Think of the operators as arrows pointing in the direction that information flows: from the stream to variables for input, or from variables to the stream for output.

Listing 5-1 shows a simple program that performs input and output.

Listing 5-1. Demonstrating Input and Output

```
import <iostream>;

int main()
{
    std::cout << "Enter a number: ";
    int x;
    std::cin >> x;
    std::cout << "Enter another number: ";
    int y;
    std::cin >> y;

    int z{x + y};
    std::cout << "The sum of " << x << " and " << y << " is " << z << "\n";
}
```

How many numbers does Listing 5-1 read from the standard input?

_____

Suppose you enter 42 and 21 as the two input values. **What do you expect for the output?**

_____

Now run the program and check your prediction. I hope you got 63. Suppose you type this as input:

42*21

What do you predict will be the output?

_____

Test your hypothesis. **What is the actual output?**

_____

Do you see what happened? If not, try xyz as the input to the program. Try 42-21. Try 42.21.

The program exhibits two distinct behaviors that you have to understand. First, to read an int, the input stream must contain a valid integer. The integer can start with a sign (- or +) but must be all digits after that; no intervening white space is allowed. The input operation stops when it reaches the first character that cannot be part of a valid integer (such as *). If at least one digit is read from the input stream, the read succeeds, and the input text is converted to an integer. The read fails if the input stream does not start with a valid integer. If the read fails, the input variable is not modified.

The second behavior is what you discovered in the previous Exploration; uninitialized int variables result in undefined behavior. In other words, if a read fails, the variable contains junk, or worse. When you learn about floating-point numbers, for example, you will learn that some bit patterns in an uninitialized floating-point variable can cause a program to terminate. On some specialized hardware, an uninitialized integer can do the same. The moral of the story is that using an uninitialized variable results in undefined behavior. That's bad. So don't do it.

Thus, when the input is xyz, both reads fail, and undefined behavior results. You probably see junk values for both numbers. When the input is 42-21, the first number is 42 and the second number is -21, so the result is correct. However, when the input is 42.21, the first number is 42, and the second number is junk, because an integer cannot start with a dot (.).

Once an input operation fails, all subsequent input attempts will also fail, unless you take remedial action. That's why the program doesn't wait for you to type a second number if the first one is invalid. C++ can tell you when an input operation fails, so your program can avoid using junk values. Also, you can reset a stream's error state, so you can resume reading after handling an error. I will cover these techniques in future Explorations. For now, make sure your input is valid and correct.

Some compilers warn you when your program leaves variables uninitialized, but it is best to be safe and initialize every variable, all the time. As you can see, even if the program immediately attempts to store a value in the variable, it might not succeed, which can give rise to unexpected behavior.

Did you think that integers could be so complicated? Surely strings are simpler, because there is no need to interpret them or convert their values. Let's see if they truly are simpler than integers. Listing 5-2 is similar to Listing 5-1, but it reads text into std::string variables.

Listing 5-2. Reading Strings

```
import <iostream>;
import <string>;

int main()
{
   std::cout << "What is your name? ";
   std::string name{};
   std::cin >> name;
   std::cout << "Hello, " << name << ", how are you? ";
   std::string response{};
   std::cin >> response;
   std::cout << "Good-bye, " << name << ". I'm glad you feel " << response << "\n";
}
```

Listing 5-2 is clearly not a model of artificial intelligence, but it demonstrates one thing well. Suppose the input is as follows:

```
Ray Lischner
Fine
```

What do you expect as the output?

_____

_____

_____

Run the program and test your hypothesis. **Were you correct?** _____

Explain.

_____

_____

Experiment with different input and try to discern the rules that C++ uses to delimit a string in the input stream. Ready? Go ahead. I'll wait until you're done.

Back so soon? **How does C++ delimit strings in an input stream?**

_____

_____

_____

Any white space character (the exact list of white space characters depends on your implementation, but typically includes blanks, tabs, newlines, and the like) ends a string, at least as far as the input operation is concerned. Specifically, C++ skips leading white space characters. Then it accumulates nonspace characters to form the string. The string ends at the next white space character.

So what happens when you mix integers and strings? **Write a program that asks for a person's name (first name only) and age (in years) and then echoes the input to the standard output.** Which do you want to ask for first? Print the information after reading it.

Table 5-1 shows some sample inputs for your program. Next to each one, **write your prediction for the program's output.** Then run the program, and **write the actual output.**

Table 5-1. *Sample Inputs for Name and Age*

Input	Predicted Output	Actual Output
Ray44		
44Ray		
Ray 44		
44 Ray		
Ray44		
44Ray		
44-Ray		
Ray-44		

Think of the standard input as a stream of characters. Regardless of how the user types those characters, the program sees them arrive one by one. (Okay, they arrive in big chunks, by the buffer load, but that's a minor implementation detail. As far as you are concerned, your program reads one character at a time, and it doesn't matter that the character comes from the buffer, not the actual input device.) Thus, the program always maintains the notion of a current position in the stream. The next read operation always starts at that position.

Before starting any input operation, if the character at the input position is a white space character, the program skips (i.e., reads and discards) that character. It keeps reading and discarding characters until it reaches a nonspace character. Then the actual read begins.

If the program attempts to read an integer, it grabs the character at the input position and checks whether it is valid for an integer. If not, the read fails, and the input position does not move. Otherwise, the input operation keeps the character and all subsequent characters that are valid elements of an integer. The input operation interprets the text as an integer and stores the value in the variable. Thus, after reading an integer, you know that the input position points to a character that is *not* a valid integer character.

When reading a string, all the characters are grabbed from the stream until a white space character is reached. Thus, the string variable does not contain any white space characters. The next read operation will skip over the white space, as described earlier.

The input stream ends at the end of the file (if reading from a file), when the user closes the console or terminal, or when the user types a special keystroke sequence to tell the operating system to end the input (such as Ctrl+D on UNIX or Ctrl+Z on DOS or Windows). Once the end of the input stream is reached, all subsequent attempts to read from the stream will fail. This is what caused the loop to end in Exploration 2.

Listing 5-3 shows my version of the name-first program. Naturally, your program will differ in the details, but the basic outline should agree with yours.

Listing 5-3. Getting the User's Name and Age

```
import <iostream>;
import <string>;

int main()
{
    std::cout << "What is your name? ";
    std::string name{};
    std::cin >> name;

    std::cout << "Hello, " << name << ", how old are you? ";
    int age{};
    std::cin >> age;

    std::cout << "Good-bye, " << name << ". You are " << age << " year";
    if (age != 1)
        std::cout << 's';
    std::cout << " old.\n";
}
```

> Now modify the program to reverse the order of the name and age and try all the input values again. Explain what you observe.

_____

_____

_____

When an input operation fails due to malformed input, the stream enters an error state; for example, the input stream contains the string "Ray" when the program tries to read an integer. All subsequent attempts to read from the stream result in an error, without actually trying to read. Even if the stream subsequently tries to read a string, which would otherwise succeed, the error state is sticky, and the string read fails too.

In other words, when the program cannot read the user's age, it won't be able to read the name either. That's why the program gets both name and age correct, or it gets both wrong.

Listing 5-4 shows my version of the age-first program.

Listing 5-4. Getting the User's Age and Then Name

```
import <iostream>;
import <string>;

int main()
{
    std::cout << "How old are you? ";
    int age{};
    std::cin >> age;

    std::cout << "What is your name? ";
    std::string name{};
    std::cin >> name;

    std::cout << "Good-bye, " << name << ". You are " << age << " year";
    if (age != 1)
        std::cout << 's';
    std::cout << " old.\n";
}
```

Table 5-2 shows a truncated version of the output (just the name and age) in each situation.

Table 5-2. Interpreting Input the C++ Way

Input	Name First	Age First
Ray44	"Ray44", 0	0, ""
44Ray	"44Ray", 0	44, "Ray"
Ray 44	"Ray", 44	0, ""
44 Ray	"44", 0	44, "Ray"
Ray44	"Ray", 44	0, ""
44Ray	"44", 0	44, "Ray"
44#Ray	"44#Ray", 0	44, "#Ray"
Ray#44	"Ray#44", 0	0, ""

Handling errors in an input stream requires some more advanced C++, but handling errors in your code is something you can take care of right now. The next Exploration helps you untangle compiler error messages.

Error Messages

By now you've seen plenty of error messages from your C++ compiler. No doubt, some are helpful and others are cryptic—a few are both. This Exploration presents a number of common errors and gives you a chance to see what kinds of messages your compiler issues for these mistakes. The more familiar you are with these messages, the easier it will be for you to interpret them in the future.

Read through Listing 6-1 and keep an eye out for mistakes.

Listing 6-1. Deliberate Errors

```
 1 #include <iosteam>
 2 // Look for errors
 3 int main()
 4 [
 5   std::cout < "This program prints a table of squares.\n";
 6           "Enter the starting value for the table: ";
 7   int start{0};
 8   std::cin >> start;
 9   std::cout << "Enter the ending value for the table: ";
10   int end(start);
11   std::cin << endl
12   std::cout << "#    #^2\n";
13   int x{start};
14   end = end + 1; // exit loop when x reaches end
15   while (x != end)
16   {
17     std:cout << x << "    " << x*x << "\n";
18     x = x + 1;
19   }
20 }
```

What errors do you expect the compiler to detect?

_____

_____

_____

_____

_____

_____

Download the source code and compile Listing 6-1.

What messages does your compiler actually issue?

_____

_____

_____

_____

_____

_____

_____

Create three groups: messages that you correctly predicted, messages that you expected but the compiler did not issue, and messages that the compiler issued but you did not expect. **How many messages are in each group?** _____

If you use command-line tools, expect to see a slew of errors running across your screen. If you use an IDE, it will help corral the error messages and associate each message with the relevant point in the source code that the compiler thinks is the cause of the error. The compiler isn't always right, but its hint is often a good starting point.

Compilers usually group problems into one of two categories: errors and warnings. An error prevents the compiler from producing an output file (an object file or program). A warning tells you that something is wrong but doesn't stop the compiler from producing its output. Modern compilers are pretty good at detecting problematic, but valid, code and issuing warnings, so get in the habit of heeding the warnings. In fact, I recommend dialing up the sensitivity to warnings. Check your compiler's documentation and look for options that direct the compiler to detect as many warnings as possible. For g++ and clang++, the switch is -Wall. Visual Studio uses /Wall. On the other hand, sometimes the compiler gets it wrong, and certain warnings are not helpful. You can usually disable a specific warning, such as my favorite for g++: -Wno-unused-local-typedefs or /wd4514 for Visual Studio.

The program actually contains seven errors, but don't fret if you missed them. Let's take them one at a time.

Misspelling

Line 1 misspells <iostream> as <iosteam>. Your compiler should give you a simple message, informing you that it could not find <iosteam>. The compiler probably cannot tell that you meant to type <iostream>, so it does not give you a suggestion. You have to know the proper spelling of the header name.

Most compilers give up completely at this point. If that happens to you, fix this one error, then run the compiler again to see some more messages.

If your compiler tries to continue, it does so without the declarations from the misspelled header. In this case, <iostream> declares std::cin and std::cout, so the compiler also issues messages about those names being unknown, as well as other error messages about the input and output operators.

Bogus Character

The most interesting error is the use of a square bracket character ([) instead of a brace character ({) in line 4. Some compilers may be able to guess what you meant, which can limit the resulting error messages. Others cannot and give a message that may be rather cryptic. For example, g++ issues many errors, none of which directly points you to the error. Instead, it issues numerous messages starting with the following:

```
list0601.cpp:6:13: error: no match for 'operator<' (operand types are 'std::ostream' {aka
'std::basic_ostream<char>'} and 'const char [41]')
    6 |    std::cout < "This program prints a table of squares.\n";
      |    ~~~~~~~~~ ^ ~~~~~~~~~~~~~~~~~~~~~~~~~~~~~~~~~~~~~~~~~~~~
      |         |          |
      |         |          const char [41]
      |         std::ostream {aka std::basic_ostream<char>}
In file included from /usr/include/c++/9/bits/stl_algobase.h:64,
                 from /usr/include/c++/9/bits/char_traits.h:39,
                 from /usr/include/c++/9/ios:40,
                 from /usr/include/c++/9/ostream:38,
                 from /usr/include/c++/9/iostream:39,
                 from list0601.cpp:2:
/usr/include/c++/9/bits/stl_pair.h:454:5: note: candidate: 'template<class _T1, class _T2>
constexpr bool std::operator<(const std::pair<_T1, _T2>&, const std::pair<_T1, _T2>&)'
  454 |    operator<(const pair<_T1, _T2>& __x, const pair<_T1, _T2>& __y)
      |    ^~~~~~~~
/usr/include/c++/9/bits/stl_pair.h:454:5: note:   template argument deduction/substitution
failed:
list0601.cpp:6:15: note:   'std::ostream' {aka 'std::basic_ostream<char>'} is not derived
from 'const std::pair<_T1, _T2>'
    6 |    std::cout < "This program prints a table of squares.\n";
      |                 ^~~~~~~~~~~~~~~~~~~~~~~~~~~~~~~~~~~~~~~~~~~~
```

When you cannot understand the error messages, look at the first message and the line number it identifies. Search for errors at or near the line number. Ignore the rest of the messages.

On other lines, you may see another error or two. After you fix them, however, a slew of messages still remains. That means you still haven't found the real culprit (which is on line 4). Different compilers issue different messages. For example, clang++ issues similar messages, but with a different format.

```
list0601.cpp:6:13: error: invalid operands to binary expression ('std::ostream' (aka
'basic_ostream<char>') and 'const char [41]')
    std::cout < "This program prints a table of squares.\n";
    ~~~~~~~~~ ^ ~~~~~~~~~~~~~~~~~~~~~~~~~~~~~~~~~~~~~~~~~~~~
/usr/lib64/gcc/x86_64-suse-linux/9/../../../../include/c++/9/system_error:208:3: note:
candidate function not viable: no known conversion from 'std::ostream' (aka 'basic_
ostream<char>') to 'const std::error_code' for 1st argument
    operator<(const error_code& __lhs, const error_code& __rhs) noexcept
    ^
```

Once you track down the square bracket and change it to a curly brace, you may get entirely different messages. This is because the substitution of [for { so thoroughly confuses the compiler, it cannot make any sense of the rest of the program. Correcting that problem straightens out the program for the compiler, but now it may find a whole new set of errors.

Unknown Operator

The input and output operators (>> and <<) are no different from any other C++ operator, such as addition (+), multiplication (*), or comparison (such as >). Every operator has a limited set of allowed operands. For example, you cannot "add" two I/O streams (e.g., std::cin + std::cout), nor can you use an output operator to "write" a number to a string (e.g., "text" << 3).

On line 5, one error is the use of < instead of <<. The compiler cannot determine that you intended to use << and instead issues a message that indicates what is wrong with <. The exact message depends on the compiler, but most likely the message is not something that helps you solve this particular problem.

Once you fix the operator, notice that the compiler does not issue any message for the other mistake, namely, the extraneous semicolon. Strictly speaking, it is not a C++ error. It is a logical error, but the result is a valid C++ program. Some compilers will issue a warning, advising you that line 6 does nothing, which is a hint that you made a mistake. Other compilers will silently accept the program.

The only sure way to detect this kind of mistake is to learn to proofread your code.

Unknown Name

An easy error for a compiler to detect is when you use a name that the compiler does not recognize at all. In this case, accidentally typing the letter l instead of a semicolon produces the name endl instead of end;. The compiler issues a clear message about this unknown name.

Fix the semicolon, and now the compiler complains about another operator. This time, you should be able to zoom in on the problem and notice that the operator is facing the wrong way (<< instead of >>). The compiler may not offer much help, however. One compiler spews out errors of the following form:

```
list0601.cxx
list0601.cxx(11) : error C2784: 'std::basic_ostream<char,_Traits> &std::operator↦
<<(std::basic_ostream<char,_Traits> &,unsigned char)' : could not deduce↦
template argument for 'std::basic_ostream<char,_Elem> &' from 'std::istream'
        C:\Program Files\Microsoft Visual C++ Toolkit 2003\include\ostream(887)↦
: see declaration of 'std::operator`<<''
list0601.cxx(11) : error C2784: 'std::basic_ostream<char,_Traits> &std::operator↦
<<(std::basic_ostream<char,_Traits> &,unsigned char)' : could not deduce↦
template argument for 'std::basic_ostream<char,_Elem> &' from 'std::istream'
        C:\Program Files\Microsoft Visual C++ Toolkit 2003\include\ostream(887)↦
: see declaration of 'std::operator`<<''
```

The line number tells you where to look, but it is up to you to find the problem.

Symbol Errors

But now you run into a strange problem. The compiler complains that it does not know what a name means (cout on line 17), but you know what it means. After all, the rest of the program uses std::cout without any difficulty. What's wrong with line 17 that it causes the compiler to forget?

Small errors can have profound consequences in C++. As it turns out, a single colon means something completely different from a double colon. The compiler sees std:cout as a statement labeled std, followed by the bare name cout. At least the error message points you to the right place. Then it's up to you to notice the missing colon.

Fun with Errors

After you have fixed all the syntax and semantic errors, compile and run the program, to make sure you truly found them all. Then introduce some new errors, just to see what happens. Some suggestions follow:

Try dropping a semicolon from the end of a statement. What happens?

_____

_____

Try dropping a double quote from the start or end of a string. What happens?

_____

_____

Try misspelling int **as iny. What happens?**

_____

_____

Now I want you to explore on your own. Introduce one error at a time and see what happens. Try making several errors at once. Sometimes, errors have a way of obscuring one another. Go wild! Have fun! How often does your teacher encourage you to make mistakes?

Now it's time to return to correct C++ code. The next Exploration introduces the for loop.

EXPLORATION 7

More Loops

Explorations 2 and 3 show some simple while loops. This Exploration introduces the while loop's big brother, the for loop.

Bounded Loops

You've already seen while loops that read from the standard input until no more input is available. That is a classic case of an *unbounded* loop. Unless you know beforehand exactly what the input stream will contain, you cannot determine the loop's bounds or limits. Sometimes you know in advance how many times the loop must run; that is, you know the bounds of the loop, making it a *bounded* loop. The for loop is how C++ implements a bounded loop.

Let's start with a simple example. Listing 7-1 shows a program that prints the first ten non-negative integers.

Listing 7-1. Using a for Loop to Print Ten Non-negative Numbers

```
import <iostream>;

int main()
{
  for (int i{0}; i != 10; i = i + 1)
    std::cout << i << '\n';
}
```

The for loop crams a lot of information in a small space, so take it one step at a time. Inside the parentheses are three parts of the loop, separated by semicolons. **What do you think these three pieces mean?**

_____

_____

_____

_____

The three parts are initialization, condition, and postiteration. Take a closer look at each part.

© Ray Lischner 2020

R. Lischner, *Exploring C++20*, https://doi.org/10.1007/978-1-4842-5961-0_7

Initialization

The first part looks similar to a variable definition. It defines an int variable named i, with an initial value of 0. Some C-inspired languages permit only an initialization expression, not a variable definition. In C++, you have a choice: expression or definition. The advantage of defining the loop control variable as part of the initialization is that you cannot accidentally refer to that variable outside the loop. The disadvantage of defining the loop control variable in the initialization part is that you cannot deliberately refer to that variable outside the loop. Listing 7-2 demonstrates the advantage of limiting the loop control variable.

Listing 7-2. You Cannot Use the Loop Control Variable Outside the Loop

```
import <iostream>;

int main()
{
  for (int i{0}; i != 10; i = i + 1)
    std::cout << i << '\n';
  std::cout << "i=" << i << '\n';          // error: i is undefined outside the loop
}
```

Another consequence of limiting the loop control variable is that you may define and use the same variable name in multiple loops, as shown in Listing 7-3.

Listing 7-3. Using and Reusing a Loop Control Variable Name

```
import <iostream>;

int main()
{
  std::cout << '+';
  for (int i{0}; i != 20; i = i + 1)
    std::cout << '-';
  std::cout << "+\n|";

  for (int i{0}; i != 3; i = i + 1)
    std::cout << ' ';
  std::cout << "Hello, reader!";

  for (int i{0}; i != 3; i = i + 1)
    std::cout << ' ';
  std::cout << "|\n+";

  for (int i{0}; i != 20; i = i + 1)
    std::cout << '-';
  std::cout << "+\n";
}
```

What does Listing 7-3 produce as output?

_____

_____

_____

If you don't have to perform any initialization, you can leave the initialization part empty, but you still need the semicolon that separates the empty initialization from the condition.

Condition

The middle part follows the same rules as a while loop condition. As you might expect, it controls the loop execution. The loop body executes while the condition is true. If the condition is false, the loop terminates. If the condition is false the first time the loop runs, the loop body never executes (but the initialization part always does).

Sometimes you will see a for loop with a missing condition. That means the condition is always true, so the loop runs without stopping. A better way to write a condition that is always true is to be explicit and use true as the condition. That way, anyone who has to read and maintain your code in the future will understand that you deliberately designed the loop to run forever. Think of it as the equivalent of a comment: "This condition deliberately left blank."

Postiteration

The last part looks like a statement, even though it lacks the trailing semicolon. In fact, it is not a full statement, but only an expression. The expression is evaluated after the loop body (hence the name *post*iteration) and before the condition is tested again. You can put anything you want here, or leave it blank. Typically, this part of the for loop controls the iteration, advancing the loop control variable as needed.

How a for Loop Works

The flow of control is as follows:

1. The initialization part runs exactly once.

2. The condition is tested. If it is false, the loop terminates, and the program continues with the statement that follows the loop body.

3. If the condition is true, the loop body executes.

4. The postiteration part executes.

5. Control jumps to 2.

Your Turn

Now it's your turn to write a for loop. Listing 7-4 shows a skeleton of a C++ program. **Fill in the missing parts to compute the sum of integers from 10 to 20, inclusive.**

Listing 7-4. Compute Sum of Integers from 10 to 20

```
import <iostream>;

int main()
{
  int sum{0};
```

```
    // Write the loop here.

    std::cout << "Sum of 10 to 20 = " << sum << '\n';
}
```

Before you test your program, you must first determine how you will know whether the program is correct. In other words, **what is the sum of the integers from 10 to 20, inclusive?** _____

Okay, now compile and run your program. **What answer does your program produce?** _____ **Is your program correct?** _____

Compare your program with that shown in Listing 7-5.

Listing 7-5. Compute Sum of Integers from 10 to 20 (Completed)

```
import <iostream>;

int main()
{
  int sum{0};
  for (int i{10}; i != 21; i = i + 1)
    sum = sum + i;
  std::cout << "Sum of 10 to 20 = " << sum << '\n';
}
```

A use of `for` loops is to format and print tables of information. To accomplish this, you need finer control over output formatting than what you have learned so far. That will be the subject of the next Exploration.

EXPLORATION 8

■ ■ ■

Formatted Output

In Exploration 4, you used tab characters to line up output neatly. Tabs are useful but crude. This Exploration introduces some of the features that C++ offers to format output nicely, such as setting the alignment, padding, and width of output fields. C++ 20 offers two very different ways to format output. This chapter presents both, and you can choose which way you prefer.

The Problem

This Exploration begins a little differently. Instead of reading a program and answering questions about it, you must write your own program to solve a problem. The task is to print a table of squares and cubes (the arithmetic variety, not the geometrical shapes) for integers from 1 to 20. The output of the program should look something like this:

N	N^2	N^3
1	1	1
2	4	8
3	9	27
4	16	64
5	25	125
6	36	216
7	49	343
8	64	512
9	81	729
10	100	1000
11	121	1331
12	144	1728
13	169	2197
14	196	2744
15	225	3375
16	256	4096
17	289	4913
18	324	5832
19	361	6859
20	400	8000

To help you get started, Listing 8-1 gives you a skeleton program. You need only fill in the loop body.

© Ray Lischner 2020
R. Lischner, *Exploring C++20*, https://doi.org/10.1007/978-1-4842-5961-0_8

Listing 8-1. Print a Table of Squares and Cubes

```
import <iomanip>;
import <iostream>;

int main()
{
  std::cout << " N   N^2    N^3\n";
  for (int i{1}; i != 21; ++i)
  {
    // write the loop body here
  }
}
```

This is a trick problem, so don't worry if you had difficulties. The point of this exercise is to demonstrate how difficult formatted output actually is. If you've learned that much, you successfully completed this exercise, even if you didn't finish the program. Perhaps you tried using tab characters at first, but that aligns the numbers on the left.

```
N    N^2   N^3
1    1     1
2    4     8
3    9     27
4    16    64
5    25    125
6    36    216
7    49    343
8    64    512
9    81    729
10   100   1000
```

Left alignment is not the way we usually write numbers. Tradition dictates that numbers should align to the right (or on decimal points, when applicable—more on that in the related section, "Alignment," later in this Exploration). Right-aligned numbers are easier to read.

C++ offers some simple but powerful techniques to format output. To format the table of powers, you have to define a field for each column. A field has a width, a fill character, and an alignment. The following sections explain these concepts in depth.

Field Width

Before exploring how you would specify alignment, first you must know how to set the width of an output field. I gave you a hint in Listing 8-1. **What is the hint?**

_____

The first line of the program is import <iomanip>;, which you have not seen before. This header declares some useful tools, including std::setw(), which sets the minimum width of an output field. For example, to print a number so that it occupies at least three character positions, call std::setw(3). If the number requires more space than that—say the value is 314159—the actual output will take up as much space as needed. In this case, the spacing turned out to be six character positions.

To use setw, call the function as part of an output statement. The statement looks like you are trying to print setw, but in fact, nothing is printed, and all you are doing is manipulating the state of the output stream. That's why setw is called an *I/O manipulator*. The <iomanip> header declares several manipulators, which you will learn about in due course.

Listing 8-2 shows the table of powers program, using setw to set the width of each field in the table.

Listing 8-2. Printing a Table of Powers the Right Way

```
import <iomanip>;
import <iostream>;

int main()
{
  std::cout << " N    N^2     N^3\n";
  for (int i{1}; i != 21; ++i)
    std::cout << std::setw(2) << i
              << std::setw(6) << i*i
              << std::setw(7) << i*i*i
              << '\n';
}
```

The first column of the table requires two positions, to accommodate numbers up to 20. The second column needs some space between columns and room for numbers up to 400; setw(6) uses three spaces between the N and the N^2 columns and three character positions for the number. The final column also uses three spaces between columns and four character positions, to allow numbers up to 8000.

The default field width is zero, which means everything you print takes up the exact amount of space it needs, no more, no less.

After printing one item, the field width automatically resets to zero. For example, if you wanted to use a uniform column width of six for the entire table, you could not call setw(6) once and leave it at that. Instead, you must call setw(6) before each output operation, as follows:

```
std::cout << std::setw(6) << i
          << std::setw(6) << i*i
          << std::setw(6) << i*i*i
          << '\n';
```

Fill Character

By default, values are padded, or filled, with space characters (' '). You can set the fill character to be any that you choose, such as zero ('0') or an asterisk ('*'). Listing 8-3 shows a fanciful use of both fill characters in a program that prints a check.

Listing 8-3. Using Alternative Fill Characters

```
import <iomanip>;
import <iostream>;

int main()
{
  using namespace std;
```

```
int day{14};
int month{3};
int year{2006};
int dollars{42};
int cents{7};

// Print date in USA order. Later in the book, you will learn how to
// handle internationalization.
cout << "Date: " << setfill('0') << setw(2) << month
                 << '/' << setw(2) << day
                 << '/' << setw(2) << year << '\n';
cout << "Pay to the order of: CASH\n";
cout << "The amount of $" << setfill('*') << setw(8) << dollars << '.'
                          << setfill('0') << setw(2) << cents << '\n';
}
```

Notice that unlike setw, setfill is sticky. That is, the output stream remembers the fill character and uses that character for all output fields until you set a different fill character.

std Prefix

Another new feature in Listing 8-3 is the declaration using namespace std;. All those std:: prefixes can sometimes make the code hard to read. The important parts of the names become lost in the clutter. By starting your program with using namespace std;, you are instructing the compiler to treat names that it doesn't recognize as though they began with std::.

As the keyword indicates, std is called a *namespace*. Almost every name in the standard library is part of the std namespace. You are not allowed to add anything to the std namespace, nor are any third-party library vendors. Thus, if you see std::, you know that what follows is part of the standard library (so you can look it up in any reliable reference). More important, you know that most names you invent in your own program will not conflict with any name in the standard library and vice versa. Namespaces keep your names separate from the standard library names. Later in this book, you will learn to create your own namespaces, which help organize libraries and manage large applications.

On the other hand, using namespace std; is a dangerous declaration, and one I use sparingly. Without the std:: qualifier before every standard library name, you have opened the door to confusion. Imagine, for example, if your program defines a variable named cout or setw. The compiler has strict rules for interpreting names and would not be confused at all, but the human reader certainly would be. It is always best to avoid names that collide with those in the standard library, with or without using namespace std;.

Alignment

C++ lets you align output fields to the right or the left. If you want to center a number, you are on your own. To force the alignment to be left or right, use the left and right manipulators, which you get for free when you include <iostream>. (The only time you need <iomanip> is when you want to use manipulators that require additional information, such as setw and setfill.)

The default alignment is to the right, which might strike you as odd. After all, the first attempt at using tab characters to align the table columns produced left-aligned values. As far as C++ is concerned, however, it knows nothing about your table. Alignment is within a field. The setw manipulator specifies the width, and the alignment determines whether the fill characters are added after the value (left alignment) or before the value (right alignment). The output stream has no memory of other values it may have printed earlier (such as on the previous line). So, for example, if you want to align a column of numbers on their decimal points, you must do that by hand (or ensure that every value in the column has the same number of digits after the decimal point).

Exploring Formatting

Now that you know the rudiments of formatting output fields, it is time to explore a little and help you develop a thorough understanding of how field width, fill character, and alignment interact. **Read the program in Listing 8-4 and predict its output.**

Listing 8-4. Exploring Field Width, Fill Character, and Alignment

```
import <iomanip>;
import <iostream>;

int main()
{
  using namespace std;
  cout << '|' << setfill('*') << setw(6) <<  1234 << '|' << '\n';
  cout << '|' << left <<        setw(6) <<  1234 << '|' << '\n';
  cout << '|' <<                setw(6) << -1234 << '|' << '\n';
  cout << '|' << right <<       setw(6) << -1234 << '|' << '\n';
}
```

What do you expect as the output from Listing 8-4?

_____

_____

_____

_____

Now write a program that will produce the following output. Don't cheat and simply print a long string. Instead, print only integers and newlines, throwing in the field width, fill character, and alignment manipulators you require to achieve the desired output.

```
000042
420000
42
-42-
```

Lots of different programs can achieve the same goal. My program, shown in Listing 8-5, is only one possibility of many.

Listing 8-5. Program to Produce Formatted Output

```cpp
import <iomanip>;
import <iostream>;

int main()
{
  using namespace std;

  cout << setfill('0') << setw(6) << 42 << '\n';
  cout << left         << setw(6) << 42 << '\n';
  cout << 42 << '\n';
  cout << setfill('-') << setw(4) << -42 << '\n';
}
```

The manipulators that take arguments, such as setw and setfill, are declared in <iomanip>. The manipulators without arguments, such as left and right, are declared in <iostream>. If you can't remember, include both modules. If you include a module that you don't really need, you won't notice any difference.

I'M LYING TO YOU

The left and boolalpha manipulators are *not* declared in <iostream>. I lied to you. They are actually declared in <ios>. But <iostream> contains <ios>, so you get everything in <ios> automatically when you include <iostream>.

I've been lying to you for some time. The input operator (>>) is actually declared in <istream>, and the output operator (<<) is declared in <ostream>. As with <ios>, the <iostream> header always includes <istream> and <ostream>. Thus, you can include <iostream> and get all the headers you need for typical input and output. Other headers, such as <iomanip>, are less commonly used, so they are not part of <iostream>.

So I wasn't really lying to you, just waiting until you could handle the truth.

Alternative Syntax

I like to use manipulators, because they are concise, clear, and easy to employ. You can also apply functions to the output stream object, using the dot operator (.). For example, to set the fill character, you can call std::cout.fill('*'). The fill function is called a *member function*, because it is a member of the output stream's type. You cannot apply it to any other kind of object. Only some types have member functions, and each type defines the member functions that it allows. A large part of any C++ library reference is taken up with the various types and their member functions. (The member functions of an output stream are declared in <ostream>, along with the output operators. An input stream's member functions are declared in <istream>. Both of these modules are imported automatically when you import <iostream>.)

When setting sticky properties, such as fill character or alignment, you might prefer using member functions instead of manipulators. You can also use member functions to query the current fill character, alignment and other flags, and field width—something you can't do with manipulators.

The member function syntax uses the stream object, a dot (.), and the function call, for example, cout.fill('0'). Setting the alignment is a little more complicated. Listing 8-6 shows the same program as Listing 8-5 but uses member functions instead of manipulators.

Listing 8-6. A Copy of Listing 8-5, but Using Member Functions

```
import <iostream>;

int main()
{
  using namespace std;

  cout.fill('0');
  cout.width(6);
  cout << 42 << '\n';
  cout.setf(ios_base::left, ios_base::adjustfield);
  cout.width(6);
  cout << 42 << '\n';
  cout << 42 << '\n';
  cout.fill('-');
  cout.width(4);
  cout << -42 << '\n';
}
```

To query the current fill character, call cout.fill(). That's the same function name you use to set the fill character, but when you call the function with no arguments, it returns the current fill character. Similarly, cout.width() returns the current field width. Obtaining the flags is slightly different. You call setf to set flags, such as the alignment, but you call flags() to return the current flags. The details are not important at this time, but if you're curious, consult any relevant library reference.

On Your Own

Now it is time for you to write a program from scratch. Feel free to look at other programs, to make sure you have all the necessary parts. Write this program to produce a multiplication table for the integers from 1 to 10, inclusive, as follows:

```
  *|   1   2   3   4   5   6   7   8   9  10
----+-----------------------------------------
  1|   1   2   3   4   5   6   7   8   9  10
  2|   2   4   6   8  10  12  14  16  18  20
  3|   3   6   9  12  15  18  21  24  27  30
  4|   4   8  12  16  20  24  28  32  36  40
  5|   5  10  15  20  25  30  35  40  45  50
  6|   6  12  18  24  30  36  42  48  54  60
  7|   7  14  21  28  35  42  49  56  63  70
  8|   8  16  24  32  40  48  56  64  72  80
  9|   9  18  27  36  45  54  63  72  81  90
 10|  10  20  30  40  50  60  70  80  90 100
```

After you finish your program and have made sure it produces the correct output, compare your program with mine, which is shown in Listing 8-7.

Listing 8-7. Printing a Multiplication Table

```cpp
import <iomanip>;
import <iostream>;

int main()
{
  using namespace std;

  int constexpr low{1};       ///< Minimum value for the table
  int constexpr high{10};     ///< Maximum value for the table
  int constexpr colwidth{4};  ///< Fixed width for all columns

  // All numbers must be right-aligned.
  cout << right;

  // First print the header.
  cout << setw(colwidth) << '*'
       << '|';
  for (int i{low}; i <= high; i = i + 1)
    cout << setw(colwidth) << i;
  cout << '\n';

  // Print the table rule by using the fill character.
  cout << setfill('-')
       << setw(colwidth) << ""              // one column's worth of "-"
       << '+'                               // the vert. & horz. intersection
       << setw((high-low+1) * colwidth) << ""   // the rest of the line
       << '\n';

  // Reset the fill character.
  cout << setfill(' ');

  // For each row...
  for (int row{low}; row <= high; row = row + 1)
  {
    cout << setw(colwidth) << row << '|';
    // Print all the columns.
    for (int col{low}; col <= high; col = col + 1)
      cout << setw(colwidth) << row * col;
    cout << '\n';
  }
}
```

My guess is that you wrote your program a little differently from how I wrote mine, or perhaps you wrote it very differently. That's okay. Most likely, you used a hard-coded string for the table rule (the line that separates the header from the table), or perhaps you used a for loop. I used I/O formatting, just to show you what is possible. Printing an empty string with a nonzero field width is a quick and easy way to print a repetition of a single character.

Another new feature I threw in for good measure is the constexpr keyword. Use this keyword in a definition to define the object as a constant instead of a variable. The compiler makes sure you do not accidentally assign anything to the object. As you know, named constants make programs easier to read and understand than littering the source code with numbers.

The format Function

New in C++ 20 is the format() function, which works similarly to Python's format() function. The first argument is a format string and subsequent arguments are values to format. The function knows how to format all the built-in types, plus types in the standard library, and you can define formatters for your custom types.

In the format string, each value to format, or field, is specified by a set of curly braces. Text outside of curly braces is copied verbatim. The format string is followed by the values to print as additional function arguments. For example,

```
std::format("x: {}, y: {}, z: {}\n", 10, 20, 30)
```

returns the following string:

```
x: 10, y: 20, z: 30
```

You can also number the fields, starting at zero. This is useful if the order in the format string does not match the order of the arguments. For example,

```
std::format("x: {2}, y: {1}, z: {0}\n", 10, 20, 30)
```

returns the following string:

```
x: 30, y: 20, z: 10
```

Do not mix numbered and unnumbered fields in a single format string.

For more control over the formatting, specify the formatting details after a colon. The details depend on the type of the argument. For standard types, the formatting specifier has the following parts. All parts are optional but if present must be in the following order:

```
fill-and-align sign # 0 width type
```

The specifier, if present, begins with an optional fill and alignment. The alignment is '<' for start adjustment, '^' for centered, and '>' for end adjustment. The fill character can be any character except '{' or '}'. If you specify a fill character, you must also specify the alignment character. By default, numbers are end-adjusted and other types are start-adjusted.

Languages that read from left to right align start-adjusted fields on the left and end-adjusted fields on the right. Languages that read from right to left reverse that so start-adjusted fields align on the right and end-adjusted fields align on the left.

After the fill and alignment is an optional sign: '+' to emit a sign for all numbers, '-' to emit a sign only for negative numbers, or a space to emit a sign for negative numbers and a blank for other values. The default is '-'.

57

Next is an optional '#' character to request an alternate form, such as a base prefix (0x for hexadecimal, 0b for binary, etc.).

The field width is next. If you don't use a fill and alignment, you can use a '0' character to start the field width, which uses the default alignment and fills with '0' characters after the sign and base. You can also use an argument as the field width by nesting a set of curly braces and an optional argument number in place of the field width.

Finally, an optional type letter further controls the formatting. For integers, you can use 'b' for binary output, 'd' for decimal, 'o' for octal, 'x' for hexadecimal, or 'c' to format the value as the equivalent character. The default for a character is 'c' and for an integer is 'd'. For example,

```
std::format("'{0:c}': {0:#04x} {0:0>#10b} |{0:{1}d}| {2:s}\n", '*', 4, "str")
```

returns the following string:

```
'*': 0x2a 0b00101010 |   42| str
```

The complete rules are slightly more complicated, but this should be enough to get you going. **Rewrite Listing 8-7 using the** `std::format()` **function.** Be sure to change the `<iomanip>` module to `<format>`. Compare your program with mine in Listing 8-8.

Listing 8-8. Printing a Multiplication Table Using the `format` Function

```cpp
import <format>;
import <iostream>;

int main()
{
  int constexpr low{1};        ///< Minimum value for the table
  int constexpr high{10};      ///< Maximum value for the table
  int constexpr colwidth{4};   ///< Fixed width for all columns

  // First print the header.
  std::cout << std::format("{1:>{0}c}|", colwidth, '*');
  for (int i{low}; i <= high; i = i + 1)
    std::cout << std::format("{1:{0}}", colwidth, i);
  std::cout << '\n';

  // Print the table rule by using the fill character.
  std::cout << std::format("{2:->{0}}+{2:->{1}}\n",
      colwidth, (high-low+1) * colwidth, "");

  // For each row...
  for (int row{low}; row <= high; row = row + 1)
  {
    std::cout << std::format("{1:{0}}|", colwidth, row);
    // Print all the columns.
    for (int col{low}; col <= high; col = col + 1)
      std::cout << std::format("{1:{0}}", colwidth, row * col);
    std::cout << '\n';
  }
}
```

Format strings are compact but can also be cryptic. Pick the style you prefer and use it uniformly in your code. Even if you prefer format( ), though, be ready to read your share of code that uses the more verbose style because that's what appears in the millions of lines of existing C++ code.

No matter how you format the output, loops are your friend. What data structure do you think of first when you think of loops? I hope you picked arrays, because that is the subject of the next Exploration.

EXPLORATION 9

Arrays and Vectors

Now that you understand the basics, it is time to start moving on to more exciting challenges. Let's write a real program, something nontrivial but still simple enough to master this early in the book. Your job is to write a program that reads integers from the standard input, sorts them into ascending order, and then prints the sorted numbers, one per line.

At this point, the book has not quite covered enough material for you to solve this problem, but it is instructive to think about the problem and the tools you may need to solve it. Your first task in this Exploration is to **write pseudo-code for the program**. Write C++ code where you can and make up whatever you need to tackle the problem.

© Ray Lischner 2020
R. Lischner, *Exploring C++20*, https://doi.org/10.1007/978-1-4842-5961-0_9

Vectors for Arrays

You need an array to store the numbers. Given only that much new information, you can write a program to read, sort, and print numbers, but only by hand-coding the sort code. Those of you who suffered through a college algorithms course may remember how to write a bubble sort or quick sort, but why should you need to muck about with such low-level code? Surely, you say, there's a better way. There is: the C++ standard library has a fast sort function that can sort just about anything. Jump straight into the solution in Listing 9-1.

Listing 9-1. Sorting Integers

```
1 import <algorithm>;
2 import <iostream>;
3 import <vector>;
4
5 int main()
6 {
7   std::vector<int> data{};      // initialized to be empty
8   int x{};
9
10  // Read integers one at a time.
11  while (std::cin >> x)
12    // Store each integer in the vector.
13    data.emplace_back(x);
14
15  // Sort the vector.
16  std::ranges::sort(data);
17
18  // Print the vector, one number per line.
19  for (int element : data)
20    std::cout << element << '\n';
21 }
```

The program introduces several new features. Let's start at line 7 and the type called vector, which is a resizable array type. The next section explains it to you.

Vectors

Line 7 defines the variable data, of type std::vector<int>. C++ has several container types, that is, data structures that can contain a bunch of objects. One of those containers is vector, which is an array that can change size. All C++ containers require an element type, that is, the type of object that you intend to store in the container. In this case, the element type is int. Specify the element type in angle brackets: <int>. That tells the compiler that you want data to be a vector and that the vector will store integers.

What's missing from the definition?

_____

The vector has no size. Instead, the vector can grow or shrink while the program runs. (If you know that you need an array of a specific, fixed size, you can use the type array. You will use vector much more often than array in most programs.) Thus, data is initially empty. Like std::string, vector is a library type, and it has a well-defined initial value, namely, empty, so you can omit the {} initializer if you wish.

You can insert and erase items at any position in the vector, although the performance is best when you add items only at the end or erase them only from the end. That's how the program stores values in data: by calling emplace_back, which adds an element to the end of a vector (line 13). The "back" of a vector is the end, with the highest index. The "front" is the beginning, so back() returns the last element of the vector, and front() returns the first. Don't call these functions if the vector is empty; that yields undefined behavior. A member function that you might find yourself calling often is size(), which returns the number of elements in the vector.

As you can tell from the std:: prefix, the vector type is part of the standard library and is not built into the compiler. Therefore, you need import <vector>, as shown on line 3. No surprises there.

All the functions mentioned so far are member functions; that is, you must supply a vector object on the left-hand side of the dot operator (.) and the function call on the right-hand side. Another kind of function does not use the dot operator and is free from any particular object. In most languages, this is the typical kind of function, but sometimes C++ programmers call them *free* functions, to distinguish them from member functions. Line 16 shows an example of a free function, std::ranges::sort.

How would you define a vector of strings?

Substitute std::string for int to get std::vector<std::string>. You can also define a vector of vectors, which is a kind of two-dimensional array: std::vector<std::vector<int>>.

Ranges and Algorithms

The std::ranges::sort function sorts stuff, as you can tell from the name. In some other object-oriented language, you might expect vector to have a sort() member function. Alternatively, the standard library could have a sort function that can sort anything the library can throw at it. The C++ library falls into the latter category.

The sort() function can sort almost anything that has a begin() and an end(). An additional requirement is to be able to access specific elements of the data. To get the third element, use data.at(2) because indexing is zero-based. That is, data.front() is similar to data.at(0) and data.back() is like data.at(data.size() - 1).

STAY SAFE

When you read C++ programs, you will most likely see square brackets (data[n]) used to access elements of a vector. The difference between square brackets and the at member function is that the at function provides an additional level of safety. If the index is out of bounds, the program will terminate cleanly. On the other hand, using square brackets with an invalid index will result in undefined behavior: you don't know what will happen. Most dangerous is that your program will not terminate but will continue to run with the bad data. That's why I recommend using at.

The sort() function can put any range of data into order as long as two elements can be compared and put in order. It has many other sibling functions to perform a wide variety of operations on data, from binary_search(), which can quickly find a value in a sorted vector or shuffle(), which puts a vector into random order.

The sort, binary_search, and shuffle functions are called *algorithms* in the C++ standard library. A C++ algorithm can operate on vectors, other containers, and many other types. An algorithm performs some operation on a *range* of data. The range can be a vector, or it could be only part of a vector. It might not be stored in a container at all. The only requirement for a range is to have a beginning, an end, and a way to get from the beginning to the end.

For a vector and other containers, the begin() member function returns the beginning of the range and the end() member function returns the end of the range. The value that begin() returns is called an *iterator* because you use it to iterate over the values of the range. An iterator offers an indirect means of accessing the values in the range. Given an iterator named (in a burst of creativity) iterator, you would use *iterator to obtain the value that iterator points to. The ++ operator advances an iterator so it points to the subsequent value in the range, as in ++iterator. To tell when an iterator reaches the end of the range, it uses a special marker for the end of the range. This marker does not denote any specific value in the range so it can mark the end of an empty range. The only thing you can do with this marker is to compare it with an iterator to determine whether the iterator has reached the end of the range. Naturally enough, data.end() returns this special end marker, called a *sentinel*. Assembling these pieces yields the following for loop to iterate over the elements of data:

```
for (std::vector<int>::iterator iter{data.begin()}; iter != data.end(); ++iter)
{ int element = *iter; std::cout << element << '\n'; }
```

And that is quite a mouthful. Don't worry that it doesn't make any sense yet because there's an easier way. The for loop on line 17 of Listing 9-1 does the same thing, much more simply. It iterates over the elements of data and assigns each successive element to the variable element. Because this style of for loop iterates over a range, it is usually called a *ranged for loop*. Figure 9-1 illustrates the nature of the begin iterator and end sentinel for the data vector.

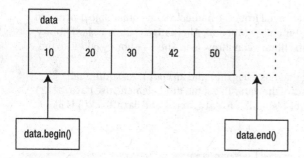

Figure 9-1. *Iterators pointing to positions in a vector*

What is the value of data.begin() if data.size() is zero?

_____

That's right. If the vector is empty, data.begin() returns the same value as data.end(), and that value is a special sentinel value that you are not allowed to dereference. In other words, *data.end() results in undefined behavior. Because you can compare two iterators or an iterator with a sentinel, one way to determine if a vector is empty is to test, as demonstrated in the following code:

```
data.begin() == data.end()
```

A better way, however, is to call data.empty(), which returns true if the vector is empty and false if the vector contains at least one element.

Ranges and iterators have many uses beyond accessing elements of a vector, and you will see them used often in this book, for input, output, and more, starting with the next Exploration.

■ ■ ■

Algorithms and Ranges

The previous Exploration introduced vectors and ranges using `std::ranges::sort` to sort a vector of integers. This Exploration examines ranges in more depth and introduces more generic algorithms, which perform useful operations on ranges of objects.

Algorithms

The `std::ranges::sort` function is an example of a generic algorithm, so named because these functions implement common algorithms and operate generically. That is, they work for just about anything you can express as a sequential range of values. Most of the standard algorithms are declared in the `<algorithm>` header, although the `<numeric>` header contains a few that are numerically oriented.

The standard algorithms run the gamut of common programming activities: sorting, searching, copying, comparing, modifying, and more. Searches can be linear or binary. A number of functions, including `std::ranges::sort`, reorder elements within a sequence. No matter what they do, nearly all generic algorithms share some common features. (A few algorithms, such as `std::max`, `std::min`, and `std::minmax`, operate on values instead of ranges.) Ranges come in different flavors, depending on the type of the iterator and the nature of the ranged data.

A vector is an example of a *sized* range, that is, a range with a size that the C++ library can determine in constant time. Suppose a program defines a range of lines of text read from a file; the number of lines cannot be known beforehand, so such a range could not be a sized range.

The flavor of range also depends on the iterator type. C++ has six different kinds of iterators, but you can broadly group them into two categories: read and write.

A *read* iterator refers to a position in a sequence of values that enables reading from the sequence. Most algorithms require a read iterator with a corresponding sentinel in order to obtain the input data. Some algorithms are read-only and others can modify the iterated values.

Most algorithms also require a *write* iterator, more commonly known as an *output* iterator. Most algorithms use only the single output iterator instead of an output range. This is because the size of the output range is not necessarily known until the algorithm has run its course over its input.

If the input range is sized, an algorithm could use that information to set the size of an output range, but not all output ranges are sized. For example, writing the values of a vector to an output stream has a sized input but not a sized output. In order to keep algorithms generic, they rarely require a sized range as input and rarely accept a range as output.

Because a typical algorithm does not and cannot check for overflow of the output iterator, you must ensure the output sequence has sufficient room to accommodate everything the algorithm will write.

For example, the `std::ranges::copy` algorithm copies values from an input range to an output iterator. The function takes two arguments: an input range and output iterator. You must ensure the output has enough capacity. Call the `resize` member function to set the size of the output vector, as shown in Listing 10-1.

© Ray Lischner 2020
R. Lischner, *Exploring C++20*, https://doi.org/10.1007/978-1-4842-5961-0_10

Listing 10-1. Demonstrating the std::ranges::copy Function

```
#include <cassert>
import <algorithm>;
import <vector>;

int main()
{
  std::vector<int> input{ 10, 20, 30 };
  std::vector<int> output{};
  output.resize(input.size());
  std::ranges::copy(input, output.begin());
  // Now output has a complete copy of input.
  assert(input == output);
}
```

The assert function is a quick way to verify that what you think is true actually is true. You assert a logical statement, and if you are wrong, the program terminates with a message that identifies the assertion. The assert function is declared differently than the rest of the standard library, using #include <cassert> instead of import. The c means the C++ library inherits this header from the C standard library, and #include is how C imports declarations. Note that assert is one of the rare exceptions to the rule that standard library members begin with std::.

If the program is correct, it runs and exits normally. But if we make a mistake, the assertion triggers, and the programs fails with a message.

Test the program in Listing 10-1. Just to see what happens when an assertion fails, **comment out the call to** std::ranges::copy **and run it again. Write down the message you get.**

_____

_____

Also note the initialization of input. Listing 10-1 demonstrates another application of "universal initialization" (as introduced in Exploration 4). The comma-separated values inside the curly braces are used to initialize the elements of the vector.

Output Iterators

Being able to call resize() is fine if the output is a vector, but you can also use an output iterator to write values to a file or console. Take an output file such as std::cout and construct a std::ostream_ iterator<int>{std::cout} object to turn it into an output iterator that prints int values. (Use import <iterator> to get declarations of the iterator-related declarations.) Even better, you can pass a string as a second argument, and the iterator writes that string after every value it writes. **Copy Listing 9-1 and replace the output loop with a call to the copy() function that copies data to the standard output.**

_____

_____

_____

_____

_____

_____

_____

_____

_____

_____

_____

_____

Compare your program with Listing 10-2.

Listing 10-2. Demonstrating the `std::ostream_iterator` Class

```
import <algorithm>;
import <iostream>;
import <iterator>;
import <vector>;

int main()
{
  std::vector<int> data;
  int element;
  while (std::cin >> element)
    data.emplace_back(element);

  std::ranges::sort(data);

  std::ranges::copy(data, std::ostream_iterator<int>{std::cout, "\n"});
}
```

Just as you can use the `ostream_iterator` to write a range to the standard output, you can also use the standard library to read values from the standard input directly into a range. What do you think the class is called?

_____

Good guess, but remember that the input is a range and the output is just an iterator. Wouldn't it be nice if the name of the class that treats the input as a range were `std::input_range`? But the name is actually `std::ranges::istream_view`. A _view_ is a kind of range that is easy to copy or assign. By naming this type a view, it tells you that you can assign an `istream_view` variable without incurring a runtime penalty.

The job is now to use the `std::ranges::copy()` function to copy a range of `int` values from `std::cin` to the `data` vector. But here we run into a problem of setting the size of `data` to match the number of input values. The `emplace_back()` function extends the size of a vector to accommodate the new value, so how do we arrange to call `emplace_back()` for every element that is read from the `istream_view`?

The answer is a special kind of output iterator called std::back_inserter. Pass data as the argument to back_inserter, and every value written to the output iterator is added to the end of data. Now you have the pieces you need to rewrite Listing 10-2 so it does not contain any loops, but instead uses range function calls to do all of its work.

_____

_____

_____

_____

_____

_____

_____

_____

_____

Compare your program with mine in Listing 10-3.

Listing 10-3. Demonstrating the std::back_inserter Function

```
1 import <algorithm>;
2 import <iostream>;
3 import <iterator>;
4 import <ranges>;
5 import <vector>;
6
7 int main()
8 {
9   std::vector<int> data;
10  std::ranges::copy(std::ranges::istream_view<int>(std::cin),
11                    std::back_inserter(data));
12  std::ranges::sort(data);
13  std::ranges::copy(data, std::ostream_iterator<int>{std::cout, "\n"});
14 }
```

Ugly C++ truth: sometimes you need parentheses and sometimes you need curly braces and sometimes you need angle brackets and sometimes you need square brackets. How do you know when to use what? By memorizing the rules of the language and library. Okay, it's not quite that bad. Square brackets are used for subscripts and angle brackets are used for types. But parentheses and curly braces can be downright confusing.

In Exploration 2, I enhorted you to use curly braces when initializing a variable. You do the same when creating an object, such as an iterator, on the fly. For example, you can create an ostream_iterator object and pass it to a function, such as copy. Because you are creating an object, you should use curly braces. But what about back_inserter? It is actually a function that takes its argument and uses it to create and return a back_insert_iterator object. By using the type (std::vector<int>) of its argument (data), back_inserter() can create the right kind of back_insert_iterator object. A result of this complication is that you need to remember what's a function and what's a type.

The standard library contains far too many functions to go into them here. Just for a taste of what is available, change the copy function on line 13 to unique_copy. How do you think this changes the program's behavior?

_____

_____

Try it. If you don't see any difference, **try the following input:**

10 42 3 1 42 5 3 10 3

Now you can see that unique_copy copies only one value when a number is repeated. So you should see the following output for the input earlier:

1
3
5
10
42

Let's try one more function. Instead of sort(), call reverse(). Be sure to change unique_copy() back to copy() because unique_copy() works correctly only if the input is sorted. The name, reverse, tells you what to expect from the program. **Try it to make sure you understand. What do you get for the same input as I?**

3
10
3
5
42
1
3
42
10

In Exploration 9, I threw an ugly for loop at you just to scare you prior to introducing the ranged for loop. It's time to start breaking down that ugly code and understand what the various pieces mean. The next Exploration takes a closer look at the handy increment (++) operator.

Increment and Decrement

This Exploration introduces the increment (++) operator, which has multiple uses in the C++ language. Not surprising, it has a counterpart to decrement values: --. This Exploration takes a closer look at these operators, which appear so often, they are part of the language name.

■ **Note**   I know that you C, Java, etc. programmers have been waiting for this Exploration ever since I wrote i = i + 1 in Exploration 7. As you saw in Exploration 9, the ++ operator means more in C++ than what you're used to. That's why I waited until now to discuss it.

Increment

The ++ operator is familiar to C, Java, Perl, and many other programmers. C was the first widespread language to introduce this operator to mean "increment" or "add 1." C++ expanded the usage it inherited from C; the standard library uses the ++ operator in several new ways, such as advancing an iterator.

The increment operator comes in two flavors: prefix and postfix. The best way to understand the difference between these two flavors is with a demonstration, as shown in Listing 11-1.

Listing 11-1. Demonstrating the Difference Between Prefix and Postfix Increment

```
import <iostream>;

int main()
{
  int x{42};

  std::cout << "x    = " << x   << "\n";
  std::cout << "++x = " << ++x << "\n";
  std::cout << "x    = " << x   << "\n";
  std::cout << "x++ = " << x++ << "\n";
  std::cout << "x    = " << x   << "\n";
}
```

© Ray Lischner 2020
R. Lischner, *Exploring C++20*, https://doi.org/10.1007/978-1-4842-5961-0_11

Predict the output of the program.

_____

_____

_____

_____

_____

What is the actual output?

_____

_____

_____

_____

_____

Explain the difference between prefix (++x) and postfix (x++) increment.

_____

_____

_____

Described briefly, the prefix operator increments the variable first: the value of the expression is the value after incrementing. The postfix operator saves the old value, increments the variable, and uses the old value as the value of the expression.

As a general rule, use prefix instead of postfix, unless you need the postfix functionality. Rarely is the difference significant, but the postfix operator must save a copy of the old value, which might impose a small performance cost. If you don't have to use postfix, why pay that price?

Decrement

The increment operator has a decrement counterpart: --. The decrement operator subtracts one instead of adding one. Decrement also has a prefix and postfix flavor. The prefix operator pre-decrements, and the postfix operator post-decrements.

You can increment and decrement any variable with a numeric type; however, only some iterators permit decrement.

For example, output iterators move forward only. You can use the increment operator (prefix or postfix), but not decrement. Test this for yourself. Write a program that uses std::ostream_iterator and try to use the decrement operator on the iterator. (If you need a hint, look at Listing 10-3. Save the ostream_iterator object in a variable. Then use the decrement operator. It doesn't matter that the program makes no sense; it won't get past the compiler anyway.)

What error message do you get?

_____

_____

Different compilers issue different messages, but the essence of the message should be that the -- operator is not defined. If you need help with the program, see Listing 11-2.

Listing 11-2. Erroneous Program That Applies Decrement to an Output Iterator

```
1 import <algorithm>;
2 import <iostream>;
3 import <iterator>;
4 import <ranges>;
5 import <vector>;
6
7 int main()
8 {
9   std::vector<int> data;
10  std::ranges::copy(std::ranges::istream_view<int>(std::cin),
11                    std::back_inserter(std::cout));
12  std::ranges::sort(data);
13  std::ostream_iterator<int> output{ std::cout, "\n" };
14  --output;
15  std::ranges::copy(input, output);
16 }
```

At the end of Exploration 10, you wrote a program that called the `std::ranges::reverse()` function. Let's take a look at how that function works. Hint: It uses increment and decrement operators.

The `std::ranges::reverse` function, like other, similar algorithms, takes a range object as an argument. It uses the range's begin iterator and end sentinel to denote the limits of the range to reverse. Most range algorithms then perform a little trick and convert the end sentinel to an end iterator. By creating a symmetry between the begin and end of the range, we can implement reverse by incrementing the begin iterator and decrementing the end iterator until they cross paths. Other algorithms don't need to decrement the end iterator, but they still devolve to an iterator-only function because all of those functions already existed in C++ 17, so it is easy to,implement a C++ 20 range function by calling a C++ 17 iterator function.

Member Types

The first thing to note is that type of an iterator for a vector of int is as follows:

```
std::vector<int>::iterator
```

You usually use the dot (.) operator for a member of an object, but a member type uses :: (called the scope operator) because types are not the same as objects. Other member types include `size_type`, which is the type used to store the value of the `size()` member function. The `value_type` member type is the type of the elements of the range; in the case of a container such as `vector`, it is the type inside the angle brackets.

Back to Iterators

You may be relieved to know that you don't need to type the full name of member types. C++ offers a shortcut, `auto`. Use `auto` as the type when you don't need to type the full type name because the type is evident from context. In this case, the `begin()` member function always returns an iterator. It turns out `end()` also returns an iterator, so we are saved from having to learn how to convert a sentinel to an iterator. (It's easy but involves some C++ that we haven't covered yet.) In this case, `end()` returns a type that can be treated transparently as an iterator and a sentinel.

In other words, you can define a variable, call it left, that holds the left-hand side iterator as follows:

```
auto left{ data.begin() };
```

Similarly, right holds the right-hand side iterator, which starts at the end of the vector:

```
auto right{ data.end() };
```

There is one difference, however. The left iterator actually points to an element of the vector (assuming the vector is not empty), but right does not. It points to an end marker. If we decrement it, it will point to the last element of the vector (i.e., back()).

To obtain the value that an iterator points to, use *left, which is known as *dereferencing* the iterator. Hence, the * operator, when used in this fashion, is known as the *dereference operator*.

The left iterator will increment and the right iterator will decrement until they meet. That means we want the for loop to iterate as long as left != right, that is, left is not equal to right, or they do not point to the same position in the range. When working with iterators, a common error is to accidentally use the dereference operator and compare values instead of comparing positions. Pay close attention to those asterisks!

The final step is to know how to reverse two elements, given two iterators. The simplest way is to create a temporary object as follows:

```
auto temporary{ *left };
*left = *right;
*right = temporary;
```

When dealing with primitive types, this may be the fastest option. But you don't want to have to rewrite your code when you change types. Instead, use the C++ function, std::iter_swap(), which exchanges the values that two iterators point to. It does so optimally, using functionality that I haven't introduced yet:

```
std::iter_swap(left, right);
```

Remember that this function swaps the values that the arguments point to and does not alter the values of the left and right variables.

You now have all the pieces you need. **Write a program that reads integers into a vector, then reverses the order of the elements in the vector (without calling the standard library's reverse function), and prints the results.**

Test your program on input with both an even and an odd number of integers. Compare your program with the one in Listing 11-3.

Listing 11-3. Reversing the Input Order

```
import <algorithm>;
import <iostream>;
import <iterator>;
import <ranges>;
import <vector>;

int main()
{
  std::vector<int> data{};
  std::ranges::copy(std::ranges::istream_view<int>(std::cin),
                    std::back_inserter(data));
```

```
for (auto start{data.begin()}, end{data.end()}; start != end; /*empty*/)
{
  --end;
  if (start != end)
  {
    std::iter_swap(start, end);
    ++start;
  }
}

std::ranges::copy(data, std::ostream_iterator<int>(std::cout, "\n"));
}
```

The start iterator points to the beginning of the data vector, and end initially points to one past the end. If the vector is empty, the for loop terminates without executing the loop body. Then the loop body decrements end so that it points to an actual element of the vector.

Notice that the program is careful to compare start != end after each increment and again after each decrement operation. If the program had only one comparison, it would be possible for start and end to pass each other. The loop condition would never be true, and the program would exhibit undefined behavior, so the sky would fall, the earth would swallow me, or worse.

Also note how the for loop has an empty postiteration part. The iteration logic appears in different places in the loop body, which is not the preferred way to write a loop but is necessary in this case.

You can rewrite the loop, so the postiteration logic appears only in the loop header. Some programmers argue that distributing the increment and decrement in the loop body makes the loop harder to understand and, in particular, harder to prove the loop terminates correctly. On the other hand, cramming everything in the loop header makes the loop condition especially tricky to understand, as you can see in Listing 11-4.

Listing 11-4. Rewriting the for Loop

```
import <algorithm>;
import <iostream>;
import <iterator>;
import <ranges>;
import <vector>;

int main()
{
  std::vector<int> data{};
  std::ranges::copy(std::ranges::istream_view<int>(std::cin),
                    std::back_inserter(data));

  for (auto start{data.begin()}, end{data.end()};
       start != end and start != --end;
       ++start)
  {
    std::iter_swap(start, end);
  }

  std::ranges::copy(data, std::ostream_iterator<int>(std::cout, "\n"));
}
```

To keep all the logic in the loop header, it was necessary to use a new operator: and. You will learn more about this operator in the next Exploration; meanwhile, just believe that it implements a logical and operation and keep reading.

Most experienced C++ programmers will probably prefer Listing 11-4, whereas most beginners will probably prefer Listing 11-3. Hiding a decrement in the middle of a condition makes the code harder to read and understand. It's too easy to overlook the decrement. As you gain experience with C++, however, you will become more comfortable with increments and decrements, and Listing 11-4 will start to grow on you.

■ **Note**   I prefer Listing 11-3 over Listing 11-4. I really don't like to bury increment and decrement operators in the middle of a complicated condition.

As you learn more C++, you will find other aspects of this program that lend themselves to improvement. I encourage you to revisit old programs and see how your new techniques can often simplify the programming task. I'll do the same as I revisit examples throughout this book.

Listing 11-4 introduced the and operator. The next Exploration takes a closer look at this operator, as well as other logical operators and their use in conditions.

■ ■ ■

Conditions and Logic

You first met the bool type in Exploration 2. This type has two possible values: true and false, which are reserved keywords (unlike in C). Although most Explorations have not needed to use the bool type, many have used logical expressions in loop and if-statement conditions. This Exploration examines the many aspects of the bool type and logical operators.

I/O and bool

C++ I/O streams permit reading and writing bool values. By default, streams treat them as numeric values: true is 1 and false is 0. The manipulator std::boolalpha (declared in <ios>, so you get it for free from <iostream>) tells a stream to interpret bool values as words. By default, the words are true and false. (In Exploration 18, you'll discover how to use a language other than English.) You use the std::boolalpha manipulator the same way you do any other manipulator (as you saw in Exploration 8). For an input stream, use an input operator with the manipulator.

Write a program that demonstrates how C++ formats and prints bool values, numerically and textually.

Compare your program with Listing 12-1.

Listing 12-1. Printing bool Values

```
import <iostream>;

int main()
{
  std::cout << "true=" << true << '\n';
  std::cout << "false=" << false << '\n';
  std::cout << std::boolalpha;
  std::cout << "true=" << true << '\n';
  std::cout << "false=" << false << '\n';
}
```

How do you think C++ handles **bool** values for input?

_____

> **Write a program to test your assumptions. Were you correct?**
> _____ **Explain how an input stream handles bool input.**
>
> _____
>
> _____

By default, when an input stream has to read a bool value, it actually reads an integer, and if the integer's value is 1, the stream interprets that as true. The value 0 is false, and any other value results in an error.

With the std::boolalpha manipulator, the input stream requires the exact text true or false. Integers are not allowed, nor are any case differences. The input stream accepts only those exact words.

Use the std::noboolalpha manipulator to revert to the default numeric Boolean values. Thus, you can mix alphabetic and numeric representations of bool in a single stream, as follows:

```
bool a{true}, b{false};
std::cin >> std::boolalpha >> a >> std::noboolalpha >> b;
std::cout << std::boolalpha << a << ' ' << std::noboolalpha << b;
```

By default, std::format() converts a bool value to a string, like boolalpha. You can also format a bool as an integer to format the value 0 or 1.

```
std::cout << std::format("{} {:d}\n", a, b);
```

Reading or writing bool values do not actually occur all that often in most programs.

Boolean Type

C++ automatically converts many different types to bool, so you can use integers, I/O stream objects, and other values whenever you need a bool, such as in a loop or if-statement condition. You can see this for yourself in Listing 12-2.

Listing 12-2. Automatic Type Conversion to bool

```
1  import <iostream>;
2
3  int main()
4  {
5    if (true)        std::cout << "true\n";
6    if (false)       std::cout << "false\n";
7    if (42)          std::cout << "42\n";
8    if (0)           std::cout << "0\n";
9    if (42.4242)     std::cout << "42.4242\n";
10   if (0.0)         std::cout << "0.0\n";
11   if (-0.0)        std::cout << "-0.0\n";
12   if (-1)          std::cout << "-1\n";
13   if ('\0')        std::cout << "'\\0'\n";
14   if ('\1')        std::cout << "'\\1'\n";
15   if ("1")         std::cout << "\"1\"\n";
16   if ("false")     std::cout << "\"false\"\n";
17   if (std::cout)   std::cout << "std::cout\n";
18   if (std::cin)    std::cout << "std::cin\n";
19 }
```

Predict the output from Listing 12-2.

_____

_____

_____

_____

_____

_____

_____

_____

_____

Check your answer. **Were you right?** _____

You may have been fooled by lines 15 and 16. C++ does not interpret the contents of string literals to decide whether to convert the string to true or false. All character strings are true, even empty ones. (The C++ language designers did not do this to be perverse. There's a good reason that strings are true, but you will have to learn quite a bit more C++ in order to understand why.)

On the other hand, character literals (lines 13 and 14) are completely different from string literals. The compiler converts the escape character '\0', which has numeric value zero, to false. All other characters are true.

Recall from many previous examples (especially in Exploration 3) that loop conditions often depend on an input operation. If the input succeeds, the loop condition is true. What is actually happening is that C++ knows how to convert a stream object (such as std::cin) to bool. Every I/O stream keeps track of its internal state, and if any operation fails, the stream remembers that fact. When you convert a stream to bool, if the stream is in a failure state, the result is false. Not all complex types can be converted to bool, however.

What do you expect to happen when you compile and run Listing 12-3?

_____

Listing 12-3. Converting a std::string to bool

```
import <iostream>;
import <string>;

int main()
{
  std::string empty{};

  if (empty)
    std::cout << "empty is true\n";
  else
    std::cout << "empty is false\n";

}
```

The compiler reports an error, because it does not know how to convert std::string to bool.

■ **Note**   Although an istream knows how to convert an input string to bool, the std::string type lacks the information it needs to interpret the string. Without knowledge of the string's context, it is unrealistic to ask a string to interpret text, such as "true," "vrai," or "richtig."

What about std::vector? **Do you think C++ defines a conversion from std::vector to bool? _____. Write a program to test your hypothesis. What is your conclusion?**

This is another case in which no general solution is feasible. Should an empty vector be false, whereas all others are true? Maybe a std::vector<bool> that contains only false elements should be false. Only the application programmer can make these decisions, so the C++ library designers wisely chose not to make them for you; therefore, you cannot convert std::vector to bool. However, there are ways of obtaining the desired result by calling member functions.

Logic Operators

Real-world conditions are often more complicated than merely converting a single value to bool. To accommodate this, C++ offers the usual logical operators: and, or, and not (which are reserved keywords). They have their usual meaning from mathematical logic, namely, that and is false, unless both operands are true; or is true, unless both operands are false; and not inverts the value of its operand.

More important, however, is that the built-in and and or operators do not evaluate their right-hand operand, unless they have to. The and operator must evaluate its right-hand operand only if the left-hand operand is true. (If the left-hand operand is false, the entire expression is false, and there is no need to evaluate the right-hand operand.) Similarly, the or operator evaluates its right-hand operand only if the left-hand operand is true. Stopping the evaluation early like this is known as *short-circuiting*.

For example, suppose you are writing a simple loop to examine all the elements of a vector to determine whether they are all equal to zero. The loop ends when you reach the end of the vector or when you find an element not equal to zero.

Write a program that reads numbers into a vector, searches the vector for a nonzero element, and prints a message about whether the vector is all zero.

You can solve this problem without using a logical operator, but try to use one, just for practice. Take a look at Listing 12-4, to see one way to solve this problem.

Listing 12-4. Using Short-Circuiting to Test for Nonzero Vector Elements

```
1 import <algorithm>;
2 import <iostream>;
3 import <iterator>;
4 import <ranges>;
5 import <vector>;
6
7 int main()
8 {
9   std::vector<int> data{};
10  std::ranges::copy(std::ranges::istream_view<int>(std::cin),
11            std::back_inserter(data));
12
13  auto iter{data.begin()}, end{data.end()};
```

```
14    for (; iter != end and *iter == 0; ++iter)
15      /*empty*/;
16    if (iter == end)
17      std::cout << "data contains all zeroes\n";
18    else
19      std::cout << "data does not contain all zeroes\n";
20  }
```

Line 14 is the key. The iterator advances over the vector and tests for zero-valued elements.

What happens when the iterator reaches the end of the vector?

_____

The condition iter != end becomes false at the end of the vector. Because of short-circuiting, C++ never evaluates the *iter == 0 part of the expression, which is good.

Why is this good? What would happen if short-circuiting did not take place?

_____

_____

Imagine that iter != end is false; in other words, the value of iter is end. That means *iter is just like *end, which is bad—really bad. You are not allowed to dereference the one-past-the-end iterator. If you are lucky, it would crash your program. If you are unlucky, your program would continue to run, but with completely unpredictable and erroneous data and, therefore, unpredictable and erroneous results.

Short-circuiting guarantees that C++ will not evaluate *iter when iter equals end, which means iter will always be valid when the program dereferences it, which is good. Some languages (such as Ada) use different operators for short-circuiting and non-short-circuiting operations. C++ does not. The built-in logical operators always perform short-circuiting, so you never accidentally use non-short-circuiting when you intended to use the short-circuiting operator.

Old-Fashioned Syntax

The logical operators have symbolic versions: && for and, || for or, and ! for not. The keywords are clearer, easier to read, easier to understand, and less error-prone. That's right, less error-prone. You see, && means and, but & is also an operator. Similarly, | is a valid operator. Thus, if you accidentally write & instead of &&, your program will compile and even run. It might seem to run correctly for a while, but it will eventually fail, because & and && mean different things. (You'll learn about & and | later in this book.) New C++ programmers aren't the only ones to make this mistake. I've seen highly experienced C++ programmers write & when they mean && or | instead of ||. Avoid this error by using only the keyword logical operators.

I was hesitant about even mentioning the symbolic operators, but I can't ignore them. Many C++ programs use the symbolic operators instead of the keyword equivalents. These C++ programmers, having grown up with the symbols, prefer to continue to use the symbols rather than the keywords. This is your chance to become a trendsetter. Eschew the old-fashioned, harder-to-read, harder-to-understand, error-prone symbols and embrace the keywords.

Comparison Operators

The built-in comparison operators always yield bool results, regardless of their operands. You have already seen == and != for equality and inequality. You also saw < for less than, and you can guess that > means greater than. Similarly, you probably already know that <= means less than or equal and >= means greater than or equal.

These operators produce the expected results when you use them with numeric operands. You can even use them with vectors of numeric types.

Write a program that demonstrates how < works with a vector of int. (If you're having trouble writing the program, take a look at Listing 12-5.) **What are the rules that govern < for a vector?**

_____

_____

_____

_____

C++ compares vectors at the element level. That is, the first elements of two vectors are compared. If one element is smaller than the other, its vector is considered less than the other. If one vector is a prefix of the other (i.e., the vectors are identical up to the length of the shorter vector), the shorter vector is less than the longer one.

Listing 12-5. Comparing Vectors

```cpp
import <iostream>;
import <vector>;

int main()
{
    std::vector<int> a{ 10, 20, 30 },  b{ 10, 20, 30 };

    if (a != b) std::cout << "wrong: a != b\n";
    if (a < b)  std::cout << "wrong: a < b\n";
    if (a > b)  std::cout << "wrong: a > b\n";
    if (a == b) std::cout << "okay: a == b\n";
    if (a >= b) std::cout << "okay: a >= b\n";
    if (a <= b) std::cout << "okay: a <= b\n";

    a.emplace_back(40);
    if (a != b) std::cout << "okay: a != b\n";
    if (a < b)  std::cout << "wrong: a < b\n";
    if (a > b)  std::cout << "okay: a > b\n";
    if (a == b) std::cout << "wrong: a == b\n";
    if (a >= b) std::cout << "okay: a >= b\n";
    if (a <= b) std::cout << "wrong: a <= b\n";

    b.emplace_back(42);
    if (a != b) std::cout << "okay: a != b\n";
    if (a < b)  std::cout << "okay: a < b\n";
    if (a > b)  std::cout << "wrong: a > b\n";
    if (a == b) std::cout << "wrong: a == b\n";
    if (a >= b) std::cout << "wrong: a >= b\n";
    if (a <= b) std::cout << "okay: a <= b\n";
}
```

C++ uses the same rules when comparing std::string types, but not when comparing two character string literals.

Write a program that demonstrates how C++ compares two std::string objects by comparing their contents.

Compare your solution with mine in Listing 12-6.

Listing 12-6. Demonstrating How C++ Compares Strings

```
import <iostream>;
import <string>;

int main()
{
  std::string a{"abc"}, b{"abc"};
  if (a != b) std::cout << "wrong: abc != abc\n";
  if (a < b)  std::cout << "wrong: abc < abc\n";
  if (a > b)  std::cout << "wrong: abc > abc\n";
  if (a == b) std::cout << "okay: abc == abc\n";
  if (a >= b) std::cout << "okay: abc >= abc\n";
  if (a <= b) std::cout << "okay: abc <= abc\n";

  a.push_back('d');
  if (a != b) std::cout << "okay: abcd != abc\n";
  if (a < b)  std::cout << "wrong: abcd < abc\n";
  if (a > b)  std::cout << "okay: abcd > abc\n";
  if (a == b) std::cout << "wrong: abcd == abc\n";
  if (a >= b) std::cout << "okay: abcd >= abc\n";
  if (a <= b) std::cout << "wrong: abcd <= abc\n";

  b.push_back('e');
  if (a != b) std::cout << "okay: abcd != abce\n";
  if (a < b)  std::cout << "okay: abcd < abce\n";
  if (a > b)  std::cout << "wrong: abcd > abce\n";
  if (a == b) std::cout << "wrong: abcd == abce\n";
  if (a >= b) std::cout << "wrong: abcd >= abce\n";
  if (a <= b) std::cout << "okay: abcd <= abce\n";
}
```

Testing how C++ compares quoted string literals is more difficult. Instead of using the contents of the string, the compiler uses the location of the strings in memory, which is a detail of the compiler's internal workings and has no bearing on anything practical. Thus, unless you know how the compiler works, you cannot predict how it will compare two quoted strings. In other words, don't do that. Make sure you create std::string objects before you compare strings. It's okay if only one operand is std::string. The other can be a quoted string literal, and the compiler knows how to compare the std::string with the literal, as demonstrated in the following example:

```
if ("help" > "hello") std::cout << "Bad. Bad. Bad. Don't do this!\n";
if (std::string("help") > "hello") std::cout << "this works\n";
if ("help" > std::string("hello")) std::cout << "this also works\n";
if (std::string("help") > std::string("hello")) std::cout << "and this works\n";
```

The next Exploration does not relate directly to Boolean logic and conditions. Instead, it shows how to write compound statements, which you need in order to write any kind of useful conditional statement.

EXPLORATION 13

Compound Statements

You have already used compound statements (i.e., lists of statements enclosed in curly braces) in many programs. Now it's time to learn some of the special rules and uses for compound statements, which are also known as *blocks*.

Statements

C++ has some hairy, scary syntax rules. By comparison though, the syntax for statements is downright simplistic. The C++ grammar defines most statements in terms of other statements. For example, the rule for while statements is

while (*condition* **)** *statement*

In this example, bold elements are required, such as the while keyword. *Italic* elements stand for other syntax rules. As you can likely deduce from the example, a while statement can have any statement as the loop body, including another while statement.

The reason most statements appear to end with a semicolon is because the most fundamental statement in C++ is just an expression followed by a semicolon.

expression **;**

This kind of statement is called an *expression statement*.

I haven't discussed the precise rules for expressions yet, but they work the way they do in most other languages, with a few differences. Most significant is that assignment is an expression in C++ (as it is in C, Java, C#, etc., but not in Pascal, Basic, Fortran, etc.). Consider the following:

```
while (std::cin >> x)
  sum = sum + x;
```

This example demonstrates a single while statement. Part of the while statement is another statement: in this case, an expression statement. The expression in the expression statement is sum = sum + x. Expressions in expression statements are often assignments or function calls, but the language permits any expression. The following, therefore, is a valid statement:

```
42;
```

© Ray Lischner 2020
R. Lischner, *Exploring C++20*, https://doi.org/10.1007/978-1-4842-5961-0_13

What do you think happens if you use this statement in a program?

_____

Try it. What actually happens?

_____

Modern compilers are usually able to detect statements that serve no useful purpose and eliminate them from the program. Typically, the compiler tells you what it's doing, but you may have to supply an extra option to tell the compiler to be extra picky. For example, try the -Wall option for g++ or /Wall for Microsoft Visual C++. (That's Wall, as in all warnings, not the thing holding up your roof.)

The syntax rule for a compound statement is

```
{ statement* }
```

where * means zero or more occurrences of the preceding rule (*statement*). Notice that the closing curly brace has no semicolon after it.

How does C++ parse the following?

```
while (std::cin >> x)
{
    sum = sum + x;
    ++count;
}
```

_____
_____
_____

Once again, you have a while statement, so the loop body must be a single statement. In this example, the loop body is a compound statement. The compound statement is a statement that consists of two expression statements. Figure 13-1 shows a tree view of the same information.

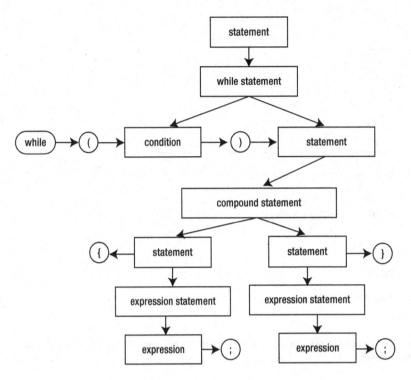

Figure 13-1. *Simplified parse tree for C++ statements*

Consider the body of main(), such as the one in Listing 13-1. What do you see? That's right, it's a compound statement. It's an ordinary block, and it follows the same rules as any other block. In case you were wondering, the body of main() must be a compound statement. This is one of the few circumstances in which C++ requires a specific kind of statement, instead of allowing any statement whatsoever.

Find and fix the errors in Listing 13-1. Visually locate as many errors as you can by reading the code. When you think you found and fixed them all, try compiling and running the program.

Listing 13-1. Finding Statement Errors

```
 1 import <iostream>;
 2 import <vector>;
 3 // find errors in this program
 4 int main()
 5 {
 6   std::vector<int> positive_data{}, negative_data{};
 7
 8   for (int x{0}; std::cin >> x ;) {
 9     if (x < 0);
10     {
11       negative_data.push_back(x)
12     };
```

```
13      else
14      {
15          positive_data.push_back(x)
16      }
17    };
18 }
```

Record all the errors in Listing 13-1.

_____

_____

_____

Did you find them all without the compiler's help? _____
The errors are

- Extra semicolon on line 9

- Extra semicolon on line 12

- Missing semicolon from the end of lines 11 and 15

- Extra semicolon on line 17

For extra credit, **which errors are not syntax violations (the compiler will not alert you to them) and do not affect the program's behavior?**

_____

_____

If you answered "the extra semicolon on line 17," give yourself a star. Strictly speaking, the extra semicolon represents an empty, do-nothing statement, called a *null statement*. Such a statement sometimes has a use in a loop, especially a for loop that does all its work in the loop header, leaving nothing for the loop body to do. (See an example in Listing 12-4.)

Thus, the way the compiler interprets line 9 is that the semicolon is the statement body for the if statement. The next statement is a compound statement, which is followed by an else, which has no corresponding if, hence the error. Every else must be a counterpart to an earlier if in the same statement. In other words, every if condition must be followed by exactly one statement, then by an optional else keyword and another statement. You cannot use else in any other way.

As written, the if statement on line 9 is followed by three statements: a null statement, a compound statement, and another null statement. The solution is to delete the null statements by deleting the semicolons on lines 9 and 12.

The statements that make up a compound statement can be any statements, including other compound statements. The next section explains why you might want to nest a compound statement within another compound statement.

Line 6 shows that you can declare more than one variable at a time, using a comma separator. I prefer to define one variable at a time but wanted to show you this style too. Each variable receives its own initializer.

Local Definitions and Scope

Compound statements do more than simply group multiple statements into a single statement. You can also group definitions within the block. Any variable that you define in a block is visible only within the confines of the block. The region where you can use a variable is known as the variable's *scope*. A good programming practice is to limit the scope to as small a region as possible. Limiting the scope of a variable serves several purposes:

- *Preventing mistakes*: You can't accidentally use a variable's name outside of its scope.

- *Communicating intent*: Anyone who reads your code can tell how a variable is used. If variables are defined at the broadest scope possible, whoever reads your code must spend more time and effort trying to determine where different variables are used.

- *Reusing names*: How many times can you use the variable i as a loop control variable? You can use and reuse it as often as you like, provided each time you limit the variable's scope to its loop.

- *Reusing memory*: When execution reaches the end of a block, all the variables defined in that block are destroyed, and the memory is available to be used again. Thus, if your code creates many large objects but needs only one at a time, you can define each variable in its own scope, so only one large object exists at a time.

Listing 13-2 shows some examples of local definitions. The lines highlighted in bold indicate local definitions.

Listing 13-2. Local Variable Definitions

```
#include <cassert>
import <algorithm>;
import <iostream>;
import <iterator>;
import <string>;
import <vector>;

int main()
{
  std::vector<int> data{};
  data.insert(data.begin(), std::istream_iterator<int>(std::cin),
                            std::istream_iterator<int>());

  // Silly way to sort a vector. Assume that the initial portion
  // of the vector has already been sorted, up to the iterator iter.
  // Find where *iter belongs in the already sorted portion of the vector.
  // Erase *iter from the vector and re-insert it at its sorted position.
  // Use binary search to speed up the search for the proper position.
  // Invariant: elements in range [begin(), iter are already sorted.
  for (auto iter{data.begin()}, end{data.end()}; iter != end; )
  {
    // Find where *iter belongs by calling the standard algorithm
    // lower_bound, which performs a binary search and returns an iterator
    // that points into data at a position where the value should be inserted.
    int value{*iter};
```

```
    auto here{std::lower_bound(data.begin(), iter, value)};
    if (iter == here)
        ++iter; // already in sorted position
    else
    {
      iter = data.erase(iter);
      // re-insert the value at the correct position.
      data.insert(here, value);
    }
}


// Debugging code: check that the vector is actually sorted. Do this by comparing
// each element with the preceding element in the vector.
for (auto iter{data.begin()}, prev{data.end()}, end{data.end()};
        iter != end;
        ++iter)
{
  if (prev != data.end())
      assert(not (*iter < *prev));
    prev = iter;
}


// Print the sorted vector all on one line. Start the line with "{" and
// end it with "}". Separate elements with commas.
// An empty vector prints as "{ }".
std::cout << '{';
std::string separator{" "};
for (int element : data)
{
  std::cout << separator << element;
  separator = ", ";
}
  std::cout << " }\n";
}
```

Listing 13-2 has a lot of new functions and features, so let's look at the code one section at a time.

The definition of data is a local definition in a block. True, almost all your definitions have been at this outermost level, but a compound statement is a compound statement, and any definition in a compound statement is a local definition. That begs the question of whether you can define a variable outside of all blocks. The answer is yes, but you rarely want to. C++ permits global variables, but no program in this book has needed to define any yet. I'll cover global variables when the time is right (which would be Exploration 52).

A for loop has its own special scope rules. As you learned in Exploration 7, the initialization part of a for loop can, and often does, define a loop control variable. The scope of that variable is limited to the for loop, as though the for statement were enclosed in an extra set of curly braces.

The value variable is also local to the for loop's body. If you try to use this variable outside of the loop, the compiler issues an error message. In this case, you have no reason to use this variable outside the loop, so define the variable inside the loop.

The lower_bound algorithm performs a binary search that tries to find a value in a range of sorted values. It returns an iterator that points to the first occurrence of the value in the range or, if the value is not found, the position where you can insert the value and keep the range in order. This is exactly what this program needs to sort the data vector.

The erase member function deletes an element from a vector, reducing the vector's size by one. Pass an iterator to erase to designate which element to delete, and save the return value, which is an iterator that refers to the new value at that position in the vector. The insert function inserts a value (the second argument) just before the position designated by an iterator (the first argument).

Notice how you can use and reuse the name iter. Each loop has its own distinct variable named iter. Each iter is local to its loop. If you were to write sloppy code and fail to initialize iter, the variable's initial value would be junk. It is not the same variable as the one defined earlier in the program, so its value is not the same as the old value of the old variable.

The separator variable holds a separator string to print between elements when printing the vector. It, too, is a local variable, but local to the main program's block. However, by defining it just before it is used, you communicate the message that this variable is not needed earlier in main. It helps prevent mistakes that can arise if you reuse a variable from one part of main in another part.

Another way you can help limit the scope of a variable such as separator is to define it in a block within a block, as shown in Listing 13-3. (This version of the program replaces the loops with calls to standard algorithms, which is a better way to write C++ programs when you are not trying to make a point.)

Listing 13-3. Local Variable Definitions in a Nested Block

```cpp
import <algorithm>;
import <iostream>;
import <iterator>;
import <string>;
import <vector>;

int main()
{
  std::vector<int> data{};
  data.insert(data.begin(), std::istream_iterator<int>(std::cin),
                            std::istream_iterator<int>());

  std::ranges::sort(data);

  {
    // Print the sorted vector all on one line. Start the line with "{" and
    // end it with "}". Separate elements with commas. An empty vector prints
    // as "{ }".
    std::cout << '{';
    std::string separator{" "};
    for (int element : data)
    {
      std::cout << separator << element;
      separator = ", ";
    }
    std::cout << " }\n";
  }
  // Cannot use separator out here.
}
```

Most C++ programmers nest blocks infrequently. As you learn more C++, you will discover a variety of techniques that improve on nested blocks and keep your main program from looking so cluttered.

Definitions in for Loop Headers

What if you did not define loop control variables inside the for loop header, but defined them outside the loop instead? Try it.

Rewrite Listing 13-2, so you don't define any variables in the for loop headers.
What do you think? **Does the new code look better or worse than the original?** _____ **Why?**

_____

_____

_____

Personally, I find for loops can become cluttered very easily. Nonetheless, keeping loop control variables local to the loop is critical for clarity and code comprehension. When faced with a large, unknown program, one of the difficulties you face in understanding that program is knowing when and how variables can take on new values. If a variable is local to a loop, you know the variable cannot be modified outside the loop. That is valuable information. If you still need convincing, try reading and understanding Listing 13-4.

Listing 13-4. Mystery Function

```cpp
#include <cassert>
import <algorithm>;
import <iostream>;
import <iterator>;
import <ranges>;
import <string>;
import <vector>;

int main()
{
  int v{};
  std::vector<int> data{};
  std::vector<int>::iterator i{}, p{};
  std::string s{};

  std::ranges::copy(std::ranges::istream_view<int>(std::cin),
          std::back_inserter(data));
  i = data.begin();

  while (i != data.end())
  {
    v = *i;
    p = std::lower_bound(data.begin(), i, v);
    if (i == p)
      ++i;
    else
    {
      i = data.erase(i);
      data.insert(p, v);
    }
  }
}
```

```
  s = " ";
  for (p = i, i = data.begin(); i != data.end(); p = i, ++i)
  {
    if (p != data.end())
      assert(not (*i < *p));
  }

  std::cout << '{';
  for (i = data.begin(); i != data.end(); ++i)
  {
    v = *p;
    std::cout << s << v;
    s = ", ";
  }
  std::cout << " }\n";
}
```

Well, that wasn't too hard, was it? After all, you recently finished reading Listing 13-2, so you can see that Listing 13-4 is intended to do the same thing but is reorganized slightly. The difficulty is in keeping track of the values of p and i and ensuring that they have the correct value at each step of the program. Try compiling and running the program. **Record your observations**.

_____

_____

_____

What went wrong?

_____

_____

_____

I made a mistake and wrote v = *p instead of v = *i. Congratulations if you spotted this error before you ran the program. If the variables had been properly defined local to their respective scopes, this error could never have occurred.

The next Exploration introduces file I/O, so your exercises can read and write files, instead of using console I/O. I'm sure your fingers will appreciate it.

■ ■ ■

Introduction to File I/O

Reading from standard input or writing to standard output works fine for many trivial programs, and it is a standard idiom for UNIX and related operating systems. Nonetheless, real programs must be able to open named files for reading, writing, or both. This Exploration introduces the basics of file I/O. Later Explorations will tackle more sophisticated I/O issues.

Reading Files

The most common file-related task in these early Explorations will involve reading from a file instead of from the standard input stream. One of the greatest benefits of this is it saves a lot of tedious typing. Some IDEs make it difficult to redirect input and output, so it's easier to read from a file and sometimes write to a file. Listing 14-1 shows a rudimentary program that reads integers from a file named *list1401.in* and writes them, one per line, to the standard output stream. If the program cannot open the file, it prints an error message.

Listing 14-1. Copying Integers from a File to Standard Output

```
#include <cerrno>
import <algorithm>;
import <fstream>;
import <iostream>;
import <iterator>;
import <system_error>;

int main()
{
  std::ifstream in{"list1401.in"};
  if (not in)
    std::cerr << "list1401.in: " <<
      std::generic_category().message(errno) << '\n';
  else
  {
    std::ranges::copy(std::ranges::istream_view<int>(in),
        std::ostream_iterator<int>{std::cout, "\n"});
    in.close();
  }
}
```

© Ray Lischner 2020
R. Lischner, *Exploring C++20*, https://doi.org/10.1007/978-1-4842-5961-0_14

The <fstream> module declares ifstream, which is the type you use to read from a file. To open a file, simply name the file in ifstream's initializer. If the file cannot be opened, the ifstream object is left in an error state, a condition for which you can test using an if statement. When you are done reading from the file, call the close() member function. After closing the stream, you cannot read from it anymore.

Once the file is open, read from it the same way you read from std::cin. All the input operators that are declared in <istream> work equally well for an ifstream, as they do for std::cin.

If the file cannot be opened, you want to issue a useful error message, and here you enter the netherworld between historic C and modern C++. Operating systems generally have a variety of error codes they can issue indicating that the file does not exist, that you don't have permission to read the file, that an electromagnetic pulse permanently scrambled the contents of your PhD thesis, and so on. The std::generic_category() (declared in <system_error>) function returns an object that can be used to get information associated with a POSIX error code, which one hopes is in the C variable, errno (no leading std:: and like <cassert>, you use #include <cerrno>). The message() function returns a string message, or you can construct a portable error_code object. The C++ standard is silent on whether or how file streams store error values in errno, but it is a realistic expectation that errno holds a useful value.

> **Run the program when you know the input file does not exist. What message does the program display?**

_____

If you can, create the input file, then change the protection on the file, so you can no longer read it. Run the program.

> **What message do you get this time?**

_____

Writing Files

As you have probably guessed, to write to a file, you define an ofstream object. To open the file, simply name the file in the variable's initializer. If the file does not exist, it will be created. If the file does exist, its old contents are discarded in preparation for writing new contents. If the file cannot be opened, the ofstream object is left in an error state, so remember to test it before you try to use it. Use an ofstream object the same way you use std::cout.

Modify Listing 14-1 to write the numbers to a named file. This time, name the input file *list1402.in* and name the output file *list1402.out*. Compare your solution with mine in Listing 14-2.

Listing 14-2. Copying Integers from a Named File to a Named File

```cpp
#include <cerrno>
import <algorithm>;
import <fstream>;
import <iostream>;
import <ranges>;
import <system_error>;

int main()
{
  std::ifstream in{"list1402.in"};
  if (not in)
    std::cerr << "list1402.in: " <<
      std::generic_category().message(errno) << '\n';
```

```
  else
  {
    std::ofstream out{"list1402.out"};
    if (not out)
      std::cerr << "list1402.out: " <<
        std::generic_category().message(errno) << '\n';
    else
    {
      std::ranges::copy(std::ranges::istream_view<int>(in),
        std::ostream_iterator<int>{out, "\n"});
      out.close();
      in.close();
    }
  }
}
```

Like ifstream, the ofstream type is declared in <fstream>.

The program opens the input file first. If that succeeds, it opens the output file. If the order were reversed, the program might create the output file, then fail to open the input file, and the result would be a wasted, empty file. Always open input files first.

Also notice that the program does not close the input file, if it cannot open the output file. Don't worry: it closes the input file just fine. When in is destroyed at the end of main, the file is automatically closed.

I know what you're thinking: if in is automatically closed, why call close at all? Why not let in close automatically in all cases? For an input file, that's actually okay. Feel free to delete the in.close(); statement from the program. For an output file, however, doing so is unwise.

Some output errors do not arise until the file is closed, and the operating system flushes all its internal buffers and does all the other cleanup it needs to do when closing a file. Thus, an output stream object might not receive an error from the operating system until you call close(). Detecting and handling these errors is an advanced skill. The first step toward developing that skill is to adopt the habit of calling close() explicitly for output files. When it comes time to add the error-checking, you will have a place where you can add it.

Try running the program in Listing 14-2 in various error scenarios. Create the output file, *list1402.out*, and then use the operating system to mark the file as read-only. **What happens?**

If you noticed that the program does not check whether the output operations succeed, congratulations for having sharp eyes! C++ offers a few different ways to check for output errors, but they all have drawbacks. The easiest is to test whether the output stream is in an error state. You can check the stream after every output operation, but that approach is cumbersome, and few people write code that way. Another way lets the stream check for an error condition after every operation and alerts your program with an exception. You'll learn about this technique in Exploration 45. A frighteningly common technique is to ignore output errors altogether. As a compromise, I recommend testing for errors after calling close(). Listing 14-3 shows the final version of the program.

Listing 14-3. Copying Integers, with Minimal Error-Checking

```
#include <cerrno>
import <algorithm>;
import <fstream>;
import <iostream>;
import <ranges>;
import <system_error>;
```

```cpp
int main()
{
  std::ifstream in{"list1403.in"};
  if (not in)
    std::cerr << "list1403.in: " <<
      std::generic_category().message(errno) << '\n';
  else
  {
    std::ofstream out{"list1403.out"};
    if (out) {
      std::ranges::copy(std::ranges::istream_view<int>(in),
        std::ostream_iterator<int>{out, "\n"});
      out.close();
    }
    if (not out)
      std::cerr << "list1403.out: " <<
        std::generic_category().message(errno) << '\n';
  }
}
```

Basic I/O is not difficult, but it can quickly become a morass of gooey, complicated code when you start to throw in sophisticated error-handling, international issues, binary I/O, and so on. Later Explorations will introduce most of these topics, but only when the time is ripe. For now, however, go back to earlier programs and practice modifying them to read and write named files instead of the standard input and output streams. For the sake of brevity (if for no other reason), the examples in the book will continue to use the standard I/O streams. If your IDE interferes with redirecting the standard I/O streams, or if you just prefer named files, you now know how to change the examples to meet your needs.

■ ■ ■

The Map Data Structure

Now that you understand the basics, it's time to move on to more exciting challenges. Let's write a real program—something nontrivial but still simple enough to master this early in the book. Your task is to write a program that reads words and counts the frequency of each unique word. For the sake of simplicity, a word is a string of nonspace characters separated by white space. Be aware, however, that, by this definition, words end up including punctuation characters, but we'll worry about fixing that problem later.

This is a complicated program, touching on everything you've learned about C++ so far. If you want to exercise your new understanding of file I/O, read from a named file. If you prefer the simplicity, read from the standard input. Before jumping in and trying to write a program, take a moment to think about the problem and the tools you need to solve it. **Write pseudo-code for the program.** Try to write C++ code where you can, and make up whatever else you need to tackle the problem. Keep it simple—and don't dwell on trying to get syntax details correct.

_____
_____
_____
_____
_____
_____
_____
_____
_____
_____
_____
_____
_____
_____

© Ray Lischner 2020
R. Lischner, _Exploring C++20_, https://doi.org/10.1007/978-1-4842-5961-0_15

Using Maps

The title of this Exploration tells you what C++ feature will help provide an easy solution to this problem. What C++ calls a *map*, some languages and libraries call a *dictionary* or *association*. A map is simply a data structure that stores pairs of keys and values, indexed by the key. In other words, it maps a key to a value. Within a map, keys are unique. The map stores keys in ascending order. Thus, the heart of the program is a map that stores strings as keys and number of occurrences as the associated value for each key.

Naturally, your program needs the <map> header. The map datatype is called std::map. To define a map, you need to specify the key and value type within angle brackets (separated by a comma), as shown in the following example:

```
std::map<std::string, int> counts;
```

You can use almost any type as the key and value types, even another map. As with vector, if you do not initialize a map, it starts out empty.

The simplest way to use a map is to look up values using square brackets. For example, counts["the"] returns the value associated with the key "the". If the key is not present in the map, it is added with an initial value of zero. If the value type were std::string, the initial value would be an empty string.

Armed with this knowledge, you can write the first part of the program—collecting the word counts—as shown in Listing 15-1. (Feel free to modify the program to read from a named file, as you learned in Exploration 14.)

Listing 15-1. Counting Occurrences of Unique Words

```cpp
import <iostream>;
import <map>;
import <string>;

int main()
{
  std::map<std::string, int> counts{};
  std::string word{};
  while (std::cin >> word)
    ++counts[word];
  // TODO: Print the results.
}
```

In Listing 15-1, the ++ operator increments the count that the program stores in counts. In other words, when counts[word] retrieves the associated value, it does so in a way that lets you modify the value. You can use it as a target for an assignment or apply the increment or decrement operator.

For example, suppose you wanted to reset a count to zero.

```cpp
counts["something"] = 0;
```

That was easy. Now all that's left to do is to print the results. Like vectors, maps also use ranges and iterators, but because an iterator refers to a key/value pair, they are a little more complicated to use than vector's iterators.

Pairs

The best way to print the map is to use a range-based for loop to iterate over the map. Each map element is a single object that contains the key and the value. The key is called first, and the value is called second.

■ **Note** The two parts of the map element's value are not named key and value, because the std::pair type is a generic part of the C++ library. The library uses this type in several different places. Thus, the names of the parts of a pair are also generic and not tied specifically to map.

Use a dot (.) operator to access a member of the pair. To keep things simple, print the output as the key, followed by a tab character, followed by the count, all on one line. Putting all these pieces together, you end up with the finished program, as presented in Listing 15-2.

Listing 15-2. Printing Word Frequencies

```cpp
import <iostream>;
import <map>;
import <string>;

int main()
{
  std::map<std::string, int> counts{};

  // Read words from the standard input and count the number of times
  // each word occurs.
  std::string word{};
  while (std::cin >> word)
    ++counts[word];

  // For each word/count pair...
  for (auto element : counts)
    // Print the word, tab, the count, newline.
    std::cout << element.first << '\t' << element.second << '\n';
}
```

When iterating over the map, you know you will use the .first and .second members, so using auto for the key/value pairs helps keep the code readable. Let the compiler worry about the details.

Using the knowledge you gained in Exploration 8, you know how to format the output nicer by adjusting two neat columns instead of using a tab. All that is required is to find the size of the longest key. In order to right-align the counts, you can try to determine the number of places required by the largest count, or you can simply use a very large number, such as 10.

Rewrite Listing 15-2 to line up the output neatly, according to the size of the longest key.

Naturally, you will need to write another loop to visit all the elements of counts and test the size of each element. In Exploration 10, you learned that vector has a size() member function that returns the number of elements in the vector. Would you be surprised to learn that map and string also have size() member functions? The designers of the C++ library did their best to be consistent with names. The size() member function returns an integer of type size_type.

Compare your program with Listing 15-3.

Listing 15-3. Aligning Words and Counts Neatly

```cpp
import <format>;
import <iostream>;
import <map>;
import <string>;

int main()
{
  std::map<std::string, int> counts{};

  // Read words from the standard input and count the number of times
  // each word occurs.
  std::string word{};
  while (std::cin >> word)
    ++counts[word];

  // Determine the longest word.
  std::string::size_type longest{};
  for (auto element : counts)
    if (element.first.size() > longest)
      longest = element.first.size();

  // For each word/count pair...
  constexpr int count_size{10}; // Number of places for printing the count
  for (auto element : counts)
    // Print the word, count, newline. Keep the columns neatly aligned.
    std::cout << std::format("{1:{0}}{3:{2}}\n",
            longest, element.first, count_size, element.second);
}
```

If you want some sample input, try the file *explore15.txt*, which you can download from this book's website. Notice how the word is left-aligned and the count is right-aligned. We expect numbers to be right-aligned, and words are customarily left-aligned (in Western cultures). And remember constexpr from Exploration 8? That simply means count_size is a constant.

Searching in Maps

A map stores its data in sorted order by key. Searching in a map, therefore, is pretty fast (logarithmic time). Because a map keeps its keys in order, you can use any of the binary search algorithms, but even better is to use map's member functions. These member functions have the same names as the standard algorithms but can take advantage of their knowledge of a map's internal structure. The member functions also run in logarithmic time, but with less overhead than the standard algorithms.

For example, suppose you want to know how many times the word *the* appears in an input stream. You can read the input and collect the counts in the usual way, then call find("the") to see if "the" is in the map, and if so, get an iterator that points to its key/value pair. If the key is not in the map, find() returns the end() iterator. If the key is present, you can extract the count. You have all the knowledge and skills you need to solve this problem, so go ahead and **write the program to print the number of occurrences of the word *the*.** Once again, you can use *explore15.txt* as sample input. If you don't want to use redirection, modify the program to read from the *explore15.txt* file.

What count does your program print when you provide this file as the input? _____ The program presented in Listing 15-4 detects ten occurrences.

Listing 15-4. Searching for a Word in a Map

```cpp
import <iostream>;
import <map>;
import <string>;

int main()
{
  std::map<std::string, int> counts{};

  // Read words from the standard input and count the number of times
  // each word occurs.
  std::string word{};
  while (std::cin >> word)
    ++counts[word];

  auto the{counts.find("the")};
  if (the == counts.end())
    std::cout << "\"the\": not found\n";
  else if (the->second == 1)
    std::cout << "\"the\": occurs " << the->second << " time\n";
  else
    std::cout << "\"the\": occurs " << the->second << " times\n";
}
```

Until now, you've used a dot (.) to access a member, such as find() or end(). An iterator is different. You have to use an arrow (->) to access a member from an iterator, hence the->second. You won't see this style much until Exploration 33.

Sometimes you don't want to use auto because you want to make sure the human reader knows a variable's type. What is the type of the variable the?

_____

The official type is std::map<std::string, int>::iterator, which is quite a keyboard-full. You can see why I prefer auto in this case. But there's another solution that preserves the explicit use of a type and maintains a sense of brevity: type synonyms, which just happens to be the subject of the next Exploration.

Type Synonyms

Using types such as `std::vector<std::string>::size_type` or `std::map<std::string, int>::iterator` can be clumsy, prone to typographical errors, and just plain annoying to type and read. C++ lets you get away with auto sometimes, but not always. Fortunately, C++ lets you define short synonyms for clumsy types. You can also use type synonyms to provide meaningful names for generic types. (The standard library has quite a few synonyms of the latter variety.) These synonyms are often referred to as typedefs, because you can define them with the `typedef` keyword, although in modern C++, the `using` keyword is more common.

`typedef` and `using` Declarations

C++ inherits the basic syntax and semantics of `typedef` from C, so you might already be familiar with this keyword. If so, please bear with me while I bring other readers up to speed.

The idea of a `typedef` is to create a synonym, or alias, for another type. There are two compelling reasons for creating type synonyms:

- They create a short synonym for a long type name. For example, you may want to use `count_iter` as a type synonym for `std::map<std::string,int>::iterator`.

- They create a mnemonic synonym. For example, a program might declare `height` as a synonym for `int`, to emphasize that variables of type `height` store a height value. This information helps the human reader understand the program.

The basic syntax for a `typedef` declaration is like defining a variable, except you start with the `typedef` keyword, and the name of the type synonym takes the place of the variable name.

```
typedef std::map<std::string,int>::iterator count_iter;
typedef int height;
```

Another way is with the `using` keyword, in which case the order is reversed, and an equal sign is thrown in for readability:

```
using count_iter = std::map<std::string, int>;
using height = int;
```

Revisit Listing 15-4 and simplify the program by using a `typedef` or `using` declaration. Compare your result with Listing 16-1.

Listing 16-1. Counting Words, with a Clean Program That Uses using

```cpp
import <iostream>;
import <map>;
import <string>;

int main()
{
  using count_map = std::map<std::string,int>;
  using count_iterator = count_map::iterator;

  count_map counts{};

  // Read words from the standard input and count the number of times
  // each word occurs.
  std::string word{};
  while (std::cin >> word)
    ++counts[word];

  count_iterator the{counts.find("the")};

  if (the == counts.end())
    std::cout << "\"the\": not found\n";
  else if (the->second == 1)
    std::cout << "\"the\": occurs " << the->second << " time\n";
  else
    std::cout << "\"the\": occurs " << the->second << " times\n";
}
```

I like the new version of this program. It's a small difference in this little program, but it offers additional clarity and readability. Now I want to throw one more new C++ feature at you. Compare Listing 16-1 with Listing 16-2.

Listing 16-2. Counting Words, Moving a Definition Inside an if Statement

```cpp
import <iostream>;
import <map>;
import <string>;

int main()
{
  using count_map = std::map<std::string,int>;
  using count_iterator = count_map::iterator;

  count_map counts{};

  // Read words from the standard input and count the number of times
  // each word occurs.
  std::string word{};
  while (std::cin >> word)
    ++counts[word];
```

```
if (count_iterator the{counts.find("the")}; the == counts.end())
  std::cout << "\"the\": not found\n";
else if (the->second == 1)
  std::cout << "\"the\": occurs " << the->second << " time\n";
else
  std::cout << "\"the\": occurs " << the->second << " times\n";
}
```

The difference is small: the definition of the variable the is now embedded in the condition of the if statement. This change tells the compiler and the human reader that the condition variable the is limited to the if statement and its else part. **Add a line to the end of the program:**

```
auto this_does_not_work{ the };
```

Compile the new program. What happens?

_____

_____

The compiler issues an error because the variable the is not available outside of the if statement. In small programs such as those in this book, the difference may not seem significant, but in real programs, it is critical to limit variables to the narrowest scope possible in order to avoid mistakes and misunderstandings.

Common typedefs

The standard library makes heavy use of typedefs, as you have already seen. For example, std::vector<int>::size_type is a typedef for an integer type. You don't know which integer type (C++ has several, which you will learn about in Exploration 26), nor does it matter. All you have to know is that size_type is the type to use if you want to store a size or index in a variable.

Most likely, size_type is a typedef for std::size_t, which is itself a typedef. The std::size_t typedef is a synonym for an integer type that is suitable for representing a size. In particular, C++ has an operator, sizeof, which returns the size in bytes of a type or object. The result of sizeof is an integer of type std::size_t; however, a compiler writer chooses to implement sizeof and std::size_t.

■ **Note**   A "byte" is defined as the size of type char. So, by definition, sizeof(char) == 1. The size of other types depends on the implementation. On most popular desktop workstations, sizeof(int) == 4, but 2 and 8 are also likely candidates.

Now let's return to the problem of counting words. This program has a number of usability flaws.

What can you think of to improve the word-counting program?

_____

_____

_____

At the top of my list are the following two items:

- Ignore punctuation marks.

- Ignore case differences.

In order to implement these additional features, you have to learn some more C++. For example, the C++ standard library has functions to test whether a character is punctuation, a digit, an uppercase letter, a lowercase letter, and so on. The next Exploration begins by exploring characters more closely.

Characters

In Exploration 2, I introduced you to character literals in single quotes, such as `'\n'`, to end a line of output, but I have not yet taken the time to explain these fundamental building blocks. Now is the time to explore characters in greater depth.

Character Type

The `char` type represents a single character. Internally, all computers represent characters as integers. The *character set* defines the mapping between characters and numeric values. Common character sets are ISO 8859-1 (also called Latin-1) and ISO 10646 (same as Unicode), but many, many other character sets are in wide use.

The C++ standard does not mandate any particular character set. The literal `'4'` represents the digit 4, but the actual value that the computer uses internally is up to the implementation. You should not assume any particular character set. For example, in ISO 8859-1 (Latin-1), `'4'` has the value 52, but in EBCDIC, it has the value 244.

Similarly, given a numeric value, you cannot assume anything about the character that value represents. If you know a `char` variable stores the value 169, the character may be `'z'` (EBCDIC), `'©'` (Unicode), or `'Љ'` (ISO 8859-5).

C++ does not try to hide the fact that a character is actually a number. You can compare `char` values with `int` values, assign a `char` to an `int` variable, or do arithmetic with `char`s. For example, C++ guarantees that any character set your compiler and library support represents digit characters with contiguous values, starting at `'0'`. Thus, for example, the following is true for all C++ implementations:

```
'0' + 7 == '7'
```

The same sequence is true for letters in the alphabet, that is, `'A' + 25 == 'Z'`, and `'q' - 'm' == 4`, but C++ makes no guarantees concerning the relative values of, say, `'A'` and `'a'`.

Read Listing 17-1. **What does the program do?** (Hint: The `get` member function reads a single character from the stream. It does not skip over white space or treat any character specially. Extra hint: What happens if you subtract `'0'` from a character that you know to be a digit?)

_____

_____

_____

_____

Listing 17-1. Working and Playing with Characters

```
import <iostream>;

int main()
{
  int value{};
  bool have_value{false};
  char ch{};
  while (std::cin.get(ch))
  {
    if (ch >= '0' and ch <= '9')
    {
      value = ch - '0';
      have_value = true;
      while (std::cin.get(ch) and ch >= '0' and ch <= '9')
        value = value * 10 + ch - '0';
    }

    if (ch == '\n')
    {
      if (have_value)
      {
        std::cout << value << '\n';
        have_value = false;
      }
    }
    else if (ch != ' ' and ch != '\t')
    {
      std::cout << '\a';
      have_value = false;

      while (std::cin.get(ch) and ch != '\n')
        /*empty*/;
    }
  }
}
```

Briefly, this program reads numbers from the standard input and echoes the values to the standard output. If the program reads any invalid characters, it alerts the user (with \a, which I describe later in this Exploration), ignores the line of input, and discards the value. Leading and trailing blank and tab characters are allowed. The program prints the saved numeric value only after reaching the end of an input line. This means if a line contains more than one valid number, the program prints only the last value. I ignore the possibility of overflow, to keep the code simple.

The get function takes a character variable as an argument. It reads one character from the input stream, then stores the character in that variable. The get function does not skip over white space. When you use get as a loop condition, it returns true if it successfully reads a character and the program should keep reading. It returns false if no more input is available or some kind of input error occurred.

All the digit characters have contiguous values, so the inner loop tests to determine if a character is a digit character by comparing it to the values for '0' and '9'. If it is a digit, subtracting the value of '0' from it leaves you with an integer in the range 0 to 9.

The final loop reads characters and does nothing with them. The loop terminates when it reads a new line character. In other words, the final loop reads and ignores the rest of the input line.

Programs that need to handle white space on their own (such as Listing 17-1) can use get, or you can tell the input stream not to skip over white space prior to reading a number or anything else. The next section discusses character I/O in more detail.

Character I/O

You just learned that the get function reads a single character without treating white space specially. You can do the same thing with a normal input operator, but you must use the std::noskipws manipulator. To restore the default behavior, use the std::skipws manipulator (declared in <ios>).

```
// Skip white space, then read two adjacent characters.
char left, right;
std::cin >> left >> std::noskipws >> right >> std::skipws;
```

After turning off the skipws flag, the input stream does not skip over leading white space characters. For instance, if you were to try to read an integer, and the stream is positioned at white space, the read would fail. If you were to try to read a string, the string would be empty, and the stream position would not advance. So you have to consider carefully whether to skip white space. Typically, you would do that only when reading individual characters.

Remember that an input stream uses the >> operator (Exploration 5), even for manipulators. Using >> for manipulators seems to break the mnemonic of transferring data to the right, but it follows the convention of always using >> with an input stream. If you forget, the compiler will remind you.

Write a program that reads the input stream one character at a time and echoes the input to the standard output stream verbatim. This is not a demonstration of how to copy streams but an example of working with characters. Compare your program with Listing 17-2.

Listing 17-2. Echoing Input to Output, One Character at a Time

```
import <iostream>;

int main()
{
  std::cin >> std::noskipws;
  char ch{};
  while (std::cin >> ch)
    std::cout << ch;
}
```

You can also use the get member function, in which case you don't need the noskipws manipulator.

Let's try something a little more challenging. Suppose you have to read a series of points. The points are defined by a pair of *x, y* coordinates, separated by a comma. White space is allowed before and after each number and around the comma. Read the points into a vector of *x* values and a vector of *y* values. Terminate the input loop if a point does not have a proper comma separator. Print the vector contents, one point per line. I know this is a bit dull, but the point is to experiment with character input. If you prefer, do something special with the data. Compare your result with Listing 17-3.

Listing 17-3. Reading and Writing Points

```
import <algorithm>;
import <iostream>;
import <limits>;
import <vector>;

int main()
{
  using intvec = std::vector<int>;
  intvec xs{}, ys{};         // store the x's and y's

  char sep{};
  // Loop while the input stream has an integer (x), a character (sep),
  // and another integer (y); then test that the separator is a comma.
  for (int x{},y{}; std::cin >> x >> sep and sep == ',' and std::cin >> y;)
  {
    xs.emplace_back(x);
    ys.emplace_back(y);
  }

  for (auto x{xs.begin()}, y{ys.begin()}; x != xs.end(); ++x, ++y)
    std::cout << *x << ',' << *y << '\n';
}
```

The first for loop is the key. The loop condition reads an integer and a character and tests to determine if the character is a comma, before reading a second integer. The loop terminates if the input is invalid or ill-formed or if the loop reaches the end-of-file. A more sophisticated program would distinguish between these two cases, but that's a side issue for the moment.

A for loop can have only one definition, not two. So I had to move the definition of sep out of the loop header. Keeping x and y inside the header avoids conflict with the variables in the second for loop, which have the same names but are distinct variables. In the second loop, the x and y variables are iterators, not integers. The loop iterates over two vectors at the same time. A range-based for loop doesn't help in this case, so the loop must use explicit iterators.

Newlines and Portability

You've probably noticed that Listing 17-3, and every other program I've presented so far, prints '\n' at the end of each line of output. We have done so without considering what this really means. Different environments have different conventions for end-of-line characters. UNIX uses a line feed ('\x0a'); macOS uses a carriage return ('\x0d'); DOS and Microsoft Windows use a combination of a carriage return, followed by a line feed ('\x0d\x0a'); and some operating systems don't use line terminators but, instead, have record-oriented files, in which each line is a separate record.

In all these cases, the C++ I/O streams automatically convert a native line ending to a single '\n' character. When you print '\n' to an output stream, the library automatically converts it to a native line ending (or terminates the record).

In other words, you can write programs that use '\n' as a line ending and not concern yourself with native OS conventions. Your source code will be portable to all C++ environments.

Character Escapes

In addition to '\n', C++ offers several other *escape sequences*, such as '\t', for horizontal tab. Table 17-1 lists all the character escapes. Remember that you can use these escapes in character literals and string literals.

Table 17-1. *Character Escape Sequences*

Escape	Meaning
\a	Alert: ring a bell or otherwise signal the user
\b	Backspace
\f	Form feed
\n	Newline
\r	Carriage return
\t	Horizontal tab
\v	Vertical tab
\\	Literal \
\'	Literal '
\"	Literal "
OOO	Octal (base 8) character value
\x*XX* . . .	Hexadecimal (base 16) character value

The last two items are the most interesting. An escape sequence of one to three octal digits (0 to 7) specifies the value of the character. Which character the value represents is up to the implementation.

Understanding all the caveats from the first section of this Exploration, there are times when you must specify an actual character value. The most common is '\0', which is the character with value zero, also called a *null character*, which you may utilize to initialize char variables. It has some other uses as well, especially when interfacing with C functions and the C standard library.

The final escape sequence (\x) lets you specify a character value in hexadecimal. Typically, you would use two hexadecimal digits, because this is all that fits in the typical, 8-bit char. (The purpose of longer \x escapes is for wide characters, the subject of Exploration 59.)

The next Exploration continues your understanding of characters by examining how C++ classifies characters according to letter, digit, punctuation, and so on.

Character Categories

Exploration 17 introduced and discussed characters. This Exploration continues that discussion with character classification (e.g., uppercase or lowercase, digit or letter), which, as you will see, turns out to be more complicated than you might have expected.

Character Sets

As you learned in Exploration 17, the numeric value of a character, such as `'A'`, depends on the character set. The compiler must decide which character set to use at compile time and at runtime. This is typically based on preferences that the end user selects in the host operating system.

Character-set issues rarely arise for the basic subset of characters—such as letters, digits, and punctuation symbols—that are used to write C++ source code. You will most likely find yourself using one or more character sets that share some common characteristics. For example, all ISO 8859 character sets use the same numeric values for the letters of the Roman alphabet, digits, and basic punctuation. Even most Asian character sets preserve the values of these basic characters.

Thus, most programmers blithely ignore the character-set issue. We use character literals, such as `'%'`, and assume the program will function the way we expect it to, on any system, anywhere in the world—and we are usually right. But not always.

Assuming the basic characters are always available in a portable manner, we can modify the word-counting program to treat only letters as characters that make up a word. The program would no longer count `right` and `right?` as two distinct words. The `string` type offers several member functions that can help us search in strings, extract substrings, and so on.

For example, you can build a string that contains only the letters and any other characters that you want to consider to be part of a word (such as `'-'`). After reading each word from the input stream, make a copy of the word but keep only the characters that are in the string of acceptable characters. Use the `find` member function to try to find each character; `find` returns the zero-based index of the character, if found, or `std::string::npos`, if not found.

Using the find function, rewrite Listing 15-3 to clean up the word string prior to inserting it in the map. Test the program with a variety of input samples. How well does it work? Compare your program with Listing 18-1.

Listing 18-1. Counting Words: Restricting Words to Letters and Letter-Like Characters

```
import <format>;
import <iostream>;
import <map>;
import <string>;
```

© Ray Lischner 2020

R. Lischner, *Exploring C++20*, https://doi.org/10.1007/978-1-4842-5961-0_18

```
int main()
{
  using count_map = std::map<std::string, int>;
  using str_size  = std::string::size_type;

  count_map counts{};
  std::string word{};

  // Characters that are considered to be okay for use in words.
  // Split a long string into parts, and the compiler joins the parts.
    std::string okay{"ABCDEFGHIJKLMNOPQRSTUVWXYZ"
                     "abcdefghijklmnopqrstuvwxyz"
                     "0123456789-_"};

  // Read words from the standard input and count the number of times
  // each word occurs.
  while (std::cin >> word)
  {
    // Make a copy of word, keeping only the characters that appear in okay.
    std::string copy{};
    for (char ch : word)
      if (okay.find(ch) != std::string::npos)
        copy.push_back(ch);
    // The "word" might be all punctuation, so the copy would be empty.
    // Don't count empty strings.
    if (not copy.empty())
      ++counts[copy];
  }

  // Determine the longest word.
  str_size longest{0};
  for (auto pair : counts)
    if (pair.first.size() > longest)
      longest = pair.first.size();

  // For each word/count pair...
  constexpr int count_size{10}; // Number of places for printing the count
  for (auto pair : counts)
    // Print the word, count, newline. Keep the columns neatly aligned.
    std::cout << std::format("{1:{0}}{3:{2}}\n",
        longest, pair.first, count_size, pair.second);
}
```

Some of you may have written a program very similar to mine. Others among you—particularly those living outside the United States—may have written a slightly different program. Perhaps you included other characters in your string of acceptable characters.

For example, if you are French and using Microsoft Windows (and the Windows-1252 character set), you may have defined the okay object as follows:

```
std::string okay{"ABCDEFGHIJKLMNOPQRSTUVWXYZÀÁÄÇÈÉÊËÎÏÔÙÛÜŒŸ"
                 "abcdefghijklmnopqrstuvwxyzàáäçèéêëîïöùûüœÿ"
                 "0123456789-_"};
```

But what if you then try to compile and run this program in a different environment, particularly one that uses the ISO 8859-1 character set (popular on UNIX systems)? ISO 8859-1 and Windows-1252 share many character codes but differ in a few significant ways. In particular, the characters 'Œ', 'œ', and 'Ÿ' are missing from ISO 8859-1. As a result, the program may not compile successfully in an environment that uses ISO 8859-1 for the compile-time character set.

What if you want to share the program with a German user? Surely that user would want to include characters such as 'Ö', 'ö', and 'ß' as letters. What about Greek, Russian, and Japanese users?

We need a better solution. Wouldn't it be nice if C++ provided a simple function that would notify us if a character is a letter, without forcing us to hard-code exactly which characters are letters? Fortunately, it does.

Character Categories

An easier way to write the program in Listing 18-1 is to call the isalnum function (declared in <locale>). This function indicates whether a character is alphanumeric in the runtime character set. The advantage of using isalnum is that you don't have to enumerate all the possible alphanumeric characters; you don't have to worry about differing character sets; and you don't have to worry about accidentally omitting a character from the approved string.

Rewrite Listing 18-1 to call isalnum instead of find. The first argument to std::isalnum is the character to test, and the second is std::locale{""}. (Don't worry yet about what that means. Have patience: I'll get to that soon.)

Try running the program with a variety of alphabetic input, including accented characters. Compare the results with the results from your original program. The files that accompany this book include some samples that use a variety of character sets. Choose the sample that matches your everyday character set and run the program again, redirecting the input to that file.

If you need help with the program, see my version of the program in Listing 18-2. For the sake of brevity, I eliminated the neat-output part of the code, reverting to simple strings and tabs. Feel free to restore the pretty output, if you desire.

Listing 18-2. Testing a Character by Calling std::isalnum

```cpp
import <iostream>;
import <locale>;
import <map>;
import <string>;

int main()
{
  using count_map = std::map<std::string, int>;
  count_map counts{};
  std::string word{};

  // Read words from the standard input and count the number of times
  // each word occurs.
  while (std::cin >> word)
  {
    // Make a copy of word, keeping only alphabetic characters.
    std::string copy{};
    for (char ch : word)
      if (std::isalnum(ch, std::locale{""}))
        copy.push_back(ch);
```

```
  // The "word" might be all punctuation, so the copy would be empty.
  // Don't count empty strings.
  if (not copy.empty())
    ++counts[copy];
}

  // For each word/count pair, print the word & count on one line.
  for (auto pair : counts)
    std::cout << pair.first << '\t' << pair.second << '\n';
}
```

Now turn your attention to the `std::locale{""}` argument. The locale directs `std::isalnum` to the character set it should use to test the character. As you saw in Exploration 17, the character set determines the identity of a character, based on its numeric value. A user can change character sets while a program is running, so the program must keep track of the user's actual character set and not depend on the character set that was active when you compiled the program.

Download the files that accompany this book and find the text files whose names begin with `sample`. **Find the one that best matches the character set you use every day, and select that file as the redirected input to the program.** Look for the appearance of the special characters in the output.

Change `locale{""}` to `locale{}` in the boldface line of Listing 18-2. Now compile and run the program with the same input. **Do you see a difference?** _____ **If so, what is the difference?**

_____

_____

Without knowing more about your environment, I can't tell you what you should expect. If you are using a Unicode character set, you won't see any difference. The program would not treat any of the special characters as letters, even when you can plainly see they are letters. This is due to the way Unicode is implemented, and Exploration 55 will discuss this topic in depth.

Other users will notice that only one or two strings make it to the output. Western Europeans who use ISO 8859-1 may notice that ÁÇÐÈ is considered a word. Greek users of ISO 8859-7 will see ΑΒΓΔΕ as a word.

Power users who know how to change their character sets on the fly can try several different options. You must change the character set that programs use at runtime and the character set that your console uses to display text.

What is most noticeable is that the characters the program considers to be letters vary from one character set to another. But after all, that's the idea of different character sets. The knowledge of which characters are letters in which character sets is embodied in the locale.

Locales

In C++, a *locale* is a collection of information pertaining to a culture, region, and language. The locale includes information about

- Formatting numbers, currency, dates, and time

- Classifying characters (letter, digit, punctuation, etc.)

- Converting characters from uppercase to lowercase and *vice versa*

- Sorting text (e.g., is 'A' less than, equal to, or greater than 'Å'?)

- Message catalogs (for translations of strings that your program uses)

Every C++ program begins with a minimal, standard locale, which is known as the *classic* or "C" locale. The `std::locale::classic()` function returns the classic locale. The unnamed locale, `std::locale{""}`, is the collection of the user's preferences that C++ obtains from the host operating system. The locale with the empty string argument is often known as the *native* locale.

The advantage of the classic locale is that its behavior is known and fixed. If your program must read data in a fixed format, you don't want the user's preferences getting in the way. By contrast, the advantage of the native format is that the user chose those preferences for a reason and wants to see program output follow that format. A user who always specifies a date as day/month/year doesn't want a program printing month/day/year simply because that's the convention in the programmer's home country.

Thus, the classic format is often used for reading and writing data files, and the native format is best used to interpret input from the user and to present output directly to the user.

Every I/O stream has its own `locale` object. To affect the stream's `locale`, call its `imbue` function, passing the `locale` object as the sole argument.

■ **Note** You read that correctly: `imbue`, not `setlocale` or `setloc`—given that the `getloc` function returns a stream's current locale—or anything else that might be easy to remember. On the other hand, `imbue` is such an unusual name for a member function; you may remember it for that reason alone.

In other words, when C++ starts up, it initializes each stream with the classic locale, as follows:

```
std::cin.imbue(std::locale::classic());
std::cout.imbue(std::locale::classic());
```

Suppose you want to change the output stream to adopt the user's native locale. Do this using the following statement at the start of your program:

```
std::cout.imbue(std::locale{""});
```

For example, suppose you have to write a program that reads a list of numbers from the standard input and computes the sum. The numbers are raw data from a scientific instrument, so they are written as digit strings. Therefore, you should continue to use the classic locale to read the input stream. The output is for the user's benefit, so the output should use the native locale.

Write the program and try it with very large numbers, so the output will be greater than 1000. What does the program print as its output? _____

See Listing 18-3 for my approach to solving this problem.

Listing 18-3. Using the Native Locale for Output

```
import <iostream>;
import <locale>;

int main()
{
  std::cout.imbue(std::locale{""});

  int sum{0};
  int x{};
  while (std::cin >> x)
```

```
    sum = sum + x;
  std::cout << "sum = " << sum << '\n';
}
```

When I run the program in Listing 18-3 in my default locale (United States), I get the following result:

```
sum = 1,234,567
```

Notice the commas that separate thousands. In some European countries, you might see this instead:

```
sum = 1.234.567
```

You should obtain a result that conforms to native customs or at least follows the preferences that you set in your host operating system.

When you use the native locale, I recommend defining a variable of type std::locale in which to store it. You can pass this variable to isalnum, imbue, or other functions. By creating this variable and distributing copies of it, your program has to query the operating system for your preferences only once, not every time you need the locale. Thus, the main loop ends up looking something like Listing 18-4.

Listing 18-4. Creating and Sharing a Single Locale Object

```
import <iostream>;
import <locale>;
import <map>;
import <string>;

int main()
{
  using count_map = std::map<std::string, int>;

  std::locale native{""};        // Get the native locale.
  std::cin.imbue(native);        // Interpret the input and output according
  std::cout.imbue(native);       // to the native locale.

  count_map counts{};
  std::string word{};

  // Read words from the standard input and count the number of times
  // each word occurs.
  while (std::cin >> word)
  {
    // Make a copy of word, keeping only alphabetic characters.
    std::string copy{};
    for (char ch : word)
      if (std::isalnum(ch, native))
        copy.push_back(ch);
    // The "word" might be all punctuation, so the copy would be empty.
    // Don't count empty strings.
```

```
   if (not copy.empty())
     ++counts[copy];
  }

  // For each word/count pair, print the word & count on one line.
  for (auto pair : counts)
     std::cout << pair.first << '\t' << pair.second << '\n';
}
```

The next step toward improving the word-counting program is to ignore case differences, so the program does not count the word The as different from the. It turns out this problem is trickier than it first appears, so it deserves an entire Exploration of its own.

■ ■ ■

Case-Folding

Picking up where we left off in Exploration 18, the next step to improving the word-counting program is to update it, so that it ignores case differences when counting. For example, the program should count The just as it does the. This is a classic problem in computer programming. C++ offers some rudimentary help but lacks some important fundamental pieces. This Exploration takes a closer look at this deceptively tricky issue.

Simple Cases

Western European languages have long made use of capital (or majuscule) letters and minuscule letters. The more familiar terms—uppercase and lowercase—arise from the early days of typesetting, when the type slugs for majuscule letters were kept in the upper cases of large racks containing all the slugs used to make a printing plate. Beneath them were the cases, or boxes, that stored the minuscule letter slugs.

In the <locale> header, C++ declares the isupper and islower functions. They take a character as the first argument and a locale as the second argument. The return value is a bool: true if the character is uppercase (or lowercase, respectively) and false if the character is lowercase (or uppercase) or not a letter.

```
std::isupper('A', std::locale{"en_US.latin1"}) == true
std::islower('A', std::locale{"en_US.latin1"}) == false
std::isupper('Æ', std::locale{"en_US.latin1"}) == true
std::islower('Æ', std::locale{"en_US.latin1"}) == false
std::islower('½', std::locale{"en_US.latin1"}) == false
std::isupper('½', std::locale{"en_US.latin1"}) == false
```

The <locale> header also declares two functions to convert case: toupper converts lowercase to uppercase. If its character argument is not a lowercase letter, toupper returns the character as is. Similarly, tolower converts to lowercase, if the character in question is an uppercase letter. Just like the category testing functions, the second argument is a locale object.

Now you can **modify the word-counting program to fold uppercase to lowercase and count all words in lowercase.** Modify your program from Exploration 18, or start with Listing 18-4. If you have difficulty, take a look at Listing 19-1.

Listing 19-1. Folding Uppercase to Lowercase Prior to Counting Words

```
import <iostream>;
import <locale>;
import <map>;
import <string>;
```

© Ray Lischner 2020
R. Lischner, *Exploring C++20*, https://doi.org/10.1007/978-1-4842-5961-0_19

```
int main()
{
  using count_map = std::map<std::string, int>;

  std::locale native{""};      // get the native locale
  std::cin.imbue(native);      // interpret the input and output according to
  std::cout.imbue(native);     // the native locale

  count_map counts{};
  std::string word{};

  // Read words from the standard input and count the number of times
  // each word occurs.
  while (std::cin >> word)
  {
    // Make a copy of word, keeping only alphabetic characters.
    std::string copy{};
    for (char ch : word)
      if (std::isalnum(ch, native))
        copy.push_back(tolower(ch, native));
    // The "word" might be all punctuation, so the copy would be empty.
    // Don't count empty strings.
    if (not copy.empty())
      ++counts[copy];
  }

  // For each word/count pair, print the word & count on one line.
  for (auto pair : counts)
    std::cout << pair.first << '\t' << pair.second << '\n';
}
```

That was easy. So what's the problem?

Harder Cases

Some of you—especially German readers—already know the problem. Several languages have letter combinations that do not map easily between uppercase and lowercase, or one character maps to two characters. The German *Eszett*, ß, is a lowercase letter; when you convert it to uppercase, you get two characters: SS. Thus, if your input file contains "ESSEN" and "eßen", you want them to map to the same word, so they're counted together, but that just isn't feasible with C++. The way the program currently works, it maps "ESSEN" to "essen", which it counts as a different word from "eßen". A naïve solution would be to map "essen" to "eßen", but not all uses of ss are equivalent to ß.

Greek readers are familiar with another kind of problem. Greek has two forms of lowercase sigma: use ς at the end of a word and σ elsewhere. Our simple program maps Σ (uppercase sigma) to σ, so some words in all uppercase will not convert to a form that matches its lowercase version.

Sometimes, accents are lost during conversion. Mapping é to uppercase usually yields É but may also yield E. Mapping uppercase to lowercase has fewer problems, in that É maps to é, but what if that E (which maps to e) really means É, and you want it to map to é? The program has no way of knowing the writer's intentions, so all it can do is map the letters it receives.

Some character sets are more problematic than others. For example, ISO 8859-1 has a lowercase ÿ but not an uppercase equivalent (Ÿ). Windows-1252, on the other hand, extends ISO 8859-1, and one of the new code points is Ÿ.

■ **Tip** *Code point* is a fancy way of saying "numeric value that represents a character." Although most programmers don't use *code point* in everyday speech, those programmers who work closely with character-set issues use it all the time, so you may as well get used to it. Mainstream programmers should become more accustomed to using this phrase.

In other words, converting case is impossible to do correctly using only the standard C++ library.

If you know your alphabet is one that C++ handles correctly, then go ahead and use `toupper` and `tolower`. For example, if you are writing a command-line interpreter, within which you have full control over the commands, and you decide that the user should be able to enter commands in any case, simply make sure the commands map correctly from one case to another. This is easy to do, as all character sets can map the 26 letters of the Roman alphabet without any problems.

On the other hand, if your program accepts input from the user and you want to map that input to uppercase or lowercase, you cannot and must not use standard C++. For example, if you are writing a word processor, and you decide you need to implement some case-folding functions, you must write or acquire a library outside the standard to implement the case-folding logic correctly. Most likely, you would need a library of character and string functions to implement your word processor. Case-folding would simply be one small part of this hypothetical library. (See this book's website for some links to non-hypothetical libraries that can help you.)

What about our simple program? It isn't always practical to handle the full, complete, correct handling of cases and characters when you just want to count a few words. The case-handling code would dwarf the word-counting code.

In this case (pun intended), you must accept the fact that your program will sometimes produce incorrect results. Our poor little program will never recognize that "ESSEN" and "eßen" are the same word but in different cases. You can work around some of the multiple mappings (such as with Greek sigma) by mapping to uppercase, then to lowercase. On the other hand, this can introduce problems with some accented characters. And I still have not touched upon the issue of whether "naïve" is the same word as "naive". In some locales, the diacritics are significant, which would cause "naïve" and "naive" to be interpreted as two different words. In other locales, they are the same word and should be counted together.

In some character sets, accented characters can be composed from separate non-accented characters followed by the desired accent. For example, maybe you can write "naïve", which is the same as "naïve".

I hope by now you are completely scared away from manipulating cases and characters. Far too many naïve programmers become entangled in this web or, worse, simply write bad code. I was tempted to wait until much later in the book before throwing all this at you, but I know that many readers will want to improve the word-counting program by ignoring case, so I decided to tackle the problem early.

Well, now you know better.

That doesn't mean you can't keep working on the word-counting program. The next Exploration returns to the realm of the realistic and feasible, as I finally show you how to write your own functions.

■ ■ ■

Writing Functions

At last, it's time to embark on the journey toward writing your own functions. In this Exploration, you'll begin by improving the word-counting program you've been crafting over the past five Explorations, writing functions to implement separate aspects of the program's functionality.

Functions

You've been using functions since the very first program you wrote. In fact, you've been writing functions too. You see, `main()` is a function, and you should view it the same as you would any other function (well, sort of, `main()` actually has some key differences from ordinary functions, but they needn't concern you yet).

A function has a return type, a name, and parameters in parentheses. Following that is a compound statement, which is the function body. If the function has no parameters, the parentheses are empty. Each parameter is like a variable declaration: type and name. Parameters are separated by commas, so you cannot declare two parameters after a single type name. Instead, you must specify the type explicitly for each parameter.

A function usually has at least one `return` statement, which causes the function to discontinue execution and return control to its caller. A `return` statement's structure begins with the `return` keyword, followed by an expression, and ends with a semicolon, as demonstrated in the following example:

```
return 42;
```

You can use a `return` statement anywhere you need a statement, and you can use as many `return` statements as you need or want. The only requirement is that every execution path through the function must have a `return` statement. Many compilers will warn you if you forget.

Some languages distinguish between functions, which return a value, and procedures or subroutines, which do not. C++ calls them all functions. If a function has no return value, declare the return type as `void`. Omit the value in the `return` statements in a `void` function:

```
return;
```

You can also omit the `return` statement entirely if the function returns `void`. In this circumstance, control returns to the caller when execution reaches the end of the function body. Listing 20-1 presents some function examples.

© Ray Lischner 2020
R. Lischner, *Exploring C++20*, https://doi.org/10.1007/978-1-4842-5961-0_20

Listing 20-1. Examples of Functions

```
import <iostream>;
import <string>;

/** Ignore the rest of the input line. */
void ignore_line()
{
  char c{};
  while (std::cin.get(c) and c != '\n')
    /*empty*/;
}


/** Prompt the user, then read a number, and ignore the rest of the line.
 * @param prompt the prompt string
 * @return the input number or 0 for end-of-file
 */
int prompted_read(std::string prompt)
{
  std::cout << prompt;
  int x{0};
  std::cin >> x;
  ignore_line();
  return x;
}

/** Print the statistics.
 * @param count the number of values
 * @param sum the sum of the values
 */
void print_result(int count, int sum)
{
  if (count == 0)
  {
    std::cout << "no data\n";
    return;
  }

  std::cout << "\ncount = " << count;
  std::cout << "\nsum   = " << sum;
  std::cout << "\nmean  = " << sum/count << '\n';
}

/** Main program.
 * Read integers from the standard input and print statistics about them.
 */
int main()
{
  int sum{0}, count{0};
  while (std::cin)
```

```
{
  if (int x{prompted_read("Value: ")}; std::cin)
  {
    sum = sum + x;
    ++count;
  }
}
print_result(count, sum);
}
```

What does Listing 20-1 do?

_____

_____

The ignore_line function reads and discards characters from std::cin until it reaches the end of the line or the end of the file. It takes no arguments and returns no values to the caller.

The prompted_read function prints a prompt to std::cout, then reads a number from std::cin. It then discards the rest of the input line. Because x is initialized to 0, if the read fails, the function returns 0. The caller cannot distinguish between a failure and a real 0 in the input stream, so the main() function tests std::cin to know when to terminate the loop. (The value 0 is unimportant; feel free to initialize x to any value.) The sole argument to the function is the prompt string. The return type is int, and the return value is the number read from std::cin.

The print_result function takes two arguments, both of type int. It returns nothing; it simply prints the results. Notice how it returns early if the input contains no data.

Finally, the main() function puts it all together, repeatedly calling prompted_read and accumulating the data. Once the input ends, main() prints the results, which, in this example, are the sum, count, and average of the integers it read from the standard input.

Function Call

In a function call, all arguments are evaluated before the function is called. Each argument is copied to the corresponding parameter in the function, then the function body begins to run. When the function executes a return statement, the value in the statement is copied back to the caller, which can then use the value in an expression, assign it to a variable, and so on.

In this book, I try to be careful about terminology: *arguments* are the expressions in a function call, and *parameters* are the variables in a function's header. I've also seen the phrase *actual argument* used for arguments and *formal argument* used for parameters. I find these confusing, so I recommend you stick with the terms *arguments* and *parameters*.

Declarations and Definitions

I wrote the functions in bottom-up fashion because C++ has to know about a function before it can compile any call to that function. The easiest way to achieve this in a simple program is to write every function before you call it—that is, write the function earlier in the source file than the point at which you call the function.

If you prefer, you can code in a top-down manner and write main() first, followed by the functions it calls. The compiler still has to know about the functions before you call them, but you don't have to provide the complete function. Instead, you provide only what the compiler requires: the return type, name, and a comma-separated list of parameters in parentheses. Listing 20-2 shows this new arrangement of the source code.

Listing 20-2. Separating Function Declarations from Definitions

```cpp
import <iostream>;
import <string>;

void ignore_line();
int prompted_read(std::string prompt);
void print_result(int count, int sum);

/** Main program.
 * Read integers from the standard input and print statistics about them.
 */
int main()
{
  int sum{0}, count{0};
  while (std::cin)
  {
    if (int x{ prompted_read("Value: ") }; std::cin)
    {
      sum = sum + x;
      ++count;
    }
  }
  print_result(count, sum);
}

/** Prompt the user, then read a number, and ignore the rest of the line.
 * @param prompt the prompt string
 * @return the input number or -1 for end-of-file
 */
int prompted_read(std::string prompt)
{
  std::cout << prompt;
  int x{-1};
  std::cin >> x;
  ignore_line();
  return x;
}

/** Ignore the rest of the input line. */
void ignore_line()
{
  char c{};
  while (std::cin.get(c) and c != '\n')
    /*empty*/;
}

/** Print the statistics.
 * @param count the number of values
 * @param sum the sum of the values
 */
```

```
void print_result(int count, int sum)
{
  if (count == 0)
  {
    std::cout << "no data\n";
    return;
  }

  std::cout << "\ncount = " << count;
  std::cout << "\nsum   = " << sum;
  std::cout << "\nmean  = " << sum/count << '\n';
}
```

Writing the function in its entirety is known as providing a *definition*. Writing the function header by itself—that is, the return type, name, and parameters, followed by a semicolon—is known as a *declaration*. In general, a declaration tells the compiler how to use a name: what part of a program the name is (typedef, variable, function, etc.), the type of the name, and anything else (such as function parameters) that the compiler requires in order to make sure your program uses that name correctly. The definition provides the body or implementation for a name. A function's declaration must match its definition: the return types, name, and the types of the parameters must be the same. However, the parameter names can differ.

A definition is also a declaration, because the full definition of an entity also tells C++ how to use that entity.

The distinction between declaration and definition is crucial in C++. So far, our simple programs have not needed to face the difference, but that will soon change. Remember: A declaration describes a name to the compiler, and a definition provides all the details the compiler requires for the entity you are defining.

In order to use a variable, such as a function parameter, the compiler needs only the declaration of its name and the type. For a local variable, however, the compiler needs a definition, so that it knows to set aside memory to store the variable. The definition can also provide the variable's initial value. Even without an explicit initial value, the compiler may generate code to initialize the variable, such as ensuring that a string or vector is properly initialized as empty.

Counting Words—Again

Your turn. **Rewrite the word-counting program (last seen in Exploration 19), this time making use of functions.** For example, you can restore the pretty-printing utility by encapsulating it in a single function. Here's a hint: you may want to use the typedef names in multiple functions. If so, declare them before the first function, following the import declarations.

Test the program to ensure that your changes have not altered its behavior.

Compare your program with Listing 20-3.

Listing 20-3. Using Functions to Clarify the Word-Counting Program

```
import <format>;
import <iostream>;
import <locale>;
import <map>;
import <string>;

using count_map  = std::map<std::string, int>; ///< Map words to counts
using count_pair = count_map::value_type;      ///< pair of a word and a count
using str_size   = std::string::size_type;     ///< String size type
```

```
/** Initialize the I/O streams by imbuing them with
 * the given locale. Use this function to imbue the streams
 * with the native locale. C++ initially imbues streams with
 * the classic locale.
 * @param locale the native locale
 */
void initialize_streams(std::locale locale)
{
  std::cin.imbue(locale);
  std::cout.imbue(locale);
}


/** Find the longest key in a map.
 * @param map the map to search
 * @returns the size of the longest key in @p map
 */
str_size get_longest_key(count_map map)
{
  str_size result{0};
  for (auto pair : map)
    if (pair.first.size() > result)
      result = pair.first.size();
  return result;
}


/** Print the word, count, newline. Keep the columns neatly aligned.
 * Rather than the tedious operation of measuring the magnitude of all
 * the counts and then determining the necessary number of columns, just
 * use a sufficiently large value for the counts column.
 * @param iter an iterator that points to the word/count pair
 * @param longest the size of the longest key; pad all keys to this size
 */
void print_pair(count_pair pair, str_size longest)
{
  constexpr int count_size{10}; // Number of places for printing the count
  std::cout << std::format("{1:{0}}{3:{2}}\n",
        longest, pair.first, count_size, pair.second);
}


/** Print the results in neat columns.
 * @param counts the map of all the counts
 */
void print_counts(count_map counts)
{
  str_size longest{get_longest_key(counts)};

  // For each word/count pair...
  for (count_pair pair : counts)
    print_pair(pair, longest);
}
```

```
/** Sanitize a string by keeping only alphabetic characters.
 * @param str the original string
 * @param loc the locale used to test the characters
 * @return a sanitized copy of the string
 */
std::string sanitize(std::string str, std::locale loc)
{
  std::string result{};
  for (char ch : str)
    if (std::isalnum(ch, loc))
      result.push_back(std::tolower(ch, loc));
  return result;
}

/** Main program to count unique words in the standard input. */
int main()
{
  std::locale native{""};              // get the native locale
  initialize_streams(native);

  count_map counts{};

  // Read words from the standard input and count the number of times
  // each word occurs.
  std::string word{};
  while (std::cin >> word)
  {
    std::string copy{ sanitize(word, native) };

    // The "word" might be all punctuation, so the copy would be empty.
    // Don't count empty strings.
    if (not copy.empty())
      ++counts[copy];
  }

  print_counts(counts);
}
```

By using functions, you can read, write, and maintain a program in smaller pieces, handling each piece as a discrete entity. Instead of being overwhelmed by one long main(), you can read, understand, and internalize one function at a time, then move on to the next function. The compiler keeps you honest by ensuring that the function calls match the function declarations, that the function definitions and declarations agree, that you haven't mistyped a name, and that the function return types match the contexts where the functions are called.

The **main()** Function

Now that you know more about functions, you can answer the question that you may have already asked yourself: **What is special about the** main() **function?**

_____

_____

One way that main() differs from ordinary functions is immediately obvious. All the main() functions in this book lack a return statement. An ordinary function that returns an int must have at least one return statement, but main() is special. If you don't supply your own return statement, the compiler inserts a return 0; statement at the end of main(). If control reaches the end of the function body, the effect is the same as return 0;, which returns a success status to the operating system. If you want to signal an error to the operating system, you can return a nonzero value from main(). How the operating system interprets the value depends on the implementation. The only portable values to return are 0, EXIT_SUCCESS, and EXIT_FAILURE. EXIT_SUCCESS means the same thing as 0—namely, success, but its actual value can be different from 0. The names are declared in <cstdlib>.

The next Exploration continues to examine functions by taking a closer look at the arguments in function calls.

EXPLORATION 21

■ ■ ■

Function Arguments

This Exploration continues the examination of functions introduced in Exploration 20, by focusing on argument passing. Take a closer look. Remember that *arguments* are the expressions that you pass to a function in a function call. *Parameters* are the variables that you declare in the function declaration. This Exploration introduces the topic of function arguments, an area of C++ that is surprisingly complex and subtle.

Argument Passing

Read through Listing 21-1, then answer the questions that follow it.

Listing 21-1. Function Arguments and Parameters

```cpp
import <algorithm>;
import <iostream>;
import <iterator>;
import <vector>;

void modify(int x)
{
  x = 10;
}

int triple(int x)
{
  return 3 * x;
}

void print_vector(std::vector<int> v)
{
  std::cout << "{ ";
  std::copy(v.begin(), v.end(), std::ostream_iterator<int>(std::cout, " "));
  std::cout << "}\n";
}
```

© Ray Lischner 2020

R. Lischner, *Exploring C++20*, https://doi.org/10.1007/978-1-4842-5961-0_21

```
void add(std::vector<int> v, int a)
{
  for (auto iter(v.begin()), end(v.end()); iter != end; ++iter)
    *iter = *iter + a;
}

int main()
{
  int a{42};
  modify(a);
  std::cout << "a=" << a << '\n';

  int b{triple(14)};
  std::cout << "b=" << b << '\n';

  std::vector<int> data{ 10, 20, 30, 40 };

  print_vector(data);
  add(data, 42);
  print_vector(data);
}
```

Predict what the program will print.

_____

_____

_____

_____

Now compile and run the program. **What does it actually print?**

_____

_____

_____

_____

Were you correct? _____ **Explain why the program behaves as it does.**

_____

_____

When I run the program, I get the following results:

```
a=42
b=42
{ 10 20 30 40 }
{ 10 20 30 40 }
```

Expanding on these results, you may have noticed the modify function does not actually modify the variable a in main(), and the add function does not modify data. Your compiler might even have issued warnings to that effect.

As you can see, C++ passes arguments *by value*—that is, it copies the argument value to the parameter. The function can do whatever it wants with the parameter, but when the function returns, the parameter goes away, and the caller never sees any changes the function made.

If you want to return a value to the caller, use a return statement, as was done in the triple function.

Rewrite the add function so it returns the modified vector to the caller.

_____

_____

_____

_____

_____

_____

_____

_____

Compare your solution with the following code block:

```cpp
std::vector<int> add(std::vector<int> v, int a)
{
  std::vector<int> result{};
  for (auto i : v)
    result.emplace_back(i + a);
  return result;
}
```

To call the new add, you must assign the function's result to a variable.

```cpp
data = add(data, 42);
```

What is the problem with this new version of add?

_____

_____

Consider what would happen when you call add with a very large vector. The function makes an entirely new copy of its argument, consuming twice as much memory as it really ought to.

Pass-by-Reference

Instead of passing large objects (such as vectors) by value, C++ lets you pass them *by reference*. Add an ampersand (&) after the type name in the function parameter declaration. **Change Listing 21-1 to pass vector parameters by reference.** Also change the modify function, but leave the other int parameters alone. **What do you predict will be the output?**

_____

_____

_____

_____

Now compile and run the program. **What does it actually print?**

_____

_____

_____

_____

Were you correct? _____ **Explain why the program behaves as it does.**

_____

_____

Listing 21-2 shows the new version of the program.

Listing 21-2. Pass Parameters by Reference

```
import <algorithm>;
import <iostream>;
import <iterator>;
import <vector>;

void modify(int& x)
{
  x = 10;
}

int triple(int x)
{
  return 3 * x;
}

void print_vector(std::vector<int>& v)
{
  std::cout << "{ ";
  std::ranges::copy(v, std::ostream_iterator<int>(std::cout, " "));
  std::cout << "}\n";
}
```

```
void add(std::vector<int>& v, int a)
{
  for (auto iter{v.begin()}, end{v.end()}; iter != end; ++iter)
    *iter = *iter + a;
}

int main()
{
  int a{42};
  modify(a);
  std::cout << "a=" << a << '\n';

  int b{triple(14)};
  std::cout << "b=" << b << '\n';

  std::vector<int> data{ 10, 20, 30, 40 };

  print_vector(data);
  add(data, 42);
  print_vector(data);
}
```

When I run the program, I get the following results:

```
a=10
b=42
{ 10 20 30 40 }
{ 52 62 72 82 }
```

This time, the program modified the x parameter in modify and updated the vector's contents in add.

Change the rest of the parameters to use pass-by-reference. What do you expect to happen?

_____

_____

Try it. **What actually happens?**

_____

_____

The compiler does not allow you to call triple(14) when triple's parameter is a reference. Consider what would happen if triple attempted to modify its parameter. You can't assign to a number, only to a variable. Variables and literals fall into different categories of expressions. In general terms, a variable is an _lvalue_, as are references. A literal is called an _rvalue_, and expressions that are built up from operators and function calls usually result in rvalues. When a parameter is a reference, the argument in the function call must be an lvalue. If the parameter is call-by-value, you can pass an rvalue.

Can you pass an lvalue to a call-by-value parameter? _____

You've seen many examples that you can pass an lvalue. C++ automatically converts any lvalue to an rvalue when it needs to. **Can you convert an rvalue to an lvalue?** _____

If you aren't sure, try to think of the problem in more concrete terms: can you convert an integer literal to a variable? That means you cannot convert an rvalue to an lvalue. Except, sometimes you can, as the next section will explain.

const References

In the modified program, the print_vector function takes its parameter by reference, but it doesn't modify the parameter. This opens a window for programming errors: you can accidentally write code to modify the vector. To prevent such errors, you can revert to call-by-value, but you would still have a memory problem if the argument is large. Ideally, you would be able to pass an argument by reference, but still prevent the function from modifying its parameter. Well, as it turns out, such a method does exist. Remember const? C++ lets you declare a function parameter const too.

```
void print_vector(std::vector<int> const& v)
{
  std::cout << "{ ";
  std::ranges::copy(v, std::ostream_iterator<int>(std::cout, " "));
  std::cout << "}\n";
}
```

Read the parameter declaration by starting at the parameter name and working your way from right to left. The parameter name is v; it is a reference; the reference is to a const object; and the object type is std::vector<int>. Sometimes, C++ can be hard to read, especially for a newcomer to the language, but with practice, you will soon read such declarations with ease.

CONST WARS

Many C++ programmers put the const keyword in front of the type, as demonstrated here:

```
void print_vector(const std::vector<int>& v)
```

For simple definitions, the const placement is not critical. For example, to define a named constant, you might use

```
const int max_width{80}; // maximum line width before wrapping
```

The difference between that and

```
int const max_width{80}; // maximum line width before wrapping
```

is small. But with a more complicated declaration, such as the parameter to print_vector, the different style is more significant. I find my technique much easier to read and understand. My rule of thumb is to keep the const keyword as close as possible to whatever it is modifying.

More and more C++ programmers are coming around to adopt the const-near-the-name style instead of const out in front. Again, this is an opportunity for you to be in the vanguard of the most up-to-date C++ programming trends. But you have to get used to reading code with const out in front, because you're going to see a lot of it.

So, v is a reference to a const vector. Because the vector is const, the compiler prevents the print_vector function from modifying it (adding elements, erasing elements, changing elements, and so on). Go ahead and try it. See what happens if you throw in any one of the following lines:

```
v.emplace_back(10); // add an element
v.pop_back();       // remove the last element
v.front() = 42;     // modify an element
```

The compiler stops you from modifying a const parameter.

Standard practice is to use references to pass any large data structure, such as vector, map, or string. If the function has no intention of making changes, declare the reference as a const. For small objects, such as int, use pass-by-value.

If a parameter is a reference to const, you can pass an rvalue as an argument. This is the exception that lets you convert an rvalue to an lvalue. To see how this works, change triple's parameter to be a reference to const.

```
int triple(int const& x)
```

Convince yourself that you can pass an rvalue (such as 14) to triple. Thus, the more precise rule is that you can convert an rvalue to a const lvalue, but not to a non-const lvalue.

const_iterator

One additional trick you have to know when using const parameters: if you need an iterator, use const_iterator instead of iterator. A const variable of type iterator is not very useful, because you cannot modify its value, so the iterator cannot advance. You can still modify the element by assigning to the dereferenced iterator (e.g., *iter). Instead, a const_iterator can be modified and advanced, but when you dereference the iterator, the resulting object is const. Thus, you can read values but not modify them. This means you can safely use a const_iterator to iterate over a const container.

```
void print_vector(std::vector<int> const& v)
{
  std::cout << "{ ";
  std::string separator{};
  for (std::vector<int>::const_iterator i{v.begin()}, end{v.end()}; i != end; ++i)
  {
    std::cout << separator << *i;
    separator = ", ";

  }
  std::cout << "}\n";
}
```

You can print the same results with a range-based for loop, but I wanted to show the use of const_iterator.

String Arguments

Strings present a unique opportunity. It is common practice to pass const strings to functions, but there is an unfortunate mismatch between C++ and its ancestor, C, when it comes to strings.

C lacks a built-in string type. Nor does it have any string type in its standard library. A quoted string literal is equivalent to a char array to which the compiler appends a NUL character ('\0') to denote the end of the string. When a program constructs a C++ std::string from a quoted literal string, the std::string object must copy the contents of the string literal. What this means is that if a function declares a parameter with type std::string const& in order to avoid copying the argument, and the caller passes a string literal, that literal gets copied anyway.

A solution to this problem was added to C++ 17 in the std::string_view class. A string_view does not copy anything. Instead, it is a small, fast way to refer to a std::string or quoted string literal. So you can use std::string_view as a function parameter type as follows:

```
int prompted_read(std::string_view prompt)
{
  std::cout << prompt;
  int x{0};
  std::cin >> x;
  ignore_line();
  return x;
}
```

In Exploration 20, calling prompted_read("Value: ") required constructing a std::string object, copying the string literal into that object, and then passing the object to the function. But the compiler can build and pass a string_view without copying any data. A string_view object is a lightweight read-only view of an existing string. You can usually treat a string_view the same way you would a const std::string. Use string_view whenever you want to pass a read-only string to a function; the function argument can be a quoted string literal, another string_view, or a std::string object. The only caveat to using string_view is that the standard library still has not caught on to string_view and there are many parts of the library that accept only string and not string_view. In this book, when you see strings passed as std::string const& instead of std::string_view, it is because the function must call some standard library function that does not handle string_view arguments.

Multiple Output Parameters

You've already seen how to return a value from a function. And you've seen how a function can modify an argument by declaring the parameter as a reference. You can use reference parameters to "return" multiple values from a function. For example, you may want to write a function that reads a pair of numbers from the standard input, as shown in the following:

```
void read_numbers(int& x, int& y)
{
  std::cin >> x >> y;
}
```

Now that you know how to pass strings, vectors, and whatnot to a function, you can begin to make further improvements to the word-counting program, as you will see in the next Exploration.

■ ■ ■

Using Ranges

As you've seen, performing some operation on a range of data is a common occurrence. So far, our programs have been simple, barely touching the possibilities that C++ offers. The main limitation has been that many of the more interesting algorithms require you to supply a function in order to do anything useful. This Exploration takes a look at these more advanced algorithms. In addition, we'll revisit some of the algorithms you already know and show how they can be used in new and wonderful ways.

Transforming Data

Several programs that you've read and written have a common theme: copying a sequence of data, such as a vector or string, and applying some kind of transformation to each element (converting to lowercase, doubling the values in an array, and so on). The standard algorithm, transform, is ideal for applying an arbitrarily complex transformation to the elements of a range.

For example, recall Listing 10-5, which doubled all the values in an array. Listing 22-1 presents a new way to write this same program, but using transform and range adaptors.

Listing 22-1. Calling transform to Apply a Function to Each Element of a Range

```
import <iostream>;
import <iterator>;
import <ranges>;

int times_two(int i)
{
  return i * 2;
}

int plus_three(int i)
{
  return i + 3;
}

int main()
{
    auto data{ std::ranges::istream_view<int>(std::cin)
             | std::ranges::views::transform(times_two)
             | std::ranges::views::transform(plus_three)
    };
```

© Ray Lischner 2020
R. Lischner, *Exploring C++20*, https://doi.org/10.1007/978-1-4842-5961-0_22

```
    for (auto element : data)
        std::cout << element << '\n';
}
```

Woah! That sure looks different from previous programs. Before diving it, **what do you think happens if you compile and run the program with the following input?**

```
1 2
3
```

I get this as output:

```
5
7
9
```

You've already seen istream_view, so you know that it reads values from an input source, such as the standard input. In this case, the values it reads are integers. It produces a sequence of values known as a range.

In addition to using a ranged for loop, a range can also feed a pipeline, as indicated by the pipe (|) operator. A range can also take a pipeline as input. In this example, transform is a range adaptor. It calls a user-supplied function for each item in the range.

A pipeline starts with a range and contains as many subsequent range adaptors or views as you wish. A range adaptor adapts a range algorithm for use in a pipeline, and the standard library supplies several in the std::ranges::views namespace, which you are free to shorten by using simply std::views.

The transform function has several flavors. This one takes two arguments: the data to transform and the name of a function. Most algorithms are declared in the <algorithm> header with help from the <ranges> header. You will often need both. Even though the data variable seems to hold the entire range, just as it did in Listing 10-5, range adaptors process their data one element at a time instead of storing any data. So the first part of the program sets up the data pipeline. The second part, the for loop, evaluates the pipeline. That's when the input is read, one integer at a time, transformed, and then printed by the loop body.

The final argument to transform is the name of a function that you must have declared or defined earlier in the source file. In this example, the functions each take one int parameter and return an int. The general rule for a transform function is that its parameter type must match the input type, which is the type of the elements in the input range. The return value is of the same or compatible type. The transform algorithm calls this function once for each element in the range and returns the new value.

Rewriting the word-counting program is a little harder. Recall from Listing 20-3 that the sanitize function transforms a string by removing non-letters and converting all uppercase letters to lowercase. The purpose of the C++ standard library is not to provide a zillion functions that cover all possible programming scenarios but, rather, to provide the tools you need to build your own functions with which you can solve your problems. Thus, you would search the standard library in vain for a single algorithm that copies, transforms, and filters. Instead, you can combine two standard functions: one that transforms and one that filters.

A further complication, however, is that you know that the filtering and transforming functions will rely on a locale. Solve the problem for now by setting your chosen locale as the global locale. Do this by calling std::local::global and passing a locale object as the sole argument. An std::locale object created with the default constructor uses the global locale, so after your program sets your chosen locale as the global locale, you can easily imbue a stream or otherwise access the chosen locale by means of std::locale{}. Any function can use the global locale without having to pass locale objects around. Listing 22-2 demonstrates how to rewrite Listing 20-3 to set the global locale to the native locale and then how to use the global locale in the rest of the program.

Listing 22-2. New main Function That Sets the Global Locale

```
import <format>;
import <iostream>;
import <locale>;
import <map>;
import <string>;
import <string_view>;

using count_map  = std::map<std::string, int>;   ///< Map words to counts
using count_pair = count_map::value_type;         ///< pair of a word and a count
using str_size   = std::string::size_type;        ///< String size type

/** Initialize the I/O streams by imbuing them with
 * the global locale. Use this function to imbue the streams
 * with the native locale. C++ initially imbues streams with
 * the classic locale.
 */
void initialize_streams()
{
  std::cin.imbue(std::locale{});
  std::cout.imbue(std::locale{});
}

/** Find the longest key in a map.
 * @param map the map to search
 * @returns the size of the longest key in @p map
 */
str_size get_longest_key(count_map const& map)
{
  str_size result{0};
  for (auto& pair : map)
    if (pair.first.size() > result)
      result = pair.first.size();
  return result;
}

/** Print the word, count, newline. Keep the columns neatly aligned.
 * Rather than the tedious operation of measuring the magnitude of all
 * the counts and then determining the necessary number of columns, just
 * use a sufficiently large value for the counts column.
 * @param pair a word/count pair
 * @param longest the size of the longest key; pad all keys to this size
 */
void print_pair(count_pair const& pair, str_size longest)
{
  int constexpr count_size{10}; // Number of places for printing the count
  std::cout << std::format("{1:{0}}{3:{2}}\n",
          longest, pair.first, count_size, pair.second);
}
```

```
/** Print the results in neat columns.
 * @param counts the map of all the counts
 */
void print_counts(count_map const& counts)
{
  str_size longest{get_longest_key(counts)};

  // For each word/count pair...
  for (count_pair pair: counts)
    print_pair(pair, longest);
}

/** Sanitize a string by keeping only alphabetic characters.
 * @param str the original string
 * @return a sanitized copy of the string
 */
std::string sanitize(std::string_view str)
{
  std::string result{};
  for (char c : str)
    if (std::isalnum(c, std::locale{}))
      result.push_back(std::tolower(c, std::locale{}));
  return result;
}

/** Main program to count unique words in the standard input. */
int main()
{
  // Set the global locale to the native locale.
  std::locale::global(std::locale{""});
  initialize_streams();

  count_map counts{};

  // Read words from the standard input and count the number of times
  // each word occurs.
  std::string word{};
  while (std::cin >> word)
  {
    std::string copy{sanitize(word)};

    // The "word" might be all punctuation, so the copy would be empty.
    // Don't count empty strings.
    if (not copy.empty())
      ++counts[copy];
  }

  print_counts(counts);
}
```

Now it's time to rewrite the sanitize function to take advantage of algorithms. Use transform to convert characters to lowercase. Use filter to keep only alphabetic characters. A string_view is a range of characters so it can feed a range pipeline.

Take a look at Listing 22-3 to see how algorithms work in code.

Listing 22-3. Sanitizing a String by Transforming and Filtering It

```
/** Test whether to keep a letter.
 * @param ch the character to test
 * @return true to keep @p ch because it may be a character that makes up a word
 */
bool keep(char ch)
{
  return std::isalnum(ch, std::locale{});
}

/** Convert to lowercase.
 * @param ch the character to test
 * @return the character converted to lowercase
 */
char lowercase(char ch)
{
  return std::tolower(ch, std::locale{});
}

/** Sanitize a string by keeping only alphabetic characters.
 * @param str the original string
 * @return a sanitized copy of the string
 */
std::string sanitize(std::string_view str)
{
  auto data{ str
             | std::views::filter(keep)
             | std::views::transform(lowercase)  };
  return std::string{ std::ranges::begin(data), std::ranges::end(data) };
}
```

The range pipeline feeds one character at a time from str and filters them so that only characters that we want to keep continue through the pipeline. Those characters are then converted to lowercase. The pipeline is stored in data.

Using a pipeline is a convenience, but in the end the sanitize() function needs to return a real string. So how do you get data from a range pipeline into a string? Fortunately, the range library also has begin() and end() functions that can be used to make a std::string object. Algorithms, even those in the std::ranges namespace, are declared in <algorithm>. Other std::ranges functions are in <ranges>.

Predicates

The keep function is an example of a *predicate*. A predicate is a function that returns a bool result. These functions have many uses in the standard library.

For example, the sort function sorts values in ascending order. What if you wanted to sort data in descending order? The sort function lets you provide a predicate to compare items. The ordering predicate (call it pred) must meet the following qualifications:

- pred(a, a) must be false (a common error is to implement <= instead of <, which violates this requirement).

- If pred(a, b) is true, and pred(b, c) is true, then pred(a, c) must also be true.

- The parameter types must match the element type to be sorted.

- The return type must be bool or something that C++ can convert automatically to bool.

If you don't provide a predicate, sort uses the < operator as the default.

Write a predicate to compare two integers for sorting in descending order.

_____

_____

_____

_____

_____

_____

Write a program to test your function. **Did it work?** _____
Compare your solution with Listing 22-4.

Listing 22-4. Sorting into Descending Order

```cpp
import <algorithm>;
import <iostream>;
import <iterator>;
import <vector>;

/** Predicate for sorting into descending order. */
int descending(int a, int b)
{
  return a > b;
}

int main()
{
  std::vector<int> data{std::istream_iterator<int>(std::cin),
                        std::istream_iterator<int>()};

  std::ranges::sort(data, descending);

  std::ranges::copy(data, std::ostream_iterator<int>(std::cout, "\n"));
}
```

148

Range pipelines are nifty, but sort() needs the entire range to be stored in a container such as std::vector. So you can use istream_view to read the data, but you still need to store the values in a vector. But you cannot make a vector object directly from an istream_view or any other range. Instead, you can initialize a vector from begin and end iterators.

The default comparison that sort uses (the < operator) is the standard for comparison throughout the standard library. The standard library uses < as the ordering function for anything and everything that can be ordered. For example, map uses < to compare keys. The lower_bound functions (which you used in Exploration 13) use the < operator to perform a binary search.

The standard library even uses < to compare objects for equality when dealing with ordered values, such as a map or a binary search. (Algorithms and containers that are not inherently ordered use ≠ to determine when two objects are equal.) To test if two items, a and b, are the same, these library functions use a < b and b < a. If both comparisons are false, then a and b must be the same, or in C++ terms, *equivalent*. If you supply a comparison predicate (pred), the library considers a and b to be equivalent if pred(a, b) is false and pred(b, a) is false.

> **Modify your descending-sort program (or Listing 22-4) to use == as the comparison operator. What do you expect to happen?**
>
> _____
>
> _____
>
> Run the new program with a variety of inputs. **What actually happens?**
>
> _____
>
> _____

Were you correct? _____

The equivalence test is broken, because descending(a,a) is true, not false. Because the predicate does not work properly, sort is not guaranteed to work properly or at all. The results are undefined. It is likely that your program crashed with a memory violation. Whenever you write a predicate, be sure the comparison is strict (i.e., you can write a valid equivalence test) and the transitive property holds (if a < b and b < c, then a < c is also true).

Other Algorithms

The standard library contains too many useful algorithms to cover in this book, but I'll take a few moments in this section to introduce you to at least some of them. Refer to a comprehensive language reference to learn about the other algorithms.

Let's explore algorithms by looking for palindromes. A palindrome is a word or phrase that reads the same forward and backward, ignoring punctuation, for example:

Madam, I'm Adam.

The program reads one line of text at a time by calling the getline function. This function reads from an input stream into a string, stopping when it reads a delimiter character. The default delimiter is '\n', so it reads one line of text. It does not skip over initial or trailing white space.

The first step is to remove non-letter characters, but you already know how to do that.

The next step is to test whether the resulting string is a palindrome. The reverse function transposes the order of elements in a range, such as characters in a string.

The equal function compares two sequences to determine whether they are the same. It takes two sequences as arguments, with an optional predicate that compares elements for equality. In this case, the comparison must be case-insensitive, so provide a predicate that converts all text to a canonical case before comparing them.

Go ahead. **Write the program.** A simple web search should deliver up some juicy palindromes with which to test your program. If you don't have access to the Web, try this:

> Eve
>
> Deed
>
> Hannah
>
> Leon saw I was Noel

If you need some hints, here are my recommendations:

- Write a function called is_palindrome that takes a std::string_view as a parameter and returns a bool.

- This function uses std::views::filter function to keep only the interesting characters.

- Use std::views::reverse to create another pipeline that iterates over the characters in reverse order.

- The std::ranges::equal() function takes two ranges and returns true if they contain the same sequence of characters.

- The main program sets the global locale to the native locale and imbues the input and output streams with the new global locale.

- The main program calls getline(std::cin, line) until the function returns false (meaning error or end-of-file), then calls is_palindrome for each line.

Listing 22-5 shows my version of the completed program.

Listing 22-5. Testing for Palindromes

```
import <algorithm>;
import <iostream>;
import <locale>;
import <ranges>;
import <string>;
import <string_view>;

/** Test for letter.
 * @param ch the character to test
 * @return true if @p ch is a letter
 */
bool letter(char ch)
{
  return std::isalpha(ch, std::locale{});
}
```

```
/** Convert to lowercase.
 * @param ch the character to test
 * @return the character converted to lowercase
 */
char lowercase(char ch)
{
  return std::tolower(ch, std::locale{});
}

/** Determine whether @p str is a palindrome.
 * Only letter characters are tested. Spaces and punctuation don't count.
 * Empty strings are not palindromes because that's just too easy.
 * @param str the string to test
 * @return true if @p str is the same forward and backward
 */
bool is_palindrome(std::string_view str)
{
  auto letters_only{ str | std::views::filter(letter) };
  auto lowercased{ letters_only | std::views::transform(lowercase) };
  auto reversed{ lowercased | std::views::reverse };
  return std::ranges::equal(lowercased, reversed);
}

int main()
{
  std::locale::global(std::locale{""});
  std::cin.imbue(std::locale{});
  std::cout.imbue(std::locale{});

  std::string line{};
  while (std::getline(std::cin, line))
    if (is_palindrome(line))
      std::cout << line << '\n';
}
```

Ranges and range adaptors are a nifty new feature of C++ 20. But as we saw in Listing 22-4, sometimes you need to use plain iterators. It is therefore instructive to see how you would implement the same programs and functions using only iterators, which is how we had to write them with C++ 17. The next Exploration takes you through the same examples, but using only iterators. See which way you prefer.

■ ■ ■

Using Iterators

In the previous Exploration, you got to see how range adaptors and ranged algorithms work. Most ranged algorithms, such as sort(), are likely implemented on top of iterator-based algorithms. Even when working with ranges, you still need to use iterators such as ostream_iterator. And sometimes, iterators are easier to use than ranges, such as initializing a vector. This Exploration visits the iterators and algorithms that offer an alternative to ranges.

Transforming Data

Several programs that you've read and written have a common theme: copying a sequence of data, such as a vector or string, and applying some kind of transformation to each element (converting to lowercase, doubling the values in an array, and so on). The standard algorithm, transform, is ideal for applying an arbitrarily complex transformation to the elements of a sequence.

For example, recall Listing 10-5, which doubled all the values in an array. Listing 23-1 presents a new way to write this same program, but using transform.

Listing 23-1. Calling transform to Apply a Function to Each Element of an Array

```
import <algorithm>;
import <iostream>;
import <iterator>;
import <vector>;

int times_two(int i)
{
  return i * 2;
}

int plus_three(int i)
{
  return i + 3;
}

int main()
{
    std::vector<int> data{std::istream_iterator<int>(std::cin),
                          std::istream_iterator<int>()};
```

```
    std::transform(data.begin(), data.end(), data.begin(), times_two);
    std::transform(data.begin(), data.end(), data.begin(), plus_three);

    std::copy(data.begin(), data.end(),
              std::ostream_iterator<int>(std::cout, "\n"));
}
```

The transform function takes four arguments: the first two specify the input range (as start and one-past-the-end iterators), the third argument is a write iterator, and the final argument is the name of a function. Like other iterator-based algorithms, transform is declared in the <algorithm> header.

Regarding the third argument, as usual, it is your responsibility to ensure the output sequence has enough room to accommodate the transformed data. In this case, the transformed data overwrite the original data, so the start of the output range is the same as the start of the input range. The fourth argument is just the name of a function that you must have declared or defined earlier in the source file. In this example, the function takes one int parameter and returns an int. The general rule for a transform function is that its parameter type must match the input type, which is the type of the element to which the read iterators refer. The return value must match the output type, which is the type to which the result iterator refers. The transform algorithm calls this function once for each element in the input range. It copies to the output range the value returned by the function.

Notice that this version of the program makes an extra pass over the range in order to apply two transformations. The ranged version of the program could perform both transformations in one pass. In order to make a single pass, you need a single function, so you could write one function that multiplies by two and then adds three. In the next Exploration, you will learn a better way to do the same thing.

Rewriting the word-counting program is straightforward. The program is essentially the same as Listing 22-2. The difference is the sanitize() function. Listing 22-3 shows the ranged version. Listing 23-2 shows the iterator version.

Listing 23-2. Sanitizing a String by Transforming and Filtering It

```
/** Test whether to keep a letter.
 * @param ch the character to test
 * @return true to keep @p ch because it may be a character that makes up a word
 */
bool keep(char ch)
{
  return std::isalnum(ch, std::locale{});
}

/** Convert to lowercase.
 * @param ch the character to test
 * @return the character converted to lowercase
 */
char lowercase(char ch)
{
  return std::tolower(ch, std::locale{});
}

/** Sanitize a string by keeping only alphabetic characters.
 * @param str the original string
 * @return a sanitized copy of the string
 */
```

```
std::string sanitize(std::string_view str)
{
  std::string result{};
  std::copy_if(str.begin(), str.end(), std::back_inserter(result), keep);
  std::transform(result.begin(), result.end(), result.begin(), lowercase);
  return result;
}
```

The copy_if function acts as a filter, copying only characters that pass the predicate. Those characters are then added to the result string. But before returning, the result string is transformed in place to lowercase. As you can see, the iterator version of sanitize() is not bad. It is clear and direct, albeit with plenty of repetition and noise that interferes slightly with the clarity. Again, the function makes an additional pass over the data. Avoiding the extra pass using iterators is more difficult than using ranges.

Another way the sanitize() function can work is to pass a std::string instead of a string_view. As noted earlier, this requires making a copy of the string, but the sanitize function is doing that anyway. Let's take a look at how sanitize could work if it is given a string to work with.

Instead of filtering, non-letters must be deleted from the string. Then it can be transformed in place, which we already know how to do. The remove_if() algorithm seems to remove characters that match a predicate, but does it, really?

Figure 23-1 illustrates how remove_if() works with a *before* and *after* view of a string. Notice how the remove_if() function does not alter the size of the string. Instead, it rearranges the string so that it appears to remove characters, and it returns the position that must be the new end of the string. But iterators cannot modify the size of the string, so it is up to the caller to do that. In this respect, working with iterators can be clumsy.

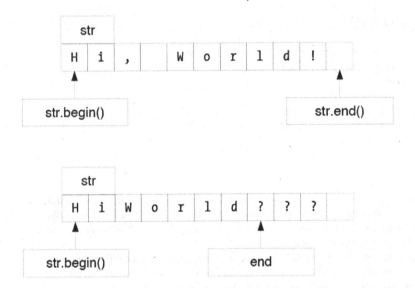

Figure 23-1. *Removing elements from a sequence*

And what about the characters left at the end of the string? They are junk. That is why you must call erase() after remove_if(). Take a look at Listing 23-3 to see how remove_if() works in code.

Listing 23-3. Sanitizing a String by Transforming It

```cpp
/** Test for non-letter.
 * @param ch the character to test
 * @return true if @p ch is not a character that makes up a word
 */
bool non_letter(char ch)
{
  return not std::isalnum(ch, std::locale());
}

/** Convert to lowercase.
 * Use a canonical form by converting to uppercase first,
 * and then to lowercase.
 * @param ch the character to test
 * @return the character converted to lowercase
 */
char lowercase(char ch)
{
  return std::tolower(ch, std::locale());
}

/** Sanitize a string by keeping only alphabetic characters.
 * @param str the original string
 * @return a sanitized copy of the string
 */
std::string sanitize(std::string str)
{
  // Remove all non-letters from the string, and then erase them.
  str.erase(std::remove_if(str.begin(), str.end(), non_letter),
            str.end());

  // Convert the remnants of the string to lowercase.
  std::transform(str.begin(), str.end(), str.begin(), lowercase);

  return str;
}
```

The erase member function takes two iterators as arguments and erases all the elements within that range. The remove_if function returns an iterator that points to one past the end of the new string, which means it also points to the first position of the elements to be erased. Passing str.end() as the end of the range instructs erase to get rid of all the removed elements.

The remove/erase idiom is common in C++, so you should get used to seeing it, at least until everyone starts to use C++ 20 ranges. The standard library has several remove-like functions, all of which work the same way. It takes a little while to get used to this approach, but once you do, you will find it quite easy to use.

Sorting with Iterators

Now that you've seen how iterators work, it should be easy to **modify Listing 22-4 to use iterators instead of ranges**. Compare your solution with Listing 23-4.

Listing 23-4. Sorting into Descending Order

```
import <algorithm>;
import <iostream>;
import <iterator>;
import <vector>;

/** Predicate for sorting into descending order. */
int descending(int a, int b)
{
  return a > b;
}

int main()
{
  std::vector<int> data{ std::istream_iterator<int>(std::cin),
                         std::istream_iterator<int>() };

  std::sort(data.begin(), data.end(), descending);

  std::copy(data.begin(), data.end(), std::ostream_iterator<int>(std::cout, "\n"));
}
```

Expanding a range into a begin/end pair is an easy transformation. What about the palindrome example? How easy is that? **Convert Listing 22-5 to use iterators.**

This is tougher. There is no filtering for iterators. Algorithms such as copy_if must store the copied characters somewhere. Using iterator algorithms requires making a new string. Alternatively, you can skip the algorithms altogether and just use iterators. Listing 23-5 shows my version of is_palindrome() function using a reverse iterator.

Listing 23-5. Testing for Palindromes

```
/** Determine whether @p str is a palindrome.
 * Only letter characters are tested. Spaces and punctuation don't count.
 * @param str the string to test
 * @return true if @p str is the same forward and backward
 */
bool is_palindrome(std::string_view str)
{
  if (str.empty())
    return true;
  for (auto left{str.begin()}, right{str.end() - 1}; left < right;) {
    if (not letter(*left))
      ++left;
    else if (not letter(*right))
      --right;
    else if (lowercase(*left) != lowercase(*right))
```

```
        return false;
    else {
        ++left;
        --right;
    }
  }
  return true;
}
```

By eliminating empty strings immediately, the for loop can initialize right with end() - 1, that is, the position of the actual last character. Each time through the loop, either the left or the right iterator advances until both point to letters. Then the letters are compared, and the iterators are moved. If the string has an even number of letters, the iterators might pass each other, but as long as they point to valid positions in the string, the < operator is safe to use.

In a large program, the predicate or transformation function might be declared far from where it is used. Often, a predicate is used only once. By defining a function just for that predicate, it makes your program harder to understand. The human reader must read all the code to ensure that the predicate truly is called in only one place. It would be nice if C++ offered a way to write the predicate in the place where it is used and thereby avoid these problems. Read the next Exploration to learn how to achieve this in C++ 20.

■ ■ ■

Unnamed Functions

One problem with calling algorithms is that sometimes the predicate or transformation function must be declared far from the place where it is called. With a properly descriptive name, this problem can be reduced, but often the function is trivial, and your program would be much easier to read if you could put its functionality directly in the call to the standard algorithm. A feature introduced in C++ 11 and expanded in subsequent standards permits exactly that.

Lambdas

C++ 20 lets you define a function as an expression. You can pass this function to an algorithm, save it in a variable, or call it immediately. Such a function is called a *lambda*, for reasons that only a computer scientist would understand or even care about. If you aren't a computer scientist, don't worry, and just realize that when the nerds talk about lambdas, they are just talking about unnamed functions. As a quick introduction, Listing 24-1 rewrites Listing 22-1 to use lambdas.

Listing 24-1. Calling `transform` to Apply a Lambda to Each Element of an Array

```
import <iostream>;
import <iterator>;
import <ranges>;

int main()
{
   auto data{ std::ranges::istream_view<int>(std::cin)
            | std::views::transform([](int i) { return i * 2; })
            | std::views::transform([](int i) { return i + 3; })
   };
   for (auto element : data)
      std::cout << element << '\n';
}
```

The lambda almost looks like a function definition. Instead of a function name, a lambda begins with square brackets. The usual function arguments and compound statement follow. **What's missing?** _____

_____

That's right, the function's return type. The compiler tries to deduce the function's type from the type of the return expression. In this case, the return type is `int`.

With a lambda, the program is slightly shorter and much easier to read. You don't have to hunt for the definition of times_two() to learn what it does. (Not all functions are named so clearly.) But lambdas are even more powerful and can do things that ordinary functions can't. Take a look at Listing 24-2 to see what I mean.

Listing 24-2. Using a Lambda to Access Local Variables

```
import <algorithm>;
import <iostream>;
import <iterator>;
import <ranges>;
import <vector>;

int main()
{
    std::cout << "Multiplier: ";
    int multiplier{};
    std::cin >> multiplier;

    auto data{
        std::ranges::istream_view<int>(std::cin)
        | std::views::transform([multiplier](int i) { return i * multiplier; })
    };

    std::cout << "Data:\n";
    std::ranges::copy(data, std::ostream_iterator<int>(std::cout, "\n"));
}
```

Predict the output if the program's input is as follows:

4 1 2 3 4 5

_____

_____

_____

_____

The first number is the multiplier, and the remaining numbers are multiplied by it, yielding

4
8
12
16
20

See the trick? The lambda is able to read the local variable, multiplier. A separate function, such as times_two() in Listing 22-1, can't do that. Of course, you can pass two arguments to times_two(), but this use of the transform algorithm calls the function with only one argument. There are ways to work around this limitation, but I won't bother showing them to you, because lambdas solve the problem simply and elegantly.

Naming an Unnamed Function

Although a lambda is an unnamed function, you can give it a name by assigning the lambda to a variable. This is a case where you probably want to declare the variable using the auto keyword, so you don't have to think about the type of the lambda that is the variable's initial value:

```
auto times_three = [](int i) { return i * 3; };
```

Once you assign a lambda to a variable, you can call that variable as though it were an ordinary function:

```
int forty_two{ times_three(14) };
```

The advantage of naming a lambda is that you can call it more than once in the same function. In this way, you get the benefit of self-documenting code with a well-chosen name and the benefit of a local definition.

If you don't want to use auto, the standard library can help. In the <functional> header is the type std::function, which you use by placing a function's return type and parameter types in angle brackets, for example, std::function<int(int)>. For example, the following defines a variable, times_two, and initializes it with a lambda that takes one argument of type int and returns int:

```
std::function<int(int)> times_two{ [](int i) { return i * 2; } };
```

The actual type of a lambda is more complicated, but the compiler knows how to convert that type to the matching std::function<> type. Using auto is preferred because calling a std::function incurs a small cost that an auto lambda does not.

Capturing Local Variables

Naming a local variable in the lambda's square brackets is called *capturing* the variable's value. If you do not capture a variable, you cannot use it in the lambda, so the lambda would be able to use only its function parameters.

Read the program in Listing 24-3. Think about how it captures the local variable multiplier.

Listing 24-3. Using a Lambda to Access Local Variables

```
import <algorithm>;
import <iostream>;
import <ranges>;
import <vector>;

int main()
{
    std::vector<int> data{ 1, 2, 3 };

    int multiplier{3};
    auto times = [multiplier](int i) { return i * multiplier; };

    std::ranges::transform(data, data.begin(), times);
```

```
    multiplier = 20;
    std::ranges::transform(data, data.begin(), times);

    std::ranges::copy(data, std::ostream_iterator<int>(std::cout, "\n"));
}
```

Listing 24-3 calls yet another flavor of transform(). Like the iterator version, it has an input and an output, but the input is a range and the output is an iterator. In this case, the transformed values overwrite data, transforming it in place. The behavior is the same as std::views::transform, calling its function arguments for every element of the range and writing that element to the output iterator. **Predict the output from Listing 24-3.**

_____

_____

_____

_____

_____

Now run the program. Was your prediction correct? _____ **Why or why not?**

_____

_____

The value of multiplier was captured by value when the lambda was defined. Thus, changing the value of multiplier later does not change the lambda, and it still multiplies by three. The transform() algorithm is called twice, so the effect is to multiply by 9, not 60.

If you need your lambda to keep track of the local variable and always use its most recent value, you can capture a variable by reference by prefacing its name with an ampersand (similar to a reference function parameter), as in the following example:

```
[&multiplier](int i) { return i * multiplier; };
```

Modify Listing 24-3 to capture multiplier by reference. Run the program to observe its new behavior.

You can choose to omit the capture name to capture all local variables. Use an equal sign to capture everything by value or just an ampersand to capture everything by reference.

```
int x{0}, y{1}, z{2};
auto capture_all_by_value = [=]() { return x + y + z; };
auto capture_all_by_reference = [&]() { x = y = z = 0; };
```

I advise against capturing everything by default, because it leads to sloppy code. Be explicit about the variables that the lambda captures. The list of captures should be short, or else you are probably doing something wrong. Nonetheless, you will likely see other programmers capture everything, if only out of laziness, so I had to show you the syntax.

If you follow best practices and list individual capture names, the default is capture-by-value, so you must supply an ampersand for each name that you want to capture by reference. Feel free to mix capture-by-value and capture-by-reference.

```
auto lambda =
   [by_value, &by_reference, another_by_value, &another_by_reference]() {
      by_reference = by_value;
      another_by_reference = another_by_value;
   };
```

const Capture

Capture-by-value has one trick up its sleeve that can take you by surprise. Consider the simple program in Listing 24-4.

Listing 24-4. Using a Lambda to Access Local Variables

```
import <iostream>;

int main()
{
   int x{0};
   auto lambda = [x](int y) {
      x = 1;
      y = 2;
      return x + y;
   };
   int local{0};
   std::cout << lambda(local) << ", " << x << ", " << local << '\n';

}
```

What do you expect to happen when you run this program?

_____

What is the surprise?

_____

You already know that function parameters are call-by-value, so the y = 2 assignment has no effect outside of the lambda, and local remains 0. A by-value capture is similar in that you cannot change the local variable that is captured (x in Listing 24-4). But the compiler is even pickier than that. It doesn't let you write the assignment x = 1. It's as though every by-value capture were declared const.

Lambdas are different from ordinary functions in that default for by-value captures is const, and to get a non-const capture, you must explicitly tell the compiler. The keyword to use is mutable, which you put after the function parameters, as shown in Listing 24-5.

Listing 24-5. Using the mutable Keyword in a Lambda

```
import <iostream>;

int main()
{
   int x{0};
   auto lambda = [x](int y) mutable {
```

163

```
        x = 1;
        y = 2;
        return x + y;
    };
    int local{0};
    std::cout << lambda(local) << ", " << x << ", " << local << '\n';
}
```

Now the compiler lets you assign to the capture, x. The capture is still by-value, so x in main() doesn't change. The output of the program is

```
3, 0, 0
```

So far, I have never found an instance when I wanted to use mutable. It's there if you need it, but you will probably never need it.

Return Type

The return type of a lambda is the type of the return expression, if the lambda body contains only a return statement. But what if the lambda is more complicated and the compiler cannot determine the return type? The syntax for a lambda does not lend itself to declaring a function return type in the usual way. Instead, the return type follows the function parameter list, with an arrow (->) between the closing parenthesis and the return type:

```
[](int i) -> int { return i * 2; }
```

In general, the lambda is easier to read without the explicit return type. The return type is usually obvious, but if it is not, go ahead and be explicit. Clarity trumps brevity.

Rewrite Listing 22-5 to take advantage of lambdas. Write functions where you think functions are appropriate, and write lambdas where you think lambdas are appropriate. Compare your solution with mine in Listing 24-6.

Listing 24-6. Testing for Palindromes

```
import <algorithm>;
import <iostream>;
import <locale>;
import <ranges>;
import <string>;
import <string_view>;

/** Determine whether @p str is a palindrome.
 * Only letter characters are tested. Spaces and punctuation don't count.
 * Empty strings are not palindromes because that's just too easy.
 * @param str the string to test
 * @return true if @p str is the same forward and backward
 */
```

```
bool is_palindrome(std::string_view str)
{
  auto letters_only{ str
     | std::views::filter([](char c) { return std::isalnum(c, std::locale{}); })
     | std::views::transform([](char c) { return std::tolower(c, std::locale{}); })
  };
  auto reversed{ letters_only | std::views::reverse };
  return std::ranges::equal(letters_only, reversed);
}

int main()
{
  std::locale::global(std::locale{""});
  std::cin.imbue(std::locale{});
  std::cout.imbue(std::locale{});

  std::string line{};
  while (std::getline(std::cin, line))
    if (is_palindrome(line))
      std::cout << line << '\n';
}
```

By now, you may have grown accustomed to seeing the same function in multiple forms, such as sort() with or without an explicit predicate. Using one name for more than one function is called *overloading*. This is the subject of the next Exploration.

■ ■ ■

Overloading Function Names

In C++, multiple functions can have the same name, provided the functions have a different number of arguments or different argument types. Using the same name for multiple functions is called *overloading* and is common in C++.

Overloading

All programming languages use overloading at one level or another. For example, most languages use + for integer addition as well as for floating-point addition. Some languages, such as Pascal, use different operators for integer division (`div`) and floating-point division (`/`), but others, such as C and Java, use the same operator (`/`).

C++ takes overloading one step further, letting you overload your own function names. Judicious use of overloading can greatly reduce complexity in a program and make your programs easier to read and understand.

For example, C++ inherits several functions from the standard C library that compute an absolute value: `abs` takes an `int` argument; `fabs` takes a floating-point argument; and `labs` takes a long integer argument.

■ **Note** Don't be concerned that I have not yet covered these other types. All that matters for the purpose of this discussion is that they are distinct from `int`. The next Exploration will begin to examine them more closely, so please be patient.

C++ also has its own `complex` type for complex numbers, which has its own absolute value function. In C++, however, they all have the same name, `std::abs`. Using different names for different types merely clutters the mental landscape and contributes nothing to the clarity of the code.

The `sort` function, just to name one example, has two overloaded forms:

```
std::sort(start, end);
std::sort(start, end, compare);
```

(The `std::ranges::sort` function is distinct due to the use of `ranges`, which will be explained in Exploration 47.) The first form sorts in ascending order, comparing elements with the `<` operator, and the second form compares elements by calling `compare`. Overloading appears in many other places in the standard library. For example, when you create a `locale` object, you can copy the global locale by passing no arguments

```
std::isalpha('X', std::locale{});
```

© Ray Lischner 2020
R. Lischner, *Exploring C++20*, https://doi.org/10.1007/978-1-4842-5961-0_25

or create a native locale object by passing an empty string argument.

```
std::isalpha('X', std::locale{""});
```

Overloading functions is easy, so why not jump in? **Write a set of functions, all named print.** They all have a void return type and take various parameters:

- One takes an int as a parameter. It prints the parameter to the standard output.

- Another takes two int parameters. It prints the first parameter to the standard output and uses the second parameter as the field width.

- Another takes a vector<int> as the first parameter, followed by three string_view parameters. Print the first string_view parameter, then each element of the vector (by calling print), with the second string_view parameter between elements, and the third string_view parameter after the vector. If the vector is empty, print the first and third string_view parameters only.

- Another has the same parameters as the vector form, but also takes an int as the field width for each vector element.

Write a program to print vectors using the print functions. Compare your functions and program with mine in Listing 25-1.

Listing 25-1. Printing Vectors by Using Overloaded Functions

```
import <iostream>;
import <string_view>;
import <vector>;

void print(int i)
{
  std::cout << i;
}

void print(int i, int width)
{
  std::cout.width(width);
  std::cout << i;
}

void print(std::vector<int> const& vec,
    int width,
    std::string_view prefix,
    std::string_view separator,
    std::string_view postfix)
{
  std::cout << prefix;

  bool print_separator{false};
  for (auto x : vec)
  {
    if (print_separator)
      std::cout << separator;
```

```
    else
      print_separator = true;
    print(x, width);
  }

  std::cout << postfix;
}

void print(std::vector<int> const& vec,
    std::string_view prefix,
    std::string_view separator,
    std::string_view postfix)
{
  print(vec, 0, prefix, separator, postfix);
}

int main()
{
  std::vector<int> data{ 10, 20, 30, 40, 100, 1000, };

  std::cout << "columnar data:\n";
  print(data, 10, "", "\n", "\n");
  std::cout << "row data:\n";
  print(data, "{", ", ", "}\n");
}
```

The C++ library often uses overloading. For example, you can change the size of a vector by calling its resize member function. You can pass one or two arguments: the first argument is the new size of the vector. If you pass a second argument, it is a value to use for new elements, in case the new size is larger than the old size.

```
data.resize(10);     // if the old size < 10, use default of 0 for new elements
data.resize(20, -42); // if the old size < 20, use -42 for new elements
```

Library writers often employ overloading, but application programmers use it less often. **Practice writing libraries by writing the following functions:**

bool is_alpha(char ch)

Returns true if ch is an alphabetic character in the global locale; if not, returns false.

bool is_alpha(std::string_view str)

Returns true if str contains only alphabetic characters in the global locale or false if any character is not alphabetic. Returns true if str is empty.

char to_lower(char ch)

Returns ch after converting it to lowercase, if possible; otherwise, returns ch. Use the global locale.

std::string to_lower(std::string_view str)

Returns a copy of str after converting its contents to lowercase, one character at a time. Copies verbatim any character that cannot be converted to lowercase.

char to_upper(char ch)

Returns ch after converting it to uppercase, if possible; otherwise, returns ch. Use the global locale.

std::string to_upper(std::string_view str)

Returns a copy of str after converting its contents to uppercase, one character at a time. Copies verbatim any character that cannot be converted to uppercase.

Compare your solution with mine, which is shown in Listing 25-2.

Listing 25-2. Overloading Functions in the Manner of a Library Writer

```
import <algorithm>;
import <iostream>;
import <locale>;
import <ranges>;
import <string>;
import <string_view>;

bool is_alpha(char ch)
{
  return std::isalpha(ch, std::locale{});
}

bool is_alpha(std::string_view str)
{
  return std::ranges::all_of(str, [](char c) { return is_alpha(c); });
}

char to_lower(char ch)
{
  return std::tolower(ch, std::locale{});
}

std::string to_lower(std::string_view str)
{
  auto data{str | std::views::transform([](char c) { return to_lower(c); })};
  return std::string{ std::ranges::begin(data), std::ranges::end(data) };
}

char to_upper(char ch)
{
  return std::toupper(ch, std::locale{});
}
```

```
std::string to_upper(std::string str)
{
  for (char& ch : str)
    ch = to_upper(ch);
  return str;
}

int main()
{
  std::string str{};
  while (std::cin >> str)
  {
    if (is_alpha(str))
      std::cout << "alpha\n";
    else
      std::cout << "not alpha\n";
    std::cout << "lower: " << to_lower(str) << "\n"
                 "upper: " << to_upper(str) << '\n';
  }
}
```

I implemented to_lower by calling the std::ranges::all_of algorithm, which calls a predicate for every element of a range and returns true if the predicate returns true for all elements. If the predicate returns false, then all_of stops iterating the range and immediately returns false.

For the sake of variety, I implemented to_upper completely differently. I used a ranged for loop with a twist. This loop actually modifies the character element while the loop iterates the string. Like a pass-by-reference function parameter, the declaration char& ch is a reference to a character in the range. Thus, assigning to ch changes the character in the string. Note that auto can also declare a reference. If each element of the range is large, you should use references to avoid making unnecessary copies. Use a const reference if you do not have to modify the element, as follows:

```
for (auto const& big_item : container_full_of_big_things)
```

The other difference is that to_upper takes a plain string as its parameter. This means the argument is passed by value, which in turn means the compiler arranges to copy the string when passing the argument to the function. The function requires the copy, so this technique helps the compiler generate optimal code for copying the argument, and it saves you a step in writing the function. It's a small trick, but a useful one. This technique will be especially useful later in the book—so don't forget it.

The is_alpha string function does not modify its parameter, so it can use the string_view type.

A common use of overloading is to overload a function for different types, including different integer types, such as a long integer. The next Exploration takes a look at these other types.

■ ■ ■

Big and Little Numbers

Another common use for overloading is to write functions that work just as well with large and small integers as with plain integers. C++ has five different integer types, ranging in size from 8 bits to 64 bits or larger, with several choices for sizes in between. This Exploration takes a look at the details.

The Long and Short of It

The size of an int is the natural size of an integer on the host platform. For your desktop computer, that probably means 32 bits or 64 bits. Not too long ago, it meant 16 bits or 32 bits. I've also used computers with 36-bit and 60-bit integers. In the realm of desktop computers and workstations, 32-bit and 64-bit processors dominate today's computing landscape, but don't forget specialized devices, such as digital signal processors (DSPs) and other embedded chips, where 16-bit architectures are still common. The purpose of leaving the standard flexible is to ensure maximum performance for your code. The C++ standard guarantees that an int can represent, at a minimum, any number in the range –32,768 to 32,767, inclusive, that is, the minimum size of int is 16 bits.

The computer you use for exercises probably implements int with a larger size than 16 bits. To discover the number of bits in an integer, use std::numeric_limits, as you did way back in Listing 2-3. **Try that same program, but substitute int for** bool. **What do you get for the output?** _____

Most likely, you got 31, although some of you may have seen 15 or 63. The reason for this is that digits does not count the sign bit. Signed integers use a representation called two's complement, which sets the most significant bit to 1 if the number is negative. Thus, for a type that represents a signed quantity, such as int, you must add one to digits, and for a type with no sign, such as bool, use digits without further modification. Fortunately, std::numeric_limits offers is_signed, which is true for a signed type and false for a type without a sign bit. **Rewrite Listing 2-3 to use is_signed to determine whether to add one to digits and print the number of bits per int and per** bool.

Check your answers. **Are they correct?** _____ Compare your program with Listing 26-1.

Listing 26-1. Discovering the Number of Bits in an Integer

```
import <iostream>;
import <limits>;

int main()
{
  std::cout << "bits per int = ";
  if (std::numeric_limits<int>::is_signed)
    std::cout << std::numeric_limits<int>::digits + 1 << '\n';
  else
    std::cout << std::numeric_limits<int>::digits << '\n';
```

© Ray Lischner 2020
R. Lischner, *Exploring C++20*, https://doi.org/10.1007/978-1-4842-5961-0_26

```
std::cout << "bits per bool = ";
if (std::numeric_limits<bool>::is_signed)
  std::cout << std::numeric_limits<bool>::digits + 1 << '\n';
else
  std::cout << std::numeric_limits<bool>::digits << '\n';
}
```

Long Integers

Sometimes, you need more bits than int can handle. In this case, add long to the definition to get a long integer.

```
long int lots_o_bits{2147483647};
```

You can even drop the int, as shown here:

```
long lots_o_bits{2147483647};
```

The standard guarantees that a long int can handle 32-bit numbers, that is, values in the range –2,147,483,648 to 2,147,483,647, but an implementation can choose a larger size. C++ does not guarantee that a long int is actually longer than a plain int. On some platforms, int might be 32 bits and long might be 64. When I first used a PC at home, an int was 16 bits and long was 32 bits. At times, I've used systems for which int and long were both 32 bits. I'm writing this book on a machine that uses 32 bits for int and 64 bits for long.

The type long long int can be even bigger (64 bits), with a range of at least –9,223,372,036,854,775,808 to 9,223,372,036,854,775,807. You can drop the int, if you wish, and programmers often do.

Use long long if you want to store numbers as large as possible and are willing to pay a small performance penalty (on some systems, or a large penalty on others). Use long if you have to ensure portability and must represent numbers larger than 16 bits.

Short Integers

Sometimes, you don't have the full range of an int, and reducing memory consumption is more important. In this case, use a short int, or just short, which has a guaranteed range of at least –32,768 to 32,767, inclusive. This is the same guaranteed range as int, but implementations often choose to make an int larger than the minimum and keep short in this range of 16 bits. But you must not assume that int is always larger than short. Both may be the exact same size.

As is done with long, you define a type as short int or short.

```
short int answer{42};
short zero{0};
```

Modify Listing 26-1 to print the number of bits in a long and a short too. How many bits are in a long on your system? _____ How many in a short? _____ long long? _____
When I run the program in Listing 26-2, I get 16 bits in a short, 32 in an int, and 64 in a long and long long. On another computer in my network, I get 16 bits in a short, 32 in an int and long, and 64 in a long long.

Listing 26-2. Revealing the Number of Bits in Short and Long Integers

```
import <iostream>;
import <limits>;

int main()
{
  std::cout << "bits per int = ";
  if (std::numeric_limits<int>::is_signed)
    std::cout << std::numeric_limits<int>::digits + 1 << '\n';
  else
    std::cout << std::numeric_limits<int>::digits << '\n';

  std::cout << "bits per bool = ";
  if (std::numeric_limits<bool>::is_signed)
    std::cout << std::numeric_limits<bool>::digits + 1 << '\n';
  else
    std::cout << std::numeric_limits<bool>::digits << '\n';

  std::cout << "bits per short int = ";
  if (std::numeric_limits<short>::is_signed)
    std::cout << std::numeric_limits<short>::digits + 1 << '\n';
  else
    std::cout << std::numeric_limits<short>::digits << '\n';

  std::cout << "bits per long int = ";
  if (std::numeric_limits<long>::is_signed)
    std::cout << std::numeric_limits<long>::digits + 1 << '\n';
  else
    std::cout << std::numeric_limits<long>::digits << '\n';

  std::cout << "bits per long long int = ";
  if (std::numeric_limits<long long>::is_signed)
    std::cout << std::numeric_limits<long long>::digits + 1 << '\n';
  else
    std::cout << std::numeric_limits<long long>::digits << '\n';
}
```

Integer Literals

When you write an integer literal (i.e., an integer constant), the type depends on its value. If the value fits in an int, the type is int; otherwise, the type is long or long long. You can force a literal to have type long by adding l or L (the letter *L* in lowercase or uppercase) after the digits. (Curiously, C++ has no way for you to type a short literal.) I always use uppercase L because a lowercase l looks too much like the digit 1. The compiler can always tell the difference, but every year it gets a little harder for me to see the difference between 1 and l. Use two consecutive Ls for a long long.

   Devise a way for a program to print int=, followed by the value, for an int literal; print long=, followed by the value, for a long literal; and print long long=, followed by the value, for a long long **literal.** (Hint: What was the topic of the previous Exploration?) Write a program to demonstrate your idea, and test it with some literals. If you can, run the program on platforms that use different sizes for int and long. Compare your program to that of Listing 26-3.

Listing 26-3. Using Overloading to Distinguish Types of Integer Literals

```cpp
import <iostream>;
import <locale>;

void print(int value)
{
  std::cout << "int=" << value << '\n';
}

void print(long value)
{
  std::cout << "long=" << value << '\n';
}

void print(unsigned long value)
{
  std::cout << "unsigned long=" << value << '\n';
}

void print(long long value)
{
  std::cout << "long long=" << value << '\n';
}

int main()
{
  std::cout.imbue(std::locale{""});
  print(0);
  print(0L);
  print(32768);
  print(-32768);
  print(2147483647);
  print(-2147483647);
  print(2147483648);
  print(9223372036854775807);
  print(-9223372036854775807);
}
```

I threw in the type unsigned long because some compilers require it. An unsigned integral type is never negative and occupies the same number of bits as its normal (or signed) equivalent. Thus, it can hold a value that is roughly twice as large as the maximum signed value. Your compiler might treat 2147483648 as an unsigned long because it is too large for plain long. Or your compiler might consider it to be a small value for a long long. Exploration 67 will have much more to say about unsigned. The actual types that your compiler chooses will vary. Your compiler may even be able to handle larger integer literals. The C++ standard sets down some guaranteed ranges for each of the integer types, so all the values in Listing 26-3 will work with a decent C++ compiler. If you stick to the guaranteed ranges, your program will compile and run everywhere; outside the range, you're taking your chances. Library writers have to be especially careful. You never know when someone working on a small, embedded processor might like your code and want to use it.

Byte-Sized Integers

The smallest integer type that C++ offers is signed char. The type name looks similar to the character type, char, but the type acts differently. It usually acts like an integer. By definition, the size of signed char is 1 byte, which is the smallest size that your C++ compiler supports for any type. The guaranteed range of signed char is –128 to 127.

In spite of the name, you should try not to think of signed char as a mutated character type; instead, think of it as a misspelled integer type. Many programs have a type declaration similar to

```
using byte = signed char;
```

to make it easier for you to think of this type as a byte-sized integer type. C++ defines its own std::byte type, but that type is for uninterpreted data, not a small integer.

There is no easy way to write a signed char literal, just as there is no way to write a simple short literal. Character literals have type char, not signed char. Besides, some characters may be out of range for signed char.

Although the compiler does its best to help you remember that signed char is not a char, the standard library is less helpful. The I/O stream types treat signed char values as characters. Somehow, you have to inform the stream that you want to print an integer, not a character. You also need a solution to create signed char (and short) literals. Fortunately, the same solution lets you use signed char constants and print signed char numbers: type casting.

Type Casting

Although you cannot write a short or arbitrary signed char literal directly, you can write a constant expression that has type short or signed char and take any suitable value. The trick is to use a plain int and tell the compiler exactly what type you want.

```
static_cast<signed char>(-1)
static_cast<short int>(42)
```

The expression does not have to be a literal, as demonstrated here:

```
int x{42};
static_cast<short>(x);
```

The static_cast expression is known as a *type cast*. The operator static_cast is a reserved keyword. It converts an expression from one type to another. The "static" in its name means the type is static, or fixed, at compile time.

You can convert any integer type to any other integer type. If the value is out of range for the target type, you get junk as a result. For example, the high-order bits may be discarded. Thus, you should always be careful when using static_cast. Be absolutely sure that you are not discarding important information.

If you cast a number to bool, the result is false if the number is zero or true if the number is not zero (just like the conversion that takes place when you use an integer as a condition).

Rewrite Listing 26-3 to overload print for short and signed char values too. Use type casting to force various values to different types and ensure that the results match your expectations. Take a look at Listing 26-4 to see one possible solution.

Listing 26-4. Using Type Casts

```
import <iostream>;
import <locale>;

using byte = signed char;

void print(byte value)
{
  // The << operator treats signed char as a mutant char, and tries to
  // print a character. In order to print the value as an integer, you
  // must cast it to an integer type.
  std::cout << "byte=" << static_cast<int>(value) << '\n';
}

void print(short value)
{
  std::cout << "short=" << value << '\n';
}

void print(int value)
{
  std::cout << "int=" << value << '\n';
}

void print(long value)
{
  std::cout << "long=" << value << '\n';
}

void print(unsigned long value)
{
  std::cout << "unsigned long=" << value << '\n';
}

void print(long long value)
{
  std::cout << "long long=" << value << '\n';
}

int main()
{
  std::cout.imbue(std::locale{""});
  print(0);
  print(0L);
  print(static_cast<short>(0));
  print(static_cast<byte>(0));
  print(static_cast<byte>(255));
  print(static_cast<short>(65535));
  print(32768);
  print(32768L);
  print(-32768);
```

```
print(2147483647);
print(-2147483647);
print(2147483648);
print(9223372036854775807);
print(-9223372036854775807);
}
```

When I run Listing 25-4, I get -1 for static_cast<short>(65535) and static_cast<byte>(255). That's because the values are out of range for the target types. The bit pattern for the largest integer is the same as the bit pattern for -1.

Make Up Your Own Literals

Although C++ does not offer a built-in way to create a short literal, you can define your own literal suffix. Just as 42L has type long, you can invent a suffix, say, _S, to mean short, so 42_S is a compile-time constant of type short. Listing 25-5 shows how you can define your own literal suffix.

Listing 26-5. User-Defined Literal

```
import <iostream>;

short operator "" _S(unsigned long long value)
{
    return static_cast<short>(value);
}

void print(short s)
{
    std::cout << "short=" << s << '\n';
}

void print(int i)
{
    std::cout << "int=" << i << '\n';
}

int main()
{
    print(42);
    print(42_S);
}
```

When the user defines a literal, it is known as a *user-defined literal,* or UDL. The name of the literal must begin with an underscore. This will let the C++ standard define additional literals that don't start with an underscore without fear of interfering with the literals you define. You can define a UDL for integer, floating-point, and string types.

Integer Arithmetic

When you use signed char and short values or objects in an expression, the compiler always turns them into type int. It then performs the arithmetic or whatever operation you want to do. This is known as *type promotion*. The compiler *promotes* a short to an int. The result of arithmetic operations is also an int.

You can mix int and long in the same expressions. C++ converts the smaller type to match the larger type, and the larger type is the type of the result. This is known as type *conversion*, which is different from type promotion. (The distinction may seem arbitrary or trivial, but it's important. The next section will explain one of the reasons.) Remember: *Promote* signed char and short to int; *convert* int to long.

```
long big{2147483640};
short small{7};
std::cout << big + small; // promote small to type int; then convert it to long;
                          // the sum has type long
```

When you compare two integers, the same promotion and conversion occurs: the smaller argument is promoted or converted to the size of the larger argument. The result is always bool.

The compiler can convert any numeric value to bool; it considers this a conversion on the same level as any other integer conversion.

Overload Resolution

The two-step type-conversion process may puzzle you. It matters when you have a set of overloaded functions, and the compiler has to decide which function to call. The first thing the compiler tries is to find an exact match. If it can't find one, it searches for a match after type promotion. Only if that fails does it search for a match allowing type conversion. Thus, it considers a match based only on type promotion to be better than type conversion. Listing 26-6 demonstrates the difference.

Listing 26-6. Overloading Prefers Type Promotion over Type Conversion

```
import <iostream>;

// print is overloaded for signed char, short, int and long
void print(signed char value)
{
  std::cout << "print(signed char = " << static_cast<int>(value) << ")\n";
}

void print(short value)
{
  std::cout << "print(short = " << value << ")\n";
}

void print(int value)
{
  std::cout << "print(int = " << value << ")\n";
}

void print(long value)
{
  std::cout << "print(long = " << value << ")\n";
}
```

```
// guess() is overloaded for bool, int, and long
void guess(bool value)
{
  std::cout << "guess(bool = " << value << ")\n";
}

void guess(int value)
{
  std::cout << "guess(int = " << value << ")\n";
}

void guess(long value)
{
  std::cout << "guess(long = " << value << ")\n";
}

// error() is overloaded for bool and long
void error(bool value)
{
  std::cout << "error(bool = " << value << ")\n";
}

void error(long value)
{
  std::cout << "error(long = " << value << ")\n";
}

int main()
{
  signed char byte{10};
  short shrt{20};
  int i{30};
  long lng{40};

  print(byte);
  print(shrt);
  print(i);
  print(lng);

  guess(byte);
  guess(shrt);
  guess(i);
  guess(lng);

  error(byte); // expected error
  error(shrt); // expected error
  error(i);    // expected error
  error(lng);
}
```

The first four lines of main call the print function. The compiler always finds an exact match and is happy. The next four lines call guess. When called with signed char and short arguments, the compiler promotes the arguments to int and finds an exact match with guess(int i).

The last four lines call the aptly named function error. The problem is that the compiler promotes signed char and short to int and then must convert int to either long or bool. It treats all conversions equally; thus, it cannot decide which function to call, so it reports an error. Delete the three lines that I marked with "expected error," and the program works just fine, or add an overload for error(int value), and everything will work.

The problem of ambiguous overload resolution is a difficult hurdle for new C++ programmers. It's also a difficult hurdle for many experienced C++ programmers. The exact rules for how C++ resolves overloaded names are complicated and subtle and will be covered in depth in Exploration 72. Avoid being clever about overloaded functions, and keep it simple. Most overloading situations are straightforward, but if you find yourself writing an overload for type long, be certain you also have an overload for type int.

Knowing about big integers helps with some programs, but others have to represent even larger numbers. The next Exploration examines how C++ works with floating-point values.

EXPLORATION 27

■ ■ ■

Very Big and Very Little Numbers

Even the longest long long cannot represent truly large numbers, such as Avogadro's number ($6.02{\times}10^{23}$) or extremely small numbers, such as the mass of an electron ($9.1{\times}10^{-31}$ kg). Scientists and engineers use scientific notation, which consists of a mantissa (such as 6.02 or 9.1) and an exponent (such as 23 or –31), relative to a base (10).

Computers represent very large and very small numbers using a similar representation, known as *floating-point*. I know many of you have been waiting eagerly for this Exploration, as you've probably grown tired of using only integers, so let's jump in.

Floating-Point Numbers

Computers use floating-point numbers for very large and very small values. By sacrificing precision, you can gain a greatly extended range. However, never forget that the range and precision are limited. Floating-point numbers are not the same as mathematical real numbers, although they can often serve as useful approximations of real numbers.

Like its scientific notation counterpart, a floating-point number has a mantissa, also called a *significand*, a sign, and an exponent. The mantissa and exponent use a common *base* or *radix*. Although integers in C++ are always binary in their representation, floating-point numbers can use any base. Binary is a popular base, but some computers use 16 or even 10 as the base. The precise details are, as always, dependent upon the implementation. In other words, each C++ implementation uses its native floating-point format for maximum performance.

Floating-point values often come in multiple flavors. C++ offers single, double, and extended precision, called float, double, and long double, respectively. The difference is that float usually has less precision and a smaller range than double, and double usually has less precision and smaller range than long double. In exchange, long double usually requires more memory and computation time than double, which usually consumes more memory and computation time than float. On the other hand, an implementation is free to use the same representation for all three types.

Use double, unless there is some reason not to. Use float when memory is at a premium and you can afford to lose precision or long double when you absolutely need the extra precision or range and can afford to give up memory and performance.

A common binary representation of floating-point numbers is the IEC 60559 standard, which is better known as IEEE 754. Most likely, your desktop system has hardware that implements the IEC 60559 standard. For the sake of convenience, the following discussion describes only IEC 60559; however, never forget that C++ permits many floating-point representations. Mainframes and DSPs, for example, may use other representations.

An IEC 60559 binary32 (C++ float) occupies 32 bits, of which 23 bits make up the mantissa and 8 bits form the exponent, leaving one bit for the mantissa's sign. The radix is 2, so the range of an IEC 60559 binary32 is roughly 2^{-127} to 2^{127} or 10^{-38} to 10^{38}. (I lied. Smaller numbers are possible, but the details are not germane to C++. If you are curious, look up *subnormal* in your favorite computer science reference.)

© Ray Lischner 2020
R. Lischner, *Exploring C++20*, https://doi.org/10.1007/978-1-4842-5961-0_27

The IEC 60559 standard reserves some bit patterns for special values. In particular, if the exponent is all one bits, and the mantissa is all zero bits, the value is considered "infinity." It's not quite a mathematical infinity, but it does its best to pretend. Adding any finite value to infinity, for example, yields an answer of infinity. Positive infinity is always greater than any finite value, and negative infinity is always smaller than finite values.

If the exponent is all one bits, and the mantissa is not all zero bits, the value is considered as not-a-number, or *NaN*. NaN comes in two varieties: quiet and signaling. Arithmetic with quiet NaN always yields a NaN result. Using a signaling NaN results in a machine interrupt. How that interrupt manifests itself in your program is up to the implementation. In general, you should expect your program to terminate abruptly. Consult your compiler's documentation to learn the details. Certain arithmetic operations that have no meaningful result can also yield NaN, such as adding positive infinity to negative infinity.

Test whether a value is NaN by calling `std::isnan` (declared in `<cmath>`). Similar functions exist to test for infinity and other properties of floating-point numbers.

A `double` (IEC 60559 `binary64`) is similar in structure to a `float`, except it takes up 64 bits: 52 bits for the mantissa, 11 bits for the exponent, and 1 sign bit. A `double` can also have infinity and NaN values, with the same structural representation (i.e., exponent all ones).

A `long double` is even longer than `double`. The IEC 60559 standard permits an extended double-precision format that requires at least 79 bits. Many desktop and workstation systems implement extended-precision, floating-point numbers using 80 bits (63 for the mantissa, 16 for the exponent, and 1 sign bit).

Floating-Point Literals

Any numeric literal with a decimal point or a decimal exponent represents a floating-point number. The decimal point is always '.', regardless of locale. The exponent starts with the letter e or E and can be signed. No spaces are permitted in a numeric literal, for example:

```
3.1415926535897
31415926535897e-13
0.000314159265e4
```

By default, a floating-point literal has type `double`. To write a `float` literal, add the letter f or F after the number. For a `long double`, use the letter l or L, as in the following examples:

```
3.141592f
31415926535897E-13l
0.000314159265E+42OL
```

As with `long int` literals, I prefer uppercase L, to avoid confusion with the digit 1. Feel free to use f or F, but I recommend you pick one and stick with it. For uniformity with L, I prefer to use F.

If a floating-point literal exceeds the range of the type, the compiler will tell you. If you ask for a value at greater precision than the type supports, the compiler will silently give you as much precision as it can. Another possibility is that you request a value that the type cannot represent exactly. In that case, the compiler gives you the next higher or lower value.

For example, your program may have the literal 0.2F, which seems like a perfectly fine real number, but as a binary floating-point value, it has no exact representation. Instead, it is approximately 0.0011001100_2. The difference between the decimal value and the internal value can give rise to unexpected results, the most common of which is when you expect two numbers to be equal and they are not. **Read Listing 27-1 and predict the outcome**.

Listing 27-1. Floating-Point Numbers Do Not Always Behave As You Expect

```
#include <cassert>
int main()
{
  float a{0.03F};
  float b{10.0F};
  float c{0.3F};
  assert(a * b == c);
}
```

What is your prediction?

_____

What is the actual outcome?

_____

Were you correct? _____

The problem is that 0.03 and 0.3 do not have exact representations in binary, so if your floating-point format is binary (and most are), the values the computer uses are approximations of the real values. Multiplying 0.03 by 10 gives a result that is very close to 0.3, but the binary representation differs from that obtained by converting 0.3 to binary. (In IEC 60559 single-precision format, 0.03 * 10.0 gives $0.0111001100110011001100100_2$ and 0.3 is $0.0111001100110011001101000_2$. The numbers are very close, but they differ in the 22nd significant bit.

Some programmers mistakenly believe that floating-point arithmetic is therefore "imprecise." On the contrary, floating-point arithmetic is exact, but not the same as arithmetic with real numbers. The problem lies only in the programmer's expectations, if you anticipate floating-point arithmetic to follow the rules of real-number arithmetic. If you realize that the compiler converts your decimal literals to other values, and computes with those other values, and if you understand the rules that the processor uses when it performs limited-precision arithmetic with those values, you can know exactly what the results will be. If this level of detail is critical for your application, you have to take the time to perform this level of analysis.

The rest of us, however, can continue to pretend that floating-point numbers and arithmetic are nearly real, without worrying overmuch about the differences. Just don't compare floating-point numbers for exact equality. (How to compare numbers for approximate equality is beyond the scope of this book. Visit the website for links and references.)

Floating-Point Traits

You can query `numeric_limits` to reveal the size and limits of a floating-point type. You can also determine whether the type allows infinity or NaN. Listing 27-2 shows some code that displays information about a floating-point type.

Listing 27-2. Discovering the Attributes of a Floating-Point Type

```
import <cmath>;
import <iostream>;
import <limits>;
import <locale>;
```

```cpp
int main()
{
  std::cout.imbue(std::locale{""});
  std::cout << std::boolalpha;
  // Change float to double or long double to learn about those types.
  using T = float;
  std::cout << "min=" << std::numeric_limits<T>::min() << '\n'
       << "max=" << std::numeric_limits<T>::max() << '\n'
       << "IEC 60559? " << std::numeric_limits<T>::is_iec559 << '\n'
       << "max exponent=" << std::numeric_limits<T>::max_exponent << '\n'
       << "min exponent=" << std::numeric_limits<T>::min_exponent << '\n'
       << "mantissa places=" << std::numeric_limits<T>::digits << '\n'
       << "radix=" << std::numeric_limits<T>::radix << '\n'
       << "has infinity? " << std::numeric_limits<T>::has_infinity << '\n'
       << "has quiet NaN? " << std::numeric_limits<T>::has_quiet_NaN << '\n'
       << "has signaling NaN? " << std::numeric_limits<T>::has_signaling_NaN << '\n';

  if (std::numeric_limits<T>::has_infinity)
  {
    T zero{0};
    T one{1};
    T inf{std::numeric_limits<T>::infinity()};
    if (std::isinf(one/zero))
      std::cout << "1.0/0.0 = infinity\n";
    if (inf + inf == inf)
      std::cout << "infinity + infinity = infinity\n";
  }
  if (std::numeric_limits<T>::has_quiet_NaN)
  {
    // There's no guarantee that your environment produces quiet NaNs for
    // these illegal arithmetic operations. It's possible that your compiler's
    // default is to produce signaling NaNs, or to terminate the program
    // in some other way.
    T zero{};
    T inf{std::numeric_limits<T>::infinity()};
    std::cout << "zero/zero = " << zero/zero << '\n';
    std::cout << "inf/inf = " << inf/inf << '\n';
  }
}
```

Modify the program so it prints information about double. Run it. Modify it again for long double, and run it. **Do the results match your expectations?** _____

Floating-Point I/O

Reading and writing floating-point values depend on the locale. In the classic locale, the input format is the same as for an integer or floating-point literal. In a native locale, you must write the input according to the rules of the locale. In particular, the decimal separator must be that of the locale. Thousands separators are optional, but if you use them, you must use the locale-specific character and correct placement.

Output is more complicated.

In addition to the field width and fill character, floating-point output also depends on the precision—the number of places after the decimal point—and the format, which can be fixed-point (without an exponent), scientific (with an exponent), or general (uses an exponent only when necessary). The default is general. Depending on the locale, the number may include separators for groups of thousands.

In the scientific and fixed formats (which you specify with a manipulator of the same name), the precision is the number of digits after the decimal point. In the general format, it is the maximum number of significant digits. Set the stream's precision with the precision member function or setprecision manipulator. The default precision is six. As usual, the manipulators that do not take arguments are declared in <ios>, so you get them for free with <iostream>, but setprecision requires that you import <iomanip>. Set the precision in a format specifier after a decimal point. The precision must appear between the minimum width and the type letter.

```
double const pi{3.141592653589793238L};
std::cout.precision(12);
std::cout << pi << '\n';
std::cout << std::setprecision(4) << pi << '\n';
std::cout << std::format("{0:.12}\n{0:.4}\n", pi);
```

In scientific format, the exponent is printed with a lowercase 'e' (or 'E', if you use the uppercase manipulator), followed by the base 10 exponent. The exponent always has a sign (+ or -) and at least two digits, even if the exponent is zero. The mantissa is written with one digit before the decimal point. The precision determines the number of places after the decimal point.

In fixed format, no exponent is printed. The number is printed with as many digits before the decimal point as needed. The precision determines the number of places after the decimal point. The decimal point is always printed.

The default format is the general format, which means printing numbers nicely without sacrificing information. If the exponent is less than or equal to -4, or if it is greater than the precision, the number is printed in scientific format. Otherwise, it is printed without an exponent. However, unlike conventional fixed-point output, trailing zeros are removed after the decimal point. If after removal of the trailing zeros the decimal point becomes the last character, it is also removed.

When necessary, values are rounded off to fit within the allotted precision.

A format introduced in C++ 11 is hexfloat (format type 'a'). The value is printed in hexadecimal, which lets you discover the exact value on systems with binary or base 16 representations. Because the letter 'e' is a valid hexadecimal value, the exponent is marked with the letters 'p' or 'P'.

The easiest way to specify a particular output format is with a manipulator: scientific, fixed, or hexfloat. Like the precision, the format persists in the stream's state until you change it. (Only width resets after an output operation.) Unfortunately, once you set the format, there is no easy way to revert to the default general format. To do that, you must use a member function, and a clumsy one at that, as shown here:

```
std::cout << std::scientific << large_number << '\n';
std::cout << std::fixed << small_number << '\n';
std::cout.unsetf(std::ios_base::floatfield);
std::cout << number_in_general_format << '\n';
std::cout << std::format("{:e}\n{:f}\n{}\n",
    large_number, small_number, number_in_general_format);
```

In a format specifier, use type 'e' for exponential or scientific, 'f' for fixed, 'g' for general, and 'a' for hexadecimal. Use an uppercase type letter to get an uppercase 'E' or 'P' for the exponent.

Complete Table 27-1, showing exactly how each value would be printed in each format, in the classic locale. I filled in the first row for your convenience.

Table 27-1. *Floating-Point Output*

Value	Precision	Scientific	Fixed	Hexfloat	General
123456.789	6	1.234568e5	123456.789000	0x1.e240cap+16	123457
1.23456789	4	_____	_____	_____	_____
123456789	2	_____	_____	_____	_____
–1234.5678e9	5	_____	_____	_____	_____

After you have filled in the table with your predictions, **write a program that will test your predictions**, then run it and see how well you did. Compare your program with Listing 27-3.

Listing 27-3. Demonstrating Floating-Point Output

```
import <format>;
import <iostream>;

/// Print a floating-point number in three different formats.
/// @param precision the precision to use when printing @p value
/// @param value the floating-point number to print
void print(int precision, float value)
{
  std::cout.precision(precision);
  std::cout << std::scientific << value << '\t'
            << std::fixed      << value << '\t'
            << std::hexfloat   << value << '\t';

  // Set the format to general.
  std::cout.unsetf(std::ios_base::floatfield);
  std::cout << value << '\n';

  std::cout << std::format("{0:.{1}e}\n{0:.{1}f}\n{0:.{1}a}\n{0:.{1}g}\n",
      value, precision);
}

/// Main program.
int main()
{
  print(6, 123456.789F);
  print(4, 1.23456789F);
  print(2, 123456789.F);
  print(5, -1234.5678e9F);
}
```

The precise values can differ from one system to another, depending on the floating-point representation. For example, float on most systems cannot support the full precision of nine decimal digits, so you should expect some fuzziness in the least significant digits of the printed result. In other words, unless you want to sit down and do some serious binary computation, you cannot easily predict exactly what the output will be in every case. Table 27-2 shows the output from Listing 27-3, when run on a typical IEC 60559–compliant system.

Table 27-2. *Results of Printing Floating-Point Numbers*

Value	Precision	Scientific	Fixed	Hexfloat	General
123456.789	6	1.234568e+05	123456.789062	0x1.e240cap+16	123457
1.23456789	4	1.2346e+00	1.2346	0x1.3c0ca4p+0	1.235
123456789	2	1.23e+08	123456792.00	0x1.d6f346p+26	1.2e+08
-1234.5678e9	5	-1.23457e+12	-1234567823360.00000	-0x1.1f71fap+40	-1.2346e+12

Some applications are never required to use floating-point numbers; others need them a lot. Scientists and engineers, for example, depend on floating-point arithmetic and math functions and must understand the subtleties of working with these numbers. C++ has everything you need for computation-intensive programming. Although the details are beyond the scope of this book, interested readers should consult a reference for the <cmath> header and the transcendental and other functions that it provides. The <cfenv> header contains functions and related declarations to let you adjust the rounding mode and other aspects of the floating-point environment. If you cannot find information about <cfenv> in a C++ reference, consult a C 99 reference for the <fenv.h> header.

The next Exploration takes a side trip to a completely different topic, explaining the strange comments—the extra slashes (///) and stars (/**)—that I've used in some programs.

■ ■ ■

Documentation

This Exploration is a little different from the others. Instead of covering part of the C++ standard, it examines a third-party tool called Doxygen. Feel free to skip this Exploration, but understand that this is where I explain the strange comments you sometimes see in the code listings.

Doxygen

Doxygen is a free (in cost and license) tool that reads your source code, looks for comments that follow a certain structure, and extracts information from the comments and from the code to produce documentation. It produces output in a number of formats: HTML, RTF (rich text format), LaTeX, UNIX man pages, and XML.

Java programmers may be familiar with a similar tool called javadoc. The javadoc tool is standard in the Java Software Development Kit, whereas Doxygen has no relationship with the C++ standard or with any C++ vendor. C++ lacks a standard for structured documentation, so you are free to do anything you want. For example, Microsoft defines its own conventions for XML tags in comments, which is fine, if you plan to work entirely within the Microsoft .NET environment. For other programmers, I recommend using tools that have more widespread and portable use. The most popular solution is Doxygen, and I think every C++ programmer should know about it, even if you decide not to use it. That's why I include this Exploration in the book.

Structured Comments

Doxygen heeds comments that follow a specific format:

- One-line comments start with an extra slash or exclamation mark: /// or //!

- Multiline comments start with an extra asterisk or exclamation mark: /** or /*!

Also, Doxygen recognizes some widespread comment conventions and decorations. For example, it ignores a line of slashes.

© Ray Lischner 2020
R. Lischner, *Exploring C++20*, https://doi.org/10.1007/978-1-4842-5961-0_28

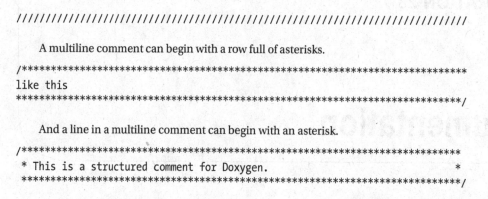

A multiline comment can begin with a row full of asterisks.

```
/*************************************************************************
like this
*************************************************************************/
```

And a line in a multiline comment can begin with an asterisk.

```
/*************************************************************************
 * This is a structured comment for Doxygen.                            *
 *************************************************************************/
```

Within a structured comment is where you document the various entities in your program: functions, types, variables, and so on.

The convention is that the comment immediately before a declaration or definition applies to the entity being declared or defined. Sometimes, you want to put the comment after the declaration, such as a one-line description of a variable. To do that, use a "less-than" (<) sign at the start of the comment.

```
double const c = 299792458.0;          ///< speed of light in m/sec
```

Documentation Tags and Markdown

Doxygen has its own markup language that utilizes *tags*. A tag can start with a backslash character (\return) or an "at sign" (@return). Some tags take arguments and some don't. In addition to its own tags, you can also use a subset of HTML or Markdown (a wiki-like syntax that is easy to read and write). The most useful tags, markup, and Markdown are as follows:

@b word

Marks up *word* in boldface. You can also use HTML markup, *phrase*, which is helpful when *phrase* contains spaces, or use Markdown, by enclosing the text in asterisks: *phrase*.

@brief one-sentence-description

Describes an entity briefly. Entities have brief and detailed documentation. Depending on how you configure Doxygen, the brief documentation can be the first sentence of the entity's full documentation, or you can require an explicit @brief tag. In either case, the rest of the comment is the detailed documentation for the entity.

@c word

Treats *word* as a code fragment and set it in a fixed-pitch typeface. You can also use HTML markup, <tt>*phrase*</tt>, or use backticks for Markdown, `phrase`.

@em word

Emphasizes *word* in italics. You can also use HTML tags, *phrase*, or underscores for Markdown: _*phrase*_.

@file file name

Presents an overview of the source file. The detailed description can describe the purpose of the file, revision history, and other global documentation. The *file name* is optional; without it, Doxygen uses the file's real name.

@link entity text @endlink

Creates a hyperlink to the named *entity*, such as a file. I use @link on my @mainpage to create a table of contents to the most important files in the project or to the sole file. Markdown offers a variety of ways to create links, such as [*text*](*entity*).

@mainpage title

Starts an overview of the entire project for the index or cover page. You can put @mainpage in any source file or even set aside a separate file just for the comment. In small projects, I place @mainpage in the same source file as the main function, but in large projects, I use a separate file, such as *main.dox*.

@p name

Sets *name* in a fixed-pitch typeface to distinguish it as a function parameter.

@par title

Starts a new paragraph. If you supply a one-line *title*, it becomes the paragraph heading. A blank line also separates paragraphs.

@param name description

Documents a function parameter named *name*. If you want to refer to this parameter elsewhere in the function's documentation, use @p *name*.

@post postcondition

Documents a postcondition for a function. A postcondition is a Boolean expression that you can assume to be true when the function returns (assuming all preconditions were true). C++ lacks any formal mechanism for enforcing postconditions (other than assert), so documenting postconditions is crucial, especially for library writers.

@pre precondition

Documents a precondition for a function. A precondition is a Boolean expression that must be true before the function is called, or else the function is not guaranteed to work properly. C++ lacks any formal mechanism for enforcing preconditions (other than assert), so documenting preconditions is crucial, especially for library writers.

@return description

Documents what a function returns.

@see xref

Inserts a cross-reference to an entity named *xref*. Doxygen looks for references to other documented entities within the structured comment. When it finds one, it inserts a hyperlink (or text cross-reference, depending on the output format). Sometimes, however, you have to insert an explicit reference to an entity that is not named in the documentation, so you can use @see.

You can suppress automatic hyperlink creation by prefacing a name with %.

@&, @@, @\, @%, @<

Escapes a literal character (&, @, \, %, or <), to prevent interpretation by Doxygen or HTML.

Doxygen is very flexible, and you have many, many ways to format your comments using native Doxygen tags, HTML, or Markdown. This book's website has links to the main Doxygen page, where you can find more information about the tool and download the software. Most Linux users already have Doxygen; other users can download Doxygen for their favorite platform.

Listing 28-1 shows a few of the many ways you can use Doxygen.

Listing 28-1. Documenting Your Code with Doxygen

```
/** @file
 * @brief Tests strings to see whether they are palindromes.
 *
 * Reads lines from the input, strip non-letters, and checks whether
 * the result is a palindrome. Ignores case differences when checking.
 * Echoes palindromes to the standard output.
 */


/** @mainpage Palindromes
 * Tests input strings to see whether they are palindromes.
 *
 * A _palindrome_ is a string that reads the same forward and backward.
 * To test for palindromes, this program needs to strip punctuation and
 * other non-essential characters from the string, and compare letters without
 * regard to case differences.
 *
 * This program reads lines of text from the standard input and echoes
 * to the standard output those lines that are palindromes.
 *
```

```
 * Source file: list2801.cpp
 *
 * @date 27-March-2020
 * @author Ray Lischner
 * @version 3.0
 */
import <algorithm>;
import <iostream>;
import <ranges>;
import <locale>;
import <ranges>;
import <string>;
import <string_view>;

/** @brief Tests for non-letter.
 *
 * Tests the character @p ch in the global locale.
 * @param ch the character to test
 * @return true if @p ch is not a letter
 */
bool non_letter(char ch)
{
  return not std::isalnum(ch, std::locale{});
}

/** @brief Converts to lowercase.
 *
 * All conversions use the global locale.
 *
 * @param ch the character to test
 * @return the character converted to lowercase
 */
char lowercase(char ch)
{
  return std::tolower(ch, std::locale{});
}

/** @brief Compares two characters without regard to case.
 *
 * @param a one character to compare
 * @param b the other character to compare
 * @return `true` if the characters are the same in lowercase,
 *         `false` if they are different.
 */
bool is_same_char(char a, char b)
{
  return lowercase(a) == lowercase(b);
}
```

```
/** @brief Determines whether @p str is a palindrome.
 *
 * Only letter characters are tested. Spaces and punctuation don't count.
 * Empty strings are not palindromes because that's just too easy.
 * @param str the string to test
 * @return `true` if @p str is the same forward and backward and
 *         `not str.empty()`
 */
bool is_palindrome(std::string_view str)
{
  auto filtered_str{ str | std::views::filter(lowercase) };
  return std::ranges::equal(filtered_str, filtered_str|std::views::reverse,
      is_same_char);
}


/** @brief Main program.
 * Sets the global locale to the user's native locale.
 * Then imbues the I/O streams with the native locale.
 */
int main()
{
  std::locale::global(std::locale{""});
  std::cin.imbue(std::locale{});
  std::cout.imbue(std::locale{});

  for (std::string line{}; std::getline(std::cin, line); /*empty*/)
    if (is_palindrome(line))
      std::cout << line << '\n';
}
```

Figure 28-1 shows the main page as it appears in a web browser.

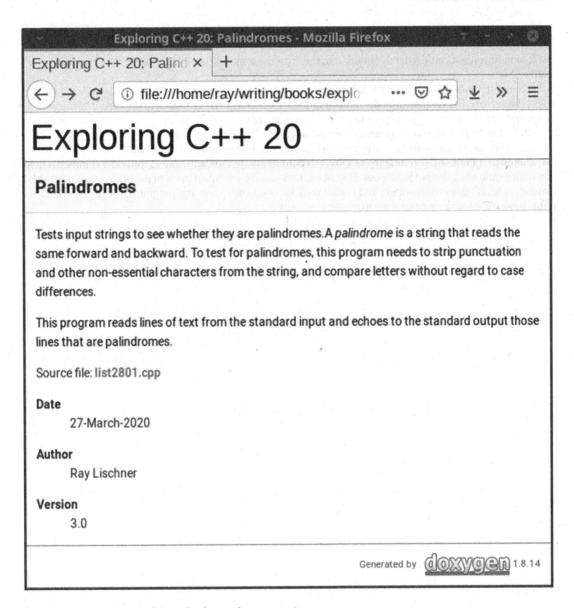

Figure 28-1. *Main page of the palindrome documentation*

Using Doxygen

Instead of taking lots of command-line arguments, Doxygen uses a configuration file, typically named
Doxyfile, in which you can put all that juicy information. Among the information in the configuration
file are the name of the project, which files to examine for comments, which output format or formats to
generate, and a variety of options you can use to tweak and adjust the output.

Because of the plethora of options, Doxygen comes with a wizard, doxywizard, to help generate a
suitable configuration file, or you can just run the command-line doxygen utility with the -g switch, to
generate a default configuration file that has lots of comments to help you understand how to customize it.

Once you have configured Doxygen, running the program is trivial. Simply run doxygen, and away it goes. Doxygen does a reasonable job at parsing C++, which is a complicated and difficult language to parse, but it sometimes gets confused. Pay attention to the error messages, to see if it had any difficulties with your source files.

The configuration file dictates the location of the output. Typically, each output format resides in its own subdirectory. For example, the default configuration file stores HTML output in the `html` directory. Open the `html/index.html` file in your favorite browser, to check out the results.

Download and install Doxygen on your system.

Add Doxygen comments to one of your programs. Configure and run Doxygen.

Future programs will continue to use Doxygen comments sporadically, when I think the comments help you understand what the program does. In general, however, I try to avoid them in the book, because the text usually explains things well enough, and I don't want to waste any space. The programs that accompany the book, however, have more complete Doxygen comments.

■ ■ ■

Project 1: Body Mass Index

It's project time! Body mass index (BMI) is a measurement some health-care professionals use to determine whether a person is overweight, and if so, by how much. To compute BMI, you need a person's weight in kilograms and height in meters. The BMI is simply weight/height^2, converted to a unitless value.

Your task is to write a program that reads records, prints the records, and computes some statistics. The program should start by asking for a threshold BMI. Only records with a BMI greater than or equal to the threshold will be printed. Each record needs to consist of a person's name (which may contain spaces), weight in kilograms, height in centimeters (not meters), and the person's sex ('M' or 'F'). Let the user enter the sex in uppercase or lowercase. Ask the user to enter the height in centimeters, so you can compute the BMI using integers. You will have to adjust the formula to allow for centimeters instead of meters.

Print each person's BMI immediately after reading his or her record. After collecting information for everyone, print two tables—one for men, one for women—based on the data. Use an asterisk after the BMI rating to mark records for which the number meets or exceeds the threshold. After each table, print the mean (average) and median BMI. (Median is the value at which half the BMI values are less than the median and half are greater than the median. If the user enters an even number of records, take the mean of the two values in the middle.) Compute individual BMI values as integers. Compute the mean and median BMI values as floating-point numbers, and print the mean with one place after the decimal point.

Listing 29-1 shows a sample user session. User input is in **boldface**.

Listing 29-1. Sample User Session with the BMI Program

```
$ bmi
This program computes Bogus Metabolic Indicator (BMI) values.
Enter threshold BMI: 25
Enter name, height (in cm), and weight (in kg) for each person:
Name 1: Ray Lischner
Height (cm): 180
Weight (kg): 90
Sex (m or f): m
BMI = 27
Name 2: A. Nony Mouse
Height (cm): 120
Weight (kg): 42
Sex (m or f): F
BMI = 29
Name 3: Mick E. Mouse
Height (cm): 30
Weight (kg): 2
Sex (m or f): M
BMI = 22
```

Name 4: **A. Nony Lischner**
Height (cm): **150**
Weight (kg): **55**
Sex (m or f): **m**
BMI = 24
Name 5: **No One**
Height (cm): **250**
Weight (kg): **130**
Sex (m or f): **f**
BMI = 20
Name 6: ^Z

Male data
Ht(cm) Wt(kg) Sex BMI Name
   180   90   M   27* Ray Lischner
    30   2   M   22 Mick E. Mouse
   150   55   M   24 A. Nony Lischner
Mean BMI = 24.3
Median BMI = 24

Female data
Ht(cm) Wt(kg) Sex BMI Name
   120   42   F   29* A. Nony Mouse
   250   130   F   20 No One
Mean BMI = 24.5
Median BMI = 24.5

Hints

Here are some hints, in case you need them:

- Keep track of the data in separate vectors, for example, heights, weights, sexes, names, bmis.

- Use the native locale for all input and output.

- Divide the program into functions, for example, compute_bmi to compute the BMI from weight and height.

- You can write this program using nothing more than the techniques that we have covered so far, but if you know other techniques, feel free to use them. The next set of Explorations will present language features that will greatly facilitate writing this kind of program.

- The complete source code for my solution is available with the other files that accompany this book, but don't peek until after you have written the program yourself.

PART II

Custom Types

■ ■ ■

Custom Types

One of the key design goals for C++ was that you should be able to define brand-new types that look and act similar to the built-in types. Do you need tri-state logic? Write your own `tribool` type. Need arbitrary-precision arithmetic? Write your own `bigint` type. Even better, let someone else write it, and you use `bigint` in the same manner as ordinary `int`. This Exploration introduces some of the language features that let you define custom types. Subsequent Explorations delve deeper into these topics.

Defining a New Type

Let's consider a scenario in which you want to define a type, `rational`, to represent rational numbers (fractions). A rational number has a numerator and a denominator, both integers. Ideally, you would be able to add, subtract, multiply, and divide rational numbers in the same fashion you can with the built-in numeric types. You should also be able to mix rational numbers and other numeric types in the same expression. (Our `rational` type is different from the `std::ratio` type, which represents a compile-time constant; our `rational` type can change value at runtime.)

The I/O streams should be able to read and write rational numbers in some reasonable manner. The input operator should accept as valid input anything the output operator produces. The I/O operators should heed the stream's flags and related settings, such as field width and fill character, so you can format neatly aligned columns of rational numbers the same way you did for integers in Exploration 8.

You should be able to assign any numeric value to a `rational` variable and convert a `rational` value to any built-in numeric type. Naturally, converting a rational number to an integer variable would result in truncation to an integer. One can argue that conversion should be automatic, similar to conversion from floating-point to integer. A counter argument is that automatic conversions that discard information were a mistake in the original C language design and one not to be duplicated. Instead, conversions that discard information should be made explicit and clear. I prefer the latter approach.

This is a lot to tackle at once, so let's begin slowly.

The first step is to decide how to store a rational number. You have to store a numerator and a denominator, both as integers. What about negative numbers? Choose a convention, such as the numerator gets the sign of the entire value, and the denominator is always positive. Listing 30-1 shows a basic `rational` type definition.

Listing 30-1. Defining a Custom `rational` Type

```
/// Represent a rational number.
struct rational
{
  int numerator;     ///< numerator gets the sign of the rational value
  int denominator;   ///< denominator is always positive
};
```

© Ray Lischner 2020
R. Lischner, *Exploring C++20*, https://doi.org/10.1007/978-1-4842-5961-0_30

The definition starts with the struct keyword. C programmers recognize this as a structure definition—but hang on, there's much more to follow.

The contents of the rational type look like definitions for variables named numerator and denominator, but they work a little differently. Remember that Listing 30-1 shows a type definition. In other words, the compiler remembers that rational names a type, but it does not allocate any memory for an object, for numerator, or for denominator. In C++ parlance, numerator and denominator are called *data members*; some other languages call them instance variables or fields.

Notice the semicolon that follows the closing curly brace. Type definitions are different from compound statements. If you forget the semicolon, the compiler will remind you, sometimes quite rudely, while referring to a line number several lines away from the line where the semicolon belongs.

When you define an object with type rational, the object stores the numerator and denominator members. Use the dot (.) operator to access the members (which you have been doing throughout this book), as shown in Listing 30-2.

Listing 30-2. Using a Custom Type and Its Members

```
import <iostream>;

/// Represent a rational number.
struct rational
{
  int numerator;     ///< numerator gets the sign of the rational value
  int denominator;   ///< denominator is always positive
};

int main()
{
  rational pi{};
  pi.numerator = 355;
  pi.denominator = 113;
  std::cout << "pi is approximately " << pi.numerator << "/" << pi.denominator << '\n';
}
```

That's not terribly exciting, is it? The rational type just sits there, lifeless. You know that many types in the standard library have member functions, such as std::ostream's width member function, which allows you to write std::cout.width(4). The next section shows how to write your own member functions.

Member Functions

Let's add a member function to rational that reduces the numerator and denominator by their greatest common divisor. Listing 30-3 shows the sample program, with the reduce() member function.

Listing 30-3. Adding the reduce Member Function

```
#include <cassert>

import <iostream>;
import <numeric>;
```

```
/// Represents a rational number.
struct rational
{
  /// Reduce the numerator and denominator by their GCD.
  void reduce()
  {
    assert(denominator != 0);
    int div{std::gcd(numerator, denominator)};
    numerator = numerator / div;
    denominator = denominator / div;
  }
  int numerator;      ///< numerator gets the sign of the rational value
  int denominator;    ///< denominator is always positive
};

int main()
{
  rational pi{};
  pi.numerator = 1420;
  pi.denominator = 452;
  pi.reduce();
  std::cout << "pi is approximately " << pi.numerator << "/" << pi.denominator << '\n';
}
```

Notice how the reduce() member function looks just like an ordinary function, except its definition appears within the rational type definition. It calls the gcd (greatest common divisor) function, which is declared in <numeric>. Also notice how reduce() can refer to the data members of rational. When you call the reduce() member function, you must supply an object as the left-hand operand of the dot (.) operator (such as pi in Listing 30-3). When the reduce() function refers to a data member, the data member is taken from that left-hand operand. Thus, numerator = numerator / div has the effect of pi.numerator = pi.numerator / div.

A member function can also call other member functions that are defined in the same type. Try it yourself: **add the assign() member function**, which takes a numerator and denominator as two parameters and assigns them to their respective data members and calls reduce(). This spares the user of rational the additional step (and possible error of neglecting the call to reduce()). Let the return type be void. **Write your member function here:**

_____

_____

_____

_____

_____

_____

Listing 30-4 presents the entire program, with my assign member function in boldface.

Listing 30-4. Adding the `assign` Member Function

```cpp
#include <cassert>
import <iostream>;
import <numeric>;

/// Represents a rational number.
struct rational
{
  /// Assigns a numerator and a denominator, then reduces to normal form.
  /// @param num numerator
  /// @param den denominator
  /// @pre denominator > 0
  void assign(int num, int den)
  {
    numerator = num;
    denominator = den;
    reduce();
  }

  /// Reduces the numerator and denominator by their GCD.
  void reduce()
  {
    assert(denominator != 0);
    int div{std::gcd(numerator, denominator)};
    numerator = numerator / div;
    denominator = denominator / div;
  }

  int numerator;      ///< numerator gets the sign of the rational value
  int denominator;    ///< denominator is always positive
};

int main()
{
  rational pi{};
  pi.assign(1420, 452);
  std::cout << "pi is approximately " << pi.numerator << "/" << pi.denominator << '\n';
}
```

Notice how simple the main program is now. Hiding details, such as `reduce()`, helps keep the code clean, readable, and maintainable.

Notice one other subtle detail: the definition of `assign()` precedes `reduce()`, even though it calls `reduce()`. We need one minor adjustment to the rule that the compiler must see at least a declaration of a name before you can use that name. Members of a `struct` can refer to other members, regardless of the order of declaration within the type. In all other situations, you must supply a declaration prior to use.

Being able to assign a numerator and denominator in one step is a fine addition to the `rational` type, but even more important is being able to initialize a `rational` object. Recall from Exploration 5 my admonition to ensure that all objects are properly initialized. The next section demonstrates how to add support for initializers to `rational`.

Constructors

Wouldn't it be nice to be able to initialize a rational object with a numerator and denominator and have them properly reduced automatically? You can do that by writing a special member function that looks and acts a little like assign, except the name is the same as the name of the type (rational), and the function has no return type or return value. Listing 30-5 shows how to write this special member function.

Listing 30-5. Adding the Ability to Initialize a rational Object

```cpp
#include <cassert>
import <iostream>;
import <numeric>;

/// Represents a rational number.
struct rational
{
  /// Constructs a rational object, given a numerator and a denominator.
  /// Always reduces to normal form.
  /// @param num numerator
  /// @param den denominator
  /// @pre denominator > 0
  rational(int num, int den)
  : numerator{num}, denominator{den}
  {
    reduce();
  }

  /// Assigns a numerator and a denominator, then reduces to normal form.
  /// @param num numerator
  /// @param den denominator
  /// @pre denominator > 0
  void assign(int num, int den)
  {
    numerator = num;
    denominator = den;
    reduce();
  }

  /// Reduces the numerator and denominator by their GCD.
  void reduce()
  {
    assert(denominator != 0);
    int div{std::gcd(numerator, denominator)};
    numerator = numerator / div;
    denominator = denominator / div;
  }

  int numerator;      ///< numerator gets the sign of the rational value
  int denominator;    ///< denominator is always positive
};
```

```
int main()
{
  rational pi{1420, 452};
  std::cout << "pi is about " << pi.numerator << "/" << pi.denominator << '\n';
}
```

Notice the definition of the pi object. The variable takes arguments in its initializer, and those two arguments are passed to the special initializer function in the same manner as function arguments. This special member function is called a *constructor*.

A constructor looks very much like a normal function, except that it doesn't have a return type. Also, you can't choose a name but must use the type name. And then there's that extra line that starts with a colon. This extra bit of code initializes the data members in the same manner as initializing a variable. After all the data members are initialized, the body of the constructor runs in the same manner as any member function body.

The initializer list is optional. Without it, data members are left uninitialized—this is a bad thing, so don't do it.

Modify the rational type so it accepts a negative denominator. If the denominator is negative, change it to positive and also change the sign of the numerator. Thus, rational{-710, -227} would have the same value as rational{710, 227}.

You can choose to perform the modification in any one of a number of places. Good software design practice dictates that the change should occur in exactly one spot, and all other functions should call that one. Therefore, I suggest modifying reduce(), as shown in Listing 30-6.

Listing 30-6. Modifying the reduce Member Function to Accept a Negative Denominator

```
/// Reduces the numerator and denominator by their GCD.
void reduce()
{
  assert(denominator != 0);
  if (denominator < 0)
  {
    denominator = -denominator;
    numerator = -numerator;
  }
  int div{std::gcd(numerator, denominator)};
  numerator = numerator / div;
  denominator = denominator / div;
}
```

Overloading Constructors

You can overload a constructor the same way you overload an ordinary function. All the overloaded constructors have the same name (i.e., the name of the type), and they must differ in the number or type of the parameters. For example, you can add a constructor that takes a single integer argument, implicitly using 1 as the denominator.

You have a choice of two ways to write an overloaded constructor. You can have one constructor call another one, or you can have the constructor initialize all the members, just like the first constructor you wrote. To call another constructor, use the type name in the initializer list.

```
rational(int num) : rational{num, 1} {}
```

Or initialize each member directly.

```
rational(int num)
: numerator{num}, denominator{1}
{}
```

When you want multiple constructors to share a common behavior, delegating the work to a common constructor makes a lot of sense. For example, you can have a single constructor call reduce(), and every other constructor can call that one constructor, thereby ensuring that no matter how you construct the rational object, you know it has been reduced.

On the other hand, when the denominator is 1, there is no need to call reduce(), so you might prefer the second form, initializing the data members directly. The choice is yours.

A constructor that calls another constructor is known as a *delegating constructor* because it delegates its work to the other constructor.

I'm sure you can see many deficiencies in the current state of the rational type. It has several that you probably missed too. Hang on; the next Exploration starts improving the type. For example, you may want to test your modification by comparing two rational objects, to see if they are equal. To do so, however, you have to write a custom == operator, which is the subject of the next Exploration.

■ ■ ■

Overloading Operators

This Exploration continues the study of writing custom types. An important aspect of making a custom type behave seamlessly with built-in types is ensuring that the custom types support all the expected operators—arithmetic types must support arithmetic operators, readable and writable types must support I/O operators, and so on. Fortunately, C++ lets you overload operators in much the same manner as overloading functions.

Comparing Rational Numbers

In the previous Exploration, you began to write a `rational` type. After making a modification to it, an important step is testing the modified type, and an important aspect of internal testing is the equality (==) operator. C++ lets you define a custom implementation for almost every operator, provided at least one operand has a custom type. In other words, you can't redefine integer division to yield a `rational` result, but you can define division of an integer by a `rational` number and vice versa.

To implement a custom operator, write a normal function, but for the function name, use the `operator` keyword, followed by the operator symbol, as shown in Listing 31-1.

Listing 31-1. Overloading the Equality Operator

```
#include <cassert>
import <iostream>;
import <numeric>;

/// Represents a rational number.
struct rational
{
  /// Constructs a rational object, given a numerator and a denominator.
  /// Always reduces to normal form.
  /// @param num numerator
  /// @param den denominator
  /// @pre denominator > 0
  rational(int num, int den)
  : numerator{num}, denominator{den}
  {
    reduce();
  }

  /// Assigns a numerator and a denominator, then reduces to normal form.
  /// @param num numerator
```

```
  /// @param den denominator
  /// @pre denominator > 0
  void assign(int num, int den)
  {
    numerator = num;
    denominator = den;
    reduce();
  }

  /// Reduces the numerator and denominator by their GCD.
  void reduce()
  {
    assert(denominator != 0);
    if (denominator < 0)
    {
      denominator = -denominator;
      numerator = -numerator;
    }
    int div{std::gcd(numerator, denominator)};
    numerator = numerator / div;
    denominator = denominator / div;
  }

  int numerator;      ///< numerator gets the sign of the rational value
  int denominator;    ///< denominator is always positive
};

/// Compares two rational numbers for equality.
/// @pre @p a and @p b are reduced to normal form
bool operator==(rational const& a, rational const& b)
{
  return a.numerator == b.numerator and a.denominator == b.denominator;
}

/// Compare two rational numbers for inequality.
/// @pre @p a and @p b are reduced to normal form
bool operator!=(rational const& a, rational const& b)
{
  return not (a == b);
}

int main()
{
  rational pi1{355, 113};
  rational pi2{1420, 452};

  if (pi1 == pi2)
    std::cout << "success\n";
  else
    std::cout << "failure\n";
}
```

212

One of the benefits of reducing all rational numbers is that it makes comparison easier. Instead of checking whether 3/3 is the same as 6/6, the constructor reduces both numbers to 1/1, so it is just a matter of comparing the numerators and denominators. Another trick is defining ! = in terms of ==. There's no point in your making extra work for yourself, so confine the actual logic of comparing rational objects to one function and call it from another function. If you worry about the performance overhead of calling an extra layer of functions, use the inline keyword, as shown in Listing 31-2.

Listing 31-2. Using inline for Trivial Functions

```
/// Compares two rational numbers for equality.
/// @pre @p a and @p b are reduced to normal form
bool operator==(rational const& a, rational const& b)
{
  return a.numerator == b.numerator and a.denominator == b.denominator;
}


/// Compares two rational numbers for inequality.
/// @pre @p a and @p b are reduced to normal form
inline bool operator!=(rational const& a, rational const& b)
{
  return not (a == b);
}
```

The inline keyword is a hint to the compiler that you would like the function expanded at the point of call. If the compiler decides to heed your wish, the resulting program will not have any identifiable function named operator!= in it. Instead, every place where you use the != operator with rational objects, the function body is expanded there, resulting in a call to operator==.

To implement the < operator, you need a common denominator. Once you implement operator<, you can implement all other relational operators in terms of <. You can choose any of the relational operators (<, >, <=, >=) as the fundamental operator and implement the others in terms of the fundamental. The convention is to start with <. Listing 31-3 demonstrates < and <=.

Listing 31-3. Implementing the < Operator for rational

```
/// Compares two rational numbers for less-than.
bool operator<(rational const& a, rational const& b)
{
  return a.numerator * b.denominator < b.numerator * a.denominator;
}


/// Compares two rational numbers for less-than-or-equal.
inline bool operator<=(rational const& a, rational const& b)
{
  return not (b < a);
}
```

Implement > and >= in terms of <.
Compare your operators with Listing 31-4.

Listing 31-4. Implementing the > and >= Operators in Terms of <

```
/// Compares two rational numbers for greater-than.
inline bool operator>(rational const& a, rational const& b)
{
  return b < a;
}

/// Compares two rational numbers for greater-than-or-equal.
inline bool operator>=(rational const& a, rational const& b)
{
  return not (b > a);
}
```

Then write a test program. To help you write your tests, download the test.cpp file and add import test to your program. Call the TEST() function as many times as you need, passing a Boolean expression as the sole argument. If the argument is true, the test passed. If the argument is false, the test failed, and the TEST function prints a suitable message. Thus, you may write tests, such as the following:

```
TEST(rational{2, 2} == rational{5, 5});
TEST(rational{6,3} > rational{10, 6});
```

The all-capital name, TEST, tells you that TEST is different from an ordinary function. In particular, if the test fails, the text of the test is printed as part of the failure message. How the TEST function works is beyond the scope of this book, but it's useful to have around; you'll use it for future test harnesses. Compare your test program with Listing 31-5.

Listing 31-5. Testing the rational Comparison Operators

```
#include <cassert>

import <iostream>;
import <numeric>;
import test;

... struct rational omitted for brevity ...

int main()
{
  rational a{60, 5};
  rational b{12, 1};
  rational c{-24, -2};
  TEST(a == b);
  TEST(a >= b);
  TEST(a <= b);
  TEST(b <= a);
  TEST(b >= a);
  TEST(b == c);
  TEST(b >= c);
  TEST(b <= c);
  TEST(a == c);
  TEST(a >= c);
  TEST(a <= c);
```

```
  rational d{109, 10};
  TEST(d < a);
  TEST(d <= a);
  TEST(d != a);
  TEST(a > d);
  TEST(a >= d);
  TEST(a != d);

  rational e{241, 20};
  TEST(e > a);
  TEST(e >= a);
  TEST(e != a);
  TEST(a < e);
  TEST(a <= e);
  TEST(a != e);
}
```

Arithmetic Operators

Comparison is fine, but arithmetic operators are much more interesting. You can overload any or all of the arithmetic operators. Binary operators take two parameters, and unary operators take one parameter. You can choose any return type that makes sense. Listing 31-6 shows the binary addition operator and the unary negation operator.

Listing 31-6. Addition Operator for the rational Type

```
rational operator+(rational const& lhs, rational const& rhs)
{
  return rational{lhs.numerator * rhs.denominator + rhs.numerator * lhs.denominator,
               lhs.denominator * rhs.denominator};
}

rational operator-(rational const& r)
{
  return rational{-r.numerator, r.denominator};
}
```

Write the other arithmetic operators: -, *, and /. Ignore for the moment the issue of division by zero. Compare your functions with mine, which are presented in Listing 31-7.

Listing 31-7. Arithmetic Operators for the rational Type

```
rational operator-(rational const& lhs, rational const& rhs)
{
  return rational{lhs.numerator * rhs.denominator - rhs.numerator * lhs.denominator,
               lhs.denominator * rhs.denominator};
}

rational operator*(rational const& lhs, rational const& rhs)
{
  return rational{lhs.numerator * rhs.numerator, lhs.denominator * rhs.denominator};
}
```

```
rational operator/(rational const& lhs, rational const& rhs)
{
  return rational{lhs.numerator * rhs.denominator, lhs.denominator * rhs.numerator};
}
```

Adding, subtracting, and so on with rational numbers is fine, but more interesting is the issue of mixing types. For example, what is the value of 3 * rational(1, 3)? **Try it.** Collect the definition of the rational type with all the operators and write a main() function that computes that expression and stores it somewhere. Choose a type for the result variable that makes sense to you, then determine how best to print that value to std::cout.

Do you expect the expression to compile without errors? _____

What is the result type of the expression? _____

What value do you expect as the result? _____

Explain your observations.

_____

_____

_____

_____

It turns out that rational's one-argument constructor tells the compiler it can construct a rational from an int anytime it needs to do so. It does so automatically, so the compiler sees the integer 3 and a multiplication of an int and a rational object. It knows about operator* between two rationals, and it knows it cannot use the built-in * operator with a rational operand. Thus, the compiler decides its best response is to convert the int to a rational (by invoking rational{3}), and then it can apply the custom operator* that multiplies two rational objects, yielding a rational result, namely, rational{1, 1}. It does all this automatically on your behalf. Listing 31-8 illustrates one way to write the test program.

Listing 31-8. Test Program for Multiplying an Integer and a Rational Number

```
#include <cassert>
import <iostream>;
import <numeric>;

... struct rational omitted for brevity ...

int main()
{
  rational result{3 * rational{1, 3}};
  std::cout << result.numerator << '/' << result.denominator << '\n';
}
```

Being able to construct a rational object automatically from an int is a great convenience. You can easily write code that performs operations on integers and rational numbers without concerning yourself with type conversions all the time. You'll find this same convenience when mixing integers and floating-point numbers. For example, you can write 1+2.0 without having to perform a type cast: static_cast<double>(1)+2.0.

On the other hand, all this convenience can be too convenient. **Try to compile the following code sample and see what your compiler reports:**

```
int a(3.14); // which one is okay,
int b{3.14}; // and which is an error?
```

I've always used curly braces to initialize a variable, but parentheses also work as long as you provide at least one argument. You also pay a cost in safety. The compiler allows conversions that lose information, such as floating-point to integer, when you use parentheses for initialization, but it reports an error when you use curly braces.

The difference is critical for the rational type. Initializing a rational number using a floating-point number in parentheses truncates the number to an integer and uses the one-argument form of constructor. This isn't what you want at all. Instead, initializing rational{3.14} should produce the same result as rational{314, 100}.

Writing a high-quality conversion from floating-point to a fraction is beyond the scope of this book. Instead, let's just pick a reasonable power of 10 and use that as the denominator. Say we choose 100,000, then rational{3.14159} would be treated as rational{static_cast<int>(3.14159 * 100000), 100000}. **Write the constructor for a floating-point number**. I recommend using a delegating constructor; that is, write the floating-point constructor so it invokes another constructor.

Compare your result with mine in Listing 31-9. A better solution uses numeric_limits to determine the number of decimal digits of precision double can support and tries to preserve as much precision as possible. An even better solution uses the radix of the floating-point implementation, instead of working in base 10.

Listing 31-9. Constructing a Rational Number from a Floating-Point Argument

```
struct rational
{
  rational(int num, int den)
  : numerator{num}, denominator{den}
  {
    reduce();
  }

  rational(double r)
  : rational{static_cast<int>(r * 100000), 100000}
  {}

  ... omitted for brevity ...

  int numerator;
  int denominator;
};
```

If you want to optimize a particular function for a particular argument type, you can do that too, by taking advantage of ordinary function overloading. You'd better make sure it's worth the extra work, however. Remember that the int operand can be the right-hand or left-hand operand, so you will have to overload both forms of the function, as shown in Listing 31-10.

Listing 31-10. Optimizing Operators for a Specific Operand Type

```
rational operator*(rational const& rat, int mult)
{
  return rational{rat.numerator * mult, rat.denominator};
}

inline rational operator*(int mult, rational const& rat)
{
  return rat * mult;
}
```

In such a simple case, it's not worth the added trouble to avoid a little extra arithmetic. However, in more complicated situations, such as division, you may have to write such code.

Math Functions

The C++ standard library offers a number of mathematical functions, such as `std::abs`, which computes absolute values (as you have already guessed). As you have seen, some math functions, such as `gcd`, are in `<numeric>`. Most of them are in `<cmath>`, and because this is inherited from the C language, you must use `#include` instead of `import`. The C++ standard prohibits you from overloading these standard functions to operate on custom types, but you can still write functions that perform similar operations. In Exploration 71, you'll learn about namespaces, which will enable you to use the real function name. Whenever you write a custom numeric type, you should consider which math functions you should provide. In this case, absolute value makes perfect sense. **Write an absolute value function that works with rational numbers. Call it absval**.

Your `absval` function should take a `rational` parameter by value and return a `rational` result. As with the arithmetic operators I wrote, you may opt to use call-by-reference for the parameter. If so, make sure you declare the reference to be `const`. Listing 31-11 shows my implementation of `absval`.

Listing 31-11. Computing the Absolute Value of a Rational Number

```
rational absval(rational const& r)
{
  return rational{std::abs(r.numerator), r.denominator};
}
```

That was easy. What about the other math functions, such as `sqrt`, for computing square roots? Most of the other functions are overloaded for floating-point arguments. If the compiler knew how to convert a rational number to a floating-point number automatically, you could simply pass a `rational` argument to any of the existing floating-point functions, with no further work. **So, which floating-point type should you use?** _____

This question has no easy answer. A reasonable first choice might be `double`, which is the "default" floating-point type (e.g., floating-point literals have type `double`). On the other hand, what if someone really wants the extra precision `long double` offers? Or what if that person doesn't need much precision and prefers to use `float`?

The solution is to abandon the possibility of automatic conversion to a floating-point type and instead offer three functions that explicitly compute the floating-point value of the rational number. **Write as_float, as_double, and as_long_double**. Each of these member functions computes and returns the floating-point approximation for the rational number. The function name identifies the return type. You will have to cast the numerator and denominator to the desired floating-point type using `static_cast`, as you learned in Exploration 26. Listing 31-12 shows how I wrote these functions, with a sample program that demonstrates their use.

Listing 31-12. Converting to Floating-Point Types

```cpp
#include <cassert>
import <iostream>;
import <numeric>;

struct rational
{
  float as_float()
  {
    return static_cast<float>(numerator) / denominator;
  }

  double as_double()
  {
    return numerator / static_cast<double>(denominator);
  }

  long double as_long_double()
  {
    return static_cast<long double>(numerator) /
           static_cast<long double>(denominator);
  }

... omitted for brevity ...

};

int main()
{
  rational pi{355, 113};
  rational bmi{90*100*100, 180*180}; // Bogus-metabolic indicator of 90kg, 180cm
  double circumference{0}, radius{10};

  circumference = 2 * pi.as_double() * radius;
  std::cout << "circumference of circle with radius " << radius << " is about "
            << circumference << '\n';
  std::cout << "bmi = " << bmi.as_float() << '\n';
}
```

As you can see, if one argument to / (or any other arithmetic or comparison operator) is floating-point, the other operand is converted to match. You can cast both operands or just one or the other. Pick the style that suits you best and stick with it.

One more task would make it easier to write test programs: overloading the I/O operators. That is the topic for the next Exploration.

■ ■ ■

Custom I/O Operators

Wouldn't it be nice to be able to read and write rational numbers directly, for example, std::cout << rational{355, 113}? In fact, C++ has everything you need, although the job is a little trickier than perhaps it should be. This Exploration introduces some of the pieces you need to accomplish this.

Input Operator

The I/O operators are just like any other operators in C++, and you can overload them the way you overload any other operator. The input operator, also known as an *extractor* (because it extracts data from a stream), takes std::istream& as its first parameter. It must be a non-const reference, because the function will modify the stream object. The second parameter must also be a non-const reference, because you will store the input value there. By convention, the return type is std::istream&, and the return value is the first parameter. That lets you combine multiple input operations in a single expression. (Go back to Listing 17-3 for an example.)

The body of the function must do the work of reading the input stream, parsing the input, and deciding how to interpret that input. Proper error-handling is difficult, but the basics are easy. Every stream has a state mask that keeps track of errors. Table 32-1 lists the available state flags (declared in <ios>).

Table 32-1. I/O State Flags

Flag	Description
badbit	Unrecoverable error
eofbit	End-of-file
failbit	Invalid input or output
goodbit	No errors

If the input is not valid, the input function sets failbit in the stream's error state. When the caller tests whether the stream is okay, it tests the error state. If failbit is set, the check fails. (The test also fails if an unrecoverable error occurs, such as a hardware malfunction, but that's not pertinent to the current topic.)

Now you have to decide on a format for rational numbers. The format should be one that is flexible enough for a human to read and write easily but simple enough for a function to read and parse quickly. The input format must be able to read the output format and might be able to read other formats too.

Let's define the format as an integer, a slash (/), and another integer. White space can appear before or after any of these elements, unless the white space flag is disabled in the input stream. If the input contains an integer that is not followed by a slash, the integer becomes the resulting value (i.e., the implicit

© Ray Lischner 2020
R. Lischner, *Exploring C++20*, https://doi.org/10.1007/978-1-4842-5961-0_32

denominator is 1). The input operator has to "unread" the character, which may be important to the rest of the program. The unget() member function does exactly that. The input operator for integers will do the same thing: read as many characters as possible until reading a character that is not part of the integer, then unget that last character.

Putting all these pieces together requires a little care, but is not all that difficult. Listing 32-1 presents the input operator. Add this operator to the rest of the rational type that you wrote in Exploration 31.

Listing 32-1. Input Operator

```
... copy the rational class from Exploration 31

std::istream& operator>>(std::istream& in, rational& rat)
{
  int n{0}, d{0};
  char sep{'\0'};
  if (not (in >> n >> sep))
    // Error reading the numerator or the separator character.
    in.setstate(std::cin.failbit);
  else if (sep != '/')
  {
    // Read numerator successfully, but it is not followed by /.
    // Push sep back into the input stream, so the next input operation
    // will read it.
    in.unget();
    rat.assign(n, 1);
  }
  else if (in >> d)
    // Successfully read numerator, separator, and denominator.
    rat.assign(n, d);
  else
    // Error reading denominator.
    in.setstate(std::cin.failbit);

  return in;
}
```

Notice how rat is not modified until the function has successfully read both the numerator and the denominator from the stream. The goal is to ensure that if the stream enters an error state, the function does not alter rat.

The input stream automatically handles white space. By default, the input stream skips leading white space in each input operation, which means the rational input operator skips white space before the numerator, the slash separator, and the denominator. If the program turns off the ws flag, the input stream does not skip white space, and all three parts must be contiguous.

Output Operator

Writing the output operator, or *inserter* (so named because it inserts text into the output stream), has a number of hurdles, due to the plethora of formatting flags. You want to heed the desired field width and alignment, and you have to insert fill characters, as needed. Like any other output operator, you want to reset the field width but not change any other format settings.

One way to write a complicated output operator is to use a temporary output stream that stores its text in a string. The std::ostringstream type is declared in the <sstream> module. Use ostringstream the way you would use any other output stream, such as cout. When you are done, the str() member function returns the finished string.

To write the output operator for a rational number, create an ostringstream, and then write the numerator, separator, and denominator. Next, write the resulting string to the actual output stream. Let the stream itself handle the width, alignment, and fill issues when it writes the string. If you had written the numerator, slash, and denominator directly to the output stream, the width would apply only to the numerator, and the alignment would be wrong. Similar to an input operator, the first parameter has type std::ostream&, which is also the return type. The return value is the first parameter. The second parameter can use call-by-value, or you can pass a reference to const, as you can see in Listing 32-2. Add this code to Listing 32-1 and the rest of the rational type that you are defining.

Listing 32-2. Output Operator

```
std::ostream& operator<<(std::ostream& out, rational const& rat)
{
  std::ostringstream tmp{};
  tmp << rat.numerator;
  if (rat.denominator != 1)
    tmp << '/' << rat.denominator;
  out << tmp.str();

  return out;
}
```

Error State

The next step is to write a test program. Ideally, the test program should be able to continue when it encounters an invalid-input error. So now is a good time to take a closer look at how an I/O stream keeps track of errors.

As you learned earlier in this Exploration, every stream has a mask of error flags (see Table 32-1). You can test these flags, set them, or clear them. Testing the flags is a little unusual, however, so pay attention.

The way most programs in this book test for error conditions on a stream is to use the stream itself or an input operation as a condition. As you learned, an input operator function returns the stream, so these two approaches are equivalent. A stream converts to a bool result by returning the inverse of its fail() function, which returns true, if failbit or badbit is set.

In the normal course of an input loop, the program progresses until the input stream is exhausted. The stream sets eofbit when it reaches the end of the input stream. The stream's state is still good, in that fail() returns false, so the loop continues. However, the next time you try to read from the stream, it sees that no more input is available, sets failbit, and returns an error condition. The loop condition is false, and the loop exits.

The loop might also exit if the stream contains invalid input, such as non-numeric characters for integer input, or the loop can exit if there is a hardware error on the input stream (such as a disk failure). Until now, the programs in this book didn't bother to test why the loop exited. To write a good test program, however, you have to know the cause.

First, you can test for a hardware or similar error by calling the bad() member function, which returns true if badbit is set. That means something terrible happened to the file, and the program can't do anything to fix the problem.

Next, test for normal end-of-file by calling the eof() member function, which is true only when eofbit is set. If bad() and eof() are both false and fail() is true, this means the stream contains invalid input. How your program should handle an input failure depends on your particular circumstances. Some programs must exit immediately; others may try to continue. For example, your test program can reset the error state by calling the clear() member function, then continue running. After an input failure, you may not know the stream's position, so you don't know what the stream is prepared to read next. This simple test program skips to the next line.

Listing 32-3 demonstrates a test program that loops until end-of-file or an unrecoverable error occurs. If the problem is merely invalid input, the error state is cleared, and the loop continues.

Listing 32-3. Testing the I/O Operators

```cpp
#include <cassert>
import <iostream>;
import <numeric>;
import <sstream>;

... omitted for brevity ...

/// Tests for failbit only
bool iofailure(std::istream& in)
{
  return in.fail() and not in.bad();
}

int main()
{
  rational r{0};

  while (std::cin)
  {
    if (std::cin >> r)
      // Read succeeded, so no failure state is set in the stream.
      std::cout << r << '\n';
    else if (not std::cin.eof())
    {
      // Only failbit is set, meaning invalid input. Clear the state,
      // and then skip the rest of the input line.
      std::cin.clear();
      std::cin.ignore(std::numeric_limits<int>::max(), '\n');
    }
  }

  if (std::cin.bad())
    std::cerr << "Unrecoverable input failure\n";
}
```

The rational type is nearly finished. The next Exploration tackles assignment operators and seeks to improve the constructors.

■ ■ ■

Assignment and Initialization

The final step needed to complete this stage of the rational type is to write assignment operators and to improve the constructors. It turns out C++ does some work for you, but you often want to fine-tune that work. Let's find out how.

Assignment Operator

Until now, all the rational operators have been free functions. The assignment operator is different. The C++ standard requires that it be a member function. One way to write this function is shown in Listing 33-1.

Listing 33-1. First Version of the Assignment Operator

```
struct rational
{
  rational(int num, int den)
  : numerator{num}, denominator{den}
  {
    reduce();
  }

  rational& operator=(rational const& rhs)
  {
    numerator = rhs.numerator;
    denominator = rhs.denominator;
    reduce();
    return *this;
  }
  int numerator;
  int denominator;
};
```

Several points require further explanation. When you implement an operator as a free function, you need one parameter per operand. Thus, binary operators require a two-parameter function, and unary operators require a one-parameter function. Member functions are different, because the object itself is an operand (always the left-hand operand), and the object is implicitly available to all member functions; therefore, you need one fewer parameter. Binary operators require a single parameter (as you can see in Listing 33-1), and unary operators require no parameters (examples to follow).

The convention for assignment operators is to return a reference to the enclosing type. The value to return is the object itself. You can obtain the object with the expression *this (this is a reserved keyword).

Because *this is the object itself, another way to refer to members is to use the dot operator (e.g., (*this).numerator) instead of the unadorned numerator. Another way to write (*this).numerator is this->numerator. The meaning is the same; the alternative syntax is mostly a convenience. Writing this-> is not necessary for these simple functions, but it's often a good idea. When you read a member function, and you have trouble discerning the members from the nonmembers, that's a signal that you have to help the reader by using this-> before all the member names. Listing 33-2 shows the assignment operator with explicit use of this->.

Listing 33-2. Assignment Operator with Explicit Use of this->

```
rational& operator=(rational const& that)
{
  this->numerator = that.numerator;
  this->denominator = that.denominator;
  reduce();
  return *this;
}
```

The right-hand operand can be anything you want it to be. For example, you may want to optimize assignment of an integer to a rational object. The way the assignment operator works with the compiler's rules for automatic conversion, the compiler treats such an assignment (e.g., r = 3) as an implicit construction of a temporary rational object, followed by an assignment of one rational object to another.

Write an assignment operator that takes an int parameter. Compare your solution with mine, which is shown in Listing 33-3.

Listing 33-3. Assignment of an Integer to a rational

```
rational& operator=(int num)
{
  this->numerator = num;
  this->denominator = 1; // no need to call reduce()
  return *this;
}
```

If you do not write an assignment operator, the compiler writes one for you. In the case of the simple rational type, it turns out that the compiler writes one that works exactly like the one in Listing 32-2, so there was actually no need to write it yourself (except for instructional purposes). When the compiler writes code for you, it is hard for the human reader to know which functions are actually defined. Also, it is harder to document the implicit functions. So C++ lets you state explicitly that you want the compiler to supply a special function for you, by following a declaration (not a definition) with =default instead of a function body.

```
rational& operator=(rational const&) = default;
```

Constructors

The compiler also writes a constructor automatically, specifically one that constructs a rational object by copying all the data members from another rational object. This is called a *copy constructor*. Any time you pass a rational argument by value to a function, the compiler uses the copy constructor to copy the argument value to the parameter. Any time you define a rational variable and initialize it with the value of another rational value, the compiler constructs the variable by calling the copy constructor.

As with the assignment operator, the compiler's default implementation is exactly what we would write ourselves, so there is no need to write the copy constructor. As with an assignment operator, you can state explicitly that you want the compiler to supply its default copy constructor.

```
rational(rational const&) = default;
```

The parameter type for the copy constructor is a reference. Think about it. The compiler uses the copy constructor when passing an argument by value, so if the copy constructor were to use call-by-value, the program would recurse infinitely the first time it tried to copy an object. So the parameter to a copy constructor must be a reference. Almost always, that reference is to a const object.

If you don't write any constructors for a type, the compiler also creates a constructor that takes no arguments, called a *default constructor*. The compiler uses the default constructor when you define a variable of a custom type and do not provide an initializer for it. The compiler's implementation of the default constructor merely calls the default constructor for each data member. If a data member has a built-in type, the member is left uninitialized. In other words, if we did not write any constructors for rational, any rational variable would be uninitialized, so its numerator and denominator would contain garbage values. That's bad—very bad. All the operators assume the rational object has been reduced to normal form. They would fail if you passed an uninitialized rational object to them. The solution is simple: don't let the compiler write its default constructor. Instead, you write one.

All you have to do is write any constructor at all. This will prevent the compiler from writing its own default constructor. (It will still write its own copy constructor.)

Early on, we wrote a constructor for the rational type, but it was not a default constructor. As a result, you could not define a rational variable and leave it uninitialized or initialize it with empty braces. (You may have run into that issue when writing your own test program.) Uninitialized data is a bad idea, and having default constructors is a good idea. So write a default constructor to make sure a rational variable that has no initializer has a well-defined value nonetheless. What value should you use? I recommend zero, which is in keeping with the spirit of the default constructors for types such as string and vector. **Write a default constructor for rational to initialize the value to zero**.

Compare your solution with mine, which is presented in Listing 33-4.

Listing 33-4. Overloaded Constructors for rational

```
rational()
: rational{0, 1}
{}
```

Putting It All Together

Before we take leave of the rational type (only temporarily; we will return), let's put all the pieces together, so you can see what you've accomplished over the past four Explorations. Listing 33-5 shows the complete definition of rational and the related operators.

Listing 33-5. Complete Definition of rational and Its Operators

```
#include <cassert>
#include <cmath>
import <iostream>;
import <numeric>;
import <sstream>;
import test;
```

```
/// Represent a rational number (fraction) as a numerator and denominator.
struct rational
{
  rational()
  : rational{0}
  {/*empty*/}

  rational(int num)
  : numerator{num}, denominator{1}
  {/*empty*/}

  rational(int num, int den)
  : numerator{num}, denominator{den}
  {
    reduce();
  }

  rational(double r)
  : rational{static_cast<int>(r * 10000), 10000}
  {/*empty*/}

  rational& operator=(rational const& that)
  {
    this->numerator = that.numerator;
    this->denominator = that.denominator;
    return *this;
  }

  float as_float()
  {
    return static_cast<float>(numerator) / denominator;
  }

  double as_double()
  {
    return static_cast<double>(numerator) / denominator;
  }

  long double as_long_double()
  {
    return static_cast<long double>(numerator) / denominator;
  }

  /// Assign a numerator and a denominator, then reduce to normal form.
  void assign(int num, int den)
  {
    numerator = num;
    denominator = den;
    reduce();
  }
```

```cpp
  /// Reduce the numerator and denominator by their GCD.
  void reduce()
  {
    assert(denominator != 0);
    if (denominator < 0)
    {
      denominator = -denominator;
      numerator = -numerator;
    }
    int div{std::gcd(numerator, denominator)};
    numerator = numerator / div;
    denominator = denominator / div;
  }

  int numerator;
  int denominator;
};

/// Absolute value of a rational number.
rational abs(rational const& r)
{
  return rational{std::abs(r.numerator), r.denominator};
}

/// Unary negation of a rational number.
rational operator-(rational const& r)
{
  return rational{-r.numerator, r.denominator};
}

/// Add rational numbers.
rational operator+(rational const& lhs, rational const& rhs)
{
  return rational{lhs.numerator * rhs.denominator + rhs.numerator * lhs.denominator,
                  lhs.denominator * rhs.denominator};
}

/// Subtraction of rational numbers.
rational operator-(rational const& lhs, rational const& rhs)
{
  return rational{lhs.numerator * rhs.denominator - rhs.numerator * lhs.denominator,
                  lhs.denominator * rhs.denominator};
}

/// Multiplication of rational numbers.
rational operator*(rational const& lhs, rational const& rhs)
{
  return rational{lhs.numerator * rhs.numerator, lhs.denominator * rhs.denominator};
}
```

```cpp
/// Division of rational numbers.
/// TODO: check for division-by-zero
rational operator/(rational const& lhs, rational const& rhs)
{
  return rational{lhs.numerator * rhs.denominator, lhs.denominator * rhs.numerator};
}


/// Compare two rational numbers for equality.
bool operator==(rational const& a, rational const& b)
{
  return a.numerator == b.numerator and a.denominator == b.denominator;
}


/// Compare two rational numbers for inequality.
inline bool operator!=(rational const& a, rational const& b)
{
  return not (a == b);
}
/// Compare two rational numbers for less-than.
bool operator<(rational const& a, rational const& b)
{
  return a.numerator * b.denominator < b.numerator * a.denominator;
}


/// Compare two rational numbers for less-than-or-equal.
inline bool operator<=(rational const& a, rational const& b)
{
  return not (b < a);
}
/// Compare two rational numbers for greater-than.
inline bool operator>(rational const& a, rational const& b)
{
  return b < a;
}


/// Compare two rational numbers for greater-than-or-equal.
inline bool operator>=(rational const& a, rational const& b)
{
  return not (b > a);
}


/// Read a rational number.
/// Format is @em integer @c / @em integer.
std::istream& operator>>(std::istream& in, rational& rat)
{
  int n{0}, d{0};
  char sep{'\0'};
  if (not (in >> n >> sep))
    // Error reading the numerator or the separator character.
    in.setstate(in.failbit);
```

```cpp
  else if (sep != '/')
  {
    // Push sep back into the input stream, so the next input operation
    // will read it.
    in.unget();
    rat.assign(n, 1);
  }
  else if (in >> d)
    // Successfully read numerator, separator, and denominator.
    rat.assign(n, d);
  else
    // Error reading denominator.
    in.setstate(in.failbit);

  return in;
}

/// Write a rational numbers.
/// Format is @em numerator @c / @em denominator.
std::ostream& operator<<(std::ostream& out, rational const& rat)
{
  std::ostringstream tmp{};
  tmp << rat.numerator << '/' << rat.denominator;
  out << tmp.str();

  return out;
}

int main()
{
    TEST(rational{1} == rational{2,2});
    ... Add tests, lots of tests
}
```

I encourage you to add tests to the program in Listing 33-5, to exercise all the latest features of the rational class. Make sure everything works the way you expect it. Then put aside rational for the next Exploration, which takes a closer look at the foundations of writing custom types.

Writing Classes

The `rational` type is an example of a *class*. Now that you've seen a concrete example of writing your own class, it's time to understand the general rules that govern all classes. This Exploration and the next four lay the foundation for this important aspect of C++ programming.

Anatomy of a Class

A class has a name and *members*—data members, member functions, and even member typedefs and nested classes. You start a class definition with the `struct` keyword. (You might wonder why you would not start a class definition with the `class` keyword. Please be patient; all will become clear in Exploration 36.) Use curly braces to surround the body of the class definition, and the definition ends with a semicolon. Within the curly braces, you list all the members. Declare data members in a manner similar to a local variable definition. You write member functions in the same manner as you would a free function. Listing 34-1 shows a simple class definition that contains only data members.

Listing 34-1. Class Definition for a Cartesian Point

```
struct point
{
  double x;
  double y;
};
```

Listing 34-2 demonstrates how C++ lets you list multiple data members in a single declaration. Except for trivial classes, this style is uncommon. I prefer to list each member separately, so I can include a comment explaining the member, what it's used for, what constraints apply to it, and so on. Even without the comment, a little extra clarity goes a long way.

Listing 34-2. Multiple Data Members in One Declaration

```
struct point
{
  double x, y;
};
```

As with any other name in a C++ source file, before you can use a class name, the compiler must see its declaration or definition. You can use the name of a class within its own definition.

Use the class name as a type name, to define local variables, function parameters, function return types, and even other data members. The compiler knows about the class name from the very start of the class definition, so you can use its name as a type name inside the class definition.

When you define a variable using a class type, the compiler sets aside enough memory so the variable can store its own copy of every data member of the class. For example, define an object with type point, and the object contains the x and y members. Define another object of type point, and that object contains its own, separate x and y members.

Use the dot (.) operator to access the members, as you have been doing throughout this book. The object is the left-hand operand, and the member name is the right-hand operand, as shown in Listing 34-3.

Listing 34-3. Using a Class and Its Members

```
import <iostream>;

struct point
{
  double x;
  double y;
};

int main()
{
  point origin{}, unity{};
  origin.x = 0;
  origin.y = 0;
  unity.x = 1;
  unity.y = 1;
  std::cout << "origin = (" << origin.x << ", " << origin.y << ")\n";
  std::cout << "unity  = (" << unity.x  << ", " << unity.y  << ")\n";
}
```

Member Functions

In addition to data members, you can have member functions. Member function definitions look very similar to ordinary function definitions, except you define them as part of a class definition. Also, a member function can call other member functions of the same class and can access data members of the same class. Listing 34-4 shows some member functions added to class point.

Listing 34-4. Member Functions for Class point

```
#include <cmath> // for sqrt and atan2

struct point
{
  /// Distance to the origin.
  double distance()
  {
    return std::sqrt(x*x + y*y);
  }
  /// Angle relative to x-axis.
```

```
double angle()
{
   return std::atan2(y, x);
}

/// Add an offset to x and y.
void offset(double off)
{
   offset(off, off);
}
/// Add an offset to x and an offset to y
void offset(double  xoff, double yoff)
{
   x = x + xoff;
   y = y + yoff;
}

/// Scale x and y.
void scale(double mult)
{
   this->scale(mult, mult);
}
/// Scale x and y.
void scale(double xmult, double ymult)
{
   this->x = this->x * xmult;
   this->y = this->y * ymult;
}
double x;
double y;
};
```

For each member function, the compiler generates a hidden parameter named this. When you call a member function, the compiler passes the object as the hidden argument. In a member function, you can access the object with the expression *this. The C++ syntax rules specify that the member operator (.) has higher precedence than the * operator, so you need parentheses around *this (e.g., (*this).x). As a syntactic convenience, another way to write the same expression is this->x, several examples of which you can see in Listing 34-4.

The compiler is smart enough to know when you use a member name, so the use of this-> is optional. If a name has no local definition, and it is the name of a member, the compiler assumes you want to use the member. Some programmers prefer to always include this-> for the sake of clarity—in a large program, you can easily lose track of which names are member names. Other programmers find the extra this-> to be clutter and use it only when necessary. My recommendation is the latter. You need to learn to read C++ classes, and one of the necessary skills is to be able to read a class definition, find the member names, and keep track of those names while you read the class definition.

A number of programmers employ a more subtle technique, which involves using a special prefix or suffix to denote data member names. For example, a common technique is to use the prefix m_ for all data members ("m" is short for *member*). Another common technique is a little less intrusive: using a plain underscore (_) suffix. I prefer a suffix to a prefix, because suffixes interfere less than prefixes, so they don't obscure the important part of a name. From now on, I will adopt the practice of appending an underscore to every data member name.

NO LEADING UNDERSCORE

If you want to use only an underscore to denote members, use it as a suffix, not a prefix. The C++ standard sets aside certain names and prohibits you from using them. The actual rules are somewhat lengthy, because C++ inherits a number of restrictions from the C standard library. For example, you should not use any name that begins with E and is followed by a digit or an uppercase letter. (That rule seems arcane, but the C standard library defines several error code names, such as ERANGE, for a range error in a math function. This rule lets the library add new names in the future and lets those who implement libraries add vendor-specific names.)

I like simplicity, so I follow three basic rules. These rules are slightly more restrictive than the official C++ rules, but not in any burdensome way:

- Do not use any name that contains two consecutive underscores (like__this).

- Do not use any name that starts with an underscore (_like_this).

- Do not use any name that is all uppercase (LIKE_THIS).

Using a reserved name results in undefined behavior. The compiler may not complain, but the results are unpredictable. Typically, a standard library implementation must invent many additional names for its internal use. By defining certain names that the application programmer cannot use, C++ ensures the library writer can use these names within the library. If you accidentally use a name that conflicts with an internal library name, the result could be chaos or merely a subtle shift in a function's implementation.

Constructor

As you learned in Exploration 30, a constructor is a special member function that initializes an object's data members. You saw several variations on how to write a constructor, and now it's time to learn a few more.

When you declare a data member, you can also provide an initializer. The initializer is a default value that the compiler uses in case a constructor does not initialize that member. Use the normal initialization syntax of providing a value or values in curly braces.

```
struct point {
  int x = 1;
  int y;
  point() {} // initializes x to 1 and y to 0
};
```

Use this style of initializing data members only when a particular member needs a single value in all or nearly all constructors. By separating the initial value from the constructor, it makes the constructor harder to read and understand. The human reader must read the constructor and the data member declarations to know how the object is initialized. On the other hand, using default initializers is a great way to ensure that data members of built-in type, such as int, are always initialized.

Recall that constructors can be overloaded, and the compiler chooses which constructor to call, based on the arguments in the initializer. I like to use curly braces to initialize an object. The values in the curly braces are passed to the constructor in the same manner as function arguments to an ordinary function. In fact, C++ 03 used parentheses to initialize an object, so an initializer looked very much like a function call.

Later versions of C++ still allow this style of initializer, but in nearly all other cases, curly braces are better. Exploration 31 demonstrated that curly braces provide greater type safety.

Another key difference with curly braces is that you can initialize a container, such as a vector, with a series of values in curly braces, as follows:

```
std::vector<int> data{ 1, 2, 3 };
```

This introduces a problem. The vector type has several constructors. For example, a two-argument constructor lets you initialize a vector with many copies of a single value. A vector with ten zeroes, for example, can be initialized as follows:

```
std::vector<int> ten_zeroes(10, 0);
```

Note that I used parentheses. What if I used curly braces? **Try it. What happens?**

_____

_____

The vector is initialized with two integers: 10 and 0. The rule is that containers treat curly braces as a series of values with which to initialize the container contents. Curly braces can be used in a few other cases, such as copying a container, but if the constructor arguments look like container values, then the compiler may interpret them that way or issue an error message about ambiguity.

Write a constructor almost the same way you would an ordinary member function, but with a few differences:

- Omit the return type.

- Use plain return; (return statements that do not return values).

- Use the class name as the function name.

- Add an initializer list after a colon to initialize the data members. An initializer can also invoke another constructor, passing arguments to that constructor. Delegating construction to a common constructor is a great way to ensure rules are properly enforced by all constructors.

Listing 34-5 shows several examples of constructors added to class point.

Listing 34-5. Constructors for Class point

```
struct point
{
  point()
  : point{0.0, 0.0}
  {}
  point(double x, double y)
  : x_{x}, y_{y}
  {}
  point(point const& pt)
  : point{pt.x_, pt.y_}
  {}
  double x_;
  double y_;
};
```

Initialization is one of the key differences between class types and built-in types. If you define an object of built-in type without an initializer, you get a garbage value, but objects of class type are always initialized by calling a constructor. You always get a chance to initialize the object's data members. The difference between built-in types and class types is also evident in the rules C++ uses to initialize data members in a constructor.

A constructor's initializer list is optional, but I recommend you always provide it, unless every data member has an initializer. The initializer list appears after a colon, which follows the closing parenthesis of the constructor's parameter list; it initializes each data member in the same order in which you declare them in the class definition, ignoring the order in the initializer list. To avoid confusion, always write the initializer list in the same order as the data members. Member initializers are separated by commas and can spill onto as many lines as you need. Each member initializer provides the initial value of a single data member or uses the class name to invoke another constructor. List the member name, followed by its initializer in curly braces. Initializing a data member is the same as initializing a variable and follows the same rules.

If you don't write any constructors for your class, the compiler writes its own default constructor. The compiler's default constructor is just like a constructor that omits an initializer list.

```
struct point {
  point() {} // x_ is initialized to 0, and y_ is uninitialized
  double x_{};
  double y_;
};
```

When the compiler writes a constructor for you, the constructor is *implicit*. If you write any constructor, the compiler suppresses the implicit default constructor. If you want a default constructor in that case, you must write it yourself.

In some applications, you may want to avoid the overhead of initializing the data members of point, because your application will immediately assign a new value to the point object. Most of the time, however, caution is best.

A *copy constructor* is one that takes a single argument of the same type as the class, passed by reference. The compiler automatically generates calls to the copy constructor when you pass objects by value to functions or when functions return objects. You can also initialize a point object with the value of another point object, and the compiler generates code to invoke the copy constructor.

```
point pt1;          // default constructor
point p2{pt1};      // copy constructor
```

If you don't write your own copy constructor, the compiler writes one for you. The automatic copy constructor calls the copy constructor for every data member, just like the one in Listing 34-5. Because I wrote one that is exactly like the one the compiler writes implicitly, there is no reason to write it explicitly. Let the compiler do its job.

To help you visualize how the compiler calls constructors, read Listing 34-6. Notice how it prints a message for each constructor use.

Listing 34-6. Visual Constructors

```
import <iostream>;

struct demo
{
  demo()       : demo{0} { std::cout << "default constructor\n"; }
  demo(int x) : x_{x} { std::cout << "constructor(" << x << ")\n"; }
  demo(demo const& that)
  : x_{that.x_}
```

```
  {
    std::cout << "copy constructor(" << x_ << ")\n";
  }
  int x_;
};

demo addone(demo d)
{
  ++d.x_;
  return d;
}

int main()
{
  demo d1{};
  demo d2{d1};
  demo d3{42};
  demo d4{addone(d3)};
}
```

Predict the output from running the program in Listing 34-6.

_____

_____

_____

_____

_____

_____

_____

Check your prediction. **Were you correct?** _____

The compiler performs some minor optimizations when passing arguments to functions and accepting return values. For example, instead of copying a demo object to the addone return value and then copying the return value to initialize d4, the C++ standard directs compilers to remove unnecessary calls to the copy constructor. When I run the program, I get this:

```
constructor(0)
default constructor
copy constructor(0)
constructor(42)
copy constructor(42)
copy constructor(43)
```

Defaulted and Deleted Constructors

If you do not supply any constructors, the compiler implicitly writes a default constructor and a copy constructor. If you write at least one constructor of any variety, the compiler does not implicitly write a default constructor, but it still gives you a copy constructor if you don't write one yourself.

You can take control over the compiler's implicit behavior without writing any of your own constructors. Write a function header without a body for the constructor, and use =default to get the compiler's implicit definition. Use =delete to suppress that function. For example, if you don't want anyone creating copies of a class, note the following:

```cpp
struct dont_copy
{
    dont_copy(dont_copy const&) = delete;
};
```

More common is letting the compiler write its copy constructor but telling the human reader explicitly. As you learn more about C++, you will learn that the rules for which constructors the compiler writes for you, and when it writes them, are more complicated than what I've presented so far. I urge you to get into the habit of stating when you ask the compiler to implicitly provide a constructor, even if it seems trivially obvious.

```cpp
struct point
{
  point() = default;
  point(point const&) = default;
  int x, y;
};
```

That was easy. The next Exploration starts with a real challenge.

EXPLORATION 35

■ ■ ■

More About Member Functions

Member functions and constructors are even more fun than what you've learned so far. This Exploration continues to uncover their mysteries.

Revisiting Project 1

What did you find most frustrating about Project 1 (Exploration 29)? If you are anything like me (although I hope you're not, for your own sake), you may have been disappointed that you had to define several separate vectors to store one set of records. However, without knowing about classes, that was the only feasible approach. Now that you've been introduced to classes, you can fix the program. **Write a class definition to store one record.** Refer back to Exploration 29 for details. To summarize, each record keeps track of an integer height in centimeters, an integer weight in kilograms, the calculated BMI (which you can round off to an integer), the person's sex (letter 'M' or 'F'), and the person's name (a string).

Next, **write a read member function that reads a single record from an istream**. It takes two arguments: an istream and an integer. Prompt the user for each piece of information by writing to std::cout. The integer argument is the record number, which you can use in the prompts. **Write a print member function that prints one record**; it takes an ostream and an integer threshold as arguments.

Finally, **modify the program to take advantage of the new class you wrote.** Compare your solution to mine, shown in Listing 35-1.

Listing 35-1. New BMI Program

```
#include <cstdlib>
import <algorithm>;
import <iomanip>;
import <iostream>;
import <limits>;
import <locale>;
import <ranges>;
import <string>;
import <vector>;

/// Compute body-mass index from height in centimeters and weight in kilograms.
int compute_bmi(int height, int weight)
{
    return static_cast<int>(weight * 10000 / (height * height) + 0.5);
}
```

© Ray Lischner 2020

R. Lischner, *Exploring C++20*, https://doi.org/10.1007/978-1-4842-5961-0_35

```cpp
/// Skip the rest of the input line.
void skip_line(std::istream& in)
{
  in.ignore(std::numeric_limits<int>::max(), '\n');
}

/// Represent one person's record, storing the person's name, height, weight,
/// sex, and body-mass index (BMI), which is computed from the height and weight.
struct record
{
  record() : height_{0}, weight_{0}, bmi_{0}, sex_{'?'}, name_{}
  {}

  /// Get this record, overwriting the data members.
  /// Error-checking omitted for brevity.
  /// @return true for success or false for eof or input failure
  bool read(std::istream& in, int num)
  {
    std::cout << "Name " << num << ": ";
    std::string name{};
    if (not std::getline(in, name))
      return false;

    std::cout << "Height (cm): ";
    int height{};
    if (not (in >> height))
      return false;
    skip_line(in);

    std::cout << "Weight (kg): ";
    int weight{};
    if (not (in >> weight))
      return false;
    skip_line(in);

    std::cout << "Sex (M or F): ";
    char sex{};
    if (not (in >> sex))
      return false;
    skip_line(in);
    sex = std::toupper(sex, std::locale());

    // Store information into data members only after reading
    // everything successfully.
    name_ = name;
    height_ = height;
    weight_ = weight;
    sex_ = sex;
    bmi_ = compute_bmi(height_, weight_);
    return true;
  }
```

```cpp
  /// Print this record to @p out.
  void print(std::ostream& out, int threshold)
  {
    out << std::setw(6) << height_
        << std::setw(7) << weight_
        << std::setw(3) << sex_
        << std::setw(6) << bmi_;
    if (bmi_ >= threshold)
      out << '*';
    else
      out << ' ';
    out << ' ' << name_ << '\n';
  }

  int height_;        ///< height in centimeters
  int weight_;        ///< weight in kilograms
  int bmi_;           ///< Body-mass index
  char sex_;          ///< 'M' for male or 'F' for female
  std::string name_;  ///< Person's name
};

/** Print a table.
 * Print a table of height, weight, sex, BMI, and name.
 * Print only records for which sex matches @p sex.
 * At the end of each table, print the mean and median BMI.
 */
void print_table(char sex, std::vector<record>& records, int threshold)
{
  std::cout << "Ht(cm) Wt(kg) Sex  BMI  Name\n";

  float bmi_sum{};
  long int bmi_count{};
  std::vector<int> tmpbmis{}; // store only the BMIs that are printed
                              // in order to compute the median
  for (auto rec : records)
  {
    if (rec.sex_ == sex)
    {
      bmi_sum = bmi_sum + rec.bmi_;
      ++bmi_count;
      tmpbmis.push_back(rec.bmi_);
      rec.print(std::cout, threshold);
    }
  }

  // If the vectors are not empty, print basic statistics.
  if (bmi_count != 0)
  {
    std::cout << "Mean BMI = "
              << std::setprecision(1) << std::fixed << bmi_sum / bmi_count
              << '\n';
```

```cpp
    // Median BMI is trickier. The easy way is to sort the
    // vector and pick out the middle item or items.
    std::ranges::sort(tmpbmis);
    std::cout << "Median BMI = ";
    // Index of median item.
    std::size_t i{tmpbmis.size() / 2};
    if (tmpbmis.size() % 2 == 0)
      std::cout << (tmpbmis.at(i) + tmpbmis.at(i-1)) / 2.0 << '\n';
    else
      std::cout << tmpbmis.at(i) << '\n';
  }
}


/** Main program to compute BMI. */
int main()
{
  std::locale::global(std::locale{""});
  std::cout.imbue(std::locale{});
  std::cin.imbue(std::locale{});

  std::vector<record> records{};
  int threshold{};

  std::cout << "Enter threshold BMI: ";
  if (not (std::cin >> threshold))
    return EXIT_FAILURE;
  skip_line(std::cin);

  std::cout << "Enter name, height (in cm),"
               " and weight (in kg) for each person:\n";
  record rec{};
  while (rec.read(std::cin, records.size()+1))
  {
    records.emplace_back(rec);
    std::cout << "BMI = " << rec.bmi_ << '\n';
  }

  // Print the data.
  std::cout << "\n\nMale data\n";
  print_table('M', records, threshold);
  std::cout << "\nFemale data\n";
  print_table('F', records, threshold);
}
```

That's a lot to swallow, so take your time. I'll wait here until you're done. When faced with a new class that you have to read and understand, start by reading the comments (if any). One approach is to first skim lightly over the class to identify the members (function and data), then reread the class to understand the member functions in depth. Tackle one member function at a time.

You may be asking yourself why I didn't overload the >> and << operators to read and write record objects. The requirements of the program are a little more complicated than what these operators offer. For example, reading a record also involves printing prompts, and each prompt includes an ordinal, so the user knows which record to type. Some records are printed differently than others, depending on the threshold. The >> operator has no convenient way to specify the threshold. Overloading I/O operators is great for simple types but usually is not appropriate for more complicated situations.

const Member Functions

Take a closer look at the print_table function. Notice anything unusual or suspicious about its parameters? The records argument is passed by reference, but the function never modifies it, so you really should pass it as a reference to const. Go ahead and make that change. **What happens?**

_____

_____

_____

You should see an error from the compiler. When records is const, the auto rec : records type must declare rec as const too. Thus, when print_table calls rec.print(), inside the print() function, this refers to a const record object. Although print() does not modify the record object, it could, and the compiler must allow for the possibility. You have to tell the compiler that print() is safe and doesn't modify any data members. Do so by adding a const modifier between the print() function signature and the function body. Listing 35-2 shows the new definition of the print member function.

Listing 35-2. Adding the const Modifier to print

```
/// Print this record to @p out.
void print(std::ostream& out, int threshold)
const
{
  out << std::setw(6) << height_
      << std::setw(7) << weight_
      << std::setw(3) << sex_
      << std::setw(6) << bmi_;
  if (bmi_ >= threshold)
    out << '*';
  else
    out << ' ';
  out << ' ' << name_ << '\n';
}
```

As a general rule, use the const modifier for any member function that does not change any data members. This ensures that you can call the member function when you have a const object. **Copy the code from Listing 34-4 and modify it to add const modifiers where appropriate**. Compare your result with mine in Listing 35-3.

Listing 35-3. const Member Functions for Class point

```
#include <cmath> // for sqrt and atan2

struct point
{
  /// Distance to the origin.
```

```cpp
  double distance()
  const
  {
    return std::sqrt(x*x + y*y);
  }
  /// Angle relative to x-axis.
  double angle()
  const
  {
    return std::atan2(y, x);
  }

  /// Add an offset to x and y.
  void offset(double off)
  {
    offset(off, off);
  }
  /// Add an offset to x and an offset to y
  void offset(double  xoff, double yoff)
  {
    x = x + xoff;
    y = y + yoff;
  }

  /// Scale x and y.
  void scale(double mult)
  {
    this->scale(mult, mult);
  }
  /// Scale x and y.
  void scale(double xmult, double ymult)
  {
    this->x = this->x * xmult;
    this->y = this->y * ymult;
  }
  double x;
  double y;
};
```

The `scale` and `offset` functions modify data members, so they cannot be const. The angle and distance member functions don't modify any members, so they are const.

Given a point variable, you can call any member function. If the object is const, however, you can call only const member functions. The most common situation is when you find yourself with a const object within another function, and the object was passed by reference to const, as illustrated in Listing 35-4.

Listing 35-4. Calling const and Non-const Member Functions

```cpp
#include <cmath>
import <iostream>;

// Use the same point definition as Listing 35-3
... omitted for brevity ...
```

```cpp
void print_polar(point const& pt)
{
  std::cout << "{ r=" << pt.distance() << ", angle=" << pt.angle() << " }\n";
}

void print_cartesian(point const& pt)
{
  std::cout << "{ x=" << pt.x << ", y=" << pt.y << " }\n";
}

int main()
{
  point p1{}, p2{};
  double const pi{3.141592653589792};
  p1.x = std::cos(pi / 3);
  p1.y = std::sin(pi / 3);
  print_polar(p1);
  print_cartesian(p1);
  p2 = p1;
  p2.scale(4.0);
  print_polar(p2);
  print_cartesian(p2);
  p2.offset(0.0, -2.0);
  print_polar(p2);
  print_cartesian(p2);
}
```

Another common use for member functions is to restrict access to data members. Imagine what would happen if a program that used the BMI record type accidentally modified the bmi_ member. A better design would let you call a bmi() function to obtain the BMI but hide the bmi_ data member, to prevent accidental modification. You can prevent such accidents, and the next Exploration shows you how.

■ ■ ■

Access Levels

Everyone has secrets, some of us more than others. Classes have secrets too. For example, throughout this book, you have used the `std::string` class without having any notion of what goes on inside the class. The implementation details are secrets—not closely guarded secrets, but secrets nonetheless. You cannot directly examine or modify any of `string`'s data members. Instead, it presents quite a few member functions that make up its public interface. You are free to use any of the publicly available member functions, but only the publicly available member functions. This Exploration explains how you can do the same with your classes.

Public vs. Private

The author of a class determines which members are secrets (for use only by the class's own member functions) and which members are freely available for use by any other bit of code in the program. Secret members are called *private*, and the members that anyone can use are *public*. The privacy setting is called the *access level*. (When you read C++ code, you may see another access level, `protected`. I'll cover that one later. Two access levels are enough to begin with.)

To specify an access level, use the `private` keyword or the `public` keyword, followed by a colon. All subsequent members in the class definition have that accessibility level until you change it with a new access-level keyword. Listing 36-1 shows the `point` class with access-level specifiers.

Listing 36-1. The point Class with Access-Level Specifiers

```
struct point
{
public:
  point() : point{0.0, 0.0} {}
  point(double x, double y) : x_{x}, y_{y} {}
  point(point const&) = default;

  double x() const { return x_; }
  double y() const { return y_; }

  double angle()   const { return std::atan2(y(), x()); }
  double distance() const { return std::sqrt(x()*x() + y()*y()); }
```

```
void move_cartesian(double x, double y)
{
  x_ = x;
  y_ = y;
}
void move_polar(double r, double angle)
{
  move_cartesian(r * std::cos(angle), r * std::sin(angle));
}

void scale_cartesian(double s)        { scale_cartesian(s, s); }
void scale_cartesian(double xs, double ys)
{
  move_cartesian(x() * xs, y() * ys);
}
void scale_polar(double r)            { move_polar(distance() * r, angle()); }
void rotate(double a)                 { move_polar(distance(), angle() + a); }
void offset(double o)                 { offset(o, o); }
void offset(double xo, double yo)     { move_cartesian(x() + xo, y() + yo); }

private:
  double x_;
  double y_;
};
```

The data members are private, so the only functions that can modify them are point's own member functions. Public member functions provide access to the position with the public x() and y() member functions.

■ **Tip** Always keep data members private, and provide access only through member functions.

To modify a position, notice that point does not let the user arbitrarily assign a new *x* or *y* value. Instead, it offers several public member functions to move the point to an absolute position or relative to the current position.

The public member functions let you work in Cartesian coordinates—that is, the familiar *x* and *y* positions, or in polar coordinates, specifying a position as an angle (relative to the *x* axis) and a distance from the origin. Both representations for a point have their uses, and both can uniquely specify any position in two-dimensional space. Some users prefer polar notation, while others prefer Cartesian. Neither user has direct access to the data members, so it doesn't matter how the point class actually stores the coordinates. In fact, you can change the implementation of point to store the distance and angle as data members by changing only a few member functions. **Which member functions would you have to change?**

_____

_____

Changing the data members from x_ and y_ to r_ and angle_ necessitates a change to the x, y, angle, and distance member functions, just for access to the data members. You also have to change the two move functions: move_polar and move_cartesian. Finally, you have to modify the constructors. No other changes are necessary. Because the scale and offset functions do not access data members directly, but instead call other member functions, they are insulated from changes to the class implementation. **Rewrite the point class to store polar coordinates in its data members.** Compare your class with mine, which is shown in Listing 36-2.

Listing 36-2. The point Class Changed to Store Polar Coordinates

```
struct point
{
public:
  point() : point{0.0, 0.0} {}
  point(double x, double y) : r_{0.0}, angle_{0.0} { move_cartesian(x, y); }
  point(point const&) = default;

  double x() const { return distance() * std::cos(angle()); }
  double y() const { return distance() * std::sin(angle()); }

  double angle()    const { return angle_; }
  double distance() const { return r_; }

  void move_cartesian(double x, double y)
  {
    move_polar(std::sqrt(x*x + y*y), std::atan2(y, x));
  }
  void move_polar(double r, double angle)
  {
    r_ = r;
    angle_ = angle;
  }

  void scale_cartesian(double s)          { scale_cartesian(s, s); }
  void scale_cartesian(double xs, double ys)
  {
    move_cartesian(x() * xs, y() * ys);
  }
  void scale_polar(double r)            { move_polar(distance() * r, angle()); }
  void rotate(double a)                 { move_polar(distance(), angle() + a); }
  void offset(double o)                 { offset(o, o); }
  void offset(double xo, double yo)     { move_cartesian(x() + xo, y() + yo); }

private:
  double r_;
  double angle_;
};
```

One small difficulty is the constructor. Ideally, point should have two constructors, one taking polar coordinates and the other taking Cartesian coordinates. The problem is that both sets of coordinates are pairs of numbers, and overloading cannot distinguish between the arguments. This means you can't use normal overloading for these constructors. Instead, you can add a third parameter: a flag that indicates whether to interpret the first two parameters as polar coordinates or Cartesian coordinates.

```
point(double a, double b, bool is_polar)
{
  if (is_polar)
    move_polar(a, b);
  else
    move_cartesian(a, b);
}
```

It's something of a hack, but it will have to do for now. Later in the book, you will learn cleaner techniques to accomplish this task.

class vs. struct

Exploration 35 hinted that the class keyword was somehow involved in class definitions, even though every example in this book so far uses the struct keyword. Now is the time to learn the truth.

The truth is quite simple. The struct and class keywords both start class definitions. The only difference is the default access level: private for class and public for struct. That's all.

By convention, programmers tend to use class for class definitions. A common (but not universal) convention is to start class definitions with the public interface, tucking away the private members at the bottom of the class definition. Listing 36-3 shows the latest incarnation of the point class, this time defined using the class keyword.

Listing 36-3. The point Class Defined with the class Keyword

```
class point
{
public:
  point() : r_{0.0}, angle_{0.0} {}

  double x() const { return distance() * std::cos(angle()); }
  double y() const { return distance() * std::sin(angle()); }

  double angle()    const { return angle_; }
  double distance() const { return r_; }

  ... other member functions omitted for brevity ...

private:
  double r_;
  double angle_;
};
```

Public or Private?

Usually, you can easily determine which members should be public and which should be private. Sometimes, however, you have to stop and ponder. Consider the rational class (last seen in Exploration 34). **Rewrite the rational class to take advantage of access levels.**

Did you decide to make reduce() public or private? I chose private, because there is no need for any outside caller to call reduce(). Instead, the only member functions to call reduce() are the ones that change the data members themselves. Thus, reduce() is hidden from outside view and serves as an implementation detail. The more details you hide, the better because it makes your class easier to use.

When you added access functions, did you let the caller change the numerator only? Did you write a function to change the denominator only? Or did you ask that the user assign both at the same time? The user of a rational object should treat it as a single entity, a number. You can't assign only a new exponent to a floating-point number, and you shouldn't be able to assign only a new numerator to a rational number. On the other hand, I see no reason not to let the caller examine only the numerator or only the denominator. For example, you may want to write your own output formatting function, which requires knowing the numerator and denominator separately.

A good sign that you have made the right choices is that you can rewrite all the operator functions easily. These functions should not have to access the data-members of rational, but use only the public functions. If you tried to access any private members, you learned pretty quickly that the compiler wouldn't let you. That's what privacy is all about.

Compare your solution with my solution, presented in Listing 36-4.

Listing 36-4. The Latest Rewrite of the rational Class

```
#include <cassert>
#include <cstdlib>
import <iostream>;
import <numeric>;
import <sstream>;

/// Represent a rational number (fraction) as a numerator and denominator.
class rational
{
public:
  rational(): rational{0}  {}
  rational(int num): numerator_{num}, denominator_{1} {} // no need to reduce
  rational(rational const&) = default;
  rational(int num, int den)
  : numerator_{num}, denominator_{den}
  {
    reduce();
  }

  rational(double r)
  : rational{static_cast<int>(r * 100000), 100000}
  {
    reduce();
  }

  int numerator()    const { return numerator_; }
  int denominator() const { return denominator_; }
  float to_float()
  const
  {
    return static_cast<float>(numerator()) / denominator();
  }
```

```
  double to_double()
  const
  {
    return static_cast<double>(numerator()) / denominator();
  }

  long double to_long_double()
  const
  {
    return static_cast<long double>(numerator()) /
           denominator();
  }

  /// Assign a numerator and a denominator, then reduce to normal form.
  void assign(int num, int den)
  {
    numerator_ = num;
    denominator_ = den;
    reduce();
  }
private:
  /// Reduce the numerator and denominator by their GCD.
  void reduce()
  {
    assert(denominator() != 0);
    if (denominator() < 0)
    {
      denominator_ = -denominator();
      numerator_ = -numerator();
    }
    int div{std::gcd(numerator(), denominator())};
    numerator_ = numerator() / div;
    denominator_ = denominator() / div;
  }

  int numerator_;
  int denominator_;
};

/// Absolute value of a rational number.
rational abs(rational const& r)
{
  return rational{std::abs(r.numerator()), r.denominator()};
}

/// Unary negation of a rational number.
rational operator-(rational const& r)
{
  return rational{-r.numerator(), r.denominator()};
}
```

```
/// Add rational numbers.
rational operator+(rational const& lhs, rational const& rhs)
{
  return rational{
          lhs.numerator() * rhs.denominator() + rhs.numerator() * lhs.denominator(),
          lhs.denominator() * rhs.denominator()};
}

/// Subtraction of rational numbers.
rational operator-(rational const& lhs, rational const& rhs)
{
  return rational{
          lhs.numerator() * rhs.denominator() - rhs.numerator() * lhs.denominator(),
          lhs.denominator() * rhs.denominator()};
}

/// Multiplication of rational numbers.
rational operator*(rational const& lhs, rational const& rhs)
{
  return rational{lhs.numerator() * rhs.numerator(),
                  lhs.denominator() * rhs.denominator()};
}

/// Division of rational numbers.
/// TODO: check for division-by-zero
rational operator/(rational const& lhs, rational const& rhs)
{
  return rational{lhs.numerator() * rhs.denominator(),
                  lhs.denominator() * rhs.numerator()};
}

/// Compare two rational numbers for equality.
bool operator==(rational const& a, rational const& b)
{
  return a.numerator() == b.numerator() and a.denominator() == b.denominator();
}

/// Compare two rational numbers for inequality.
inline bool operator!=(rational const& a, rational const& b)
{
  return not (a == b);
}
/// Compare two rational numbers for less-than.
bool operator<(rational const& a, rational const& b)
{
  return a.numerator() * b.denominator() < b.numerator() * a.denominator();
}
```

```
/// Compare two rational numbers for less-than-or-equal.
inline bool operator<=(rational const& a, rational const& b)
{
  return not (b < a);
}
/// Compare two rational numbers for greater-than.
inline bool operator>(rational const& a, rational const& b)
{
  return b < a;
}

/// Compare two rational numbers for greater-than-or-equal.
inline bool operator>=(rational const& a, rational const& b)
{
  return not (b > a);
}


/// Read a rational number.
/// Format is @em integer @c / @em integer.
std::istream& operator>>(std::istream& in, rational& rat)
{
  int n{}, d{};
  char sep{};
  if (not (in >> n >> sep))
    // Error reading the numerator or the separator character.
    in.setstate(in.failbit);
  else if (sep != '/')
  {
    // Push sep back into the input stream, so the next input operation
    // will read it.
    in.unget();
    rat.assign(n, 1);
  }
  else if (in >> d)
    // Successfully read numerator, separator, and denominator.
    rat.assign(n, d);
  else
    // Error reading denominator.
    in.setstate(in.failbit);

  return in;
}
```

```
/// Write a rational numbers.
/// Format is @em numerator @c / @em denominator.
std::ostream& operator<<(std::ostream& out, rational const& rat)
{
  std::ostringstream tmp{};
  tmp << rat.numerator() << '/' << rat.denominator();
  out << tmp.str();

  return out;
}
```

Classes are one of the fundamental building blocks of object-oriented programming. Now that you know how classes work, you can see how they apply to this style of programming, which is the subject of the next Exploration.

■ ■ ■

Understanding Object-Oriented Programming

This Exploration takes a break from C++ programming to turn to the topic of object-oriented programming (OOP). You may already be familiar with this topic, but I urge you to continue reading. You may learn something new. To everyone else, this Exploration introduces some of the foundations of OOP in general terms. Later Explorations will show how C++ implements OOP principles.

Books and Magazines

What is the difference between a book and a magazine? Yes, I really want you to write down your answer. Write down as many differences as you can think of.

_____

_____

_____

What are the similarities between books and magazines? Write down as many similarities as you can think of.

_____

_____

_____

If you can, compare your lists with the lists that other people write. They don't have to be programmers; everyone knows what books and magazines are. Ask your friends and neighbors; stop strangers at the bus stop and ask them. Try to find a core set of commonalities and differences.

Many items on the lists will be qualified. For instance, "most books have at least one author," "many magazines are published monthly," and so on. That's fine. When solving real problems, we often map "maybe" and "sometimes" into "never" or "always," according to the specific needs of the problem at hand. Just remember that this is an OOP exercise, not a bookstore or library exercise.

© Ray Lischner 2020
R. Lischner, *Exploring C++20*, https://doi.org/10.1007/978-1-4842-5961-0_37

Now categorize the commonalities and the differences. I'm not telling you how to categorize them. Just try to find a small set of categories that covers the diverse items on your lists. Some less useful categorizations are group by number of words, group by last letter. **Try to find useful categories. Write them down.**

_____

_____

_____

_____

I came up with two broad categories: attributes and actions. _Attributes_ describe the physical characteristics of books and magazines:

- Books and magazines have size (number of pages) and cost.

- Most books have an ISBN (International Standard Book Number).

- Most magazines have an ISSN (International Standard Serial Number).

- Magazines have a volume number and issue number.

Books and magazines have a title and publisher. Books have authors. Magazines typically don't. (Magazine articles have authors, but a magazine as a whole rarely lists an author.)

Actions describe how a book or magazine acts or how you interact with them:

- You can read a book or magazine. A book or magazine can be open or closed.

- You can purchase a book or magazine.

- You can subscribe to a magazine.

The key distinction between attributes and actions is that attributes are specific to a single object. Actions are shared by all objects of a common class. Sometimes, actions are called _behaviors_. All dogs exhibit the behavior called panting; they all pant in pretty much the same manner and for the same reasons. All dogs have the attribute color, but one dog is golden, another dog is black, and the dog over there next to the tree is white with black spots.

In programming terms, a _class_ describes the behaviors or actions and the types of attributes for all the objects of that class. Each _object_ has its own values for the attributes that the class enumerates. In C++ terms, member functions implement actions and provide access to attributes, and data members store attributes.

Classification

Books and magazines don't do much on their own. Instead, their "actions" depend on how we interact with them. A bookstore interacts with books and magazines by selling, stocking, and advertising them. A library's actions include lending and accepting returns. Other kinds of objects have actions they initiate on their own. For example, **what are some of the behaviors of a dog?**

_____

_____

_____

_____

_____

What are the attributes of a dog?

_____

_____

_____

_____

_____

What about a cat? **Do cats and dogs have significantly different behaviors?** _____ **Attributes?**
_____ **Summarize the differences.**

_____

_____

I don't own dogs or cats, so my observations are limited. From where I sit, dogs and cats have many similar attributes and behaviors. I expect that many readers are much more astute observers than I and can enumerate quite a few differences between the two animals.

Nonetheless, I maintain that once you consider the differences closely, you will see that many of them are not attributes or behaviors unique to one type of animal or the other but are merely different values of a single attribute or different details of a single behavior. Cats may be more fastidious, but dogs and cats both exhibit grooming behavior. Dogs and cats come in different colors, but they both have colored furs (with rare exceptions).

In other words, when trying to enumerate the attributes and behaviors of various objects, your job can be made simpler by classifying similar objects together. For critters, biologists have already done the hard work for us, and they have devised a rich and detailed taxonomy of animals. Thus, a species (_catus_ or _familiaris_) belongs to a genus (_Felis_ or _Canis_), which is part of a family (Felidae or Canidae). These are grouped yet further into an order (Carnivora), a class (Mammalia), and so on, up to the animal (Metazoa) kingdom. (Taxonomists, please forgive my oversimplification.)

So what happens to attributes and behaviors as you ascend the taxonomic tree? **Which attributes and behaviors are the same across all mammals?**

_____

_____

_____

_____

All animals?

_____

_____

_____

_____

As the classification became broader, the attributes and behavior also became more general. Among the attributes of dogs and cats are color of fur, length of tail, weight, and much more. Not all mammals have fur or tails, so you need broader attributes for the entire class. Weight still works, but instead of overall length, you may want to use size. Instead of color of fur, you need only generic coloring. For all animals, the attributes are quite broad: size, weight, single cell vs. multicell, and so on.

Behaviors are similar. You may list that cats purr, dogs pant, both animals can walk and run, and so on. All mammals eat and drink. Female mammals nurse their young. For all animals, you are left with a short, general list: eat and reproduce. It's hard to be more specific than that when you are trying to list the behaviors common to all animals, from amoebae to zebras.

A classification tree helps biologists understand the natural world. Class trees (or *class hierarchies*, as they are often called, because big words make us feel important) help programmers model the natural world in software (or model the unnatural world, as so often happens in many of our projects). Instead of trying to name each level of the tree, programmers prefer a local, recursive view of any class hierarchy. Going up the tree, each class has a *base* class, also called a superclass or parent class. Thus, *animal* is a base class of *mammal*, which is a base class of *dog*. Going downward are *derived* classes, also called subclasses or child classes. *Dog* is a derived class of *mammal*. Figure 37-1 illustrates a class hierarchy. Arrows point from derived class to base class.

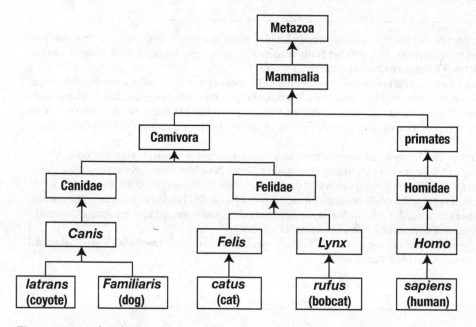

Figure 37-1. A class diagram

An *immediate* base class is one with no intervening base classes. For example, the immediate base class of *catus* is *Felis*, which has an immediate base class of Felidae, which has an immediate base class of Carnivora. Metazoa, Mammalia, Carnivora, Felidae, and *Felis* are all base classes of *catus*, but only *Felis* is its immediate base class.

Inheritance

Just as a mammal has all the attributes and behaviors of an animal, and a dog has the attributes and behaviors of all mammals, in an OOP language, a derived class has all the behaviors and attributes of all of its base classes. The term most often used is *inheritance*: the derived class *inherits* the behaviors and attributes of its base class. This term is somewhat unfortunate, because OOP inheritance is nothing like real-world inheritance. When a derived class inherits behaviors, the base class retains its behaviors. In the real world, classes don't inherit anything; objects do.

In the real world, a person object inherits the value of certain attributes (cash, stock, real estate, etc.) from a deceased ancestor object. In the OOP world, a person class inherits behaviors from a base class, such as primate, by sharing the single copy of those behavior functions that are defined in the base class. A person class inherits the attributes of a base class, so objects of the derived class contain values for all the attributes defined in its class and in all of its base classes. In time, the inheritance terminology will become natural to you.

Because inheritance creates a tree structure, tree terminology also pervades discussion of inheritance. As is so common in programming, tree diagrams are drawn upside down, with the root at the top, and leaves at the bottom (as you saw in Figure 36-1). Some OOP languages (Java, Smalltalk, Delphi) have a single root, which is the ultimate base class for all classes. Others, such as C++, do not. Any class can be the root of its own inheritance tree.

So far, the main examples for inheritance involved some form of specialization. *Cat* is more specialized than *mammal*, which is more specialized than *animal*. The same is true in computer programming. For example, class frameworks for graphical user interfaces (GUIs) often use a hierarchy of specialized classes. Figure 37-2 shows a selection of some of the more important classes that make up wxWidgets, which is an open source C++ framework that supports many platforms.

Even though C++ does not require a single root class, some frameworks do; wxWidgets is one that does require a single root class. Most wxWidgets classes derive from wxObject. Some objects are straightforward, such as wxPen and wxBrush. Interactive objects derive from wxEvtHandler (short for "event handler"). Thus, each step in the class tree introduces another degree of specialization.

Later in the book, you will see other uses for inheritance, but the most common and most important use is to create specialized derived classes from more general base classes.

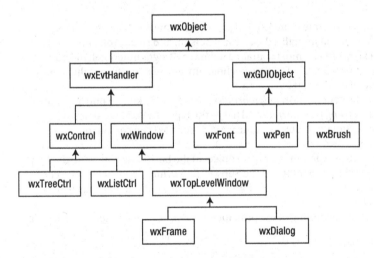

Figure 37-2. Excerpt from the wxWidgets class hierarchy

Liskov's Substitution Principle

When a derived class specializes the behavior and attributes of a base class (which is the common case), any code that you write involving the base class should work equally well with an object of the derived class. In other words, the act of feeding a mammal is, in broad principles, the same, regardless of the specific kind of animal.

Barbara Liskov and Jeannette Wing formalized this fundamental principle of object-oriented programming, which is often known today as the Substitution Principle or Liskov's Substitution Principle. Briefly, the Substitution Principle states that if you have base class *B* and derived class *D*, in any situation that calls for an object of type *B*, you can substitute an object of type *D*, with no ill effects. In other words, if you need a mammal, any mammal, and someone hands you a dog, you should be able to use that dog. If someone hands you a cat, a horse, or a cow, you can use that animal. If someone hands you a fish, however, you are allowed to reject the fish in any manner that you deem suitable.

The Substitution Principle helps you write programs, but it also imposes a burden. It helps because it frees you to write code that depends on base class behavior without concerning yourself about any derived classes. For example, in a GUI framework, the base `wxEvtHandler` class might be able to recognize a mouse click and dispatch it to an event handler. The click handler does not know or care whether the control is actually a `wxListCtrl` control, a `wxTreeCtrl` control, or a `wxButton`. All that matters is that `wxEvtHandler` accepts a click event, acquires the position, determines which mouse button was clicked, and so on and then dispatches this event to the event handler.

The burden is on the authors of the `wxButton`, `wxListCtrl`, and `wxTreeCtrl` classes to ensure that their click behavior meets the requirements of the Substitution Principle. The easiest way to meet the requirements is to let the derived class inherit the behavior of the base class. Sometimes, however, the derived class has additional work to do. Instead of inheriting, it provides new behavior. In that case, the programmer must ensure that the behavior is a valid substitution for the base class behavior. The next few Explorations will show concrete examples of this abstract principle.

Type Polymorphism

Before returning to C++-land, I want to present one more general principle. Suppose I hand you a box labeled "Mammal." Inside the box can be any mammal: a dog, a cat, a person, and so on. You know the box cannot contain a bird, a fish, a rock, or a tree. It must contain a mammal. Programmers call the box *polymorphic*, from the Greek meaning "many forms." The box can hold any one of many forms, that is, any one mammal, regardless of which form of mammal it is.

Although many programmers use the general term *polymorphism*, this specific kind of polymorphism is *type polymorphism*, also known as *subtyping polymorphism*. That is, the type of a variable (or a box) determines which kinds of objects it can contain. A polymorphic variable (or box) can contain one of a number of types of objects.

In particular, a variable with a base class type can refer to an object of the base class type or to an object of any type that is derived from that base class. According to the Substitution Principle, you can write code to use the base class variable, calling any of the member functions of the base class, and that code will work, regardless of the object's true, derived type.

Now that you have a fundamental understanding of the principles of OOP, it is time to see how they play out in C++.

EXPLORATION 38

■ ■ ■

Inheritance

The previous Exploration introduced general OOP principles. Now it's time to see how to apply those principles to C++.

Deriving a Class

Defining a derived class is just like defining any other class, except that you include a base class access level and name after a colon. See Listing 38-1 for an example of some simple classes to support a library. Every item in the library is a work of some kind: a book, a magazine, a movie, and so on. To keep things simple, the class work has only two derived classes, book and periodical.

Listing 38-1. Defining a Derived Class

```cpp
import <iostream>;
import <string>;
import <string_view>;

class work
{
public:
  work() = default;
  work(work const&) = default;
  work(std::string_view id, std::string_view title) : id_{id}, title_{title} {}
  std::string const& id()    const { return id_; }
  std::string const& title() const { return title_; }
private:
  std::string id_;
  std::string title_;
};

class book : public work
{
public:
  book() : work{}, author_{}, pubyear_{} {}
  book(book const&) = default;
  book(std::string_view id, std::string_view title, std::string_view author,
       int pubyear)
```

```
  : work{id, title}, author_{author}, pubyear_{pubyear}
  {}
  std::string const& author() const { return author_; }
  int pubyear()              const { return pubyear_; }
private:
  std::string author_;
  int pubyear_; ///< year of publication
};
```

```
class periodical : public work
{
public:
  periodical() : work{}, volume_{0}, number_{0}, date_{} {}
  periodical(periodical const&) = default;
  periodical(std::string_view id, std::string_view title, int volume,
             int number,
 std::string_view date)
  : work{id, title}, volume_{volume}, number_{number}, date_{date}
  {}
  int volume()              const { return volume_; }
  int number()              const { return number_; }
  std::string const& date() const { return date_; }
private:
  int volume_;       ///< volume number
  int number_;       ///< issue number
  std::string date_; ///< publication date
};
```

```
int main()
{
    book b{"1", "Exploring C++ 20", "Ray Lischner", 2020};
    periodical p{"2", "The C++ Times", 1, 1, "Jan 1, 2020"};
    std::cout << b.title() << '\n' <<
                 p.title() << '\n';
}
```

When you define a class using the struct keyword, the default access level is public. For the class keyword, the default is private. These keywords also affect derived classes. Except in rare circumstances, public is the right choice here, which is what I used to write the classes in Listing 37-1.

Also in Listing 38-1, note that there is something new about the initializer lists. A derived class can (and should) initialize its base class by listing the base class name and its initializer. You can call any constructor by passing the right arguments. If you omit the base class from the initializer list, the compiler uses the base class's default constructor.

> **What do you think happens if the base class does not have a default constructor?**

_____

Try it. Change work's default constructor from = default to = delete and try to compile the code for Listing 38-1. **What happens?**

_____

That's right; the compiler complains. The exact error message or messages you receive vary from compiler to compiler. I get something like the following:

```
$ g++ -ansi -pedantic list3801err.cpp
list3801err.cpp: In constructor 'book::book()':
list3801err.cpp:17:41: error: use of deleted function 'work::work()'
   book() : work{}, author_{}, pubyear_{0} {}
                                        ^
list3801err.cpp:4:3: error: declared here
   work() = delete;
   ^
list3801err.cpp: In constructor 'periodical::periodical()':
list3801err.cpp:33:56: error: use of deleted function 'work::work()'
   periodical() : work{}, volume_{0}, number_{0}, date_{} {}
                                                      ^
list3801err.cpp:4:3: error: declared here
   work() = delete;
   ^
```

Base classes are always initialized before members, starting with the root of the class tree. You can see this for yourself by writing classes that print messages from their constructors, as demonstrated in Listing 38-2.

Listing 38-2. Printing Messages from Constructors to Illustrate Order of Construction

```
import <iostream>;

class base
{
public:
  base() { std::cout << "base\n"; }
};

class middle : public base
{
public:
  middle() { std::cout << "middle\n"; }
};

class derived : public middle
{
public:
  derived() { std::cout << "derived\n"; }
};

int main()
{
  derived d;
}
```

What output do you expect from the program in Listing 38-2?

_____

_____

_____

Try it. **What output did you actually get?**

_____

_____

_____

Were you correct? _____ In the interest of being thorough, I receive this:

```
base
middle
derived
```

Remember that if you omit the base class from the initializers, or you omit the initializer list entirely, the base class's default constructor is called. Listing 38-2 contains only default constructors, so what happens is the constructor for `derived` first invokes the default constructor for `middle`. The constructor for `middle` invokes the default constructor for `base` first, and the constructor for `base` has nothing to do except execute its function body. Then it returns, and the constructor body for `middle` executes and returns, finally letting `derived` run its function body.

Member Functions

A derived class inherits all members of the base class. This means a derived class can call any public member function and access any public data member. So can any users of the derived class. Thus, you can call the `id()` and `title()` functions of a `book` object, and the `work::id()` and `work::title()` functions are called.

The access levels affect derived classes, so a derived class cannot access any private members of a base class. (In Exploration 69, you will learn about a third access level that shields members from outside prying eyes while granting access to derived classes.) Thus, the `periodical` class cannot access the `id_` or `title_` data members, and so a derived class cannot accidentally change a `work`'s identity or title. In this way, access levels ensure the integrity of a class. Only the class that declares a data member can alter it, so it can validate all changes, prevent changes, or otherwise control who changes the value and how.

If a derived class declares a member function with the same name as the base class, the derived class function is the only one visible in the derived class. The function in the derived class is said to _shadow_ the function in the base class. As a rule, you want to avoid this situation, but there are several cases in which you very much want to use the same name, without shadowing the base class function. In the next Exploration, you will learn about one such case. Later, you will learn others.

Destructors

When an object is destroyed—perhaps because the function in which it is defined ends and returns—sometimes you have to do some cleanup. A class has another special member function that performs cleanup when an object is destroyed. This special member function is called a _destructor_.

Like constructors, destructors do not have return values. A destructor name is the class name preceded by a tilde (~). Listing 38-3 adds destructors to the example classes from Listing 38-2.

Listing 38-3. Order of Calling Destructors

```
import <iostream>;

class base
{
public:
  base()  { std::cout << "base\n"; }
  ~base() { std::cout << "~base\n"; }
};

class middle : public base
{
public:
  middle()  { std::cout << "middle\n"; }
  ~middle() { std::cout << "~middle\n"; }
};

class derived : public middle
{
public:
  derived()  { std::cout << "derived\n"; }
  ~derived() { std::cout << "~derived\n"; }
};

int main()
{
  derived d;
}
```

What output do you expect from the program in Listing 37-3?

_____

_____

_____

_____

_____

_____

Try it. **What do you actually get?**

_____

_____

_____

_____

_____

_____

Were you correct? _____ When a function returns, it destroys all local objects in the reverse order of construction. When a destructor runs, it destroys the most-derived class first, by running the destructor's function body. It then invokes the immediate base class destructor. Hence, the destructors run in opposite order of construction in the following example:

```
base
middle
derived
~derived
~middle
~base
```

If you don't write a destructor, the compiler writes a trivial one for you. Whether you write your own or the compiler implicitly writes the destructor, after every destructor body finishes, the compiler arranges to call the destructor for every data member and then execute the destructor for the base classes, starting with the most derived. For simple classes in these examples, the compiler's destructors work just fine. Later, you will find more interesting uses for destructors. For now, the main purpose is just to visualize the life cycle of an object.

Read Listing 38-4 carefully.

Listing 38-4. Constructors and Destructors

```cpp
import <iostream>;

class base
{
public:
  base(int value) : value_{value} { std::cout << "base(" << value << ")\n"; }
  base() : base{0} { std::cout << "base()\n"; }
  base(base const& copy)
  : value_{copy.value_}
  { std::cout << "copy base(" << value_ << ")\n"; }

  ~base() { std::cout << "~base(" << value_ << ")\n"; }
  int value() const { return value_; }
  base& operator++()
  {
    ++value_;
    return *this;
  }
private:
  int value_;
};

class derived : public base
{
public:
  derived(int value): base{value} { std::cout << "derived(" << value << ")\n"; }
  derived() : base{} { std::cout << "derived()\n"; }
  derived(derived const& copy)
  : base{copy}
```

```
    { std::cout << "copy derived(" << value() << "\n"; }
    ~derived() { std::cout << "~derived(" << value() << ")\n"; }
};

derived make_derived()
{
  return derived{42};
}

base increment(base b)
{
  ++b;
  return b;
}

void increment_reference(base& b)
{
  ++b;
}

int main()
{
  derived d{make_derived()};
  base b{increment(d)};
  increment_reference(d);
  increment_reference(b);
  derived a(d.value() + b.value());
}
```

Fill in the left-hand column of Table 38-1 with the output you expect from the program.

Table 38-1. *Expected and Actual Results of Running the Program in Listing 38-4*

Expected Output	Actual Output

Try it. Fill in the right-hand column of Table 38-1 with the actual output and compare the two columns. **Did you get everything correct?** _____

What follows is the output generated on my system, along with some commentary. Remember that compilers have some leeway in optimizing away extra calls to the copy constructor. You may get one or two extra copy calls in the mix.

```
base(42)         // inside make_derived()
derived(42)      // finish constructing in make_derived()
copy base(42)    // copy to b in call to increment()
copy base(43)    // copy return value from increment to b in main
~base(43)        // destroy temporary return value
base(87)         // construct a in main
```

```
derived(87)                    // construct a in main
~derived(87)                   // end of main: destroy a
~base(87)                      // destroy a
~base(44)                      // destroy b
~derived(43)                   // destroy d
~base(43)                      // finish destroying d
```

Note how pass-by-reference (increment_reference) does not invoke any constructors, because no objects are being constructed. Instead, references are passed to the function, and the referenced object is incremented.

By the way, I have not yet shown you how to overload the increment operator, but you probably guessed that's how it works (in class base). Decrement is similar.

Access Level

At the start of this Exploration, I advised you to use public before the base class name but never explained why. Now is the time to fill you in on the details.

Access levels affect inheritance the same way they affect members. *Public inheritance* occurs when you use the struct keyword to define a class or use the public keyword before the base class name. Public inheritance means the derived class inherits every member of the base class at the same access level that the members have in the base class. Except in rare circumstances, this is exactly what you want.

Private inheritance occurs when you use the private keyword, and it is the default when you define a class using the class keyword. Private inheritance keeps every member of the base class private and inaccessible to users of the derived class. The compiler still calls the base class constructor and destructor when necessary, and the derived class still inherits all the members of the base class. The derived class can call any of the base class's public member functions, but no one else can call them through the derived class. It's as though the derived class re-declares all inherited members as private. Private inheritance lets a derived class make use of the base class without being required to meet the Substitution Principle. This is an advanced technique, and I recommend that you try it only with proper adult supervision.

If the compiler complains about inaccessible members, most likely you forgot to include a public keyword in the class definition. Try compiling Listing 38-5 to see what I mean.

Listing 38-5. Accidentally Inheriting Privately

```
class base
{
public:
  base(int v) : value_{v} {}
  int value() const { return value_; }
private:
  int value_;
};

class derived : base
{
public:
  derived() : base{42} {}
};
```

```
int main()
{
  base b{42};
  int x{b.value()};
  derived d{};
  int y{d.value()};
}
```

The compiler issues an error message, complaining that base is private or not accessible from derived, or something along those lines.

Programming Style

When in doubt, make data members and member functions private, unless and until you know you need to make a member public. Once a member is part of the public interface, anyone using your class is free to use that member, and you have one more code dependency. Changing a public member means finding and fixing all those dependencies. Keep the public interface as small as possible. If you have to add members later, you can, but it's much harder to remove a member or change it from public to private. Anytime you have to add members to support the public interface, make the supporting functions and data members private.

Use public, not private, inheritance. Remember that inherited members also become part of the derived class's public interface. If you change which class is the base class, you may have to write additional members in the derived class, to make up for members that were in the original base class but are missing from the new base class. The next Exploration continues the discussion of how derived classes work with base classes to provide important functionality.

EXPLORATION 39

■ ■ ■

Virtual Functions

Deriving classes is fun, but there's not a lot you can do with them—at least, not yet. The next step is to see how C++ implements type polymorphism, and this Exploration starts you on that journey.

Type Polymorphism

Recall from Exploration 37 that type polymorphism is the ability of a variable of type B to take the "form" of any class derived from B. The obvious question is "How?" The key in C++ is to use a magic keyword to declare a member function in a base class and also implement the function in a derived class with a different magic word. The magic keyword tells the compiler that you want to invoke type polymorphism, and the compiler implements the polymorphism magic. Define a variable of type reference-to-base class and initialize it with an object of derived class type. When you call the polymorphic function for the object, the compiled code checks the object's actual type and calls the derived class implementation of the function. The magic word to turn a function into a polymorphic function is `virtual`. Derived classes are marked with `override`.

For example, suppose you want to be able to print any kind of work in the library (see Listing 38-1) using standard (more or less) bibliographical format. For books, I use the format

> *author, title, year.*

For periodicals, I use

> *title, volume(number), date.*

Add a `print` member function to each class, to print this information. Because this function has different behavior in each derived class, the function is polymorphic, so use the `virtual` keyword before the base class declaration of `print` and `override` after each derived class declaration, as shown in Listing 39-1.

Listing 39-1. Adding a Polymorphic print Function to Every Class Derived from work

```
class work
{
public:
  work() = default;
  work(work const&) = default;
  work(std::string_view id, std::string_view title) : id_{id}, title_{title} {}
  virtual ~work() {}
  std::string const& id()    const { return id_; }
  std::string const& title() const { return title_; }
  virtual void print(std::ostream&) const {}
```

© Ray Lischner 2020
R. Lischner, *Exploring C++20*, https://doi.org/10.1007/978-1-4842-5961-0_39

```cpp
private:
  std::string id_;
  std::string title_;
};

class book : public work
{
public:
  book() : work{}, author_{}, pubyear_{0} {}
  book(book const&) = default;
  book(std::string_view id, std::string_view title, std::string_view author,
       int pubyear)
  : work{id, title}, author_{author}, pubyear_{pubyear}
  {}
  std::string const& author() const { return author_; }
  int pubyear()              const { return pubyear_; }
  void print(std::ostream& out)
  const override
  {
    out << author() << ", " << title() << ", " << pubyear() << ".";
  }
private:
  std::string author_;
  int pubyear_; ///< year of publication
};

class periodical : public work
{
public:
  periodical() : work{}, volume_{0}, number_{0}, date_{} {}
  periodical(periodical const&) = default;
  periodical(std::string_view id, std::string_view title, int volume,
             int number,
 std::string_view date)
  : work{id, title}, volume_{volume}, number_{number}, date_{date}
  {}
  int volume()               const { return volume_; }
  int number()               const { return number_; }
  std::string const& date() const { return date_; }
  void print(std::ostream& out)
  const override
  {
    out << title() << ", " << volume() << '(' << number() << "), " <<
        date() << ".";
  }
private:
  int volume_;        ///< volume number
  int number_;        ///< issue number
  std::string date_; ///< publication date
};
```

▓ Tip   When writing a stub function, such as print(), in the base class, omit the parameter name or names. The compiler requires only the parameter types. Some compilers warn you if a parameter or variable is not used, and even if the compiler doesn't issue a warning, it is a clear message to the human who reads your code that the parameters are not used.

A program that has a reference to a work object can call the print member function to print that work, and because print is polymorphic, or virtual, the C++ environment performs its magic to ensure that the correct print is called, depending on whether the work object is actually a book or a periodical. To see this demonstrated, read the program in Listing 39-2.

Listing 39-2 Calling the print Function

```cpp
import <iostream>;
import <string>;
import <string_view>;

// All of Listing 39-1 belongs here
... omitted for brevity ...

void showoff(work const& w)
{
  w.print(std::cout);
  std::cout << '\n';
}

int main()
{
  book sc{"1", "The Sun Also Crashes", "Ernest Lemmingway", 2000};
  book ecpp{"2", "Exploring C++", "Ray Lischner", 2020};
  periodical pop{"3", "Popular C++", 13, 42, "January 1, 2000"};
  periodical today{"4", "C++ Today", 1, 1, "January 13, 1984"};

  showoff(sc);
  showoff(ecpp);
  showoff(pop);
  showoff(today);
}
```

What output do you expect?

_____

_____

_____

_____

Try it. **What output do you actually get?**

_____

_____

_____

_____

The showoff function does not have to know about the book or periodical classes. As far as it is concerned, w is a reference to a work object. The only member functions you can call are those declared in the work class. Nonetheless, when showoff calls print, it will invoke book's print or periodical's print, if the object's true type is book or periodical.

Write an output operator (operator<<) that prints a work object by calling its print member function. Compare your solution with my solution, as shown in Listing 39-3.

Listing 39-3. *Output Operator for Class work*

```cpp
std::ostream& operator<<(std::ostream& out, work const& w)
{
  w.print(out);
  return out;
}
```

Writing the output operator is perfectly normal. Just be certain you declare w as a reference. Polymorphic magic does not occur with ordinary objects, only references. With this operator, you can write any work-derived object to an output stream, and it will print using its print function.

■ **Tip** The const keyword, if present, always comes before override. Although the specifiers, such as virtual, can be mixed freely with the function's return type (even if the result is strange, such as int virtual long function()), the const qualifier and override specifier must follow a strict order.

Virtual Functions

A polymorphic function is called a *virtual function* in C++, owing to the virtual keyword. Once a function is defined as virtual, it remains so in every derived class. The virtual function must have the same name, the same return type, and the same number and type of parameters (but the parameters can have different names) in the derived class.

A derived class is not required to implement a virtual function. If it doesn't, it inherits the base class function the same way it does for a non-virtual function. When a derived class implements a virtual function, it is said to *override* the function, because the derived class's behavior overrides the behavior that would have been inherited from the base class.

In the derived class, the override specifier is optional but helps to prevent mistakes. If you accidentally mistype the function's name or parameters in the derived class, the compiler might think you are defining a brand-new function. By adding override, you tell the compiler that you intend to override a virtual function that was declared in the base class. If the compiler cannot find a matching function in the base class, it issues an error message.

Add a class, movie, to the library classes. The movie class represents a movie or film recording on tape or disc. Like book and periodical, the movie class derives from work. For the sake of simplicity, define a movie as having an integer running time (in minutes), in addition to the members it inherits from work. Do not override print yet. Compare your class to Listing 39-4.

Listing 39-4. Adding a Class movie

```
class movie : public work
{
public:
  movie() : work{}, runtime_{0} {}
  movie(movie const&) = default;
  movie(std::string_view id, std::string_view title, int runtime)
  : work{id, title}, runtime_{runtime}
  {}
  int runtime() const { return runtime_; }
private:
  int runtime_; ///< running length in minutes
};
```

Now modify the test program from Listing 39-2 to create and print a movie object. If you want, you can take advantage of the new output operator, instead of calling showoff. Compare your program with Listing 39-5.

Listing 39-5. Using the New movie Class

```
import <iostream>;
import <string>;
import <string_view>;

// All of Listing 39-1 belongs here
// All of Listing 39-3 belongs here
// All of Listing 39-4 belongs here
... omitted for brevity ...

int main()
{
  book sc{"1", "The Sun Also Crashes", "Ernest Lemmingway", 2000};
  book ecpp{"2", "Exploring C++", "Ray Lischner", 2006};
  periodical pop{"3", "Popular C++", 13, 42, "January 1, 2000"};
  periodical today{"4", "C++ Today", 1, 1, "January 13, 1984"};
  movie tr{"5", "Lord of the Token Rings", 314};

  std::cout << sc << '\n';
  std::cout << ecpp << '\n';
  std::cout << pop << '\n';
  std::cout << today << '\n';
  std::cout << tr << '\n';
}
```

What do you expect as the last line of output?

_____

Try it. What do you get?

_____

Because movie does not override print, it inherits the implementation from the base class, work. The definition of print in the work class does nothing, so printing the tr object prints nothing.

Fix the problem by adding print to the movie class. Now your movie class should look something like Listing 39-6.

Listing 39-6. Adding a print Member Function to the movie Class

```
class movie : public work
{
public:
  movie() : work{}, runtime_{0} {}
  movie(movie const&) = default;
  movie(std::string_view id, std::string_view title, int runtime)
  : work{id, title}, runtime_{runtime}
  {}
  int runtime() const { return runtime_; }
  void print(std::ostream& out)
  const override
  {
    out << title() << " (" << runtime() << " min)";
  }
private:
  int runtime_; ///< running length in minutes
};
```

The override keyword is optional in the derived class but highly recommended. Some programmers also use the virtual keyword in the derived classes. In C++ 03, this served as a reminder to the human reader that the derived class function overrides a virtual function. The override specifier was added in C++ 11 and has the added feature of telling the compiler the same thing, so the compiler can check your work and complain if you make a mistake. I urge you to use override everywhere it belongs.

EVOLUTION OF A LANGUAGE

You may find it odd that the virtual keyword appears at the start of a function header and override appears at the end. You are witnessing the compromises that are often necessary when a language evolves.

The override specifier was added to the language after its initial standardization. One way to add the override specifier would have been to add it to the list of function specifiers, like virtual. But adding a new keyword to a language is fraught with difficulty. Every existing program that uses override as a variable or other user-defined name would break. Programmers all over the world would have to check and possibly modify their software to avoid this new keyword.

So the C++ standards committee devised a way to add `override` without making it a reserved keyword. The syntax of a function declaration puts the `const` qualifier in a special place. No other identifiers are allowed there, so it is easy to add `override` to the syntax for member functions in a manner similar to `const`, and with no risk of breaking existing code.

Other new language features use existing keywords in new ways, such as `=default` and `=delete` for constructors. But a few new keywords were added, and they bring with them the risk of breaking existing code. So the committee tried to choose names that would be less likely to conflict with existing user-chosen names. You will see examples of some of these new keywords later in the book as well as other novel uses of special words in special contexts that avoid reserving those special words as keywords.

References and Slices

The `showoff` function in Listing 39-2 and the output operator in Listing 39-3 declare their parameter as a reference to const `work`. **What do you expect would happen if you were to change them to pass-by-value?**

_____

_____

_____

Try it. Delete the ampersand in the declaration of the output operator, as shown here:

```
std::ostream& operator<<(std::ostream& out, work w)
{
  w.print(out);
  return out;
}
```

Run the test program from Listing 39-5. **What is the actual output?**

_____

_____

_____

_____

_____

Explain what happened.

_____

_____

_____

When you pass an argument by value or assign a derived class object to a base class variable, you lose polymorphism. For instance, instead of a book, the result is an honest-to-goodness, genuine, no-artificial-ingredients work—with no memory of book-ness whatsoever. Thus, the output operator ends up calling work's version of print every time the output operator calls it. That's why the program's output is a bunch of empty lines. When you pass a book object to the output operator, not only do you lose polymorphism, but you also lose all sense of book-ness. In particular, you lose the author_ and pubyear_ data members. The data members that a derived class adds are *sliced* away when the object is copied to a base class variable. Another way to look at it is this: because the derived class members are sliced away, what is left is only a work object, so you cannot have polymorphism. The same thing occurs with assignment.

```
work w;
book nuts{"7", "C++ in a Nutshell", "Ray Lischner", 2003};
w = nuts; // slices away the author_ and pubyear_; copies only id_ and title_
```

Slicing is easy to avoid when writing functions (pass all arguments by reference) but harder to cope with for assignment. The techniques you need to manage assignment come much later in this book. For now, I will focus on writing polymorphic functions.

Pure Virtual Functions

The class work defines the print function, but the function doesn't do anything useful. In order to be useful, every derived class must override print. The author of a base class, such as work, can ensure that every derived class properly overrides a virtual function, by omitting the body of the function and substituting the tokens, = 0, instead. These tokens mark the function as a *pure virtual function*, which means the function has no implementation to inherit, and derived classes must override the function.

Modify the work class to make print a pure virtual function. Then delete the book class's print function, just to see what happens. What does happen?

_____

_____

The compiler enforces the rules for pure virtual functions. A class that has at least one pure virtual function is said to be *abstract*. You cannot define an object of abstract type. **Fix the program.** The new work class should look something like Listing 39-7.

Listing 39-7. Defining work As an Abstract Class

```
class work
{
public:
  work() = default;
  work(work const&) = default;
  work(std::string_view id, std::string_view title) : id_(id), title_(title) {}
  virtual ~work() {}
  std::string const& id()    const { return id_; }
  std::string const& title() const { return title_; }
  virtual void print(std::ostream& out) const = 0;
private:
  std::string id_;
  std::string title_;
};
```

Virtual Destructors

Although most classes you are writing at this time do not require destructors, I want to mention an important implementation rule. Any class that has virtual functions must declare its destructor to be virtual too. This rule is a programming guideline, not a semantic requirement, so the compiler will not help you by issuing a message when you break it (although some compilers may issue a warning). Instead, you must enforce this rule yourself, through discipline.

I will repeat the rule when you begin to write classes that require destructors. If you try any experiments on your own, please be mindful of this rule, or else your programs could be subject to subtle problems—or not-so-subtle crashes.

The next Exploration continues the discussion of classes and their relationship in the C++ type system.

EXPLORATION 40

■ ■ ■

Classes and Types

One of the main design goals for C++ was to give the programmer the ability to define custom types that look and act nearly identically to the built-in types. The combination of classes and overloaded operators gives you that power. This Exploration takes a closer look at the type system and how your classes can best fit into the C++ world.

Classes vs. typedefs

Suppose you are writing a function to compute Bogus Metabolic Index (BMI) from an integer height in centimeters and an integer weight in kilograms. You have no difficulty writing such a function (which you can copy from your work in Explorations 29 and 35). For added clarity, you decide to add typedefs for height and weight, which allows the programmer to define variables for storing and manipulating these values with extra clarity to the human reader. Listing 40-1 shows a simple use of the compute_bmi() function and the associated typedefs.

Listing 40-1. Computing BMI

```
import <iostream>;

using height = int;
using weight = int;
using bmi = int;

bmi compute_bmi(height h, weight w)
{
  return w * 10000 / (h * h);
}

int main()
{
  std::cout << "Height in centimeters: ";
  height h{};
  std::cin >> h;

  std::cout << "Weight in kilograms: ";
  weight w{};
  std::cin >> w;

  std::cout << "Bogus Metabolic Index = " << compute_bmi(w, h) << '\n';
}
```

© Ray Lischner 2020
R. Lischner, *Exploring C++20*, https://doi.org/10.1007/978-1-4842-5961-0_40

Test the program. **What's wrong?**

_____

_____

If you haven't spotted it yet, take a closer look at the call to compute_bmi(), on the last line of code in main(). Compare the arguments with the parameters in the function definition. Now do you see the problem?

In spite of the extra clarity that the height and weight using declarations offer, I still made a fundamental mistake and reversed the order of the arguments. In this case, the error is easy to spot, because the program is small. Also, the program's output is so obviously wrong that testing quickly reveals the problem. Don't relax too much, though; not all mistakes are so obvious.

The problem here is that a using declaration does not define a new type but instead creates an alias for an existing type. The original type and its alias are completely interchangeable. Thus, a height is the same as an int is the same as a weight. Because the programmer is able to mix up height and weight, the using declaration doesn't actually help much.

More useful would be to create distinct types called height and weight. As distinct types, you would not be able to mix them up, and you would have full control over the operations that you allow. For example, dividing two weights should yield a plain, unitless int. Adding a height to a weight should result in an error message from the compiler. Listing 40-2 shows simple height and weight classes that impose these restrictions.

Listing 40-2. Defining Classes for height and weight

```
import <iostream>;

/// Height in centimeters
class height
{
public:
  height(int h) : value_{h} {}
  int value() const { return value_; }
private:
  int value_;
};

/// Weight in kilograms
class weight
{
public:
  weight(int w) : value_{w} {}
  int value() const { return value_; }
private:
  int value_;
};

std::istream& operator>>(std::istream& stream, height& ht)
{
  int tmp;
  if (stream >> tmp)
```

```
    ht = height{tmp};
  return stream;
}

std::istream& operator>>(std::istream& stream, weight& wt)
{
  int tmp;
  if (stream >> tmp)
    wt = weight{tmp};
  return stream;
}

/// Body-mass index
class bmi
{
public:
  bmi() : value_{0} {}
  bmi(height h, weight w)
  : value_{(w.value() * 10000) / (h.value() * h.value())}
  {}
  int value() const { return value_; }
private:
  int value_;
};

std::ostream& operator<<(std::ostream& out, bmi x)
{
  return out << x.value();
}

int main()
{
  std::cout << "Height in centimeters: ";
  height h{0};
  std::cin >> h;

  std::cout << "Weight in kilograms: ";
  weight w{0};
  std::cin >> w;

  std::cout << "Bogus metabolic index = " << bmi(h, w) << '\n';
}
```

The new classes prevent mistakes, such as that in Listing 40-1, but at the expense of more code. For example, you have to write suitable I/O operators. You also have to decide which arithmetic operators to implement. In this trivial application, we implemented only the operators needed for this one program. To represent a logical weight in a larger program, you may need to implement all of the possible operations that can be performed on a weight, such as adding two weights, subtracting, dividing, and so on. And don't forget the comparison operators. Most of these functions are trivial to write, but you can't neglect them. In many applications, however, the work will pay off many times over, by removing potential sources of error.

I'm not suggesting that you do away with unadorned integers and other built-in types and replace them with wrapper classes. In fact, I agree with you (don't ask how I know what you're thinking) that the BMI example is rather artificial. If I were writing a real, honest-to-goodness program for computing and managing BMIs, I would use plain int variables and rely on careful coding and proofreading to prevent and detect errors. I use wrapper classes, such as height and weight, when they add some primary value. A big program in which heights and weights figured prominently would offer many opportunities for mistakes. In that case, I would want to use wrapper classes. I could also add some error-checking to the classes, impose constraints on the domain of values they can represent, or otherwise help myself to do my job as a programmer. Nonetheless, it's best to start simple and add complexity slowly and carefully. The next section explains in greater detail what behavior you must implement to make a useful and meaningful custom class.

Value Types

The height and weight types are examples of *value types*—that is, types that behave as ordinary values. Contrast them with the I/O stream types, which behave very differently. For example, you cannot copy or assign streams; you must pass them by reference to functions. Nor can you compare streams or perform arithmetic on them. Value types, by design, behave similarly to the built-in types, such as int and float. One of the important characteristics of value types is that you can store them in containers, such as vector and map. This section explains the general requirements for value types.

The basic guideline is to make sure your type behaves "like an int." When it comes to copying, comparing, and performing arithmetic, avoid surprises, by making your custom type look, act, and work as much like the built-in types as possible.

Copying

Copying an int yields a new int that is indistinguishable from the original. Your custom type should behave the same way.

Consider the example of string. Many implementations of string are possible. Some of these use copy-on-write to optimize frequent copying and assignment. In a copy-on-write implementation, the actual string contents are kept separate from the string object. Copies of the string object do not copy the contents until and unless a copy is needed, which happens when the string contents must be modified. Many uses of strings are read-only, so copy-on-write avoids unnecessary copies of the contents, even when the string objects themselves are copied frequently.

Other implementations optimize for small strings by using the string object to store their contents but storing large strings separately. Copying small strings is fast, but copying large strings is slower. Most programs use only small strings. In spite of these differences in implementation, when you copy a string (such as passing a string by value to a function), the copy and the original are indistinguishable, just like an int.

Usually, the compiler's automatic copy constructor does what you want, and you don't have to write any code. Nonetheless, you have to think about copying and assure yourself that the compiler's automatic (also called *implicit*) copy constructor does exactly what you want.

Assigning

Assigning objects is similar to copying them. After an assignment, the target and source must contain identical values. The key difference between assignment and copying is that copying starts with a blank slate: an object under construction. Assignment begins with an existing object, and you may have to clean up the old value before you can assign the new value. Simple types such as height have nothing to clean up, but later in this book, you will learn how to implement more complicated types, such as string, which require careful cleanup.

Most simple types work just fine with the compiler's implicit assignment operator, and you don't have to write your own. Nonetheless, you must consider the possibility and make sure the implicit assignment operator is exactly what you want.

Moving

Sometimes, you don't want to make an exact copy. I know I wrote that assignment should make an exact copy, but you can break that rule by having assignment *move* a value from the source to the target. The result leaves the source in an unknown state (typically empty), and the target gets the original value of the source.

Force a move assignment by calling std::move (declared in <utility>):

```
std::string source{"string"}, target{};
target = std::move(source);
```

After the assignment, source is in an unknown, but valid, state. Typically, it will be empty, but you cannot write code that assumes it is empty. In practical terms, the string contents of source are moved into target without copying any of the string contents. Moving is fast and independent of the amount of data stored in a container.

You can also move an object in an initializer, as follows:

```
std::string source{"string"};
std::string target{std::move(source)};
```

Moving works with strings and most containers, including std::vector. Consider the program in Listing 40-3.

Listing 40-3. Copying vs. Moving

```
import <iostream>;
import <utility>;
import <vector>;

void print(std::vector<int> const& vector)
{
  std::cout << "{ ";
  for (int i : vector)
    std::cout << i << ' ';
  std::cout << "}\n";
}

int main()
{
  std::vector<int> source{1, 2, 3 };
  print(source);
  std::vector<int> copy{source};
  print(copy);
  std::vector<int> move{std::move(source)};
  print(move);
  print(source);
}
```

Predict the output of the program in Listing 40-3.

_____

_____

_____

_____

When I run the program, I get this:

```
{ 1 2 3 }
{ 1 2 3 }
{ 1 2 3 }
{ }
```

The first three lines print { 1 2 3 }, as expected. But the last line is interesting, because source was moved into move. After moving an object, the only thing you are allowed to do is to assign a new value or reset the object to known state, so printing it is not guaranteed to do what you expect, and your C++ library might do something different from the one I used.

Writing a move constructor is advanced and will have to wait until later in this book, but you can take advantage of move constructors and move assignment operators in the standard library by calling std::move().

Comparing

I defined copying and assignment in a way that requires meaningful comparison. If you can't determine whether two objects are equal, you can't verify whether you copied or assigned them correctly. C++ has a few ways to check whether two objects are the same:

- The first and most obvious way is to compare objects with the == operator. Value types should overload this operator. Make sure the operator is transitive—that is, if a == b and b == c, then a == c. Make sure the operator is commutative, that is, if a == b, then b == a. Finally, the operator should be reflexive: a == a.

- Standard algorithms such as find compare items by one of two methods: with operator== or with a caller-supplied predicate. Sometimes, you may want to compare objects with a custom predicate, for example, a person class might have operator== that compares every data member (name, address, etc.), but you want to search a container of person objects by checking only last names, which you do by writing your own comparison function. The custom predicate must obey the same transitive and reflexive restrictions as the == operator. If you are using the predicate with a specific algorithm, that algorithm calls the predicate in a particular way, so you know the order of the arguments. You don't have to make your predicate commutative, and in some cases, you wouldn't want to.

- Containers such as map store their elements in sorted order. Some standard algorithms, such as binary_search, require their input range to be in sorted order. The ordered containers and algorithms use the same conventions. By default, they use the < operator, but you can also supply your own comparison predicate. These containers and algorithms never use the == operator to determine whether two objects are the same. Instead, they check for equivalence—that is, a is equivalent to b if a < b is false and b < a is false.

If your value type can be ordered, you should overload the < operator. Ensure that the operator is transitive (if a < b and b < c, then a < c). Also, the ordering must be strict, that is, a < a is always false.

- Containers and algorithms that check for equivalence also take an optional custom predicate instead of the < operator. The custom predicate must obey the same transitive and strictness restrictions as the < operator.

Not all types are comparable with a less-than relationship. If your type cannot be ordered, do not implement the < operator, but you must also understand that you will not be able to store objects of that type in a map or use any of the binary search algorithms. Sometimes, you may want to impose an artificial order, just to permit these uses. For example, a color type may represent colors such as red, green, or yellow. Although nothing about red or green inherently defines one as being "less than" another, you may want to define an arbitrary order, just so you can use these values as keys in a map. One immediate suggestion is to write a comparison function that compares colors as integers, using the < operator.

On the other hand, if you have a value that should be compared (such as rational), you should implement operator== and operator<. You can then implement all other comparison operators in terms of these two. (See Exploration 33 for an example of how the rational class does this.)

If you have to store unordered objects in a map, you can use std::unordered_map. It works almost exactly the same as std::map, but it stores values in a hash table instead of a binary tree. Ensuring that a custom type can be stored in std::unordered_map is more advanced and won't be covered until much later.

Implement a color class that describes a color as three components: red, green, and blue, which are integers in the range 0 to 255. Define a comparison function, order_color, to permit storing colors as map keys. **For extra credit, devise a suitable I/O format and overload the I/O operators too.** Don't worry about error-handling yet—for example, what if the user tries to set red to 1000, blue to 2000, and green to 3000. You'll get to that soon enough.

Compare your solution with mine, which is presented in Listing 40-4.

Listing 40-4. The color Class

```
import <iomanip>;
import <iostream>;
import <sstream>;

class color
{
public:
  color() : color{0, 0, 0} {}
  color(color const&) = default;
  color(int r, int g, int b) : red_{r}, green_{g}, blue_{b} {}
  int red() const { return red_; }
  int green() const { return green_; }
  int blue() const { return blue_; }
  /// Because red(), green(), and blue() are supposed to be in the range [0,255],
  /// it should be possible to add them together in a single long integer.
  /// TODO: handle out of range
  long int combined() const { return ((red() * 256L + green()) * 256) + blue(); }
private:
  int red_, green_, blue_;
};
```

```
inline bool operator==(color const& a, color const& b)
{
  return a.combined() == b.combined();
}

inline bool operator!=(color const& a, color const& b)
{
  return not (a == b);
}

inline bool order_color(color const& a, color const& b)
{
  return a.combined() < b.combined();
}

/// Write a color in HTML format: #RRGGBB.
std::ostream& operator<<(std::ostream& out, color const& c)
{
  std::ostringstream tmp{};
  // The hex manipulator tells a stream to write or read in hexadecimal (base 16).
  // Use a temporary stream in case the out stream has its own formatting,
  // such as width, adjustment.
  tmp << '#' << std::hex << std::setw(6) << std::setfill('0') << c.combined();
  out << tmp.str();
  return out;
}

class ioflags
{
public:
  /// Save the formatting flags from @p stream.
  ioflags(std::basic_ios<char>& stream) : stream_{stream}, flags_{stream.flags()} {}
  ioflags(ioflags const&) = delete;
  /// Restore the formatting flags.
  ~ioflags() { stream_.flags(flags_); }
private:
  std::basic_ios<char>& stream_;
  std::ios_base::fmtflags flags_;
};

std::istream& operator>>(std::istream& in, color& c)
{
  ioflags flags{in};

  char hash{};
  if (not (in >> hash))
    return in;
  if (hash != '#')
  {
    // malformed color: no leading # character
    in.unget();                        // return the character to the input stream
```

```
    in.setstate(in.failbit);    // set the failure state
    return in;
  }
  // Read the color number, which is hexadecimal: RRGGBB.
  int combined{};
  in >> std::hex >> std::noskipws;
  if (not (in >> combined))
    return in;
  // Extract the R, G, and B bytes.
  int red, green, blue;
  blue = combined % 256;
  combined = combined / 256;
  green = combined % 256;
  combined = combined / 256;
  red = combined % 256;

  // Assign to c only after successfully reading all the color components.
  c = color{red, green, blue};

  return in;
}

int main()
{
  color c;
  while (std::cin >> c)
  {
    if (c == color{})
      std::cout << "black\n";
    else
      std::cout << c << '\n';
  }
}
```

Listing 40-3 introduces a new trick with the ioflags class. The next section explains all.

Resource Acquisition Is Initialization

A programming idiom that goes by the name of Resource Acquisition Is Initialization (RAII) takes advantage of constructors, destructors, and automatic destruction of objects when a function returns. Briefly, the RAII idiom means that a constructor acquires a resource: it opens a file, connects to a network, or even just copies some flags from an I/O stream. The acquisition is part of the object's initialization. The destructor releases the resource: closes the file, disconnects from the network, or restores any modified flags in the I/O stream.

To use an RAII class, all you have to do is define an object of that type. That's all. The compiler takes care of the rest. The RAII class's constructor takes whatever arguments it needs to acquire its resources. When the surrounding function returns, the RAII object is automatically destroyed, thereby releasing the resources. It's that simple.

You don't even have to wait until the function returns. Define an RAII object in a compound statement, and the object is destroyed when the statement finishes and control leaves the compound statement.

The ioflags class in Listing 40-4 is an example of using RAII. It throws some new items at you; let's take them one at a time:

- The std::basic_ios<char> class is the base class for all I/O stream classes, such as istream and ostream. Thus, ioflags works the same with input and output streams.

- The std::ios_base::fmtflags type is the type for all the formatting flags.

- The flags() member function with no arguments returns all the current formatting flags.

- The flags() member function with one argument sets all the flags to its argument.

The way to use ioflags is simply to define a variable of type ioflags in a function or compound statement, passing a stream object as the sole argument to the constructor. The function can change any of the stream's flags. In this case, the input operator sets the input radix (or base) to hexadecimal with the std::hex manipulator. The input radix is stored with the formatting flags. The operator also turns off the skipws flag. By default, this flag is enabled, which instructs the standard input operators to skip initial white space. By turning this flag off, the input operator does not permit any white space between the pound sign (#) and the color value.

When the input function returns, the ioflags object is destroyed, and its destructor restores the original formatting flags. Without the magic of RAII, the operator>> function would have to restore the flags manually at all four return points, which is burdensome and prone to error.

It makes no sense to copy an ioflags object. If you copy it, which object would be responsible for restoring the flags? Thus, the class deletes the copy constructor. If you accidentally write code that would copy the ioflags object, the compiler will complain.

RAII is a common programming idiom in C++. The more you learn about C++, the more you will come to appreciate its beauty and simplicity.

As you can see, our examples are becoming more complicated, and it's becoming harder and harder for me to fit entire examples in a single code listing. Your next task is to understand how to separate your code into multiple files, which makes my job and yours much easier. The first step for this new task is to take a closer look at declarations, definitions, and the distinctions between them.

EXPLORATION 41

■ ■ ■

Declarations and Definitions

Exploration 20 introduced the distinction between declarations and definitions. This is a good time to remind you of the difference and to explore declarations and definitions of classes and their members.

Declaration vs. Definition

Recall that a *declaration* furnishes the compiler with the basic information it needs, so that you can use a name in a program. In particular, a function declaration tells the compiler about the function's name, return type, parameter types, and modifiers, such as const and override.

A *definition* is a particular kind of declaration that also provides the full implementation details for an entity. For example, a function definition includes all the information of a function declaration, plus the function body. Classes, however, add another layer of complexity, because you can declare or define the class's members independently of the class definition itself. A class definition must declare all of its members. Sometimes, you can also define a member function as part of a class definition (which is the style I've been using so far), but most programmers prefer to declare member functions inside the class and to define the member functions separately, outside of the class definition.

As with any function declaration, a member function declaration includes the return type (possibly with a virtual specifier), the function name, the function parameters, and an optional const or override modifier. If the function is a pure virtual function, you must include the = 0 token marks as part of the function declaration, and you don't define the function.

The function definition is like any other function definition, with a few exceptions. The definition must follow the declaration—that is, the member function definition must come later in the source file than the class definition that declares the member function. In the definition, omit the virtual and override specifiers. The function name must start with the class name, followed by the scope operator (::) and the function name, so that the compiler knows which member function you are defining. Write the function body the same way you would write it if you provided the function definition inside the class definition. Listing 41-1 shows some examples.

Listing 41-1. Declarations and Definitions of Member Functions

```
class rational
{
public:
  rational();
  rational(int num);
  rational(int num, int den);
  void assign(int num, int den);
  int numerator() const;
```

```
  int denominator() const;
  rational& operator=(int num);
private:
  void reduce();
  int numerator_;
  int denominator_;
};

rational::rational()
: rational{0}
{}

rational::rational(int num)
: numerator_{num}, denominator_{1}
{}

rational::rational(int num, int den)
: numerator_{num}, denominator_{den}
{
  reduce();
}

void rational::assign(int num, int den)
{
  numerator_ = num;
  denominator_ = den;
  reduce();
}

void rational::reduce()
{
  assert(denominator_ != 0);
  if (denominator_ < 0)
  {
    denominator_ = -denominator_;
    numerator_ = -numerator_;
  }
  int div{std::gcd(numerator_, denominator_)};
  numerator_ = numerator_ / div;
  denominator_ = denominator_ / div;
}

int rational::numerator()
const
{
  return numerator_;
}

int rational::denominator()
const
{
```

```
    return denominator_;
}

rational& rational::operator=(int num)
{
  numerator_ = num;
  denominator_ = 1;
  return *this;
}
```

Because each function name begins with the class name, the full constructor name is `rational::rational`, and member function names have the form `rational::numerator`, `rational::operator=`, and so on. The C++ term for the complete name is *qualified name*.

Programmers have many reasons to define member functions outside the class. The next section presents one way that functions differ depending on where they are defined, and the next Exploration will focus on this thread in detail.

inline Functions

In Exploration 31, I introduced the `inline` keyword, which is a hint to the compiler that it should optimize speed over size by trying to expand a function at its point of call. You can use `inline` with member functions too. Indeed, for trivial functions, such as those that return a data member and do nothing else, making the function `inline` can improve speed and program size.

When you define a function inside the class definition, the compiler automatically adds the `inline` keyword. If you separate the definition from the declaration, you can still make the function `inline` by adding the `inline` keyword to the function declaration or definition. Common practice is to place the `inline` keyword only on the definition, but I recommend putting the keyword in both places, to help the human reader.

Remember that `inline` is just a hint. The compiler does not have to heed the hint. Modern compilers are becoming better and better at making these decisions for themselves.

My personal guideline is to define one-line functions in the class definition. Longer functions or functions that are complicated to read usually belong outside the class definition. Some functions are too long to fit in the class definition but are short and simple enough that they should be `inline`. Organizational coding styles usually include guidelines for `inline` functions. For example, directives for large projects may eschew `inline` functions because they increase coupling between software components. Thus, `inline` may be allowed only on a function-by-function basis, when performance measurements demonstrate their need.

Rewrite the rational class from Listing 41-1 to use inline functions judiciously. Compare your solution with that of mine, shown in Listing 41-2.

Listing 41-2. The rational Class with inline Member Functions

```
class rational
{
public:
  rational(int num) : numerator_{num}, denominator_{1} {}
  rational(rational const&) = default;
  inline rational(int num, int den);
  void assign(int num, int den);
  int numerator() const            { return numerator_; }
  int denominator() const          { return denominator_; }
  rational& operator=(int num);
```

```
private:
  void reduce();
  int numerator_;
  int denominator_;
};

inline rational::rational(int num, int den)
: numerator_{num}, denominator_{den}
{
  reduce();
}

void rational::assign(int num, int den)
{
  numerator_ = num;
  denominator_ = den;
  reduce();
}

void rational::reduce()
{
  assert(denominator_ != 0);
  if (denominator_ < 0)
  {
    denominator_ = -denominator_;
    numerator_ = -numerator_;
  }
  int div{std::gcd(numerator_, denominator_)};
  numerator_ = numerator_ / div;
  denominator_ = denominator_ / div;
}

rational& rational::operator=(int num)
{
  numerator_ = num;
  denominator_ = 1;
  return *this;
}
```

Don't agonize over deciding which functions should be inline. When in doubt, don't bother. Make functions inline only if performance measures show that the function is called often and the function call overhead is significant. In all other aspects, I regard the matter as one of aesthetics and clarity: I find one-line functions are easier to read when they are inside the class definition.

Variable Declarations and Definitions

Ordinary data members have declarations, not definitions. Local variables in functions and blocks have definitions, but not separate declarations. This can be a little confusing, but don't be concerned, I'll unravel it and make it clear.

A definition of a named object instructs the compiler to set aside memory for storing the object's value and to generate the necessary code to initialize the object. Some objects are actually sub-objects—not entire objects on their own (entire objects are called *complete* objects in C++ parlance). A sub-object doesn't get its own definition; instead, its memory and lifetime are dictated by the complete object that contains it. That's why a data member or base class doesn't get a definition of its own. Instead, the definition of an object with class type causes memory to be set aside for all of the object's data members. Thus, a class definition contains declarations of data members but not definitions.

You define a variable that is local to a block. The definition specifies the object's type, name, whether it is const, and the initial value (if any). You can't declare a local variable without defining it, but there are other kinds of declarations.

You can declare a local reference as a synonym for a local variable. Declare the new name as a reference in the same manner as a reference parameter, but initialize it with an existing object. If the reference is const, you can use any expression (of a suitable type) as the initializer. For a non-const reference, you must use an lvalue (remember those from Exploration 21?), such as another variable. Listing 41-3 illustrates these principles.

Listing 41-3. Declaring and Using References

```cpp
import <iostream>;

int main()
{
  int answer{42};      // definition of a named object, also an lvalue
  int& ref{answer};    // declaration of a reference named ref
  ref = 10;            // changes the value of answer
  std::cout << answer << '\n';
  int const& cent{ref * 10}; // declaration; must be const to initialize with expr
  std::cout << cent << '\n';
}
```

A local reference is not a definition, because no memory is allocated, and no initializers are run. Instead, the reference declaration creates a new name for an old object. One common use for a local reference is in a ranged for loop. Listing 41-4 shows a simple program that reads a series of words into a vector and then looks for the longest word in the vector. It illustrates the use and limitations of a local reference.

Listing 41-4. Finding the Longest String in a Data Set

```cpp
import <algorithm>;
import <iostream>;
import <iterator>;
import <string>;
import <vector>;

int main()
{
  std::vector<std::string> data{
    std::istream_iterator<std::string>(std::cin),
    std::istream_iterator<std::string>()
  };
```

```
// Ensure at least one string to measure.
if (data.empty()) data.emplace_back();
auto longest{ std::ranges::max(data,
  [](std::string const& a, std::string const& b)
  {
    return a.size() < b.size();
  })
};
std::cout << "Longest string is \"" << longest << "\"\n";
}
```

If you were to define string as an ordinary variable instead of declaring it as a reference, the program would work just fine, but it would also make an unneeded copy of every element of data. In this program, the extra copy is irrelevant and unnoticeable, but in other programs, the cost savings can add up.

So if local references are so nifty, why isn't longest also a reference? If you are feeling adventurous, go ahead and try changing the definition of longest to be a reference. **What happens?**

_____

_____

Remember that a reference is just another name for something else. You must initialize a reference or else it would be the name of nothing at all, and that is simply not allowed. Besides, if you were to assign a string to a reference, the assignment would modify the object behind the name. In other words, there is no way to make a reference refer to a different object. In the for loop, string is the name for an element of data and it seems to be able to refer to a different element every time through the loop, but it does so because it is created anew every iteration. Within the loop body, you have no way to make string refer to any other element or data or any other string. Because longest is outside the loop, a reference could have only one value no matter how many times the loop iterates. It cannot be redefined. This means we must make a copy of the longest string, which seems wasteful. Fortunately, there is a solution. Unfortunately, it will have to wait because the solution opens a can of big, ugly, scary worms.

Static Variables

Local variables are *automatic*. This means that when the function begins or a local block (compound statement) is entered, memory is allocated, and the object is constructed. When the function returns or when control exits the block, the object is destroyed, and memory is reclaimed. All automatic variables are allocated on the program stack, so memory allocation and release is trivial and typically handled by the host platform's normal function call instructions.

Remember that main() is like a function and follows many of the same rules as other functions. Thus, variables that you define in main() seem to last for the entire lifetime of the program, but they are automatic variables, allocated on the stack, and the compiler treats them the same as it treats any other automatic variables.

The behavior of automatic variables permits idioms such as RAII (see Exploration 40) and greatly simplifies typical programming tasks. Nonetheless, it is not suited for every programming task. Sometimes you need a variable's lifetime to persist across function calls. For example, suppose you need a function that generates unique identification numbers for a variety of objects. It starts a serial counter at 1 and increments the counter each time it issues an ID. Somehow, the function must keep track of the counter value, even after it returns. Listing 41-5 demonstrates one way to do it.

Listing 41-5. Generating Unique Identification Numbers

```
int generate_id()
{
  static int counter{0};
  ++counter;
  return counter;
}
```

The `static` keyword informs the compiler that the variable is not automatic but *static*. The first time the program calls `generate_id()`, the variable `counter` is initialized. The memory is not automatic and is not allocated on the program stack. Instead, all static variables are kept off to the side somewhere, so they don't go away until the program shuts down. When `generate_id()` returns, `counter` is not destroyed and, therefore, retains its value.

Write a program to call `generate_id()` multiple times, to see that it works and generates new values each time you call it. Compare your program with mine, which is shown in Listing 41-6.

Listing 41-6. Calling generate_id to Demonstrate Static Variables

```
import <iostream>;

int generate_id()
{
  static int counter{0};
  ++counter;
  return counter;
}

int main()
{
  for (int i{0}; i != 10; ++i)
    std::cout << generate_id() << '\n';
}
```

You can also declare a variable outside of any function. Because it is outside of all functions, it is not inside any block; thus, it cannot be automatic, and so its memory must be static. You don't have to use the `static` keyword for such a variable. **Rewrite Listing 40-6 to declare `counter` outside of the `generate_id` function**. Do not use the `static` keyword. Assure yourself that the program still works correctly. Listing 41-7 shows my solution.

Listing 41-7. Declaring counter Outside of the generate_id Function

```
import <iostream>;

int counter;

int generate_id()
{
  ++counter;
  return counter;
}
```

```
int main()
{
  for (int i{0}; i != 10; ++i)
    std::cout << generate_id() << '\n';
}
```

Unlike automatic variables, all static variables without initializers start out filled with zero, even if the variable has a built-in type. If the class has a custom constructor, the default constructor is then called to initialize static variables of class type. Thus, you don't have to specify an initializer for counter, but you can if you want to.

All names in C++ are lexically scoped; a name is visible only within its scope. The scope for a name declared within a function is the block that contains the declaration (including the statement header of for, if, and while statements). The scope for a name declared outside of any function is a little trickier. The name of a variable or function is global and can be used only for that single entity throughout the program. On the other hand, you can use it only in the source file where it is declared, from the point of declaration to the end of the file. (The next Exploration will go into more detail about working with multiple source files.)

The common term for variables that you declare outside of all functions is *global variables*. That's not the standard C++ terminology, but it will do for now.

If you declare counter globally, you can refer to it and modify it anywhere else in the program, which may not be what you want. It's always best to limit the scope of every name as narrowly as possible. By declaring counter inside generate_id, you guarantee that no other part of the program can accidentally change its value. In other words, if only one function has to access a static variable, keep the variable's definition local to the function. If multiple functions must share the variable, define the variable globally.

Static Data Members

The static keyword has many uses. You can use it before a member declaration in a class to declare a *static data member*. A static data member is one that is not part of any objects of the class but, instead, is separate from all objects. All objects of that class type (and derived types) share a sole instance of the data member. A common use for static data members is to define useful constants. For example, the std::string class has a static data member, npos, which roughly means "no position." Member functions return npos when they cannot return a meaningful position, such as find when it cannot find the string for which it was looking. You can also use static data members to store shared data the same way a globally static variable can be shared. By making the shared variable a data member, however, you can restrict access to the data member using the normal class access levels.

Define a static data member the way you would any other global variable but qualify the member name with the class name. Use the static keyword only in the data member's declaration, not in its definition. Because static data members are not part of objects, do not list them in a constructor's initializer list. Instead, initialize static data members the way you would an ordinary global variable, but remember to qualify the member name with the class name. Qualify the name when you use a static data member too. Listing 41-8 shows some simple uses of static data members.

Listing 41-8. Declaring and Defining Static Data Members

```
import <iostream>;
import <numeric>;

class rational {
public:
  rational();
  rational(int num);
```

```
  rational(int num, int den);
  int numerator() const { return numerator_; }
  int denominator() const { return denominator_; }
  // Some useful constants
  static const rational zero;
  static const rational one;
  static const rational pi;
private:
  void reduce()
  {
    int div{std::gcd(numerator_, denominator_)};
    numerator_ = numerator_ / div;
    denominator_ = denominator_ / div;
  }

  int numerator_;
  int denominator_;
};

rational::rational() : rational{0, 1} {}
rational::rational(int num) : numerator_{num}, denominator_{1} {}
rational::rational(int num, int den)
: numerator_{num}, denominator_{den}
{
  reduce();
}

std::ostream& operator<<(std::ostream& out, rational const& r)
{
  return out << r.numerator() << '/' << r.denominator();
}

const rational rational::zero{};
const rational rational::one{1};
const rational rational::pi{355, 113};

int main()
{
  std::cout << "pi = " << rational::pi << '\n';
}
```

Listing 41-9 shows some examples of static data members in a more sophisticated ID generator. This one uses a prefix as part of the IDs it produces and then uses a serial counter for the remaining portion of each ID. In certain situations, such as initializing an integer, you can provide the initial value in the class definition. For a const value, you would not need to provide a separate definition because the compiler uses the value at compile time. For a static data member that is not const, the compiler still needs to set aside memory for the data member, so it still needs a separate definition. Using a different prefix for every run is fine for production software but greatly complicates testing. Therefore, this version of the program uses the fixed quantity 1. A comment shows the intended code.

Listing 41-9. Using Static Data Members for an ID Generator

```cpp
import <iostream>;

class generate_id
{
public:
  generate_id() : counter_{0} {}
  long next();
private:
  short counter_;
  static short prefix_;
  static short const max_counter_ = 32767;
};

short generate_id::prefix_{1};

long generate_id::next()
{
  if (counter_ == max_counter_)
    counter_ = 0;
  else
    ++counter_;
  return static_cast<long>(prefix_) * (max_counter_ + 1) + counter_;
}

int main()
{
  generate_id gen;          // Create an ID generator
  for (int i{0}; i != 10; ++i)
    std::cout << gen.next() << '\n';
}
```

Declarators

As you've already seen, you can define multiple variables in a single declaration, as demonstrated in the following:

```cpp
int x{42}, y{}, z{x+y};
```

The entire declaration contains three *declarators*. Each declarator declares a single name, whether that name is for a variable, function, or type. Most C++ programmers don't use this term in everyday conversation, but C++ experts often do. You have to know official C++ terminology, so that if you have to ask for help from the experts, you can understand them.

The most important reason to know about separating declarations from definitions is so you can put a definition in one source file and a declaration in another. The next Exploration shows how to work with multiple source files.

EXPLORATION 42

■ ■ ■

Modules

Real programs rarely fit into a single source file, and I know you've been champing at the bit, eager to explore how C++ works with multiple source files that make up a single program. This Exploration shows you the basics. A warning, though: this chapter discusses brand-new features in C++ 20, and although compiler developers are working at implementing all of the new features, they have many features to implement, and all that hard work takes time. What you read in this chapter might not work in your compiler, at least not until some future release. Not to worry, Exploration 43 takes you back to the old-fashioned way of working with multiple source files, a way that has worked from the very first days of C++. But for now, let's step boldly into the future.

Introducing Modules

Put simply, you write a large program by dividing it into modules. A module is the C++ 20 way of working with multiple source files. Just as a function has a declaration and a definition, a module has an interface (declaration) and an implementation (definition). Because a module can contain multiple functions, classes, and more, they have ways to divide one module into multiple files as an implementation detail.

Let's start with a simple example. Let's define a function, world(), in a module, hello. Our main() program will call that function. So what do we need? First, define the module as shown in Listing 42-1.

Listing 42-1. Writing a Module

```
export module hello;
import <iostream>;
export void world()
{
    std::cout << "hello, world\n";
}
```

Well, that was easy. The module keyword informs the compiler that this file is part of a module. The export keyword says that this is an interface, that is, this file is exporting symbols. In particular, the module exports the world() function. The module imports <iostream> so world() can do its work, but that is an implementation detail. The only information that is visible from outside of the module are exported declarations, which in this case is world(). Armed with just this interface, you can write a program that imports the hello module and calls the world() function. Listing 42-2 shows you how.

© Ray Lischner 2020
R. Lischner, *Exploring C++20*, https://doi.org/10.1007/978-1-4842-5961-0_42

Listing 42-2. Importing a Module

```
import hello;
int main()
{
    world();
}
```

The `import` declaration imports a module, which makes every symbol that the module exports available in the file that does the importing. You can use any of the names that the module exports just as though you had written those functions in the file doing the importing. The name `hello` has no further significance after the `import` declaration. This means you do not need to qualify the name of the `world()` function. Just call it normally as you would if you had defined it in the same file as `main()`.

A `module` declaration is optional, but if present must be the first declaration in a file. Then come any `import` declarations. After the imports, you may not use any further `module` or `import` declarations in the file. These simple restrictions mean you can use `module` and `import` as ordinary names elsewhere in your program, which is great for existing programs that use those names, but new code should not use them in order to avoid confusion.

If a file has no `module` declaration, it is the same as though the file began with an unnamed module declaration:

```
module;
```

The unnamed module is also called the *global* module. A program's `main()` function lives in the global module, and any module can contribute declarations to the global module by starting the file with an unnamed module header, followed by ordinary declarations, and then a named module declaration.

All of the standard library headers (except those imported from the C programming language) can be imported as modules. That's why the code listings for this book use `import` for `<iostream>` and `#include` for `<cassert>`. Because modules are new features in C++ 20, all the zillions of lines of existing code use `#include` for all headers. Get used to seeing `#include` for a while.

The C++ 20 standard does not take modules any farther into the library implementation, but you can expect library authors to begin to tinker with implementations of the standard library as a suite of modules. For example, Microsoft Visual C++ lets you import `std.core` to import nearly the entire standard library at once. A future version of the standard may adopt that or a similar module name for packaging and arranging the standard library, but for now stick to the standard and look forward to libraries starting to arrive neatly bundled with a ribbon and a module.

Classes and Modules

Let's try a more challenging example: the `rational` class. This is easy to do, but introduces unseen twists. Listing 42-3 illustrates how to define a `rat` module that contains the `rational` class from Listing 41-2. You can fill in the rest of the details yourself.

Listing 42-3. Defining the rational Class in a Module

```
export module rat1;
#include <cassert>
import <numeric>;
export class rational
{
```

```
public:
  rational(int num) : numerator_{num}, denominator_{1} {}
  rational(rational const&) = default;
  inline rational(int num, int den);
  void assign(int num, int den);
  int numerator() const          { return numerator_; }
  int denominator() const        { return denominator_; }
  rational& operator=(int num);
private:
  void reduce();
  int numerator_;
  int denominator_;
};

inline rational::rational(int num, int den)
: numerator_{num}, denominator_{den}
{
  reduce();
}

void rational::assign(int num, int den)
{
  numerator_ = num;
  denominator_ = den;
  reduce();
}

void rational::reduce()
{
  assert(denominator_ != 0);
  if (denominator_ < 0)
  {
    denominator_ = -denominator_;
    numerator_ = -numerator_;
  }
  int div{std::gcd(numerator_, denominator_)};
  numerator_ = numerator_ / div;
  denominator_ = denominator_ / div;
}

rational& rational::operator=(int num)
{
  numerator_ = num;
  denominator_ = 1;
  return *this;
}
```

The std::gcd() function is declared in the <numeric> header, which you can include the old way, #include <numeric>, or the new way, import <numeric>. There is no difference to the rational class or its use of std::gcd(). It is mostly a choice of style, and because you are writing a module so you can live on the cutting edge of C++ modernization, you may as well import the <numeric> header.

307

Throwing in a module declaration and an export keyword is only the first step. Recall from Exploration 41 that any member function defined inside the class is automatically inline. That is true outside of a module, but within a module, it is no longer the case. The only way a function in a module can be inline is for you to make it so explicitly with the inline keyword, which you can see in Listing 42-4.

Listing 42-4. Defining the rational Class in One Declaration in a Module

```cpp
export module rat2;
#include <cassert>
import <numeric>;
export class rational
{
public:
  inline rational(int num) : numerator_{num}, denominator_{1} {}
  inline rational(rational const&) = default;
  inline rational(int num, int den)
  : numerator_{num}, denominator_{den}
  {
    reduce();
  }
  void assign(int num, int den)
  {
    numerator_ = num;
    denominator_ = den;
    reduce();
  }
  inline int numerator() const            { return numerator_; }
  inline int denominator() const          { return denominator_; }
  rational& operator=(int num)
  {
    numerator_ = num;
    denominator_ = 1;
    return *this;
  }
private:
  void reduce()
  {
    assert(denominator_ != 0);
    if (denominator_ < 0)
    {
      denominator_ = -denominator_;
      numerator_ = -numerator_;
    }
    int div{std::gcd(numerator_, denominator_)};
    numerator_ = numerator_ / div;
    denominator_ = denominator_ / div;
  }
  int numerator_;
  int denominator_;
};
```

As you can see, I did more than just add `inline` keywords. I also moved all of the member functions into the class definition. This style of defining a class may be familiar to readers familiar with Java, Eiffel, and similar languages. The idea is to put everything about the class in one self-contained piece.

Also, `inline` is not needed on a defaulted function, in this case the copy constructor. When the compiler automatically fills in any constructor or function, it always automatically adds the `inline` qualifier. Remember that `inline` is just a suggestion to the compiler, not a requirement.

This style of defining a simple class suits `rational`, but more complicated classes sometimes require more complicated solutions. Let's take a step in that direction by hiding the non-inline functions in a different part of the module.

Hiding the Implementation

You can divide a module into multiple parts. The simplest division is just into interface and implementation. Start by removing the definitions of the non-inline functions, as you can see in Listing 42-5.

Listing 42-5. Defining the `rational` Class in a Module Interface

```
export module rat3;
export class rational
{
public:
  inline rational(int num) : numerator_{num}, denominator_{1} {}
  inline rational(rational const&) = default;
  inline rational(int num, int den)
  : numerator_{num}, denominator_{den}
  {
    reduce();
  }
  void assign(int num, int den);
  inline int numerator() const        { return numerator_; }
  inline int denominator() const      { return denominator_; }
  rational& operator=(int num);
private:
  void reduce();
  int numerator_;
  int denominator_;
};
```

Notice how `#include` and `import` are no longer needed in the module interface. Only the `reduce()` function needs those declarations. This is one of the ways that separating the implementation helps keep the interface module cleaner.

When the compiler must import a module, it needs only the module interface. This includes the definitions of every inline function; otherwise, it would not be able to compile the functions inline. The definitions of the non-inline functions live in a separate file, the module implementation. This looks very much like a module interface, but without the `export` keyword. Listing 42-6 shows the `rat3` module implementation.

Listing 42-6. Writing a Module Implementation

```
module rat3;
#include <cassert>
import <numeric>;
void rational::assign(int num, int den)
{
  numerator_ = num;
  denominator_ = den;
  reduce();
}
void rational::reduce()
{
  assert(denominator_ != 0);
  if (denominator_ < 0)
  {
    denominator_ = -denominator_;
    numerator_ = -numerator_;
  }
  int div{std::gcd(numerator_, denominator_)};
  numerator_ = numerator_ / div;
  denominator_ = denominator_ / div;
}
rational& rational::operator=(int num)
{
  numerator_ = num;
  denominator_ = 1;
  return *this;
}
```

The function definitions look just like they did in Listing 42-3. The module implementation must use the same module name as the module interface. Any function, variable, or type defined in the module implementation is hidden from all users of the module unless the module interface exports that symbol.

The main advantage of separating the implementation is that changes to the implementation do not affect the interface. For example, maybe you want to change the assert() to issue a more helpful error message. It is conceivable that compilers will be able to compile a single module in such a way that changing the assert() call will not affect how the interface is compiled. But by separating the implementation module, you also tell the human reader what changes will affect the users of the module and what changes are hidden from them.

Modules Exporting Modules

One module can import another. In doing so, it can hide the imported module as an implementation detail, or it can expose the imported module as though that module were part of the exported interface. For example, consider the vital_stats class (similar to the record class in Listing 35-1, for recording a person's vital statistics, including body mass index) in Listing 42-7.

Listing 42-7. The vital_stats Class to Record a Person's Vital Statistics

```
export module stats;
import <istream>;
import <ostream>;
export import <string>;
```

```
export class vital_stats
{
public:
  inline vital_stats() : height_{0}, weight_{0}, bmi_{0}, sex_{'?'}, name_{}
  {}

  bool read(std::istream& in, int num);
  void print(std::ostream& out, int threshold) const;

private:
  int compute_bmi() const; ///< Return BMI, based on height_ and weight_
  int height_;             ///< height in centimeters
  int weight_;             ///< weight in kilograms
  int bmi_;                ///< Body-mass index
  char sex_;               ///< 'M' for male or 'F' for female
  std::string name_;       ///< Person's name
};
```

Because the vital_stats class uses std::string, the stats module must import <string>. Similarly, std::istream is defined in <istream> and std::ostream in <ostream>. But any user of the stats module must be able to create a std::string and so will also need to use the <string> module, so stats also exports it. It does not export <istream> and <ostream> because any user of stats will have its own import declarations, such as <iostream> to pick up std::cin and std::cout, which also imports <istream> and <ostream>. So there is no need for stats to do the same. By exporting all the necessary modules in the stats module, you remove one burden from the programmer who makes use it. By not importing too much, stats avoids burdening its consumer with too many extraneous symbols.

More often than exporting a standard header, a large library that has modules A, B, and C will export part A from parts B and C, for example. **Write a set of simple modules so that the const double pi = 3.14159265358979323 is exported from module a; module b imports and exports a and also exports a function, area(), to compute the area of a circle. Module c imports and exports a and exports circumference() to compute the circumference of a circle. Write a main() program to demonstrate all three modules.**

_____

_____

_____

_____

_____

_____

_____

_____

_____

_____

_____

_____

_____

_____

_____

_____

_____

_____

_____

_____

_____

_____

_____

_____

_____

_____

_____

Listing 42-8 shows module a; Listing 42-9 shows module b; Listing 42-10 shows module c; and Listing 42-11 shows the main program.

Listing 42-8. Module a Exports pi

```
export module a;
export double constexpr pi = 3.14159265358979323;
```

Listing 42-9. Module b Exports area()

```
export module b;
export import a;
export double area(double radius)
{
    return pi * radius * radius;
}
```

Listing 42-10. Module c Exports circumference()

```
export module c;
export import a;
export double circumference(double radius)
{
    return 2.0 * pi * radius;
}
```

Listing 42-11. Main Program Imports a, b, and c

```
module;
import b;
import c;
import <iostream>;

int main()
{
    while (std::cin)
    {
        std::cout << "pi=" << pi << '\n';
        std::cout << "Radius=";
        double radius{};
        if (std::cin >> radius)
        {
            std::cout << "Area = " << area(radius) << '\n';
            std::cout << "Circumference = " << circumference(radius) << '\n';
        }
    }
}
```

Compiling Modules

Because modules are brand new, every compiler vendor supports them in slightly different ways. Gone are the old, simpler times of libraries of compiled object files. Now we must confront precompiled modules, module maps, and other complexities.

Because every compiler vendor does things a little bit differently, I can offer only general advice here. First of all, check whether your tools support modules yet. They may be available if you pass a special option to the compiler, such as -fmodules. Or you may have to wait for a newer release of your favorite compiler.

Due to the separation of interface and implementation, even if both are in the same source file, somehow the compiler needs to store the interface portion of the module in a manner that makes it available to any importer. The implementation portion can be compiled into a traditional object file, with some extra information, but most likely it will be stored separately. When compiling a file that imports a module, the compiler must be able to find the compiled module interface. This is tricky because a module interface can actually come in multiple pieces. I omitted this complexity from the Exploration because modules are complicated enough, and only module authors need to be aware of this capability. Module importers always get the entire module, and that means the compiler needs to be able to find and collect all the modules' pieces in order to make them available to the importer, that is, unless the compiler is compiling one piece of the implementation that imports another piece of the implementation. As I said, partitioning a module into pieces is too complicated to cover in this book.

Your best bet is to use an IDE that understands modules and let it handle the difficulties for you. If the IDE is closely tied to the compiler, it should know where module interface files are stored and how to retrieve them when modules are imported. This is an entirely new way to working with C++, so even IDE vendors may need to make changes to accommodate modules smoothly.

It is possible that your compiler implements modules, but the standard library has not yet been updated so it can be imported. You may be able to compile and run the examples in this Exploration after changing imports of the standard library but not other import declarations.

Now that you have glimpsed the future of C++ programming, I regret to inform you that billions of lines of C++ code have been written without the benefit of modules, and you, my friend, will have to maintain your tiny corner of those billions. You need to learn how to write your code not as modules but as mere #include files, the subject of the next Exploration.

■ ■ ■

Old-Fashioned "Modules"

Modules are the way of the future, but until the future arrives, we are stuck with #include files. Billions of lines of C++ code currently use #include files, so you need to know how they work. With a little bit of discipline, you can still separate interface from implementation and achieve much of what modules offer.

Interfaces As Headers

The basic principle is that you can define any function or global object in any source file. The compiler does not care which file contains what. As long as it has a declaration for every name it needs, it can compile a source file to an object file. (In this unfortunate case of convergent terminology, *object* files are unrelated to *objects* in a C++ program.) To create the final program, you have to link all the object files together. The linker doesn't care which file contains which definition; it simply has to find a definition for every name reference that the compiler generates.

The previous Exploration presented the rational class as an interface (Listing 42-5) and an implementation (Listing 42-6). Let's rewrite the program to put the rational class interface in one file called rational.hpp and the implementation in a another called rational.cpp. Listing 43-1 shows the rational.hpp file.

Listing 43-1. The Interface Header for rational in rational.hpp

```
#ifndef RATIONAL_HPP_
#define RATIONAL_HPP_

#include <iosfwd>
class rational
{
public:
  inline rational(int num) : numerator_{num}, denominator_{1} {}
  inline rational(rational const&) = default;
  inline rational(int num, int den)
  : numerator_{num}, denominator_{den}
  {
    reduce();
  }
  void assign(int num, int den);
  inline int numerator() const          { return numerator_; }
  inline int denominator() const        { return denominator_; }
  rational& operator=(int num);
```

```
private:
  void reduce();
  int numerator_;
  int denominator_;
};

std::ostream& operator<<(std::ostream&, rational const&);
#endif // RATIONAL_HPP_
```

Listing 43-2 shows rational.cpp.

Listing 43-2. The rational Implementation in rational.cpp

```
#include "rational.hpp"
#include <cassert>
#include <numeric>
#include <ostream>
void rational::assign(int num, int den)
{
  numerator_ = num;
  denominator_ = den;
  reduce();
}
void rational::reduce()
{
  assert(denominator_ != 0);
  if (denominator_ < 0)
  {
    denominator_ = -denominator_;
    numerator_ = -numerator_;
  }
  int div{std::gcd(numerator_, denominator_)};
  numerator_ = numerator_ / div;
  denominator_ = denominator_ / div;
}
rational& rational::operator=(int num)
{
  numerator_ = num;
  denominator_ = 1;
  return *this;
}
std::ostream& operator<<(std::ostream& stream, rational const& r)
{
    return stream << r.numerator() << '/' << r.denominator();
}
```

To use the rational class, you must #include "rational.hpp", as demonstrated in Listing 43-3.

Listing 43-3. The main Function Using the rational Class in the main.cpp File

```
#include <iostream>
#include "rational.hpp"

int main()
{
  rational pi{3927, 1250};
  std::cout << "pi approximately equals " << pi << '\n';
}
```

Now compile main.cpp and rational.cpp, then link them together to produce a working C++ program. An IDE takes care of the details for you, provided both source files are part of the same project. If you are using command-line tools, you can invoke the same compiler, but instead of listing source file names on the command line, list only the object file names. Alternatively, you can compile and link at the same time, by listing all the source file names in one compilation.

That's the basic idea, but the details, of course, are a little trickier. For the remainder of this Exploration, we'll take a closer look at those details.

Inline or Not Inline

Because Listing 42-1 is not a module, functions defined inside the class declaration are implicitly inline. But I declared them with the inline keyword anyway. This is a good practice to remind the human reader that these functions are inline. It also promotes a hybrid style of programming.

As much fun as it would be to leap forward into the future and embrace modules 100%, we must maintain existing code and write new code. We want to move forward and not lock our code in the past, so the ideal would be write code that can live in both worlds. It turns out this is easy to do with modules and headers. The first step is to be explicit with the inline keyword. Now the class definition works in a module and in a header. Then create a module from the header as shown in Listing 43-4.

Listing 43-4. Creating a Module from a Header

```
export module rat;
export {
    #include "rational.hpp"
}
```

Once again, working with modules makes coding easy. The export keyword can apply to all declarations in a brace-enclosed block. In this case, the #included header contains a single class declaration, but it can include much, much more.

Quotes and Brackets

All of the standard library's #include directives used angle brackets, such as <iostream>, but #include "rational.hpp" uses double quotes. The difference is that you should use angle brackets only for the standard library and system headers, although some third-party libraries recommend the use of angle brackets too. Use double quotes for everything else. The C++ standard is deliberately vague and recommends that angle brackets be used for headers that are provided with the system and quotes be used for other headers. Vendors of add-on libraries have all taken different approaches concerning naming their library files and whether they require angle brackets or double quotes.

For your own files, the important aspect is that the compiler must be able to find all your #include files. The easiest way to do that is to keep them in the same directory or folder as your source files. As your projects become larger and more complex, you probably will want to move all the #include files to a separate area. In this case, you have to consult your compiler documentation, to learn how to inform the compiler about that separate area. Users of g++ and other UNIX and UNIX-like command-line tools typically use the -I (capital letter *I*) option. Microsoft's command-line compiler uses /I. IDEs have a project option with which you can add a directory or folder to the list of places to search for #include files.

For many compilers, the only difference between angle brackets and quotes is where it looks for the file. A few compilers have additional differences that are specific to that compiler.

In a source file, I like to list all the standard headers together, in alphabetical order, and list them first, followed by the #include files that are specific to the program (also in alphabetical order). This organization makes it easy for me to determine whether a source file #includes a particular header and helps me add or remove #include directives as needed.

Include Guards

One very important difference between modules and #include files is that a module can be imported multiple times with no ill effect. But #include-ing the same file more than once might repeat all the declarations in that file, which is not allowed. Listing 43-1 protects against this possible mistake with #ifndef RATIONAL_HPP_. The directive #ifndef is short for "if not defined," so the first line tests whether RATIONAL_HPP_ is not defined, which is isn't. The second line goes about defining it. An #endif closes the conditional at the end of the file. If the same file is #included again, RATIONAL_HPP_ is now defined, so the #ifndef is false, and the entire file is skipped, down to #endif. This *include guard*, as it is known, is a common idiom in header files. It is not needed in a module, but is harmless. (And remember from Exploration 34 not to begin the guard name with an underscore. I use a trailing underscore to ensure the name does not conflict with any real name that the header might declare.)

Forward Declarations

The <istream> header contains the full declaration of std::istream and other, related declarations, and <ostream> declares std::ostream. These are large classes in large headers. Sometimes, you don't need the full class declarations. For example, declaring an input or output function in an interface requires informing the compiler that std::istream and std::ostream are classes, but the compiler needs to know the full class definitions only in the implementation file.

The header <iosfwd> is a small header that declares the names std::istream, std::ostream, and so on, without providing the complete class declarations. Thus, you can reduce compilation time for any file that includes a header by changing <istream> and <ostream> to <iosfwd>.

You can do the same for your own classes by declaring the class name after the class keyword, with nothing else describing the class:

```
class rational;
```

This is known as a *forward* declaration. You can use a forward declaration when the compiler has to know a name is a class but doesn't have to know the size of the class or any of the class's members. A common case is using a class solely as a reference function parameter.

If your header uses <iosfwd> or other forward declarations, be sure to include the full class declarations (e.g., <iostream>) in the .cpp source file.

extern Variables

Global variables are usually a bad idea, but global constants can be extremely helpful. If you define a constexpr constant, you can put that in a header and not worry about it again. But not all constant objects can be constexpr. If you need to define a global constant and cannot make it constexpr, you need to declare it in a header and define it in a separate source file, which you link with the rest of your program. Use the extern keyword to declare the constant in the header. Another reason to separate the declaration and definition of a global constant is when you may need to change the value of the constant but do not want to recompile the entire program.

For example, suppose you need to define some global constants for use in a larger program. The program name and global version number will not change often or will change when the program is rebuilt anyway, so they can be made constexpr and declared in globals.hpp. But you also want to declare a string called credits, which contains citations and credits for the entire project. You don't want to rebuild your component just because someone else added a credit to the string. So the definition of credits goes into a separate globals.cpp file. **Start by writing globals.hpp, with include guards and using constexpr for globals with values and extern for globals without values.** Compare your file with Listing 43-5.

Listing 43-5. Simple Header for Global Constants

```
#ifndef GLOBALS_HPP_
#define GLOBALS_HPP_

#include <string_view>

constexpr std::string_view program_name{ "The Ultimate Program" };
constexpr std::string_view program_version{ "1.0" };

extern const std::string_view program_credits;

#endif
```

One source file in the project must define program_credits. Name the file globals.cpp. **Write globals.cpp.** Compare your file with Listing 43-6.

Listing 43-6. Definitions of Global Constants

```
#include "globals.hpp"

std::string_view const program_credits{
    "Ray Lischner\n"
    "Jane Doe\n"
    "A. Nony Mouse\n"
};
```

Invent a program to test the globals. Link your main.cpp with globals.cpp to create the program. Listing 43-7 shows an example of such a program.

Listing 43-7. A Trivial Demonstration of `globals.hpp`

```cpp
#include <iostream>
#include "globals.hpp"

int main()
{
  std::cout << "Welcome to " << program_name << ' ' << program_version << '\n';
  std::cout << program_credits;
}
```

One-Definition Rule

The compiler enforces the rule that permits one definition of a class, function, or object per source file. Another rule is that you can have only one definition of a function or global object in the entire program. You can define a class in multiple source files, provided the definition is the same in all source files.

Inline functions follow different rules than ordinary functions. You can define an inline function in multiple source files. Each source file must have no more than one definition of the inline function, and every definition in the program must be the same.

These rules are collectively known as the One-Definition Rule (ODR).

The compiler enforces the ODR within a single source file. However, the standard does not require a compiler or linker to detect any ODR violations that span multiple source files. If you make such a mistake, the problem is all yours to find and fix.

Imagine that you are maintaining a program, and part of the program is the header file shown in Listing 43-8.

Listing 43-8. The Original point.hpp File

```cpp
#ifndef POINT_HPP_
#define POINT_HPP_
class point
{
public:
  point() : point{0, 0} {}
  point(int x, int y) : x_{x}, y_{y} {}
  int x() const { return x_; }
  int y() const { return y_; }
private:
  int y_, x_;
};
#endif // POINT_HPP_
```

The program works just fine. One day, however, you upgrade compiler versions, and when recompiling the program, the new compiler issues a warning, as follows, that you've never seen before:

```
point.hpp: In constructor 'point::point()':
point.hpp:13: warning: 'point::x_' will be initialized after
point.hpp:13: warning:    'int point::y_'
point.hpp:8: warning:   when initialized here
```

The problem is that the order of the data member declarations is different from the order of the data members in the constructors' initializer lists. It's a minor error, but one that can lead to confusion, or worse, in more complicated classes. It's a good idea to ensure the orders are the same. Suppose you decide to fix the problem by reordering the data members.

Then you recompile the program, but the program fails in mysterious ways. Some of your regression tests pass and some fail, including trivial tests that have never failed in the past.

What went wrong?

_____

_____

With such limited information, you can't determine for certain what went wrong, but the most likely scenario is that the recompilation failed to capture all the source files. Some part of the program (not necessarily the part that is failing) is still using the old definition of the point class, and other parts of the program use the new definition. The program fails to adhere to the ODR, resulting in undefined behavior. Specifically, when the program passes a point object from one part of the program to another, one part of the program stores a value in x_, and another part reads the same data member as y_.

This is only one small example of how ODR violations can be both subtle and terrible at the same time. By ensuring that all class definitions are in their respective header files, and that any time you modify a header file you recompile all dependent source files, you can avoid most accidental ODR violations.

Modules do not make ODR problems vanish, but they greatly reduce the likelihood that you will run into one. Because modules are distinct entities that the compiler knows about and have semantics of their own, the compiler can do more error-checking than it can with #include headers, which are just files and carry no additional semantic information. So when using modules, the compiler might be able to tell you that the implementation was compiled with a different version of the interface or that the interface for a particular class changed since the last time you compiled the implementation.

■ **Tip** If you can write your own modules, I recommend that you do so, even if your tools do not fully support standard library modules yet. Judging from prereleases, it looks like importing standard library modules, such as import <iostream>, may be the last aspect of modules to be implemented. Just don't let that stop you from writing your own.

Now that you have the tools needed to start writing some serious programs, it's time to embark on some more advanced techniques. The next Exploration introduces function objects—a powerful technique for using the standard algorithms.

■ ■ ■

Function Objects

Classes have many, many uses in C++ programs. This Exploration introduces one powerful use of classes to replace functions. This style of programming is especially useful with the standard algorithms.

The Function Call Operator

The first step is to take a look at an unusual "operator," the function call operator, which lets an object behave as a function. Overload this operator the same way you would any other. Its name is operator(). It takes any number of parameters and can have any return type. Listing 44-1 shows another iteration of the generate_id class (last seen in Listing 41-5), this time replacing the next() member function with the function call operator. In this case, the function has no parameters, so the first set of empty parentheses is the operator name, and the second set is the empty parameter list.

Listing 44-1. Rewriting generate_id to Use the Function Call Operator

```
export module generate_id;
/// Class for generating a unique ID number.
export class generate_id
{
public:
  generate_id() : counter_{0} {}
  long operator()();
private:
  short counter_;
  static short prefix_;
  static short constexpr max_counter_{32767};
};
```

Listing 44-2 displays the implementation of the function call operator (and prefix_, which also requires a definition).

Listing 44-2. Implementation of the generate_id Function Call Operator

```
module generate_id;

short generate_id::prefix_{1};

long generate_id::operator()()
{
```

© Ray Lischner 2020
R. Lischner, *Exploring C++20*, https://doi.org/10.1007/978-1-4842-5961-0_44

```
  if (counter_ == max_counter_)
    counter_ = 0;
  else
    ++counter_;
  return static_cast<long>(prefix_) * (max_counter_ + 1) + counter_;
}
```

In order to use the function call operator, you must first declare an object of the class type, then use the object name as though it were a function name. Pass arguments to this object the way you would to an ordinary function. The compiler sees the use of the object name as a function and invokes the function call operator. Listing 44-3 shows a sample program that uses a generate_id function call operator to generate ID codes for new library works. (Remember the work class from Exploration 39? Collect work and its derived classes into a single module file and add the necessary import declarations. Call the module library. Or download a complete library.cpp from the book's website.) Assume that int_to_id converts an integer identification into the string format that work requires, for example, it calls std::to_string().

Listing 44-3. Using a generate_id Object's Function Call Operator

```
import <iostream>;

import generate_id;
import library;

bool get_movie(std::string& title, int& runtime)
{
  std::cout << "Movie title: ";
  if (not std::getline(std::cin, title))
    return false;
  std::cout << "Runtime (minutes): ";
  if (not (std::cin >> runtime))
    return false;
  return true;
}

int main()
{
  generate_id gen{};            // Create an ID generator
  std::string title{};
  int runtime{};
  while (get_movie(title, runtime))
  {
    movie m(int_to_id(gen()), title, runtime);
    std::cout << "new movie: " << m << '\n';
  }
}
```

Function Objects

A *function object* or *functor* is an object of class type for a class that overloads the function call operator. Informally, programmers sometimes also speak of the class as a "function object," with the understanding that the actual function objects are the variables defined with that class type.

C++ 03 programs often used functors, but C++ 11 has lambdas, which are much easier to read and write. (Recall lambdas from Exploration 23?) So what do functors offer that lambdas lack? To answer that question, consider the following problem.

Suppose you need a vector that contains integers of increasing value. For example, a vector of size 10 would contain the values 1, 2, 3, ..., 8, 9, 10. The std::generate algorithm takes an iterator range and calls a function or functor for each element of the range, assigning the result of the functor to successive elements. **Write a lambda to use as the final argument to std::generate.** (Construct a vector of a specific size by passing the desired size to a constructor. Remember to use parentheses instead of curly braces to call the right constructor.) Compare your solution with mine in Listing 44-4.

Listing 44-4. A Program for Generating Successive Integers

```
import <algorithm>;
import <iostream>;
import <iterator>;
import <vector>;

int main()
{
  std::vector<int> vec(10);
  int state;
  std::ranges::generate(vec, [&state]() { return ++state; });
  // Print the resulting integers, one per line.
  std::ranges::copy(vec, std::ostream_iterator<int>(std::cout, "\n"));
}
```

Okay, that was easy, but the solution is not very general. The lambda cannot be reused anywhere else. It needs the state variable, and you can have only one such lambda per state variable. Can you think of a way to write a lambda such that you can have more than one generator, each with its own state? That's much harder to do with lambdas, but easy with functors. **Write a functor class to generate successive integers, so the functor can be used with the generate algorithm**. Name the class sequence. The constructor takes two arguments: the first specifies the initial value of the sequence, and the second is the increment. Each time you call the function call operator, it returns the generator value, then increments that value, which will be the value returned on the next invocation of the function call operator. Listing 44-5 shows the main program. Write your solution in a separate module, sequence.

Listing 44-5. Another Program for Generating Successive Integers

```
import <algorithm>;
import <iostream>;
import <iterator>;
import <vector>;

import sequence;

int main()
{
  int size{};
  std::cout << "How many integers do you want? ";
  std::cin >> size;
  int first{};
  std::cout << "What is the first integer? ";
```

```
  std::cin >> first;
  int step{};
  std::cout << "What is the interval between successive integers? ";
  std::cin >> step;

  std::vector<int> data(size);
  // Generate the integers to fill the vector.
  std::ranges::generate(data, sequence(first, step));

  // Print the resulting integers, one per line.
  std::ranges::copy(data, std::ostream_iterator<int>(std::cout, "\n"));
}
```

Compare your solution with mine, shown in Listing 44-6.

Listing 44-6. The sequence Module

```
export module sequence;
/// Generate a sequence of integers.
export class sequence
{
public:
  /// Construct the functor.
  /// @param start the first value the generator returns
  /// @param step increment the value by this much for each call
  inline sequence(int start, int step ) : value_{start}, step_{step} {}
  inline sequence(int start) : sequence{start, 1} {}
  inline sequence() : sequence{0} {}

  /// Return the current value in the sequence, and increment the value.
  int operator()()
  {
    int result(value_);
    value_ = value_ + step_;
    return result;
  }
private:
  int value_;
  int const step_;
};
```

The generate algorithm has a partner, generate_n, which specifies an input range with an iterator for the start of the range and an integer for the size of the range. The next Exploration examines this and several other useful algorithms.

EXPLORATION 45

■ ■ ■

Useful Algorithms

The standard library includes a suite of functions, which the library calls *algorithms*, to simplify many programming tasks that involve repeated application of operations over data ranges. The data can be a container of objects, a portion of a container, values read from an input stream, or any other sequence of objects that you can express with iterators. I've introduced a few algorithms when appropriate. This Exploration takes a closer look at a number of the most useful algorithms.

All of the algorithms in this Exploration are defined in the `<algorithm>` module.

Ranges and Iterators

Most of the algorithms used so far use ranges, but as you learned in Exploration 23, sometimes it is useful to use iterators. In most cases, the same algorithm is available in both flavors. But because the range algorithms tend to be easier to use for most programming situations, this Exploration focuses on them. Just remember that the same algorithm is usually available in an iterator flavor, too. And some exist only in iterator form.

The range-flavored algorithms live in the `std::ranges` namespace, which helps keep the algorithms organized. For example, the following are the two forms of the `copy` algorithm, both copying the contents of data to the standard output:

```
std::copy(data.begin(), data.end(), std::ostream_iterator<int>(std::cout));
std::ranges::copy(data, std::ostream_iterator<int>(std::cout));
```

Helper iterators, such `std::ostream_iterator`, are declared in the `<iterator>` module. Range helpers, such as `std::ranges::istream_view`, are declared in the `<ranges>` module.

Searching

The standard algorithms include many flavors of searching, divided into two broad categories: linear and binary. The linear searches examine every element in a range, starting from the first and proceeding to subsequent elements until reaching the end (or the search ends because it is successful). The binary searches require the elements be sorted in ascending order, using the `<` operator, or according to a custom predicate, that is, a function, functor, or lambda that returns a Boolean result.

© Ray Lischner 2020

R. Lischner, *Exploring C++20*, https://doi.org/10.1007/978-1-4842-5961-0_45

Linear Search Algorithms

The most basic linear search is the find function. It searches a range of read iterators for a value. It returns an iterator that refers to the first matching element in the range. If find cannot find a match, it returns a copy of the end iterator. Listing 45-1 shows an example of its use. The program reads integers into a vector, searches for the value 42, and if found, changes that element to 0.

Listing 45-1. Searching for an Integer

```
import <algorithm>;
import <iostream>;

import data;

int main()
{
  intvector data{};
  read_data(data);
  write_data(data);
  if(auto iter{std::ranges::find(data, 42)}; iter == data.end())
    std::cout << "Value 42 not found\n";
  else
  {
    *iter = 0;
    std::cout << "Value 42 changed to 0:\n";
    write_data(data);
  }
}
```

Listing 45-2 shows the *data* module, which provides a few utilities for working with vectors of integers. Most of the examples in this Exploration will import this module.

Listing 45-2. The data Module to Support Integer Data

```
export module data;

import <algorithm>;
import <iostream>;
import <iterator>;
export import <vector>;

/// Convenient shorthand for a vector of integers.
export using intvector = std::vector<int>;

/// Read a series of integers from the standard input into @p data,
/// overwriting @p data in the process.
/// @param[in,out] data a vector of integers
export void read_data(intvector& data)
{
  data.clear();
  data.insert(data.begin(), std::istream_iterator<int>(std::cin),
                            std::istream_iterator<int>());
}
```

```
/// Write a vector of integers to the standard output. Write all values on one
/// line, separated by single space characters, and surrounded by curly braces,
/// e.g., { 1 2 3 }.
/// @param data a vector of integers
export void write_data(intvector const& data)
{
  std::cout << "{ ";
  std::ranges::copy(data, std::ostream_iterator<int>(std::cout, " "));
  std::cout << "}\n";
}
```

A companion to the find algorithm is find_if. Instead of searching for a matching value, find_if takes a predicate function or function object (from now on, I will write *functor* to indicate a free function, a function object, or a lambda). It calls the functor for every element in the range, until the functor returns true (or any value that can be converted automatically to true, such as a nonzero numeric value). If the functor never returns true, find_if returns the end iterator.

Every search algorithm comes in two forms. The first compares items using an operator (== for linear searches and < for binary searches). The second form uses a caller-supplied functor instead of the operator. For most algorithms, the functor is an additional argument to the algorithm, so the compiler can distinguish the two forms. In a few cases, both forms take the same number of arguments, and the library uses distinct names, because the compiler could not otherwise distinguish between the two forms. In these cases, the functor form has _if added to the name, such as find and find_if.

Suppose you want to search a vector of integers, not for a single value, but for any value that falls within a certain range. You can write a custom predicate to test a hard-coded range, but a more useful solution is to write a general-purpose functor that compares an integer against any range. Use this functor by supplying the range limits as argument to the constructor. **Is this best implemented as a free function, function object, or lambda?** _____ Because it must store state, I recommend writing a functor.

A lambda is good when you need to search for specific values, but a functor is easier if you want to write a generic comparator that can store the limits. **Write the intrange functor.** The constructor takes two int arguments. The function call operator takes a single int argument. It returns true, if the argument falls within the inclusive range specified in the constructor, or false, if the argument lies outside the range.

Listing 45-3 shows my implementation of intrange. This range is inclusive of the low and high ends, which differs from the C++ convention of using a half-open range. But it is the simplest way to ensure that a range can span the entire set of integers. In a half-open range, a range in which the low and high have the same value is the typical way to represent an empty range. With intrange, an empty range occurs when high < low.

Listing 45-3. Functor intrange to Generate Integers in a Certain Range

```
export module intrange;

import <algorithm>;

/// Check whether an integer lies within an inclusive range.
export class intrange
{
public:
  /// Construct an integer range.
  /// If the parameters are in the wrong order,
  /// swap them to the right order.
  /// @param low the lower bound of the inclusive range
  /// @param high the upper bound of the inclusive range
```

```
inline intrange(int low, int high)
: low_{low}, high_{high}
{}

/// Check whether a value lies within the inclusive range.
/// @param test the value to test
inline bool operator()(int test)
const
{
  return test >= low_ and test <= high_;
}
private:
int const low_;
int const high_;
};
```

Write a test program that reads integers from the standard input and then uses find_if and intrange to find the first value that lies within the range [10, 20]. Compare your solution with mine in Listing 45-4.

Listing 45-4. Using find_if and intrange to Find an Integer That Lies Within a Range

```
import <algorithm>;
import <iostream>;
import <ranges>;

import data;
import intrange;

int main()
{
  intvector data{};
  read_data(data);
  write_data(data);
  if (auto iter{std::ranges::find_if(data, intrange{10, 20})}; iter == data.end())
    std::cout << "No values in [10,20] found\n";
  else
    std::cout << "Value " << *iter << " in range [10,20].\n";
}
```

A few of the following examples generate random data and apply algorithms to the data. The standard library has a rich, complicated library for generating pseudo-random numbers. The details of this library are beyond the scope of this book. Only the mathematically adventuresome should crack open the details of the <random> module. For your convenience, Listing 45-5 presents the randomint module, which defines the randomint class, which generates random integers in a caller-supplied range.

Listing 45-5. Generating Random Integers

```
export module randomint;

import <algorithm>;
import <random>;

/// Generate uniformly distributed random integers in a range.
export class randomint
{
public:
  using result_type = std::default_random_engine::result_type;

  /// Construct a random-number generator to produce numbers in the range [`low`, `high`].
  /// If @p low > @p high the values are reversed.
  randomint(result_type low, result_type high)
  : prng_{},
    distribution_{std::min(low, high), std::max(low, high)}
  {}

  /// Generate the next random number generator.
  result_type operator()()
  {
    return distribution_(prng_);
  }

private:
  // implementation-defined pseudo-random-number generator
  std::default_random_engine prng_;
  // Map random numbers to a uniform distribution.
  std::uniform_int_distribution<result_type> distribution_;
};
```

The search function is similar to find, except it searches for a matching subrange. That is, you supply a range in which to search and a range of values to find. The search algorithm looks for the first occurrence of a sequence of elements that equals the entire match range and returns a subrange that is actually a pair of iterators that point into the search range for where it found the first match. If not found, the subrange is empty, which evaluates as false in an if statement. Listing 45-6 shows a silly program that generates a large vector of random integers in the range 0 to 9 and then searches for a subrange that matches the first four digits of π.

Listing 45-6. Finding a Subrange That Matches the First Four Digits of π

```
import <algorithm>;
import <iostream>;
import <iterator>;
import <vector>;

import data;
import randomint;
```

```
int main()
{
  intvector pi{ 3, 1, 4, 1 };
  intvector data(10000, 0);
  // The randomint functor generates random numbers in the range [0, 9].
  std::ranges::generate(data, randomint{0, 9});

  auto match{std::ranges::search(data, pi)};
  if (not match)
    std::cout << "The integer range does not contain the digits of pi.\n";
  else
  {
    std::cout << "Easy as pi: ";
    std::ranges::copy(match, std::ostream_iterator<int>(std::cout, " "));
    std::cout << '\n';
  }
}
```

Other useful linear functions include count, which takes a range and value and returns the number of occurrences of the value in the range. Its counterpart count_if takes a predicate instead of a value and returns the number of times the predicate returns true.

Three more algorithms have a common pattern. They apply a predicate to every element in a range and return a bool:

- all_of(range, predicate) returns true if predicate(element) returns true for every element in range.

- any_of(range, predicate) returns true if predicate(element) returns true for at least one element in range.

- none_of(range, predicate) returns true if predicate(element) returns false for every element in range.

The min, max, and minmax algorithms live in the iterator world and are equally home on the range. Prior to C++ 20, the min() function compared two values and returned the smaller; the min_element algorithm took two iterators and found the position of the smallest value. Now, the std::ranges::min() function returns the minimum value of a range, and std::ranges::min_element() also returns the minimum value of a range. Ditto for max(). You can guess what minmax returns: a pair of iterators for the minimum and maximum values in the range. All three come in the usual overloaded forms: one uses the < operator, and the other takes an additional argument for a comparison predicate.

Binary Search Algorithms

The map container stores its elements in sorted order, so you can use any of the binary search algorithms, but map also has member functions that can take advantage of access to the internal structure of a map and, so, offer improved performance. Thus, the binary search algorithms are typically used on sequential containers, such as vector, when you know that they contain sorted data. If the input range is not properly sorted, the results are undefined: you might get the wrong answer; the program might crash; or something even worse might happen.

The binary_search function simply tests whether a sorted range contains a particular value. By default, values are compared using only the < operator. Another form of binary_search takes a comparison functor as an additional argument to perform the comparison.

WHAT'S IN A NAME?

The find function performs a linear search for a single item. The search function performs a linear search for a matching series of items. So why isn't binary_search called binary_find? On the other hand, find_end searches for the match that is furthest right in a range of values, so why isn't it called search_end? The equal function is completely different from equal_range, in spite of the similarity in their names.

The C++ standards committee did its best to apply uniform rules for algorithm names, such as appending _if to functions that take a functor argument but cannot be overloaded, but it faced some historical constraints with a number of names. What this means for you is that you have to keep a reference close at hand. Don't judge a function by its name, but read the description of what the function does and how it does it, before you decide whether it's the right function to use.

The lower_bound function is similar to binary_search, except it exists only in iterator form. It takes two iterators to delimit an input range, and it returns an iterator that points somewhere in that range. The returned iterator points to the first occurrence of the value, or it points to a position where the value belongs if you want to insert the value into the range and keep the values in sorted order. The upper_bound function is similar to lower_bound, except it returns an iterator that points to the last position where you can insert the value and keep it in sorted order. If the value is found, that means upper_bound points to one position past the last occurrence of the value in the range. To put it another way, the range [lower_bound, upper_bound) is the subrange of every occurrence of the value in the sorted range. As with any range, if lower_bound == upper_bound, the result range is empty, which means the value is not in the search range.

Listing 45-7 shows a slow way to arrange for sorted input. Reading integers into a vector and then calling sort() is faster. This is just an example of using lower_bound() and upper_bound(). As a bonus, Listing 45-7 inserts a value only if it is not already present in the vector.

Listing 45-7. Using lower_bound to Create a Sorted Vector

```
import <algorithm>;
import <iostream>;
import <ranges>;

import data;

int main()
{
  intvector data{};
  int value;
  while (std::cin >> value)
  {
    auto lb{std::lower_bound(data.begin(), data.end(), value)};
    auto ub{std::upper_bound(data.begin(), data.end(), value)};
    if (lb == ub)
        // Not in data, so insert.
        data.insert(ub, value);
    // else value is already in the vector
  }
  write_data(data);
}
```

To better understand how lower_bound and upper_bound really work, it helps to write a test program. The program can read some integers from the user into a vector, sort the vector, and then test some values using lower_bound and upper_bound. To help you understand exactly what these functions return, call the distance function to determine an iterator's position in a vector, as follows:

```
auto iter{std::lower_bound(data.begin(), data.end(), 42)};
std::cout << "Index of 42 is " << std::distance(data.begin(), iter) << '\n';
```

The distance function (declared in <iterator>) takes an iterator range and returns the number of elements in the range. The return type is an integer type, although the exact type (e.g., int or long int) depends on the implementation.

Write the test program to test the values 3, 4, 8, 0, and 10. Then run the program with the following sample input:

```
9 4 2 1 5 4 3 6 2 7 4
```

What should the program print as the sorted vector?

_____

Fill in Table 45-1 with the expected values for the lower and upper bounds of each value. Then run the program to check your answers.

Table 45-1. *Results of Testing Binary Search Functions*

Value	Expected Lower Bound	Expected Upper Bound	Actual Lower Bound	Actual Upper Bound
3				
4				
8				
0				
10				

Compare your test program with mine in Listing 45-8.

Listing 45-8. Exploring the lower_bound and upper_bound Functions

```
import <algorithm>;
import <iostream>;
import <ranges>;
import <vector>;

import data;

int main()
{
  intvector data{};
  read_data(data);
  std::ranges::sort(data);
  write_data(data);
```

```
for (int test : { 3, 4, 8, 0, 10 })
{
  auto lb{std::lower_bound(data.begin(), data.end(), test)};
  auto ub{std::upper_bound(data.begin(), data.end(), test)};
  std::cout << "bounds of " << test << ": { "
        << std::distance(data.begin(), lb) << ", "
        << std::distance(data.begin(), ub) << " }\n";
}
}
```

An even better way to write this program is to call equal_range, which finds the lower and upper bounds in one pass over the data. It returns a pair of iterators: the first member of the pair is the lower bound, and the second is the upper bound.

Comparing

To check whether two ranges are equal, that is, that they contain the same values, call the equal algorithm. This algorithm takes a start and one-past-the-end iterator for one range and the start of the second range. You must ensure that the two ranges have the same size. If every element of the two ranges is equal, it returns true. If any element doesn't match, it returns false. The function has two forms: pass only the iterators to equal, and it compares elements with the == operator; pass a comparison functor as the last argument, and equal compares elements by calling the functor. The first argument to the functor is the element from the first range, and the second argument is the element from the second range.

The mismatch function is the opposite. It compares two ranges and returns a single object that holds two iterators that refer to the first elements that do not match. The in1 member in the pair is an iterator that refers to an element in the first range, and the in2 member is an iterator that refers to the second range. If the two ranges are equal, the return value is a pair of end iterators.

The lexicographical_compare algorithm used to set the record for the longest algorithm name. It compares two ranges and determines whether the first range is "less than" the second. It does this by comparing the ranges one element at a time. If the ranges are equal, the function returns false. If the ranges are equal up to the end of one range, and the other range is longer, the shorter range is less than the longer range. If an element mismatch is found, whichever range contains the smaller element is the smaller range. All elements are compared using the < operator (or a caller-supplied predicate) and checked for equivalence, not equality. Recall that elements a and b are equivalent if the following is true:

```
not (a < b) and not (b < a)
```

If you apply lexicographical_compare to two strings, you get the expected less-than relationship, which explains the name. In other words, if you call this algorithm with the strings "hello" and "help", it returns true; if you call it with "help" and "hello", it returns false; and if you call it with "hel" and "hello", it returns true. If you were curious, it lost the longest-name crown to its cousin, lexicographical_compare_three_way, which is similar but can compare for equality and greater-than at one time.

Write a test program that reads two sequences of integers into separate vectors. You can do this by putting a non-number string between the two sets of data. Reading the first set of numbers fails when it reaches the non-number string. Call std::cin.clear() to clear the fail status, read and discard the separator string, and then read the second set of data. Then test the equal, mismatch, and lexicographical_compare functions on the two ranges.

Table 45-2 lists some suggested input data sets.

Table 45-2. *Suggested Data Sets for Testing Comparison Algorithms*

Data Set 1	Data Set 2
1 2 3 4 5	1 2 3
1 2 3	1 2 3 4 5
1 2 3 4 5	1 2 4 5
1 2 3	1 2 3

Compare your test program with mine in Listing 45-9.

Listing 45-9 Testing Various Comparison Algorithms

```
import <algorithm>;
import <iostream>;
import <ranges>;
import <vector>;

import data;

int main()
{
  intvector data1{};
  intvector data2{};

  read_data(data1);

  std::cin.clear();
  std::string discard;
  std::cin >> discard;

  read_data(data2);

  std::cout << "data1: ";
  write_data(data1);
  std::cout << "data2: ";
  write_data(data2);

  std::cout << std::boolalpha;
  std::cout << "equal(data1, data2) = " << std::ranges::equal(data1, data2) << '\n';

  auto result{std::ranges::mismatch(data1, data2)};
  std::cout << "mismatch(data1, data2) = index " <<
   std::distance(data1.begin(), result.in2) << '\n';

  std::cout << "lex_comp(data1, data2) = " <<
    std::ranges::lexicographical_compare(data1, data2) << '\n';
}
```

336

Rearranging Data

You've already seen the sort algorithm many times. Other algorithms are also adept at rearranging values in a range. The merge algorithm merges two sorted input ranges into a single output range. As always, you must ensure the output range has sufficient room to accept the entire merged result from both input ranges. The two input ranges can be different sizes, so merge takes five or six arguments: two for the first input range, two for the second input range, one for the start of the output range, and an optional argument for a functor to use instead of the < operator.

The replace algorithm scans an input range and replaces every occurrence of an old value with a new value. The replacement occurs in place, so you specify the usual range but no write iterator. The replace_if function is similar but takes a predicate instead of an old value. **Write a program that reads a vector of integers and replaces all occurrences of values in the range [10, 20] with 0.** Reuse the intrange functor class or write a lambda. Compare your program with mine in Listing 45-10.

Listing 45-10. Using replace_if and intrange to Replace All Integers in [10, 20] with 0

```
import <algorithm>;

import data;
import intrange;

int main()
{
  intvector data{};
  read_data(data);
  write_data(data);
  std::ranges::replace_if(data, intrange{10, 20}, 0);
  write_data(data);
}
```

Listing 45-11 shows the same program using a lambda.

Listing 45-11. Using replace_if and a Lambda to Replace All Integers in [10, 20] with 0

```
import <algorithm>;
import <ranges>;

import data;

int main()
{
  intvector data{};
  read_data(data);
  write_data(data);
  std::ranges::replace_if(data, [](int x) { return x >= 10 and x <= 20; }, 0);
  write_data(data);
}
```

A fun algorithm is shuffle, which shuffles elements in place into random order. This function takes two arguments, specifying the range to shuffle and a pseudo-random number generator. For the second argument, use the same std::default_random_engine as used in Listing 45-5.

337

Use the *sequence* module (from Listing 44-6) and generate a vector of 100 sequential integers. Then shuffle it into random order and print it. Compare your solution with mine in Listing 45-12.

Listing 45-12. Shuffling Integers into Random Order

```
import <algorithm>;
import <random>;

import data;
import sequence;

int main()
{
  intvector data(100);
  std::ranges::generate(data, sequence{1, 1});
  write_data(data);
  std::ranges::shuffle(data, std::default_random_engine{});
  write_data(data);
}
```

The generate algorithm repeatedly calls a functor with no arguments and copies the return value into an output range. It calls the functor once per element in the range, overwriting every element. The generate_n function takes an iterator for the start of a range and an integer for the size of the range. It then calls a functor (the third argument) once for each element of the range, copying the return value into the range. It is your responsibility to ensure that the range actually has that many elements in it. To use generate_n instead of generate in Listing 45-12, you could write

```
std::generate_n(data.begin(), data.size(), sequence{1, 1});
```

If you don't have to call a functor for every item of a range but instead want to fill a range with copies of the same value, call fill, passing a range and a value. The value is copied into every element in the range. The fill_n function takes a starting iterator and an integer size to specify the target range.

The transform algorithm modifies items by calling a functor for each item in an input range. It writes the transformed results to an output range, which can be the same as the input range, resulting in modifying the range in place. You've seen this algorithm at work already, so I won't add much to what you already know. The function has two forms: unary and binary. The unary form takes one input range, the start of an output range, and a functor. It calls the functor for each element of the input range, copying the result to the output range. The output range can be the same as the input range, or it can be a separate range. As with all algorithms, you must ensure that the output range is large enough to store the results.

The binary form of transform takes two input ranges, the start of an output range, and a binary functor. The functor is called for each element in the input ranges; the first argument comes from the first input range, and the second argument comes from the second input range. As with the unary form, the function copies the result to the output range, which can be the same as either input range. Note that the types of the two input ranges do not have to be the same.

Copying Data

Some algorithms operate in place, and others copy their results to an output range. For example, reverse reverses items in place, and reverse_copy leaves the input range intact and copies the reversed items to an output range. If a copying form of an algorithm exists, its name has _copy appended. (Unless it is also a predicate form of a function, in which case it has _if appended after _copy, as in replace_copy_if.)

In addition to just plain copy, which you've seen many times already, the standard library offers copy_
backward, which makes a copy but starts at the end and works toward the beginning, preserving the original
order; copy_n, which takes the start of a range, a count, and a write iterator; and copy_if, which is like copy
but takes a predicate and copies an element only if the predicate returns true. Distinguish copy_backward
from reverse_copy. The latter starts at the beginning and works toward the end of the input range but copies
the values into reverse order.

If you have to move elements instead of copy them, call std::move or std::move_backward. This
std::move is different from the one you encountered in Exploration 40. This one is declared in <algorithm>.
Like copy, the move algorithm takes an input range and a write iterator. It calls the other form of std::move
for each element of the input range, moving the element into the output range.

As with all algorithms that write output, it is your responsibility to ensure the output range is large
enough to handle everything you write to it. Some implementations of the standard library offer debugging
modes to help detect violations of this rule. If your library offers such a feature, by all means, take full
advantage of it.

Deleting Elements

The trickiest algorithms to use are those that "remove" elements. As you learned in Exploration 23,
algorithms such as remove don't actually delete anything. Instead, they rearrange the elements in the range,
so that all the elements slated for removal are packed at the end of the range. The removal algorithm returns
a subrange object that contains the remaining elements of the range.

The remove function takes an iterator range and a value, and it removes all elements equal to that value.
You can also use a predicate with remove_if to remove all elements for which a predicate returns true. These
two functions also have copying counterparts that don't rearrange anything but merely copy the elements
that are not being removed: remove_copy copies all the elements that are not equal to a certain value and
remove_copy_if copies all elements for which a predicate returns false.

Another algorithm that removes elements is unique (and unique_copy). It takes an input range and
removes all adjacent duplicates, thereby ensuring that every item in the range is unique. (If the range is
sorted, then all duplicates are adjacent.) Both functions can take a comparison functor instead of using the
default == operator.

When remove() returns a subrange, the return value actually holds two iterators that delimit the range
of elements to erase. The only data copied are the values that are "removed" from the original range by
reorganizing the vector. All of the algorithms treat any range the same way, whether the range is a vector, a
pair of iterator endpoints, or anything else that you can express by means of two endpoints.

**Write a program that reads integers into a vector, sorts the values into descending order, erases all
even elements, and copies to a vector while removing duplicates. Print the resulting vector.** Test for even
number with the modulus (%) operator: x is even when x % 2 == 0. My solution is in Listing 45-13.

Listing 45-13. Erasing Elements from a Vector

```
import <algorithm>;
import <iterator>;
import <ranges>;

import data;
import intrange;
```

```
int main()
{
  intvector data{};
  read_data(data);
  // sort into descending order
  std::ranges::sort(data, [](int a, int b) { return b < a; });
  auto odd{ std::ranges::remove_if(data, [](int x) { return x % 2 == 0; }) };
  intvector uniquely_odd{};
  std::unique_copy(begin(data), begin(odd), std::back_inserter(uniquely_odd));
  write_data(uniquely_odd);
}
```

Iterators

Algorithms, ranges, and iterators are closely related. I waved my hands a lot when describing how to use the algorithms with various kinds of iterators, ranges, and subranges. Before examining ranges in depth, we need to take a closer look at iterators and how to use them effectively, which is the topic of the next Exploration.

EXPLORATION 46

■ ■ ■

More About Iterators

Iterators provide element-by-element access to a sequence of things. The things can be numbers, characters, or objects of almost any type. The standard containers, such as vector, provide iterator access to the container contents, and other standard iterators let you access input streams and output streams, for example. One way to think of a range is as a pair of iterators. Standard algorithms require iterators for operating on sequences of things.

Until now, your view and use of iterators has been somewhat limited. Sure, you've used them, but do you really understand them? This Exploration helps you understand what's really going on with iterators.

Kinds of Iterators

So far, you have seen that iterators come in multiple varieties, in particular, read and write. You saw that you can construct a vector from a pair of iterators, such as std::istream_iterator. The std::ranges::copy function requires a write iterator for the copy destination.

All this time, however, I've oversimplified the situation by referring to "read" and "write" iterators. In fact, C++ has six different categories of iterators: input, output, forward, bidirectional, random access, and contiguous. And each category has additional traits to further describe what a particular iterator can or cannot do. Input and output iterators have the least functionality, and contiguous has the most. You can substitute an iterator with more functionality anywhere that calls for an iterator with less. Figure 46-1 illustrates the substitutability of iterators. Don't be misled by the figure, however. It does not show class inheritance. What makes an object an iterator is its behavior. If it fulfills all the requirements of an input iterator, for example, it is an input iterator, regardless of its type.

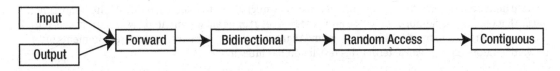

Figure 46-1. *Substitution tree for iterators*

All iterators can be copied and assigned freely. The result of a copy or an assignment is a new iterator that refers to the same item as the original iterator. The other characteristics depend on the iterator category, as described in the following sections.

R. Lischner, *Exploring C++20*, https://doi.org/10.1007/978-1-4842-5961-0_46

Input Iterators

An input iterator, unsurprisingly, supports only input. You can read from the iterator (using the unary *
operator) only once per iteration. You cannot modify the item that the iterator refers to. The ++ operator
advances to the next input item. You can compare iterators for equality and inequality, but the only
meaningful comparison is to compare an iterator with an end iterator. You cannot, in general, compare two
input iterators to see if they refer to the same item.

That's about it. Input iterators are quite limited, but they are also extremely useful. Many standard
algorithms express their inputs in terms of input iterators. The istream_iterator type is an example of an
input iterator. You can also treat any container's iterator as an input iterator, for example, the iterator that a
vector's begin() member function returns.

Output Iterators

An output iterator supports only output. You can assign to an iterator item by applying the * operator to the
iterator on the left-hand side of an assignment, but you cannot read from the iterator. You can modify the
iterator value only once per iteration. The ++ operator advances to the next output item.

You *cannot* compare output iterators for equality or inequality.

In spite of the limitations on output iterators, they, too, are widely used by the standard algorithms.
Every algorithm that copies data to an output range takes an output iterator to specify the start of the range.

One caution when dealing with output iterators is that you must ensure that wherever the iterator is
actually writing has enough room to store the entire output. Any mistakes result in undefined behavior.
Some implementations offer debugging iterators that can check for this kind of mistake, and you should
certainly take advantage of such tools when they are available. Don't rely solely on debugging libraries,
however. Careful code design, careful code implementation, and careful code review are absolutely
necessary to ensure safety when using output (and other) iterators.

The ostream_iterator type is an example of an output iterator. You can also treat many container's
iterators as output iterators, for example, the iterator that a vector's begin() member function returns.

Forward Iterators

A forward iterator has all the functionality of an input iterator and an output iterator, and a little bit more.
You can freely read from, and write to, an iterator item (still using the unary * operator), and you can do so
as often as you wish. The ++ operator advances to the next item, and the == and != operators can compare
iterators to see if they refer to the same item or to the end position.

Some algorithms require forward iterators instead of input iterators. I glossed over that detail in the
previous Explorations, because it rarely affects you. For example, the binary search algorithms require
forward iterators to specify the input range, because they might have to refer to a particular item more than
once. That means you cannot directly use an istream_iterator as an argument to, say, lower_bound, but
then you aren't likely to try that in a real program. All the containers' iterators meet the requirements of
forward iterators, so in practical terms, this restriction has little impact.

Bidirectional Iterators

A bidirectional iterator has all the functionality of a forward iterator, but it also supports the -- operator,
which moves the iterator backward one position to the previous item. As with any iterator, you are
responsible for ensuring that you never advance the iterator past the end of the range or before the
beginning.

The reverse and reverse_copy algorithms (and a few others) require bidirectional iterators. Most of the containers' iterators meet at least the requirements of bidirectional iterators, so you rarely have to worry about this restriction.

Random Access Iterators

A random access iterator has all the functionality of all other iterators, plus you can move the iterator an arbitrary amount by adding or subtracting an integer.

You can subtract two iterators (provided they refer to the same sequence of objects) to obtain the distance between them. Recall from Exploration 45 that the distance function returns the distance between two iterators. If you pass forward or bidirectional iterators to the function, it advances the starting iterator one step at a time, until it reaches the end iterator. Only then will it know the distance. If you pass random access iterators, it merely subtracts the two iterators and immediately returns the distance between them.

You can compare random access iterators for equality or inequality. If the two iterators refer to the same sequence of objects, you can also use any of the relational operators. For random access iterators, a < b means a refers to an item earlier in the sequence than b.

Algorithms such as sort require random access iterators. The vector type provides random access iterators, but not all containers do. The list container, for example, implements a doubly linked list, so it has only bidirectional iterators. Because you can't use the sort algorithm, the list container has its own sort member function. Learn more about list in Exploration 56.

Contiguous Iterators

A contiguous iterator has all the functionality of all other iterators, plus it applies to elements that are stored in adjacent memory locations. A vector or array has contiguous iterators, but other containers do not.

Now that you know that vectors supply contiguous iterators, and you can compare contiguous (and random access) iterators using relational operators, revisit Listing 10-4. Can you think of an easier way to write that program? (Hint: Consider a loop condition of start < end.) See my rewrite in Listing 46-1.

Listing 46-1. Comparing Iterators by Using the < Operator

```
import <algorithm>;
import <iostream>;
import <iterator>;
import <vector>;

int main()
{
  std::vector<int> data{
    std::istream_iterator<int>(std::cin),
    std::istream_iterator<int>()
  };

  for (auto start{data.begin()}, end{data.end()}; start < end; ++start)
  {
    --end; // now end points to a real position, possibly start
    std::iter_swap(start, end); // swap contents of two iterators

  }
```

```
std::copy(data.begin(), data.end(),
          std::ostream_iterator<int>(std::cout, "\n"));
}
```

This time I used `std::copy()`, which uses a pair of iterators instead of a range, just to show how iterator pairs work for input and output.

So input, forward, bidirectional, random access, and contiguous iterators all qualify as "read" iterators, and output, forward, bidirectional, random access, and contiguous iterators all qualify as "write" iterators. An algorithm, such as copy, might require only input and output iterators. That is, the input range requires two input iterators. You can use any iterator that meets the requirements of an input iterator: input, forward, bidirectional, random access, or contiguous. For the start of the output range, use any iterator that meets the requirements of an output iterator: output, forward, bidirectional, random access, or contiguous.

Working with Iterators

The most common sources for iterators are the `begin()` and `end()` member functions that all containers (such as map and vector) provide. The `begin()` member function returns an iterator that refers to the first element of the container, and `end()` returns an iterator that refers to the position of the one-past-the-end element of the container.

What does begin() return for an empty container?

_____

If the container is empty, `begin()` returns the same value as `end()`, that is, a special value that represents "past the end" and cannot be dereferenced. One way to test whether a container is empty is to test whether `begin() == end()`. (Even better, especially when you are writing a real program and not trying to illustrate the nature of iterators, is to call the `empty()` member function, which every container provides.)

Each container implements its iterator differently. All that matters to you is that the iterator fulfills the requirements of one of the standard categories.

The exact category of iterator depends on the container. A `vector` returns contiguous iterators. A `map` returns bidirectional iterators. Any library reference will tell you exactly what category of iterator each container supports.

A number of algorithms and container member functions also return iterators. For example, almost every function that performs a search returns an iterator that refers to the desired item. If the function cannot find the item, it returns the end iterator. The type of the return value is usually the same as the type of the iterators in the input range. Algorithms that copy elements to an output range return the result iterator.

Once you have an iterator, you can dereference it with * to obtain the value that it refers to (except for an output iterator, which you dereference only to assign a new value, and the end iterators, which you can never dereference). If the iterator refers to an object, and you want to access a member of the object, you can use the shorthand `->` notation.

```
std::vector<std::string> lines(2, "hello");
std::string first{*lines.begin()};         // dereference the first item
std::size_t size{lines.begin()->size()};   // dereference and call a member function
```

You can advance an iterator to a new position by calling the next or advance function (declared in `<iterator>`). The advance function modifies the iterator that you pass as the first argument. The next function takes the iterator by value and returns a new iterator value. The second argument is the integer distance to advance the iterator. The second argument is optional for next; default is one. If the iterator is random access, the function adds the distance to the iterator. Any other kind of iterator must apply its increment (++) operator multiple times to advance the desired distance, for example:

```
std::vector<int> data{ 1, 2, 3, 4, 5 };
auto iter{ data.begin() };
std::cout << "4 == " << *std::next(iter, 3) << '\n';
```

For a vector, std::next() is just like addition, but for other containers, such as std::map, it applies the increment operator multiple times to reach the desired destination. If you have a reverse iterator, you can pass a negative distance or call std::prev(). If the iterator is bidirectional, the second argument can be negative to go backward. You can advance an input iterator but not an output iterator. Reusing the sequence functor from Exploration 44, read the program in Listing 46-2.

Listing 46-2. Advancing an Iterator

```
import <algorithm>;
import <iostream>;
import <iterator>;
import <vector>;

import data;       // see Listing 45-2.
import sequence;   // see Listing 44-6.

int main()
{
   intvector data(10);
   // fill with even numbers
   std::generate(data.begin(), data.end(), sequence{0, 2});
   auto iter{data.begin()};
   std::advance(iter, 4);
   std::cout << *iter << ", ";
   iter = std::prev(iter, 2);
   std::cout << *iter << '\n';
}
```

What does the program print?_____

_____

The data vector is filled with even numbers, starting at 0. The iterator, iter, initially refers to the first element of the vector, namely, 0. The iterator advances four positions, to value 8, and then back two positions, to 4. So the output is

8, 4

Declaring variables to store iterators is clumsy. The type names are long and cumbersome. Therefore, I often use auto to define a variable. Sometimes you need to name an iterator type explicitly. This is usually done with a member type name. Listing 46-3 illustrates some uses of member types for iterators.

Listing 46-3. Demonstrating Iterator Member Types

```cpp
import <iostream>;
import <string>;
import <vector>;

int main()
{
  std::vector<std::string> lines{2, "hello"};

  std::vector<std::string>::iterator iter{lines.begin()};
  *iter = "good-bye";              // dereference and modify the first item
  std::size_t size{iter->size()};  // dereference and call a member function

  std::vector<std::string>::const_iterator citer{lines.cbegin()};
  std::cout << *citer << '\n';
  std::cout << size << '\n';
}
```

The member type `const_iterator` yields const elements of the container. The `iterator` type yields modifiable members. The next section examines `const_iterator` more closely.

const_iterator vs. const iterator

A minor source of confusion is the difference between a `const_iterator` and `const iterator`. An output iterator (and any iterator that also meets the requirements of an output iterator, namely, forward, bidirectional, random access, and contiguous) lets you modify the item it references. For some forward iterators (and bidirectional, random access, and contiguous), you want to treat the data in the range as read-only. Even though the iterator itself meets the requirements of a forward iterator, your immediate need might be only for an input iterator.

You might think that declaring the iterator const would help. After all, that's how you ask the compiler to help you, by preventing accidental modification of a variable: declare the variable with the const specifier. What do you think? **Will it work?** _____

If you aren't sure, try a test. Read Listing 46-4 and **predict its output**. Use the same data module as in Exploration 45.

Listing 46-4. Printing the Middle Item of a Series of Integers

```cpp
import <iostream>;
import <iterator>;
import data;

int main()
{
  intvector data{};
  read_data(data);
  const intvector::iterator iter{data.begin()};
  std::advance(iter, data.size() / 2); // move to middle of vector
  if (not data.empty())
    std::cout << "middle item = " << *iter << '\n';
}
```

Can you see why the compiler refuses to compile the program? Maybe you can't see the precise reason, buried in the compiler's error output. (The next section will discuss this problem at greater length.) The error is that the variable iter is const. You cannot modify the iterator, so you cannot advance it to the middle of the vector.

Instead of declaring the iterator itself as const, you have to tell the compiler that you want the iterator to refer to const data. If the vector itself were const, the begin() function would return exactly such an iterator. You could freely modify the iterator's position, but you could not modify the value that the iterator references. The name of the iterator that this function returns is const_iterator (with underscore).

In other words, every container actually has two different begin() functions. One is a const member function and returns const_iterator. The other is not a const member function; it returns a plain iterator. As with any const or non-const member function, the compiler chooses one or the other, depending on whether the container itself is const. If the container is not const, you get the non-const version of begin(), which returns a plain iterator, and you can modify the container contents through the iterator. If the container is const, you get the const version of begin(), which returns a const_iterator, which prevents you from modifying the container's contents. You can also force the issue by calling cbegin(), which always returns const_iterator, even for a non-const object.

Rewrite Listing 46-4 to use a const_iterator. Your program should look something like Listing 46-5.

Listing 46-5. Really Printing the Middle Item of a Series of Integers

```
import <iostream>;
import <iterator>;
import data;

int main()
{
  intvector data{};
  read_data(data);
  intvector::const_iterator iter{data.begin()};
  std::advance(iter, data.size() / 2); // move to middle of vector
  if (not data.empty())
    std::cout << "middle item = " << *iter << '\n';
}
```

Prove to yourself that you cannot modify the data when you have a const_iterator. **Make a further modification to your program to negate the middle value.** Now your program should look like Listing 46-6.

Listing 46-6. Negating the Middle Value in a Series of Integers

```
import <iostream>;
import <iterator>;
import data;

int main()
{
  intvector data{};
  read_data(data);
  intvector::const_iterator iter{data.begin()};
  std::advance(iter, data.size() / 2); // move to middle of vector
  if (not data.empty())
    *iter = -*iter;
  write_data(data);
}
```

If you change const_iterator to iterator, the program works. **Do it.**

Error Messages

When you compiled Listing 46-4, the compiler issued an error message, or *diagnostic*, as the C++ standard writers call it. For example, the compiler that I use every day, g++, prints this:

```
In file included from /usr/include/c++/10/bits/stl_algobase.h:66,
                 from /usr/include/c++/10/bits/char_traits.h:39,
                 from /usr/include/c++/10/ios:40,
                 from /usr/include/c++/10/ostream:38,
                 from /usr/include/c++/10/iostream:39,
                 from list4604.cc:3:
/usr/include/c++/10/bits/stl_iterator_base_funcs.h: In instantiation of 'constexpr void
std::__advance(_RandomAccessIterator&, _Distance, std::random_access_iterator_tag) [with
_RandomAccessIterator = const __gnu_cxx::__normal_iterator<int*, std::vector<int> >; _
Distance = long int]':
/usr/include/c++/10/bits/stl_iterator_base_funcs.h:206:21:   required from 'constexpr void
std::advance(_InputIterator&, _Distance) [with _InputIterator = const __gnu_cxx::__normal_
iterator<int*, std::vector<int> >; _Distance = long unsigned int]'
list4604.cc:11:37:   required from here
/usr/include/c++/10/bits/stl_iterator_base_funcs.h:181:2: error: passing 'const __gnu_
cxx::__normal_iterator<int*, std::vector<int> >' as 'this' argument discards qualifiers
[-fpermissive]
  181 |   ++__i;
      |   ^~~~~
In file included from /usr/include/c++/10/bits/stl_algobase.h:67,
                 from /usr/include/c++/10/bits/char_traits.h:39,
                 from /usr/include/c++/10/ios:40,
                 from /usr/include/c++/10/ostream:38,
                 from /usr/include/c++/10/iostream:39,
                 from list4604.cc:3:
/usr/include/c++/10/bits/stl_iterator.h:975:7: note:   in call to 'constexpr __gnu_
cxx::__normal_iterator<_Iterator, _Container>& __gnu_cxx::__normal_iterator<_Iterator,
_Container>::operator++() [with _Iterator = int*; _Container = std::vector<int>]'
  975 |       operator++() _GLIBCXX_NOEXCEPT
      |       ^~~~~~~~~
In file included from /usr/include/c++/10/bits/stl_algobase.h:66,
                 from /usr/include/c++/10/bits/char_traits.h:39,
                 from /usr/include/c++/10/ios:40,
                 from /usr/include/c++/10/ostream:38,
                 from /usr/include/c++/10/iostream:39,
                 from list4604.cc:3:
/usr/include/c++/10/bits/stl_iterator_base_funcs.h:183:2: error: passing 'const __gnu_
cxx::__normal_iterator<int*, std::vector<int> >' as 'this' argument discards qualifiers
[-fpermissive]
```

So what does all that gobbledygook mean? Although a C++ expert can figure it out, it may not be much help to you. Buried in the middle is the line number and source file that identify the source of the error. That's where you have to start looking. The compiler didn't detect the error until it started working through various modules. The file names depend on the implementation of the standard library, so you can't always tell from those file names what is the actual error.

In this case, the error arises from within the std::advance function when it tries to apply the ++ operator to the iterator. That's when the compiler detects that it has a const iterator, but it does not have any functions that work with a const iterator. The message about "discards qualifiers" means the only way the compiler could proceed were if it could get rid of the const qualifier on the iter object.

Don't give up hope for ever understanding C++ compiler error messages. By the end of the book, you will have gained quite a bit more knowledge that will help you understand how the compiler and library really work, and that understanding will help you make sense of these error messages.

My advice for dealing with the deluge of confusing error messages is to start by finding the first mention of your source file. That should tell you the line number that gives rise to the problem. Check the source file. You might see an obvious mistake. If not, check the error message text. Ignore the "instantiated from here" and similar messages. Try to find the real error message, which often starts with error: instead of warning: or note:.

Specialized Iterators

The <iterator> header defines a number of useful, specialized iterators, such as back_inserter, which you've seen several times already. Strictly speaking, back_inserter is a function that returns an iterator, but you rarely have to know the exact iterator type.

In addition to back_inserter, you can also use front_inserter, which also takes a container as an argument and returns an output iterator. Every time you assign a value to the dereferenced iterator, it calls the container's push_front member function to insert the value at the start of the container.

The inserter function takes a container and an iterator as arguments. It returns an output iterator that calls the container's insert function. The insert member function requires an iterator argument, specifying the position at which to insert the value. The inserter iterator initially passes its second argument as the insertion position. After each insertion, it updates its internal iterator, so subsequent insertions go into subsequent positions. In other words, inserter just does the right thing.

Other specialized iterators include istream_iterator and ostream_iterator, which you've also seen. An istream_iterator is an input iterator that extracts values from a stream when you dereference the iterator. With no arguments, the istream_iterator constructor creates an end-of-stream iterator. An iterator is equal to the end-of-stream iterator when an input operation fails.

An ostream_iterator is an output iterator. The constructor takes an output stream and an optional string as arguments. Assigning to the dereferenced iterator writes a value to the output stream, optionally followed by the string (from the constructor).

Another specialized iterator is the reverse_iterator class. It adapts an existing iterator (called the *base* iterator), which must be bidirectional (or random access or contiguous). When the reverse iterator goes forward (++), the base iterator goes backward (--). Containers that support bidirectional iterators have rbegin() and rend() member functions, which return reverse iterators. The rbegin() function returns a reverse iterator that points to the last element of the container, and rend() returns a special reverse iterator value that represents one position before the beginning of the container. Thus, you treat the range [rbegin(), rend()) as a normal iterator range, expressing the values of the container in reverse order.

C++ doesn't permit an iterator to point to one position before the beginning, so reverse iterators have a somewhat funky implementation. Ordinarily, implementation details don't matter, but reverse_iterator exposes this particular detail in its base() member function, which returns the base iterator.

I could tell you what the base iterator actually is, but that would deprive you of the fun. **Write a program to reveal the nature of the reverse_iterator's base iterator.** (Hint: Fill a vector with a sequence of integers. Use a reverse iterator to get to the middle value. Compare with the value of the iterator's base() iterator.)

> **If a reverse_iterator points to position x of a container, what does its base()
> iterator point to?**

_____

If you did not answer $x + 1$, try running the program in Listing 46-7.

Listing 46-7. Revealing the Implementation of reverse_iterator

```
import <algorithm>;
import <iostream>;

import data;
import sequence;

int main()
{
  intvector data(10);
  std::generate(data.begin(), data.end(), sequence(1));
  write_data(data);                            // prints { 1 2 3 4 5 6 7 8 9 10 }
  intvector::iterator iter{data.begin()};
  iter = iter + 4;                             // iter is contiguous
  std::cout << *iter << '\n';                  // prints 5

  intvector::reverse_iterator rev{data.rbegin()};
  std::cout << *rev << '\n';                   // prints 10
  rev = rev + 4;                               // rev is also contiguous
  std::cout << *rev << '\n';                   // prints 6
  std::cout << *rev.base() << '\n';            // prints 7
  std::cout << *data.rend().base() << '\n';    // prints 1
}
```

Now do you see? The base iterator always points to one position *after* the reverse iterator's position. That's the trick that allows rend() to point to a position "before the beginning," even though that's not allowed. Under the hood, the rend() iterator actually has a base iterator that points at the first item in the container, and the reverse_iterator's implementation of the * operator performs the magic of taking the base iterator, retreating one position, and then dereferencing the base iterator.

As you can see, iterators are a little more complicated than they initially seem to be. Once you understand how they work, however, you will see that they are actually quite simple, powerful, and easy to use. Iterators form the basis of the range library. You can think of a range as a pair of iterators, but they are slightly more complicated than that, as the next Exploration explains.

■ ■ ■

Ranges, Views, and Adaptors

From early in this book, I have talked about "ranges" with little more than a vague description of what a range truly is. In part because ranges are defined using fairly advanced features of C++ that I haven't covered yet, and in part because the way C++ uses ranges, you don't need to know much more about them. This Exploration starts to unravel the mystery of ranges and gives you some more fun adventures you can have with them, including some very powerful coding techniques that use range views and range adaptors.

Ranges

So far, you have encountered two kinds of ranges: vectors and iterator pairs. A vector is a range because it stores a series of values, and the range is one way to access those values. A pair of iterators can also express a range by dereferencing and incrementing the start iterator until it equals the end iterator.

More precisely, a range is characterized by a start iterator and an end sentinel. A *sentinel* can be an end iterator but it doesn't have to be. A sentinel might be some other type that represents the end of the range. A common implementation of linked lists uses a sentinel node to mark the end of the list because that can make the code simpler to write than trying to define an end iterator. Unless you want to implement a range type, you don't need to concern yourself with sentinels other than to know that they exist.

So a range has a starting iterator and ending sentinel. The `std::ranges::begin()` function returns the start of the range, and `std::ranges::end()` returns the sentinel. Some code examples used `data.begin()` and `data.end()`, which work for vectors, but not every range. The `std::ranges` functions work for all range types. Just as the `cbegin()` member function returns a const_iterator, the `std::ranges::cbegin()` function does the same for any range.

If a range has a known size, such as a vector, the `std::ranges::size()` function returns that size. The function is defined only for range types that can return their size quickly. Others, such as as `istream_view`, simply do not have a corresponding `std::ranges::size()` function. Similarly, `std::ranges::empty()` returns true if a range is empty, but is defined only if that can be determined without modifying the range. So you can't use it to test whether an instance of `std::ranges::istream_view` is empty, but you can use it to test a vector.

Listing 47-1 demonstrates some of these range functions.

Listing 47-1. Demonstrating Range Functions

```
import <algorithm>;
import <iostream>;
import <ranges>;
import <vector>;
```

© Ray Lischner 2020
R. Lischner, *Exploring C++20*, https://doi.org/10.1007/978-1-4842-5961-0_47

```
int main()
{
    std::vector<int> data;
    std::cout << "Enter some numbers:\n";
    std::ranges::copy(std::ranges::istream_view<int>(std::cin),
        std::back_inserter(data));

    std::cout << "You entered " << std::ranges::size(data) << " values\n";
    if (not std::ranges::empty(data))
    {
        std::ranges::sort(data);
        auto start{ std::ranges::cbegin(data) };
        auto middle{ start + std::ranges::size(data) / 2 };
        std::cout << "The median value is " << *middle << '\n';
    }
}
```

Given an iterator and a compatible sentinel, you can define a range by constructing a `std::ranges::subrange` object by passing the iterator and sentinel to the constructor. The subrange does not copy any elements from the source range. It just holds onto the iterator and sentinel. Just as `std::advance` advances an iterator and `std::next()` returns a new iterator, the subrange class implements the `advance()` member function to advance the start iterator. The `next()` member function returns a new subrange with a start position advanced by one. Both functions take an argument to advance by more than one position. For example, the following prints the numbers 3, 4, and 5 to the standard output:

```
std::vector<int> data{ 1, 2, 3, 4, 5 };
std::ranges::subrange sub{ std::ranges::begin(data), std::ranges::end(data) };
std::ranges::copy(sub.next(2), std::ostream_iterator<int>(std::cout, "\n"));
```

Just as iterators come in different flavors, so do ranges. An input range is one with an input iterator as its start iterator. An output range has a starting output iterator. The other iterator types also have corresponding range types: forward_range, bidirectional_range, random_access_range, and contiguous_range. The behavior and restrictions on a range are the same as they are for their respective iterators.

Ranges have additional characteristics, such as common_range, which is when the sentinel type is the same as the starting iterator type. All of the container types in the standard library (such as vector) are common ranges. A viewable_range is a range that can be used as a view, which is the topic of the next section.

Range Views

A view is a special kind of range that features lightweight copying. Copying a view just makes another view that looks the same as the original view. Destroying a view (such as when the view goes out of scope) is instant because no elements in the viewed range are destroyed. A subrange is a kind of view, and other kinds of view include single_view, which takes a single object and makes it look like a range of size one.

The `std::ranges::iota_view` type is similar to the sequence class of Listing 44-5. It takes one or two arguments and yields a range of integers with a starting value and an optional sentinel value. Without the sentinel value, the range goes on forever until the integer value wraps around and repeats.

One interesting aspect of the view types is that you can construct one in two different ways. Calling `std::ranges::view::iota(start)` function is equivalent to constructing `std::ranges::iota_view{start}`. Ditto for passing two arguments.

Experiment with std::ranges::single_view. **Write a program that reads a single integer from the user, constructs a single_view, and uses a ranged for loop to print every element of the view.** Compare your program with mine in Listing 47-2.

Listing 47-2. Demonstrating Range Functions

```
import <iostream>;
import <ranges>;

int main()
{
    std::cout << "Enter an integer: ";
    int input{};
    if (std::cin >> input)
    {
        for (auto x : std::ranges::single_view{input}) {
            std::cout << x << '\n';
        }
    }
}
```

Range Pipelines

Range views are cute, but what good are they? The standard library defines the vertical bar operator (|) as a pipeline operator, capable of piping data from a range into a pipeline of views. For example, suppose you are writing the scoring software for a judging event. The rules for scoring are to discard the high and low scores and compute the mean of the remaining scores. You can do this with iterators, but it would be clumsy adjusting the start and end iterators. Or you could just modify the vector that stores the scores to remove the first and last. Or you can use views, as shown in Listing 47-3.

Listing 47-3. Computing Scores by Using Views

```
import <algorithm>;
import <iostream>;
import <ranges>;
import <vector>;

int main()
{
    std::cout << "Enter the scores: ";
    std::vector<int> scores{};
    std::ranges::copy(std::ranges::istream_view<int>(std::cin),
        std::back_inserter(scores));
    std::ranges::sort(scores);
    auto drop_high{ scores | std::ranges::views::take(scores.size() - 1) };
    auto remaining_scores{ drop_high | std::ranges::views::drop(1) };

    int sum{0};
    int count{0};
    for (int score : remaining_scores)
```

```
    {
        ++count;
        sum += score;
    }
    std::cout << "mean score is " << sum / count << '\n';
}
```

What is noteworthy about the `take` and `drop` views, as with other views, is that the vector of scores is never copied. Instead, the vector is traversed once, and the relevant scores are tallied with little overhead. What makes these pipelines so effective are special views that perform processing on their data. These special views are called *range adaptors*, which are the subject of the next section.

Range Adaptors

A range adaptor is another way to create a view when given a range. The standard library includes several useful range adaptors, and third parties are likely to add many more.

The `drop` View

The `std::ranges::view::drop` adaptor takes an integer argument and skips over that many elements of the input range, passing through all subsequent elements, for example, to skip the first two characters of a string (which is a range of characters, after all):

```
std::string string{"string"};
auto ring = string | std::ranges::views::drop(2);
```

The `drop_while` adaptor is similar, but it takes a predicate instead of a count. It skips elements until the predicate returns true and iterates that element followed by all remaining elements after that.

The `filter` View

Use `std::ranges::view::filter(predicate)` to select only elements of the input range that pass a predicate. As usual, this can be a function, functor, or lambda, for example, to select only values greater than zero:

```
auto positives = data
    | std::ranges::views::filter([](auto value) { return value > 0; });
```

The `join` View

Flatten a range of ranges into a single range with `std::ranges::view::join`. A common use of join is to join a range of strings into a single range of characters, for example:

```
std::vector<std::string> words{ "this", " ", "is an", " ", "example" };
auto sentence = words | std::ranges::views::join;
```

The **keys** View

Iterating over a map yields a pair of a key and a value for each element. Often, you need to iterate only over the keys, which you can do with std::ranges::view::keys, for example:

```
std::map<std::string, int> barn{ {"horse", 3}, {"dog", 4}, {"cat", 0} };
for (auto const& animal : barn | std::ranges::views::keys)
    std::cout << animal << '\n';
```

The **reverse** View

If a range is bidirectional, the std::ranges::views::reverse adaptor iterates it in reverse order, for example:

```
std::map<std::string, int> barn{ {"horse", 3}, {"dog", 4}, {"cat", 0} };
auto animals{ barn | std::ranges::views::reverse | std::ranges::views::keys };
for (auto const& animal : animals)
    std::cout << animal << '\n';
```

The **transform** View

The std::ranges::view::transform adaptor takes a function or lambda argument and passes each element of the range to that function, replacing the element with the value returned from the function, for example, to change a range of strings into a range of integer string lengths and then to keep only lengths greater than three:

```
std::vector<std::string> strings{"string", "one", "two", "testing" };
auto sizes = strings
    | std::ranges::views::transform([](auto&& str) { return str.size(); })
    | std::ranges::views::filter([](auto size) { return size > 3; });
```

The **take** View

The std::ranges::view::take adaptor takes an integer argument and yields that many elements of the input range, starting with the first, for example, to keep only the first three characters of a string:

```
std::string string{"string"};
std::ranges::copy(string | std::ranges::views::take(3),
    std::ostreambuf_iterator(std::cout));
```

The take_while adaptor is similar, but it takes a predicate instead of a count. The take_while adaptor iterates elements until the predicate returns false, after which it stops iterating for the remainder of the input range.

The **values** View

Iterating over a map yields a pair of a key and a value for each element. Often, you need to iterate only over the values, which you can do with std::ranges::view::values, for example:

```
std::map<std::string, int> barn{ {"horse", 3}, {"dog", 4}, {"cat", 0} };
int total{0};
for (auto count : barn | std::ranges::views::values)
    total += count;
```

This was not an exhaustive list, although it covered most view adaptors. The examples illustrated a few of the ways that view adaptors can be assembled using pipelines. C++ offers a little flexibility if you prefer function call syntax. The following pipelines all do the same thing, create a view of [2, 7):

```
auto data{ std::ranges::views::iota(0, 10) }; // [0, 10)

auto demo1 = data | std::ranges::views::drop(2) | std::ranges::views::take(5);
auto demo2 = std::ranges::views::drop(data, 2) | std::ranges::views::take(5);
auto demo3 = std::ranges::views::take(std::ranges::views::drop(data, 2), 5);
auto demo4 = std::ranges::views::take(5)(std::ranges::views::drop(2)(data));
```

So many programs involve iterating over a range. It is, perhaps, the most fundamental aspect of programming. Languages offer a variety of constructs for iterating over a range, and C++ has three different kinds of loops. In the end, you can do everything with a ranged for loop, ranges, views, and adaptors.

Now it's time to pick up a few more important C++ programming techniques. The next Exploration introduces exceptions and exception handling, necessary topics for properly handling programmer and user errors.

EXPLORATION 48

Exceptions

You may have been dismayed by the lack of error-checking and error-handling in the Explorations so far. That's about to change. C++, like most modern programming languages, supports exceptions as a way to jump out of the normal flow of control in response to an error or other exceptional condition. This Exploration introduces exceptions: how to throw them, how to catch them, when the language and library use them, and when and how you should use them.

Introducing Exceptions

Exploration 9 introduced vector's at member function, which retrieves a vector element at a particular index. At the time, I wrote that most programs you read would use square brackets instead. Now is a good time to examine the difference between square brackets and the at function. First, take a look at two programs. Listing 48-1 shows a simple program that uses a vector.

Listing 48-1. Accessing an Element of a Vector

```cpp
import <iostream>;
import <vector>;

int main()
{
  std::vector<int> data{ 10, 20 };
  data.at(5) = 0;
  std::cout << data.at(5) << '\n';
}
```

What do you expect to happen when you run this program?

_____

Try it. **What actually happens?**

_____

The vector index, 5, is out of bounds. The only valid indices for data are 0 and 1, so it's no wonder that the program terminates with a nastygram. Now consider the program in Listing 48-2.

© Ray Lischner 2020
R. Lischner, *Exploring C++20*, https://doi.org/10.1007/978-1-4842-5961-0_48

Listing 48-2. A Bad Way to Access an Element of a Vector

```
import <iostream>;
import <vector>;

int main()
{
  std::vector<int> data{ 10, 20 };
  data[5] = 0;
  std::cout << data[5] << '\n';
}
```

What do you expect to happen when you run this program?

_____

Try it. **What actually happens?**

_____

The vector index, 5, is still out of bounds. If you still receive a nastygram, you get a different one than before. On the other hand, the program might run to completion without indicating any error. You might find that disturbing, but such is the case of undefined behavior. Anything can happen.

That, in a nutshell, is the difference between using subscripts ([ ]) and the at member function. If the index is invalid, the at member function causes the program to terminate in a predictable, controlled fashion. You can write additional code and avoid termination, take appropriate actions to clean up prior to termination, or let the program end.

The subscript operator, on the other hand, results in undefined behavior if the index is invalid. Anything can happen, so you have no control—none whatsoever. If the software is controlling, say, an airplane, then "anything" involves many options that are too unpleasant to imagine. On a typical desktop workstation, a more likely scenario is that the program crashes, which is a good thing, because it tells you that something went wrong. The worst possible consequence is that nothing obvious happens, and the program silently uses a garbage value and keeps running.

The at member function, and many other functions, can *throw exceptions* to signal an error. When a program throws an exception, the normal, statement-by-statement progression of the program is interrupted. Instead, a special exception-handling system takes control of the program. The standard gives some leeway in how this system actually works, but you can imagine that it forces functions to end and destroys local objects and parameters, although the functions do not return a value to the caller. Instead, functions are forcefully ended, one at a time, and a special code block *catches* the exception. Use the try-catch statement to set up these special code blocks in a program. A catch block is also called an *exception handler*. Normal code execution resumes after the handler finishes its work:

```
try {
  throw std::runtime_error("oops");
} catch (std::runtime_error const& ex) {
  std::cerr << ex.what() << '\n';
}
```

When a program throws an exception (with the throw keyword), it throws a value, called an exception object, which can be an object of nearly any type. By convention, exception types, such as std::runtime_error, inherit from the std::exception class or one of several subclasses that the standard library provides. Third-party class libraries often introduce their own exception base class.

An exception handler also has an object declaration, which has a type, and the handler accepts only exception objects of a matching type. If no exception handler has a matching type, or if you don't write any handler at all, the program terminates, as happens with Listing 48-1. The remainder of this Exploration examines each aspect of exception handling in detail.

EXPLORATION 48 ■ EXCEPTIONS

Catching Exceptions

An exception handler is said to *catch* an exception. Write an exception handler at the end of a try: the try keyword is followed by a compound statement (it must be compound), followed by a series of *handlers*. Each handler starts with a catch keyword, followed by parentheses that enclose the declaration of an exception-handler object. After the parentheses is a compound statement that is the body of the exception handler.

When the type of the exception object matches the type of the exception-handler object, the handler is deemed a match, and the handler object is initialized with the exception object. The handler declaration is usually a reference, which avoids copying the exception object unnecessarily. Most handlers don't have to modify the exception object, so the handler declaration is typically a reference to const. A "match" is when the exception object's type is the same as the handler's declared type or a class derived from the handler's declared type, ignoring whether the handler is const or a reference.

The exception-handling system destroys all objects that it constructed in the try part of the statement prior to throwing the exception, then it transfers control to the handler, so the handler's body runs normally, and control resumes with the statement after the end of the entire try-catch statement, that is, after the statement's last catch handler. The handler types are tried in order, and the first match wins. Thus, you should always list the most specific types first and base class types later.

A base class exception-handler type matches any exception object of a derived type. To handle all exceptions that the standard library might throw, write the handler to catch std::exception (declared in <exception>), which is the base class for all standard exceptions. Listing 48-3 demonstrates some of the exceptions that the std::string class can throw. Try out the program by typing strings of varying length.

Listing 48-3. Forcing a string to Throw Exceptions

```cpp
import <cstdlib>;
import <exception>;
import <iostream>;
import <stdexcept>;
import <string>;

int main()
{
  std::string line{};
  while (std::getline(std::cin, line))
  {
    try
    {
      line.at(10) = ' ';                        // can throw out_of_range
      if (line.size() < 20)
        line.append(line.max_size(), '*');      // can throw length_error
      for (std::string::size_type size(line.size());
           size < line.max_size();
           size = size * 2)
      {
        line.resize(size);                      // can throw bad_alloc
      }
      line.resize(line.max_size());             // can throw bad_alloc
      std::cout << "okay\n";
    }
```

```
    catch (std::out_of_range const& ex)
    {
        std::cout << ex.what() << '\n';
        std::cout << "string index (10) out of range.\n";
    }
    catch (std::length_error const& ex)
    {
        std::cout << ex.what() << '\n';
        std::cout << "maximum string length (" << line.max_size() << ") exceeded.\n";
    }
    catch (std::exception const& ex)
    {
        std::cout << "other exception: " << ex.what() << '\n';
    }
    catch (...)
    {
        std::cout << "Unknown exception type. Program terminating.\n";
        std::abort();
    }
  }
}
```

If you type a line that contains 10 or fewer characters, the line.at(10) expression throws a std::out_of_range exception. If the string has more than 10 characters, but fewer than 20, the program tries to append the maximum string size repetitions of an asterisk ('*'), which results in std::length_error. If the initial string is longer than 20 characters, the program tries to increase the string size, using ever-growing sizes. Most likely, the size will eventually exceed available memory, in which case the resize() function will throw std::bad_alloc. If you have lots and lots of memory, the next error situation forces the string size to the limit that string supports and then tries to add another character to the string, which causes the push_back function to throw std::length_error. (The max_size member function returns the maximum number of elements that a container, such as std::string, can contain.)

The base class handler catches any exceptions that the first two handlers miss; in particular, it catches std::bad_alloc. The what() member function returns a string that describes the exception. The exact contents of the string vary by implementation. Any nontrivial application should define its own exception classes and hide the standard library exceptions from the user. In particular, the strings returned from what() are implementation-defined and are not necessarily helpful. Catching bad_alloc is especially tricky, because if the system is running out of memory, the application might not have enough memory to save its data prior to shutting down. You should always handle bad_alloc explicitly, but I wanted to demonstrate a handler for a base class.

The final catch handler uses an ellipsis (...) instead of a declaration. This is a catch-all handler that matches any exception. If you use it, it must be last, because it matches every exception object, of any type. Because the handler doesn't know the type of the exception, it has no way to access the exception object. This catch-all handler prints a message and then calls std::abort() (declared in <cstdlib>), which immediately ends the program. Because the std::exception handler catches all standard library exceptions, the final catch-all handler is not really needed, but I wanted to show you how it works.

Throwing Exceptions

A *throw expression* throws an exception. The expression consists of the throw keyword followed by an expression, namely, the exception object. The standard exceptions all take a string argument, which becomes the value returned from the what() member function.

```
throw std::out_of_range("index out of range");
```

The messages that the standard library uses for its own exceptions are implementation-defined, so you cannot rely on them to provide any useful information.

You can throw an exception anywhere an expression can be used, sort of. The type of a throw expression is void, which means it has no type. Type void is not allowed as an operand for any arithmetic, comparison, or other operator. Thus, realistically, a throw expression is typically used in an expression statement, all by itself.

You can throw an exception inside a catch handler, which low-level code and libraries often do. Instead of using the throw keyword, call std::throw_with_nested(), passing the new exception object as the argument. The throw_with_nested() function combines your exception object with the currently thrown exception object and bubbles both out to the next exception handler. Catch a nested exception normally, but if you see that the exceptions are nested, the handler must peel them off one at a time, as illustrated in Listing 48-4.

Listing 48-4. Nested Exceptions

```
import <exception>;
import <fstream>;
import <iomanip>;
import <iostream>;
import <stdexcept>;

void print_exception(const std::exception& e, int level = 0)
{
  std::cerr << std::setw(level) << ' ' << "exception: " << e.what() << '\n';
  try {
    std::rethrow_if_nested(e);
  } catch(const std::exception& e) {
    // caught a nested exception
    print_exception(e, level+1);
  } catch(...) {}
}

int main()
{
  std::string const filename{ "nonexistent file" };
  std::ifstream file;
  file.exceptions(std::ios_base::failbit);
  try
  {
    file.open(filename);
  }
  catch (std::ios_base::failure const&)
  {
    std::throw_with_nested(std::runtime_error{"Cannot open: " + filename});
  }
```

```
  catch (...)
  {
    file.close();
    throw;
  }
}
```

Opening file streams will be covered later. Here it is just an example of a common way to throw an I/O exception when the handler can add some useful information to the exception, specifically the name of the file being opened. The way nested exception work is that each level of nesting embeds an exception object, and `rethrow_if_nested()` actually throws that object as a new exception. So the handler recursively unpeels the exception onion one layer at a time.

If you just want perform some cleanup and rethrow the same exception, use the `throw` keyword without any expression. A common case for rethrowing an exception is inside a catch-all handler. The catch-all handler performs some important cleanup work and then propagates the exception so the program can handle it.

Program Stack

To understand what happens when a program throws an exception, you must first understand the nature of the *program stack*, sometimes called the *execution stack*. Procedural and similar languages use a stack at runtime to keep track of function calls, function arguments, and local variables. The C++ stack also helps keep track of exception handlers.

When a program calls a function, the program pushes a *frame* onto the stack. The frame has information such as the instruction pointer and other registers, arguments to the function, and possibly some memory for the function's return value. When a function starts, it might set aside some memory on the stack for local variables. Each local scope pushes a new frame onto the stack. (The compiler might be able to optimize away a physical frame for some local scopes or even an entire function. Conceptually, however, the following applies.)

While a function executes, it typically constructs a variety of objects: function arguments, local variables, temporary objects, and so on. The compiler keeps track of all the objects the function must create, so it can properly destroy them when the function returns. Local objects are destroyed in the opposite order of their creation.

Frames are dynamic, that is, they represent function calls and the flow of control in a program, not the static representation of source code. Thus, a function can call itself, and each call results in a new frame on the stack, and each frame has its own copy of all the function arguments and local variables.

When a program throws an exception, the normal flow of control stops, and the C++ exception-handling mechanism takes over. The exception object is copied to a safe place, off the execution stack. The exception-handling code looks through the stack for a `try` statement. When it finds a `try` statement, it checks the types for each handler in turn, looking for a match. If it doesn't find a match, it looks for the next `try` statement, farther back in the stack. It keeps looking until it finds a matching handler or it runs out of frames to search.

When it finds a match, it pops frames off the execution stack, calling destructors for all local objects in each popped frame, and continues to pop frames until it reaches the handler. Popping frames from the stack is also called *unwinding* the stack.

After unwinding the stack, the exception object initializes the handler's exception object, and then the `catch` body is executed. After the `catch` body exits normally, the exception object is freed, and execution continues with the statement that follows the end of the last sibling `catch` block.

If the handler throws an exception, the search for a matching handler starts anew. A handler cannot handle an exception that it throws, nor can any of its sibling handlers in the same `try` statement.

If no handler matches the exception object's type, the std::terminate function is called, which aborts the program. Some implementations will pop the stack and free local objects prior to calling terminate, but others won't.

Listing 48-5 can help you visualize what is going on inside a program when it throws and catches an exception.

Listing 48-5. Visualizing an Exception

```
1  import <exception>;
2  import <iostream>;
3  import <string>;
4
5  /// Make visual the construction and destruction of objects.
6  class visual
7  {
8  public:
9    visual(std::string const& what)
10   : id_{serial_}, what_{what}
11   {
12     ++serial_;
13     print("");
14   }
15   visual(visual const& ex)
16   : id_{ex.id_}, what_{ex.what_}
17   {
18     print("copy ");
19   }
20   ~visual()
21   {
22     print("~");
23   }
24   void print(std::string const& label)
25   const
26   {
27     std::cout << label << "visual(" << what_ << ": " << id_ << ")\n";
28   }
29  private:
30   static int serial_;
31   int const id_;
32   std::string const what_;
33  };
34
35  int visual::serial_{0};
36
37  void count_down(int n)
38  {
39    std::cout << "start count_down(" << n << ")\n";
40    visual v{"count_down local"};
41    try
42    {
43      if (n == 3)
44        throw visual("exception");
```

```
45      else if (n > 0)
46        count_down(n - 1);
47    }
48    catch (visual ex)
49    {
50      ex.print("catch on line 50 ");
51      throw;
52    }
53    std::cout << "end count_down(" << n << ")\n";
54 }
55
56 int main()
57 {
58    try
59    {
60      count_down(2);
61      std::cout << "--------------------\n";
62      count_down(4);
63    }
64    catch (visual const ex)
65    {
66      ex.print("catch on line 66 ");
67    }
68    std::cout << "All done!\n";
69 }
```

The visual class helps show when and how objects are constructed, copied, and destroyed. The count_down function throws an exception when its argument equals 3, and it calls itself when its argument is positive. The recursion stops for non-positive arguments. To help you see function calls, it prints the argument upon entry to, and exit from, the function.

The first call to count_down does not trigger the exception, so you should see normal creation and destruction of the local visual object. **Write exactly what the program should print as a result of line 60 (count_down(2)).**

_____

_____

_____

_____

_____

_____

_____

_____

_____

_____

_____

The next call to count_down from main (line 62) allows count_down to recurse once before throwing an exception. So count_down(4) calls count_down(3). The local object, v, is constructed inside the frame for count_down(4), and a new instance of v is constructed inside the frame for count_down(3). Then the exception object is created and thrown. (See Figure 48-1.)

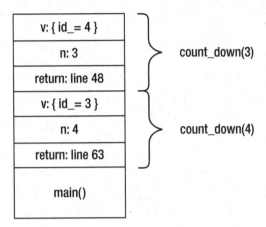

Figure 48-1. *Program stack when the exception is thrown*

The exception is caught inside count_down, so its frame is not popped. The exception object is then copied to ex (line 48), and the exception handler begins. It prints a message and then rethrows the original exception object (line 51). The exception-handling mechanism treats this exception the same way it treats any other: the try statement's frame is popped, and then the count_down function's frame is popped. Local objects are destroyed (including ex and v). The final statement in count_down does not execute.

The stack is unwound, and the try statement inside the call to count_down(4) is found, and once again, the exception object is copied to a new instance of ex. (See Figure 48-2.) The exception handler prints a message and rethrows the original exception. The count_down(4) frame is popped, returning control to the try statement in main. Again, the final statement in count_down does not execute.

```
ex: visual { id_ = 5 }

main()
```

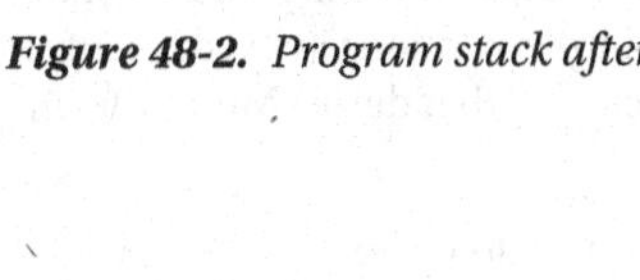

Figure 48-2. *Program stack after rethrowing exception*

The exception handler in main gets its turn, and this handler prints the exception object one last time (line 66). After the handler prints a message, and the catch body reaches its end, the local exception object and the original exception object are destroyed. Execution then continues normally on line 68. The final output is

```
start count_down(2)
visual(count_down local: 0)
start count_down(1)
visual(count_down local: 1)
start count_down(0)
visual(count_down local: 2)
end count_down(0)
~visual(count_down local: 2)
end count_down(1)
~visual(count_down local: 1)
end count_down(2)
~visual(count_down local: 0)
--------------------
start count_down(4)
visual(count_down local: 3)
start count_down(3)
visual(count_down local: 4)
visual(exception: 5)
copy visual(exception: 5)
catch on line 50 visual(exception: 5)
~visual(exception: 5)
~visual(count_down local: 4)
copy visual(exception: 5)
catch on line 50 visual(exception: 5)
~visual(exception: 5)
~visual(count_down local: 3)
copy visual(exception: 5)
catch on line 66 visual(exception: 5)
~visual(exception: 5)
~visual(exception: 5)
All done!
```

Standard Exceptions

The standard library defines several standard exception types. The base class, exception, is declared in the <exception> header. Most of the other exception classes are defined in the <stdexcept> header. If you want to define your own exception class, I recommend deriving it from one of the standard exceptions in <stdexcept>.

The standard exceptions are divided into two categories (with two base classes that derive directly from exception):

- Runtime errors (std::runtime_error) are exceptions that you cannot detect or prevent merely by examining the source code. They arise from conditions that you can anticipate, but not prevent.

- Logic errors (std::logic_error) are the result of programmer error. They represent violations of preconditions, invalid function arguments, and other errors that the programmer should prevent in code.

366

The other standard exception classes in <stdexcept> derive from these two. Most standard library exceptions are logic errors. For example, out_of_range inherits from logic_error. The at member function and others throw out_of_range when the index is out of range. After all, you should check indices and sizes, to be sure your vector and string usage are correct, and not rely on exceptions. The exceptions are there to provide clean, orderly shutdown of your program when you do make a mistake (and we all make mistakes).

Your library reference tells you which functions throw which exceptions, such as at can throw out_of_range. Many functions might throw other, undocumented exceptions too, depending on the library's and compiler's implementation. In general, however, the standard library uses few exceptions. Instead, most of the library yields undefined behavior when you provide bad input. The I/O streams do not ordinarily throw any exceptions, but you can arrange for them to throw exceptions when bad errors happen, as I explain in the next section.

I/O Exceptions

You learned about I/O stream state bits in Exploration 32. State bits are important, but checking them repeatedly is cumbersome. In particular, many programs fail to check the state bits of output streams, especially when writing to the standard output. That's just plain, old-fashioned laziness. Fortunately, C++ offers an avenue for programmers to gain I/O safety without much extra work: the stream can throw an exception when I/O fails.

In addition to state bits, each stream also has an *exception mask*. The exception mask tells the stream to throw an exception if a corresponding state bit changes value. For example, you could set badbit in the exception mask and never write an explicit check for this unlikely occurrence. If a serious I/O error were to occur, causing badbit to become set, the stream would throw an exception. You can write a handler at a high level to catch the exception and terminate the program cleanly, as shown in Listing 48-6.

Listing 48-6. Using an I/O Stream Exception Mask

```
import <iostream>;

int main()
{
  std::cin.exceptions(std::ios_base::badbit);
  std::cout.exceptions(std::ios_base::badbit);

  int x{};
  try
  {
    while (std::cin >> x)
      std::cout << x << '\n';
    if (not std::cin.eof()) // failure without eof means invalid input
      std::cerr << "Invalid integer input. Program terminated.\n";
  }
  catch(std::ios_base::failure const& ex)
  {
    std::cerr << "Major I/O failure! Program terminated.\n" <<
                ex.what() << '\n';
    std::terminate();
  }
}
```

As you can see, the exception class is named `std::ios_base::failure`. Also note a new output stream: `std::cerr`. The `<iostream>` header actually declares several standard I/O streams. So far, I've used only `cin` and `cout`, because that's all we've needed. The `cerr` stream is an output stream dedicated to error output. In this case, separating normal output (to `cout`) from error output (to `cerr`) is important, because `cout` might have a fatal error (say, a disk is full), so any attempt to write an error message to `cout` would be futile. Instead, the program writes the message to `cerr`. There's no guarantee that writing to `cerr` would work, but at least there's a chance; for example, the user might redirect the standard output to a file (and thereby risk encountering a disk-full error) while allowing the error output to appear on a console.

Recall that when an input stream reaches the end of the input, it sets `eofbit` in its state mask. Although you can also set this bit in the exception mask, I can't see any reason why you would want to. If an input operation does not read anything useful from the stream, the stream sets `failbit`. The most common reason that the stream might not read anything is end-of-file (`eofbit` is set) or an input formatting error (e.g., text in the input stream when the program tries to read a number). Again, it's possible to set `failbit` in the exception mask, but most programs rely on ordinary program logic to test the state of an input stream. Exceptions are for exceptional conditions, and end-of-file is a normal occurrence when reading from a stream.

The loop ends when `failbit` is set, but you have to test further to discover whether `failbit` is set, because of a normal end-of-file condition or because of malformed input. If `eofbit` is also set, you know the stream is at its end. Otherwise, `failbit` must be owing to malformed input.

As you can see, exceptions are not the solution for every error situation. Thus, `badbit` is the only bit in the exception mask that makes sense for most programs, especially for input streams. An output stream sets `failbit` if it cannot write the entire value to the stream. Usually, such a failure occurs because of an I/O error that sets `badbit`, but it's at least theoretically possible for output failure to set `failbit` without also setting `badbit`. In most situations, any output failure is cause for alarm, so you might want to throw an exception for `failbit` with output streams and `badbit` with input streams.

```
std::cin.exceptions(std::ios_base::badbit);
std::cout.exceptions(std::ios_base::failbit);
```

Custom Exceptions

Exceptions simplify coding by removing exceptional conditions from the main flow of control. You can and should use exceptions for many error situations. For example, the `rational` class (most recently appearing in Exploration 41) has, so far, completely avoided the issue of division by zero. A better solution than invoking undefined behavior (which is what happens when you divide by zero) is to throw an exception anytime the denominator is zero. Define your own exception class by deriving from one of the standard exception base classes, as shown in Listing 48-7. By defining your own exception class, any user of `rational` can easily distinguish its exceptions from other exceptions.

Listing 48-7. Throwing an Exception for a Zero Denominator

```
export module rational;
import <stdexcept>;
import <string>;

export class rational
{
public:
  class zero_denominator : public std::logic_error
  {
  public:
```

```
    using std::logic_error::logic_error;
  };

  rational() : rational{0} {}
  rational(int num) : numerator_{num}, denominator_{1} {}
  rational(int num, int den) : numerator_{num}, denominator_{den}
  {
    if (denominator_ == 0)
      throw zero_denominator{"zero denominator"};
    reduce();
  }
... omitted for brevity ...
};
```

Notice how the zero_denominator class nests within the rational class. The nested class is a perfectly ordinary class. It has no connection with the outer class (as with a Java inner class), except the name. The nested class gets no special access to private members in the outer class, nor does the outer class get special access to the nested class name. The usual rules for access levels determine the accessibility of the nested class. Some nested classes are private helper classes, so you would declare them in a private section of the outer class definition. In this case, zero_denominator must be public, so that callers can use the class in exception handlers.

To use a nested class name outside the outer class, you must use the outer class and the nested class names, separated by a scope operator (::). The nested class name has no significance outside of the outer class's scope. Thus, nested classes help avoid name collisions. They also provide clear documentation for the human reader who sees the type in an exception handler:

```
catch (rational::zero_denominator const& ex) {
  std::cerr << "zero denominator in rational number\n";
}
```

Find all other places in the rational class that have to check for a zero denominator and add appropriate error-checking code to throw zero_denominator.

All roads lead to reduce(), so one approach is to put the check for a zero denominator and throw the exception there. You don't have to modify any other functions, and even the extra check in the constructor (illustrated in Listing 48-6) is unnecessary. Listing 48-8 shows the latest implementation of reduce().

Listing 48-8. Checking for a Zero Denominator in reduce()

```
void rational::reduce()
{
  if (denominator_ == 0)
    throw zero_denominator{"denominator is zero"};
  if (denominator_ < 0)
  {
    denominator_ = -denominator_;
    numerator_ = -numerator_;
  }
  int div{std::gcd(numerator_, denominator_)};
  numerator_ = numerator_ / div;
  denominator_ = denominator_ / div;
}
```

When a Function Doesn't Throw Exceptions

Certain functions should never throw an exception. For example, the numerator() and denominator() functions simply return an integer. There is no way they can throw an exception. If the compiler knows that the functions never throw an exception, it can generate more efficient object code. With these specific functions, the compiler probably expands the functions inline to access the data members directly, so in theory, it doesn't matter. But maybe you decide not to make the functions inline (for any of the reasons listed in Exploration 31). You still want to be able to tell the compiler that the functions cannot throw any exceptions. Enter the noexcept qualifier.

To tell the compiler that a function does not throw an exception, add the noexcept qualifier after the function parameters (after const but before override).

```
int numerator() const noexcept;
```

What happens if you break the contact? **Try it.** Write a program that calls a trivial function that is qualified as noexcept, but throws an exception. Try to catch the exception in main(). **What happens?**

_____

If your program looks anything like mine in Listing 48-9, the catch is supposed to catch the exception, but it doesn't. The compiler trusted noexcept and did not generate the normal exception-handling code. As a result, when function() throws an exception, the only thing the program can do is terminate immediately.

Listing 48-9. Throwing an Exception from a noexcept Function

```cpp
import <iostream>;
import <exception>;

void function() noexcept
{
  throw std::exception{};
}

int main()
{
  try {
    function();
  } catch (std::exception const& ex) {
    std::cout << "Gotcha!\n";
  }
}
```

Use noexcept judiciously. If function a() calls only functions that are marked noexcept, the author of a() might decide to make a() noexcept too. But if one of those functions, say, b(), changes and is no longer noexcept, then a() is in trouble. If b() throws an exception, the program unceremoniously terminates. So use noexcept only if you can guarantee that the function cannot throw an exception now and will never change in the future to throw an exception. So it is probably safe for numerator() and denominator() to be noexcept in the rational class, as well as the default and single-argument constructors, but I can't think of any other member function that can be noexcept.

System Errors

Exploration 14 introduced the <system_error> header to display an error message when a program could not open a file. The intent of <system_error> is to provide a portable means of managing error codes, conditions, and messages. It supports the POSIX standard error codes well, but leaves other operating systems up to the implementation. So read your documentation to learn about your operating system's support.

An std::error_category defines the error codes and messages that your system supports. The standard library defined two global error categories: generic and system. The std::generic_category() function returns an error_category object for POSIX errors, and std::system_category() returns an error_category for implementation-defined errors.

An std::error_code represents a low-level error code as an integer tied to a specific error_category. Obtain the integer error number from errno (no std:: prefix), which is declared in the C header, <cerrno>. You can construct an error_code object as follows:

```
auto ec{ std::error_code(errno, std::system_category()) };
```

But if you only need the associated text message, the error category returns it directly with the message() member functions:

```
std::cerr << std::system_category().message(errno) << '\n';
```

To throw an exception that uses an error code, throw the system_error exception. You can pass an error_code object or pass errno and an error_category as arguments to the system_error constructor. You can also pass an optional string, such as a file name. Listing 48-10 shows a silly program that tries to open a nonexistent file and throws an exception when the open fails.

Listing 48-10. Throwing system_error for a File-Open Error

```
#include <cerrno>
import <fstream>;
import <iostream>;
import <string>;
import <system_error>;

std::size_t count_words(std::string const& filename)
{
  std::ifstream file(filename);
  if (not file)
    throw std::system_error(errno, std::system_category(), filename);
  std::size_t count{0};
  std::string word;
  while (file >> word)
    ++count;
  return count;
}

int main()
{
  try
  {
    std::cout << count_words("Not a Real File Name") << '\n';
  }
```

```
catch (std::exception const& ex)
{
    std::cerr << ex.what() << '\n';
}
}
```

Exceptional Advice

The basic mechanics of exceptions are easy to grasp, but their proper use is more difficult. The application programmer has three distinct tasks: catching exceptions, throwing exceptions, and avoiding exceptions.

You should write your programs to catch all exceptions, even the unexpected ones. One approach is for your main program to have a master try statement around the entire program body. Within the program, you might use targeted try statements to catch specific exceptions. The closer you are to the source of the exception, the more contextual information you have, and the better you can ameliorate the problem, or at least present the user with more useful messages.

This outermost try statement catches any exceptions that other statements miss. It is a last-ditch attempt to present a coherent and helpful error message before the program terminates abruptly. At a minimum, tell the user that the program is terminating because of an unexpected exception.

In an event-driven program, such as a GUI application, exceptions are more problematic. The outermost try statement shuts down the program, closing all windows. Most event handlers should have their own try statement to handle exceptions for that particular menu pick, keystroke event, and so on.

Within the body of your program, better than catching exceptions is avoiding them. Use the at member function to access elements of a vector, but you should write the code so you are confident that the index is always valid. Index and length exceptions are signs of programmer error.

When writing low-level code, throw exceptions for most error situations that should not happen or that otherwise reflect programmer error. Some error conditions are especially dangerous. For example, in the rational class, a denominator should never be zero or negative after reduce() returns. If a condition arises when the denominator is indeed zero or negative, the internal state of the program is corrupt. If the program were to attempt a graceful shutdown, saving all files, and so on, it might end up writing bad data to the files. Better to terminate immediately and rely on the most recent backup copy, which your program made while its state was still known to be good. Use assertions, not exceptions, for such emergencies.

Ideally, your code should validate user input, check vector indices, and make sure all arguments to all functions are valid before calling the functions. If anything is invalid, your program can tell the user with a clear, direct message and avoid exceptions entirely. Exceptions are a safety net when your checks fail or you forget to check for certain conditions.

As a general rule, libraries should throw exceptions, not catch them. Applications tend to catch exceptions more than throw them. As programs grow more complex, I will highlight situations that call for exceptions, throwing or catching.

Now that you know how to write classes, overload operators, and handle errors, you need only learn about some additional operators before you can start implementing fully functional classes of your own. The next Exploration revisits some familiar operators and introduces a few new ones.

■ ■ ■

More Operators

C++ has lots of operators. Lots and lots. So far, I've introduced the basic operators that you require for most programs: arithmetic, comparison, assignment, subscript, and function call. Now it's time to introduce some more: additional assignment operators, the conditional operator (which is like having an if statement in the middle of an expression), and the comma operator (most often used in for loops).

Conditional Operator

The conditional operator is a unique entry in the C++ operator bestiary, being a ternary operator, that is, an operator that takes three operands.

```
condition ? true-part : false-part
```

The *condition* is a Boolean expression. If it evaluates to true, the result of the entire expression is the *true-part*. If the condition is false, the result is the *false-part*. As with an if statement, only one part is evaluated; the branch not taken is skipped. For example, the following statement is perfectly safe:

```
std::cout << (x == 0 ? 0 : y / x);
```

If x is zero, the y / x expression is not evaluated, and division by zero never occurs. The conditional operator has very low precedence, so you often see it written inside parentheses. A conditional expression can be the source of an assignment expression. So the following expression assigned 42 or 24 to x, depending on whether test is true.

```
x = test ? 42 : 24;
```

And an assignment expression can be the *true-part* or *false-part* of a conditional expression, that is, the following expression

```
x ? y = 1 : y = 2;
```

is parsed as

```
x ? (y = 1) : (y = 2);
```

© Ray Lischner 2020

R. Lischner, *Exploring C++20*, https://doi.org/10.1007/978-1-4842-5961-0_49

The *true-part* and *false-part* are expressions that have the same or compatible types, that is, the compiler can automatically convert one type to the other, ensuring that the entire conditional expression has a well-defined type. For example, you can mix an integer and a floating-point number; the expression result is a floating-point number. The following statement prints 10.000000 if x is positive:

```
std::cout << std::fixed << (x > 0 ? 10 : 42.24) << '\n';
```

Do not use the conditional operator as a replacement for if statements. If you have a choice, use an if statement, because a statement is almost always easier to read and understand than a conditional expression. Use conditional expressions in situations when if statements are infeasible. Initializing a data member in a constructor, for example, does not permit the use of an if statement. Although you can use a member function for complicated conditions, you can also use a conditional expression for simple conditions.

The rational class (last seen in Exploration 47), for example, takes a numerator and a denominator as constructor arguments. The class ensures that its denominator is always positive. If the denominator is negative, it negates the numerator and denominator. In past Explorations, I loaded the reduce() member function with additional responsibilities, such as checking for a zero denominator and a negative denominator to reverse the signs of the numerator and denominator. This design has the advantage of centralizing all code needed to convert a rational number to canonical form. An alternate design is to separate the responsibility and let the constructor check the denominator prior to calling reduce(). If the denominator is zero, the constructor throws an exception; if the denominator is negative, the constructor negates the numerator and the denominator. This alternative design makes reduce() simpler, and simple functions are less error-prone than complicated functions. Listing 49-1 shows how you can do this using conditional operators.

Listing 49-1. Using Conditional Expressions in a Constructor's Initializer

```
/// Construct a rational object from a numerator and a denominator.
/// If the denominator is zero, throw zero_denominator. If the denominator
/// is negative, normalize the value by negating the numerator and denominator.
/// @post denominator_ > 0
/// @throws zero_denominator
rational::rational(int num, int den)
: numerator_{den < 0 ? -num : num},
  denominator_{den == 0 ? throw zero_denominator("0 denominator") :
                          (den < 0 ? -den : den)}
{
  reduce();
}
```

A throw expression has type void, but the compiler knows it doesn't return, so you can use it as one (or both) of the parts of a conditional expression. The type of the overall expression is that of the non-throwing part (or void, if both parts throw an exception).

In other words, if den is zero, the *true-part* of the expression throws an exception. If the condition is false, the *false-part* executes, which is another conditional expression, which evaluates the absolute value of den. The initializer for the numerator also tests den, and if negative, it negates the numerator too.

Like me, you might find that the use of conditional expressions makes the code harder to read. The conditional operator is widely used in C++ programs, so you must get used to reading it. If you decide that the conditional expressions are just too complicated, write a separate, private member function to do the work, and initialize the member by calling the function, as shown in Listing 49-2.

Listing 49-2. Using a Function and Conditional Statements Instead of Conditional Expressions

```
/// Construct a rational object from a numerator and a denominator.
/// If the denominator is zero, throw zero_denominator. If the denominator
/// is negative, normalize the value by negating the numerator and denominator.
/// @post denominator_ > 0
/// @throws zero_denominator
rational::rational(int num, int den)
: numerator_{den < 0 ? -num : num}, denominator_{init_denominator(den)}
{
  reduce();
}

/// Return an initial value for the denominator_ member. This function is used
/// only in a constructor's initializer list.
int rational::init_denominator(int den)
{
  if (den == 0)
    throw zero_denominator("0 denominator");
  else if (den < 0)
    return -den;
  else
    return den;
}
```

When writing new code, use the technique that you like best, but get used to reading both programming styles.

Short-Circuit Operators

C++ lets you overload the and and or operators, but you must resist the temptation. By overloading these operators, you defeat one of their key benefits: short-circuiting.

Recall from Exploration 12 that the and and or operators do not evaluate their right-hand operands if they don't have to. That's true of the built-in operators, but not if you overload them. When you overload the Boolean operators, they become normal functions, and C++ always evaluates function arguments before calling a function. Therefore, overloaded and and or operators behave differently from the built-in operators, and this difference makes them significantly less useful.

■ **Tip**   Do not overload the and and or operators.

Comma Operator

The comma (,) serves many roles: it separates arguments in a function call, parameters in a function declaration, declarators in a declaration, and initializers in a constructor's initializer list. In all these cases, the comma is a punctuator, that is, a symbol that is part of the syntax that serves only to show where one thing (argument, declarator, etc.) ends and another thing begins. It is also an operator in its own right, which is a completely different use for the same symbol. The comma as operator separates two expressions;

it causes the left-hand operand to be evaluated, and then the right-hand operand is evaluated, which becomes the result of the entire expression. The value of the left-hand operand is ignored.

At first, this operator seems a little pointless. After all, what's the purpose of writing, say,

```
x = 1 + 2, y = x + 3, z = y + 4
```

instead of

```
x = 1 + 2;
y = x + 3;
z = y + 4;
```

The comma operator is not meant to be a substitute for writing separate statements. There is one situation, however, when multiple statements are not possible, but multiple expressions have to be evaluated. I speak of none other than the for loop.

Suppose you want to implement the iterator-based search algorithm. Implementing a fully generic algorithm requires techniques that you haven't learned yet, but you can write this function so that it works with iterators but lacks any verification that its arguments are proper iterators. The basic idea is simple, search looks through a search range, trying to find a sequence of elements that are equal to elements in a match range. It steps through the search range one element at a time, testing whether a match starts at that element. If so, it returns an iterator that refers to the start of the match. If no match is found, search returns the end iterator. To check for a match, use a nested loop to compare successive elements in the two ranges. Listing 49-3 shows one way to implement this function.

Listing 49-3. Searching for a Matching Subrange Using Iterators

```
auto search(auto first1, auto last1, auto first2, auto last2)
{
  // s1 is the size of the untested portion of the first range
  // s2 is the size of the second range
  // End the search when s2 > s1 because a match is impossible if the
  // remaining portion of the search range is smaller than the test range.
  // Each iteration of the outer loop shrinks the search range by one,
  // and advances the first1 iterator. The inner loop searches
  // for a match starting at first1.
  for (auto s1{last1-first1}, s2{last2-first2}; s2 <= s1; --s1, ++first1)
  {
    // Is there a match starting at first1?
    auto f2{first2};
    for (auto f1{first1};
         f1 != last1 and f2 != last2 and *f1 == *f2;
         ++f1, ++f2)
    {
      // The subsequence matches so far, so keep checking.
      // All the work is done in the loop header, so the body is empty.
    }
    if (f2 == last2)
      return first1;      // match starts at first1
  }
  // no match
  return last1;
}
```

The boldface lines demonstrate the comma operator. The initialization portion of the first for loop does not invoke the comma operator. The comma in the declaration is only a separator between declarators. The comma operator appears in the postiteration part of the loops. Because the postiteration part of a for loop is an expression, you cannot use multiple statements to increment multiple objects. Instead, you have to do it in a single expression, hence the need for the comma operator.

On the other hand, some programmers prefer to avoid the comma operator, because the resulting code can be hard to read. **Rewrite Listing 49-3 so that it does not use the comma operator. Which version of the function do you prefer?** _____ Listing 49-4 shows my version of search without the comma operator.

Listing 49-4. The search Function Without Using the Comma Operator

```
auto search(auto first1, auto last1, auto first2, auto last2)
{
  // s1 is the size of the untested portion of the first range
  // s2 is the size of the second range
  // End the search when s2 > s1 because a match is impossible if the
  // remaining portion of the search range is smaller than the test range.
  // Each iteration of the outer loop shrinks the search range by one,
  // and advances the first1 iterator. The inner loop searches
  // for a match starting at first1.
  for (auto s1{last1-first1}, s2{last2-first2}; s2 <= s1; --s1)
  {
    // Is there a match starting at first1?
    auto f2{first2};
    for (auto f1{first1}; f1 != last1 and f2 != last2 and *f1 == *f2; )
    {
      ++f1;
      ++f2;
    }
    if (f2 == last2)
      return first1;       // match starts at first1
    ++first1;
  }
  // no match
  return last1;
}
```

The comma operator has very low precedence, even lower than assignment and the conditional operator. If a loop has to advance objects by steps of 2, for example, you can use assignment expressions with the comma operator.

```
for (int i{0}, j{size-1}; i < j; i += 2, j -= 2) do_something(i, j);
```

By the way, C++ lets you overload the comma operator, but you shouldn't take advantage of this feature. The comma is so basic, C++ programmers quickly grasp its standard use. If the comma does not have its usual meaning, readers of your code will be confused, bewildered, and stymied when they try to understand it.

Arithmetic Assignment Operators

In addition to the usual arithmetic operators, C++ has assignment operators that combine arithmetic with assignment: +=, -=, *=, /=, and %=. The assignment operator x += y is shorthand for x = x + y, and the same applies to the other special assignment operators. Thus, the following three expressions are all equivalent if x has a numeric type:

```
x = x + 1;
x += 1;
++x;
```

The advantage of the special assignment operator is that x is evaluated only once, which can be a boon if x is a complicated expression. If data has type std::vector<int>, which of the following two equivalent expressions do you find easier to read and understand?

```
data.at(data.size() / 2) = data.at(data.size() / 2) + 10;
data.at(data.size() / 2) += 10;
```

Listing 49-5 shows a sample implementation of *= for the rational class.

Listing 49-5. Implementing the Multiplication Assignment Operator

```
rational const& rational::operator*=(rational const& rhs)
{
  numerator_ *= rhs.numerator();
  denominator_ *= rhs.denominator();
  reduce();
  return *this;
}
```

The return type of operator*= is a reference, rational&. The return value is *this. Although the compiler lets you use any return type and value, the convention is for assignment operators to return a reference to the object, that is, an lvalue. Even if your code never uses the return value, many programmers use the result of an assignment, so don't use void as a return type. On the other hand, assigning to the result of an assignment leads to madness, so returning a const lvalue makes a lot of sense.

```
rational r;
while ((r += rational{1,10}) != 2) do_something(r);
```

Often, implementing an arithmetic operator, such as +, is easiest to do by implementing the corresponding assignment operator first. Then implement the free operator in terms of the assignment operator, as shown in Listing 49-6 for the rational class.

Listing 49-6. Reimplementing Multiplication in Terms of an Assignment Operator

```
rational operator*(rational const& lhs, rational const& rhs)
{
  rational result{lhs};
  result *= rhs;
  return result;
}
```

Implement the /=, +=, and -= operators for class rational. You can implement these operators in many ways. I recommend putting the arithmetic logic in the assignment operators and reimplementing the /, +, and - operators to use the assignment operators, as I did with the multiplication operators. My solution appears in Listing 49-7.

Listing 49-7. Other Arithmetic Assignment Operators

```cpp
rational const& rational::operator+=(rational const& rhs)
{
  numerator_ = numerator() * rhs.denominator() + rhs.numerator() * denominator();
  denominator_ *= rhs.denominator();
  reduce();
  return *this;
}

rational const& rational::operator-=(rational const& rhs)
{
  numerator_ = numerator() * rhs.denominator() - rhs.numerator() * denominator();
  denominator_ *= rhs.denominator();
  reduce();
  return *this;
}

rational const& rational::operator/=(rational const& rhs)
{
  if (rhs.numerator() == 0)
    throw zero_denominator{"divide by zero"};
  numerator_ *= rhs.denominator();
  denominator_ *= rhs.numerator();
  if (denominator_ < 0)
  {
    denominator_ = -denominator_;
    numerator_ = -numerator_;
  }
  reduce();
  return *this;
}
```

Because reduce() no longer checks for a negative denominator, any function that might change the denominator to negative must check. Because the denominator is always positive, you know that operator+= and operator-= cannot cause the denominator to become negative. Only operator/= introduces that possibility, so only that function needs to check.

Increment and Decrement

Let's add increment (++) and decrement (--) operators to the rational class. Because these operators modify the object, I suggest implementing them as member functions, although C++ lets you use free functions too. **Implement the prefix increment operator for class rational.** Compare your function with mine in Listing 49-8.

Listing 49-8. The Prefix Increment Operator for rational

```
rational const& rational::operator++()
{
  numerator_ += denominator_;
  return *this;
}
```

I am confident that you can implement the decrement operator with no additional help. Like the arithmetic assignment operators, the prefix operator++ returns the object as a reference.

That leaves the postfix operators. Implementing the body of the operator is easy and requires only one additional line of code. However, you must take care with the return type. The postfix operators cannot simply return *this, because they return the original value of the object, not its new value. Thus, these operators cannot return a reference. Instead, they must return a plain rational rvalue.

But how do you declare the function? A class can't have two separate functions with the same name (operator++) and arguments. Somehow, you need a way to tell the compiler that one implementation of operator++ is prefix and another is postfix.

The solution is that when the compiler calls a custom postfix increment or decrement operator, it passes the integer 0 as an extra argument. The postfix operators don't need the value of this extra parameter; it's just a placeholder to distinguish prefix from postfix.

Thus, when you declare operator++ with an extra parameter of type int, you are declaring the postfix operator. When you declare the operator, omit the name for the extra parameter. That tells the compiler that the function doesn't use the parameter, so the compiler won't bother you with messages about unused function parameters. **Implement the postfix increment and decrement operators for** rational. Listing 49-9 shows my solution.

Listing 49-9. Postfix Increment and Decrement Operators

```
rational rational::operator++(int)
{
  rational result{*this};
  numerator_ += denominator_;
  return result;
}

rational rational::operator--(int)
{
  rational result{*this};
  numerator_ -= denominator_;
  return result;
}
```

Once all the dust settles from our rehabilitation project, behold the new, improved rational class definition in Listing 49-10.

Listing 49-10. The rational Class Definition

```cpp
export module rat;
import <iostream>;
import <stdexcept>;

/// Represent a rational number (fraction) as a numerator and denominator.
export class rational
{
public:
  class zero_denominator : public std::logic_error
  {
  public:
    using std::logic_error::logic_error;
  };
  rational() noexcept : rational{0} {}
  rational(int num) noexcept : numerator_{num}, denominator_{1} {}
  rational(int num, int den);
  rational(double r);

  int numerator()            const noexcept { return numerator_; }
  int denominator()          const noexcept { return denominator_; }
  float as_float()           const;
  double as_double()         const;
  long double as_long_double() const;

  // optimization to avoid an unneeded call to reduce()
  rational const& operator=(int) noexcept;

  rational const& operator+=(rational const& rhs);
  rational const& operator-=(rational const& rhs);
  rational const& operator*=(rational const& rhs);
  rational const& operator/=(rational const& rhs);
  rational const& operator++();
  rational const& operator--();
  rational operator++(int);
  rational operator--(int);

private:
  /// Reduce the numerator and denominator by their GCD.
  void reduce();
  /// Reduce the numerator and denominator, and normalize the signs of both,
  /// that is, ensure denominator is not negative.
  void normalize();
  /// Return an initial value for denominator_. Throw a zero_denominator
  /// exception if @p den is zero. Always return a positive number.
  int init_denominator(int den);
  int numerator_;
  int denominator_;
};
```

```
export rational abs(rational const& r);
export rational operator-(rational const& r);
export rational operator+(rational const& lhs, rational const& rhs);
export rational operator-(rational const& lhs, rational const& rhs);
export rational operator*(rational const& lhs, rational const& rhs);
export rational operator/(rational const& lhs, rational const& rhs);

export bool operator==(rational const& a, rational const& b);
export bool operator<(rational const& a, rational const& b);

export inline bool operator!=(rational const& a, rational const& b)
{
  return not (a == b);
}

export inline bool operator<=(rational const& a, rational const& b)
{
  return not (b < a);
}

export inline bool operator>(rational const& a, rational const& b)
{
  return b < a;
}

export inline bool operator>=(rational const& a, rational const& b)
{
  return not (b > a);
}

export std::istream& operator>>(std::istream& in, rational& rat);
export std::ostream& operator<<(std::ostream& out, rational const& rat);
```

The next Exploration is your second project. Now that you know about classes, inheritance, operator overloading, and exceptions, you are ready to tackle some serious C++ coding.

EXPLORATION 50

■ ■ ■

Project 2: Fixed-Point Numbers

Your task for Project 2 is to implement a simple fixed-point number class. The class represents fixed-point numbers using an integer type. The number of places after the decimal point is a fixed constant, four. For example, represent the number 3.1415 as the integer 31415 and 3.14 as 31400. You must overload the arithmetic, comparison, and I/O operators to maintain the fixed-point fiction.

The fixed Class

Name the class fixed. It should have the following public members:

value_type

A type alias for the underlying integer type, such as int or long. By using value_type throughout the fixed class, you can easily switch between int and long by changing only the declaration of value_type.

places

A static const int equal to 4, or the number of places after the decimal point. By using a named constant instead of hard-coding the value 4, you can easily change the value to 2 or something else in the future.

places10

A static const int equal to places10, or the scale factor for the fixed-point values. Divide the internal integer by places10 to obtain the true value. Multiply a number by places10 to scale it to an integer that the fixed object stores internally.

fixed()

Default constructor.

fixed(value_type integer, value_type fraction)

A constructor to make a fixed-point value from an integer part and a fractional part. For example, to construct the fixed-point value 10.0020, use fixed{10, 20}.

© Ray Lischner 2020
R. Lischner, *Exploring C++20*, https://doi.org/10.1007/978-1-4842-5961-0_50

Throw std::invalid_argument if fraction < 0. If fraction >= places10, then the constructor should discard digits to the right, rounding off the result. For example, fixed{3, 14159} == fixed{3, 1416} and fixed{31, 415926} == fixed{31, 4159}.

fixed(double val)

A constructor to make a fixed-point value from a floating-point number. Round off the fraction and discard excess digits. Thus, fixed{12.3456789} == fixed{12, 3456789} == fixed{12, 3457}.

Implement the arithmetic operators, arithmetic assignment operators, comparison operators, and I/O operators. Don't concern yourself with overflow. Do your best to check for errors when reading fixed-point numbers. Be sure to handle integers without decimal points (42) and values with too many decimal points (3.14159).

Implement a member function to convert the fixed-point value to std::string.

to_string()

Convert the value to a string representation; for example, 3.1416 becomes "3.1416" and –21 becomes "-21.0000".

To convert to an integer means discarding information. To make it abundantly clear to the user, call the function round(), to emphasize that the fixed-point value must be rounded off to become an integer.

round()

Round off to the nearest integer. If the fractional part is exactly 5000, round to the nearest even integer (banker's rounding). Be sure to handle negative and positive numbers.

Other useful member functions give you access to the raw value (good for debugging, implementing additional operations, etc.) or the parts of the fixed-point value: the integer part and the fractional part.

integer()

Return just the integer part, without the fractional part.

fraction()

Return just the fraction part, without the integer part. The fraction part is always in the range [0, places10].

Implement the fixed class in a module also named fixed. You decide whether to write separate interface and implementation modules or to write a single module file. Decide which member functions should be inline (if any), and be sure to define all inline functions in the module interface. After you finish, review your solution carefully and run some tests, comparing your results to mine, which you can download from the book's website.

If you need help testing your code, try linking your fixed module with the test program in Listing 50-1. The test program makes use of the test and test_equal functions, declared in the test module. The details are beyond the scope of this book. Just call test with a Boolean argument. If the argument is true, the test passed. Otherwise, the test failed, and test prints a message. The test_equal function takes two arguments and prints a message if they are not equal. Thus, if the program produces no output, all tests passed.

Listing 50-1. Testing the `fixed` Class

```
import <iostream>;
import <sstream>;
import <stdexcept>;

import test;
import fixed;

int main()
{
  fixed f1{};
  test_equal(f1.value(), 0);
  test_equal(f1.to_string(), "0.0000");
  fixed f2{1};
  test_equal(f2.value(), 10000);
  test_equal(f2.to_string(), "1.0000");
  fixed f3{3, 14162};
  test_equal(f3.value(), 31416);
  fixed f4{2, 14159265};
  test_equal(f4.value(), 21416);
  test_equal(f2 + f4, f1 + f3);
  test(f2 + f4 <= f1 + f3);
  test(f2 + f4 >= f1 + f3);
  test(f1 < f2);
  test(f1 <= f2);
  test(f1 != f2);
  test(f2 > f1);
  test(f2 >= f1);
  test(f2 != f1);

  test_equal(f2 + f4, f3 - f1);
  test_equal(f2 * f3, f3);
  test_equal(f3 / f2, f3);
  f4 += f2;
  test_equal(f3, f4);
  f4 -= f1;
  test_equal(f3, f4);
  f4 *= f2;
  test_equal(f3, f4);
  f4 /= f2;
  test_equal(f3, f4);

  test_equal(-f4, f1 - f4);
  test_equal(-(-f4), f4);
  --f4;
  test_equal(f4 + 1, f3);
  f4--;
  test_equal(f4 + 2, f3);
  ++f4;
  test_equal(f4 + 1, f3);
  f4++;
```

```
test_equal(f4, f3);
++f3;
test_equal(++f4, f3);
test_equal(f4--, f3);
test_equal(f4++, --f3);
test_equal(--f4, f3);

test_equal(f4 / f3, f2);
test_equal(f4 - f3, f1);

test_equal(f4.to_string(), "3.1416");
test_equal(f4.integer(), 3);
f4 += fixed{0,4584};
test_equal(f4, 3.6);
test_equal(f4.integer(), 3);
test_equal(f4.round(), 4);

test_equal(f3.integer(), 3);
test_equal((-f3).integer(), -3);
test_equal(f3.fraction(), 1416);
test_equal((-f3).fraction(), 1416);

test_equal(fixed{7,4999}.round(), 7);
test_equal(fixed{7,5000}.round(), 8);
test_equal(fixed{7,5001}.round(), 8);
test_equal(fixed{7,4999}.round(), 7);
test_equal(fixed{8,5000}.round(), 8);
test_equal(fixed{8,5001}.round(), 9);

test_equal(fixed{123,2345500}, fixed(123,2346));
test_equal(fixed{123,2345501}, fixed(123,2346));
test_equal(fixed{123,2345499}, fixed(123,2345));
test_equal(fixed{123,2346500}, fixed(123,2346));
test_equal(fixed{123,2346501}, fixed(123,2347));
test_equal(fixed{123,2346499}, fixed(123,2346));
test_equal(fixed{123,2346400}, fixed(123,2346));
test_equal(fixed{123,2346600}, fixed(123,2347));

test_equal(fixed{-7,4999}.round(), -7);
test_equal(fixed{-7,5000}.round(), -8);
test_equal(fixed{-7,5001}.round(), -8);
test_equal(fixed{-7,4999}.round(), -7);
test_equal(fixed{-8,5000}.round(), -8);
test_equal(fixed{-8,5001}.round(), -9);

test_equal(fixed{-3.14159265}.value(), -31416);
test_equal(fixed{123,456789}.value(), 1234568);
test_equal(fixed{123,4}.value(), 1230004);
test_equal(fixed{-10,1111}.value(), -101111);
```

```
    std::ostringstream out{};
    out << f3 << " 3.14159265 " << fixed(-10,12) << " 3 421.4 end";
    fixed f5{};
    std::istringstream in{out.str()};
    test(in >> f5);
    test_equal(f5, f3);
    test(in >> f5);
    test_equal(f5, f3);
    test(in >> f5);
    test_equal(f5.value(), -100012);
    test(in >> f5);
    test_equal(f5.value(), 30000);
    test(in >> f5);
    test_equal(f5.value(), 4214000);
    test(not (in >> f5));

    test_equal(fixed{31.4159265}, fixed{31, 4159});
    test_equal(fixed{31.41595}, fixed{31, 4160});

    bool okay{false};
    try {
      fixed f6{1, -1};
    } catch (std::invalid_argument const&) {
      okay = true;
    } catch (...) {
    }
    test(okay);
    test_exit();
}
```

If you need a hint, I implemented fixed so that it stores a single integer, with an implicit decimal place places10 positions from the right. Thus, I store the value 1 as 10000. Addition and subtraction are easy. When multiplying or dividing, you have to scale the result. (Even better is to scale the operands prior to multiplication, which avoids some overflow situations, but you have to be careful about not losing precision.)

PART III

Generic Programming

■ ■ ■

Function Templates

You saw in Exploration 25 that the magic of overloading lets C++ implement an improved interface to the absolute value function. Instead, of three different names (abs, labs, and fabs), C++ has a single name for all three functions. Overloading helps the programmer who needs to call the abs function, but it doesn't help the implementer much, who still has to write three separate functions that all look and act the same. Wouldn't it be nice if the library author could write the abs function once instead of three times? After all, the three implementations may be identical, differing only in the return type and parameter type. This Exploration introduces this style of programming, called generic programming.

Generic Functions

Sometimes, you want to provide overloaded functions for integer and floating-point types, but the implementation is essentially the same. Absolute value is one example; for any type T, the function looks the same (I'm using the name absval, to avoid any confusion or conflict with the standard library's abs), as shown in Listing 51-1.

Listing 51-1. Writing an Absolute Value Function

```
T absval(T x)
{
  if (x < 0)
    return -x;
  else
    return x;
}
```

Substitute int for T, double for T, or use any other numeric type. You can even substitute rational for T, and the absval function still works the way you expect it to. So why waste your precious time writing, rewriting, and re-rewriting the same function? With a simple addition to the function definition, you can turn the function into a generic function, that is, a function that works with any suitable type T, which you can see in Listing 51-2.

© Ray Lischner 2020

R. Lischner, *Exploring C++20*, https://doi.org/10.1007/978-1-4842-5961-0_51

Listing 51-2. Writing a Function Template

```
template<class T>
T absval(T x)
{
  if (x < 0)
    return -x;
  else
    return x;
}
```

The first line is the key. The `template` keyword means that what follows is a template, in this case, a *function template* definition. The angle brackets delimit a comma-separated list of template parameters. A function template is a pattern for creating functions, according to the parameter type, T. Within the function template definition, T represents a type, potentially any type. The caller of the `absval` function determines the template argument that will substitute for T.

When you define a function template, the compiler remembers the template but does not generate any code. The compiler waits until you use the function template, and then it generates a real function. You can imagine the compiler taking the source text of the template, substituting the template argument, such as `int`, for the template parameter, T, and then compiling the resulting text. The next section tells you more about how to use a function template.

Using Function Templates

Using a function template is easy, at least in most situations. Just call the `absval` function, and the compiler will automatically determine the template argument based on the function argument type. It might take you a little while to get comfortable with the notion of template parameters and template arguments, which are quite different from function parameters and function arguments.

In the case of `absval`, the template parameter is T, and the template argument must be a type. You can't pass a type as a function argument, but templates are different. You aren't really "passing" anything in the program. Template magic occurs at compile time. The compiler sees the template definition of `absval`, and later it sees an invocation of the `absval` function template. The compiler examines the type of the function argument and, from the function argument's type, determines the template argument. The compiler substitutes that template argument for T and generates a new instance of the `absval` function, customized for the template argument type. Thus, in the following example, the compiler sees that x has type `int`, so it substitutes `int` for T.

```
int x{-42};
int y{absval(x)};
```

The compiler generates a function just as though the library implementer had written the following:

```
int absval(int x)
{
  if (x < 0)
    return -x;
  else
    return x;
}
```

Later, in the same program, perhaps you call absval on a rational object:

```
rational r{-420, 10};
rational s{absval(r)};
```

The compiler generates a new instance of absval:

```
rational absval(rational x)
{
  if (x < 0)
    return -x;
  else
    return x;
}
```

In this new instance of absval, the < operator is the overloaded operator that takes rational arguments. The negation operator is also a custom operator that takes a rational argument. In other words, when the compiler generates an instance of absval, it does so by compiling the source code pretty much as the template author wrote it.

Write a sample program that contains the absval function template definition and some test code to call absval with a variety of argument types. Convince yourself that function templates actually work. Compare your test program with mine in Listing 51-3.

Listing 51-3. Testing the absval Function Template

```
import <iostream>;
import rational;  // Listing 49-10

template<class T>
T absval(T x)
{
  if (x < 0)
    return -x;
  else
    return x;
}

int main()
{
  std::cout << absval(-42) << '\n';
  std::cout << absval(-4.2) << '\n';
  std::cout << absval(42) << '\n';
  std::cout << absval(4.2) << '\n';
  std::cout << absval(-42L) << '\n';
  std::cout << absval(rational{42, 5}) << '\n';
  std::cout << absval(rational{-42, 5}) << '\n';
  std::cout << absval(rational{42, -5}) << '\n';
}
```

Writing Function Templates

Writing function templates is harder than writing ordinary functions. When you write a template such as absval, the problem is that you don't know what type or types T will actually be. So, the function must be generic. The compiler will prevent you from using certain types for T. Its restrictions are implicit by the way the template body uses T.

In particular, absval imposes the following restrictions on T:

- T *must be copyable.* That means you must be able to copy an object of type T, so arguments can be passed to the function and a result can be returned. If T is a class type, the class must have an accessible copy constructor, that is, the copy constructor must not be private.

- T *must be comparable with* 0 *using the* < *operator.* You might overload the < operator, or the compiler can convert 0 to T or T to an int.

- *Unary* operator- *must be defined for an operand of type* T. The result type must be T or something the compiler can convert automatically to T.

The built-in numeric types all meet these requirements. The rational type also meets these requirements, because of the custom operators it supports. The string type, just to name one example, does not, because it lacks a comparison operator when the right-hand operand is an integer, and it lacks a unary negation (-) operator. Suppose you tried to call absval on a string.

```
std::string test{"-42"};
std::cout << absval(test) << '\n';
```

What do you think would happen?

_____

_____

Try it. What really happens?

_____

_____

The compiler complains about the lack of the comparison and negation operators for std::string. One difficulty in delivering helpful error messages when working with templates is whether to give you the line number where the template is used or the line number in the template definition. Sometimes, you will get both. Sometimes, the compiler cannot report an error in the template definition unless you try to use the template. Other errors it can report immediately. **Read Listing 51-4 carefully.**

Listing 51-4. Mystery Function Template

```
template<class T>
T add(T lhs, T rhs)
{
  return lhs(rhs);
}

int main()
{
}
```

What is the error?

_____

Does your compiler report it?

_____

Because the compiler does not know the type T, it cannot tell what lhs(rhs) means. It is possible to define a type for which that expression is valid, but that probably wouldn't match the function name of add. We know that we want to use a numeric type for T, so lhs(rhs) is silly. After all, what does 3(4) mean?

How can you force your compiler to report the error?

_____

Add a line of code to use the template. For example, add this to main:

```
return add(0, 0);
```

Every compiler will now report the not-really-a-function-call expression in the template definition.

Template Parameters

Whenever you see T in a C++ program, most likely, you are looking at a template. Look backward in the source file until you find the template header, that is, the part of the declaration that starts with the template keyword. That's where you should find the template parameters. The use of T as a template parameter name is merely a convention, but its use is nearly universal. The use of class to declare T may seem a little strange, especially because you've seen several examples when the template argument is not, in fact, a class.

Instead of class to declare a template parameter type, some programmers use an alternate keyword, typename, which means the same thing in this one context. The advantage of typename over class is that it avoids any confusion over nonclass types. The disadvantage is that typename has more than one use in a template context, which can confuse human readers in more complicated template definitions. Learn to read both styles, but I prefer to use class when I write my own templates, and class appears much more often than typename in most C++ code.

Sometimes, you will see parameter names that are more specific than T. If the template has more than one parameter, every parameter must have a unique name, so you will definitely see names other than T. For example, the std::ranges::copy algorithm is a function template with two template parameters: the input range type and the output iterator type. The definition of copy, therefore, might look something like Listing 51-5.

Listing 51-5. One Way to Implement the copy Algorithm

```
template<class InputRange, class OutputIterator>
OutputIterator copy(InputRange range, OutputIterator output)
{
  for (auto const& item : range)
    *output++ = item;
  return output;
}
```

Pretty simple, isn't it? (The real copy function is more complicated, with checking for valid arguments and optimizations for certain types. Underneath the complexity, however, is probably a function that looks just like Listing 51-5, albeit with different parameter names.)

When you use the copy algorithm, the compiler determines the value of InputRange and OutputIterator according to the function argument types. As you saw with absval, the function's requirements on the template arguments are all implicit. Because InputRange must be a range, std::ranges::begin(range) must return the start iterator and std::ranges::end(range) must return the sentinel. The start iterator must meet the requirements of an input iterator, namely, operator * returns an item, operator++ advances the iterator, and the iterator must be comparable with the sentinel. OutputIterator must also implement * and ++ in the manner of an output iterator.

Write a simple implementation of the find **algorithm.** The range form of this algorithm raises some thorny issues, so let's implement the iterator form of the function. (If you are curious, think about the range version of find(). What is its return type? The template parameter is the range type, and std::ranges::begin() returns an iterator, which is the desired return type of find(). But if the value is not found, find() must return the sentinel value of std::ranges::end(), even if that has a different type. So find() must convert the sentinel value to the iterator type. You will learn more about templates in the coming Explorations, which will help you master these problems. Now we return to the iterator form of find().)

The template has two parameters: InputIterator and T. The function has three arguments. The first two are of type InputIterator and specify the range to search. The third argument is of type T and is the value to search for. Compare your solution with Listing 51-6.

Listing 51-6. Implementing the find Algorithm

```
template<class InputIterator, class T>
InputIterator find(InputIterator start, InputIterator end, T value)
{
   for ( ; start != end; ++start)
      if (*start == value)
         return start;
   return end;
}
```

Many of the standard algorithms are quite simple at their heart. Modern implementations are heavily optimized, and as is the nature of hand-optimized code, the results often bear little resemblance to the original code, and the optimized code can be much harder to read. Nonetheless, the simplicity remains in the architecture of the standard library, which relies extensively on templates.

Template Arguments

Templates are easiest to use when the compiler automatically deduces the template arguments from the function arguments. It can't always do so, however, so you might have to tell the compiler explicitly what you want. The simple form of the min, max, and mixmax standard algorithms, for example, takes a single template parameter. Listing 51-7 shows one possible implementation of the min function, for reference.

Listing 51-7. The std::min Algorithm

```
template<class T>
T min(T a, T b)
{
   if (b < a)
      return b;
   else
      return a;
}
```

If both argument types are the same, the compiler can deduce the desired type, and everything just works.

```
int x{10}, y{20}, z{std::min(x, y)};
```

On the other hand, if the function argument types are different, the compiler can't tell which type to use for the template argument.

```
int x{10}; •
long y{20};
std::cout << std::min(x, y); // error
```

Why is that? Suppose you wrote your own function as a non-template.

```
long my_min(long a, long b)
{
  if (b < a)
    return b;
  else
    return a;
}
```

The compiler could handle my_min(x, y) by converting x from an int to a long. As a template, however, the compiler does not perform any automatic type conversion. The compiler cannot read your mind and know that you want the template parameter to have the type of the first function argument or the second, or sometimes the first and sometimes the second. Instead, the compiler requires you to write exactly what you mean. In this case, you can tell the compiler what type to use for the template parameter by enclosing the desired type in angle brackets.

```
int x{10};
long y{20};
std::cout << std::min<long>(x, y); // okay: compiler converts x to type long
```

If a template takes multiple arguments, separate the arguments with a comma. For example, Listing 51-8 shows the input_sum function, which reads items from the standard input and accumulates them by means of the += operator. The accumulator can have a different type than the item type. Because the item and accumulator types are not used in the function arguments, the compiler cannot deduce the parameter arguments, so you must supply them explicitly.

Listing 51-8. Multiple Template Arguments

```
import <iostream>;

template<class T, class U>
U input_sum(std::istream& in)
{
  T x{};
  U sum{0};
  while (in >> x)
    sum += x;
  return sum;
}
```

```
int main()
{
  long sum{input_sum<int, long>(std::cin)};
  std::cout << sum << '\n';
}
```

Write a function, isprime, to be a function template, so that you can use the same function template for int, short, or long arguments. The function determines whether its argument is a prime number, that is, a number divisible only by 1 and itself. Compare your solution with mine in Listing 51-9.

Listing 51-9. The isprime Function Template

```
template<class T>
bool isprime(T n)
{
    if (n < 2)
        return false;
    else if (n <= 3)
        return true;
    else if (n % 2 == 0)
        return false;
    else
    {
        for (T test{3}, limit{n / 2}; test < limit; test += 2)
            if (n % test == 0)
                return false;
        return true;
    }
}
```

Abbreviated Function Templates

A shorter way to write certain templates is to use the auto keyword as a function parameter type, similar to the way it can be used to define local variables. Using auto for any function parameter type changes the function into a function template. Each auto parameter is like adding a template parameter. For example, you can rewrite Listing 51-5 using auto, as shown in Listing 51-10.

Listing 51-10. Another Way to Implement the copy Algorithm

```
auto copy(auto range, auto output)
{
  for (auto const& item : range)
    *output++ = item;
  return output;
}
```

The return type is also auto, which tells the compiler to determine the return type from the return statement or statements in the function. In this case, the return type is the same as the type of the output parameter, which is exactly what we want.

It is much harder to use `auto` for the iterator form of `copy` (Listing 51-6) because each `auto` function parameter has as its type a separate template parameter. Forcing two parameters to have the same type is easiest to do with an ordinary function template. But when a function template has a separate template parameter for every function parameter, the abbreviated form can be a compact way to write a function template.

Declarations and Definitions

I can't seem to stop talking about declarations and definitions. Templates introduce yet another twist to this plot. When you work with templates, the rules change. The compiler has to see more than just a declaration before you can use a function template. The compiler usually requires the full function template definition. In other words, if you define a template in a module, that module must include the body of that function template. Suppose you want to share the `isprime` function among many projects. Ordinarily, you would put the function declaration in a module, say, `prime`, and you might want a separate module implementation.

When you convert `isprime` to a function template, however, you must put the definition in the module interface so the compiler can create concrete functions from the template, say, for `isprime<int>` or `isprime<long>`.

Member Function Templates

In Exploration 36, we wrote three nearly identical functions for the `rational` class: `to_long_double`, `to_double`, and `to_float`. They all do the same thing: divide the numerator by the denominator after converting to the destination type. Whenever you have multiple functions doing the same thing, in the same way, using the same code, you have a candidate for a template, such as this:

```
template<class T, class R>
T convert(R const& r)
{
  return static_cast<T>(r.numerator()) / r.denominator();
}
```

As with any function template, the only requirement on R is that objects of type R have member functions named `numerator()` and `denominator()` and that these functions have return types suitable for use with `operator/` (which could be overloaded). To use the `convert` function, you must supply the target type, T, as an explicit template argument, but you can let the compiler deduce R from the function argument:

```
rational r{42, 10};
double d{ convert<double>(r) };
```

You can omit template arguments that the compiler can deduce, starting from the right-most argument. As you saw earlier in this Exploration, if the compiler can deduce all the arguments, you can leave out the angle brackets entirely.

A function template can be a member function too. Instead of passing the `rational` object as an argument, you might prefer to use a member function template, as follows:

```
rational r{42, 10};
double d{ r.convert<double>() };
```

A member function template avoids collisions with other free functions that might be named convert. But it also restricts the utility of your function. As a nonmember function (also called a free function), it works with any type that looks like a rational type with a numerator and a denominator. Even if it's a type you haven't seen before, as long as it meets the basic restrictions of the convert() function, it works just fine. But as a member function, it is tied inextricably to your rational type and no one else's. You will see that the standard C++ library has many free functions that are designed to work with a wide range of user-written types. This is just plain good design.

Generic programming is a powerful technique, and as you learn more about it in the next several Explorations, you will see how expressive and useful this programming paradigm is.

■ ■ ■

Class Templates

A class can be a template, which makes all of its members templates. Every program in this book has used class templates, because much of the standard library relies on templates: the standard I/O streams, strings, vectors, and maps are all class templates. This Exploration takes a look at simple class templates.

Parameterizing a Type

Consider a simple point class, which stores an x and y coordinate. A graphics device driver might use int for the member types.

```
class point {
public:
    point(int x, int y) : x_{x}, y_{y} {}
    int x() const { return x_; }
    int y() const { return y_; }
private:
    int x_, y_;
};
```

On the other hand, a calculus tool probably prefers to use double.

```
class point {
public:
    point(double x, double y) : x_{x}, y_{y} {}
    double x() const { return x_; }
    double y() const { return y_; }
private:
    double x_, y_;
};
```

Imagine adding much more functionality to the point classes: computing distances between two point objects, rotating one point around another by some angle, and so on. The more functionality you dream up, the more code you must duplicate in both classes.

Wouldn't your job be simpler if you could write the point class once and use that single definition for both of these situations and for others not yet dreamed of? Templates to the rescue. Listing 52-1 shows the point class template.

© Ray Lischner 2020
R. Lischner, *Exploring C++20*, https://doi.org/10.1007/978-1-4842-5961-0_52

Listing 52-1. *The point Class Template*

```
template<class T>
class point {
public:
    point(T x, T y) : x_{x}, y_{y} {}
    T x() const { return x_; }
    T y() const { return y_; }
    /// Move to absolute coordinates (x, y).
    void move_to(T x, T y);
    /// Add (x, y) to current position.
    void move_by(T x, T y);
private:
    T x_, y_;
};

template<class T>
void point<T>::move_to(T x, T y)
{
    x_ = x;
    y_ = y;
}
```

Just as with function templates, the `template` keyword introduces a class template. The class template is a pattern for making classes, which you do by supplying template arguments, for example, `point<int>`.

The member functions of a class template are themselves function templates, using the same template parameters, except that you supply the template arguments to the class, not the function, as you can see in the `point<T>::move_to` function. **Write the move_by member function.** Compare your solution with Listing 52-2.

Listing 52-2. *The move_by Member Function*

```
template<class T>
void point<T>::move_by(T x, T y)
{
    x_ += x;
    y_ += y;
}
```

Every time you use a different template argument, the compiler generates a new class instance, with new member functions. That is, `point<int>::move_by` is one function, and `point<double>::move_by` is another, which is exactly what would happen if you had written the functions by hand. If two different source files both use `point<int>`, the compiler and linker ensure that they share the same template instance.

Parameterizing the rational Class

A simple `point` class is easy. What about something more complicated, such as the `rational` class? Suppose someone likes your `rational` class but wants more precision. You decide to change the type of the numerator and denominator from `int` to `long`. Someone else then complains that `rational` takes up too much memory and asks for a version that uses `short` as the base type. You could make three copies of the source code, one each for types `short`, `int`, and `long`. Or you could define a class template, as illustrated by the simplified `rational` class template in Listing 52-3.

Listing 52-3. The rational Class Template

```cpp
template<class T>
class rational
{
public:
  using value_type = T;
  rational() : rational{0} {}
  rational(value_type num) : numerator_{num}, denominator_{1} {}
  rational(value_type num, value_type den);

  void assign(value_type num, value_type den);

  rational const& operator +=(rational const& rhs);
  rational const& operator -=(rational const& rhs);
  rational const& operator *=(rational const& rhs);
  rational const& operator /=(rational const& rhs);

  template<class U>
  U convert()
  const
  {
    return static_cast<U>(numerator()) / static_cast<U>(denominator());
  }

  value_type const& numerator() const { return numerator_; }
  value_type const& denominator() const { return denominator_; }
private:
  void reduce();
  value_type numerator_;
  value_type denominator_;
};

template<class T>
rational<T>::rational(value_type num, value_type den)
: numerator_{num}, denominator_{den}
{
  reduce();
}

template<class T>
void rational<T>::assign(value_type num, value_type den)
{
  numerator_ = num;
  denominator_ = den;
  reduce();
}
```

```
template<class T>
bool operator==(rational<T> const& a, rational<T> const& b)
{
  return a.numerator() == b.numerator() and
         a.denominator() == b.denominator();
}

template<class T>
inline bool operator!=(rational<T> const& a, rational<T> const& b)
{
  return not (a == b);
}
```

The value_type member type is a useful convention. Many class templates that use a template parameter as some kind of subordinate type expose the parameter under a well-defined name. For example, vector<char>::value_type is a member type for its template parameter, namely, char.

Look at the definition of the constructor. When you define a member outside of its class template, you have to repeat the template header. The full name of the type includes the template parameter, rational<T>, in this case. Inside the class scope, use only the class name, without the template parameter. Also, once the compiler sees the fully qualified class name, it knows it is inside the class scope, and you can also use the template parameter by itself, which you can see in the parameter declarations. Inside a member function definition, you can call any other member functions and use member types, such as value_type.

Because the name T is already in use, the convert member function (line 12) needs a new name for its template parameter. U is a common convention, provided you don't take it too far. More than two or three single-letter parameters, and you start to need more meaningful names, just to help keep straight which parameter goes with which template.

In addition to the class template itself, you have to convert all the free functions that support the rational type to be function templates. Listing 52-3 keeps things simple by showing only operator== and operator!=. Other operators work similarly.

Using Class Templates

Unlike function templates, the compiler cannot deduce the template argument of a class template. This means you must supply the argument explicitly, inside angle brackets.

```
rational<short> zero{};
rational<int> pi1{355, 113};
rational<long> pi2{80143857L, 25510582L};
```

Notice anything familiar? Does rational<int> look like vector<int>? All the collection types, such as vector and map, are class templates. The standard library makes heavy use of templates throughout, and you will discover other templates when the time is right.

If a class template takes multiple arguments, separate the arguments with a comma, as in map<long, int>. A template argument can even be another template, such as

```
std::vector<std::vector<int>> matrix;
```

Starting with rational<> from Listing 52-3, **add the I/O operators**. (See Listing 36-4 for the non-template versions of the operators.) Write a simple test program that reads rational objects and echoes the values, one per line, to the standard output. Try changing the template argument to different types (short, int, long). Your test program might look something like Listing 52-4.

Listing 52-4. Simple I/O Test of the `rational` Class Template

```
import <iostream>;
import rational;

int main()
{
  rational<int> r{};
  while (std::cin >> r)
    std::cout << r << '\n';
}
```

Now modify the test program to print only nonzero values. The program should look something like Listing 52-5.

Listing 52-5. Testing `rational` Comparison Operator

```
import <iostream>;
import rational;

int main()
{
  static const rational<int> zero{};
  rational<int> r{};
  while (std::cin >> r)
    if (r != zero)
      std::cout << r << '\n';
}
```

Remember that with the old `rational` class, the compiler knew how to construct a `rational` object from an integer. Thus, it could convert the 0 to `rational(0)` and then call the overloaded == operator to compare two rational objects. So everything is fine. Right? So why doesn't it work?

Overloaded Operators

Remember from the previous Exploration that the compiler does not perform automatic type conversion for a function template. That means the compiler will not convert an int to a `rational<int>`. To solve this problem, you have to add some additional comparison operators, such as

```
template<class T> bool operator==(rational<T> const& lhs, T rhs);
template<class T> bool operator==(T lhs, rational<T> const& rhs);
template<class T> bool operator!=(rational<T> const& lhs, T rhs);
template<class T> bool operator!=(T lhs, rational<T> const& rhs);
```

and so on, for all of the comparison and arithmetic operators. On the other hand, you have to consider whether that's what you really want. To better understand the limitations of this approach, go ahead and try it. You don't need all the comparison operators yet, just `operator!=`, so you can compile the test program. After adding the two new overloaded `operator!=` functions, compile Listing 52-5 again, to be sure it works. Next, compile the test program with a template parameter of `long`. What happens?

_____

_____

Once again, the compiler complains that it can't find any suitable function for the != operator. The problem is that an overloaded != operator exists for the template parameter, namely, type long, but the type of the literal 0 is int, not long. You can try to solve this problem by defining operators for all the built-in types, but that quickly gets out of hand. So your choices are as follows:

- Define only operators that take two rational arguments. Force the caller to convert arguments to the desired rational type.

- Define operators in triples: one that takes two rational arguments and two others that mix one rational and one base type (T).

- Define operators to cover all the bases—for the built-in types (signed char, char, short, int, long), plus some types that I haven't covered yet. Thus, each operator requires 11 functions.

You might be interested in knowing how the C++ standard library addresses this issue. Among the types in the standard library is a class template, complex, which represents a complex number. The standardization committee opted for the second choice, that is, three overloaded function templates.

```
template<class T> bool operator==(complex<T> const& a, complex<T> const& b);
template<class T> bool operator==(complex<T> const& a, T const& b);
template<class T> bool operator==(T const& a, complex<T> const& b);
```

This solution works well enough, and later in the book, you'll learn techniques to reduce the amount of work involved in defining all these functions.

Another dimension to this problem is the literal 0. Using a literal of type int is fine when you know the base type of rational is also int. How do you express a generic zero for use in a template? The same issue arises when testing for a zero denominator. That was easy when you knew that the type of the denominator was int. When working with templates, you don't know the type. Recall from Listing 47-6 that the division assignment operator checked for a zero divisor and threw an exception in that case. If you don't know the type T, how do you know how to express the value zero? You can try using the literal 0 and hope that T has a suitable constructor (single argument of type int). A better solution is to invoke the default constructor for type T, as shown in Listing 52-6.

Listing 52-6. Invoking a Default Constructor of a Template Parameter

```
template<class T>
rational<T> const& rational<T>::operator/=(rational const& rhs)
{
  if (rhs.numerator() == T{})
      throw zero_denominator("divide by zero");
  numerator_ *= rhs.denominator();
  denominator_ *= rhs.numerator();
  if (denominator_ < T{})
  {
      denominator_ = -denominator_;
      numerator_ = -numerator_;
  }
  reduce();
  return *this;
}
```

If the type T is a class type, T{} yields an object that is initialized using T's default constructor. If T is a built-in type, the value of T{} is zero (i.e., 0, 0.0, or false). Initializing the local variables in the input operator is a little trickier.

Mixing Types

As you know, you can assign an int value to a long object or *vice versa*. It seems reasonable, therefore, that you should be able to assign a rational<int> value to a rational<long> object. Try it. **Write a simple program to perform an assignment that mixes base types.** Your program might look a little bit like Listing 52-7, but many other programs are equally reasonable.

Listing 52-7. Trying to Mix rational Base Types

```
import rational;

int main()
{
  rational<int> little{};
  rational<long> big{};
  big = little;
}
```

What happens when you compile your program?

_____

_____

The only assignment operator for the new rational class template is the compiler's implicit operator. Its parameter type is rational<T> const, so the base type of the source expression must be the same as the base type of the assignment target. You can fix this easily with a member function template. Add the following declaration to the class template:

```
template<class U>
rational& operator=(rational<U> const& rhs);
```

Inside the rational class template, the unadorned name, rational, means the same thing as rational<T>. The complete name of the class includes the template argument, so the proper name of the constructor is rational<T>. Because rational means the same as rational<T>, I was able to shorten the constructor name and many other uses of the type name throughout the class template definition. But the assignment operator's parameter is rational<U>. It uses a completely different template argument. Using this assignment operator, you can freely mix different rational types in an assignment statement.

Write the definition of the assignment operator. Don't worry about overflow that might result from assigning large values to small. It's a difficult problem and distracts from the main task at hand, which is practicing writing class templates and function templates. Compare your solution with Listing 52-8.

Listing 52-8. Defining the Assignment Operator Function Template

```
template<class T>
template<class U>
rational<T>& rational<T>::operator=(rational<U> const& rhs)
{
  assign(rhs.numerator(), rhs.denominator());
  return *this;
}
```

The first template header tells the compiler about the rational class template. The next template header tells the compiler about the assignment operator function template. Note that the compiler will be able to deduce the template argument for U from the type of the assignment source (rhs). After adding this operator to the rational class template, you should now be able to make your test program work.

Add a member template constructor that works similarly to the assignment operator. In other words, add to rational a constructor that looks like a copy constructor but isn't really. A copy constructor copies only objects of the same type, or rational<T>. This new constructor copies rational objects with a different base type, rational<U>. Compare your solution with Listing 52-9.

Listing 52-9. Defining a Member Constructor Template

```
template<class T>
template<class U>
rational<T>::rational(rational<U> const& copy)
: numerator_{copy.numerator()}, denominator_{copy.denominator()}
{}
```

Notice how the template headers stack up. The class template header comes first, followed by the constructor template header. **Finish the rational class by completing all the operators.** The new class is too big to include here, but as always, you can download the completed module from the book's website.

Template Variables

A variable can also be a template. Imagine how you expect a template variable definition to work. The <numbers> header defines several template constants for commonly used mathematical constants, such as π, e (natural logarithm base), $\sqrt{2}$, and more. The convention that the standard uses is to define the template name with a suffix of _v, then drop the suffix to instantiate the template with a double template argument, for example:

```
template<class T> constexpr T pi_v = 3.1415926535897932384626433832795002884L;
constexpr double pi = pi_v<double>;
```

Define a pi template for rational. It is actually trickier than a floating-point template because the floating-point template can rely on the compiler to convert the long double constant to double or float as needed. For rational, if you try to define an approximation that requires a long long template argument, the argument won't work for smaller argument types. So for now, keep it simple and use 31416 and 10000, which works for short and larger types. Compare your variable definition with Listing 52-10.

Listing 52-10. Defining a Variable Template

```
template<class T>
inline const rational<T> pi{ 31416, 10000 };
```

Because the two-argument constructor is not constexpr, the pi variable cannot be constexpr. But it can be inline, which is like an inline function. The compiler tries to use the variable's value immediately, rather than fetching it from memory.

Programming with templates and type parameters opens a new world of programming power and flexibility. A template lets you write a function or class once and lets the compiler generate actual functions and classes for different template arguments. Sometimes, however, one size does not fit all, and you have to grant exceptions to the rule. The next Exploration takes a look at how you do that by writing template specializations.

EXPLORATION 53

■ ■ ■

Template Specialization

Perhaps the most powerful feature of C++ is the ability to write a template and then use that template multiple times, with different template arguments each time. The ability to carve out exceptions to the rule magnifies that power. That is, you can tell the compiler to use a template for most template arguments, except that for certain argument types, it should use a different template definition. This Exploration introduces this feature.

Instantiation and Specialization

Template terminology is tricky. When you use a template, it is known as *instantiating* the template. A *template instance* is a concrete function or class that the compiler creates by applying the template arguments to the template definition. Another name for a template instance is a *specialization*. Thus, rational<int> is a specialization of the template rational<>.

Therefore, specialization is the realization of a template for a specific set of template arguments. C++ lets you define a custom specialization for one particular set of template arguments; that is, you can create an exception to the rule set down by the template. When you define the specialization—instead of letting the compiler instantiate the template for you—it is known as *explicit specialization*. Thus, a specialization that the compiler creates automatically would be an *implicit specialization*. (Explicit specialization is also called *full specialization*, for reasons that will become clear in the next Exploration.)

For example, the standard library's <type_traits> module supports a number of class templates that describe, characterize, and query a type's capabilities. Let's start with a very simple template, is_void<>, which simply indicates whether its template argument is the void type. Listing 53-1 shows one possible implementation. The primary template inherits from std::false_type, and the specialization for the void type derives from std::true_type.

Listing 53-1. The is_void Class Template

```
template<class T>
class is_void : public std::false_type
{};

template<>
class is_void<void> : public std::true_type
{};
```

When you write your own template class, you can use is_void<T>::value to determine whether the type T is the void type. As you can see, an explicit specialization begins with template<> (notice the empty angle brackets). Next is the definition. Notice how the class name is the full specialized template name: is_void<void>. That's how the compiler knows what you are specializing. The initial template definition is called the *primary* template, to distinguish it from template specializations.

Your explicit specialization completely replaces the template declaration for that template argument (or arguments; if the template takes multiple arguments, you must supply a specific value for each one). In general, a full specialization will implement the same members, just differently, but that is convention, not a language rule. Sometimes, a specialization might be very different from the primary template.

Let's say that a customer likes your rational class template but wants to use it in their own template and sometimes their template argument type will be void, so they want rational<void> to do something useful. You cannot have a data member of type void, so the compiler will reject rational<void> unless you write an explicit specialization. **What makes sense?**

_____

All I can think of is to represent the numeric value 0/1. **Write an explicit specialization for rational<void>.** Listing 53-2 shows one way to write it.

Listing 53-2. Specializing rational<void>

```cpp
import rational;

template<>
class rational<void>
{
public:
  using value_type = void;
  rational() {}

  int numerator() const { return 0; }
  int denominator() const { return 1; }
};
```

You do not need to implement reduce() or anything like that because rational<void> has only one value, namely, zero. The numerator() and denominator() functions always return the same values. This is not a particularly useful class, but it shows how a specialization may look very different from the primary template.

Custom Comparators

The map container lets you provide a custom comparator. The default behavior is for map to use a template class, std::less<>, which is a functor that uses the < operator to compare keys. If you want to store a type that cannot be compared with <, you can specialize std::less for your type. For example, suppose you have a person class, which stores a person's name, address, and telephone number. You want to store a person in a map, ordered by name. All you need to do is write a template specialization, std::less<person>, as shown in Listing 53-3.

Listing 53-3. Specializing `std::less` to Compare person Objects by Name

```
import <functional>;
import <iostream>;
import <map>;
import <string>;
import <string_view>;

class person {
public:
   person() : name_{}, address_{}, phone_{} {}
   person(std::string_view name,
          std::string_view address,
          std::string_view phone)
   : name_{name}, address_{address}, phone_{phone}
   {}
   std::string const& name()    const { return name_; }
   std::string const& address() const { return address_; }
   std::string const& phone()   const { return phone_; }
private:
   std::string name_, address_, phone_;
};

namespace std {
   template<>
   struct less<person> {
      bool operator()(person const& a, person const& b) const {
         return a.name() < b.name();
      }
   };
}

int main()
{
   std::map<person, int> people;
   people[person{"Ray", "123 Erewhon", "555-5555"}] = 42;
   people[person{"Arthur", "456 Utopia", "123-4567"}]= 10;
   std::cout << people.begin()->first.name() << '\n';
}
```

You are allowed to specialize class templates (but not function templates) that are defined in the `std` namespace, but you cannot add new declarations to `std`. The `std::less` template is declared in the `<functional>` module. This module defines comparator templates for all the relational and equality operators, and quite a bit more besides. Consult a language reference for details. What matters right now is what the `std::less` primary template looks like, that is, the primary template that C++ uses when it cannot find an explicit specialization (such as `std::less<person>`). Write the definition of a class template, `less`, that would serve as a primary template to compare any comparable objects with the `<` operator. Compare your solution with Listing 53-4.

Listing 53-4. The Primary std::less Class Template

```
template<class T>
struct less
{
    bool operator()(T const& a, T const& b) const { return a < b; }
};
```

If you can find the source code, take a peek into your standard library's <functional> module. It might be more complicated than Listing 53-4, but you should be able to find something that you can recognize and understand.

Specializing Function Templates

You can specialize a function template, but you should prefer overloading to templates. For example, let's keep working with the template form of absval (Exploration 50). Suppose you have an arbitrary-precision integer class, integer, and it has an efficient absolute value function (i.e., it simply clears the sign bit, so there's no need for a comparison). Instead of the template form of absval, you want to use the efficient method for taking the absolute value of integer. Although C++ permits you to specialize the absval<> function template, a better solution is to override the absval function (not template):

```
integer absval(integer i)
{
    i.clear_sign_bit();
    return i;
}
```

When the compiler sees a call to absval, it examines the type of the argument. If the type matches the parameter type used in a non-template function, the compiler arranges to call that function. If it can't match the argument type with the parameter type, it checks template functions. The precise rules are complicated, and I will discuss them later in the book. For now, just remember that the compiler prefers non-template functions to template functions, but it will use a template function instead of a non-template function if it can't find a good match between the argument types and the parameter types of the non-template function.

Sometimes, however, you have to write a template function, even if you just want to overload the absval function. For example, suppose you want to improve the absolute value function for the rational<T> class template. There is no need to compare the entire value with zero; just compare the numerator, and avoid unnecessary multiplications.

```
template<class T>
rational<T> absval(rational<T> const& r)
{
  if (r.numerator() < 0) // to avoid unnecessary multiplications in operator<
    return -r;
  else
    return r;
}
```

When you call absval, pass it an argument in the usual way. If you pass an int, double, or other built-in numeric type, the compiler instantiates the original function template. If you pass an integer object, the compiler calls the overloaded non-template function, and if you pass a rational object, the compiler instantiates the overloaded function template.

Traits

Earlier in this exploration, I introduced you to the <type_traits> module, which has a plethora of ways to examine a type. You've also seen another example of a traits template: std::numeric_limits. The <limits> module defines a class template named std::numeric_limits. The primary template is rather dull, saying that the type has zero digits of precision, a radix of zero, and so on. The only way this template makes any sense is to specialize it. Thus, the <limits> module also defines explicit specializations of the template for all the built-in types. Thus, you can discover the smallest int by calling std::numeric_limits<int>::min() or determine the floating-point radix of double with std::numeric_limits<double>::radix and so on. Every specialization declares the same members, but with values that are particular to the specialization. (Note that the compiler does not enforce the fact that every specialization declares the same members. The C++ standard mandates this requirement for numeric_limits, and it is up to the library author to implement the standard correctly, but the compiler provides no help.)

You can define your own specialization when you create a numeric type, such as rational. Defining a template of a template involves some difficulties that I will cover in the next Exploration, so for now, go back to Listing 49-10 and the old-fashioned non-template rational class, which hard-coded int as the base type. Listing 53-5 shows how to specialize numeric_limits for this rational class.

Listing 53-5. Specializing numeric_limits for the rational Class

```
namespace std {
template<>
class numeric_limits<rational>
{
public:
  static constexpr bool is_specialized{true};
  static constexpr rational min() noexcept {
    return rational(numeric_limits<int>::min());
  }
  static constexpr rational max() noexcept {
    return rational(numeric_limits<int>::max());
  }
  static rational lowest() noexcept { return -max(); }
  static constexpr int digits{ 2 * numeric_limits<int>::digits };
  static constexpr int digits10{ numeric_limits<int>::digits10 };
  static constexpr int max_digits10{ numeric_limits<int>::max_digits10 };
  static constexpr bool is_signed{ true };
  static constexpr bool is_integer{ false };
  static constexpr bool is_exact{ true };
  static constexpr int radix{ 2 };
  static constexpr bool is_bounded{ true };
  static constexpr bool is_modulo{ false };
  static constexpr bool traps{ std::numeric_limits<int>::traps };

  static rational epsilon() noexcept
      { return rational{1, numeric_limits<int>::max()-1}; }
  static rational round_error() noexcept
      { return rational{1, numeric_limits<int>::max()}; }

  // The following are meaningful only for floating-point types.
  static constexpr int min_exponent{ 0 };
  static constexpr int min_exponent10{ 0 };
```

```
static constexpr int max_exponent{ 0 };
static constexpr int max_exponent10{ 0 };
static constexpr bool has_infinity{ false };
static constexpr bool has_quiet_NaN{ false };
static constexpr bool has_signaling_NaN{ false };
static constexpr float_denorm_style has_denorm {denorm_absent};
static constexpr bool has_denorm_loss {false};
// The following are meant only for floating-point types, but you have
// to define them, anyway, even for nonfloating-point types. The values
// they return do not have to be meaningful.
static constexpr rational infinity() noexcept { return max(); }
static constexpr rational quiet_NaN() noexcept { return rational{}; }
static constexpr rational signaling_NaN() noexcept { return rational{}; }
static constexpr rational denorm_min() noexcept { return rational{}; }
static constexpr bool is_iec559{ false };
static constexpr bool tinyness_before{ false };
static constexpr float_round_style round_style{ round_toward_zero };
};
} // namespace std
```

This example has a few new things. They aren't important right now, but in C++, you have to get all the tiny details right or the compiler voices its stern disapproval. The first line, which starts namespace std, is how you specialize templates in the standard library. You are not allowed to add new names to the standard library, but you are allowed to specialize templates that the standard library has already defined. Notice the opening curly brace for the namespace, which has a corresponding closing curly brace on the last line of the listing. (This topic will be covered in more depth in Exploration 56.)

The member functions all have noexcept between their names and bodies. This tells the compiler that the function does not throw any exceptions (recall from Exploration 48).

The constexpr specifier is similar to const, but it tells the compiler that the function is callable at compile time. In order for a function to be constexpr, the compiler imposes a number of restrictions. Any functions that it calls must also be constexpr. Function parameter and return type must be built-in or types that can be constructed with constexpr constructors. If any restriction is violated, the function cannot be declared constexpr. Thus, the gcd() function cannot be constexpr, so reduce() cannot be constexpr, so the two-argument constructor cannot be constexpr. The value of being able to write a function that is called at compile time is extremely useful, and we will return to constexpr in the future.

■ **Tip**   When writing a template for the first time, start with a non-template version. It is much easier to debug a non-template function or class. Once you get the non-template version working, then change it into a template.

Template specialization has many other uses, but before we get carried away, the next Exploration takes a look at a particular kind of specialization, where your specialization still requires template parameters, called partial specialization.

■ ■ ■

Partial Template Specialization

Explicit specialization requires you to specify a template argument for every template parameter, leaving no template parameters in the template header. Sometimes, however, you want to specify only some of the template arguments, leaving one or more template parameters in the header. C++ lets you do just that and more, but only for class templates, as this Exploration describes.

Degenerate Pairs

The standard library defines the `std::pair<T, U>` class template in the `<utility>` header. This class template is a trivial holder of a pair of objects. The template arguments specify the types of these two objects. Listing 54-1 depicts a common definition of this simple template. (I omitted some members that involve more advanced programming techniques, just to keep this Exploration manageable.)

Listing 54-1. The pair Class Template

```
template<class T, class U>
struct pair
{
    using first_type = T;
    using second_type = U;
    T first;
    U second;
    pair();
    pair(T const& first, U const& second);
    template<class T2, class U2>
    pair(pair<T2, U2> const& other);
};
```

Remember that the keyword `struct` means the same as `class`. The difference is that the default access level is `public`. Many simple classes use `struct`, but I like to use `class` all the time just for the sake of constancy. But the standard describes `std::pair` using `struct`, so I chose the same for Listing 54-1. Even when defined using the `struct` keyword, I still call the type a "class" because it is.

As you can tell, the `pair` class template doesn't do much. The `std::map` class template can use `std::pair` to store keys and values. A few functions, such as `std::equal_range`, return a `pair` in order to return two pieces of information. In other words, `pair` is a useful, if dull, part of the standard library.

What happens if T or U is void?

_____

© Ray Lischner 2020

R. Lischner, *Exploring C++20*, https://doi.org/10.1007/978-1-4842-5961-0_54

Although void has popped up here and there, usually as a function's return type, I haven't discussed it much. The void type means "no type." That's useful for returning from a function that does not return a value, but you cannot declare an object with void type, nor does the compiler permit you to use void for a data member. Thus, pair<int, void> results in an error.

As you start to use templates more and more, you will find yourself in unpredictable situations. A template might contain a template, which might contain another template, and suddenly you find a template, such as pair, being instantiated with template arguments that you never imagined before, such as void. So let's add specializations for pair that permit one or two void template arguments, just for the sake of completeness. The standard permits specializations of library templates only if a template argument is a user-defined type. Therefore, specializing std::pair for the void type results in undefined behavior. So we will specialize our own pair class template, not the std::pair template in the standard library.

Write an explicit specialization for pair<void, void>. It cannot store anything, but you can declare objects of type pair<void, void>. To test your solution, the compiler needs to see the primary template first, then the specialization, so remember to include both in your test code. Compare your solution with Listing 54-2.

Listing 54-2. Specializing pair<> for Two void Arguments

```
template<>
struct pair<void, void>
{
    using first_type = void;
    using second_type = void;
    pair(pair const&) = default;
    pair() = default;
    pair& operator=(pair const&) = default;
};
```

The constructors have nothing to do, and the template specialization cannot define any data members, so this specialization is basic and relies on the compiler's own default definitions of the constructors and assignment operator. More difficult is the case of one void argument. You still need a template parameter for the other part of the pair. That calls for *partial specialization*.

Partial Specialization

When you write a template specialization that involves some, but not all, of the template arguments, it is called *partial specialization*. Some programmers call explicit specialization *full specialization* to help distinguish it from partial specialization. Partial specialization is explicit, so the phrase full specialization is more descriptive, and I will use it for the rest of this book.

Begin a partial specialization with a template header that lists the template parameters you are not specializing. Then define the specialization. As with full specialization, name the class that you are specializing by listing all the template arguments. Some of the template arguments depend on the specialization's parameters, and some are fixed with specific values. That's what makes this specialization partial.

As with full specialization, the definition of the specialization completely replaces the primary template for a particular set of template arguments. By convention, you keep the same interface, but the actual implementation is up to you.

Listing 54-3 shows a partial specialization of pair if the first template argument is void.

Listing 54-3. Specializing pair for One void Argument

```
template<class U>
struct pair<void, U>
{
    typedef void first_type;
    typedef U second_type;
    U second;
    pair() = default;
    pair(pair const&) = default;
    pair(U const& second) : second{second} {}
    template<class U2>
    pair(pair<void, U2> const& other);
};
```

Based on Listing 54-3, **write a partial specialization of pair with a void** second argument. Compare your solution with Listing 54-4.

Listing 54-4. Specializing pair for the Other void Argument

```
template<class T>
struct pair<T, void>
{
    typedef T first_type;
    typedef void second_type;
    T first;
    pair() = default;
    pair(pair const&) = default;
    pair(T const& first) : first{first} {}
    template<class T2>
    pair(pair<T2, void> const& other);
};
```

Regardless of the presence or absence of any partial or full specializations, you still use the pair template the same way: always with two type arguments. The compiler examines those template arguments and determines which specialization to use.

The template arguments to a partial template specialization do not need to be arguments to the template itself. They can be any arguments to any template being specialized. For example, Listing 53-5 shows a full specialization of std::numeric_limits<rational> assuming that rational was hard-coded to use an int type. But more useful is the rational<> class template. In that case, you would need a partial specialization of numeric_limits, as sketched in Listing 54-5.

Listing 54-5. Partially Specializing numeric_limits for rational

```
namespace std {
template<class T>
class numeric_limits<rational<T>>
{
public:
    static constexpr bool is_specialized{true};
    static constexpr rational<T> min() noexcept {
        return rational<T>(numeric_limits<T>::min());
    }
```

```
  static constexpr rational<T> max() noexcept {
    return rational<T>(numeric_limits<T>::max());
  }
  static rational<T> lowest() noexcept { return -max(); }
  static constexpr int digits{ 2 * numeric_limits<T>::digits };
  static constexpr int digits10{ numeric_limits<T>::digits10 };
  static constexpr int max_digits10{ numeric_limits<T>::max_digits10 };
  static constexpr bool is_signed{ numeric_limits<T>::is_signed };
  static constexpr bool is_integer{ false };
  static constexpr bool is_exact{ true };
  static constexpr int radix{ 2 };
  static constexpr bool is_bounded{ numeric_limits<T>::is_bounded };
  static constexpr bool is_modulo{ false };
  static constexpr bool traps{ std::numeric_limits<T>::traps };
  ... omitted for brevity
};
} // namespace std
```

Partially Specializing Function Templates

You cannot partially specialize a function template. Full specialization is allowed, as described in the previous Exploration, but partial specialization is not. Sorry. Use overloading instead, which is usually better than template specialization anyway.

Value Template Parameters

Before I present the next example of partial specialization, I want to introduce a new template feature. Templates typically use types as parameters, but they can also use values. Declare a value template parameter with a type and optional name, much the same way that you would declare a function parameter. Value template parameters are limited to types for which you can specify a compile-time constant: bool, char, int, and so on, but string literals and most classes are not allowed.

For example, suppose you want to modify the fixed class that you wrote for Exploration 50 so that the developer can specify the number of digits after the decimal place. While you're at it, you can also use a template parameter to specify the underlying type, as shown in Listing 54-6.

Listing 54-6. Changing fixed from a Class to a Class Template

```
template<class T, int N>
class fixed
{
public:
    using value_type = T;
    static constexpr int places{N};
    static constexpr int places10{ipower(10, N)};
    fixed();
    fixed(T const& integer, T const& fraction);
    fixed& operator=(fixed const& rhs);
    fixed& operator+=(fixed const& rhs);
```

```
    fixed& operator*=(fixed const& rhs);
    ... and so on...
private:
    T value_; // scaled to N decimal places
};

template<class T, int N>
fixed<T, N>::fixed(value_type const& integer, value_type const& fraction)
: value_(integer * places10 + fraction)
{}

template<class T1, int N1, class T2, int N2>
bool operator==(fixed<T1,N1> const& a, fixed<T2,N2> const& b);

... and so on...
```

The key challenge in converting the fixed class to a class template is defining places10 in terms of places. C++ has no exponentiation operator, but you can write a constexpr function to compute an integer power. See Listing 54-7 for the compile-time ipower function.

Listing 54-7. Computing a Power of 10 at Compile Time

```
/// Compute base to the exp-th power at compile time.
template<class Base, class Exp>
Base constexpr ipower(Base base, Exp exp)
{
    if (exp < Exp{})
        throw std::domain_error("No negative powers of 10");
    if (exp == Exp{})
    {
        if (base == Base{})
            throw std::domain_error("0 to 0th power is not allowed");
        return Base{1};
    }

    Base power{base};
    for (Exp e{1}; e != exp;)
    {
        // invariant(power == base ** e)
        if (e + e < exp)
        {
            power *= power;
            e += e;
        }
        else
        {
            power *= base;
            ++e;
        }
    }
    return power;
}
```

Suppose you have an application that instantiates fixed<long, 0>. This degenerate case is no different from a plain long, but with overhead and complexity for managing the implicit decimal point. Suppose further that performance measurements of your application reveal that this overhead has a measurable impact on the overall performance of the application. Therefore, you decide to use partial specialization for the case of fixed<T, 0>. Use a partial specialization, so that the template still takes a template argument for the underlying type.

You might wonder why the application programmer doesn't simply replace fixed<long, 0> with plain long. In some cases, that is the correct solution. Other times, however, the use of fixed<long, 0> might be buried inside another template. The issue, therefore, becomes one of which template to specialize. For the sake of this Exploration, we are specializing fixed.

Remember that any specialization must provide a full implementation. You don't have to specialize the free functions too. By specializing the fixed class template, we get the performance boost we need. Listing 54-8 shows the partial specialization of fixed.

Listing 54-8. Specializing fixed for N == 0

```
template<class T>
class fixed<T, 0>
{
public:
    using value_type = T;
    static constexpr T places{0};
    static constexpr T places10{1};
    fixed() : value_{} {}
    fixed(T const& integer, T const&);
    fixed& operator=(fixed const& rhs) { value_ = rhs; }
    fixed& operator+=(fixed const& rhs) { value_ += rhs; }
    fixed& operator*=(fixed const& rhs) { value_ *= rhs; }
    ... and so on...
private:
    T value_; // no need for scaling
};

template<class T>
fixed<T, 0>::fixed(value_type const& integer, value_type const&)
: value_(integer)
{}
```

What if the template argument to rational or fixed is not an integer? What if the user accidentally tries to use, say, std::string? Of course, disaster would ensue, and the user would be bombarded by error messages. Buried deep within those messages would be the true reason, but how easy would it be for the user to discover the problem? C++ 20 offers an easy way for the author of a template to specify requirements on a template argument, and that is the topic of the next Exploration.

■ ■ ■

Template Constraints

One drawback to templates is that they are open to misuse, and accidentally using the wrong type as a template argument can confuse a compiler to such a degree that the error messages it issues require an advanced degree in C++ to decipher. Not to worry, though, because a template author can specify constraints on template arguments. This Exploration describes how to write constraints on your templates.

Constraining a Function Template

Consider what would happen if you were to pass a string to the ipower() function (Listing 54-7), or a floating-point value. The function works correctly only for integral arguments, but because C++ has several different integral types, writing a template makes more sense than writing the same function multiple times, once per integral type. What we really want is a way to restrict the template arguments to only the integral types. Listing 55-1 shows how to limit the arguments to integral types.

Listing 55-1. Requiring Template Argument Types to Be Integral

```cpp
/// Compute base to the exp-th power at compile time.
template<class Base, class Exp>
Base constexpr ipower(Base base, Exp exp)
    requires std::integral<Base> and std::integral<Exp>
{
    if (exp < Exp{})
        throw std::domain_error("No negative powers of 10");
    if (exp == Exp{})
    {
        if (base == Base{})
            throw std::domain_error("0 to 0th power is not allowed");
        return Base{1};
    }

    Base power{base};
    for (Exp e{1}; e != exp;)
    {
        // invariant(power == base ** e)
        if (e + e < exp)
        {
            power *= power;
            e += e;
        }
    }
```

© Ray Lischner 2020
R. Lischner, *Exploring C++20*, https://doi.org/10.1007/978-1-4842-5961-0_55

```
        else
        {
            power *= base;
            ++e;
        }
    }
    return power;
}
```

Now if you try to pass a string or floating-point value, the compiler tells you that the integral constraint has been violated. **Try calling ipower() with different argument types and see what kinds of messages your compiler issues.**

The requires modifier follows a function template declaration or the function header in a definition. What follows requires looks like a Boolean expression, but is slightly different. Constraints can be combined with logical operators (and, or, not), and, like a Boolean expression, the compiler evaluates constraints with short-circuits. If the left-hand constraint of an and is false, the constraint fails without evaluating the right-hand constraint. And if the left-hand constraint of an or is true, the constraint passes without evaluating the right-hand constraint. You can use parentheses for complicated constraints.

You can also use constraints to distinguish among overloaded functions. For example, the std::vector<> template has several functions named insert to insert one or more values into the vector. One insert function is a member function template that takes two iterators as argument and copies a range of values into the vector at a specific position:

```
template<class InputIterator>
iterator insert(const_iterator pos, InputIterator first, InputIterator last);
```

There is also a function that inserts multiple copies of a single value:

```
iterator insert(const_iterator pos, size_type count, T const& value);
```

How does the compiler interpret the following code?

```
std::vector<int> v;
v.insert(v.end(), 10, 20);
```

_____

_____

_____

_____

Because the type of 10 and 20 is int, the template function is invoked with the InputIterator type set to int. Obviously, 10 and 20 are not iterators and the compiler would end up issuing numerous errors. So the iterator form of the function is constrained as follows:

```
template<class InputIterator>
iterator insert(const_iterator pos, InputIterator first, InputIterator last)
    requires std::input_iterator<InputIterator>;
```

The <iterator> header defines std::input_iterator.

Now it's your turn. **Modify the** copy() **function in Listing 51-5 to add suitable constraints on the template parameters.** The <iterator> header provides std::output_iterator<I, T>, where I is the iterator to test and T is the value type. The <ranges> header provides std::ranges::input_range<R> as well as std::ranges::range_value_t<R>, which yields the value type for a range R. Compare your function with Listing 55-2.

Listing 55-2. Constraining the copy Function's Arguments

```
template<class Input, class Output>
Output copy(Input input, Output output)
    requires
        std::ranges::input_range<Input> and
        std::output_iterator<Output, std::ranges::range_value_t<Input>>
{
    for (auto const& item : input)
        *output++ = item;
    return output;
}
```

Another way to specify constraints is to dictate the operations that you need to perform on the function arguments. For example, suppose you want to implement an operator to multiply a rational<T> value by any numeric scalar value, and you want to permit user-defined types (std::integral<T> and std::floating_point<T> work only for built-in types). Listing 55-3 shows how to define the constraints in terms of the multiplication and division operations.

Listing 55-3. Constraining a Multiplication Operator

```
template<class T, class U>
U operator*(rational<T> const& lhs, U const& rhs)
    requires
        requires(T lhs, U rhs) {
            (lhs * rhs) / lhs;
        }
{
    return lhs.numerator() * rhs / lhs.denominator();
}
```

The second requires keyword starts a requires expression. This requires expression is followed by what looks like function parameters. Within the curly braces is a sequence of requirements, each terminated by a semicolon. In Listing 55-3, the requirement is simply an expression. If the expression is valid, the requirement is true. If the user were to, say, try to pass a string to the * operator, the compiler would report that the (lhs * rhs) / lhs constraint was violated.

Another kind of requirement that can appear in the list is a type requirement, which is just the name of a type such as a member type name or a template specialization. If the type is valid, the requirement is true. For example, all of the standard containers have a member type named size_type. If you wanted to write a size() function that checks for a size_type member and a size() member function, you could write it as shown in Listing 55-4.

Listing 55-4. Constraining the `size` Function

```
template<class T>
auto size(T const& container)
    requires
        requires(T container) {
            container.size();
            typename T::size_type;
            { container.size() } -> std::same_as<typename T::size_type>;
        }
{
    return container.size();
}
```

The `container.size()` constraint checks that the expression is valid, which means the `size()` member function is valid. If it is valid, that is, the compiler know how to call the `size()` member function, the compiler checks the second requirement, or `typename T::size_type`, which checks that the template argument has a `size_type` type member. If the second requirement is true, the compiler checks the third requirement. This checks that `container.size()` is valid and that the return type is `T::size_type`, using the standard `std::same_as` concept. The final requirement subsumes the first two, but Listing 55-4 shows all three just to demonstrate the three flavors of requirement expressions.

An alternative syntax is for the template constraint to follow immediately after the template header. Listing 55-5 shows the same constraints as Listing 55-4, but with this different syntax.

Listing 55-5. Constraining the `size` Function

```
template<class T>
requires
    requires(T container) {
        container.size();
        typename T::size_type;
        { container.size() } -> std::same_as<typename T::size_type>;
    }
auto size(T const& container)
{
    return container.size();
}
```

Constraining a Class Template

You can also apply constraints to a class template. For example, the `rational` template requires that its template argument be an integral type:

```
template<class T>
requires std::integral<T>
class rational;
```

The constraints are the same as for function templates. Within a class definition, you can also apply constraints to individual member functions that are templates.

To further abbreviate a template header, instead of using `class` to introduce a parameter name, you can use a concept, for example:

```
template<std::integral T>
class rational;
```

Standard Concepts

As you've seen, the C++ standard library provides many useful constraint tests. These tests are called *concepts*. Many fundamental concepts are defined in the `<concepts>` header, with additional concepts defined in `<iterator>` and `<ranges>`. Among the concepts defined in the `<concepts>` header are the following:

std::equality_comparable<T>

Yields a true constraint if values of type T can be compared for equality. with the `==` operator. The `find()` algorithm requires elements be `equality_comparable` if the caller does not provide a predicate.

std::floating_point<T>

Yields a true constraint if T is one of the built-in floating-point types (`float`, `double`, or `long double`).

std::integral<T>

Yields a true constraint if T is one of the built-in integral types (`char`, `short`, `int`, `long`, or `long long`).

predicate<T>

Yields a true constraint if T is a predicate, that is a function that returns a Boolean result. Many algorithms, such as `copy_if()`, require a predicate argument.

std::strict_weak_order<T>

Yields a true constraint if values of type T can be compared for with the `<` operator, and the result is a strict, weak ordering. This is the requirement for using T as the key type in a `map`. The term *strict* means that an expression `x < x` is always false, and weak ordering is essentially the ability to say that.

Iterator Concepts

The `<iterator>` header defines a concept for each iterator category, plus some finer-grained concepts.

std::bidirection_iterator<I>

Yields a true constraint if I is bidirectional, random access, or contiguous.

std::contiguous_iterator<I>

Yields a true constraint if I is contiguous.

std::forward_iterator<I>

Yields a true constraint if I is forward, bidirectional, random access, or contiguous.

std::indirectly_readable<I>

Yields a true constraint if I is any read iterator, that is, it is possible to read a value indirectly or via the dereference operator (*).

std::indirectly_writable<I>

Yields a true constraint if I is any write iterator, that is, it is possible to write a value indirectly or via the dereference operator (*).

std::input_iterator<I>

Yields a true constraint if I is input, forward, bidirectional, random access, or contiguous.

std::input_or_output_iterator<I>

Yields a true constraint if I is an input or output iterator. These two iterator types share the common trait that they are incrementable and code must dereference the iterator once between iterations.

std::output_iterator<I>

Yields a true constraint if I is output, forward, bidirectional, random access, or contiguous.

std::permutable<I>

Yields a true constraint if I can be used to reorder data in the iterable range. A permuting algorithm may move or swap data.

std::random_access_iterator<I>

Yields a true constraint if I is random access or contiguous.

std::sortable<I>

Yields a true constraint if I can be used to order data in the iterable range. A sorting algorithm may move or swap data and must be able to compare elements in a strict, weak ordering.

Range Concepts

The `<range>` header defines a concept for each iterator category, plus some finer-grained concepts.

std::ranges::bidirectional_range<R>

Yields a true constraint if R is a bidirectional, random access, or contiguous range, such as a linked list, array, or vector.

std::ranges::contiguous_range<R>

Yields a true constraint if R is a contiguous range, such as an array or vector.

std::ranges::forward_range<R>

Yields a true constraint if R is a forward, bidirectional, random access, or contiguous range, such as an input view or standard container.

std::ranges::input_range<R>

Yields a true constraint if R is an input, forward, bidirectional, random access, or contiguous range, such as an input view.

std::ranges::output_range<R>

Yields a true constraint if R is an output, forward, bidirectional, random access, or contiguous range. So far in this book, we have used an output iterator, not an output range. An example of an output range is a vector that has been presized to accommodate the expected output.

std::ranges::random_access_range<R>

Yields a true constraint if R is a random access or contiguous range, such as an array or vector.

std::ranges::range<R>

Yields a true constraint if R is any range, such as a pair of iterators, a view, or a standard container.

std::ranges::sized_range<R>

Yields a true constraint if R is a range with a known size and the size can be determined in constant time (not by iterating the range).

`std::ranges::view<R>`

Yields a true constraint if R is a view. To be a view, a range must be lightweight, that is, movable and destroyable in constant time. To be destroyable in constant time means the view cannot own any elements in the range because destroying the range requires destroying the objects in the range.

Writing Your Own Concept

A constraint can be a Boolean expression related to a template argument. Most often that expression makes use of a special kind of template just for writing template constraints, called a *concept*. For example, suppose you want a constraint for any integral type, including user-defined types. The requirement is that if the user defines an integral type, the `std::numeric_limits` template must be specialized for that type:

```
template<class T>
concept any_integral = std::numeric_limits<T>::is_integer;
```

Let's see an application of concepts in writing a range-oriented class. The `join` view takes a range of ranges and flattens them into a single range. A practical application of this is to take a range of strings and join them into a single string. But it doesn't quite finish the job. The end result is a view into a range, which can be used to construct a new string, but that generally requires saving the joined view to a variable and then using the variable's `begin()` and `end()` to construct a string. Listing 55-6 shows a class that can be used at the end of a view pipeline to make the `std::string` object for us.

Listing 55-6. *Defining the store Function Template*

```
import <algorithm>;
import <concepts>;
import <iostream>;
import <ranges>;
import <string>;
import <vector>;

template<class Range>
concept can_reserve =
        std::ranges::sized_range<Range> and
        requires(Range r) {
            r.reserve(0);
        };

template<class Container>
concept can_insert_back =
    requires(Container c) {
        std::back_inserter(c);
    };

template<can_insert_back Container>
class store_t
{
```

```
public:
    using container_type = Container;
    using value_type = std::ranges::range_value_t<container_type>;
    store_t(container_type& output) : output_{output} {}

    template<can_reserve Range>
    Container& operator()(Range const& input) const {
        output_.reserve(std::ranges::size(output_)+std::ranges::size(input));
        std::ranges::copy(input, std::back_inserter(output_));
        return output_;
    }

    template<class Range>
    requires (not can_reserve<Range>)
    Container& operator()(Range const& input) const {
        std::ranges::copy(input, std::back_inserter(output_));
        return output_;
    }
private:
    container_type& output_;
};

template<class T>
store_t<T> store(T& container) { return store_t<T>(container); }

template<class In, class Out>
Out& operator|(In range, store_t<Out> const& storer)
{
    return storer(std::forward<In>(range));
}

int main() {
    std::vector<std::string> strings{ "this" " is ", "a", " test", ".\n" };
    std::string str;
    std::ranges::views::join(strings) | store(str);
    std::cout << str;
}
```

Even though the can_insert_back concept has only one use, defining a separate concept instead of using a local template constraint has two advantages:

- By assigning a name to the constraint, it provides some documentation to the human reader and maintainer.

- A separate constraint means the class declaration has less clutter, which makes it slightly easier to read.

The advantages are all for the human reader. The compiler doesn't care. The can_reserve concept is similar. It reduces the clutter around the function call operators so it is easier to see that one applies to situations when it is possible to preallocate memory for the copy (say, for a vector), and the other applies to situations when the output range will be extended one element at a time (say, for a linked list).

Template constraints and concepts are a wonderful addition to C++ 20, and you should expect future versions of the language to expand the use of constraints through the rest of the standard library. Third-party libraries will also start to adopt constraints, which will make them much easier to use.

The next Exploration introduces a language feature that helps you manage your custom types: namespaces.

EXPLORATION 56

■ ■ ■

Names and Namespaces

Nearly every name in the standard library begins with `std::`, and only names in the standard library are permitted to start with `std::`. For your own names, you can define other prefixes, which is a good idea and an excellent way to avoid name collisions. Libraries and large programsf in particular benefit from proper partitioning and naming. However, templates and names have some complications, and this Exploration helps clarify the issues.

Namespaces

The name `std` is an example of a *namespace*, which is a C++ term for a named scope. A namespace is a way to keep names organized. When you see a name that begins with `std::`, you know it's in the standard library. Good third-party libraries use namespaces. The open source Boost project (`www.boost.org`), for example, uses the `boost` namespace to ensure names, such as `boost::container::vector`, do not interfere with similar names in the standard library, such as `std::vector`. Applications can take advantage of namespaces too. For example, different project teams can place their own names in different namespaces, so members of one team are free to name functions and classes without the need to check with other teams. For example, the GUI team might use the namespace `gui` and define a `gui::tree` class, which manages a tree widget in a user interface. The database team might use the `db` namespace. Thus, `db::tree` might represent a tree data structure that is used to store database indices on disk. A database debugging tool can use both `tree` classes, because there is no clash between `db::tree` and `gui::tree`. The namespaces keep the names separate.

To create a namespace and declare names within it, you must define the namespace. A namespace definition begins with the `namespace` keyword, followed by an optional identifier that names the namespace. This, in turn, is followed by declarations within curly braces. Unlike a class definition, a namespace definition does not end with a semicolon after the closing curly brace. All the declarations within the curly braces are in the scope of the namespace. You must define a namespace outside of any function. Listing 56-1 defines the namespace `numeric` and, within it, the `rational` class template.

Listing 56-1. Defining the `rational` Class Template in the `numeric` Namespace

```
namespace numeric
{
  template<class T>
  class rational
  {
    ... you know what goes here...
  };
  template<class T>
  bool operator==(rational<T> const& a, rational<T> const& b);
```

```
template<class T>
rational<T> operator+(rational<T> const& a, rational<T> const& b);
... and so on...
} // namespace numeric
```

Namespace definitions can be discontiguous. This means that you can have many separate namespace blocks that all contribute to the same namespace. Therefore, multiple modules can each define the same namespace, and every definition adds names to the same, common namespace. In a module interface, you can export an entire namespace or only certain names in a namespace. Listing 56-2 illustrates how to define the fixed class template within the same numeric namespace, even in a different module (say, fixed).

Listing 56-2. Defining the fixed Class Template in the numeric Namespace

```
export module fixed;
namespace numeric
{
  export template<class T, int N>
  class fixed
  {
    ... copied from Exploration 54...
  };

  export template<class T, int N>
  bool operator==(fixed<T,N> const& a, fixed<T,N> const& b);

  export template<class T, int N>
  fixed<T,N> operator+(fixed<T,N> const& a, fixed<T,N> const& b);
  // and so on...
} // namespace numeric
```

A module that imports the fixed module will import numeric::fixed even though the numeric namespace is not explicitly exported. Because the namespace is not exported, every free function requires an export declaration if you want to be able to call it from other modules. The free functions and operators related to fixed must be defined in the numeric namespace. I'll explain exactly why later in the Exploration, but I wanted to point it out now, because it's very important.

When you declare but don't define an entity (such as a function) in a namespace, you have a choice for how to define that entity, as described here:

- Use the same or another namespace definition and define the entity within the namespace definition.

- Define the entity outside of the namespace and prefix the entity name with the namespace name and the scope operator (::).

Listing 56-3 illustrates both styles of definition. (The declarations are in Listings 56-1 and 56-2.)

Listing 56-3. Defining Entities in a Namespace

```
namespace numeric
{
  template<class T>
  rational<T> operator+(rational<T> const& a, rational<T> const& b)
```

```
{
    rational<T> result{a};
    result += b;
    return result;
  }
}

template<class T, int N>
numeric::fixed<T, N> numeric::operator+(fixed<T, N> const& a, fixed<T, N> const& b)
{
    fixed<T, N> result{a};
    result += b;
    return result;
}
```

The first form is straightforward. As always, the definition must follow the declaration. This is the form you will see most often.

The second form may be used when there are few definitions. The compiler sees the namespace name (numeric), followed by the scope operator, and knows to look up the subsequent name (operator*) in that namespace. The compiler considers the rest of the function to be in the namespace scope, so you don't have to specify the namespace name in the remainder of the declaration (i.e., the function parameters and the function body). The function's return type comes before the function name, which places it outside the namespace scope, so you still have to use the namespace name. To avoid ambiguity, you are not allowed to have a namespace and a class with the same name in a single namespace.

An alternative style of writing a function return type that I touched on in Exploration 24 lets you write the return type without repeating the namespace scope, because the function name establishes the scope for you. Instead of beginning the function header with the return type, use the auto keyword, and place the return type after the function parameters, using -> to indicate the return type, as shown in Listing 56-4.

Listing 56-4. Alternative Style of Function Declaration

```
template<class T, int N>
auto numeric::operator+(fixed<T, N> const& a, fixed<T, N> const& b) -> fixed<T, N>
{
    fixed<T, N> result{a};
    result += b;
    return result;
}
```

Traditionally, when you define a namespace in a module, the module contains a single namespace definition, which contains all the necessary declarations and definitions. When you implement functions and other entities in a separate source file, I find it most convenient to write an explicit namespace and define the functions inside the namespace, but some programmers prefer to omit the namespace definition. Instead, they use the namespace name and scope operator when defining the entities. An entity name that begins with the namespace name and scope operator is an example of a *qualified* name—that is, a name that explicitly tells the compiler where to look to find the name's declaration.

The name rational<int>::value_type is qualified, because the compiler knows to look up value_type in the class template rational, specialized for int. The name std::vector is a qualified name, because the compiler looks up vector in the namespace std. On the other hand, where does the compiler look up the name std? Before I can answer that question, I have to delve into the general subject of nested namespaces.

Nested Namespaces

Namespaces can nest, that is, you can define a namespace inside another namespace, as demonstrated here:

```
namespace exploring_cpp
{
  namespace numeric {
    template<class T> class rational
    {
      ... and so on ...
    };
  }
}
```

To use a nested namespace, the qualifier lists all the namespaces in order, starting from the outermost namespace. Separate each namespace with the scope operator (::), for example:

```
exploring_cpp::numeric::rational<int> half{1, 2};
std::ranges::copy(source, destination);
```

A top-level namespace, such as `std` or `exploring_cpp`, is actually a nested namespace. Its outer namespace is called the *global namespace*. All entities that you declare outside of any function are in a namespace—in an explicit namespace or in the global namespace. Thus, names outside of functions are said to be at *namespace scope*. The phrase *global scope* refers to names that are declared in the implicit global namespace, which means outside of any explicit namespace. Qualify a global name by prefixing the name with a scope operator.

```
::exploring_cpp::numeric::rational<int> half{1, 2};
::std::ranges::copy(source, destination);
```

Most programs you read will not use an explicit global scope operator. Instead, programmers tend to rely on the normal C++ rules for looking up names, letting the compiler find global names on its own. So far, every function you've written has been global; every call to these functions has been unqualified. The compiler has never had a problem with the unqualified names. If you have a situation in which a local name hides a global name, you can refer to the global name explicitly. Listing 56-5 demonstrates the kind of trouble you can wreak through poor choice of names and how to use qualified names to extricate yourself.

Listing 56-5. Coping with Conflicting Names

```
 1 import <cmath>;
 2 import <numeric>;
 3 import <vector>;
 4
 5 namespace stats {
 6   // Really bad name for a functor to compute sum of squares,
 7   // for use in determining standard deviation.
 8   class std
 9   {
10   public:
11     std(double mean) : mean_{mean} {}
12     double operator()(double acc, double x)
13     const
```

```
14    {
15      return acc + square(x - mean_);
16    }
17    double square(double x) const { return x * x; }
18  private:
19    double mean_;
20  };
21
22  // Really bad name for a function in the stats namespace.
23  // It computes standard deviation.
24  double stats(::std::vector<double> const& data)
25  {
26    double std{0.0}; // Really, really bad name for a local variable
27    if (not data.empty())
28    {
29      double sum{::std::accumulate(data.begin(), data.end(), 0.0)};
30      double mean{sum / data.size()};
31      double sumsq{::std::accumulate(data.begin(), data.end(), 0.0,
32                   stats::std(mean))};
33      double variance{sumsq / data.size() - mean * mean};
34      std = ::std::sqrt(variance);
35    }
36    return std;
37  }
38 }
```

The local variable std does not conflict with the namespace of the same name because the compiler knows that only class and namespace names can appear on the left-hand side of a scope operator. On the other hand, the class std does conflict, so the use of a bare std:: qualifier is ambiguous. You must use ::std (for the standard library namespace) or stats::std (for the class). References to the local variable must use a plain std.

The name stats on line 24 names a function, so it does not conflict with the namespace stats. Therefore, the use of stats::std on line 32 is not ambiguous.

The accumulate algorithm, called on lines 29 and 31, does exactly what its name suggests. It adds all the elements in a range to a starting value, either by invoking the + operator or by calling a binary functor that takes the sum and a value from the range as arguments.

Remove the global scope operators from ::std::accumulate (lines 29 and 31) to give std::accumulate. Recompile the program. **What messages does your compiler give you?**

_____

_____

_____

Restore the file to its original form. **Remove the first :: qualifier from ::std::vector (line 24). What message does the compiler give you?**

_____

_____

_____

Restore the file to its original form. **Remove the `stats::` qualifier from `stats::std` (line 32). What message does the compiler give you?**

_____

_____

_____

Sane and rational people do not deliberately name a class `std` in a C++ program, but we all make mistakes. (Maybe you have a class that represents a building element in an architectural CAD system, and you accidentally omitted the letter u from `stud`.) By seeing the kinds of messages that the compiler issues when it runs into name conflicts, you can better recognize these errors when you accidentally create a name that conflicts with a name invented by a third-party library or another team working on your project.

Most application programmers don't have to use the global scope prefix, because you can be careful about choosing names that don't conflict. Library authors, on the other hand, never know where their code will be used or what names that code will use. Therefore, cautious library authors often use the global scope prefix.

Global Namespace

Names that you declare outside of all namespaces are _global_. In the past, I used _global_ to mean "outside of any function," but that was before you knew about namespaces. C++ programmers refer to names declared at _namespace scope_, which is our way of saying "outside of any function." Such a name can be declared in a namespace or outside of any explicit namespace.

A program's `main` function must be global, that is, at namespace scope, but not in any namespace. If you define another function named `main` in a namespace, it does not interfere with the global `main`, but it will confuse anyone who reads your program.

The std Namespace

As you know, the standard library uses the `std` namespace. You are not allowed to define any names in the `std` namespace, but you can specialize templates that are defined in `std`, provided at least one template argument is a user-defined type.

The C++ standard library inherits some functions, types, and objects from the C standard library. You can recognize the C-derived headers, because their names begin with an extra letter c; for example, `<cmath>` is the C++ equivalent of the C header `<math.h>`. Some C names, such as `EOF`, do not follow namespace rules. These names are usually written in all capital letters, to warn you that they are special. You don't have to concern yourself with the details; just be aware that you cannot use the scope operator with these names, and the names are always global. When you look up a name in a language reference, these special names are called _macros_.

The C++ standard grants some flexibility in how a library implementation inherits the C standard library. The specific rule is that a C header of the form `<header.h>` (for some C headers, such as `math`) declares its names in the global namespace, and the implementation decides whether the names are also in the `std` namespace. The C header with the form `<cheader>` declares its names in the `std` namespace, and the implementation may also declare them in the global namespace. Regardless of the style you choose, all C standard functions are reserved to the implementation, which means you are not free to use any C standard function name in the global namespace. If you want to use the same name, you must declare it in a different namespace. Some people like `<cstddef>` and `std::size_t`, and others prefer `<stddef.h>` and `size_t`. Pick a style and stick with it.

My recommendation is not to get caught up in which names originate in the C standard library and which are unique to C++. Instead, consider any name in the standard library off-limits. The only exception is when you want to use the same name for the same purpose, but in your own namespace. For example, you may want to overload the abs function to work with rational or fixed objects. Do so in their respective namespaces, alongside all the overloaded operators and other free functions.

■ **Caution** Many C++ references omit the C portions of the standard library. As you can see, however, the C portions are most problematic when it comes to name clashes. Thus, make sure your C++ reference is complete or supplement your incomplete C++ reference with a complete C 18 library reference.

Using Namespaces

In order to use any name, the C++ compiler must be able to find it, which means identifying the scope in which it is declared. The most direct way to use a name from a namespace, such as rational or fixed, is to use a qualified name—that is, the namespace name as a prefix, for example, numeric, followed by the scope operator(::).

```
numeric::rational<long> pi_r{80143857L, 25510582L};
numeric::fixed<long, 6> pi_f{3, 141593};
```

When the compiler sees the namespace name and the double colons (::), it knows to look up the subsequent name in that namespace. There is no chance of a collision with the same entity name in a different namespace.

Sometimes, however, you end up using the namespace a lot, and brevity becomes a virtue. The next two sections describe a few options.

Namespace Alias

If you have deeply nested namespace or long namespace names, you can come up with your own abbreviation, or alias, such as

```
namespace rng = std::ranges;
rng::copy(source, destination);
```

Just be sure to pick an alias that will not conflict with other names. This technique is best used within a scope to keep its effect as limited as possible and to avoid surprises.

The using Directive

You've seen a using directive before, but in case you need a refresher, take a look at this:

```
using namespace std;
```

The syntax is as follows: the `using` keyword, the `namespace` keyword, and a namespace name. A `using` directive instructs the compiler to treat all the names in the namespace as though they were global. (The precise rule is slightly more complicated. However, unless you have a nested hierarchy of namespaces, the simplification is accurate.) You can list multiple `using` directives, but you run the risk of introducing name collisions among the namespaces. A `using` directive affects only the scope in which you place it. Because it can have a big impact on name lookup, restrict `using` directives to the narrowest scope you can; typically this would be an inner block.

Although a `using` directive has its advantages—and I use them in this book—you must be careful. They hinder the key advantage of namespaces: avoidance of name collisions. Names in different namespaces don't ordinarily collide, but if you try to mix namespaces that declare a common name, the compiler will complain.

If you are careless with `using` directives, you can accidentally use a name from the wrong namespace. If you're lucky, the compiler will tell you about your mistake, because your code uses the wrong name in a way that violates language rules. If you aren't lucky, the wrong name will coincidentally have the same syntax, and you won't notice your mistake until much, much later.

Never place a `using` directive in a module interface. That ruins namespaces for everyone who imports your module. Keep `using` directives as local as possible, in the smallest scope possible.

In general, I try to avoid `using` directives. You should get used to reading fully qualified names. On the other hand, sometimes long names interfere with easy comprehension of complicated code. Rarely do I use more than one `using` directive in the same scope. So far, the only time I've ever done so is when all the namespaces are defined by the same library, so I know they work together, and I won't run into naming problems. Listing 56-6 illustrates how `using` directives work.

Listing 56-6. *Examples of using Directives*

```
1 import <iostream>;
2
3 void print(int i)
4 {
5   std::cout << "int: " << i << '\n';
6 }
7
8 namespace labeled
9 {
10   void print(double d)
11   {
12     std::cout << "double: " << d << '\n';
13   }
14 }
15
16 namespace simple
17 {
18   void print(int i)
19   {
20     std::cout << i << '\n';
21   }
22   void print(double d)
23   {
24     std::cout << d << '\n';
25   }
26 }
27
```

```
28 void test_simple()
29 {
30   using namespace simple;
31   print(42);                // ???
32   print(3.14159);           // finds simple::print(double)
33 }
34
35 void test_labeled()
36 {
37   using namespace labeled;
38   print(42);                // find ::print(int)
39   print(3.14159);           // finds labeled::print(double)
40 }
41
42 int main()
43 {
44   test_simple();
45   test_labeled();
46 }
```

What will happen if you try to compile Listing 56-6?

_____

_____

_____

The error is on line 31. The using directive effectively merges the simple namespace with the global namespace. Thus, you now have two functions named print that take a single int argument, and the compiler doesn't know which one you want. Fix the problem by qualifying the call to print(42) (on line 32), so it calls the function in the simple namespace. **What do you expect as the program output?**

_____

_____

_____

_____

Try it. Make sure you get what you expect. Line 31 should now look like this:

```
simple::print(42);
```

The using Declaration

More specific, and therefore less dangerous, than a using directive is a using declaration. A using declaration imports a single name from another namespace into a local scope, as demonstrated here:

```
using numeric::rational;
```

A using declaration adds the name to the local scope as though you had declared it explicitly. Thus, within the scope where you place the using declaration, you can use the declared name without qualification (e.g., rational). Listing 56-7 shows how using declarations help avoid the problems you encountered with *using* directives in Listing 56-6.

Listing 56-7 Examples of using Declarations with Namespaces

```
 1 import <iostream>;
 2
 3 void print(int i)
 4 {
 5   std::cout << "int: " << i << '\n';
 6 }
 7
 8 namespace labeled
 9 {
10   void print(double d)
11   {
12     std::cout << "double: " << d << '\n';
13   }
14 }
15
16 namespace simple
17 {
18   void print(int i)
19   {
20     std::cout << i << '\n';
21   }
22   void print(double d)
23   {
24     std::cout << d << '\n';
25   }
26 }
27
28 void test_simple()
29 {
30   using simple::print;
31   print(42);
32   print(3.14159);
33 }
34
35 void test_labeled()
36 {
37   using labeled::print;
38   print(42);
39   print(3.14159);
40 }
41
42 int main()
43 {
44   test_simple();
45   test_labeled();
46 }
```

Predict the program's output.

_____

_____

_____

_____

This time, the compiler can find `simple::print(int)`, because the `using` declaration injects names into the local scope. Thus, the local names do not conflict with the global `print(int)` function. On the other hand, the compiler does not call `::print(int)` for line 38. Instead, it calls `labeled::print(double)`, converting 42 to 42.0.

Are you puzzled by the compiler's behavior? Let me explain. When the compiler tries to resolve an overloaded function or operator name, it looks for the first scope that declares a matching name. It then collects all overloaded names from that scope, and only from that scope. Finally, it resolves the name by choosing the best match (or reporting an error, if it cannot find exactly one good match). Once the compiler finds a match, it stops looking in other scopes or outer namespaces.

In this case, the compiler sees the call to `print(42)` and looks for the name `print` first in the local scope, where it finds a function named `print` that was imported from the `labeled` namespace. So it stops looking for namespaces and tries to resolve the name `print`. It finds one function, which takes a `double` argument. The compiler knows how to convert an `int` to a `double`, so it deems this function a match and calls it. The compiler never even looks at the global namespace.

How would you instruct the compiler to also consider the global `print` function?

_____

Add a `using` declaration for the global `print` function. Between lines 37 and 38, insert the following:

```
using ::print;
```

When the compiler tries to resolve `print(int)`, it finds `labeled::print(double)` and `::print(int)`, both imported into the local scope. It then resolves the overload by considering both functions. The `print(int)` function is the best match for an `int` argument.

Now add `using simple::print;` at the same location. **What do you expect to happen when you compile this example now?**

_____

Now the compiler has too many choices—and they conflict. A `using` directive doesn't cause this kind of conflict, because it simply changes the namespaces where the compiler looks for a name. A `using` declaration, however, adds a declaration to the local scope. If you add too many declarations, those declarations can conflict, and the compiler would complain.

When a `using` declaration names a template, the template name is brought into the local scope. The compiler keeps track of full and partial specializations of a template. The `using` declaration affects only whether the compiler finds the template at all. Once it finds the template and decides to instantiate it, the compiler will find the proper specialization. That's why you can specialize a template that is defined in the standard library—that is, in the `std` namespace.

A key difference between a `using` directive and a `using` declaration is that a `using` directive does not affect the local scope. A `using` declaration, however, introduces the unqualified name into the local scope. This means you cannot declare your own name in the same scope. Listing 56-8 illustrates the difference.

Listing 56-8. Comparing a using Directive with a using Declaration

```
import <iostream>;

void demonstrate_using_directive()
{
   using namespace std;
   typedef int ostream;
   ostream x{0};
   std::cout << x << '\n';
}

void demonstrate_using_declaration()
{
   using std::ostream;
   typedef int ostream;
   ostream x{0};
   std::cout << x << '\n';
}
```

The local declaration of ostream interferes with the using declaration, but not the using directive. A local scope can have only one object or type with a particular name, and a using declaration adds the name to the local scope, whereas a using directive does not.

The using Declaration in a Class

A using declaration can also import a member of a class. This is different from a namespace using declaration, because you can't just import any old member into any old class, but you can import a name from a base class into a derived class. There are several reasons why you may want to do this. Two immediate reasons are

- The base class declares a function, and the derived class declares a function with the same name, and you want overloading to find both functions. The compiler looks for overloads only in a single class scope. With a using declaration to import the base class function into the derived class scope, overloading can find both functions in the derived class scope and so choose the best match.

- When inheriting privately, you can selectively expose members by placing a using declaration in a public section of the derived class.

Listing 56-9 illustrates using declarations. You will learn more advantages of using declarations as you learn more advanced C++ techniques.

Listing 56-9. Examples of using Declarations with Classes

```
import <iostream>;

class base
{
public:
  void print(int i) { std::cout << "base: " << i << '\n'; }
};
```

```
class derived1 : public base
{
public:
  void print(double d) { std::cout << "derived: " << d << '\n'; }
};

class derived2 : public base
{
public:
  using base::print;
  void print(double d) { std::cout << "derived: " << d << '\n'; }
};

int main()
{
  derived1 d1{};
  derived2 d2{};

  d1.print(42);
  d2.print(42);
}
```

Predict the output from the program.

_____

_____

The class derived1 has a single member function named print. Calling d1.print(42) converts 42 to 42.0 and calls that function. Class derived2 imports print from the base class. Thus, overloading determines the best match for d2.print(42) and calls print in the base class. The output appears as follows:

```
derived: 42
base: 42
```

Name Lookup

In the absence of namespaces, looking up a function or operator name is simple. The compiler looks in the local block first, then in the outer blocks and the inner namespace before the outer namespace, until, finally, the compiler searches global declarations. It stops searching in the first block that contains a matching declaration. If the compiler is looking for a function or operator, the name may be overloaded, so the compiler considers all the matching names that are declared in the same scope, regardless of parameters.

Looking up a member function is slightly different. When the compiler looks up an unqualified name in a class context, it starts by searching in the local block and enclosing blocks, as described earlier. The search continues by considering members of the class, then its base class, and so on for all ancestor classes. Again, when looking up an overloaded name, the compiler considers all the matching names that it finds in the same scope—that is, the same class or block.

443

Namespaces complicate the name lookup rules. Suppose you want to use the rational type, which is defined in the exploring_cpp::numeric namespace. You know how to use a qualified name for the type, but what about, for instance, addition or the I/O operators, such as those in the following:

```
exploring_cpp::numeric::rational<int> r;
std::cout << r + 1 << '\n';
```

The full name of the addition operator is exploring_cpp::numeric::operator+. But normally, you use the addition operator without specifying the namespace. Therefore, the compiler needs some help to determine which namespace contains the operator declaration. The trick is that the compiler checks the types of the operands and looks for the overloaded operator in the namespaces that contain those types. This is known as argument-dependent lookup (ADL).

The compiler collects several sets of scopes to search. It first determines which scopes to search using the ordinary lookup rules, described at the beginning of this section. For each function argument or operator operand, the compiler also collects a set of namespaces based on the argument types. If a type is a class type, the compiler selects the namespace that contains the class declaration and the namespaces that contain all of its ancestor classes. If the type is a specialization of a class template, the compiler selects the namespace that contains the primary template and the namespaces of all the template arguments. The compiler forms the union of all these scopes and then searches them for the function or operator. As you can see, the goal of ADL is to be inclusive. The compiler tries hard to discover which scope declares the operator or function name.

To better understand the importance of ADL, take a look at Listing 56-10.

Listing 56-10. Reading and Writing Tokens

```
import <algorithm>;
import <iostream>;
import <iterator>;
import <string>;
import <vector>;

namespace parser
{
  class token
  {
  public:
    token() : text_{} {}
    token(std::string& s) : text_{s} {}
    token& operator=(std::string const& s) { text_ = s; return *this; }
    std::string text() const { return text_; }
  private:
    std::string text_;
  };
}

std::istream& operator>>(std::istream& in, parser::token& tok)
{
  std::string str{};
  if (in >> str)
    tok = str;
  return in;
}
```

```
std::ostream& operator<<(std::ostream& out, parser::token const& tok)
{
  out << tok.text();
  return out;
}

int main()
{
  using namespace parser;
  using namespace std;

  vector<token> tokens{};
  ranges::copy(ranges::istream_view<token>(std::cin), back_inserter(tokens));
  ranges::copy(tokens, ostream_iterator<token>(cout, "\n"));
}
```

What will happen when you compile the program?

_____

_____

Some compilers, trying to be helpful, fill your console with messages. The core of the problem is that istream_iterator and ostream_iterator invoke the standard input (>>) and output (<<) operators. In the case of Listing 52-10, the compiler locates the operators through ordinary lookup as member functions of the istream and ostream classes. The standard library declares these member function operators for the built-in types, so the compiler cannot find a match for an argument of type parser::token. Because the compiler finds a match in a class scope, it never gets around to searching the global scope, so it never finds the custom I/O operators.

The compiler applies ADL and searches the parser namespace because the second operand to << and >> has type parser::token. It searches the std namespace because the first operand has type std::istream or std::ostream. It cannot find a match for the I/O operators in these namespaces, because the operators are in the global scope.

Now you see why it's vital that you declare all associated operators in the same namespace as the main type. If you don't, the compiler cannot find them. **Move the I/O operators into the parser namespace and see that the program now works.** Compare your program with Listing 56-11.

Listing 56-11. Move the I/O Operators into the parser Namespace

```
import <algorithm>;
import <iostream>;
import <iterator>;
import <string>;
import <string_view>;
import <vector>;

namespace parser
{
  class token
  {
  public:
    token() : text_{} {}
    token(std::string_view s) : text_{s} {}
```

```
    token& operator=(std::string_view s) { text_ = s; return *this; }
    std::string text() const { return text_; }
  private:
    std::string text_;
  };

  std::istream& operator>>(std::istream& in, parser::token& tok)
  {
    std::string str{};
    if (in >> str)
      tok = str;
    return in;
  }

  std::ostream& operator<<(std::ostream& out, parser::token const& tok)
  {
    out << tok.text();
    return out;
  }
}

int main()
{
  using namespace parser;
  using namespace std;

  vector<token> tokens{};
  ranges::copy(ranges::istream_view<token>(std::cin), back_inserter(tokens));
  ranges::copy(tokens, ostream_iterator<token>(cout, "\n"));
}
```

To see how the compiler extends its ADL search, **modify the program to change the container from a vector to a map, and count the number of occurrences of each token.** (Remember Exploration 23?) Because a map stores pair objects, write an output operator that prints pairs of tokens and counts. This means ostream_iterator calls the << operator with two arguments from namespace std. Nonetheless, the compiler finds your operator (in the parser namespace), because the template argument to std::pair is in parser. Your program may end up looking something like Listing 56-12.

Listing 56-12. Counting Occurrences of Tokens

```
import <algorithm>;
import <iostream>;
import <iterator>;
import <map>;
import <string>;
import <string_view>;

namespace parser
{
  class token
  {
```

```
  public:
    token() : text_{} {}
    token(std::string_view s) : text_{s} {}
    token& operator=(std::string_view s) { text_ = s; return *this; }
    std::string text() const { return text_; }
  private:
    std::string text_;
  };

  // To store tokens in a map.
  bool operator<(token const& a, token const& b)
  {
    return a.text() < b.text();
  }

  std::istream& operator>>(std::istream& in, parser::token& tok)
  {
    std::string str{};
    if (in >> str)
      tok = str;
    return in;
  }

  std::ostream& operator<<(std::ostream& out, parser::token const& tok)
  {
    out << tok.text();
    return out;
  }

  std::ostream& operator<<(std::ostream& out,
                           std::pair<const token, long> const& count)
  {
    out << count.first.text() << '\t' << count.second << '\n';
    return out;
  }
}

int main()
{
  using namespace parser;
  using namespace std;

  map<token, long> tokens{};
  token tok{};
  while (cin >> tok)
    ++tokens[tok];
  ranges::copy(tokens,
      ostream_iterator<pair<const token, long>>(cout));
}
```

Now that you know about templates and namespaces, it's time to look at some of their practical uses. The next several Explorations take a closer look at parts of the standard library, beginning with the standard containers.

■ ■ ■

Containers

So far, the only standard containers you've used have been vector and map. I mentioned array in Exploration 9 and list in Exploration 46 but never went into depth. This Exploration introduces the remaining containers and discusses the general nature of containers. When third-party libraries implement additional containers, they usually follow the pattern set by the standard library and make their containers follow the same requirements.

Properties of Containers

The container types implement familiar data structures, such as trees, lists, arrays, and so on. They all serve the common purpose of storing a collection of similar objects in a single container object. You can treat the container as a single entity: compare it, copy it, assign it, and so on. You can also access the individual items in the container. What distinguishes one container type from another is how the container stores the items within it, which in turn affects the speed of accessing and modifying items in the container.

The standard containers fall into two broad categories: sequence and associative. The difference is that you can control the order of items in a sequence container but not in an associative container. As a result, associative containers offer improved performance for accessing and modifying their contents. The standard sequence containers are array (fixed size), deque (double-ended queue), forward_list (singly linked list), list (doubly linked list), and vector (variable-length array). The forward_list type works differently from the other containers (due to the nature of singly linked lists) and is for specialized uses. This book does not cover forward_list, but you can find it in any C++ reference.

The associative containers have two subcategories: ordered and unordered. Ordered containers store keys in a data-dependent order, which is given by the < operator or a caller-supplied functor. Although the standard does not specify any particular implementation, the complexity requirements pretty much dictate that ordered associative containers are implemented as balanced binary trees. Unordered containers store keys in a hash table, so the order is unimportant to your code and is subject to change as you add items to the container.

Another way to divide the associative containers is into sets and maps. Sets are like mathematical sets: they have members and can test for membership. Maps are like sets that store key/value pairs. Sets and maps can require unique keys or permit duplicate keys. The set types are set (unique key, ordered), multiset (duplicate key, ordered), unordered_set, and unordered_multiset. The map types are map, multimap, unordered_map, and unordered_multimap.

Different containers have different characteristics. For example, vector permits rapid access to any item, but insertion in the middle is slow. A list, on the other hand, offers rapid insertion and erasure of any item but provides only bidirectional iterators, not random access.

© Ray Lischner 2020
R. Lischner, *Exploring C++20*, https://doi.org/10.1007/978-1-4842-5961-0_57

The C++ standard defines container characteristics in terms of *complexity*, which is written in big-O notation. Remember from your introductory algorithms course that $O(1)$ is constant complexity, but without any indication of what the constant might be. $O(n)$ is linear complexity: if the container has n items, performing an $O(n)$ operation takes time proportional to n. Operations on sorted data are often logarithmic: $O(\log n)$.

Table 57-1 summarizes all the containers and their characteristics. The Insert, Erase, and Lookup columns show the average-case complexity for these operations, where N is the number of elements in the container. Lookup for a sequence container means looking for an item at a particular index. For an associative container, it means looking for a specific item by value. "No" means the container does not support that operation at all.

Table 57-1. *Summary of Containers and Their Characteristics*

Type	Header	Insert	Erase	Lookup	Iterator
array	`<array>`	No	No	$O(1)$	Contiguous
deque	`<deque>`	$O(N)$*	$O(N)$*	$O(1)$	Random access
forward_list	`<forward_list>`	$O(1)$	$O(1)$	$O(N)$	Forward
list	`<list>`	$O(1)$	$O(1)$	$O(N)$	Bidirectional
map	`<map>`	$O(\log N)$	$O(\log N)$	$O(\log N)$	Bidirectional
multimap	`<map>`	$O(\log N)$	$O(\log N)$	$O(\log N)$	Bidirectional
multiset	`<set>`	$O(\log N)$	$O(\log N)$	$O(\log N)$	Bidirectional
set	`<set>`	$O(\log N)$	$O(\log N)$	$O(\log N)$	Bidirectional
unordered_map	`<unordered_map>`	$O(1)$	$O(1)$	$O(1)$	Forward
unordered_multimap	`<unordered_map>`	$O(1)$	$O(1)$	$O(1)$	Forward
unordered_multiset	`<unordered_set>`	$O(1)$	$O(1)$	$O(1)$	Forward
unordered_set	`<unordered_set>`	$O(1)$	$O(1)$	$O(1)$	Forward
vector	`<vector>`	$O(N)$*	$O(N)$*	$O(1)$	Contiguous

Complexity is $O(N)$ for insertion and erasure in the middle of the container but is $O(1)$ at the end of the container, when amortized over many operations. A deque also allows amortized $O(1)$ insertion and erasure at the beginning of the container.

Member Types

Every container provides a number of useful types and typedefs as members of the container. This section makes frequent use of several of them:

value_type

This is a synonym for the type that the container stores. For example, `value_type` for `vector<double>` is `double` and `std::list<char>::value_type` is `char`. Using a standard member type makes it easier to write and read container code. The rest of this Exploration uses `value_type` extensively.

The mapped containers store key/value pairs, so `value_type` for `map<Key, T>` (and `multimap`, `unordered_map`, and `unordered_multimap`) is `std::pair<const Key, T>`. The key type is `const`, because you cannot change the key after adding an item to an associative container. The internal structure of the container depends on the keys, so changing the keys would violate the ordering constraints.

key_type

The associative containers declare `key_type` as a typedef for the first template parameter—for example, `map<int, double>::key_type` is `int`. For the set types, `key_type` and `value_type` are the same.

reference

This is a synonym for a reference to `value_type`. Except in very rare cases, `reference` is identical to `value_type&`.

const_reference

`const_reference` is a synonym for a reference to `const value_type`. Except in very rare cases, `const_reference` is identical to `value_type const&`.

iterator

This is the iterator type. It might be a typedef, but more likely, it is a class, the definition of which is implementation-dependent. All that matters is that this type meets the requirements of an iterator. Each container type implements a specific category of iterator, as described in Table 57-1.

const_iterator

`const_iterator` is the iterator type for `const` items. It might be a typedef, but more likely, it is a class, the definition of which is implementation-dependent. All that matters is that this type meets the requirements of an iterator of `const` items. Each container type implements a specific category of iterator, as described in Table 57-1.

size_type

`size_type` is a typedef for one of the built-in integer types (which one depends on the implementation). It represents an index for a sequence container or a container size.

What Can Go into a Container

In order to store an item in a container, the item's type must meet some basic requirements. You must be able to copy or move the item and assign it using copy or move. For the built-in types, this is automatic. For a class type, you usually have that capability. The compiler even writes the constructors and assignment operators for you. So far, all the classes in this book meet the basic requirements; you won't have to concern yourself with non-conforming classes until Exploration 63.

Sequence containers themselves do not have to compare items for equality; they just copy or move elements as required. When they have to make copies, they assume that copies are identical to the original.

Ordered associative containers require an ordering functor. By default, they use a standard functor called std::less<key_type>, which in turn uses the < operator. You can supply a custom functor, provided it implements *strict weak ordering*, which is defined by the following requirements:

- If *a* < *b* and *b* < *c*, then *a* < *c*.

- *a* < *a* is always false.

- The order does not change after an item is stored in a container.

A common error among new C++ programmers is to violate rule 2, typically by implementing <= instead of <. Violations of the strict weak ordering rule result in undefined behavior. Some libraries have a debugging mode that checks your functor to ensure that it is valid. If your library has such a mode, use it.

Unordered associative containers need a hash functor and an equality functor. The default hash functor is std::hash<key_type> (declared in <functional>). The standard library provides specializations for the built-in types and string. If you store a custom class in an unordered container, you have to provide your own hash functor. The simplest way to do that is to specialize hash. Listing 57-1 shows how to specialize hash for the rational type. You have to provide only the function call operator, which must return type std::size_t (an implementation-defined integer type).

Listing 57-1. Specializing the hash Template for the rational Type

```
import <functional>;
import rational;
namespace std {

template<class T>
class hash<rational<T>>
{
public:
  std::size_t operator()(rational<T> const& r)
  const
  {
    return hasher_(r.numerator() * r.denominator());
  }
private:
  std::hash<T> hasher_;
};
} // end of std
```

Although the standard library provides a std::hash<> specialization for all built-in types, it does not provide any effective way to combine multiple hash values. The method shown in Listing 57-1 does not give good results. (One-half and two share the same hash value, for example.) But writing effective hash functions is not in the scope of this book; visit the book's website for information on writing better hash functions.

The default equality functor is std::equal_to<T> (declared in <functional>), which uses the == operator. If two items are equal, their hash values must also be equal (but the reverse is not necessarily true).

When you insert an item in a container, the container keeps a copy of the item, or you can move an object into a container. When you erase an item, the container destroys the item. When you destroy a container, it destroys all of its elements. The next section discusses insertion and erasure at greater length.

Inserting and Erasing

I've presented a number of examples of inserting and erasing elements in vectors and maps. This section explores this topic in greater depth. Except for array and forward_list, the container types follow some basic patterns. The array type has a fixed size, so it provides none of the insertion or erasure functions. And forward_list has its own way of doing things, because a singly linked list cannot insert or erase items directly. All the other containers follow the specification described in this section.

Inserting in a Sequence Container

You have a choice of several member functions with which to insert an item into a sequence container. The most fundamental function is emplace, which constructs an item in place in the container. It has the following form:

iterator emplace(const_iterator here, args...)

Inserts a newly constructed item into the collection immediately before the position here and returns an iterator that refers to the newly added item. The args can be zero or more arguments that are passed to the value_type constructor. If here is end(), the item is constructed at the end of the container.

reference emplace_back(args...)

Appends a newly constructed item to the collection and returns a reference to the constructed item. The args can be zero or more arguments that are passed to the value_type constructor. Containers that allow fast insertion to the front of the container (deque, list) also have emplace_front().

If you have objects that are already constructed, call insert, which has four overloaded forms:

iterator insert(const_iterator here, value_type item)

Inserts item by copying or moving it into the collection immediately before the position here and returns an iterator that refers to the newly added item. If here is end(), item is appended to the end of the container.

iterator insert(const_iterator here, size_type n, value_type const& item)

Inserts n copies of item immediately before the position to which here refers. If here is end(), the items are appended to the end of the container. Returns an iterator to the first item inserted.

iterator insert(const_iterator here, std::initializer_list<value_type> brace_enclosed_list)

An initializer list is a list of values in curly braces. The compiler constructs a range of values, and this function copies those values into the container, starting at the position immediately before here. Returns an iterator to the first item inserted.

template<class InputIterator>
iterator insert(const_iterator here, InputIterator first, InputIterator last)

Copies the values from the range [first, last) into the container, starting at the position immediately before here. Returns an iterator to the first item inserted.

453

Erasing from a Sequence Container

The erase function erases, or deletes, items from a container. Sequence containers implement two forms of erase:

iterator erase(const_iterator pos)

Erases the item to which pos refers and returns an iterator that refers to the subsequent item. Returns end() if the last item is erased. The behavior is undefined if you try to erase end() or if pos is an iterator for a different container object.

iterator erase(const_iterator first, const_iterator last)

Erases all the items in the range [first, last) and returns an iterator that refers to the item that immediately followed the last item erased. Returns end() if the last item in the container is erased. The behavior is undefined if the iterators are in the wrong order or refer to a different container object.

The clear() function erases all elements from the container. In addition to the basic erasure functions, sequence containers also provide pop_front to erase the first element and pop_back to erase the last element of a collection. A container implements these two functions only if it can do so with constant complexity. **Which sequence containers implement pop_back?**

_____

Which sequence containers implement pop_front?

_____

As with the emplacement functions, vector provides pop_back, and list and deque provide both pop_back and pop_front.

Inserting in an Associative Container

All the insertion functions for associative containers follow a common pattern for return types. The duplicate-key containers (multimap, multiset, unordered_multimap, unordered_multiset) return an iterator for the newly added item. The unique-key containers (map, set, unordered_map, unordered_set) return a pair<iterator, bool>: the iterator refers to the item in the container, and the bool is true if the item was added or false if the item was already present. In this section, the return type is shown as _return_. If the item was already present, the existing item is untouched, and the new item is ignored.

Construct a new item in an associative container by calling one of the two emplace functions:

return emplace(args...)

Constructs a new element at the correct position in the container, passing args to the value_type constructor.

iterator emplace_hint(iterator hint, args...)

Constructs a new element as close to hint as possible, passing args to the value_type constructor.

For an ordered container, if the item's position is immediately after hint, the item is added with constant complexity. Otherwise, the complexity is logarithmic. If you have to store many items in an ordered container, and the items are already in order, you can save some time by using the position of the most recently inserted item as the hint.

As with sequence containers, you can also call the `insert` function to insert into an associative container. One key difference from the sequence containers is that you don't have to provide a position (one form does let you provide a position as a hint).

> **return insert(value_type item)**

Moves or copies `item` into the container.

> **iterator insert(const_iterator hint, value_type item)**

Moves or copies `item` into the container as close to `hint` as possible, as described earlier with `emplace_hint`.

> **template<class InputIterator>**
> **void insert(InputIterator first, InputIterator last)**

Copies the values from the range [`first`, `last`) into the container. For the ordered containers, you get optimal performance if the range [`first`, `last`) is already sorted. Again, there is no range form of insert.

Write a program that reads a list of strings from the standard input into a set of strings. Use the `emplace_hint` function. Save the return value to pass as the hint when inserting the next item. Find a large list of strings to use as input. Make two copies of the list, one in sorted order and one in random order. (See this book's website if you need help locating or preparing the input files.) **Compare the performance of your program reading the two input files.**

Write another version of the same program, this time using the simple, one-argument `emplace` function. Again, run the program with both input files. Compare the performance of all four variations: hinted and unhinted insert, sorted and unsorted input.

Listing 57-2 shows a simple form of the program that uses `emplace_hint`.

Listing 57-2. Using a Hint Position when Inserting into a Set

```
import <iostream>;
import <set>;
import <string>;

int main()
{
  std::set<std::string> words{};

  std::set<std::string>::iterator hint{words.begin()};
  std::string word{};
  while(std::cin >> word)
    hint = words.emplace_hint(hint, std::move(word));

  std::cout << "stored " << words.size() << " unique words\n";
}
```

When I run the program with a file of more than 200,000 words, the hinted program with sorted input executes in about 1.6 seconds. The unhinted form takes 2.2 seconds. With randomly ordered inputs, both programs run in about 2.3 seconds. As you can see, the hint can make a difference when the input is already sorted. The details depend on the library implementation; your mileage may vary.

The node-based containers (set, map, list, multiset, and multimap) allow you to extract nodes from one container and add them to another. Refer to a language reference for details about these advanced capabilities.

Erasing from an Associative Container

The erase function erases, or deletes, items from a container. Associative containers implement three forms of erase:

iterator erase(const_iterator pos)

Erases the item to which pos refers; complexity is constant, possibly amortized over many calls. Returns an iterator that refers to the successor value (or end()). The behavior is undefined if pos is not a valid iterator for the container.

iterator erase(const_iterator first, const_iterator last)

Erases all the items in the range [first, last). Returns an iterator that refers to the item that follows the last item erased. Returns end() if the last item in the container is erased. The behavior is undefined if [first, last) is not a valid iterator range for the container.

iterator erase(value_type const& value)

Erases all occurrences of value from the container. Returns the number of items erased, which can be zero.

As with sequence containers, clear() erases all elements of the container.

Exceptions

The containers do their best to keep order if an exception is thrown. Exceptions have two potential sources: the container itself and the items in the containers. Most member functions do not throw exceptions for invalid arguments, so the most common source of exceptions from the container itself is std::bad_alloc if the container runs out of memory and cannot insert a new item.

If you try to insert a single item into a container, and the operation fails (perhaps because the item's copy constructor throws an exception, or the container ran out of memory), the container is unchanged.

If you try to insert multiple items, and one of those items throws an exception while it is being inserted into a container (e.g., the item's copy constructor throws an exception), most containers do not roll back the change. Only the list and forward_list types roll back to their original state. The other containers leave the container in a valid state, and the items that have been inserted successfully remain in the container.

When erasing one or many items, the containers do not throw exceptions themselves, but they may have to move (or in the case of ordered containers, compare) items; if an item's move constructor throws an exception (a highly unlikely event), the erasure may be incomplete. No matter what, however, the container remains in a valid state.

In order for these guarantees to remain valid, destructors must not throw exceptions.

■ **Tip** Never throw an exception from a destructor.

Iterators and References

When using containers, one important point that I have not yet covered is the validity of iterators and references. The issue is that when you insert or erase items in a container, some or all iterators for that container can become invalid, and references to items in the container can become invalid. The details of which iterators and references become invalid and under what circumstances depend on the container.

Iterators and references becoming invalid reflect the internal structure of the container. For example, vector stores its elements in a single, contiguous chunk of memory. Therefore, inserting or erasing any elements shifts all the elements at higher indices, which invalidates all iterators and references to those elements at higher indices. As a vector grows, it may have to allocate a new internal array, which invalidates all extant iterators and references for that vector. You never know when that can occur, so it is safest never to hold onto a vector's iterators or references while adding items to the vector. (But look up the reserve member function in a library reference, if you must keep those iterators and references lying around.)

A list, on the other hand, implements a doubly linked list. Inserting or erasing an element is simply a matter of inserting or deleting a node, which has no effect on iterators and references to other nodes. For all containers, if you erase a node that an iterator refers to, that iterator necessarily becomes invalid, just as a reference to the erased element must become invalid.

In practical terms, you must take care when inserting and erasing elements. These functions often return iterators that you can use to help maintain your program's logic. Listing 57-3 shows a function template, erase_unsorted, which marches through a container and calls erase for any element that is greater than the value that precedes it. It is a function template, and it works with any class that meets the requirements of a sequence container.

Listing 57-3. Erasing Elements from a Sequence Container

```
template<class Container>
void erase_unsorted(Container& cont)
{
  auto prev{cont.end()};
  auto next{cont.begin()};
  while (next != cont.end())
  {
    // invariant: std::is_sorted(cont.begin(), prev);
    if (prev != cont.end() and *next < *prev)
      next = cont.erase(next);
    else
    {
      prev = next;
      ++next;
    }
  }
}
```

Notice how erase_less moves the iterator, iter, through the container. The prev iterator refers to the previous item (or container.end(), when the loop first begins and there is no previous item). As long as *prev is less than *iter, the loop advances by setting prev to iter and incrementing iter. If the container is in ascending order, nothing happens to it. If an item is out of place, however, *prev < *iter is false, and the item at position iter is erased. The value that erase returns is an iterator that refers to the item that follows iter prior to its erasure. That's exactly where we want iter to point, so we just set iter to the return value and let the loop continue.

Write a test program to see that erase_unsorted works with a list and with a vector. Make sure it works with ascending data, descending data, and mixed data. Listing 57-4 shows my simple test program.

Listing 57-4. Testing the erase_unsorted Function Template

```
import <algorithm>;
import <iostream>;
import <initializer_list>;
import <iterator>;
import <ranges>;
import <vector>;

import erase_unsorted; // Listing 57-3

/// Print items from a container to the standard output.
template<class Container>
requires std::ranges::range<Container>
void print(std::string const& label, Container const& container)
{
  std::cout << label;
  using value_type = std::ranges::range_value_t<Container>;
  std::ranges::copy(container,
      std::ostream_iterator<value_type>(std::cout, " "));
  std::cout << '\n';
}

/// Test erase_unsorted by extracting integers from a string into a container
/// and calling erase_unsorted. Print the container before and after.
/// Double-check that the same results obtain with a list and a vector.
void test(std::initializer_list<int> numbers)
{
  std::vector<int> data{numbers};
  erase_unsorted(data);
  if (not std::is_sorted(data.begin(), data.end()))
      print("FAILED", data);
}

int main()
{
  test({2, 3, 7, 11, 13, 17, 23, 29, 31, 37});
  test({37, 31, 29, 23, 17, 13, 11, 7, 3, 2});
  test({});
  test({42});
  test({10, 30, 20, 40, 0, 50});
}
```

The net effect of the erase_unsorted function is to leave the container in sorted order. So the test() function calls std::is_sorted to verify that the function is indeed sorted. If not, it prints a message and the list of numbers for debugging. The tests include number sequences that are already in order (including one-element and empty sequences), in reverse order, and in mixed order.

Sequence Containers

In this book, the most common use of a container has been to add items to the end of vector. A program might then use standard algorithms to change the order, such as sorting into ascending order, shuffling into random order, and so on. In addition to vector, the other sequence containers are array, deque, and list.

The primary distinguishing feature of the sequence containers is their complexity characteristics. If you often have to insert and erase from the middle of the sequence, you probably want list. If you have to insert and erase only off one end, use vector. If the container's size is a fixed, compile-time constant, use array. If the elements of the sequence must be stored contiguously (in a single block of memory), use array or vector.

The following sections include some more details about each container type. Each section presents the same program for comparison. The program constructs a deck of playing cards, then randomly selects a card for itself and a card for you. The card with the highest value wins. The program plays ten times, then exits. The program plays without replacement—that is, it does not return used cards to the deck after each game. In order to pick a random card, the programs use the randomint class, from Listing 45-5. Save the class definition in a file named randomint.hpp or download the file from the book's website. Listing 57-5 shows the card class, which the sample programs use. For the full class definition, download card.hpp from the book's website.

Listing 57-5. The card Class, to Represent a Playing Card

```
export module cards;
import <iosfwd>;

/// Represent a standard western playing card.
export class card
{
public:
  using suit = char;
  static constexpr suit const spades   {4};
  static constexpr suit const hearts   {3};
  static constexpr suit const clubs    {2};
  static constexpr suit const diamonds {1};

  using rank = char;
  static constexpr rank const ace   {14};
  static constexpr rank const king  {13};
  static constexpr rank const queen {12};
  static constexpr rank const jack  {11};

  constexpr card() : rank_{0}, suit_{0} {}
  constexpr card(rank r, suit s) : rank_{r}, suit_{s} {}

  constexpr void assign(rank r, suit s);
  constexpr suit get_suit() const { return suit_; }
  constexpr rank get_rank() const { return rank_; }
private:
  rank rank_;
  suit suit_;
};
```

```
export bool operator==(card a, card b);
export bool operator!=(card a, card b);
export std::ostream& operator<<(std::ostream& out, card c);
export std::istream& operator>>(std::istream& in, card& c);

/// In some games, Aces are high. In other Aces are low. Use different
/// comparison functors depending on the game.
export bool acehigh_less(card a, card b);
export bool acelow_less(card a, card b);

/// Generate successive playing cards, in a well-defined order,
/// namely, 2-10, J, Q, K, A. Diamonds first, then Clubs, Hearts, and Spades.
/// Roll-over and start at the beginning again after generating 52 cards.
export class card_generator
{
public:
  card_generator();
  card operator()();
private:
  card card_;
};
```

The array Class Template

The array type is a fixed-size container, so you cannot call insert or erase. To use array, specify a base type and a size as a compile-time constant expression, as shown here:

```
std::array<double, 5> five_elements;
```

If you initialize an array with fewer values than the array size, remaining values are initialized to zero. If you omit the initializer altogether, the compiler calls the default initializer if the value type is a class type; otherwise, it leaves the array elements uninitialized. Because an array cannot change size, you can't simply erase the cards after playing. In order to keep the code simple, the program returns cards to the deck after each game. Listing 57-6 shows the high-card program with replacement.

Listing 57-6. Playing High-Card with array

```
import <algorithm>;
import <array>;
import <iostream>;

import card;
import randomint; // Listing 45-5

int main()
{
  std::array<card, 52> deck;
  std::ranges::generate(deck, card_generator{});
```

```
  randomint picker{0, deck.size() - 1};
  for (int i{0}; i != 10; ++i)
  {
    card const& computer_card{deck.at(picker())};
    std::cout << "I picked " << computer_card << '\n';

    card const& user_card{deck.at(picker())};
    std::cout << "You picked " << user_card << '\n';

    if (acehigh_less(computer_card, user_card))
      std::cout << "You win.\n";
    else
      std::cout << "I win.\n";
  }
}
```

The deque Class Template

A deque (pronounced "deck") represents a double-ended queue. Insertion and erasure from the beginning or the end is fast, but the complexity is linear, if you have to insert or erase anywhere else. Most of the time, you can use deque the same way you would use a vector, so **apply your experience with vector to write the high-card program.** Play without replacement: that is, after each game, discard the two cards by erasing them from the container. Listing 57-7 shows how I wrote the high-card program using a deque.

Listing 57-7. Playing High-Card with a deque

```
import <algorithm>;
import <deque>;
import <iostream>;

import card;
import randomint;

int main()
{
  std::deque<card> deck(52);
  std::ranges::generate(deck, card_generator{});

  for (int i{0}; i != 10; ++i)
  {
    auto pick{deck.begin() + randomint{0, deck.size()-1}()};
    card computer_card{*pick};
    deck.erase(pick);

    std::cout << "I picked " << computer_card << '\n';

    pick = deck.begin() + randomint{0, deck.size() - 1}();
    card user_card{*pick};
    deck.erase(pick);

    std::cout << "You picked " << user_card << '\n';
```

```
    if (acehigh_less(computer_card, user_card))
      std::cout << "You win.\n";
    else
      std::cout << "I win.\n";
  }
}
```

The list Class Template

A list represents a doubly linked list. Insertion and erasure is fast at any point in the list, but random access is not supported. Thus, the high-card program uses iterators and the advance function (Exploration 46). **Write the high-card program to use list.** Compare your solution with that of mine in Listing 57-8.

Listing 57-8. Playing High-Card with a list

```
import <algorithm>;
import <iostream>;
import <list>;

import card;
import randomint;

int main()
{
  std::list<card> deck(52);
  std::ranges::generate(deck, card_generator{});

  for (int i{0}; i != 10; ++i)
  {
    auto pick{deck.begin()};
    std::advance(pick, randomint{0, deck.size() - 1}());
    card computer_card{*pick};
    deck.erase(pick);

    std::cout << "I picked " << computer_card << '\n';

    pick = std::next(deck.begin(), randomint{0, deck.size() - 1}());
    card user_card{*pick};
    deck.erase(pick);

    std::cout << "You picked " << user_card << '\n';

    if (acehigh_less(computer_card, user_card))
      std::cout << "You win.\n";
    else
      std::cout << "I win.\n";
  }
}
```

The deque type supports random access iterators, so it could add an integer to begin() to pick a card. But list uses bidirectional iterators, so it must call advance() or next(); Listing 57-8 demonstrates both. Note that you can call advance() or next() for deques, too, and the implementation would still use addition.

The vector Class Template

A vector is an array that can change size at runtime. Appending to the end or erasing from the end is fast, but complexity is linear when inserting or erasing anywhere else in the vector. **Compare deque and list versions of the high-card program. Pick the one you prefer and modify it to work with vector.** My version of the program is displayed in Listing 57-9.

Listing 57-9. Playing High-Card with vector

```
import <algorithm>;
import <iostream>;
import <vector>;

import card;
import randomint;

int main()
{
  std::vector<card> deck(52);
  std::ranges::generate(deck, card_generator{});

  for (int i{0}; i != 10; ++i)
  {
    auto pick{deck.begin() + randomint{0, deck.size()-1}()};
    card computer_card{*pick};
    deck.erase(pick);

    std::cout << "I picked " << computer_card << '\n';

    pick = deck.begin() + randomint{0, deck.size() - 1}();
    card user_card{*pick};
    deck.erase(pick);

    std::cout << "You picked " << user_card << '\n';

    if (acehigh_less(computer_card, user_card))
      std::cout << "You win.\n";
    else
      std::cout << "I win.\n";
  }
}
```

Notice how you can change the program to use vector instead of deque, just by changing the type names. Their usage is quite similar. One key difference is that deque offers fast (constant complexity) insertion at the beginning of the container, something that vector lacks. The other key difference is that vector supports contiguous iterators, and deque uses random access iterators. Neither of these factors matters here.

Associative Containers

The associative containers offer rapid insertion, deletion, and lookup, by controlling the order of elements in the container. The ordered associative containers store elements in a tree, ordered by a comparison functor (default is std::less, which uses <), so insertion, erasure, and lookup occur with logarithmic complexity. The unordered containers use hash tables (according to a caller-supplied hash functor and equality functor) for access with constant complexity in the average case, but with a linear worst-case complexity. Consult any textbook on data structures and algorithms for more information regarding trees and hash tables.

Sets store keys, and maps store key/value pairs. Multisets and multimaps allow duplicate keys. All equivalent keys are stored at adjacent locations in the container. Plain sets and maps require unique keys. If you try to insert a key that is already in the container, the new key is not inserted. Remember that equivalence in an ordered container is determined solely by calling the comparison functor: compare(a, b) is false, and compare(b, a) is false means a and b are equivalent.

Unordered containers call their equality functor to determine whether a key is a duplicate. The default is std::equal_to (declared in <functional>), which uses the == operator.

Because associative arrays store keys in an order that depends on the keys' contents, you cannot modify the contents of a key that is stored in an associative container. This means you cannot use an associative container's iterators as output iterators. Thus, if you want to implement the high-card program using an associative container, you can use the inserter function to create an output iterator that fills the container. Listing 57-10 shows how to use set to implement the high-card program.

Listing 57-10. Playing High-Card with set

```
import <algorithm>;
import <iostream>;
import <iterator>;
import <set>;
import <utility>;

import card;
import randomint;

int main()
{
  using cardset = std::set<card, std::function<bool(card, card)>>;
  cardset deck(acehigh_less);
  std::generate_n(std::inserter(deck, deck.begin()), 52, card_generator{});

  for (int i{0}; i != 10; ++i)
  {
    auto pick{deck.begin()};
    std::advance(pick, randomint{0, deck.size() - 1}());
    card computer_card{*pick};
    deck.erase(pick);

    std::cout << "I picked " << computer_card << '\n';

    pick = deck.begin();
    std::advance(pick, randomint{0, deck.size() - 1}());
    card user_card{*pick};
    deck.erase(pick);

    std::cout << "You picked " << user_card << '\n';
```

```
    if (acehigh_less(computer_card, user_card))
      std::cout << "You win.\n";
    else
      std::cout << "I win.\n";
  }
}
```

When using associative containers, you may experience some difficulty when you use a custom compare functor (for ordered containers) or custom equality and hash functors (for unordered containers). You must specify the functor type as a template argument. When you construct a container object, pass a functor as an argument to the constructor. The functor must be an instance of the type that you specified in the template specialization.

For example, Listing 57-10 uses the acehigh_less function, which it passes to the constructor for deck. Because acehigh_less is a function, you must specify a function type as the template argument. The easiest way to declare a function type is with the std::function template. The template argument looks somewhat like a nameless function header—supply the return type and parameter types:

```
std::function<bool(card, card)>
```

Another approach is to specialize the std::less class template for type card. The explicit specialization would implement the function call operator to call acehigh_less. Taking advantage of the specialization, you could use the default template argument and constructor arguments. Follow the pattern of functors in the <functional> header. The functor should provide a function call operator that uses the argument and return types and implements the strict weak ordering function for your container. Listing 57-11 demonstrates yet another version of the high-card program, this time using a specialization of less. The only real difference is how the deck is initialized.

Listing 57-11. Playing High-Card Using an Explicit Specialization of std::less

```
import <algorithm>;
import <functional>;
import <iostream>;
import <iterator>;
import <set>;

import card;
import randomint;

namespace std
{
  template<>
  class less<card>
  {
  public:
    bool operator()(card a, card b) const { return acehigh_less(a, b); }
  };
}

int main()
{
  using cardset = std::set<card>;
  cardset deck{};
  std::generate_n(std::inserter(deck, deck.begin()), 52, card_generator{});
```

```
for (int i{0}; i != 10; ++i)
{
    auto pick{deck.begin()};
    std::advance(pick, randomint{0, deck.size() - 1}());
    card computer_card{*pick};
    deck.erase(pick);

    std::cout << "I picked " << computer_card << '\n';

    pick = deck.begin();
    std::advance(pick, randomint{0, deck.size() - 1}());
    card user_card{*pick};
    deck.erase(pick);

    std::cout << "You picked " << user_card << '\n';

    if (acehigh_less(computer_card, user_card))
        std::cout << "You win.\n";
    else
        std::cout << "I win.\n";
}
}
```

To use an unordered container, you must write an explicit specialization of std::hash<card>. Listing 57-1 should be able to help. The *card* module already declares operator== for card, so you should be ready to **rewrite the high-card program one last time, this time for unordered_set.** Compare your solution with Listing 57-12. All these programs are remarkably similar, in spite of the different container types, a feat made possible through the judicious use of iterators, algorithms, and functors.

Listing 57-12. Playing High-Card with unordered_set

```
import <algorithm>;
import <functional>;
import <iostream>;
import <iterator>;
import <unordered_set>;

import card;
import randomint;

namespace std
{
    template<>
    class hash<card>
    {
    public:
        std::size_t operator()(card a)
        const
```

```
    {
      return hash<int>{}(a.get_suit() * 64 + a.get_rank());
    }
  };
} // namespace std

int main()
{
  using cardset = std::unordered_set<card>;
  cardset deck{};
  std::generate_n(std::inserter(deck, deck.begin()), 52, card_generator{});

  for (int i(0); i != 10; ++i)
  {
    auto pick{deck.begin()};
    std::advance(pick, randomint{0, deck.size() - 1}());
    card computer_card{*pick};
    deck.erase(pick);

    std::cout << "I picked " << computer_card << '\n';

    pick = deck.begin();
    std::advance(pick, randomint{0, deck.size() - 1}());
    card user_card{*pick};
    deck.erase(pick);

    std::cout << "You picked " << user_card << '\n';

    if (acehigh_less(computer_card, user_card))
      std::cout << "You win.\n";
    else
      std::cout << "I win.\n";
  }
}
```

In the next Exploration, you will embark on a completely different journey, one involving world travels to exotic locations, where natives speak exotic languages and use exotic character sets. The journey also touches on new and interesting uses for templates.

EXPLORATION 58

■ ■ ■

Locales and Facets

As you saw in Exploration 18, C++ offers a complicated system to support internationalization and localization of your code. Even if you don't intend to ship translations of your program in a multitude of languages, you must understand the locale mechanism that C++ uses. Indeed, you have been using it all along, because C++ always sends formatted I/O through the locale system. This Exploration will help you understand locales better and make more effective use of them in your programs.

The Problem

The story of the Tower of Babel resonates with programmers. Imagine a world that speaks a single language and uses a single alphabet. How much simpler programming would be if we didn't have to deal with character-set issues, language rules, or locales.

The real world has many languages, numerous alphabets and syllabaries, and multitudinous character sets, all making life far richer and more interesting and making a programmer's job more difficult. Somehow, we programmers must cope. It isn't easy, and this Exploration cannot give you all the answers, but it's a start.

Different cultures, languages, and character sets give rise to different methods to present and interpret information, different interpretations of character codes (as you learned in Exploration 18), and different ways of organizing (especially sorting) information. Even with numeric data, you may find that you have to write the same number in several ways, depending on the local environment, culture, and language. Table 58-1 presents just a few examples of the ways to write a number according to various cultures, conventions, and locales.

Table 58-1. *Various Ways to Write a Number*

Number	Culture
123456.7890	Default C++
123,456.7890	United States
123 456.7890	International scientific
Rs. 1,23,456.7890	Indian currency*
123.456,7890	Germany

Yes, the commas are correct.

Other cultural differences can include

- 12-hour *vs.* 24-hour clock

- Time zones

- Daylight saving time practices

- How accented characters are sorted relative to non-accented characters (does 'a' come before or after 'á'?)

- Date formats: month/day/year, day/month/year, or year-month-day

- Formatting of currency (¥123,456 or 99¢)

Somehow, the poor application programmer must figure out exactly what is culturally dependent, collect the information for all the possible cultures where the application might run, and use that information appropriately in the application. Fortunately, the hard work has already been done for you and is part of the C++ standard library.

Locales to the Rescue

C++ uses a system called *locales* to manage this disparity of styles. Exploration 18 introduced locales as a means to organize character sets and their properties. Locales also organize formatting of numbers, currency, dates, and times (plus some more stuff that I won't get into).

C++ defines a basic locale, known as the *classic* locale, which provides minimal formatting. Each C++ implementation is then free to provide additional locales. Each locale typically has a name, but the C++ standard does not mandate any particular naming convention, which makes it difficult to write portable code. You can rely on only two standard names:

- The *classic* locale is named "C". The classic locale specifies the same basic formatting information for all implementations. When a program starts, the classic locale is the initial locale.

- An empty string ("") means the *default*, or native, locale. The default locale obtains formatting and other information from the host operating system in a manner that depends on what the OS can offer. With traditional desktop operating systems, you can assume that the default locale specifies the user's preferred formatting rules and character-set information. With other environments, such as embedded systems, the default locale may be identical to the classic locale.

A number of C++ implementations use ISO and POSIX standards for naming locales: an ISO 639 code for the language (e.g., fr for French, en for English, ko for Korean), optionally followed by an underscore and an ISO 3166 code for the region (e.g., CH for Switzerland, GB for Great Britain, HK for Hong Kong). The name is optionally followed by a dot and the name of the character set (e.g., utf8 for Unicode UTF-8, Big5 for Chinese Big 5 encoding). Thus, I use en_US.utf8 for my default locale. A native of Taiwan might use zh_TW.Big5; developers in French-speaking Switzerland might use fr_CH.latin1. Read your library documentation to learn how it specifies locale names. **What is your default locale? _____ What are its main characteristics?**

_____

_____

_____

Every C++ application has a global `locale` object. Unless you explicitly change a stream's locale, it starts off with the global locale. (If you later change the global locale, that does not affect streams that already exist, such as the standard I/O streams.) Initially, the global locale is the classic locale. The classic locale is the same everywhere (except for the parts that depend on the character set), so a program has maximum portability with the classic locale. On the other hand, it has minimum local flavor. The next section explores how you can change a stream's locale.

Locales and I/O

Recall from Exploration 18 that you *imbue* a stream with a locale in order to format I/O according to the locale's rules. Thus, to ensure that you read input in the classic locale and that you print results in the user's native locale, you need the following:

```
std::cin.imbue(std::locale::classic()); // standard input uses the classic locale
std::cout.imbue(std::locale{""});        // imbue with the user's default locale
```

The standard I/O streams initially use the classic locale. You can imbue a stream with a new locale at any time, but it makes the most sense to do so before performing any I/O.

Typically, you would use the classic locale when reading from, or writing to, files. You usually want the contents of files to be portable and not dependent on a user's OS preferences. For ephemeral output to a console or GUI window, you may want to use the default locale, so the user can be most comfortable reading and understanding it. On the other hand, if there is any chance that another program might try to read your program's output (as happens with UNIX pipes and filters), you should stick with the classic locale, in order to ensure portability and a common format. If you are preparing output to be displayed in a GUI, by all means, use the default locale.

Facets

The way a stream interprets numeric input and formats numeric output is by making requests of the imbued locale. A `locale` object is a collection of pieces, each of which manages a small aspect of internationalization. For example, one piece, called numpunct, provides the punctuation symbols for numeric formatting, such as the decimal point character (which is `'.'` in the United States, but `','` in France). Another piece, num_get, reads from a stream and parses the text to form a number, using information it obtains from numpunct. The pieces such as num_get and numpunct are called *facets*.

For ordinary numeric I/O, you never have to deal with facets. The I/O streams automatically manage these details for you: the operator<< function uses the num_put facet to format numbers for output, and operator>> uses num_get to interpret text as numeric input. For currency, dates, and times, I/O manipulators use facets to format values. But sometimes you need to use facets yourself. The isalpha, toupper, and other character-related functions about which you learned in Exploration 18 use the ctype facet. Any program that has to do a lot of character testing and converting can benefit by managing its facets directly.

Like strings and I/O streams, facets are class templates, parameterized on the character type. So far, the only character type you have used is char; you will learn about other character types in Exploration 59. The principles are the same, regardless of character type (which is why facets use templates).

To obtain a facet from a locale, call the use_facet function template. The template argument is the facet you seek, and the function argument is the `locale` object. The returned facet is const and is not copyable, so the best way to use the result is to initialize a const reference, as demonstrated here:

```
auto const& mget{ std::use_facet<std::money_get<char>>(std::locale{""}) };
```

471

Reading from the inside outward, the object named mget is initialized to the result of calling the use_facet function, which is requesting a reference to the money_get<char> facet. The default locale is passed as the sole argument to the use_facet function. The type of mget is a reference to a const money_get<char> facet. It's a little daunting to read at first, but you'll get used to it—eventually.

Using facets directly can be complicated. Fortunately, the standard library offers a few I/O manipulators (declared in <iomanip>) to simplify the use of the time and currency facets. Listing 58-1 shows a simple program that imbues the standard I/O streams with the native locale and then reads and writes currency values.

Listing 58-1. Reading and Writing Currency Using the Money I/O Manipulators

```
import <iomanip>;
import <iostream>;
import <locale>;
import <string>;

int main()
{
  std::locale native{""};
  std::cin.imbue(native);
  std::cout.imbue(native);

  std::cin >> std::noshowbase;   // currency symbol is optional for input
  std::cout << std::showbase;    // always write the currency symbol for output

  std::string digits;
  while (std::cin >> std::get_money(digits))
  {
    std::cout << std::put_money(digits) << '\n';
  }
  if (not std::cin.eof())
    std::cout << "Invalid input.\n";
}
```

The locale manipulators work like other manipulators, but they invoke the associated facets. The manipulators use the stream to take care of the error flags, iterators, fill character, and so on. The get_time and put_time manipulators read and write dates and times; consult a library reference for details.

Character Categories

This section continues the examination of character sets and locales that you began in Exploration 18. In addition to testing for alphanumeric characters or lowercase characters, you can test for several different categories. Table 58-2 lists all the classification functions and their behavior in the classic locale. They all take a character as the first argument and a locale as the second; they all return a bool result.

Table 58-2. *Character Classification Functions*

Function	Description	Classic Locale
isalnum	Alphanumeric	'a'-'z', 'A'-'Z', '0'-'9'
isalpha	Alphabetic	'a'-'z', 'A'-'Z'
iscntrl	Control	Any non-printable character*
isdigit	Digit	'0'-'9' (in all locales)
isgraph	Graphical	Printable character other than ' '*
islower	Lowercase	'a'-'z'
isprint	Printable	Any printable character in the character set*
ispunct	Punctuation	Printable character other than alphanumeric or white space*
isspace	White space	' ', '\f', '\n', '\r', '\t', '\v'
isupper	Uppercase	'A'-'Z'
isxdigit	Hexadecimal digit	'a'-'f', 'A'-'F', '0'-'9' (in all locales)

Behavior depends on the character set, even in the classic locale.

The classic locale has fixed definitions for some categories (such as isupper). Other locales, however, can expand these definitions to include other characters, which may (and probably will) depend on the character set too. Only isdigit and isxdigit have fixed definitions for all locales and all character sets.

However, even in the classic locale, the precise implementation of some functions, such as isprint, depends on the character set. For example, in the popular ISO 8859-1 (Latin-1) character set, '\x80' is a control character, but in the equally popular Windows-1252 character set, it is printable. In UTF-8, '\x80' is invalid, so all the categorization functions would return false.

The interaction between the locale and the character set is one of the areas where C++ underperforms. The locale can change at any time, which potentially sets a new character set, which in turn can give new meaning to certain character values. But, the compiler's view of the character set is fixed. For instance, the compiler treats 'A' as the uppercase Roman letter *A* and compiles the numeric code according to its idea of the runtime character set. That numeric value is then fixed forever. If the characterization functions use the same character set, everything is fine. The isalpha and isupper functions return true; isdigit returns false; and all is right with the world. If the user changes the locale and by so doing changes the character set, those functions may not work with that character variable any more.

Let's consider a concrete example as shown in Listing 58-2. This program encodes locale names, which may not work for your environment. Read the comments and see if your environment can support the same kind of locales, albeit with different names. You will need the ioflags class from Listing 40-4. Copy the class to its own module called ioflags or download the file from the book's website. After reading Listing 58-2, **what do you expect as the result?**

_____

_____

Listing 58-2. Exploring Character Sets and Locales

```
import <format>;
import <iostream>;
import <locale>;
import <ostream>;
```

```
import ioflags;  // from Listing 40-4

/// Print a character's categorization in a locale.
void print(int c, std::string const& name, std::locale loc)
{
  // Don't concern yourself with the & operator. I'll cover that later
  // in the book, in Exploration 63. Its purpose is just to ensure
  // the character's escape code is printed correctly.
  std::cout << std::format("\\x{:02x} is {} in {}\n", c & 0xff, name, loc.name());
}

/// Test a character's categorization in the locale, @p loc.
void test(char c, std::locale loc)
{
  ioflags save{std::cout};
  if (std::isalnum(c, loc))
    print(c, "alphanumeric", loc);
  else if (std::iscntrl(c, loc))
    print(c, "control", loc);
  else if (std::ispunct(c, loc))
    print(c, "punctuation", loc);
  else
    print(c, "none of the above", loc);
}

int main()
{
  // Test the same code point in different locales and character sets.
  char c{'\xd7'};

  // ISO 8859-1 is also called Latin-1 and is widely used in Western Europe
  // and the Americas. It is often the default character set in these regions.
  // The country and language are unimportant for this test.
  // Choose any that support the ISO 8859-1 character set.
  test(c, std::locale{"en_US.iso88591"});

  // ISO 8859-5 is Cyrillic. It is often the default character set in Russia
  // and some Eastern European countries. Choose any language and region that
  // support the ISO 8859-5 character set.
  test(c, std::locale{"ru_RU.iso88595"});

  // ISO 8859-7 is Greek. Choose any language and region that
  // support the ISO 8859-7 character set.
  test(c, std::locale{"el_GR.iso88597"});

  // ISO 8859-8 contains some Hebrew. The character set is no longer widely used.
  // Choose any language and region that support the ISO 8859-8 character set.
  test(c, std::locale{"he_IL.iso88598"});
}
```

What do you get as the actual response?

_____

_____

_____

_____

In case you had trouble identifying locale names or other problems running the program, the following are the results I get when I run it on my system:

```
\xd7 is punctuation in en_US.iso88591
\xd7 is alphanumeric in ru_RU.iso88595
\xd7 is alphanumeric in el_GR.iso88597
\xd7 is none of the above in he_IL.iso88598
```

As you can see, the same character has different categories, depending on the locale's character set. Now imagine that the user has entered a string, and your program has stored the string. If your program changes the global locale or the locale used to process that string, you may end up misinterpreting the string.

In Listing 58-2, the categorization functions reload their facets every time they are called, but you can rewrite the program so it loads its facet only once. The character type facet is called ctype. It has a function named is that takes a category mask and a character as arguments and returns a bool: true if the character has a type in the mask. The mask values are specified in std::ctype_base.

Note   Notice the convention that the standard library uses throughout. When a class template needs helper types and constants, they are declared in a non-template base class. The class template derives from the base class and so gains easy access to the types and constants. Callers gain access to the types and constants by qualifying with the base class name. By avoiding the template in the base class, the standard library avoids unnecessary instantiations just to use a type or constant that is unrelated to the template argument.

The mask names are the same as the categorization functions, but without the leading is. Listing 58-3 shows how to rewrite the simple character-set demonstration to use a single cached ctype facet.

Listing 58-3. Caching the ctype Facet

```cpp
import <format>;
import <iostream>;
import <locale>;

import ioflags;  // from Listing 40-4

void print(int c, std::string const& name, std::locale loc)
{
    // Don't concern yourself with the & operator. I'll cover that later
    // in the book. Its purpose is just to ensure the character's escape
    // code is printed correctly.
    std::cout << std::format("\\x{:02x} is {} in {}\n", c & 0xff, name, loc.name());
}
```

```
/// Test a character's categorization in the locale, @p loc.
void test(char c, std::locale loc)
{
  ioflags save{std::cout};

  std::ctype<char> const& ctype{std::use_facet<std::ctype<char>>(loc)};

  if (ctype.is(std::ctype_base::alnum, c))
    print(c, "alphanumeric", loc);
  else if (ctype.is(std::ctype_base::cntrl, c))
    print(c, "control", loc);
  else if (ctype.is(std::ctype_base::punct, c))
    print(c, "punctuation", loc);
  else
    print(c, "none of the above", loc);
}

int main()
{
  // Test the same code point in different locales and character sets.
  char c{'\xd7'};

  // ISO 8859-1 is also called Latin-1 and is widely used in Western Europe
  // and the Americas. It is often the default character set in these regions.
  // The country and language are unimportant for this test.
  // Choose any that support the ISO 8859-1 character set.
  test(c, std::locale{"en_US.iso88591"});

  // ISO 8859-5 is Cyrillic. It is often the default character set in Russia
  // and some Eastern European countries. Choose any language and region that
  // support the ISO 8859-5 character set.
  test(c, std::locale{"ru_RU.iso88595"});

  // ISO 8859-7 is Greek. Choose any language and region that
  // support the ISO 8859-7 character set.
  test(c, std::locale{"el_GR.iso88597"});

  // ISO 8859-8 contains some Hebrew. It is no longer widely used.
  // Choose any language and region that support the ISO 8859-8 character set.
  test(c, std::locale{"he_IL.iso88598"});
}
```

The ctype facet also performs case conversions with the toupper and tolower member functions, which take a single character argument and return a character result. Recall the word-counting problem from Exploration 22. **Rewrite your solution (see Listings 23-2 and 23-3) and change the sanitize() function to use a cached facet**. I recommend replacing the function with a sanitizer class so the class can store the facet in a data member. Compare your program with Listing 58-4.

Listing 58-4. Counting Words Again, This Time with Cached Facets

```cpp
import <format>;
import <iostream>;
import <locale>;
import <map>;
import <ranges>;
import <string>;
import <string_view>;

using count_map  = std::map<std::string, int>;   ///< Map words to counts
using count_pair = count_map::value_type;        ///< pair of a word and a count
using str_size   = std::string::size_type;       ///< String size type

void initialize_streams()
{
  std::cin.imbue(std::locale{});
  std::cout.imbue(std::locale{});
}

class sanitizer
{
public:
  sanitizer(std::locale const& locale)
  : ctype_{ std::use_facet<std::ctype<char>>(locale) }
  {}

  bool keep(char ch) const { return ctype_.is(ctype_.alnum, ch); }
  char tolower(char ch) const { return ctype_.tolower(ch); }

  std::string operator()(std::string_view str)
  const
  {
    auto data{ str
      | std::ranges::views::filter([this](char ch) { return keep(ch); })
      | std::ranges::views::transform([this](char ch) { return tolower(ch); }) };
    return std::string{ std::ranges::begin(data), std::ranges::end(data) };
  }
private:
  std::ctype<char> const& ctype_;
};

str_size get_longest_key(count_map const& map)
{
  str_size result{0};
  for (auto const& pair : map)
    if (pair.first.size() > result)
      result = pair.first.size();
  return result;
}
```

```cpp
void print_pair(count_pair const& pair, str_size longest)
{
  int constexpr count_size{10}; // Number of places for printing the count
  std::cout << std::format("{0:{1}} {2:{3}}\n", pair.first, longest, pair.second,
  count_size);
}

void print_counts(count_map const& counts)
{
  auto longest{get_longest_key(counts)};

  // For each word/count pair...
  for (count_pair pair: counts)
    print_pair(pair, longest);
}

int main()
{
  // Set the global locale to the native locale.
  std::locale::global(std::locale{""});
  initialize_streams();

  count_map counts{};
  sanitizer sanitize{std::locale{""}};

  // Read words from the standard input and count the number of times
  // each word occurs.
  std::string word{};
  while (std::cin >> word)
  {
    std::string copy{sanitize(word)};

    // The "word" might be all punctuation, so the copy would be empty.
    // Don't count empty strings.
    if (not copy.empty())
      ++counts[copy];
  }

  print_counts(counts);
}
```

Notice how most of the program is unchanged. The simple act of caching the ctype facet reduces this program's runtime by about 15% on my system.

Collation Order

You can use the relational operators (such as <) with characters and strings, but they don't actually compare characters or code points; they compare storage units. Most users don't care whether a list of names is sorted in ascending numerical order by storage unit. They want a list of names sorted in ascending alphabetical order, according to their native collation rules.

For example, which comes first: *ångstrom* or *angle*? The answer depends on where you live and what language you speak. In Scandinavia, *angle* comes first, and *ångstrom* follows *zebra*. The collate facet compares strings according to the locale's rules. Its compare function is somewhat clumsy to use, so the locale class template provides a simple interface for determining whether one string is less than another in a locale: use the locale's function call operator. In other words, you can use a locale object itself as the comparison functor for standard algorithms, such as sort. Listing 58-5 shows a program that demonstrates how collation order depends on locale. In order to get the program to run in your environment, you may have to change the locale names.

Listing 58-5. Demonstrating How Collation Order Depends on Locale

```
import <algorithm>;
import <iostream>;
import <iterator>;
import <locale>;
import <string>;
import <vector>;

void sort_words(std::vector<std::string> words, std::locale loc)
{
  std::ranges::sort(words, loc);
  std::cout << loc.name() << ":\n";
  std::ranges::copy(words,
          std::ostream_iterator<std::string>(std::cout, "\n"));
}

int main()
{
  std::vector<std::string> words{
    "circus",
    "\u00e5ngstrom",      // ångstrom
    "\u00e7irc\u00ea",    // çircê
    "angle",
    "essen",
    "ether",
    "\u00e6ther",         // æther
    "aether",
    "e\u00dfen"           // eßen
  };
  sort_words(words, std::locale::classic());
  sort_words(words, std::locale{"en_GB.utf8"});  // Great Britain
  sort_words(words, std::locale{"no_NO.utf8"});  // Norway
}
```

The \uNNNN characters are a portable way to express Unicode characters. The NNNN must be four hexadecimal digits, specifying a Unicode code point. You will learn more in the next Exploration.

The boldface line shows how the locale object is used as a comparison functor to sort the words. Table 58-3 lists the results I get for each locale. Depending on your native character set, you may get different results.

Table 58-3. *Collation Order for Various Locales*

Classic	Great Britain	Norway
aether	aether	aether
angle	æther	angle
circus	angle	çircê
essen	ångstrom	circus
ether	çircê	essen
eßen	circus	eßen
ångstrom	essen	ether
æther	eßen	æther
çircê	ether	ångstrom

The next Exploration takes a closer look at Unicode, international character sets, and related challenges.

EXPLORATION 59

■ ■ ■

International Characters

Explorations 17–19 discussed characters, but only hinted at bigger things to come. Exploration 58 started to examine these bigger issues with locales and facets. The next topic to explore is how to wrangle character sets and character encodings in an international setting.

This Exploration introduces wide characters, which are like ordinary (or *narrow*) characters, except that they usually occupy more memory. This means the wide character type can potentially represent many more characters than plain char. During your exploration of wide characters, you will also get to know more about Unicode.

Why Wide?

As you saw in Exploration 18, the meaning of a particular character value depends on the locale and character set. For instance, in one locale, you can handle Greek characters, while in another locale, Cyrillic, depending on the character set. Your program needs to know the locale and the character set in order to determine which characters are letters, which are punctuation, which are uppercase or lowercase, and how to convert uppercase to lowercase and *vice versa*.

What if your program has to handle Cyrillic and Greek? What if this program needs to handle them both at the same time? And what about Asian languages? Chinese does not use a Western-style alphabet but instead uses thousands of distinct ideographs. Several Asian languages have adopted some Chinese ideographs for their own use. The typical implementation of the char type reaches its limit at only 256 distinct characters, which is woefully inadequate for international demands.

In other words, you can't use plain char and string types if you want to support the majority of the world's population and their languages. C++ solves this problem with *wide characters*, which it represents using several types: wchar_t, char16_t, and char32_t. (Unlike C's definition of wchar_t, the type names in C++ are reserved keywords and built-in types, not typedefs.) The intent is that wchar_t is a native type that can represent characters that don't fit into a char. With larger characters, a program can support Asian character sets, for example. The char16_t and char32_t are Unicode types. The type char8_t is also for Unicode but is a narrow character type. The Exploration begins by examining wchar_t.

Using Wide Characters

In true C++ fashion, the size and other characteristics of wchar_t are left to the implementation. The only guarantees are that wchar_t is at least as big as char and that wchar_t is the same size as one of the built-in integer types. The <cwchar> header declares a typedef, std::wint_t, for that built-in type. In some implementations, wchar_t may be identical to char, but most desktop and workstation environments use 16 or 32 bits for wchar_t.

© Ray Lischner 2020
R. Lischner, *Exploring C++20*, https://doi.org/10.1007/978-1-4842-5961-0_59

Dig up Listing 26-2 and modify it to reveal the size of wchar_t and wint_t in your C++ environment. **How many bits are in wchar_t?** _____ **How many are in wint_t?** _____ They should be the same number. **How many bits are in char?** _____

Wide string objects use the std::wstring type (declared in <string>). A wide string is a string composed of wide characters. In all other ways, wide strings and narrow strings behave similarly; they have the same member functions, and you use them the same way. For example, the size() member function returns the number of characters in the string, regardless of the size of each character.

Wide character and string literals look like their narrow equivalents, except that they start with a capital L and they contain wide characters. The best way to express a wide character in a character or string literal is to specify the character's hexadecimal value with the \x escape (introduced in Exploration 17). Thus, you have to know the wide character set that your C++ environment uses, and you have to know the numeric value of the desired character in that character set. If your editor and compiler permit it, you may be able to write wide characters directly in a wide character literal, but your source code will not be portable to other environments. You can also write a narrow character in a wide character or string literal, and the compiler automatically converts the narrow characters to wide ones, as shown here:

```
wchar_t capital_a{'A'};        // the compiler automatically widens narrow characters
std::wstring ray{L"Ray"};
wchar_t pi{L'π'};              // if your tools let you type π as a character
wchar_t pi_unicode{L'\x03c0'}; // if wchar_t uses a Unicode encoding, such as UTF-32
std::wstring price{L"\x20ac" L"12345"};        // Unicode Euro symbol: €12345
```

Notice how in the last line of the example I divided the string into two parts. Recall from Exploration 17 that the \x escape starts an escape sequence that specifies a character by its value in hexadecimal (base 16). The compiler collects as many characters as it can that form a valid hexadecimal number—that is, digits and the letters A through F (in uppercase or lowercase). It then uses that numeric value as the representation of a single character. If the last line were left as one string, the compiler would try to interpret the entire string as the \x escape. This means the compiler would think the character value is the hexadecimal value $20AC12345_{16}$. By separating the strings, the compiler knows when the \x escape ends, and it compiles the character value $20AC_{16}$, followed by the characters 1, 2, 3, 4, and 5. Just like narrow strings, the compiler assembles adjacent wide strings into a single wide string. (You are not allowed to place narrow and wide strings next to each other, however. Use all wide strings or all narrow strings, not a mixture of the two.)

Wide Strings

Everything you know about string also applies to wstring. They are just instances of a common template, basic_string. The <string> header declares string to be a typedef for basic_string<char> and wstring as a typedef for basic_string<wchar_t>. The magic of templates takes care of the details.

Because the underlying implementation of string and wstring is actually a template, any time you write some utility code to work with strings, you should consider making that code a template too. For example, suppose you want to rewrite the is_palindrome function (from Listing 22-5) so that it operates with wide characters. Instead of replacing char with wchar_t, let's turn it into a function template. Begin by rewriting the supporting functions to be function templates, taking a character type as a template argument. **Rewrite the supporting functions for is_palindrome so that they function with narrow and wide strings and characters.** My solution is presented in Listing 59-1.

Listing 59-1. Supporting Cast for the is_palindrome Function Template

```
import <locale>;

template<class Char>
auto const& ctype{ std::use_facet<std::ctype<Char>>(std::locale()) };

/** Test for non-letter.
 * @param ch the character to test
 * @return true if @p ch is not a letter
 */
template<class Char>
bool isletter(Char ch)
{
  return ctype<Char>.is(std::ctype_base::alpha, ch);
}


/** Convert to lowercase.
 * @param ch the character to test
 * @return the character converted to lowercase
 */
template<class Char>
Char lowercase(Char ch)
{
  return ctype<Char>.tolower(ch);
}

/** Compare two characters without regard to case. */
template<class Char>
bool same_char(Char a, Char b)
{
  return lowercase(a) == lowercase(b);
}
```

The next task is to rewrite is_palindrome itself. The basic_string template actually takes three template arguments, and basic_string_view takes two. The first is the character type, and the next two are details that needn't concern us at this time. All that matters is that if you want to templatize your own function that deals with strings, you should handle all three of the template parameters.

Before starting, however, you must be aware of a minor hurdle when dealing with functions as arguments to standard algorithms: the argument must be a real function, not the name of a function template. In other words, if you have to work with function templates, such as lowercase and non_letter, you must instantiate the template and pass the template instance. When you pass non_letter and same_char to the remove_if and equal algorithms, be sure to pass the correct template argument too. If Char is the template parameter for the character type, use non_letter<Char> as the functor argument to remove_if.

Rewrite the is_palindrome function as a function template with two template parameters. The first template parameter is the character type: call it Char. Call the second template parameter Traits. You will have to use both arguments to the std::basic_string_view template. Listing 59-2 shows my version of the is_palindrome function, converted to a template, so that it can handle narrow and wide strings.

Listing 59-2. Changing is_palindrome to a Function Template

```
import <ranges>;
import <string_view>;

/** Determine whether @p str is a palindrome.
 * Only letter characters are tested. Spaces and punctuation don't count.
 * Empty strings are not palindromes because that's just too easy.
 * @param str the string to test
 * @return true if @p str is the same forward and backward
 */
template<class Char, class Traits>
bool is_palindrome(std::basic_string_view<Char, Traits> str)
{
  auto letters_only{ str | std::views::filter(isletter<Char>) };
  auto reversed{ letters_only | std::ranges::views::reverse };
  return std::equal(
    std::ranges::begin(letters_only), std::ranges::end(letters_only),
    std::ranges::begin(reversed),     std::ranges::end(reversed),
    same_char<Char>);
}
```

The is_palindrome function never uses the Traits template parameter, except to pass it along to basic_string_view. If you're curious about that parameter, consult a language reference, but be warned that it's a bit advanced.

Calling is_palindrome is easy, because the compiler uses automatic type deduction to determine whether you are using narrow or wide strings and instantiates the templates accordingly. Thus, the caller doesn't have to bother with templates at all.

Without further ado, the isletter and lowercase function templates work with wide character arguments. That's because locales are templates, parameterized on the character type, just like the string and I/O class templates.

However, in order to use wide characters, you do have to perform I/O with wide characters, which is the subject of the next section.

Wide Character I/O

You read wide characters from the standard input by reading from std::wcin. Write wide characters by writing to std::wcout or std::wcerr. Once you read or write anything to or from a stream, the character width of the corresponding narrow and wide streams is fixed, and you cannot change it—you must decide whether to use narrow or wide characters and stay with that choice for the lifetime of the stream. So, a program must use cin or wcin, but not both. Ditto for the output streams. The <iostream> header declares the names of all the standard streams, narrow and wide. The <istream> header defines all the input stream classes and operators; <ostream> defines the output classes and operators. More precisely, <istream> and <ostream> define templates, and the character type is the first template parameter.

The <istream> header defines the std::basic_istream class template, parameterized on the character type. The same header declares two typedefs, as follows:

```
using istream = basic_istream<char>;
using wistream = basic_istream<wchar_t>;
```

As you can guess, the <ostream> header is similar, defining the basic_ostream class template and the ostream and wostream typedefs.

The <fstream> header follows the same pattern—basic_ifstream and basic_ofstream are class templates, with typedefs, as in the following:

```
using ifstream  = basic_ifstream<char>;
using wifstream = basic_ifstream<wchar_t>;
using ofstream  = basic_ofstream<char>;
using wofstream = basic_ofstream<wchar_t>;
```

Rewrite the main program from Listing 22-5 to test the is_palindrome function template with wide character I/O. Modern desktop environments should be able to support wide characters, but you may have to learn some new features to figure out how to get your text editor to save a file with wide characters. You may also have to load some additional fonts. Most likely, you can supply an ordinary, narrow-text file as input, and the program will work just fine. If you're having difficulty finding a suitable input file, try the palindrome files that you can download with the other examples in this book. The file names indicate the character set. For example, palindrome-utf8.txt contains UTF-8 input. You have to determine what format your C++ environment expects when reading a wide stream and pick the correct file. My solution is shown in Listing 59-3.

Listing 59-3. The main Program for Testing is_palindrome

```
int main()
{
  std::locale::global(std::locale{""});
  std::wcin.imbue(std::locale{});
  std::wcout.imbue(std::locale{});

  std::wstring line{};
  while (std::getline(std::wcin, line))
    if (is_palindrome(std::wstring_view{line}))
      std::wcout << line << L'\n';
}
```

Reading wide characters from a file or writing wide characters to a file is different from reading or writing narrow characters. All file I/O passes through an additional step of character conversion. C++ always interprets a file as a series of bytes. When reading or writing narrow characters, the conversion of a byte to a narrow character is a no-op, but when reading or writing wide characters, the C++ library has to interpret the bytes to form wide characters. It does so by accumulating one or more adjacent bytes to form each wide character. The rules for deciding which bytes are elements of a wide character and how to combine the characters are specified by the encoding rules for a *multi-byte character set*.

Multi-byte Character Sets

Multi-byte character sets originated in Asia, where demand for characters exceeded the few character slots available in a single-byte character set, such as ASCII. European nations managed to fit their alphabets into 8-bit character sets, but languages such as Chinese, Japanese, Korean, and Vietnamese require far more bits to represent thousands of ideographs, syllables, and native characters.

The requirements of Asian languages spurred the development of character sets that used two bytes to encode a character—hence the common term *double-byte character set* (DBCS), with the generalization to *multi-byte character sets* (MBCS). Many DBCSes were invented, and sometimes a single character had multiple encodings. For example, in Chinese Big 5, the ideograph 丁 has the double-byte value "\xA4\x42". In the EUC-KR character set (which is popular in Korea), the same ideograph has a different encoding: "\xEF\xCB".

The typical DBCS uses characters with the most significant bit set (in an 8-bit byte) to represent double characters. Characters with the most significant bit clear would be taken from a single-byte character set (SBCS). Some DBCSes mandate a particular SBCS; others leave it open, so you get different conventions for different combinations of DBCS and SBCS. Mixing single- and double-byte characters in a single character stream is necessary to represent the common use of character streams that mix Asian and Western text. Working with multi-byte characters is more difficult than working with single-byte characters. A string's size() function, for example, doesn't tell you how many characters are in a string. You must examine every byte of the string to learn the number of characters. Indexing into a string is more difficult, because you must take care not to index into the middle of a double-byte character.

Sometimes a single character stream needs more flexibility than simply switching between one particular SBCS and one particular DBCS. Sometimes the stream has to mix multiple double-byte character sets. The ISO 2022 standard is an example of a character set that allows shifting between other, subsidiary character sets. *Shift sequences* (also called *escape sequences*, not to be confused with C++ backslash escape sequences) dictate which character set to use. For example, ISO 2022-JP is widely used in Japan and allows switching between ASCII, JIS X 0201 (a SBCS), and JIS X 0208 (a DBCS). Each line of text begins in ASCII, and a shift sequence changes character sets mid-string. For example, the shift sequence "\x1B$B" switches to JIS X 0208-1983.

Seeking to an arbitrary position in a file or text stream that contains shift sequences is clearly problematic. A program that has to seek in a multi-byte text stream must keep track of shift sequences in addition to stream positions. Without knowing the most recent shift sequence in the stream, a program has no way of knowing which character set to use to interpret the subsequent characters.

A number of variations on ISO 2022-JP permit additional character sets. The point here is not to offer a tutorial on Asian character sets but to impress on you the complexities of writing a truly open, general, and flexible mechanism that can support the world's rich diversity in character sets and locales. These and similar problems gave rise to the Unicode project.

Unicode

Unicode is an attempt to get out of the whole character-set mess by unifying all major variations into one, big, happy character set. To a large degree, the Unicode Consortium has succeeded. The Unicode character set has been adopted as an international standard as ISO 10646. However, the Unicode project includes more than just the character set; it also specifies rules for case-folding, character collation, and more.

Unicode provides 1,114,112 possible character values (called *code points*). So far, the Unicode Consortium has assigned about 100,000 code points to characters, so there's plenty of room for expansion. The simplest way to represent a million code points is to use a 32-bit integer, and indeed, this is a common encoding for Unicode. It is not the only encoding, however. The Unicode standard also defines encodings that let you represent a code point using one or two 16-bit integers and one to four 8-bit integers.

The standard way to denote a Unicode code point is U+, followed by the code point as a hexadecimal number of at least four places. Thus, '\x41' is the C++ encoding of U+0041 (Latin capital *A*) and Greek π has code point U+03C0. A musical eighth note (♪) has code point U+266A or U+1D160; the former code point is in a group of miscellaneous symbols, which happens to include an eighth note. The latter code point is part of a group of musical symbols, which you will need for any significant work with music-related characters.

UTF-32 is the name of the encoding that stores a code point as a 32-bit integer. To represent a UTF-32 code point in C++, preface the character literal with U (uppercase letter *U*). Such a character literal has type char32_t. For example, to represent the letter *A*, use U'A'; for a lowercase Greek π, use U'\x03c0'; and for a musical eighth note (♪), use U'\x266a' or U'\x1d160'. Do the same for a character string literal, and the standard library defines the type std::u32string for a string of char32_t. For example, to represent the characters π ≈ 3.14, use the following:

```
std::u32string pi_approx_3_14{ U"\x03c0 \x2248 3.14" };
```

Another common encoding for Unicode uses one to four 8-bit units to make up a single code point. Common characters in Western European languages can usually be represented in a single byte, and many other characters take only two bytes. Less common characters require three or four. The result is an encoding that supports the full range of Unicode code points and almost always consumes less memory than other encodings. This character set is called UTF-8. UTF-8 characters are written in the manner of ordinary character literals prefaced with u8. The type of a UTF-8 string literal is char8_t. A UTF-8 string has type std::u8string.

Representing a Greek letter π requires only two bytes, but with different values than the two low-order bytes in UTF-32: u8"\xcf\x80". An eighth note (♪) requires three or four bytes, again with a different encoding than that used in UTF-32: u8"\xe2\x99\xaa" or u8"\xf0\x9d\x85\xa0".

The primary difficulty when dealing with UTF-8 in a program is that the only way to know how many code points are in a string is to scan the entire string. The size() member function returns the number of storage units in the string, but each code point requires one to four storage units. On the other hand, UTF-8 has the advantage that you can seek to an arbitrary position in a UTF-8 byte stream and know whether that position is in the middle of a multi-byte character because multi-byte characters always have their most significant bit set. By examining the encoding, you can tell whether a byte is the first byte of a multi-byte character or a following byte.

UTF-8 is a common encoding for files and network transmissions. It has become the *de facto* standard for many desktop environments, word processors (including the one I am using to write this book), web pages, and other everyday applications.

Some other environments use UTF-16, which represents a code point using one or two 16-bit integers. The C++ type for a UTF-16 character literal is char16_t, and the string type is std::u16string. Write such a character literal with the u prefix (lowercase letter *u*), for example, u'\x03c0'.

Unicode's designers kept the most common code points in the lower 16-bit region (called the *Basic Multilingual Plane*, or BMP). When a code point is outside the BMP, that is, its value exceeds U+FFFF, it requires two storage units in UTF-16 and is called a *surrogate pair*. For example, ⊤ requires two 16-bit storage units: u"\xD834\xDD1E".

Thus, you have the same problem as UTF-8, namely, that one storage unit does not necessarily represent a single code point, so UTF-16 is less than ideal as an in-memory representation. But the vast majority of code points that most programs deal with fit in a single UTF-16 storage unit, so UTF-16 usually requires half the memory as UTF-32, and in many cases, a u16string's size() is the number of code points in the string (although you can't be sure without scanning the string).

Some programmers cope with the difficulty of working with UTF-16 by ignoring surrogate pairs completely. They assume that size() does indeed return the number of code points in the string, so their programs work correctly only if all code points are from the BMP. This means you lose access to ancient scripts, specialized alphabets and symbols, and infrequently used ideographs.

UTF-8 has an advantage over UTF-16 and UTF-32 encodings for external representations, because you don't have to deal with endianness. The Unicode standard defines a mechanism for encoding and revealing the endianness of a stream of UTF-16 or UTF-32 text, but that just makes extra work for you.

■ **Note** The position of the most significant byte is called "endianness." A "big-endian" platform is one with the most significant byte first. A "little-endian" platform puts the least significant byte first. The popular Intel x86 platform is little-endian.

Universal Character Names

Unicode makes another official appearance in the C++ standard. You can specify a character using its Unicode code point. Use \uXXXX or \UXXXXXXXX, replacing XXXX or XXXXXXXX with the hexadecimal code point. Unlike the \x escape, you must use exactly four hexadecimal digits with \u or eight with \U. These character constructs are called *universal character names*.

Thus, a better way to encode international characters in a string is to use a universal character name. This helps to insulate you against vagaries in the native character set. On the other hand, you have no control over the compiler's actions if it cannot map a Unicode code point to a native character. Therefore, if your native character set is ISO 8859-7 (Greek), the following code should initialize the variable pi with the value '\xf0', but if your native character set is ISO 8859-1 (Latin-1), the compiler cannot map it and so might give you a space or a question mark, or the compiler may refuse to compile it:

```
char pi{'\u03c0'};
```

Also note that \u and \U are not escape sequences (unlike \x). You can use them anywhere in a program, not only in a character or string literal. Using a Unicode character name lets you use UTF-8 and UTF-16 strings without knowing the encoding details. Thus, a better way to write the UTF-8 string for Greek lowercase π is u8"\u03c0", and the compiler will store the encoded bytes "\xcf\x80".

If you are fortunate, you will be able to avoid universal character names. Instead, your tools will let you edit Unicode characters directly. Instead of dealing with Unicode encoding issues, the editor simply reads and writes universal character names. Thus, the programmer edits WYSIWYG international text, and the source code retains maximum portability. Because universal character names are allowed anywhere, you can use international text in comments too. If you really want to have fun, try using international letters in identifier names. Not all compilers support this feature, although the standard requires it. Thus, you would write a declaration

```
double π{3.14159265358979};
```

and your smart editor would store the following in the source file:

```
double \u03c0{3.14159265358979};
```

and your standard-compliant compiler would accept it and let you use π as an identifier. I don't recommend using extended characters in identifiers unless you know that everyone reading your code is using tools that are aware of universal character names. Otherwise, they make the code much harder to read, understand, and maintain.

Does your compiler support universal character names in strings? _____ **Does your compiler support universal character names in identifiers?** _____

Unicode Difficulties

For all the seeming benefits of Unicode, C++ support remains minimal. Although you can write Unicode character literals and string literals, the standard library offers no useful support. Try this exercise: modify the palindrome program to use char32_t instead of wchar_t. **What happens?**

It doesn't work. There are no I/O stream classes for Unicode. Template specializations for isalnum and so on don't exist for char8_t, char16_t, or char32_t. Although the standard library offers some functions for converting Unicode strings to and from wstring, the support ends there.

If you have to work with international characters in any meaningful way, you need a third-party library. The most widely used library is International Components for Unicode (ICU). See the book's website for a current link.

The next and final topic in Part 3 is to further your understanding of text I/O.

■ ■ ■

Text I/O

Input and output have two basic flavors: text and binary. Binary I/O introduces subtleties that are beyond the scope of this book, so all discussion of I/O herein is text-oriented. This Exploration presents a variety of topics related to textual I/O. You've already seen how the input and output operators work with the built-in types as well as with the standard library types, when it makes sense. You've also seen how you can write your own I/O operators for custom types. This Exploration offers some additional details about file modes, reading and writing strings, and converting values to and from strings.

File Modes

Exploration 14 briefly introduced the file stream classes `ifstream` and `ofstream`. The basic behavior is to take a file name and open it. You gain a little more control than that by passing a second argument, which is a file mode. The default mode for an `ifstream` is `std::ios_base::in`, which opens the file for input. The default mode for `ofstream` is `std::ios_base::out | std::ios_base::trunc`. (The | operator combines certain values, such as modes. Exploration 68 will cover this in depth.) The out mode opens the file for output. If the file doesn't exist, it is created. The `trunc` mode means to truncate the file, so you always start with an empty file. If you explicitly specify the mode and omit `trunc`, the old contents (if any) remain. Therefore, by default, writing to the output stream overwrites the old contents. If you want to position the stream at the end of the old contents, use the `ate` mode (short for *at-end*), which sets the stream's initial position to the end of the existing file contents. The default is to position the stream at the start of the file.

Another useful mode for output is app (short for *append*), which causes every write to append to the file. That is, app affects every write, whereas `ate` affects only the starting position. The app mode is useful when writing to a log file.

Write a **debug()** function that takes a single string as an argument and writes that string to a file named **"debug.txt"**. Listing 60-1 shows the interface module.

Listing 60-1. Module That Declares a Trivial Debugging Function

```
export module debug;
import <string_view>;

/** @brief Write a debug message to the file @c "debug.txt"
 * @param msg The message to write
 */
export void debug(std::string_view msg);
```

Append every log message to the file, terminating each message with a newline. To ensure that the debugging information is properly recorded, even if the program crashes, open the file anew every time the debug() function is called. Listing 60-2 shows my implementation module.

Listing 60-2. Implementing the Debug Function

```
module debug;
import <fstream>;
import <ostream>;
import <stdexcept>;

void debug(std::string_view str)
{
    std::ofstream stream{"debug.txt", std::ios_base::out | std::ios_base::app};
    if (not stream)
        throw std::runtime_error("cannot open debug.txt");
    stream.exceptions(std::ios_base::failbit);
    stream << str << '\n';
    stream.close();
}
```

String Streams

In addition to file streams, C++ offers string streams. The <sstream> header defines istringstream and ostringstream. A string stream reads from and writes to a std::string object. For input, supply the string as an argument to the istringstream constructor. For output, you can supply a string object, but the more common usage is to let the stream create and manage the string for you. The stream appends to the string, allowing the string to grow as needed. After you are finished writing to the stream, call the str() member function to retrieve the final string.

Suppose you have to read pairs of numbers from a file representing a car's odometer reading and the amount of fuel needed to fill the tank. The program computes the miles per gallon (or liters per kilometer, if you prefer) at each fill-up and overall. The file format is simple: each line has the odometer reading, followed by the fuel amount, on one line, separated by white space.

Write the program. Listing 60-3 demonstrates the miles-per-gallon approach.

Listing 60-3. Computing Miles per Gallon

```
import <iostream>;

int main()
{
    double total_fuel{0.0};
    double total_distance{0.0};
    double prev_odometer{0.0};
    double fuel{}, odometer{};
    while (std::cin >> odometer >> fuel)
    {
        if (fuel != 0)
        {
            double distance{odometer - prev_odometer};
```

```
        std::cout << distance / fuel << '\n';
        total_fuel += fuel;
        total_distance += distance;
        prev_odometer = odometer;
    }
}
if (total_fuel != 0)
    std::cout << "Net MPG=" << total_distance / total_fuel << '\n';
}
```

Listing 60-4 shows the equivalent program, but computing liters per kilometer. For the remainder of this Exploration, I will use miles per gallon. Readers who don't use this method can consult the files that accompany the book for hundred liters per kilometer.

Listing 60-4. Computing Liters per Kilometer

```
import <iostream>;

int main()
{
    double total_fuel{0.0};
    double total_distance{0.0};
    double prev_odometer{0.0};
    double fuel{}, odometer{};
    while (std::cin >> odometer >> fuel)
    {
        fuel *= 100.0;
        double distance{odometer - prev_odometer};
        if (distance != 0)
        {
            std::cout << fuel / distance << '\n';
            total_fuel += fuel;
            total_distance += distance;
            prev_odometer = odometer;
        }
    }
    if (total_distance != 0)
        std::cout << "Net 100LPK=" << total_fuel / total_distance << '\n';
}
```

What happens if the user accidentally forgets to record the fuel on one line of the file?

_____

The input loop doesn't know or care about lines. It resolutely skips over white space in its quest to fulfill each input request. Thus, it reads the subsequent line's odometer reading as a fuel amount. Naturally, the results will be incorrect.

A better solution would be to read each line as a string and extract two numbers from the string. If the string is not formatted correctly, issue an error message and ignore that line. You read a line of text into a std::string by calling the std::getline function (declared in <string>). This function takes an input stream as the first argument and a string object as the second argument. It returns the stream, which means it returns a true value if the read succeeds or a false one if the read fails, so you can use the call to getline as a loop condition.

Once you have the string, open an `istringstream` to read from the string. Use the string stream the same way you would any other input stream. Read two numbers from the string stream. If the string stream does not contain any numbers, ignore that line. If it contains only one number, issue a suitable error message. Listing 60-5 presents the new program.

Listing 60-5. Rewriting the Miles-per-Gallon Program to Parse a String Stream

```cpp
import <iostream>;
import <sstream>;
import <string>;

int main()
{
   double prev_odometer{0.0};
   double total_fuel{0.0};
   double total_distance{0.0};
   std::string line{};
   int linenum{0};
   bool error{false};
   while (std::getline(std::cin, line))
   {
      ++linenum;
      std::istringstream input{line};
      double odometer{};
      if (input >> odometer)
      {
         double fuel{};
         if (not (input >> fuel))
         {
            std::cerr << "Missing fuel consumption on line " << linenum << '\n';
            error = true;
         }
         else if (fuel != 0)
         {
            double distance{odometer - prev_odometer};
            std::cout << distance / fuel << '\n';
            total_fuel += fuel;
            total_distance += distance;
            prev_odometer = odometer;
         }
      }
   }
   if (total_fuel != 0)
   {
      std::cout << "Net MPG=" << total_distance / total_fuel;
      if (error)
         std::cout << " (estimated, due to input error)";
      std::cout << '\n';
   }
}
```

Most text file formats allow some form of annotation or commentary. The file format already allows one form of commentary, as a side effect of the program's implementation. **How can you add comments to the input file?**

After the program reads the fuel amount from a line, it ignores the rest of the string. You can add comments to any line that contains the proper odometer and fuel data. But that's a sloppy side effect. A better design requires the user to insert an explicit comment marker. Otherwise, the program might misinterpret erroneous input as a valid input, followed by a comment, such as accidentally inserting an extra space, as illustrated here:

```
123   21 10.23
```

Let's modify the file format. Any line that begins with a pound sign (#) is a comment. Upon reading a comment character, the program skips the entire line. **Add this feature to the program.** A useful function is an input stream's unget() function. After reading a character from the stream, unget() returns that character to the stream, causing the subsequent read operation to read that character again. In other words, after reading a line, read a character from the line, and if it is '#', skip the line. Otherwise, call unget() and continue as before. Compare your result with mine, as shown in Listing 60-6.

Listing 60-6. Parsing Comments in the Miles-per-Gallon Data File

```cpp
import <iostream>;
import <sstream>;
import <string>;

int main()
{
   double total_fuel{0.0};
   double total_distance{0.0};
   double prev_odometer{0.0};
   std::string line{};
   int linenum{0};
   bool error{false};
   while (std::getline(std::cin, line))
   {
      ++linenum;
      std::istringstream input{line};
      char comment{};
      if (input >> comment and comment != '#')
      {
         input.unget();
         double odometer{};
         if (input >> odometer)
         {
            double fuel{};
            if (not (input >> fuel))
            {
               std::cerr << "Missing fuel consumption on line " << linenum << '\n';
               error = true;
            }
```

```
            else if (fuel != 0)
            {
                double distance{odometer - prev_odometer};
                std::cout << distance / fuel << '\n';
                total_fuel += fuel;
                total_distance += distance;
                prev_odometer = odometer;
            }
        }
    }
}
if (total_fuel != 0)
{
    std::cout << "Net MPG=" << total_distance / total_fuel;
    if (error)
        std::cout << " (estimated, due to input error)";
    std::cout << '\n';
}
}
```

More complicated still is allowing the comment marker to appear anywhere on a line. A comment extends from the # character to the end of the line. The comment marker can appear anywhere on a line, but if the line contains any data, it must contain two valid numbers prior to the comment marker. **Enhance the program to allow comment markers anywhere**. Consider using the find() member function of std::string. It has many forms, one of which takes a character as an argument and returns the zero-based index of the first occurrence of that character in the string. The return type is std::string::size_type. If the character is not in the string, find() returns the magic constant std::string::npos.

Once you find the comment marker, you can delete the comment by calling erase() or copy the non-comment portion of the string by calling substr().String member functions work with zero-based indices. Substrings are expressed as a starting position and a count of the number of characters affected. Usually, the count can be omitted to mean the rest of the string. Compare your solution with mine, presented in Listing 60-7.

Listing 60-7. Allowing Comments Anywhere in the Miles-per-Gallon Data File

```
import <iostream>;
import <sstream>;
import <string>;

int main()
{
    double total_fuel{0.0};
    double total_distance{0.0};
    double prev_odometer{0.0};
    std::string line{};
    int linenum{0};
    bool error{false};
    while (std::getline(std::cin, line))
```

```
{
    ++linenum;
    std::string::size_type comment{line.find('#')};
    if (comment != std::string::npos)
        line.erase(comment);
    std::istringstream input{line};
    double odometer{};
    if (input >> odometer)
    {
        double fuel{};
        if (not (input >> fuel))
        {
            std::cerr << "Missing fuel consumption on line " << linenum << '\n';
            error = true;
        }
        else if (fuel != 0)
        {
            double distance{odometer - prev_odometer};
            std::cout << distance / fuel << '\n';
            total_fuel += fuel;
            total_distance += distance;
            prev_odometer = odometer;
        }
    }
}
if (total_fuel != 0)
{
    std::cout << "Net MPG=" << total_distance / total_fuel;
    if (error)
        std::cout << " (estimated, due to input error)";
    std::cout << '\n';
}
}
```

Now that the file format allows explicit comments on each line, you should add some more error-checking to make sure that each line contains only two numbers, and nothing more (after removing comments). One way to check is to read a single character after reading the two numbers. If the read succeeds, the line contains erroneous text. **Add error-checking to detect lines with extra text**. Compare your solution with my solution, shown in Listing 60-8.

Listing 60-8. Adding Error-Checking for Each Line of Input

```
import <iostream>;
import <sstream>;
import <string>;

int main()
{
    double total_fuel{0.0};
    double total_distance{0.0};
    double prev_odometer{0.0};
    std::string line{};
```

```
    int linenum{0};
    bool error{false};
    while (std::getline(std::cin, line))
    {
        ++linenum;
        std::string::size_type comment{line.find('#')};
        if (comment != std::string::npos)
            line.erase(comment);
        std::istringstream input{line};
        double odometer{};
        if (input >> odometer)
        {
            double fuel{};
            char check{};
            if (not (input >> fuel))
            {
                std::cerr << "Missing fuel consumption on line " << linenum << '\n';
                error = true;
            }
            else if (input >> check)
            {
                std::cerr << "Extra text on line " << linenum << '\n';
                error = true;
            }
            else if (fuel != 0)
            {
                double distance{odometer - prev_odometer};
                std::cout << distance / fuel << '\n';
                total_fuel += fuel;
                total_distance += distance;
                prev_odometer = odometer;
            }
        }
    }
    if (total_fuel != 0)
    {
        std::cout << "Net MPG=" << total_distance / total_fuel;
        if (error)
            std::cout << " (estimated, due to input error)";
        std::cout << '\n';
    }
}
```

Text Conversion

Let me put on my clairvoyance cap for a moment. I can see that you have many unanswered questions about C++; and one of those questions is "How can I convert a number to a string easily, and *vice versa*?"

The standard library offers some simple functions: std::to_string() takes an integer and returns a string representation. To convert a string to an integer, choose from several functions, depending on the desired return type: std::stoi() returns an int, and std::stod() returns double.

But these functions offer little flexibility. You know that I/O streams offer lots of flexibility and control over formatting. Surely, you say, you can create functions that are just as easy to use with suitable defaults, but also offer some flexibility in formatting (such as floating-point precision, fill characters, etc.).

Now that you know how to use string streams, the way forward is clear: use an istringstream to read a number from a string, or use an ostringstream to write a number to a string. The only task is to wrap up the functionality in an appropriate function. Even better is to use a template. After all, reading or writing an int is essentially the same as reading or writing a long and others.

Listing 60-9 shows the from_string function template, which has a single template parameter, T—the type of object to convert. The function returns type T and takes a single function argument: a string to convert.

Listing 60-9. The from_string Function Extracts a Value from a String

```
import <istream>;
import <sstream>;
import <stdexcept>;
import <string>;

template<class T>
requires
  requires(T value, std::istream stream) {
    stream >> value;
  }
T from_string(std::string const& str)
{
  std::istringstream in{str};
  T result{};
  if (in >> result)
    return result;
  else
    throw std::runtime_error{str};
}
```

T can be any type that permits reading from an input stream with the >> operator, including any custom operators and types that you write.

Now what about the advertised flexibility? Let's add some. As written, the from_string function does not check for text that follows the value. Plus, it skips over leading white space. **Modify the function to take a bool argument: skipws**. If true, from_string skips leading white space and allows trailing white space. If false, it does not skip leading white space, and it does not permit trailing white space. In both cases, it throws runtime_error, if invalid text follows the value. Compare your solution with mine in Listing 60-10.

Listing 60-10. Enhancing the from_string Function

```
import <istream>;
import <sstream>;
import <stdexcept>;
import <string>;

template<class T>
requires
  requires(T value, std::istream stream) {
    stream >> value;
  }
```

```
T from_string(std::string const& str, bool skipws = true)
{
  std::istringstream in{str};
  if (not skipws)
    in >> std::noskipws;
  T result{};
  char extra;
  if (not (in >> result))
    throw std::runtime_error{str};
  else if (in >> extra)
    throw std::runtime_error{str};
  else
    return result;
}
```

I threw in a new language feature. The function parameter skipws is followed by = true, which looks like an assignment or initialization. It lets you call from_string with one argument, just as before, using true as the second argument. This is how file streams specify a default file mode, in case you were wondering. If you decide to declare default argument values, you must supply them starting with the right-most argument in the argument list. I don't use default arguments often, and in Exploration 73, you will learn about some subtleties related to default arguments and overloading. For now, use them when they help, but use them sparingly.

Your turn to write a function from scratch. **Write the to_string function template**, which takes a single template argument and declares the to_string function to take a single function argument of that type. The function converts its argument to a string by writing it to a string stream and returns the resulting string. Compare your solution with mine, presented in Listing 60-11.

Listing 60-11. The to_string Function Converts a Value to a String

```
import <ostream>;
import <sstream>;
import <string>;

template<class T>
requires
  requires(T value, std::ostream stream) {
    stream << value;
  }
std::string to_string(T const& obj)
{
  std::ostringstream out{};
  out << obj;
  return out.str();
}
```

Can you see any particular drawback to these functions? _____ **If so, what?**

_____

No doubt, you can see many problems, but in particular, the one I want to point out is that they don't work with wide characters. It would be a shame to waste all that effort you spent in understanding wide characters, so let's add another template parameter for the character type. The std::string class template has three template parameters: the character type, the character traits, and an allocator object to manage any heap memory that the string might use. You don't have to know any of the details of these three types; you need only pass them to the basic_string class template. The basic_ostringstream class template takes the first two template arguments.

Your first attempt at implementing to_string may look a little bit like Listing 60-12.

Listing 60-12. Rewriting to_string As a Template Function

```
import <ostream>;
import <sstream>;
import <string>;

template<class T, class Char, class Traits, class Allocator>
requires
  requires(T value, std::ostream stream) {
    stream << value;
  }
std::basic_string<Char, Traits, Allocator> to_string(T const& obj)
{
  std::basic_ostringstream<Char, Traits> out{};
  out << obj;
  return out.str();
}
```

This implementation works. It's correct, but it's clumsy. Try it. **Try to write a simple test program that converts an integer to a narrow string and the same integer to a wide string**. Don't be discouraged if you can't figure out how to do it. This exercise is a demonstration of how templates in the standard library can lead you astray if you aren't careful. Take a look at my solution in Listing 60-13.

Listing 60-13. Demonstrating the Use of to_string

```
import <iostream>;
import to_string;
import from_string;

int main()
{
    std::string str{
      to_string<int, char, std::char_traits<char>, std::allocator<char>>(42)
    };
    int value{from_string<int>(str)};
    std::cout << value << '\n';
}
```

Do you see what I mean? How were you supposed to know what to provide as the third and fourth template arguments? Don't worry, we can find a better solution.

One alternative approach is not to return the string, but to take it as an output function argument. The compiler could then use argument-type deduction, and you wouldn't have to specify all those template arguments. **Write a version of to_string that takes the same template parameters** but also two function arguments: the value to convert and the destination string. **Write a demonstration program** to show how much simpler this function is to use. Listing 60-14 shows my solution.

Listing 60-14. Passing the Destination String As an Argument to to_string

```
import <iostream>;
import <sstream>;
import <string>;
import from_string;

template<class T, class Char, class Traits, class Allocator>
requires
  requires(T value, std::ostream stream) {
    stream << value;
  }
void to_string(T const& obj, std::basic_string<Char, Traits, Allocator>& result)
{
  std::basic_ostringstream<Char, Traits> out{};
  out << obj;
  result = out.str();
}

int main()
{
    std::string str{};
    to_string(42, str);
    int value(from_string<int>(str));
    std::cout << value << '\n';
}
```

On the other hand, if you want to use the string in an expression, you still have to declare a temporary variable just to hold the string.

Another way to approach this problem is to specify std::string or std::wstring as the sole template argument. The compiler can deduce the type of the object you want to convert. The basic_string template has member types for its template parameters, so you can use those to discover the traits and allocator types. The to_string function returns the string type and takes an argument of the object type. Both types have to be template parameters. **Which parameter should be first?** Listing 60-15 shows the latest incarnation of to_string, which now takes two template parameters: the string type and the object type.

Listing 60-15. Improving the Calling Interface of to_string

```
import <ostream>;
import <sstream>;

template<class String, class T>
requires
  requires(T value, std::ostream stream) {
    stream << value;
    typename String::value_type;
    typename String::traits_type;
  }
```

EXPLORATION 60 ■ TEXT I/O

```
String to_string(T const& obj)
{
  std::basic_ostringstream<typename String::value_type,
                           typename String::traits_type> out{};
  out << obj;
  return out.str();
}
```

Remember typename from Exploration 57? The compiler doesn't know that String::value_type names a type. A specialization of basic_ostringstream could declare it to be anything. The typename keyword tells the compiler that you know the name is for a type. Calling this form of to_string is straightforward.

```
to_string<std::string>(42);
```

This form seems to strike the best balance between flexibility and ease of use. But can we add some more formatting flexibility? Should we add width and fill characters? Field adjustment? Hexadecimal or octal? What if to_string takes std::ios_base::fmtflags as an argument and the caller can specify any formatting flags? What should be the default? Listing 60-16 shows what happens when the author goes overboard.

Listing 60-16. Making to_string Too Complicated

```
import <iostream>;
import <sstream>;

template<class String, class T>
requires
  requires(T value, std::ostream stream) {
    stream << value;
    typename String::value_type;
    typename String::traits_type;
  }
String to_string(T const& obj,
  std::ios_base::fmtflags flags = std::ios_base::fmtflags{},
  int width = 0,
  char fill = ' ')
{
  std::basic_ostringstream<typename String::value_type,
                           typename String::traits_type> out{};
  out.flags(flags);
  out.width(width);
  out.fill(fill);
  out << obj;
  return out.str();
}
```

Listing 60-17 shows some examples of calling this form of to_string.

Listing 60-17. Calling the Complicated Version of to_string

```
import <iostream>;
import <string>;
import to_string;

int main()
{
  std::cout << to_string<std::string>(42, std::ios_base::hex) << '\n';
  std::cout << to_string<std::string>(42.0, std::ios_base::scientific, 10) << '\n';
  std::cout << to_string<std::string>(true, std::ios_base::boolalpha) << '\n';
}
```

You should see the following as output:

```
2a
4.200000e+01
true
```

This version of to_string has too many arguments to be easy to use and it ends up being too verbose to achieve any kind of formatting. The standard library offers a completely different approach with the <format> module. You will need a language reference for a complete explanation, but the basic idea is to write a formatting string that describes the desired format, and pass arguments that match the format string. Format strings work similarly to the way they do in Python. You can pass any number of arguments and format all of them at one time. Listing 60-18 demonstrates how a single call to the format() function can format all three values of Listing 60-17.

Listing 60-18. Calling std::format to Format a String

```
import <format>;
import <iostream>;

int main()
{
  std::cout << std::format("{0:x}\n{1:.10e}\n{2}\n", 42, 42.0, true);
}
```

Pass a wide string as the format string to produce a wide string result. You can also call std::format_to() with an output iterator as the first argument to write the formatted string to the iterator instead of constructing a string. This is a more efficient way to format text output. **Modify Listing 60-17 to write to an iterator that writes to std::cout, thereby eliminating the need for a temporary string**. Because the format_to() function does all the formatting and yields characters, you can use std::ostreambuf_iterator<char> instead of ostream_iterator. Listing 60-19 shows my solution.

Listing 60-19. Calling `std::format_to` to Format Output

```
import <format>;
import <iostream>;
import <iterator>;

int main()
{
  std::format_to(std::ostreambuf_iterator<char>(std::cout),
     "{0:x}\n{1:.10e}\n{2}\n", 42, 42.0, true);
}
```

That concludes Part 3. Time for a project.

■ ■ ■

Project 3: Currency Type

It's time for another project. You're going to continue building on the fixed type from Project 2 and incorporate what you've learned about locales and I/O. Your task this time is to write a currency type. The value is stored as a fixed-point value. I/O is formatted using the get_money and put_money manipulators.

Make sure you can add two currency amounts to get a currency value, subtract two currency amounts to get currency, multiply and divide currency by an integer or rational value to get a currency result, and divide two currency values to get a rational result.

As with any project, start small and add functionality as you go. For example, start with the basic data representation, then add I/O operators. Add arithmetic operators one at a time. Write each test function before you implement the feature.

© Ray Lischner 2020
R. Lischner, *Exploring C++20*, https://doi.org/10.1007/978-1-4842-5961-0_61

PART IV

Real Programming

EXPLORATION 62

■ ■ ■

Pointers

Few topics cause more confusion, especially for programmers new to C++, than pointers. Necessary, powerful, and versatile, pointers can also be dangerous and the underlying cause of so many bugs that they are both bane and blessing. Pointers are hard at work behind many of the standard library's features, and any serious application or library inevitably uses pointers in some fashion. Most application programmers do not work with pointers directly, but they affect the entire C++ standard in ways that you cannot ignore.

A Programming Problem

Before diving into syntax and semantics, consider the following problem. Real-life C++ projects typically contain multiple source files, and each source file imports multiple modules. While you are working, you will compile and recompile the project many times. Each time, it's preferable to recompile only those files that have changed or import a module whose interface has changed. Different development environments have different tools to decide which files to recompile. An IDE typically makes these decisions itself; in other environments, a separate tool, such as make, jam, or scons, examines the files in your project and decides which ones to recompile. (I use cmake to compile and test all of the code listings in this book.)

The problem to tackle in this and following Explorations is to write a simple tool that decides which files to compile and pretends to compile them. (Actually invoking an external program is beyond the scope of this book, so you won't learn how to write an entire build tool.)

The essential idea is simple: to make an executable program, you must compile source files into object files and link the object files to form the program. The executable program is said to *depend on* the object files, which in turn depend on the source files. Other terminology has the program as the *target*, with the object files as its *dependencies*. An object file, in turn, can be a target, with a source file and the module interface files that it imports as dependencies.

As you know, to compile a single source file into a single object file, the compiler may be required to read many additional module files. Each of these module files is a dependency of the object file. Thus, one module file can be a dependency of many object files. In more technical terms, targets and dependencies form a directed acyclic graph (DAG), which I will call the *dependency graph*.

■ **Note**   A cyclic graph, such that A depends on B and B depends on A, is a bad idea in the real world and often indicates a faulty or poorly considered design. For the sake of simplicity, I will ignore this error condition in this and subsequent Explorations.

Anyone who's been around large projects knows that dependency graphs can become extremely complex. Some module files may be generated by other programs, so the module files are targets, with the generating programs as dependencies, and the generating programs are targets with their own dependencies.

IDEs and programs, such as make, analyze the dependency graph and determine which targets must be built first to ensure that every target's dependencies are fulfilled. Thus, if A depends on B and B depends on C, make must build C first (if it is a target), then B, and finally A. The key algorithm that make employs to find the correct order in which to build targets is a *topological sort*.

Topological sorts are not included in the typical algorithms coursework of many computer science majors. Nor does the algorithm appear in many textbooks. However, any comprehensive algorithms book includes topological sort.

■ **Note** A good text on topological sort is *Introduction to Algorithms*, third ed., by T. H. Cormen, C. E. Leiserson, and R. L. Rivest (MIT Press, 2009). My solution implements exercise 22.4-5.

The C++ standard library does not include a topological sort algorithm, because it is not a sequential algorithm. It operates on a graph, and the C++ library has no standard graph classes.

We'll begin this Exploration by writing a pseudo-make program—that is, a program that reads a *makefile*: a file that describes a set of targets and their dependencies, performs a topological sort to find the order for building targets, and prints the targets in proper build order. In order to simplify the program somewhat, restrict the input to a text file that declares dependencies as pairs of strings, one pair on a line of text. The first string is the name of a target, and the second string is the name of a dependency. If a target has multiple dependencies, the input file must list the target on multiple lines, one per dependency. A target can be a dependency of another target. The order of lines within the input file is not important. The goal is to write a program that will print the targets in order, so that a make-like program can build the first target first, and proceed in order, such that all targets are built before they are needed as dependencies.

To help clarify terminology, I use the term *artifact* for a string that can be a target, a dependency, or both. If you already know an algorithm for topological sort, go ahead and implement the program now. Otherwise, keep reading to see one implementation of `topological_sort`. To represent the dependency graph, use a map of sets. The map key is a dependency, and the value is the set of targets that list the key as a dependency. This seems inside out from the way you may usually think about organizing targets and dependencies, but as you can see in Listing 62-1, it makes the topological sort quite easy to implement. Because the `topological_sort` function is reusable, it is a template function and works with *nodes* instead of artifacts, targets, and dependencies.

Listing 62-1. Topological Sort of a Directed Acyclic Graph

```
export module topsort;
import <deque>;
import <ranges>;
import <stdexcept>;

// Helper function for topological_sort().
template<class Graph, class Nodes>
requires
    std::ranges::range<Graph> and
    requires {
        typename Graph::value_type;
        typename Graph::key_type;
    }
```

```
void topsort_clean_graph(Graph& graph, Nodes& nodes)
{
  for (auto iter{std::ranges::begin(graph)}; iter != std::ranges::end(graph);)
  {
    if (iter->second.empty())
    {
      nodes.push_back(iter->first);
      graph.erase(iter++);  // advance iterator before erase invalidates it
    }
    else
      ++iter;
  }
}

/// Topological sort of a directed acyclic graph.
/// A graph is a map keyed by nodes, with sets of nodes as values.
/// Edges run from values to keys. The sorted list of nodes
/// is copied to an output iterator in reverse order.
/// @param graph The graph
/// @param sorted The output iterator
/// @throws std::runtime_error if the graph contains a cycle
/// @pre Graph::key_type == Graph::mapped_type::key_type
export template<class Graph, class OutIterator>
requires
    std::ranges::range<Graph> and
    requires {
        typename Graph::value_type;
        typename Graph::key_type;
    }
    and
    std::output_iterator<OutIterator, typename Graph::key_type>
void topological_sort(Graph graph, OutIterator sorted)
{
  std::deque<typename Graph::key_type> nodes{};
  // Start with the set of nodes with no incoming edges.
  topsort_clean_graph(graph, nodes);

  while (not nodes.empty())
  {
    // Grab the first node to process, output it to sorted,
    // and remove it from the graph.
    auto n{nodes.front()};
    nodes.pop_front();
    *sorted = n;
    ++sorted;

    // Erase n from the graph
    for (auto& node : graph)
    {
      node.second.erase(n);
    }
```

513

```
    // After removing n, find any nodes that no longer
    // have any incoming edges.
    topsort_clean_graph(graph, nodes);
  }
  if (not graph.empty())
    throw std::runtime_error("Dependency graph contains cycles");
}
```

Now that you have the topological_sort function, **implement the pseudo-make program** to read and parse the input, build the dependency graph, call topological_sort, and print the sorted result. Keep things simple and treat artifacts (targets and dependencies) as strings. Thus, the dependency graph is a map with std::string as the key type and std::unordered_set<std::string> as the value type. (The map and set do not need to be in alphabetical order, so use unordered containers.) Compare your solution with Listing 62-2.

Listing 62-2. First Draft of the Pseudo-make Program

```cpp
#include <cstdlib>
import <algorithm>;
import <iostream>;
import <iterator>;
import <sstream>;
import <stdexcept>;
import <string>;
import <unordered_map>;
import <unordered_set>;
import <vector>;

import topsort;

using artifact = std::string; ///< A target, dependency, or both

class dependency_graph
{
public:
  using graph_type=std::unordered_map<artifact, std::unordered_set<artifact>>;

  void store_dependency(artifact const& target, artifact const& dependency)
  {
    graph_[dependency].insert(target);
    graph_[target]; // ensures that target is in the graph
  }

  graph_type const& graph() const { return graph_; }

  template<class OutIter>
  requires std::output_iterator<OutIter, artifact>
  void sort(OutIter sorted)
  const
  {
    topological_sort(graph_, sorted);
  }
```

```
private:
  graph_type graph_;
};

int main()
{
  dependency_graph graph{};

  std::string line{};
  while (std::getline(std::cin, line))
  {
    std::string target{}, dependency{};
    std::istringstream stream{line};
    if (stream >> target >> dependency)
      graph.store_dependency(target, dependency);
    else if (not target.empty())
      // Input line has a target with no dependency,
      // so report an error.
      std::cerr << "malformed input: target, " << target <<
                   ", must be followed by a dependency name\n";
    // else ignore blank lines
  }

  try {
    // Get the artifacts in dependency order.
    std::vector<artifact> sorted{};
    graph.sort(std::back_inserter(sorted));
    // Print in build order, which is reverse of dependency order.
    for (auto const& artifact: sorted | std::ranges::views::reverse)
      std::cout << artifact << '\n';
  } catch (std::runtime_error const& ex) {
    std::cerr << ex.what() << '\n';
    return EXIT_FAILURE;
  }
}
```

So what do DAGs and topological sorts have to do with the topic of this Exploration? I thought you'd never ask. Let's construct a slightly more complicated problem by making it a little more realistic.

A real make program has to keep track of more information about an artifact, especially the time when it was last modified. A target also has a list of actions to perform, if any dependency is newer than the target. Thus, a class makes more sense than a string for representing an artifact. You can add to the class whatever functionality you need for your make program.

Query a file's modification type with std::filesystem::last_write_time(), which is declared in <filesystem>. The time returned has type std::filesystem::file_time_type, which you can compare with an ordinary comparison operators. Ignoring the build() action, you might define the artifact type as shown in Listing 62-3.

Listing 62-3. New Definition of an Artifact

```
export module artifact;
import <filesystem>;
import <string>;
import <system_error>;

export class artifact
{
public:
  using file_time_type = std::filesystem::file_time_type;
  artifact() : name_{}, mod_time_{file_time_type::min()} {}
  artifact(std::string const& name)
  : name_{name}, mod_time_{get_mod_time()}
  {}

  std::string const& name() const { return name_; }
  file_time_type mod_time() const { return mod_time_; }

  /// Builds a target.
  /// After completing the actions (not yet implemented),
  /// update the modification time.
  void build();

  /// Looks up the modification time of the artifact.
  /// Returns file_time_type::min() if the artifact does not
  /// exist (and therefore must be built) or if the time cannot
  /// be obtained for any other reason.
  file_time_type get_mod_time()
  {
    std::error_code ec;
    auto time{ std::filesystem::last_write_time(name_, ec) };
    if (ec)
        return file_time_type::min();
    else
        return time;
  }
private:
  std::string name_;
  file_time_type mod_time_;
};
```

Now we run into a problem. In the first draft of this program, what made two strings refer to the same artifact is that the strings had the same content. The target named "program" is the same artifact as the dependency named "program," because they are spelled the same. That scheme falls down now that an artifact is more than just a string. When you build a target and update its modification time, you want all uses of that artifact to be updated. Somehow, every use of an artifact name must be associated with a single artifact object for that name.

Got any ideas? It can be done with your current understanding of C++, but you may have to stop and think about it.

Need a hint? How about storing all artifacts in one big vector? Then make a dependency graph that contains indices into the vector, instead of artifact names. **Try it**. Rewrite the program in Listing 62-2 to use the new artifact module from Listing 62-3. When an artifact name is read from the input file, look up that name in a vector of all artifacts. If the artifact is new, add it to the end. Store vector indices in the dependency graph. Print the final list by looking up the numbers in the vector. Compare your solution with Listing 62-4.

■ **Note**   If the performance of linear lookups concerns you, congratulations for sharp thinking. Not to worry, however, because the program will continue to grow and evolve throughout this Exploration, and we will eliminate the performance issue before we finish.

Listing 62-4. Second Draft, After Adding Modification Times to Artifacts

```
#include <cstdlib>
import <algorithm>;
import <iostream>;
import <iterator>;
import <sstream>;
import <stdexcept>;
import <string>;
import <unordered_map>;
import <unordered_set>;
import <vector>;

import artifact;
import topsort;

using artifact_index = std::size_t;

class dependency_graph
{
public:
  using graph_type = std::unordered_map<artifact_index,
      std::unordered_set<artifact_index>>;

  void store_dependency(artifact_index target, artifact_index dependency)
  {
    graph_[dependency].insert(target);
    graph_[target]; // ensures that target is in the graph
  }

  graph_type const& graph() const { return graph_; }

  template<class OutIter>
  requires std::output_iterator<OutIter, artifact_index>
  void sort(OutIter sorted)
```

```
  const
  {
    topological_sort(graph_, sorted);
  }

private:
  graph_type graph_;
};

std::vector<artifact> artifacts{};

artifact_index lookup_artifact(std::string const& name)
{
  auto iter{ std::find_if(artifacts.begin(), artifacts.end(),
    [&name](artifact const& a) { return a.name() == name; })
  };
  if (iter != artifacts.end())
    return iter - artifacts.begin();
  // Artifact not found, so add it to the end.
  artifacts.emplace_back(name);
  return artifacts.size() - 1;
}

int main()
{
  dependency_graph graph{};

  std::string line{};
  while (std::getline(std::cin, line))
  {
    std::string target_name{}, dependency_name{};
    std::istringstream stream{line};
    if (stream >> target_name >> dependency_name)
    {
      artifact_index target{lookup_artifact(target_name)};
      artifact_index dependency{lookup_artifact(dependency_name)};
      graph.store_dependency(target, dependency);
    }
    else if (not target_name.empty())
      // Input line has a target with no dependency,
      // so report an error.
      std::cerr << "malformed input: target, " << target_name <<
                  ", must be followed by a dependency name\n";
    // else ignore blank lines
  }

  try {
    // Get the artifact indices in dependency order.
    std::vector<artifact_index> sorted{};
    graph.sort(std::back_inserter(sorted));
```

```
  // Print in build order, which is reverse of dependency order.
  for (auto index: sorted | std::ranges::views::reverse)
    std::cout << artifacts.at(index).name() << '\n';
} catch (std::runtime_error const& ex) {
  std::cerr << ex.what() << '\n';
  return EXIT_FAILURE;
}
}
```

Well, that works, but it's ugly. Looking up indices is sloppy programming. Much better would be to store references to the artifact objects directly in the graph. Ah, there's the rub. You can't store a reference in a standard container. Containers are for storing objects—real objects. The container must be able to copy and assign the elements in the container, but it can't do that with references. Copying a reference actually copies the object to which it refers. A reference is not a first-class entity that a program can manipulate.

Wouldn't it be nice if C++ had a language feature that acts like a reference but lets you copy and assign the reference itself (not the referred-to object)? Let's pretend we are inventing the C++ language, and we have to add this language feature.

The Solution

Let's devise a new language feature to solve this programming problem. This new feature is similar to references but permits use with standard containers. Let's call this feature a *flex-ref*, short for "flexible reference."

If a and b are both flex-refs that refer to type int, the statement

```
a = b;
```

means the value of a changes so that a now refers to the same int object to which b refers. Passing a as an argument to a function passes the value of a, so if the function assigns a new value to a, that change is local to the function (just as with any other function argument). Using a suitable operator, however, the function can obtain the int object to which a refers and read or modify that int.

You need a way to obtain the referred-to value, so we have to invent a new operator. Look at iterators for inspiration: given an iterator, the unary * operator returns the item to which the iterator refers. Let's use the same operator for flex-refs. Thus, the following prints the int value to which a refers:

```
std::cout << *a;
```

In the spirit of the * operator, declare a flex-ref by using * in the same manner that you use & for references.

```
int *a, *b;
```

Use the same syntax when declaring a container. For example, declare a vector of flex-refs that refer to type int.

```
std::vector<int*> vec;
vec.push_back(a);
b = vec.front();
```

All that's left is to provide a way to make a flex-ref refer to an object. For that, let's turn to ordinary references for inspiration and use the & operator. Supposing that c is of type int, the following makes a refer to c:

```
a = &c;
```

As you've guessed by now, flex-refs are pointers. The variables a and b are called "pointers to int." A pointer is an honest-to-goodness lvalue. It occupies memory. The values that are stored in that memory are addresses of other lvalues. You can freely change the value stored in that memory, which has the effect of making the pointer refer to a different object.

A pointer can point to a const object, or it can be a const pointer, or both. The following shows pointer to const int:

```
int const* p;
p = &c;
```

Define a const pointer—that is, a pointer that is itself const and therefore cannot be the target of an assignment, but the dereferenced object can be the target.

```
int * const q{&c};
*q = 42;
```

Like any const object, you must supply an initializer, and you cannot modify the pointer. However, you can modify the object to which the pointer points.

You can define a reference to a pointer, just as you can define a reference to anything (except another reference).

```
int const*&r{p};
```

Read this declaration the way you would read any other declaration: start by finding the declarator, r. Then read the declaration from the inside, working your way outward. To the left, see &, telling you that r is a reference. To the right is the initializer, {p}; r is a reference to p (r is another name for the object p). Continuing to the left, you see *, so r is a reference to a pointer. Then you see const, so you know r is a reference to a pointer to a const something. Finally, int tells you that r is a reference to a pointer to const int. Thus, the initializer is valid, because its type is pointer to int.

What about the other way around? Can you define a pointer to a reference? The short answer is that you can't. A pointer to a reference makes as little sense as a reference to a reference. References and pointers must refer or point to a real object. When you use the & operator on a reference, you get the address of the referenced object.

You can define a pointer to a pointer, or a pointer to a pointer to a pointer to a pointer. Just keep track of the exact type of your pointer. The compiler ensures that you assign only expressions of the correct type, as shown here:

```
int x;
int *y;
int **z;
y = &x;
z = &y;
```

Try z = &x and y = z. What happens?

Because x has type int, &x has type int*; y has type int*, too, so you can assign &x to y but not to z, which has type int**. The types must match, so you can't assign z to y either.

It took me long enough to get to the point, but now you can see how pointers help solve the problem of writing the dependency graph. Before we dive into the code, however, let's take a moment to clarify some terminology.

Addresses vs. Pointers

Programmers are sticklers for details. The compilers and other tools we use daily force us to be. So let's be absolutely clear about addresses and pointers.

An *address* is a memory location. In C++ parlance, it is an rvalue, so you cannot modify or assign to an address. When a program takes the address of an object (with the & operator), the result is a constant for the lifetime of that object. Like every other rvalue, an address in C++ has a type, which must be a pointer type.

A *pointer type* is more properly called an *address type*, because the range of values represented by the type are addresses. Nonetheless, the term *pointer type* is more common, because a pointer object has a pointer type.

A pointer type can denote multiple levels of indirection—it can denote a pointer to a pointer, or a pointer to a pointer to a pointer, and so on. You must declare each level of pointer indirection with an asterisk. In other words, int* is the type "pointer to int" and int** is "pointer to pointer to int."

A *pointer* is an lvalue that has a pointer type. A pointer object, like any object, has a location in memory in which the program can store a value. The value must have a type that is compatible with the pointer's type; the value must be an address of the correct type.

Dependency Graphs

Now let's get back to the dependency graph. The graph can store pointers to artifacts. Each external file corresponds to a single artifact object in the program. That artifact can have many nodes in the graph pointing to it. If you update that artifact, all nodes that point to the artifact see the update. Thus, when a build rule updates an artifact, the file modification time may change. All nodes for that artifact in the graph immediately see the new time, because they all point to a single object.

All that's left to figure out is where these artifacts reside. For the sake of simplicity, I recommend a map, keyed by artifact name. The mapped values are artifact objects (not pointers). Take the address of an artifact in the map to obtain pointers to store in the graph. **Go ahead; don't wait for me.** Using the topsort and artifact modules, **rewrite Listing 62-4** to store artifact objects in a map and artifact pointers in the graph. Compare your solution with Listing 62-5.

Listing 62-5. Storing Pointers in the Dependency Graph

```
#include <cstdlib>
import <algorithm>;
import <iostream>;
import <iterator>;
import <map>;
import <sstream>;
import <stdexcept>;
import <string>;
import <unordered_map>;
import <unordered_set>;
import <vector>;
```

```
import artifact;
import topsort;

class dependency_graph
{
public:
  using graph_type = std::unordered_map<artifact*,
                        std::unordered_set<artifact*>>;

  void store_dependency(artifact* target, artifact* dependency)
  {
    graph_[dependency].insert(target);
    graph_[target]; // ensures that target is in the graph
  }

  graph_type const& graph() const { return graph_; }

  template<class OutIter>
  requires std::output_iterator<OutIter, artifact*>
  void sort(OutIter sorted)
  const
  {
    topological_sort(graph_, sorted);
  }

private:
  graph_type graph_;
};

std::map<std::string, artifact> artifacts{};

artifact* lookup_artifact(std::string const& name)
{
  auto a( artifacts.find(name) );
  if (a != artifacts.end())
    return &a->second;
  else
  {
    auto [iterator, inserted]{ artifacts.emplace(name, name) };
    return &iterator->second;
  }
}

int main()
{
  dependency_graph graph{};

  std::string line{};
  while (std::getline(std::cin, line))
  {
    std::string target_name{}, dependency_name{};
    std::istringstream stream{line};
```

```
    if (stream >> target_name >> dependency_name)
    {
        artifact* target{lookup_artifact(target_name)};
        artifact* dependency{lookup_artifact(dependency_name)};
        graph.store_dependency(target, dependency);
    }
    else if (not target_name.empty())
        // Input line has a target with no dependency, so report an error.
        std::cerr << "malformed input: target, " << target_name <<
                     ", must be followed by a dependency name\n";
    // else ignore blank lines
}

try {
    // Get the sorted artifacts.
    std::vector<artifact*> sorted{};
    graph.sort(std::back_inserter(sorted));
    // Print in build order, which is reverse of dependency order.
    for (auto artifact : sorted | std::ranges::views::reverse)
    {
        std::cout << artifact->name() << '\n';
    }
} catch (std::runtime_error const& ex) {
    std::cerr << ex.what() << '\n';
    return EXIT_FAILURE;
}
}
```

Overall, the program requires minimal changes, and the changes are mostly simplifications. As the program grows more complicated (as real programs inevitably do), the simplicity and elegance of pointers become more and more evident.

One new feature is a curious statement in lookup_artifact:

```
auto [iterator, inserted]{ artifacts.emplace(name, name) };
```

This is a declaration that defines two variables, iterator and inserted. The initial value of these variables is the value returned from the emplace() function, which returns a std::pair. The compiler unpacks the pair and initializes iterator with the first member of the pair and initializes inserted with the second member. This kind of declaration is called a *structured binding*.

The artifact objects are stored in a std::map instead of unordered_map because the pointers to the artifacts must remain valid as artifacts are added to the map. In the case of unordered_map, it may need to increase the size of its hash table, which might mean moving all of the artifact objects around in memory. That invalidates all the pointers that the dependency graph holds on to. Because std::map uses a tree structure, adding nodes to the tree does not require changing where existing artifacts are stored. We will revisit this consideration, but first let's beef up the parser. The next Exploration looks at how to use regular expressions to parse the makefile.

■ ■ ■

Regular Expressions

All modern languages support regular expressions in one fashion or another. Some scripting languages feature them prominently in the language syntax. C++ provides basic support for regular expressions with its <regex> module. This Exploration covers only the C++ classes and functions and does not delve into regular expression syntax. Many resources in print and online can help you if you need to brush up on regular expression syntax. C++ supports multiple regular expression styles; the default is the RegeExp object in ECMAScript 2019 (better known as JavaScript).

Parsing with Regular Expressions

Writing a parser often calls for parser-generator tools, but our dependency tool has such a simple language, we can use regular expressions to parse the input. The input of two strings on one line of text is easily matched by the regular expression, or *regex*:

```
^[ \t]*(\S+)[ \t]+(\S+)[ \t]*$
```

Let's make the input a little bit more like the make program and add a colon to separate the target from its dependency:

```
^[ \t]*(\S+)[ \t]*:[ \t]*(\S+)[ \t]*$
```

We can also add optional comments that start with a # character or allow the line to be blank:

```
^[ \t]*(?:#.*|(\S+)[ \t]*:[ \t]*(\S+)[ \t]*(?:#.*)?)?$
```

Construct a std::regex object to compile the regular expression. If the regular expression contains an error, the constructor throws std::regex_error. Remember that backslash (\) has a special meaning in strings and is used as a metacharacter in regular expressions, so you must repeat it for \\S. Leave a single backslash in \t because it is an ordinary tab character. The regex_match() function tests a string against a regex and, depending on the arguments you pass, can return the capture groups, too. Copying Listing 62-5 and changing the parser to use a regular expression results in Listing 63-1.

Listing 63-1. Parsing with a Regular Expression

```
#include <cstdlib>
import <iostream>;
import <iterator>;
import <map>;
import <ranges>;
```

© Ray Lischner 2020
R. Lischner, *Exploring C++20*, https://doi.org/10.1007/978-1-4842-5961-0_63

```cpp
import <regex>;
import <sstream>;
import <stdexcept>;
import <string>;
import <unordered_map>;
import <unordered_set>;
import <vector>;

import artifact;
import topsort;

class dependency_graph
{
public:
  using graph_type = std::unordered_map<artifact*,
                          std::unordered_set<artifact*>>;

  void store_dependency(artifact* target, artifact* dependency)
  {
    graph_[dependency].insert(target);
    graph_[target]; // ensures that target is in the graph
  }

  graph_type const& graph() const { return graph_; }

  template<class OutIter>
  requires std::output_iterator<OutIter, artifact*>
  void sort(OutIter sorted)
  const
  {
    topological_sort(graph_, sorted);
  }

  artifact* lookup_artifact(std::string const& name)
  {
    auto a( artifacts_.find(name) );
    if (a != artifacts_.end())
      return &a->second;
    else
    {
      auto [iterator, inserted]{ artifacts_.emplace(name, name) };
      return &iterator->second;
    }
  }

private:
  graph_type graph_;
  std::map<std::string, artifact> artifacts_;
};
```

```cpp
int main()
{
  dependency_graph graph{};

  static const std::regex regex{
      "^[ \t]*(?:#.*|(\\S+)[ \t]*:[ \t]*(\\S+)[ \t]*(?:#.*)?)?$"
  };

  std::string line{};
  std::size_t line_number{};
  while (std::getline(std::cin, line))
  {
    ++line_number;
    std::smatch match;
    if (std::regex_match(line, match, regex))
    {
      // Skip comments and blank lines.
      if (match[1].matched) {
        auto target{graph.lookup_artifact(match[1].str())};
        auto dependency{graph.lookup_artifact(match[2].str())};
        graph.store_dependency(target, dependency);
      }
    }
    else
      // Input line cannot be parsed.
      std::cerr << "line " << line_number << ": parse error\n";
  }

  try {
    // Get the sorted artifacts.
    std::vector<artifact*> sorted{};
    graph.sort(std::back_inserter(sorted));
    // Print in build order, which is reverse of dependency order.
    for (auto artifact : sorted | std::ranges::views::reverse)
    {
      std::cout << artifact->name() << '\n';
    }
  } catch (std::runtime_error const& ex) {
    std::cerr << ex.what() << '\n';
    return EXIT_FAILURE;
  }
}
```

Now that we have some more power in our parser, we can start to add features. Let's add variables. A variable definition has the form variable=value. A variable reference has the form $(variable) and is replaced by the value of variable. Two adjacent dollar signs ($$) are replaced by a single dollar sign. An unknown variable expands to an empty string. After replacing all variable expansions, a string is rescanned to see if there are more expansions to be made. Thus, $$(var$(n)) expands first by converting $$ to $ and looking up variable n. Assume n has the value 42. After replacing $$ by $ and $(n) by the value of n, the resulting string $(var42) is then expanded by looking up var42.

Before jumping into rewriting the parser, let's move the dependency_graph class to its own module. Determine which modules it must import and write a depgraph module that exports dependency_graph. Change store_dependency so it takes two strings as arguments and handles all the artifact pointers locally so main() doesn't need to concern itself with how artifacts are actually managed. Write the depgraph module. Compare yours with mine in Listing 63-2.

Listing 63-2. The depgraph Module

```
export module depgraph;

import <iterator>;
import <map>;
import <string>;
import <unordered_map>;
import <unordered_set>;

import artifact;
import topsort;

export class dependency_graph
{
public:
  using graph_type = std::unordered_map<artifact*,
                        std::unordered_set<artifact*>>;

  void store_dependency(std::string const& target_name,
      std::string const& dependency_name)
  {
    auto target{ lookup_artifact(target_name) };
    auto dependency{ lookup_artifact(dependency_name) };
    store_dependency(target, dependency);
  }

  graph_type const& graph() const { return graph_; }

  template<class OutIter>
  requires std::output_iterator<OutIter, artifact*>
  void sort(OutIter sorted)
  const
  {
    topological_sort(graph_, sorted);
  }

  artifact* lookup_artifact(std::string const& name)
  {
    auto a{ artifacts_.find(name) };
    if (a != artifacts_.end())
      return &a->second;
```

```
    else
    {
      auto [iterator, inserted]{ artifacts_.emplace(name, name) };
      return &iterator->second;
    }
  }

private:
  void store_dependency(artifact* target, artifact* dependency)
  {
    graph_[dependency].insert(target);
    graph_[target]; // ensures that target is in the graph
  }

  graph_type graph_;
  std::map<std::string, artifact> artifacts_;
};
```

You will need to store and retrieve variables. Write a variables module that exports functions to define, look up, and expand variables. For expanding variables, we'll use a regex_iterator to find all the variables in the input string. The iterator value is an smatch object. Be brave and try your hand at writing the variables module, or just look at Listing 63-3.

Listing 63-3. The variables Module

```
export module variables;

import <ranges>;
import <regex>;
import <string>;
import <unordered_map>;

std::unordered_map<std::string, std::string> variables;

export void define_variable(std::string const& name, std::string const& value)
{
    variables[name] = value;
}

std::string const empty_string;

export std::string const& lookup_variable(std::string const& name)
{
    if (auto var = variables.find(name); var == variables.end())
        return empty_string;
    else
        return var->second;
}
```

```
export std::string expand_variables(std::string const& input)
{
    static const std::regex regex{ "\\$(?:\\$|\\(([\\w.-_]+)\\))" };
    std::string result{};
    auto prefix_begin{ input.begin() };
    auto begin{ std::sregex_iterator{input.begin(), input.end(), regex} };
    auto end{ std::sregex_iterator{} };
    bool matched{false};
    using subrange = std::ranges::subrange<std::sregex_iterator>;
    for (auto const& match: subrange(begin, end)){
        // Copy the string prior to the match
        result.append(prefix_begin, match[0].first);
        prefix_begin = match[0].second;
        if (match[1].matched)
        {
            result += lookup_variable(match[1].str());
            matched = true;
        }
        else
            result += '$'; // no variable, so the regex matched $$
    }
    // copy rest of unmatched string
    result.append(prefix_begin, input.end());
    if (not matched)
        return result;

    // try matching again.
    return expand_variables(result);
}
```

Armed with the new depgraph and variables modules, it's time to revisit the parser in main(). **You can do this on your own**. After parsing the target and dependency names, expand variables in them, and add them to the dependency graph. Compare your program with mine in Listing 63-4.

Listing 63-4. New Program Using depgraph and variables Modules

```
#include <cstdlib>
import <iostream>;
import <iterator>;
import <ranges>;
import <regex>;
import <string>;
import <vector>;

import artifact;
import depgraph;
import variables;
```

```cpp
int main()
{
  dependency_graph graph{};

  static const std::regex regex{
      "^[ \t]*(?:#.*|[ \t]*(\\S+)[ \t]*=[ \t]*(.*)|(\\S+)[ \t]*:[ \t]*(\\S+)[ \t]*
      (?:#.*)?)?$"
  };

  std::string line{};
  std::size_t line_number{};
  while (std::getline(std::cin, line))
  {
    ++line_number;
    std::smatch match;
    if (std::regex_match(line, match, regex))
    {
      if (match[1].matched)
        // variable definition
        define_variable(match[1].str(), match[2].str());
      else if (match[3].matched) {
        // target: dependency
        auto target{expand_variables(match[3].str())};
        auto dependency{expand_variables(match[4].str())};
        graph.store_dependency(target, dependency);
      }
      // else comment or blank line
    }
    else
      // Input line cannot be parsed.
      std::cerr << "line " << line_number << ": parse error\n";
  }

  try {
    // Get the sorted artifacts.
    std::vector<artifact*> sorted{};
    graph.sort(std::back_inserter(sorted));
    // Print in build order, which is reverse of dependency order.
    for (auto artifact : sorted | std::ranges::views::reverse)
    {
      std::cout << artifact->name() << '\n';
    }
  } catch (std::runtime_error const& ex) {
    std::cerr << ex.what() << '\n';
    return EXIT_FAILURE;
  }
}
```

531

The next step is to permit per-target variables. That is, if the input starts with a target name and colon, but what follows is a variable definition instead of a dependency name, then the variable definition applies only to that target, for example:

```
NUM=1
target$(NUM) : SRC=1
target$(NUM) : source$(SRC)
target2      : source$(NUM)
target2      : source$(SRC)
```

The NUM variable is global, so target2 depends on source1. The SRC variable applies only to target1, so target1 depends on source1. On the other hand, the last line says that target2 depends on source, not source2, because target2 does not have a SRC variable, and unknown variables expand to an empty string.

Let's start by adding a local variable map to every artifact. Later, we will refine the implementation to distinguish between targets and dependencies so that only targets have variable maps. Let's start by revisiting the variables module. Because we now have local variables and global variables, it seems like a good idea to write a variables class that can serve both purposes. But there's a catch.

When looking up a variable name, it needs to be looked up in a target-specific map and in the global map. So lookup depends on what kind of map it is. **Modify the variables module to define a base class that implements the map logic, with two derived classes for local and global variables, which differ only in their lookup functions**. Compare your module with mine in Listing 63-5.

Listing 63-5. Adding Local and Global Maps to the variables Module

```
export module variables;

import <ranges>;
import <regex>;
import <string>;
import <unordered_map>;

class base
{
public:
    virtual ~base() = default;
    virtual std::string const& lookup(std::string const& name) const = 0;

    void define(std::string const& name, std::string const& value)
    {
        map_[name] = value;
    }

    std::string expand(std::string const& input)
    const
    {
        static const std::regex regex{ "\\$(?:\\$|\\(([\\w.-_]+)\\))" };
        std::string result{};
        auto prefix_begin{ input.begin() };
        auto begin{ std::sregex_iterator{input.begin(), input.end(), regex} };
        auto end{ std::sregex_iterator{} };
        bool matched{false};
        using subrange = std::ranges::subrange<std::sregex_iterator>;
```

```cpp
        for (auto const& match: subrange(begin, end)){
            // Copy the string prior to the match
            result.append(prefix_begin, match[0].first);
            prefix_begin = match[0].second;
            if (match[1].matched)
            {
                result += lookup(match[1].str());
                matched = true;
            }
            else
                result += '$'; // no variable, so the regex matched $$
        }
        // copy rest of unmatched string
        result.append(prefix_begin, input.end());
        if (not matched)
            return result;

        // try matching again.
        return expand(result);
    }

protected:
    base() = default;
    static const std::string empty_string;
    std::unordered_map<std::string, std::string> map_;
};

const std::string base::empty_string;

class global : public base
{
public:
    std::string const& lookup(std::string const& name)
    const override
    {
        if (auto var = map_.find(name); var == map_.end())
            return empty_string;
        else
            return var->second;
    }
};

// Global variables
export global global_variables;

// Target-specific variables
export class variables : public base
{
public:
    std::string const& lookup(std::string const& name)
    const override
```

```
        {
            if (auto var = map_.find(name); var == map_.end())
                return global_variables.lookup(name);
            else
                return var->second;
        }
};
```

Add a **variables** data member to **artifact** (from Listing 62-3). To hide the variables object, let the artifact class provide its own define() and expand() member functions to forward to the variables member. Compare your module with mine in Listing 63-6.

Listing 63-6. The New artifact Module

```
export module artifact;
import <filesystem>;
import <string>;
import <system_error>;

import variables;

export class artifact
{
public:
  using file_time_type = std::filesystem::file_time_type;
  artifact() : name_{}, mod_time_{file_time_type::min()}, vars_{} {}
  artifact(std::string const& name)
  : name_{name}, mod_time_{get_mod_time()}, vars_{}
  {}

  std::string const& name() const { return name_; }
  file_time_type mod_time() const { return mod_time_; }

  /// Builds a target.
  /// After completing the actions (not yet implemented),
  /// update the modification time.
  void build();

  /// Looks up the modification time of the artifact.
  /// Returns file_time_type::min() if the artifact does not
  /// exist (and therefore must be built) or if the time cannot
  /// be obtained for any other reason.
  file_time_type get_mod_time()
  {
    std::error_code ec;
    auto time{ std::filesystem::last_write_time(name_, ec) };
    if (ec)
        return file_time_type::min();
    else
        return time;
  }
```

```
  void define(std::string const& name, std::string const& value)
  {
    vars_.define(name, value);
  }

  std::string expand(std::string const& input)
  const
  {
    return vars_.expand(input);
  }

private:
  std::string name_;
  file_time_type mod_time_;
  variables vars_;
};
```

Now you are ready to update the parser. The regular expression is getting ugly, and this is the point at which you should start considering other parser options. Standard C++ doesn't help, but you can look at parser generators or third-party parser libraries. Sticking to standard C++, we will just make our regex a little more complicated. But we can make it a little easier to read by taking advantage of the fact that the compiler automatically concatenates adjacent strings. Split the regex into key parts and put each part in its own string. Add suitable space between the strings to enhance readability.

Write a parser module that exports a parse function. The function should take an istream and a dependency_graph argument, both passed by reference. Does yours resemble mine in Listing 63-7?

Listing 63-7. The parser Module

```
export module parser;

import <iostream>;
import <regex>;
import <string>;

import artifact;
import depgraph;

const std::regex regex{
    "^[ \t]*"
    "(?:"
        "#.*"                                        "|"
        "[ \t]*(\\S+)[ \t]*=[ \t]*(.*)"              "|"
        "(\\S+)[ \t]*:[ \t]*(\\S+)[ \t]*=[ \t]*(.*)" "|"
        "(\\S+)[ \t]*:[ \t]*(\\S+)[ \t]*(?:#.*)?"
    ")?$"
    };

export void parse(std::istream& stream, dependency_graph& graph)
{
  bool okay{true};
  std::string line{};
  std::size_t line_number{};
```

```
  while (std::getline(stream, line))
  {
    ++line_number;
    std::smatch match;
    if (std::regex_match(line, match, regex))
    {
      if (match[1].matched)
        // var=value
        global_variables.define(match[1].str(), match[2].str());
      else if (match[3].matched) {
        // target: var=value
        auto target_name{ global_variables.expand(match[3].str()) };
        auto target{graph.lookup_artifact(target_name)};
        target->define(match[4].str(), target->expand(match[5].str())));
      }
      else if (match[6].matched) {
        // target: dependency
        auto target_name{ global_variables.expand(match[6].str()) };
        auto target{target_name};
        auto dependency{
            graph.lookup_artifact(target)->expand(match[7].str())
        };
        graph.store_dependency(target, dependency);
      }
      // else comment or blank line
    }
    else
    {
      // Input line cannot be parsed.
      std::cerr << "line " << line_number << ": parse error\n";
      okay = false;
      // Keep going in case there are more errors.
    }
  }

  if (not okay)
    throw std::runtime_error("Cannot continue due to parse errors");
}
```

Now the main program is even simpler. Write the new main program. My take on it is in Listing 63-8.

Listing 63-8. New Program Using the parser Module

```
#include <cstdlib>
import <iostream>;
import <iterator>;
import <ranges>;
import <stdexcept>;
import <vector>;
```

```
import artifact;
import depgraph;
import parser;

int main()
{
  try {
    dependency_graph graph{};
    parse(std::cin, graph);

    // Get the sorted artifacts.
    std::vector<artifact*> sorted{};
    graph.sort(std::back_inserter(sorted));
    // Print in build order, which is reverse of dependency order.
    for (auto artifact : sorted | std::ranges::views::reverse)
    {
      std::cout << artifact->name() << '\n';
    }
  } catch (std::runtime_error const& ex) {
    std::cerr << ex.what() << '\n';
    return EXIT_FAILURE;
  }
}
```

Before moving on to the next steps in the pseudo-make program, it is time finally to delve into the magic of std::move(), which I introduced in Exploration 40 without explanation. The next Exploration finally explains std::move() and its importance in C++ programming.

■ ■ ■

Moving Data with Rvalue References

In Exploration 40, I introduced `std::move()` without explaining what it really does or how it works. Somehow it moves data, such as a string, from one variable to another, instead of copying the string contents, but you must be wondering how it works its wonders. The function itself is surprisingly simple. The concepts that underlie that simple implementation are more complicated, which is why I have waited until now to introduce the complexities and subtleties involved.

Copying vs. Moving

As you know, the std::vector type stores an array of values. As you add more values to the vector, it might have to allocate a new array to hold more values. When that happens, it must copy the old array into the new. If the values are large objects, this can be an expensive, time-consuming operation. If the value type permits it, however, the vector will move the values instead of copying them. Imagine if you bought a copy of *War and Peace* and you had to copy its contents to take the book home instead of moving it from the bookstore to your home.

The trick is for the compiler to know when it can move data and when it must make a copy. Ordinary assignment, for example, requires making a copy of the assignment source, so the target of the assignment ends up with an accurate copy of the source. Passing an argument to a function also requires making a copy of the argument, unless the parameter is declared as a reference type.

But sometimes, a function argument is temporary and the compiler knows it is temporary. The compiler knows that it doesn't have to copy data out of the temporary object. The temporary is about to be destroyed; it doesn't need to retain its data, so the data can be moved to the destination without copying.

To help you visualize what happens when objects are copied, let's create a new class that wraps `std::string` and shows you when its copy constructor and assignment operator are called. Then create a trivial program that reads strings from `std::cin` and adds them to a vector. **Write the program** and compare your program with mine in Listing 64-1.

Listing 64-1. Exposing How Strings Are Copied

```
import <iostream>;
import <string>;
import <vector>;
```

© Ray Lischner 2020

R. Lischner, *Exploring C++20*, https://doi.org/10.1007/978-1-4842-5961-0_64

```
class mystring : public std::string
{
public:
    mystring() : std::string{} { std::cout << "mystring()\n"; }
    mystring(mystring const& copy) : std::string{copy} {
        std::cout << "mystring copy(\"" << *this << "\")\n";
    }
};

std::vector<mystring> read_data()
{
    std::vector<mystring> strings{};
    mystring line{};
    while (std::getline(std::cin, line))
        strings.push_back(line);
    return strings;
}

int main()
{
    std::vector<mystring> strings{};
    strings = read_data();
}
```

Try running the program with a few lines of input. **How many times is each string copied?** _____ The program copies line into the vector in push_back(). When the compiler returns the strings variable to the caller, it knows that it doesn't have to copy the vector. It can move it instead. Thus, you don't get any extra copies there.

How can we reduce the number of times the strings are copied? The line variable stores temporary data. The program has no reason to retain the value in line after calling push_back(). So we know it is safe to move the string contents out of line and into data. Call std::move() to tell the compiler that it can move the string into the vector. You also have to add a move constructor to mystring. See the new program in Listing 64-2. **Now how many times is each string copied?** _____

Listing 64-2. Moving Strings Instead of Copying Them

```
import <iostream>;
import <string>;
import <utility>;
import <vector>;

class mystring : public std::string
{
public:
    mystring() : std::string{} { std::cout << "mystring()\n"; }
    mystring(mystring const& copy) : std::string{copy} {
        std::cout << "mystring copy(\"" << *this << "\")\n";
    }
    mystring(mystring&& move) noexcept
    : std::string{std::move(move)} {
        std::cout << "mystring move(\"" << *this << "\")\n";
    }
};
```

```
std::vector<mystring> read_data()
{
    std::vector<mystring> strings{};
    mystring line{};
    while (std::getline(std::cin, line))
        strings.emplace_back(std::move(line));
    return strings;
}

int main()
{
    std::vector<mystring> strings;
    strings = read_data();
}
```

The new constructor declares its parameters with a double ampersand (&&). It looks sort of like a reference. Notice that the parameter is not const. That's because moving data from an object must necessarily modify that object. Finally, recall from Exploration 48 that the noexcept specifier tells the compiler that the constructor cannot throw an exception. Notice also that the mystring constructor calls std::move() to move its parameter into the std::string constructor. You must call std::move() for any named object, even if that object is a special && reference.

The exact output depends on your library's implementation, but most start with a small amount of memory for the vector and grow slowly at first, to avoid wasting memory. Thus, adding just a few strings should reveal how the vector moves or copies its strings when reallocating its array. Table 64-1 shows the output from Listing 64-1 and Listing 64-2, when I supply three lines of input.

Table 64-1. *Comparing Output of Listing 64-1 and Listing 64-2*

Listing 60-1	Listing 60-2
mystring()	mystring()
mystring copy("one")	mystring move("one")
mystring copy("two")	mystring move("two")
mystring copy("one")	mystring move("one")
mystring copy("three")	mystring move("three")
mystring copy("two")	mystring move("two")
mystring copy("one")	mystring move("one")

The rest of this Exploration explains how C++ implements this move functionality.

Lvalues, Rvalues, and More

Recall from Exploration 21 that an expression falls into one of two categories: lvalue or rvalue. Informally, lvalues can appear on the left-hand side of an assignment, and rvalues appear on the right-hand side. At least that was the origin for the "l" and "r" names. More specifically, lvalues have identifiers and are stored somewhere in memory. Rvalues are not required to have either, although they might. Passing arguments to functions is similar to assignment: the function parameter takes on the role of lvalue, and the argument is an rvalue.

541

One key way to tell the difference between an lvalue and an rvalue is that you can take the address of an lvalue (using operator &). The compiler does not let you take the address of an rvalue, which makes sense. What is the address of 42?

The compiler automatically converts an lvalue to an rvalue whenever it has to, say, when passing an lvalue as an argument to a function or using an lvalue as the right-hand side of an assignment. The only situation in which the compiler turns an rvalue into an lvalue is when the lvalue's type is reference to const. For example, a function that declares its parameter as std::string const& can take an rvalue std::string as an argument, and the compiler turns that rvalue into an lvalue. But except for that one case, you cannot turn an rvalue into an lvalue.

The distinction between an lvalue and an rvalue is important when you consider the lifetime of an object. You know that the scope of a variable determines its lifetime, so any lvalue with a name (e.g., a variable or function parameter) has a lifetime determined by the name's scope. An rvalue, on the other hand, is temporary. Unless you bind a name to that rvalue (remember the name's type must be a reference to const), the compiler will destroy the temporary object as soon as it can.

For example, in the following expression, two temporary std::string objects are created and then passed to operator+ to concatenate the strings. The operator+ function binds its std::string const& parameters to the corresponding arguments, thereby guaranteeing that the arguments will live at least until the function returns. The operator+ function returns a new temporary std::string, which is then printed to std::cout:

```
std::cout << std::string("concat") + std::string("enate");
```

Once the statement finishes executing, the temporary std::string objects can be destroyed. The std::move() function lets you distinguish between the lifetime of an object and the data it contains, such as the characters that make up a string or the elements of a vector. The function takes an lvalue, whose lifetime is dictated by the scope, and turns it into an rvalue, so the contents can be treated as temporary. Thus, in Listing 64-1, the lifetime of line is determined by the scope. But in Listing 64-2, by calling std::move(), you are saying that it is safe to treat the string contents of line as temporary.

Because std::move() turns an lvalue into an rvalue, the return type (using the double ampersand) is called an *rvalue reference*. The parameters to the mystring move constructor also use double ampersands, so their types are rvalue references. A single-ampersand reference type is called an lvalue reference, to clearly distinguish it from rvalue references.

In a somewhat confusing turn of terminology, an expression with an rvalue reference type falls into both the rvalue expression category and the lvalue category. To reduce the confusion somewhat, a special name is given to this kind of expression: *xvalue*, for "eXpiring value." That is, the expression is still an lvalue and can appear on the left-hand side of an assignment, but it is also an rvalue, because it is near the end of its lifetime, so you are free to steal its contents.

A different name is given to rvalues that are not also xvalues: *pure rvalue*, or *prvalue*. Pure rvalues are expressions such as numeric literals, arithmetic expressions, function calls (if the return type is not a reference type), and so on. With a complete lack of symmetry, there are no pure lvalues. Instead, the term *lvalue* is used for the class of lvalues that are not also xvalues. The new term *generalized lvalue*, or *glvalue*, applies to all lvalues and xvalues. Figure 64-1 depicts the various expression categories.

So it turns out std::move() is actually a trivial function. It takes an lvalue reference as an argument and turns it into an rvalue reference. The difference is important to the compiler in how it treats the expression, but std::move() does not generate any code and has no impact on performance.

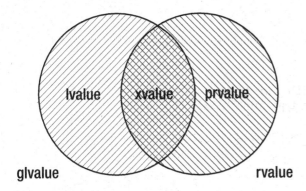

Figure 64-1. *Expression categories*

To summarize:

- Calling a function that returns a type of lvalue reference returns an expression of category lvalue.

- Calling a function that returns a type of rvalue reference returns an expression of category xvalue.

- Calling a function that returns a non-reference type returns an expression of category prvalue.

- The compiler matches an rvalue (xvalue or prvalue) argument with a function parameter of type rvalue reference. It matches an lvalue argument with an lvalue reference.

- A named object has category lvalue, even if the object's type is rvalue reference.

- Declare a parameter with an rvalue reference type (using a double ampersand) to move data from the argument.

- Call std::move() as the source of an assignment or to pass an argument to a function when you want to move the data from an lvalue. This transforms an lvalue reference into an rvalue reference.

Implementing Move

Implementing a constructor for the mystring class is easy, because it simply moves its argument to its base class's move constructor. But how does a class such as std::string or std::vector implement move functionality? Go back to the artifact class in Listing 63-6. It should be possible to move an artifact. Think about how you might go about moving an artifact. What, exactly, needs to be moved? How?

Write a move constructor for the artifact class. Then compare your solution with mine in Listing 64-3.

Listing 64-3. Adding a Move Constructor to the artifact Class

```
export module artifact;
import <filesystem>;
import <string>;
import <system_error>;
```

```
import variables;

export class artifact
{
public:
  using file_time_type = std::filesystem::file_time_type;
  artifact() : name_{}, mod_time_{file_time_type::min()}, vars_{} {}
  artifact(std::string name)
  : name_{std::move(name)}, mod_time_{get_mod_time()}, vars_{}
  {}
  artifact(artifact&& src) noexcept
  : name_{std::move(src.name_)},
    mod_time_{std::move(src.mod_time_)},
    vars_{std::move(src.vars_)}
  {}

  std::string const& name() const { return name_; }
  file_time_type mod_time() const { return mod_time_; }

  file_time_type get_mod_time();

  void define(std::string const& name, std::string const& value);

  std::string expand(std::string const& input) const;

private:
  std::string name_;
  file_time_type mod_time_;
  variables vars_;
};
```

Rvalue or Lvalue?

All these xyzvalues can get confusing. To help you understand what's going on, Listing 64-4 shows a number of different expressions passed as arguments to overloaded print() functions.

Listing 64-4. Examining Expression Categories

```
import <iostream>;
import <string>;
import <utility>;

void print(std::string&& move)
{
    std::cout << "move: " << std::move(move) << '\n';
}

void print(std::string const& copy)
{
    std::cout << "copy: " << copy << '\n';
}
```

```
int main()
{
  std::string a{"a"}, b{"b"}, c{"c"};

  print(a);
  print(a + b);
  print(a + b + c);
  print(std::move(a + b));
  print(a + std::move(b));
  print(std::move(a));
}
```

Predict the output.

_____

_____

_____

_____

_____

_____

When I run the program, I get the following:

```
copy: a
move: ab
move: abc
move: ab
move: ab
move: a
```

You cannot create a reference to a reference. If a type is already a reference, say as a typedef, then adding an additional reference in a declaration collapses to a single level of reference. If the type is an lvalue reference, you always get an lvalue reference. If the original type is an rvalue reference, then you get the same type as the original reference, for example:

```
using lvalue = int&;
using rvalue = int&&;
int i;
lvalue& ref1 = i;      // ref1 has type int&
lvalue&& ref2 = i;     // ref2 has type int&
rvalue& ref3 = i;      // ref3 has type int&
rvalue&& ref4 = 42;    // ref4 has type int&&
```

When using an auto declaration and you don't know whether the source type is a reference type or what kind of reference it is, then always make the auto declaration an rvalue reference. For example, item will have an lvalue reference type if the range iterators return lvalue references and it will have an rvalue reference type if the range iterators return rvalue references. If the iterators return non-reference types, then item will be a reference to a temporary const value:

```
for (auto&& item : range) do_something(item);
```

545

Special Member Functions

When you write a move constructor, you should also write a move assignment operator and *vice versa*. You must also consider whether and how to write a copy constructor and copy assignment operator. The compiler will help you by implicitly writing default implementations or deleting the special member functions. This section takes a closer look at the compiler's implicit behavior and guidelines for writing your own special member functions (constructors, assignment operators, and destructor).

The compiler can implicitly create any or all of the following:

- Default constructor, for example, `name()`

- Copy constructor, for example, `name(name const&)`

- Move constructor, for example, `name(name&&)`

- Copy assignment operator, for example, `name& operator=(name const&)`

- Move assignment operator, for example, `name& operator=(name&&)`

- Destructor, for example, `~name()`

A good guideline is that if you write any one of these special functions, you should write them all. You might decide that the compiler's implicit function is exactly what you want, in which case, you should say so explicitly with `=default`. That helps the human who maintains the code to know your intentions. If you know that the compiler would suppress a special member, note that explicitly with `= delete`.

As you know, the compiler deletes its implicit default constructor if you explicitly write any constructor. The implicit default constructor leaves pointers uninitialized, so if you have any pointer-type data member, you should write your own default constructor to initialize pointers to `nullptr` or delete the default constructor.

The compiler deletes its copy constructor and copy assignment operator if you explicitly provide a move constructor or move assignment operator.

The compiler deletes its move constructor if you explicitly provide any of the following special member functions: move assignment, copy constructor, copy assignment, or destructor.

The compiler deletes the move assignment operator if you explicitly provide any of the following special member functions: move constructor, copy constructor, copy assignment, or destructor.

The compiler's default behavior is to ensure safety. It will implicitly create copy and move functions if all the data members and base classes permit it. But if you start to write your own special members, the compiler assumes that you know best and suppresses anything that may be unsafe. It is then up to you to add back the special members that make sense for your class. When the compiler implicitly supplies any special member function, it also supplies the `noexcept` specifier when it is safe and correct to do so, that is, when all the data members and base classes also declare that function `noexcept` (or are built-in types).

Whenever a class uses an external resource, such as allocating heap memory or opening a file, you must consider all the special member functions to ensure that the resource is managed properly. Usually, the C++ class that provides the interface to the resource takes care of the details for you. For example, the standard `<fstream>` classes implement move logic and inhibit copying; they close files when the stream object is destroyed.

Ensure that pointer-type data members are always initialized. Ensure that move constructors and assignment operators correctly set the source pointers to `nullptr`. If you must implement a copy constructor or copy assignment operator, implement the appropriate deep copy or otherwise ensure that two objects are not both holding the same pointer. Make sure everything the class allocates gets deleted.

The requirements of data members apply to the class. Thus, if a data member lacks a copy constructor, then the compiler suppresses the implicit copy constructor for the containing class. After all, how could it copy the class if it can't copy all the members? Ditto for move functions.

All of these complications apply only to the author of a class that actually manages the resource. Even then, you can take advantage of the C++ library to make your job easier. Let's make the artifact class a little more interesting. Suppose the variables map is a large, unwieldy object, even when empty. (It's not, but let's pretend.) So you want to create one only when the user actually defines a variable for a target. Most targets will not have a variables map. So the variables map becomes a special resource to be managed.

To change artifact so that it sometimes has a variables map and sometimes doesn't, we change it to a pointer, but a special kind of pointer call unique_ptr. What makes the pointer unique is that it has a unique owner, that is, one artifact owns a particular variables object. If you write a copy constructor for artifact, it cannot copy the unique_ptr because the two artifact objects would "own" the same variables map, so the owner would not be unique. But you can move a unique_ptr, transferring ownership from one owner to another in a move constructor.

To create a new variables object, call std::make_unique<variables>(). When the owner of the unique pointer is destroyed, then the variables object will be destroyed. Modify the artifact class to use std::unique_ptr for the variables map. Compare your solution with Listing 64-5.

Listing 64-5. Using a Unique Pointer for the variables Member

```
export module artifact;
import <filesystem>;
import <memory>;
import <string>;
import <system_error>;

import variables;

export class artifact
{
public:
  using file_time_type = std::filesystem::file_time_type;
  artifact() : name_{}, mod_time_{file_time_type::min()}, vars_{} {}
  artifact(std::string name)
  : name_{std::move(name)}, mod_time_{get_mod_time()}, vars_{}
  {}
  artifact(artifact const&) = delete; // move-only
  artifact& operator=(artifact const&) = delete; // move-only
  artifact(artifact&&) = default;
  artifact& operator=(artifact&&) = default;
  ~artifact() = default;

  std::string const& name() const { return name_; }
  file_time_type mod_time() const { return mod_time_; }

  file_time_type get_mod_time();

  void define(std::string const& name, std::string const& value)
  {
    if (not vars_)
      vars_ = std::make_unique<variables>();
    vars_->define(name, value);
  }
```

```
std::string expand(std::string const& input)
const
{
    if (vars_)
        return vars_->expand(input);
    else
        return global_variables.expand(input);
}

private:
  std::string name_;
  file_time_type mod_time_;
  std::unique_ptr<variables> vars_;
};
```

The variables table is constructed lazily, when it is needed. The expand() function checks whether it exists and, if not, uses only the global variables to expand the input string. The unique_ptr class implements all the logic for moving the pointer, so ensuring proper handling of the variables resource is easy to accomplish.

The unique_ptr class is not the only smart pointer in the C++ standard library. The next Exploration takes you deeper into the pointer jungle.

EXPLORATION 65

■ ■ ■

Smart Pointers

One challenge that I have glossed over with respect to pointers is the inherent danger in their use. The map that holds all of the artifact objects must outlive all uses of artifact pointers in the program. So far, this has not been a problem, but as the program grows in size and complexity, the bookkeeping involved may obscure how pointers are used. So let's explore a slight change to the program to ensure that no matter how the program evolves, all the pointers will be safe to use. This Exploration takes a closer look at pointers, their problems, and how to avoid them.

Pointers and Iterators

Perhaps you've noticed the similarity between iterator syntax and pointer syntax. The C++ committee deliberately designed iterators to mimic pointers. Indeed, a pointer meets all the requirements of a contiguous iterator, so you can use all the standard algorithms with a C-style array, as follows:

```
int data[4];
std::ranges::fill(data, 42);
```

Thus, iterators are a form of smart pointer. Iterators are especially smart, because they come in six distinct flavors (see Exploration 44 for a reminder). Contiguous iterators are just like pointers; other kinds of iterators have less functionality, so they are smart by being dumb.

Iterators can be just as dangerous as pointers. In their pure form, iterators are nearly as unchecked, wild, and raw as pointers. After all, iterators do not prevent you from advancing too far, from dereferencing an uninitialized iterator, from comparing iterators that point to different containers, and so on. The list of unsafe practices with iterators is quite extensive.

Because these errors result in undefined behavior, a library implementer is free to choose any result for each kind of error. In the interest of performance, most libraries do not implement additional safety checks and push that back on the programmer, who can decide on his or her preference for a safety/performance trade-off.

If the programmer prefers safety to performance, some library implementations offer a debugging version that implements a number of safety checks. The debugging version of the standard library can check that iterators refer to the same container when comparing the iterators and throw an exception if they do not. An iterator is allowed to check that it is valid before honoring the dereference (*) operator. An iterator can ensure that it does not advance past the end of a container.

Thus, iterators are smart pointers, because they can be really, really smart. I highly recommend that you take full advantage of all safety features that your standard library offers. Remove checks one by one only after you have measured the performance of your program and found that one particular check degrades performance significantly, and you have the reviews and tests in place to give you confidence in the less safe code.

© Ray Lischner 2020

R. Lischner, *Exploring C++20*, https://doi.org/10.1007/978-1-4842-5961-0_65

More About `unique_ptr`

Exploration 64 introduced `unique_ptr` as a way to manage dynamically allocated objects. The `unique_ptr` class template overloads the dereference (`*`) and member access (`->`) operators and lets you use a `unique_ptr` object the same way you would use a pointer. At the same time, it extends the behavior of an ordinary pointer, such that when the `unique_ptr` object is destroyed, it automatically deletes the pointer it holds. That's why `unique_ptr` is called a *smart pointer*—it's just like an ordinary pointer, only smarter. Using `unique_ptr` helps ensure that memory is properly managed, even in the face of unexpected exceptions.

When used properly, the key feature of `unique_ptr` is that exactly one `unique_ptr` object owns a particular pointer. You can move `unique_ptr` objects. Each time you do, the target of the move becomes the new owner of the pointer.

Call the `reset` member function to set the `unique_ptr` to a null pointer.

```
auto ap{std::make_unique<int>(42)};
ap.reset();                // deletes the pointer to 42
```

The `get()` member function retrieves the raw pointer without affecting the `unique_ptr`'s ownership. The `unique_ptr` template also overloads the dereference (`*`) and member (`->`) operators, so that they work the way they do with ordinary pointers. These functions do not affect ownership of the pointer.

```
auto rp{std::make_unique<rational>(420, 10)};
int n{rp->numerator()};
rational r{*rp};
sendto(socket, rp.get(), sizeof(r), n, nullptr, 0);
```

In order to enforce its ownership semantics, `unique_ptr` has a move constructor and move assignment operator but deletes its copy constructor and copy assignment operator. If you use `unique_ptr` for data members in a class, the compiler implicitly deletes the class's copy constructor and copy assignment operator.

Thus, using `unique_ptr` may free you from thinking about your class's destructor, but you are not excused from thinking about the constructors and assignment operators. This is a minor tweak to the guideline that if you have to deal with one, you must deal with all special members. The compiler's default behavior is usually correct, but you might want to implement a copy constructor that performs a deep copy or other non-default behavior.

Copyable Smart Pointers

Sometimes, you don't want exclusive ownership. There are circumstances when multiple objects will share ownership of a pointer. When no objects own the pointer, the memory is automatically reclaimed. The `std::shared_ptr` smart-pointer type implements shared ownership.

Once you deliver a pointer to a `shared_ptr`, the `shared_ptr` object owns that pointer. When the `shared_ptr` object is destroyed, it will delete the pointer. The difference between `shared_ptr` and `unique_ptr` is that you can freely copy and assign `shared_ptr` objects with normal semantics. Unlike `unique_ptr`, `shared_ptr` has a copy constructor and copy assignment operator. The `shared_ptr` object keeps a reference count, so assignment merely increments the reference count, without having to transfer ownership. When a `shared_ptr` object is destroyed, it decrements the reference count. When the count reaches zero, the pointer is deleted. Thus, you can make as many copies as you like, store `shared_ptr` objects in a container, pass them to functions, return them from functions, copy them, move them, assign them, and carry on to your heart's content. It's that simple. Listing 65-1 shows that copying `shared_ptr` works in ways that don't work with `unique_ptr`.

Listing 65-1. Working with `shared_ptr`

```
import <iostream>;
import <memory>;
import <vector>;

class see_me
{
public:
  see_me(int x) : x_{x} { std::cout <<  "see_me(" << x_ << ")\n"; }
  ~see_me()             { std::cout << "~see_me(" << x_ << ")\n"; }
  int value() const     { return x_; }
private:
  int x_;
};

std::shared_ptr<see_me> does_this_work(std::shared_ptr<see_me> x)
{
  std::shared_ptr<see_me> y{x};
  return y;
}

int main()
{
  std::shared_ptr<see_me> a{}, b{};
  a = std::make_shared<see_me>(42);
  b = does_this_work(a);
  std::vector<std::shared_ptr<see_me>> v{};
  v.push_back(a);
  v.push_back(b);
}
```

The best way to create a `shared_ptr` is to call `make_shared`. The template argument is the type you want to create, and the function arguments are passed directly to the constructor. Due to implementation details, constructing a new `shared_ptr` instance any other way is slightly less efficient in space and time.

Using `shared_ptr`, you can reimplement the program from Listing 63-8. The old program used the `artifact` map to manage the lifetime of all artifacts. Although convenient, there is no reason to tie artifacts to this map, because the map is used only for parsing. In a real program, most of its work lies in the actual building of targets, not parsing the input. All the parsing objects should be freed and long gone by the time the program is building targets.

Rewrite the artifact-lookup portion of Listing 63-8 to allocate artifact objects dynamically, using shared_ptr throughout to refer to artifact pointers. See Listing 65-2 for my solution.

Listing 65-2. Using Smart Pointers to Manage Artifacts

```
std::unordered_map<std::string, std::shared_ptr<artifact>> artifacts;

std::shared_ptr<artifact>
lookup_artifact(std::string const& name)
{
  std::shared_ptr<artifact> a{artifacts[name]};
```

```
  if (a.get() == nullptr)
  {
    a = std::make_shared<artifact>(name);
    artifacts[name] = a;
  }
  return a;
}
```

I changed the map to unordered_map because it no longer matters that the address of every artifact object never change. Storing smart pointers alleviates us of that restriction. With a little more care, you could use unique_ptr instead of shared_ptr, but that results in greater changes to the rest of the code. You should prefer unique_ptr to shared_ptr, due to the overhead of maintaining the reference count. But if you require shared ownership, shared_ptr is your choice. In all cases, there is no reason to use raw pointers instead of a smart pointer.

Smart Arrays

Allocating a single object is completely different from allocating an array of objects. Thus, smart pointers must also distinguish between a smart pointer to a single object and a smart pointer to an array of objects. When a smart pointer holds a pointer to an array (i.e., the template argument is an array type, e.g., unique_ptr<int[ ]>), it supports the subscript operator instead of * and ->.

Pimpls

No, that's not a spelling error. Although programmers have spoken for years about pimples and warts in their programs, often referring to unsightly but unavoidable bits of code, Herb Sutter associated the phrase *pointer-to-implementation* with these pimples to come up with the *pimpl* idiom.

In short, a pimpl is a class that hides implementation details in an implementation class, and the public interface object holds only a pointer to that implementation object. Instead of forcing the user of your class to allocate and de-allocate objects, manage pointers, and keep track of object lifetimes, you can expose a class that is easier to use. Specifically, the user can treat instances of the class as values, in the manner of int and other built-in types.

The pimpl wrapper manages the lifetime of the pimpl object. It typically implements the special member functions: copy and move constructors, copy and move assignment operators, and destructor. It delegates most of its other member functions to the pimpl object. The user of the wrapper never has to be concerned with any of this.

Thus, we will rewrite the artifact class so that it wraps a pimpl—that is, a pointer to an artifact_impl class. The artifact_impl class will do the real work, and artifact will merely forward all functions through its pimpl. The module interface has only a forward declaration for artifact_impl. The declaration doesn't provide the compiler with anything more about the class, so the class type is *incomplete*. You face a number of restrictions on what you can do with an incomplete type. In particular, you cannot define any objects or data members of that type, nor can you use an incomplete class as a function parameter or return type. You cannot refer to any members of an incomplete class. But you can use pointers or references to the type when you define objects, data members, function parameters, and return types. In particular, you can use a pointer to artifact_impl in the artifact class.

A normal class definition is a *complete* type definition. You can mix forward declarations with a class definition of the same class name. A common pattern is for a module interface to declare a forward declaration, and the implementation module fills in the complete class definition.

The definition of the artifact class, therefore, can have a data member that is a smart pointer to artifact_impl, even though the compiler knows only that artifact_impl is a class but doesn't know any details about it. The interface module contains only the forward declaration. The implementation details are tucked away in a separate file for the implementation module, and the rest of your program can make use of the artifact class completely insulated from artifact_impl. In large projects, this kind of barrier is tremendously important.

Writing the artifact interface module is not difficult. Start with a forward declaration of artifact_impl. In the artifact class, the declarations of the member functions are the same as in the original class. Change the data members to a single pointer to artifact_impl. Read Listing 65-3 to see one possible implementation of this module.

Listing 65-3. Defining an artifact Pimpl Wrapper Class

```
export module artifact;
import <filesystem>;
import <memory>;
import <string>;

class artifact_impl;

export class artifact
{
public:
  using file_time_type = std::filesystem::file_time_type;
  artifact();
  artifact(std::string name);
  artifact(artifact const&) = default;
  artifact(artifact&&) = default;
  artifact& operator=(artifact const&) = default;
  artifact& operator=(artifact&&) = default;
  ~artifact() = default;

  std::string const& name() const;
  file_time_type mod_time() const;
  std::string expand(std::string const& str) const;

  void build() const;
  file_time_type get_mod_time() const;

  void define(std::string const& name, std::string const& value);

private:
  std::shared_ptr<artifact_impl> pimpl_;
};

export bool operator==(artifact const& lhs, artifact const& rhs) {
    return lhs.name() == rhs.name();
}

namespace std {
  template<>
  export struct hash<artifact> : std::hash<std::string> {
```

```
    using super = std::hash<std::string>;
    std::size_t operator()(artifact const& a) const {
      return super::operator()(a.name());
    }
  };
}
```

The module defines the artifact class with only a forward declaration of artifact_impl and the pimpl_ data member. Because the dependency graph will no longer store pointers but artifact objects, the compiler needs to know how to hash an artifact object and how to compare them for equality in order to store them in an unordered container. Both functions merely delegate the artifact's name.

The next step is to write the implementation module. This is where the compiler needs the full definition of the artifact_impl class, thus making artifact_impl a *complete class*. The artifact class doesn't do much on its own. Instead, it just delegates every action to the artifact_impl class. See the details in Listing 65-4.

Listing 65-4. Implementing the artifact Module

```
module artifact;

import <filesystem>;
import <memory>;
import <string>;
import <system_error>;

import variables;

class artifact_impl
{
public:
  using file_time_type = std::filesystem::file_time_type;
  artifact_impl() : name_{}, mod_time_{file_time_type::min()}, vars_{} {}
  artifact_impl(std::string name)
  : name_{std::move(name)}, mod_time_{get_mod_time()}, vars_{}
  {}

  std::string const& name() const { return name_; }
  file_time_type mod_time() const { return mod_time_; }

  file_time_type get_mod_time()
  const
  {
    std::error_code ec;
    auto time{ std::filesystem::last_write_time(name(), ec) };
    if (ec)
        return file_time_type::min();
    else
        return time;
  }
```

```
  void define(std::string const& name, std::string const& value)
  {
     if (not vars_)
        vars_ = std::make_unique<variables>();
     vars_->define(name, value);
  }

  std::string expand(std::string const& input)
  const
  {
     if (vars_)
        return vars_->expand(input);
     else
        return global_variables.expand(input);
  }

private:
  std::string name_;
  file_time_type mod_time_;
  std::unique_ptr<variables> vars_;
};

artifact::artifact() : pimpl_{std::make_shared<artifact_impl>()} {}

artifact::artifact(std::string name)
: pimpl_(std::make_shared<artifact_impl>(std::move(name)))
{}

std::string const& artifact::name()
const
{
   return pimpl_->name();
}

artifact::file_time_type artifact::mod_time()
const
{
   return pimpl_->mod_time();
}

std::string artifact::expand(std::string const& str)
const
{
   return pimpl_->expand(str);
}

artifact::file_time_type artifact::get_mod_time()
const
{
   return pimpl_->get_mod_time();
}
```

```
void artifact::define(std::string const& name, std::string const& value)
{
    pimpl_->define(name, value);
}
```

The `artifact_impl` class is unsurprising. The implementation is just like the old `artifact` implementation from Listing 64-5.

Now it's time to modify the depgraph module. This time, the `artifacts` map stores `artifact` objects directly. Modify Listing 63-2 for the new artifact class. See Listing 65-5 for one way to rewrite the program.

Listing 65-5. Rewriting the depgraph Module

```
export module depgraph;

import <iterator>;
import <map>;
import <string>;
import <unordered_map>;
import <unordered_set>;

import artifact;
import topsort;

export class dependency_graph
{
public:
  using graph_type = std::unordered_map<artifact,
                            std::unordered_set<artifact>>;

  void store_dependency(std::string const& target_name,
      std::string const& dependency_name)
  {
    auto target{ lookup_artifact(target_name) };
    auto dependency{ lookup_artifact(dependency_name) };
    store_dependency(target, dependency);
  }

  graph_type const& graph() const { return graph_; }

  template<class OutIter>
  requires std::output_iterator<OutIter, artifact>
  void sort(OutIter sorted)
  const
  {
    topological_sort(graph_, sorted);
  }

  artifact lookup_artifact(std::string const& name)
  {
    auto a{ artifacts_.find(name) };
    if (a != artifacts_.end())
      return a->second;
```

```
    else
    {
      auto [iterator, inserted]{ artifacts_.emplace(name, name) };
      return iterator->second;
    }
  }

private:
  void store_dependency(artifact target, artifact dependency)
  {
    graph_[dependency].insert(target);
    graph_[target]; // ensures that target is in the graph
  }

  graph_type graph_;
  std::map<std::string, artifact> artifacts_;
};
```

As you can see, the code that uses artifact objects is simpler and easier to read. The complexity of managing pointers is pushed down into the artifact and artifact_impl classes. In this manner, the complexity is kept contained in one place and not spread throughout the application. Because the code that uses artifact is now simpler, it is less likely to contain errors. Because the complexity is localized, it is easier to review and test thoroughly. The cost is a little more development time, to write two classes instead of one, and a little more maintenance effort, because anytime a new function is needed in the artifact public interface, that function must also be added to artifact_impl. In many, many situations, the benefits far outweigh the costs, which is why this idiom is so popular.

The new artifact class is easy to use, because you can use it the same way you use an int. That is, you can copy it, assign it, store it in a container, and so on, without concern about the size of an artifact object or the cost of copying it. Instead of treating an artifact as a big, fat object, or as a dangerous pointer, you can treat it as a value. Defining a class with *value semantics* makes it easy to use. Although it was more work to implement, the value artifact is the easiest incarnation to use for writing the application.

One advantage of the new design is the independence of the dependency graph and the build system. (Of course, we haven't written a build system, but presumably that would be the major part of any real make-like program.) Listing 65-6 shows a small change to the main program that demonstrates this separability.

Listing 65-6. New Program Using the parser Module

```
import <iostream>;
import <iterator>;
import <ranges>;
import <stdexcept>;
import <vector>;

import artifact;
import depgraph;
import parser;

std::vector<artifact> get_dependency_order()
{
    dependency_graph graph{};
    parse(std::cin, graph);
```

```
    std::vector<artifact> sorted;
    graph.sort(std::back_inserter(sorted));
    return sorted;
}

int main()
{
  try {
    std::vector<artifact> build_list{ get_dependency_order() };

    // Print in build order, which is reverse of dependency order.
    for (auto artifact : build_list | std::ranges::views::reverse)
    {
      std::cout << artifact.name() << '\n';
    }
  } catch (std::runtime_error const& ex) {
    std::cerr << ex.what() << '\n';
    return EXIT_FAILURE;
  }
}
```

A couple of notes. Returning an entire vector from a function seems like to might be expensive, but in fact the vector is moved to the caller, not copied. So this is a reasonable way to return a list of strings from a function. But more important is the fact that the dependency graph is now a temporary variable in the get_dependency_order() function. Before, it had to live the full lifetime of the program because of all the artifact pointers that pointed back to the map stored in the graph. Now, thanks to shared pointers and pimpls, separate parts of the program are indeed separate.

Dumb Arrays

There is one place where smart pointers and all the power and majesty of C++ fail to help us. The main() function holds us back, tying us to the old C way of doing things. In its simplest form, with no arguments, we are fine. But for a program to learn the command-line arguments that the operating system or command shell is passing to the program, there is another signature for main(). Listing 65-7 shows a trivial echo-like program, demonstrating how a program accesses command-line arguments.

Listing 65-7. Demonstrating Command-Line Arguments

```
#include <cstring>
import <iostream>;

int main(int argc, char **argv)
{
    if (argc > 1) {
        if (std::strcmp(argv[1], "--help") == 0)
            std::cout << "usage: " << argv[0] << " [ARGS...]";
        else {
            std::cout << argv[1];
```

```
        for (int argn{2}; argn < argc; ++argn)
            std::cout << ' ' << argv[argn];
    }
  }
  std::cout << '\n';
}
```

As with any function, the names of the function parameters are up to you. The names argc and argv are merely convention. As you can see and guess, the first function argument (argc) is the number of command-line arguments, the first being the program name (argv[0]). The declaration of the second function argument, argv, is a pointer to an array of pointers to the command-line argument strings, each string being a NUL-terminated array of char, which is how C represents strings.

The std::strcmp() function is how C compares NUL-terminated strings. It is declared in <cstring>, but because it is a C header, not C++, you must use the C #include directive.

The argv array has one additional entry, nullptr, which follows the final command-line argument, so an alternative way to iterate the arguments is just to loop until reaching nullptr. Listing 65-8 shows the echo program using this style.

Listing 65-8. Alternative Style of Accessing Command-Line Arguments

```
import <iostream>;
import <string_view>;

int main(int, char **argv)
{
    if (argv[1] != nullptr) {
        if (std::string_view{argv[1]} == "--help")
            std::cout << "usage: " << argv[0] << " [ARGS...]";
        else {
            std::cout << *++argv;
            while (*++argv != nullptr)
                std::cout << ' ' << *argv;
        }
    }
    std::cout << '\n';
}
```

Constructing a std::string_view from a NUL-terminated C string is the best way to deal with these relics in a C++ program. The string_view holds a pointer to the C string without copying its contents, so there is no performance penalty, and you get all the convenience of a C++ string. Figure 65-1 illustrates how C organizes its command-line arguments.

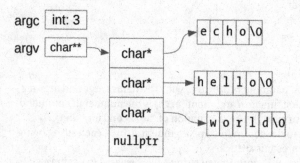

Figure 65-1. *Command-line arguments*

This completes your tour of pointers and memory. Now that you know how to read command-line arguments, you are ready to tackle files and filesystems.

EXPLORATION 66

■ ■ ■

Files and File Names

In addition to reading and writing files, the C++ standard library has functions for manipulating entire files, such as copying, renaming, and deleting files. It also has a portable way to work with file and directory names. Let's take a look at what the file system library has to offer.

Everything in this Exploration is declared in `<filesystem>` and is in the `std::filesystem` namespace. Although I prefer to use fully qualified names, as I have done throughout the previous 60 Explorations, this name is just too long. For this and subsequent Explorations, assume the following namespace alias:

```
namespace fsys = std::filesystem;
```

Portable File Names

The key to the `<filesystem>` library is a means of representing file names and paths using a portable API, or at least as portable as is possible given the many different file systems in use, from sophisticated networked storage devices to lightbulbs and other Internet-of-Things (IoT) devices. The class that makes this possible is `fsys::path`.

The `fsys::path` class abstracts a path name in terms of a root name, a root directory, and a relative path. A relative path is a sequence of file names and separators. You can use the preferred separator for the file system or `'/'`, which is called the fallback separator. It also happens to be the preferred separator for UNIX, POSIX, and similar operating systems. On Microsoft Windows, the preferred separator is `'\\'`, which causes all manner of trouble in C++ strings, so using `'/'` is usually easier, even on Windows.

Most modern file systems for desktop workstations and servers can handle Unicode file names using UTF-8 or UTF-16 encoding, but going back to the IoT and similar devices, they may not. If you need to ensure portability across as many environments as possible, you should restrict file names to alphanumeric characters, underscore (`'_'`), hyphen (`'-'`), and period (`'.'`), which constitute the POSIX Portable Filename Character Set.

A root name may be a DOS drive letter and colon or two separators to denote a network name. It could be a host name followed by a colon. The presence of a root name is part of the portable path API, but the meaning of it depends entirely on the local environment. Directories are hierarchical, starting at the root, which is denoted by an initial separator.

A single path object may hold a complete path name or a partial path name. If the path contains a separator, the portion of the path after the final separator is called the *filename*. The filename can have a *stem* followed by an *extension*. The extension is the right-most period followed by non-period characters. But if the only period is the first character, the filename equals the stem and the extension is empty.

You can construct a path object from a string or you can build one from multiple path elements. The / operator is overloaded to combine paths with an intervening directory separator. Given a path object, you can deconstruct it into its constituent parts, modify parts, and add filenames.

Listing 66-1 demonstrates various uses of a path object.

R. Lischner, *Exploring C++20*, https://doi.org/10.1007/978-1-4842-5961-0_66

Listing 66-1. Demonstrating the path Class

```cpp
import <filesystem>;
import <iostream>;

namespace fsys = std::filesystem;

int main()
{
    std::string line;
    while (std::getline(std::cin, line))
    {
        fsys::path path{line};
        std::cout <<
            "root-name:      " << path.root_name() << "\n"
            "root-directory: " << path.root_directory() << "\n"
            "relative-path:  " << path.relative_path() << "\n"
            "parent-path:    " << path.parent_path() << "\n"
            "filename:       " << path.filename() << "\n"
            "stem:           " << path.stem() << "\n"
            "extension:      " << path.extension() << "\n"
            "generic path:   " << path.generic_string() << "\n"
            "native path:    " << path.string() << '\n';

        fsys::path newpath;
        newpath = path.root_path() / "top" / "subdir" / "stem.ext";
        std::cout << "newpath = " << newpath << '\n';
        newpath.replace_filename("newfile.newext");
        std::cout << "newpath = " << newpath << '\n';
        newpath.replace_extension(".old");
        std::cout << "newpath = " << newpath << '\n';
        newpath.remove_filename();
        std::cout << "newpath = " << newpath << '\n';
    }
}
```

Some namespace-scope functions perform other operations on path names:

> path absolute(path const& p) converts p to an absolute path. If the operating system has the notion of a current working directory, current_path() returns that directory as a path object, and absolute() may use current_path() as a prefix to the argument p.

> path canonical(path const& p) converts p to a canonical path by eliminating directory names of "." (the current directory) and ".." (the parent directory) and by resolving symbolic links.

> path relative(path const& p, path const& base=current_path()) converts p to a path that is relative to base.

Path name is another place where you are likely to encounter international character sets (Exploration 59). The path type is actually a specialization of basic_path for the host environment, which would typically be char or wchar_t. The path class converts strings to paths and back again in a manner that depends on the operating system.

Working with Files

In addition to file names, the standard library offers numerous functions that manipulate entire files and their attributes. Querying and manipulating file attributes such as permissions, dates and times, and so on in a portable manner is a challenge, and this book cannot cover all of the complexities in the <filesystem> module. This section hits some of the highlights.

In general, the standard C++ library takes its cues from the POSIX standards. For example, file permissions are direct mappings from POSIX permissions and complexities such as Access Control Lists are not supported. Similarly, C++ file types are mappings of POSIX file types, such as sockets, pipes, and character devices, although implementations are allowed to add other file types.

POSIX offers two ways for a single file to have multiple names. Both ways are called *links*, distinguished as *hard* links and *soft* links. Soft links are also called *symbolic* links or *symlinks* for short. A hard link is a directory entry that points directly to the file contents. Two hard links for the same file contents are indistinguishable. The fsys::hard_link_count() function returns the number of hard links that point to the same file. The fsys::create_hard_link() function creates a new hard link.

A symbolic link is a directory entry that contains the path to another file. The path may be absolute or relative to the directory that contains the soft link. Using a symbolic link introduces the possibility that the target path does not exist. To create a new symlink, call fsys::create_directory_symlink() to link to a directory and fsys::create_symlink() to link to a file. The fsys::read_symlink() function can read the contents of either kind of symbolic link.

To query a file's attributes, call status(), which returns an fsys::file_status object, which in turn has a permissions() member function to return a file permissions and type() to return the file type, such as fsys::file_type::regular. If the file is a symbolic link, the status of the target file is returned. Call fsys::symlink_status() to get the status of the symlink itself; if the file is not a symlink, symlink_status() is like status(). Also, fsys::is_regular_file() and similar functions exist to directly query a file type.

A file's modification time can be queried and set with fsys::last_write_time(). The C++ standard library has a rich and complicated date and time library in the <chrono> module. Its use is beyond the scope of this book. The std::format() function understands file times. After the colon, use {:%F %T} for ISO date and time or {:%x %X} for locale-specific date and time formatting. Many other options are also possible. Consult an up-to-date reference for details.

Listing 66-2 demonstrates the use of many of these functions by presenting a very simple file listing program, similar to POSIX ls or DOS dir commands. For this first program, it takes only one file name on the command line. We will expand the capability of this little program as this Exploration progresses.

Listing 66-2. Demonstrating the path Class

```
import <filesystem>;
import <format>;
import <iostream>;
import <iterator>;

namespace fsys = std::filesystem;

void print_file_type(std::ostream& stream, fsys::path const& path)
{
    auto status{ fsys::symlink_status(path) };
    if (fsys::is_symlink(status)) {
        auto link{ fsys::read_symlink(path) };
        stream << " -> " << link.generic_string();
    }
```

```
    else if (fsys::is_directory(status))
        stream << '/';
    else if (fsys::is_fifo(status))
        stream << '|';
    else if (fsys::is_socket(status))
        stream << '=';
    else if (fsys::is_character_file(status))
        stream << "(c)";
    else if (fsys::is_block_file(status))
        stream << "(b)";
    else if (fsys::is_other(status))
        stream << "?";
}

void print_file_info(std::ostream& stream, fsys::path const& path)
{
    std::format_to(std::ostreambuf_iterator<char>(stream),
        "{0:>16} {1:%F %T} ",
        fsys::file_size(path),
        fsys::last_write_time(path));
    stream << path.generic_string();
    print_file_type(stream, path);
    stream << '\n';
}

int main(int, char** argv)
{
    if (argv[1] == nullptr)
    {
        std::cerr << "usage: " << argv[0] << " FILENAME\n";
        return EXIT_FAILURE;
    }
    fsys::path path{ argv[1] };
    try
    {
        print_file_info(std::cout, path);
    }
    catch(fsys::filesystem_error const& ex)
    {
        std::cerr << ex.what() << '\n';
    }
}
```

The fsys::copy_symlink() function does as its name suggests and creates a new symlink that contains a copy of an existing symlink. The fsys::copy_file() function creates a new file and copies the content of an existing file to the new file. An optional final argument lets you control whether to allow overwriting an existing file. The fsys::copy() function combines the other copy functions and more. The copy options direct how it should treat symlinks and directories, even permitting the recursive copying of an entire directory tree.

To rename a file, call fsys::rename(), and to delete a file, call fsys::remove(). To delete an entire directory tree, call fsys::remove_all(). Many other file-level functions exist; consult a good reference for details.

Errors

If you have tried running the program in Listing 66-2 or experimented on your own, you may have found that the file system library throws exceptions for any kind of error or unusual result. Often, you expect certain problems, such as a missing file if the user mistypes a file name. Permission errors are common, and so on. So the library lets you decide whether it should throw an exception or return an error code.

When you expect that errors are common, pass a std::error_code object as an additional, final argument to any of the filesystem functions. The function will always store a result instead of throwing an exception, which will be zero for success or some other value that indicates an error. Treating the error_code as a Boolean value means true for an error or false for success. If that bothers you, the .value() member function returns the code as an integer, which you can explicitly compare with zero.

Rewrite Listing 66-2 to use an error_code instead of relying on exceptions. This also means that it makes sense to accept multiple command-line arguments. The program can issue an error message for each argument instead of dying on the first error. You can print the error_code itself to an output stream, but that shows you only the numeric code. The message() member function returns the corresponding string message. See my rewrite in Listing 66-3.

Listing 66-3. Examining Errors with error_code

```
import <filesystem>;
import <format>;
import <iostream>;
import <iterator>;
import <string_view>;
import <system_error>;

namespace fsys = std::filesystem;

void print_file_type(std::ostream& stream, fsys::path const& path, fsys::file_status status)
{
    if (fsys::is_symlink(status)) {
        std::error_code ec;
        auto link{ fsys::read_symlink(path, ec) };
        if (ec)
            stream << ": " << ec.message();
        else
            stream << " -> " << link.generic_string();
    }
    else if (fsys::is_directory(status))
        stream << '/';
    else if (fsys::is_fifo(status))
        stream << '|';
    else if (fsys::is_socket(status))
        stream << '=';
    else if (fsys::is_character_file(status))
        stream << "(c)";
    else if (fsys::is_block_file(status))
        stream << "(b)";
    else if (fsys::is_other(status))
        stream << "?";
}
```

```cpp
// There may be many reasons why a file has no size, e.g., it is
// a directory. So don't treat it as an error--just return zero.
uintmax_t get_file_size(fsys::path const& path)
{
    std::error_code ec;
    auto size{ fsys::file_size(path, ec) };
    if (ec.value() != 0)
        return 0;
    else
        return size;
}

// Similarly, return a false timestamp for any error.
fsys::file_time_type get_last_write_time(fsys::path const& path)
{
    std::error_code ec;
    auto time{ fsys::last_write_time(path, ec) };
    if (ec)
        return fsys::file_time_type{};
    else
        return time;
}

void print_file_info(std::ostream& stream, fsys::path const& path)
{
    std::error_code ec;
    auto status{ fsys::symlink_status(path, ec) };
    if (ec)
        stream << path.generic_string() << ": " << ec.message();
    else
    {
        std::format_to(std::ostreambuf_iterator<char>(stream),
            "{0:>16} {1:%F %T} {2}",
            get_file_size(path),
            get_last_write_time(path),
            path.generic_string());
        print_file_type(stream, path, status);
    }
    stream << '\n';
}

int main(int, char** argv)
{
    if (argv[1] == nullptr or std::string_view(argv[1]) == "--help")
    {
        std::cerr << "usage: " << argv[0] << " FILENAME\n";
        return EXIT_FAILURE;
    }
```

```
while (*++argv != nullptr)
{
    fsys::path path{ *argv };
    print_file_info(std::cout, path);
}
}
```

The next task is to recurse into directories. The next section covers directory entries and iterators.

Navigating Directories

A directory (often called a folder) contains file entries, which may be any kind of file, including another directory. To discover the entries in a directory, construct a directory iterator. Use fsys::directory_iterator to see the entries in a single directory, or use fsys::recursive_directory_iterator to iterate over entries in subdirectories, too. Construct either iterator type with the path to the directory with an optional error_code argument, as usual. Even though a directory iterator is an iterator, it can also be used as a range in a ranged for loop or ranged function.

The value type for a directory iterator is fsys::directory_entry, which has the name, status, and other information about the file. All operating systems and file systems differ in their details, but usually the act of iterating a directory retrieves information about a file so there is no need to make separate system calls to obtain the same information. The directory_entry, therefore, stores the file status, modification time, and so on, which you would otherwise have to call fsys functions to obtain.

Based on this information, you can now **modify Listing 66-3 to descend into directories**. My version is in Listing 66-4. Notice how I use directory_entry for files named on the command line, too. This simplifies the code by having one way to display file information.

Listing 66-4. Recursing into Directories

```
import <filesystem>;
import <format>;
import <iostream>;
import <iterator>;
import <system_error>;

namespace fsys = std::filesystem;

void print_file_type(std::ostream& stream, fsys::directory_entry const& entry)
{
    auto status{ entry.symlink_status() };
    if (fsys::is_symlink(status)) {
        std::error_code ec;
        auto link{ fsys::read_symlink(entry.path(), ec) };
        if (ec)
            stream << ": " << ec.message();
        else
            stream << " -> " << link.generic_string();
    }
    else if (fsys::is_directory(status))
        stream << '/';
    else if (fsys::is_fifo(status))
        stream << '|';
```

```
        else if (fsys::is_socket(status))
            stream << '=';
        else if (fsys::is_character_file(status))
            stream << "(c)";
        else if (fsys::is_block_file(status))
            stream << "(b)";
        else if (fsys::is_other(status))
            stream << "?";
}


// There may be many reasons why a file has no size, e.g., it is
// a directory. So don't treat it as an error--just return zero.
uintmax_t get_file_size(fsys::directory_entry const& entry)
{
    std::error_code ec;
    auto size{ entry.file_size(ec) };
    if (ec)
        return 0;
    else
        return size;
}


// Similarly, return a false timestamp for any error.
fsys::file_time_type get_last_write_time(fsys::directory_entry const& entry)
{
    std::error_code ec;
    auto time{ entry.last_write_time(ec) };
    if (ec)
        return fsys::file_time_type{};
    else
        return time;
}


void print_file_info(std::ostream& stream, fsys::directory_entry const& entry)
{
    std::format_to(std::ostreambuf_iterator<char>(stream),
        "{0:>16} {1:%F %T} {2}",
        get_file_size(entry),
        get_last_write_time(entry),
        entry.path().generic_string());
    print_file_type(stream, entry);
    stream << '\n';
    if (not entry.is_symlink() and entry.is_directory())
    {
        for (auto&& entry : fsys::directory_iterator{entry.path()})
            print_file_info(stream, entry);
    }
}
```

```
int main(int, char** argv)
{
    if (argv[1] == nullptr or std::string_view(argv[1]) == "--help")
    {
        std::cerr << "usage: " << argv[0] << " FILENAME\n";
        return EXIT_FAILURE;
    }
    while (*++argv != nullptr)
    {
        fsys::path path{ *argv };
        std::error_code ec;
        fsys::directory_entry entry{ path, ec };
        if (ec)
            std::cout << *argv << ": " << ec.message() << '\n';
        else
            print_file_info(std::cout, entry);
    }
}
```

The next topic gets down into the bits and bytes of C++.

EXPLORATION 67

■ ■ ■

Working with Bits

This Exploration begins a series of Explorations that cover more advanced topics in the C++ type system. The series kicks off with an examination of how to work with individual bits. This Exploration begins with operators that manipulate integers at the bit level, then introduces bitfields—a completely different way of working with bits. The final topic is the bitset class template, which lets you work with bitsets of any size.

Integer As a Set of Bits

A common idiom in computer programming is to treat an integer as a bitmask. The bits can represent a set of small integers, such that a value n is a member of the set if the bit at position n is one; n is not in the set if the corresponding bit is zero. An empty set has the numeric value zero, because all bits are zero. To better understand how this works, consider the I/O stream formatting flags (introduced in Exploration 39).

Typically, you use manipulators to set and clear flags. For example, Exploration 17 introduced the skipws and noskipws manipulators. These manipulators set and clear the std::ios_base::skipws flag by calling the setf and unsetf member functions. In other words, the following statement

```
std::cin >> std::noskipws >> read >> std::skipws;
```

is exactly equivalent to

```
std::cin.unsetf(std::ios_base::skipws);
std::cin >> read;
std::cin.setf(std::ios_base::skipws);
```

Other formatting flags include boolalpha (introduced in Exploration 12), showbase (Exploration 58), showpoint (displays a decimal point even when it would otherwise be suppressed), and showpos (shows a plus sign for positive numbers). Consult a C++ reference to learn about the remaining formatting flags.

A simple implementation of the formatting flags is to store the flags in an int and assign a specific bit position to each flag. A common way to write flags that you define in this manner is to use hexadecimal notation, as shown in Listing 67-1. Write a hexadecimal integer literal with 0x or 0X, followed by the base 16 value. Letters A through F in uppercase or lowercase represent 10 through 15. (The C++ standard does not mandate any particular implementation of the formatting flags. Your library probably implements the formatting flags differently.)

Listing 67-1. An Initial Definition of Formatting Flags

```
using fmtflags = int;
fmtflags const showbase   = 0x01;
fmtflags const boolalpha  = 0x02;
fmtflags const skipws     = 0x04;
fmtflags const showpoint  = 0x08;
fmtflags const showpos    = 0x10;
// etc. for other flags...
```

© Ray Lischner 2020

R. Lischner, *Exploring C++20*, https://doi.org/10.1007/978-1-4842-5961-0_67

The next step is to write the setf and unsetf functions. The former function sets specific bits in a flags_ data member (of the std::ios_base class), and the latter clears bits. To set and clear bits, C++ provides some operators that manipulate individual bits in an integer. Collectively, they are called the *bitwise* operators.

The bitwise operators perform the usual arithmetic promotions and conversions (Exploration 26). The operators then perform their operation on successive bits in their arguments. The & operator implements bitwise *and*; the | operator implements bitwise inclusive *or*; and the ~ operator is a unary operator to perform bitwise complement. Figure 67-1 illustrates the bitwise nature of these operators (using & as an example).

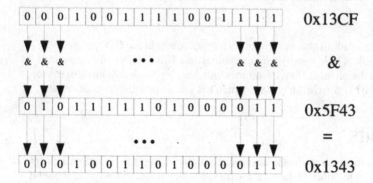

Figure 67-1. How the & (bitwise and) operator works

OPERATOR ABUSE

It may seem strange to you (it certainly does to me) that C++ uses the same operator to obtain the address of an object and to perform bitwise *and*. There are only so many characters to go around. The logical *and* operator is also used for rvalue references. The asterisk does double duty for multiplication and dereferencing a pointer or iterator. The difference is whether the operator is unary (one operand) or binary (two operands). So there is no ambiguity, just unusual syntax. Later in this Exploration, you will learn that the I/O operators are repurposed shift operators. But don't worry, you will get used to it. Eventually.

Implement the setf function. This function takes a single fmtflags argument and sets the specified flags in the flags_ data member. Listing 67-2 shows a simple solution.

Listing 67-2. A Simple Implementation of the setf Member Function

```
void setf(fmtflags f)
{
    flags_ = flags_ | f;
}
```

The unsetf function is slightly more complicated. It must clear flags, which means setting the corresponding bits to zero. In other words, the argument specifies a bitmask in which each 1 bit means to clear (set to 0) the bit in flags_. **Write the unsetf function**. Compare your solution with Listing 67-3.

Listing 67-3. A Simple Implementation of the unsetf Member Function

```
void unsetf(fmtflags f)
{
    flags_ = flags_ & ~f;
}
```

Recall from Exploration 49 that various assignment operators combine an arithmetic operator with assignment. Assignment operators also exist for the bitwise functions, so you can write these functions even more succinctly, as shown in Listing 67-4.

Listing 67-4. Using Assignment Operators in the Flags Functions

```
void setf(fmtflags f)
{
    flags_ |= f;
}

void unsetf(fmtflags f)
{
    flags_ &= ~f;
}
```

Recall from Exploration 50 that the | operator combines I/O mode flags. Now you know that the flags are bits, and the I/O mode is a bitmask. Should the need arise, you can use any of the bitwise operators on I/O modes.

Bitmasks

Not all the flags are individual bits. The alignment flags, for example, can be left, right, or internal. The floating-point style can be fixed, scientific, hexfloat, or general. To represent three or four values, you need two bits. For these situations, C++ has a two-argument form of the setf function. The first argument specifies a mask of bits to set within the field, and the second argument specifies a mask of which bits to affect.

Using the same bitwise operators, you can define adjustfield as a two-bit-wide bitmask, for example, 0x300. If both bits are clear, that could mean left adjustment; one bit set means right adjustment; the other bit could mean "internal" alignment (align after a sign or 0x in a hexadecimal value). That leaves one more possible value (both bits are set), but the standard library defines only three different alignment values.

Listing 67-5 shows one possible implementation of the adjustfield and floatfield masks and their associated values.

Listing 67-5. Declarations for Formatting Fields

```
fmtflags static constexpr adjustfield = 0x300;
fmtflags static constexpr left        = 0x000;
fmtflags static constexpr right       = 0x100;
fmtflags static constexpr internal    = 0x200;
fmtflags static constexpr floatfield  = 0xC00;
fmtflags static constexpr scientific  = 0x400;
fmtflags static constexpr fixed       = 0x800;
fmtflags static constexpr hexfloat    = 0xC00;
// general does not have a name; its value is zero
```

Thus, to set the alignment to right, one calls setf(right, adjustfield). **Write the two-argument form of the setf function**. Compare your solution with Listing 67-6.

Listing 67-6. Two-Argument Form of the setf Function

```
void setf(fmtflags flags_to_set, fmtflags field)
{
   flags_ &= ~field;
   flags_ |= flags_to_set;
}
```

One difficulty with defining bitfields in this fashion is that the numeric values can be hard to read, unless you've spent a lot of time working with hexadecimal values. Another solution is to use more familiar integers for all flags and fields and let the computer do the hard work by shifting those values into the correct positions.

Shifting Bits

Listing 67-7 shows another way to define the formatting fields. They represent the exact same values as shown in Listing 67-1, but they are a little easier to proofread.

Listing 67-7. Using Shift Operators to Define the Formatting Fields

```
int static constexpr boolalpha_pos = 0;
int static constexpr showbase_pos  = 1;
int static constexpr showpoint_pos = 2;
int static constexpr showpos_pos   = 3;
int static constexpr skipws_pos    = 4;
int static constexpr adjust_pos    = 5;
int static constexpr adjust_size   = 2;
int static constexpr float_pos     = 7;
int static constexpr float_size    = 2;

fmtflags static constexpr boolalpha   = 1 << boolalpha_pos;
fmtflags static constexpr showbase    = 1 << showbase_pos;
fmtflags static constexpr showpos     = 1 << showpos_pos;
fmtflags static constexpr showpoint   = 1 << showpoint_pos;
fmtflags static constexpr skipws      = 1 << showpoint_pos;
fmtflags static constexpr adjustfield = 3 << adjust_pos;
fmtflags static constexpr floatfield  = 3 << float_pos;

fmtflags static constexpr left     = 0 << adjust_pos;
fmtflags static constexpr right    = 1 << adjust_pos;
fmtflags static constexpr internal = 2 << adjust_pos;

fmtflags static constexpr fixed      = 1 << float_pos;
fmtflags static constexpr scientific = 2 << float_pos;
fmtflags static constexpr hexfloat = 3 << float_pos;
```

The << operator (which looks just like the output operator) is the left-shift operator. It shifts its left-hand operator (which must be an integer) by the number of bit positions specified by the right-hand operator (also an integer). Vacated bits are filled with zero.

```
1 << 2 == 4
10 << 3 == 80
```

Although this style is more verbose, you can clearly see that the bits are defined with adjacent values. You can also easily see the size of multibit bitmasks. If you have to add a new flag, you can do so without the need to recompute any other fields or flags.

What is the C++ right-shift operator? _____ That's right: >>, which is also the input operator.

If the right-hand operand is negative, that reverses the direction of the shift. That is, a left shift by a negative amount is the same as right-shifting by a positive amount and *vice versa*. You can use the shift operators on integers but not on floating-point numbers. The right-hand operand cannot be greater than the number of bits in the left-hand operand. (Use the numeric_limits class template, introduced in Exploration 26, to determine the number of bits in a type, such as int.)

The C++ standard library overloads the shift operators for the I/O stream classes to implement the I/O operators. Thus, the >> and << operators were designed for shifting bits in an integer and were later usurped for I/O. As a result, the operator precedence is not quite right for I/O. In particular, the shift operators have a higher precedence than the bitwise operators, because that makes the most sense for manipulating bits. As a consequence, if, for instance, you want to print the result of a bitwise operation, you must enclose the expression in parentheses.

```
std::cout << "5 & 3 = " << (5 & 3) << '\n';
```

One caution when using the right-shift operator: The value of the bits that are filled in is implementation-defined. This can be particularly problematic with negative numbers. The value -1 >> 1 may be positive on some implementations and negative on others. Fortunately, C++ has a way to avoid this uncertainty, as the next section explains.

Safe Shifting with Unsigned Types

Every primitive integer type has a corresponding type that you declare with the unsigned keyword. These types are known—not surprisingly—as *unsigned* types. One key difference between ordinary (or signed) integer types and their unsigned equivalents is that unsigned types always shift in a zero when right-shifting. For this reason, unsigned types are preferable to signed types for implementing bitmasks.

```
using fmtflags = unsigned int;
```

Write a program to determine how your C++ environment right-shifts negative values. Compare this with shifting unsigned values. Your program will certainly look different from mine, which is shown in Listing 67-8, but you should be able to recognize the key similarities.

Listing 67-8. Exploring How Negative and Unsigned Values Are Shifted

```
import <iostream>;
import <string_view>;

template<class T>
void print(std::string_view label, T value)
```

```
{
    std::cout << label << " = ";
    std::cout << std::dec << value << " = ";
    std::cout.width(8);
    std::cout.fill('0');
    std::cout << std::hex << std::internal << std::showbase << value << '\n';
}

int main()
{
    int i{~0}; // all bits set to 1; on most systems, ~0 == -1
    unsigned int u{~0u}; // all bits set to 1
    print("int >> 15", i >> 15);
    print("unsigned >> 15", u >> 15);
}
```

On my Linux x86 system, I see the following output

```
int >> 15 = -1 = 0xffffffff
unsigned >> 15 = 131071 = 0x01ffff
```

which means right-shifting a signed value fills in the vacated bits with copies of the sign bit (a process known as *sign extensio*n), and that right-shifting an unsigned value works correctly by shifting in zero bits.

Signed and Unsigned Types

The plain int type is shorthand for signed int. That is, the int type has two sign flavors: signed int and unsigned int, the default being signed int. Similarly, short int is the same as signed short int, and long int is the same as signed long int. Thus, you have no reason to use the signed keyword with the integer types.

Like too many rules, however, this one has an exception: signed char. The char type comes in three flavors, not two: char, signed char, and unsigned char. All three types occupy the same amount of space (one byte). The plain char type has the same representation as either signed char or unsigned char, but it remains a distinct type. The choice is left to the compiler; consult your compiler's documentation to learn the equivalent char type for your implementation. Thus, the signed keyword has a use for the signed char type; the most common use for signed char is to represent a tiny, signed integer when conserving memory is important. Use plain char for text, signed char for tiny integers, and unsigned char for tiny bitmasks.

Unfortunately, the I/O stream classes treat signed char and unsigned char as text, not tiny integers or bitmasks. Thus, reading or writing tiny integers is harder than it should be. Instead of reading or writing an integer, the I/O stream classes read or write a single character, casting the signed char or unsigned char to char. An easy solution for output is to call std::format('{0}', byte) because format() avoids the sin of the streams and formats char as a character, bool as bool, and all other integral types as numbers. Input is harder. Your best solution may be to write your own function to read an integer and cast it to the desired byte-sized integral type.

Unsigned Literals

If an integer literal does not fit in a signed int, the compiler tries to make it fit into an unsigned int. If that works, the literal's type is unsigned int. If the value is too big for unsigned int, the compiler tries long, and then unsigned long, then long long, and finally unsigned long long, before giving up and issuing an error message.

You can force an integer to be unsigned with the u or U suffix. The U and L suffixes can appear in any order for an unsigned long literal. Use ULL for unsigned long long. (Remember that C++ permits lowercase l, but I recommend uppercase L to avoid confusion with numeral 1.)

```
1234u
4321UL
0xFFFFLu
```

One consequence of this flexibility is that you can't always know the type of an integer literal. For example, the type of 0xFFFFFFFF might be int on a 64-bit system. On some 32-bit systems, the type might be unsigned int, and on others, it might be unsigned long. The moral is to make sure you write code that works correctly, regardless of the precise type of an integer literal, which isn't difficult. For example, all the programs and fragments in this book work on any C++ compiler, regardless of the size of an int.

Type Conversions

A signed type and its unsigned counterpart always occupy the same amount of space. You can use static_cast (Exploration 26) to convert one to the other, or you can let the compiler implicitly perform the conversion, which can result in surprises, if you aren't careful. Consider the example in Listing 67-9.

Listing 67-9. Mixing Signed and Unsigned Integers

```
import <iostream>;
void show(unsigned u)
{
    std::cout << u << '\n';
}

int main()
{
    int i{-1};
    std::cout << i << '\n';
    show(i);
}
```

This results in the following output on my system:

```
-1
4294967295
```

If you mix signed and unsigned values in an expression (usually a bad idea), the compiler converts the signed value to unsigned, which often results in more surprises. This kind of surprise often arises in comparisons. Most compilers will at least warn you about the problem.

Listing 67-10. Mystery Program

```
import <algorithm>;
import <iostream>;
import <iterator>;
import <vector>;

template<class T>
void append(std::vector<T>& data, const T& value, int max_size)
{
  if (data.size() < max_size - 1)
    data.push_back(value);
}

int main()
{
  std::vector<int> data{};
  append(data, 10, 3);
  append(data, 20, 2);
  append(data, 30, 1);
  append(data, 40, 0);
  append(data, 50, 0);
  std::ranges::copy(data, std::ostream_iterator<int>(std::cout, " "));
  std::cout << '\n';
}
```

Before you run the program, **predict what Listing 67-10 will print**.

_____

_____

_____

Try it. Were you correct? _____ **Explain what the program does.**

_____

_____

_____

The program succeeds in appending 10 to data because the vector size is zero, which is less than 2. The next call to append, however, does nothing, because the vector size is 1, and max_size - 1 is also 1. The next call fails for a similar reason. So why does the next call succeed in appending 40 to data? Because max_size is 0, you might think the comparison would be with -1, but -1 is signed, and data.size() is unsigned. Therefore, the compiler converts -1 to unsigned, which is an implementation-defined conversion. On typical workstations, -1 converts to the largest unsigned integer, so the test succeeds.

The first moral of the story is to avoid expressions that mix signed and unsigned values. Your compiler might help you here by issuing warnings when you mix signed and unsigned values. A common source for unsigned values is from the size() member functions in the standard library, which all return an unsigned result. You can reduce the chances for surprises by using one of the standard typedefs for sizes, such as std::size_t, which is an implementation-defined unsigned integer type. The standard containers all define a member type, size_type, to represent sizes and similar values for that container. Use these typedefs for your variables when you know you have to store sizes, indices, or counts.

"That's easy!" you say. "Just change the declaration of `max_size` to `std::vector<T>::size_type`, and problem solved!" Maybe you can avoid this kind of problem by sticking with the standard member typedefs, such as `size_type` and `difference_type` (Exploration 55). Take a gander at Listing 67-11 and see what you think.

Listing 67-11. Another Mystery Program

```
import <algorithm>;
import <iostream>;
import <iterator>;
import <vector>;

/** Return the index of a value in a range.
 * Look for the first occurrence of @p value in the range
 * [<tt>first</tt>, <tt>last</tt>), and return the zero-based
 * index or -1 if @p value is not found.
 * @param first The start of the range to search
 * @param last One past the end of the range to search
 * @param value The value to search for
 * @return [0, size), such that size == last-first, or -1
 */
template<class Range>
    requires std::ranges::forward_range<Range>
std::ranges::range_difference_t<Range>
index_of(Range const& range, std::ranges::range_value_t<Range> const& value)
{
    auto iter{std::ranges::find(range, value)};
    if (iter == std::ranges::end(range))
        return -1;
    else
        return std::distance(std::ranges::begin(range), iter);
}

/** Determine whether the first occurrence of a value in a container is
 * in the last position in the container.
 * @param container Any standard container
 * @param value The value to search for.
 * @return true if @p value is at the last position,
 *         or false if @p value is not found or at any other position.
 */
template<class T>
bool is_last(T const& container, typename T::value_type const& value)
{
    return index_of(container, value) == container.size() - 1;
}

int main()
{
    std::vector<int> data{};
    if (is_last(data, 10))
        std::cout << "10 is the last item in data\n";
}
```

Predict the output before you run the program in Listing 67-11.

Try it. What do you actually get?

I get "10 is the last item in data," even though data is clearly empty. Can you spot the conceptual error that I committed? In a standard container, the `difference_type` typedef is always a signed integral type. Thus, `index_of()` always returns a signed value. I made the mistake of thinking that the signed value `-1` would always be less than any unsigned value because they are always 0 or more. Thus, `is_last()` would not have to check for an empty container as a special case.

What I failed to take into account is that when a C++ expression mixes signed and unsigned values, the compiler converts the signed value to unsigned. Thus, the signed result from `index_of` becomes unsigned, and `-1` becomes the largest possible unsigned value. If the container is empty, `size()` is zero, and `size()` - 1 (which the compiler interprets as `size()` - `1u`) is also the largest possible unsigned integer.

If you are fortunate, your compiler issues a warning about comparing signed and unsigned values. That gives you a hint that something is wrong. **Fix the program. Compare your solution with Listing 67-12.**

Listing 67-12. Fixing the Second Mystery Program

```
import <algorithm>;
import <iostream>;
import <iterator>;
import <vector>;

/** Return the index of a value in a range.
 * Look for the first occurrence of @p value in the range
 * [<tt>first</tt>, <tt>last</tt>), and return the zero-based
 * index or -1 if @p value is not found.
 * @param first The start of the range to search
 * @param last One past the end of the range to search
 * @param value The value to search for
 * @return [0, size), such that size == last-first, or -1
 */
template<class Range>
    requires std::ranges::forward_range<Range>
std::ranges::range_difference_t<Range>
index_of(Range const& range, std::ranges::range_value_t<Range> const& value)
{
    auto iter{std::ranges::find(range, value)};
    if (iter == std::ranges::end(range))
        return -1;
    else
        return std::distance(std::ranges::begin(range), iter);
}

/** Determine whether the first occurrence of a value in a container is
 * in the last position in the container.
 * @param container Any standard container
 * @param value The value to search for.
 * @return true if @p value is at the last position,
 *         or false if @p value is not found or at any other position.
 */
template<class T>
```

```
bool is_last(T const& container, typename T::value_type const& value)
{
    auto index{ index_of(container, value) };
    decltype(index) last{ container.size() - 1 };
    return index == last;
}

int main()
{
    std::vector<int> data{};
    if (is_last(data, 10))
        std::cout << "10 is the last item in data\n";
}
```

There are many ways to ensure that both sides of the comparison have the same type. The decltype() operator takes an expression and yields the expression's type without evaluating the expression. In this case, it is used just to match the type of the index variable.

The second moral of the story is not to use unsigned types if you don't have to. Most of the time, signed types work just as well. Just because a type's range of legal values happens to be non-negative is not a reason to use an unsigned type. Doing so only complicates any code that must cooperate with the unsigned type.

But, I hear you say, every class with a size() member function returns an unsigned std::size_t value. How can I avoid mixing signed and unsigned types when the C++ standard library itself does not heed this excellent advice? As one small step toward addressing this problem, you can call std::ranges::ssize() for any container or range that knows its size. Thus, function returns the size as a signed integer. Maybe if ssize() becomes popular, a future revision to the C++ standard will mandate it for all containers.

■ **Tip** When using the standard library, make use of the typedefs and member typedefs that it provides. When you have control over the types, use signed types for all numeric types, including sizes, and reserve the unsigned types for bitmasks. And always be very, very careful every time you write an expression that uses an unsigned type with other integers.

Overflow

Until now, I've told you to ignore arithmetic overflow. That's because it's a difficult topic. Strictly speaking, if an expression involving signed integers or floating-point numbers overflows, the results are unspecified. In reality, your typical desktop system wraps integer overflow (so adding two positive numbers can yield a negative result). Overflow of floating-point numbers can yield infinity, or the program may terminate.

If you must prevent overflow, you should check values before evaluating an expression, to ensure the expression will not overflow. Use std::numeric_limits<> to check the min() and max() values for the type.

If you explicitly cast a signed value to a type, such that the value overflows the destination type, the results are not so dire. Most implementations simply discard the excess bits. Therefore, for maximum safety and portability, you should check for overflow. Use numeric_limits (Exploration 26) to learn the maximum or minimum value of a type.

Unsigned integers are different. The standard explicitly permits unsigned arithmetic to overflow. The result is to discard any extra high-order bits. Mathematically speaking, this means unsigned arithmetic is modulo 2^n, where n is the number of bits in the unsigned type. If you have to perform arithmetic that you know may overflow, and you want the values to wrap around without reporting an error, use static_cast to cast to the corresponding unsigned types, perform the arithmetic, and static_cast back the original types. The static_casts have no impact on performance, but they clearly tell the compiler and the human what's going on.

Rotating Integers

Although C++ has operators for bit-shifting, it lacks operators for rotations. But it has functions in <bit> for rotating bits, counting bits, and so on. Listing 67-13 illustrates a few such functions.

Listing 67-13. Examples from the <bit> Module

```
import <bit>;
import <iostream>;

int main()
{
    std::cout << std::hex << std::showbase <<
        "std::rotl(0x12345678U, 8) = " << std::rotl(0x12345678U, 8) <<
        "std::rotr(0x12345678U, 8) = " << std::rotr(0x12345678U, 8) <<
        std::dec <<
        "std::popcount(0x0110110U) = " << std::popcount(0x0110110U) <<
        "std::bit_width(0x00ffffU) = " << std::bit_width(0x00ffffU) <<
        '\n';
}
```

The <bit> module has a few other bit-fiddling functions for counting bits in an integer, testing endianness, and so on.

Introducing Bitfields

A *bitfield* is a way to partition an integer within a class into individual bits or masks of adjacent bits. Declare a bitfield using an unsigned integer type or bool, the field name, a colon, and the number of bits in the field. Listing 67-14 shows how you might store the I/O formatting flags using bitfields.

Listing 67-14. Declaring Formatting Flags with Bitfields

```
struct fmtflags
{
    bool skipws_f :        1;
    bool boolalpha_f:      1;
    bool showpoint_f:      1;
    bool showbase_f:       1;
    bool showpos_f:        1;
    unsigned adjustfield_f: 2;
    unsigned floatfield_f: 2;

    static unsigned constexpr left     = 0;
    static unsigned constexpr right    = 1;
    static unsigned constexpr internal = 2;
```

```
    static unsigned constexpr fixed      = 1;
    static unsigned constexpr scientific = 2;
    static unsigned constexpr hexfloat = 3;
};
```

Use a bitfield member the way you would use any other data member. For example, to set the skipws flag, use

```
flags.skipws_f = true;
```

and to clear the flag, use the following:

```
flags.skipws_f = false;
```

To select scientific notation, try the line that follows:

```
flags.floatfield_f = fmtflags::scientific;
```

As you can see, code that uses bitfields is easier to read and write than the equivalent code using shift and bitwise operators. That's what makes bitfields popular. On the other hand, it is hard to write functions such as setf and unsetf. It is hard to get or set multiple, nonadjacent bits at one time. That's why your library probably doesn't use bitfields to implement I/O formatting flags.

Another limitation is that you cannot take the address of a bitfield (with the & operator), because an individual bit is not directly addressable in the C++ memory model.

Nonetheless, the clarity that bitfields offer puts them at the top of the list when choosing an implementation. Sometimes, other factors knock them off the list, but you should always consider bitfields first. With bitfields, you don't have to be concerned with bitwise operators, shift operators, mixed-up operator precedence, and so on.

Portability

The C++ standard leaves several details up to each implementation. In particular, the order of bits in a field is left up to the implementation. A bitfield cannot cross a word boundary where the definition of a *word* is also left up to the implementation. Popular desktop and workstation computers often use 32 bits or 64 bits, but there is no guarantee that a word is the same size as an int. An unnamed bitfield of size zero tells the compiler to insert pad bits, so that the subsequent declaration aligns on a word boundary.

```
class demo {
  unsigned bit0 : 1;
  unsigned bit1 : 1;
  unsigned bit2 : 3;
  unsigned      : 0;
  unsigned word1: 2;
};
```

The size of a demo object depends on the implementation. Whether bit0 is the least or most significant bit of a demo's actual implementation also varies from one system to another. The number of pad bits between bit2 and word1 also depends on the implementation.

Most code does not have to know the layout of the bits in memory. On the other hand, if you are writing code that interprets the bits in a hardware control register, you have to know the order of bits, the exact nature of padding bits, and so on. But you probably aren't expecting to write highly portable code, anyway. In the most common case, when you are trying to express a compact set of individual set members or small bitmasks, bitfields are wonderful. They are easy to write and easy to read. They are limited, however, to a single word, often 32 bits. For larger bitfields, you must use a class, such as std::bitset.

The `bitset` Class Template

Sometimes you have to store more bits than can fit in an integer. In that case, you can use the std::bitset class template, which implements a fixed-size string of bits of any size.

The std::bitset class template takes one template argument: the number of bits in the set. Use a bitset object the way you would any other value. It supports all the bitwise and shift operators, plus a few member functions for further convenience. Another nifty trick that bitset can perform is the subscript operator, which lets you access individual bits in the set as discrete objects. The right-most (least significant) bit is at index zero. Construct a bitset from an unsigned long (to set the least significant bits of the bitset, initializing the remaining bits to zero) or from a string of '0' and '1' characters, as illustrated in Listing 67-15.

Listing 67-15. Example of Using std::bitset

```
import <bitset>;
import <iostream>;

/** Find the first 1 bit in a bitset, starting from the most significant bit.
 * @param bitset The bitset to examine
 * @return A value in the range [0, bitset.size()-1) or
 *         size_t(-1) if bitset.none() is true.
 */
template<std::size_t N>
std::size_t first(std::bitset<N> const& bitset)
{
    for (std::size_t i{bitset.size()}; i-- != 0;)
        if (bitset.test(i))
            return i;
    return std::size_t(-1);
}

int main()
{
    std::bitset<50> lots_o_bits{"10110111011110111110111111101111111"};
    std::cout << "bitset: " << lots_o_bits << '\n';
    std::cout << "first 1 bit: " << first(lots_o_bits) << '\n';
    std::cout << "count of 1 bits: " << lots_o_bits.count() << '\n';
    lots_o_bits[first(lots_o_bits)] = false;
    std::cout << "new first 1 bit: " << first(lots_o_bits) << '\n';
    lots_o_bits.flip();
    std::cout << "bitset: " << lots_o_bits << '\n';
    std::cout << "first 1 bit: " << first(lots_o_bits) << '\n';
}
```

In Exploration 25, I presented static_cast<> as a way to convert one integer to a different type. Listing 67-14 demonstrates another way to convert integer types, using constructor and initializer syntax: std::size_t(-1) or std::size{-1}. For a simple type conversion, this syntax is often easier to read than static_cast<>. I recommend using this syntax only when converting literals; use static_cast<> for more complicated expressions.

Unlike working with bitfields, most of the behavior of bitset is completely portable. Thus, every implementation gives the same results when running the program in Listing 67-14. The following output displays those results:

```
bitset: 000000000000000010110111011110111110111111101111111
first 1 bit: 33
count of 1 bits: 28
new first 1 bit: 31
bitset: 111111111111111111001000100001000001000000010000000
first 1 bit: 49
```

Write a function template, find_pair, that takes two arguments: a bitset to search and a bool value to compare. The function searches for the first pair of adjacent bits that are equal to the second argument and returns the index of the most significant bit of the pair. **What should the function return if it cannot find a matching pair of bits? Write a simple test program too.**

Compare your solution with mine, which is presented in Listing 67-16.

Listing 67-16. The find_pair Function and Test Program

```cpp
import <bitset>;
import <iostream>;

template<std::size_t N>
std::size_t find_pair(std::bitset<N> const& bitset, bool value)
{
   if (bitset.size() >= 2)
      for (std::size_t i{bitset.size()}; i-- != 1; )
         if (bitset[i] == value and bitset[i-1] == value)
            return i;
   return std::size_t(-1);
}

void test(bool condition) {
   if (not condition)
      throw std::logic_error("test failure");
}

int main()
{
   auto constexpr static not_found{static_cast<std::size_t>(-1)};
   std::bitset<0> bs0{};
   std::bitset<1> bs1{};
   std::bitset<2> bs2{};
   std::bitset<3> bs3{};
   std::bitset<100> bs100{};
```

```
    test(find_pair(bs0, false) == not_found);
    test(find_pair(bs0, true) == not_found);
    test(find_pair(bs1, false) == not_found);
    test(find_pair(bs1, true) == not_found);
    test(find_pair(bs2, false) == 1);
    test(find_pair(bs2, true) == not_found);
    bs2[0] = true;
    test(find_pair(bs2, false) == not_found);
    test(find_pair(bs2, true) == not_found);
    bs2.flip();
    test(find_pair(bs2, false) == not_found);
    test(find_pair(bs2, true) == not_found);
    bs2[0] = true;
    test(find_pair(bs2, false) == not_found);
    test(find_pair(bs2, true) == 1);
    test(find_pair(bs3, false) == 2);
    test(find_pair(bs3, true) == not_found);
    bs3[2].flip();
    test(find_pair(bs3, false) == 1);
    test(find_pair(bs3, true) == not_found);
    bs3[1].flip();
    test(find_pair(bs3, false) == not_found);
    test(find_pair(bs3, true) == 2);
    test(find_pair(bs100, false) == 99);
    test(find_pair(bs100, true) == not_found);
    bs100[50] = true;
    test(find_pair(bs100, true) == not_found);
    bs100[51] = true;
    test(find_pair(bs100, true) == 51);
    std::cout << "pass\n";
}
```

Although bitset is not widely used, when you need it, it can be extremely helpful. The next Exploration covers a language feature that is much more widely used than bitset: enumerations.

EXPLORATION 68

■ ■ ■

Enumerations

The final mechanism for defining types in C++ is the enum keyword, which is short for *enumeration*. Enumerations come in two flavors. One flavor originated in C and has some strange quirks. The other flavor addresses those quirks and will probably make more sense to you. This Exploration starts with the new flavor.

Scoped Enumerations

An enumerated type is a user-defined type that defines a set of identifiers as the values of the type. Define an enumerated type with the enum class keywords, followed by the name of your new type, followed by an optional colon and integer type, followed by the enumerated literals in curly braces. Feel free to substitute struct for class; they are interchangeable in an enum declaration. The following code shows some examples of enumerated types:

```
enum class color { black, red, green, yellow, blue, magenta, cyan, white };
enum class sign : char { negative, positive };
enum class flags : unsigned { boolalpha, showbase, showpoint, showpos, skipws };
enum class review : int { scathing = -2, negative, neutral, positive, rave };
```

A scoped enum definition defines a brand-new type that is distinct from all other types. The type name is also a scope name, and the names of all the enumerators are declared in that scope. Because enumerators are scoped, you can use the same enumerator name in multiple scoped enumerations.

The type after the colon must be an integral type. If you omit the colon and type, the compiler implicitly uses int. This type is called the *underlying type*. The enumerated value is stored as though it were a value of the underlying type.

Each enumerator names a compile-time constant. The type of each enumerator is the enumeration type. You can obtain the integral value by casting the enumerated type to its underlying type, and you can cast an integral type to the enumerated type. The compiler will *not* perform these conversions automatically. Listing 68-1 shows one way to implement the std::ios_base::openmode type (refresh your memory in Exploration 14). The type must support the bitwise operators to combine out, trunc, app, and so on, which it can provide by converting enumerated value to unsigned, performing the operation, and casting back to openmode.

© Ray Lischner 2020

R. Lischner, *Exploring C++20*, https://doi.org/10.1007/978-1-4842-5961-0_68

Listing 68-1. One Way to Implement openmode Type

```
enum class openmode : unsigned char {
    in=1, out=2, binary=4, trunc=8, app=16, ate=32
};

openmode operator|(openmode lhs, openmode rhs)
{
    return static_cast<openmode>(
      static_cast<unsigned>(lhs) | static_cast<unsigned>(rhs) );
}

openmode operator&(openmode lhs, openmode rhs)
{
    return static_cast<openmode>(
      static_cast<unsigned>(lhs) & static_cast<unsigned>(rhs) );
}

openmode operator~(openmode arg)
{
    return static_cast<openmode>( ~static_cast<unsigned>(arg) );
}
```

When you declare an enumerator, you can provide an integral value by following the enumerator name with an equal sign and a constant expression. The expression can use enumerators declared earlier in the same type as integral constants. If you omit a value, the compiler adds one to the previous value. If you omit a value for the first enumerator, the compiler uses zero, for example:

```
enum class color : unsigned { black, red=0xff0000, green=0x00ff00, blue=0x0000ff,
    cyan = blue|green, yellow=red|green, magenta=red|blue, white=red|blue|green };
```

You can forward declare an enumerated type, similar to the way you can forward declare a class type. If you omit the curly-braced list of enumerators, it tells the compiler the type name and its underlying type, so you can use the type to declare function parameters, data members, and so on. You can provide the enumerators in a separate declaration:

```
enum class deferred : short;
enum class deferred : short { example, of, forward, declared, enumeration };
```

A forward-declared enumeration is also called an *opaque declaration*. One way to use an opaque declaration is to declare the type in a module interface, but provide the enumerators in the module implementation. If the opaque type is declared in a class or namespace, be sure to qualify the type's name when you provide the full type definition, for example, if the header contains

```
export module demo;
export struct demo {
  enum hidden : unsigned;
};
```

The source file might declare enumerators that are for use solely by the implementation and not the user of the class as follows:

```
module demo;
enum demo::hidden : unsigned { a, b, c };
```

The compiler implicitly defines the comparison operators for enumerators. As you probably expect, they work by comparing the underlying integral values. The compiler provides no other operators, such as I/O, increment, decrement, and so on.

Scoped enumerations pretty much work the way one would expect an enumerated type to work. Given the name "scoped" enumerations, you must surely be asking yourself, "What is an unscoped enumeration?" You are in for a surprise.

Unscoped Enumerations

An unscoped enumerated type defines a new type, distinct from other types. The new type is an integer bitmask type, with a set of predefined mask values. If you do not specify an underlying type, the compiler chooses one of the built-in integral types; the exact type is implementation-defined. Define an unscoped enumeration in the same manner as a scoped enumeration, except you must omit the class (or struct) keyword.

The compiler does not define the arithmetic operators for enumerated types, leaving you free to define these operators. The compiler implicitly converts an unscoped enumerated value to its underlying integer value, but to convert back, you must use an explicit type cast. Use the enumerated type name in the manner of a constructor with an integer argument or use static_cast.

```
enum color { black, blue, green, cyan, red, magenta, yellow, white };
int c1{yellow};
color c2{ color(c1 + 1) };
color c3{ static_cast<color>(c2 + 1) };
```

Calling an enum a "bitmask" may strike you as odd, but that is how the standard defines the implementation of an unscoped enumeration. Suppose you define the following enumeration:

```
enum sample { low=4, high=256 };
```

The permissible values for an object of type sample are all values in the range [sample(0), sample(511)]. The permissible values are all the bitmask values that fit into a bitfield that can hold the largest and smallest bitmask values among the enumerators. Thus, in order to store the value 256, the enumerated type must be able to store up to 9 bits. As a side effect, any 9-bit value is valid for the enumerated type, or integers up to 511.

You can use an enumerated type for a bitfield (Exploration 66). It is your responsibility to ensure that the bitfield is large enough to store all the possible enumeration values, as demonstrated in the following:

```
struct demo {
  color okay  : 3; // big enough
  color small : 2; // oops, not enough bits, but valid C++
};
```

The compiler will let you declare a bitfield that is too small; if you are fortunate, your compiler will warn you about the problem.

C++ inherits this definition of enum from C. The earliest implementations lacked a formal model, so when the standards committee tried to nail down the formal semantics, the best they could do was to capture the behavior of extant compilers. They later invented scoped enumerators to try to provide a rational way to define enumerations.

Strings and Enumerations

One deficiency of scoped and unscoped enumerations is I/O support. C++ does not implicitly create any I/O operators for enumerations. You are on your own. Unscoped enumerators can be implicitly promoted to the underlying type and printed as an integer, but that's all. If you want to use the names of the enumerators, you must implement the I/O operators yourself. One difficulty is that C++ gives you no way to discover the literal names with any reflection or introspection mechanism.

In order to implement I/O operators that can read and write strings, you must be able to map strings to enumerated values and *vice versa*. Most enumerated types have a limited number of literals, so it is often feasible to create a map with names as keys as literals as values. To map a value to a string, search all the values linearly for a match. This is easy and for small maps, not too costly.

> **How would you implement a type that behaves as a map but also allows reverse lookups?**
>
> _____
>
> _____

I recommend deriving a class from std::unordered_map, adding a few member functions for the reverse lookup. **Go ahead and write a template class**, taking an enumerated type as a template argument and deriving from std::unordered_map. What methods do you want to add? Listing 68-2 shows one way to do this.

Listing 68-2. Defining a Type That Maps Strings to and from Enumerations

```
export module enums;

import <algorithm>;
import <initializer_list>;
import <stdexcept>;
import <string>;
import <type_traits>;
import <unordered_map>;

export template<class T>
concept is_enum = std::is_enum_v<T>;

export template<class Enum>
requires is_enum<Enum>
class enum_map : public std::unordered_map<std::string, Enum>
{
public:
    using enum_type = Enum;
    using super = std::unordered_map<std::string, enum_type>;
    using value_type = super::value_type;
    using key_type = super::key_type;
    using mapped_type = super::mapped_type;
    using const_iterator = super::const_iterator;
```

```
    // All the same constructors as the super class.
    using super::super;
    // But initializer lists require a distinct constructor.
    enum_map(std::initializer_list<value_type> list) : super(list) {}

    using super::find;
    // Lookup by enum value. Return iterator or end().
    const_iterator find(mapped_type value) const {
        return std::ranges::find_if(*this, [value](auto& pair)
        {
            return pair.second == value;
        });
    }

    using super::at;
    // Lookup by enum value. Return reference to key or throw
    key_type const& at(mapped_type value) const {
        if (auto iter = find(value); iter != this->end())
            return iter->first;
        else
            throw std::out_of_range("enum_map::at()");
    }
};
```

When a derived class defines a member function that is also defined in a base class, the derived class hides or shadows the base class function because the compiler stops looking once it finds the function in the derived class. Even if the base class would have a better (or correct) match for the function arguments, the search stops as soon as the compiler finds any function with the correct name. The using declarations bring the base class functions into the derived class so the compiler can find all of them and then pick the one that fits best. Because we know the key type is a string and the mapped type is an enumeration, there is no ambiguity calling find() or at(). If the argument is a string, the regular unordered_map function is called, and if the argument is an enumeration, the new enum_map function is called.

Given the enum_map type, write template I/O functions. The stream operators don't help because in order to read and write a string or enumerated value, the enum_map object is also needed. **So write read() and write() functions instead.** See if your functions look anything like mine in Listing 68-3.

Listing 68-3. Defining a Type That Maps Strings to and from Enumerations

```
import <istream>;
import <ostream>;

template<class Enum>
std::istream& read(std::istream& stream, enum_map<Enum> const& map, Enum& value)
{
    std::string token;
    if (stream >> token)
    {
        value = map.at(token);
    }
    return stream;
}
```

```
template<class Enum>
std::ostream& write(std::ostream& stream, enum_map<Enum> const& map, Enum value)
{
    stream << map.at(value);
    return stream;
}
```

Test your code with a simple enumerated type. Suppose you define a language type that enumerates your favorite computer languages. Write a program that initializes a const enum_map object, reads some values from cin, and writes them back to cout. Catch and report exceptions and continue the loop. My sample program is Listing 68-4.

Listing 68-4. Demonstrating the enum_map Type

```
import <iostream>;
import enums;

enum class language { apl, low=apl, cpp, haskell, lisp, scala, high=scala };

enum_map<language> const languages{
    { "apl", language::apl },
    { "c++", language::cpp },
    { "haskell", language::haskell },
    { "lisp", language::lisp },
    { "scala", language::scala }
};

int main()
{
    language lang;
    while (std::cin)
    {
        try {
            if (read(std::cin, languages, lang)) {
                write(std::cout, languages, lang);
                std::cout << '\n';
            }
        }
        catch (std::out_of_range const& ex) {
            std::cout << ex.what() << '\n';
        }
    }
}
```

Spaceships

No, this section does not address spaceship avionics. Rather, it informs you of the so-called "spaceship" operator, <=>. More formally, this operator's name is the three-way comparison operator, but spaceship is more fun. This comparison operator returns an enumerated value (which is why I have not mentioned it yet).

The spaceship operator compares two values and tells you in one go whether one object is less-than, greater-than, or equal to the other object. It also allows for the possibility that the objects cannot be compared (say, two not-a-number floating-point values).

If the operand types permit it, the operator returns a std::strong_ordering value, which can be less, equal, or greater. The other possibility is std::partial_ordering, which also provides the less, equal, and greater literals, as well as unordered. Both types are scoped, so you need to qualify the literals. The types are defined in <compare>.

A type can overload the operator. For example, rational can implement strong ordering, as shown in Listing 68-5.

Listing 68-5. Implementing Three-Way Comparison for rational

```
import <compare>;

template<class T>
std::strong_ordering operator<=>(rational<T> const& lhs, rational<T> const& rhs)
{
  if (lhs.denominator() == rhs.denominator())
    // The easy case.
    return lhs.numerator() <=> rhs.numerator();
  else
    return lhs.numerator()*rhs.denominator() <=> lhs.denominator()*rhs.numerator();
}

template<class T>
bool operator<(rational<T> const& lhs, rational<T> const& rhs)
{
  return std::strong_ordering::less == (lhs <=> rhs);
}
```

Revisiting Projects

Now that you know all about enumerations, consider how you could improve some previous projects. For example, in Exploration 36, we wrote a constructor for the point class that uses a bool to distinguish between Cartesian and polar coordinate systems. Because it is not obvious whether true means Cartesian or polar, a better solution is to use an enumerated type, such as the following:

```
enum class coordinate_system : bool { cartesian, polar };
```

Another example that can be improved with enumerations is the card class, from Listing 57-5. Instead of using int constants for the suits, use an enumeration. You can also use an enumeration for the rank. The enumeration has to specify enumerators: the number cards and ace, jack, queen, and king. Choose appropriate values so that you can cast an integer in the range [2, 10] to rank and get the desired value. You will have to implement operator++ for suit and rank. One major improvement by using enumerations is that it is no longer possible to mistake the suit and rank types. Write your new, improved card class and compare it with my solution in Listing 68-6.

Listing 68-6. Improving the card Class with Enumerations

```
export module card;

import <istream>;
import <ostream>;

export enum class suit { diamonds, clubs, hearts, spades };
export enum class rank { r2=2, r3, r4, r5, r6, r7, r8, r9, r10, jack, queen, king, ace };

export suit& operator++(suit& s)
{
   if (s == suit::spades)
      s = suit::diamonds;
   else
      s = static_cast<suit>(static_cast<int>(s) + 1);
   return s;
}

export rank operator++(rank& r)
{
   if (r == rank::ace)
      r = rank::r2;
   else
      r = static_cast<rank>(static_cast<int>(r) + 1);
   return r;
}

/// Represent a standard western playing card.
export class card
{
public:
   constexpr card() : rank_(rank::ace), suit_(suit::spades) {}
   constexpr card(rank r, suit s) : rank_{r}, suit_{s} {}

   constexpr void assign(rank r, suit s);
   constexpr suit get_suit() const { return suit_; }
   constexpr rank get_rank() const { return rank_; }
private:
   rank rank_;
   suit suit_;
};

export bool operator==(card a, card b);
export bool operator!=(card a, card b);
export std::ostream& operator<<(std::ostream& out, card c);
export std::istream& operator>>(std::istream& in, card& c);

/// In some games, Aces are high. In other Aces are low. Use different
/// comparison functors depending on the game.
export bool acehigh_compare(card a, card b);
export bool acelow_compare(card a, card b);
```

```
/// Generate successive playing cards, in a well-defined order,
/// namely, 2-10, J, Q, K, A. Diamonds first, then Clubs, Hearts, and Spades.
/// Roll-over and start at the beginning again after generating 52 cards.
export class card_generator
{
public:
  card_generator();
  card operator()();
private:
  card card_;
};
```

What other projects can you improve with enumerations?

■ ■ ■

Multiple Inheritance

Unlike some other object-oriented languages, C++ lets a class have more than one base class. This feature is known as *multiple inheritance*. Several other languages permit a single base class and introduce a variety of mechanisms for pseudo-inheritance, such as Java interfaces and Ruby mix-ins and modules. Multiple inheritance in C++ is a superset of all these other behaviors.

Multiple Base Classes

Declare more than one base class by listing all the base classes in a comma-separated list. Each base class gets its own access specifier, as demonstrated here:

```
class derived : public base1, private base2, public base3
{};
```

As with single inheritance, the derived class has access to all the non-private members of all of its base classes. The derived class constructor initializes all the base classes in order of declaration. If you have to pass arguments to any base class constructor, do so in the initializer list. As with data members, the order of initializers does not matter. Only the order of declaration matters, as illustrated in Listing 69-1.

Listing 69-1. Demonstrating the Order of Initialization of Base Classes

```
import <iostream>;
import <string>;
import <utility>;

class visible {
public:
    visible(std::string msg) : msg_{std::move(msg)} { std::cout << msg_ << '\n'; }
    std::string const& msg() const { return msg_; }
private:
    std::string msg_;
};

class base1 : public visible {
public:
    base1(int x) : visible{"base1 constructed"}, value_{x} {}
    int value() const { return value_; }
private:
    int value_;
};
```

© Ray Lischner 2020
R. Lischner, *Exploring C++20*, https://doi.org/10.1007/978-1-4842-5961-0_69

```cpp
class base2 : public visible {
public:
    base2(std::string const& str) : visible{"base2{" + str + "} constructed"} {}
};

class base3 : public visible {
public:
    base3() : visible{"base3 constructed"} {}
    int value() const { return 42; }
};

class derived : public base1, public base2, public base3 {
public:
    derived(int i, std::string const& str) : base3{}, base2{str}, base1{i} {}
    int value() const { return base1::value() + base3::value(); }
    std::string msg() const
    {
        return base1::msg() + "\n" + base2::msg() + "\n" + base3::msg();
    }
};

int main()
{
    derived d{42, "example"};
}
```

Your compiler may issue a warning when you compile the program, pointing out that the order of base classes in derived's initializer list does not match the order in which the initializers are called. Running the program demonstrates that the order of the base classes controls the order of the constructors, as shown in the following output:

```
base1 constructed
base2{example} constructed
base3 constructed
```

Figure 69-1 illustrates the class hierarchy of Listing 69-1. Notice that each of the base1, base2, and base3 classes has its own copy of the visible base class. Don't be concerned now, but this point will arise later, so pay attention.

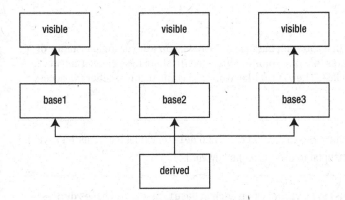

Figure 69-1. *UML diagram of classes in Listing 69-1*

If two or more base classes have a member with the same name, you must indicate to the compiler which of them you mean, if you want to access that particular member. Do this by qualifying the member name with the desired base class name when you access the member in the derived class. See the examples in the derived class in Listing 69-1. **Change the main() function to the following:**

```
int main()
{
   derived d{42, "example"};
   std::cout << d.value() << '\n' << d.msg() << '\n';
}
```

Predict the output from the new program.

_____

_____

_____

_____

_____

_____

_____

Compare your results with the following output I got:

```
base1 constructed
base2{example} constructed
base3 constructed
84
base1 constructed
base2{example} constructed
base3 constructed
```

Virtual Base Classes

Sometimes you don't want a separate copy of a common base class. Instead, you want a single instance of the common base class, and every class shares that one common instance. To share base classes, insert the virtual keyword when declaring the base class. The virtual keyword can come before or after the access specifier; convention is to list it first.

■ **Note** C++ overloads certain keywords, such as static, virtual, and delete. Virtual base classes have no relationship with virtual functions. They just happen to use the same keyword.

Imagine changing the visible base class to be virtual when each of base1, base2, and base3 derives from it. **Can you think of any difficulty that might arise?**

Notice that each of the classes that inherit from visible passes a different value to the constructor for visible. If you want to share a single instance of visible, you have to pick one value and stick with it. To enforce this rule, the compiler ignores all the initializers for a virtual base class, except the one that it requires in the most-derived class (in this case, derived). Thus, to change visible to be virtual, not only must you change the declarations of base1, base2, and base3, but you must also change derived. When derived initializes visible, it initializes the sole, shared instance of visible. **Try it.** Your modified program should look something like Listing 69-2.

Listing 69-2. Changing the Inheritance of Visible to Virtual

```
import <iostream>;
import <string>;
import <utility>;

class visible {
public:
    visible(std::string msg) : msg_{std::move(msg)} { std::cout << msg_ << '\n'; }
    std::string const& msg() const { return msg_; }
private:
    std::string msg_;
};

class base1 : virtual public visible {
public:
    base1(int x) : visible{"base1 constructed"}, value_{x} {}
    int value() const { return value_; }
private:
    int value_;
};

class base2 : virtual public visible {
public:
    base2(std::string const& str) : visible{"base2{" + str + "} constructed"} {}
};
```

```
class base3 : virtual public visible {
public:
    base3() : visible{"base3 constructed"} {}
    int value() const { return 42; }
};

class derived : public base1, public base2, public base3 {
public:
    derived(int i, std::string const& str)
    : base3{}, base2{str}, base1{i}, visible{"derived"}
    {}
    int value() const { return base1::value() + base3::value(); }
    std::string msg() const
    {
        return base1::msg() + "\n" + base2::msg() + "\n" + base3::msg();
    }
};

int main()
{
    derived d{42, "example"};
    std::cout << d.value() << '\n' << d.msg() << '\n';
}
```

Predict the output from Listing 69-2.

_____

_____

_____

_____

_____

_____

_____

Notice that the visible class is now initialized only once and that the derived class is the one that initializes it. Thus, every class message is "derived". This example is unusual because I want to illustrate how virtual base classes work. Most virtual base classes define only a default constructor. This frees authors of derived classes from concerning themselves with passing arguments to the virtual base class constructor. Instead, every derived class invokes the default constructor; it doesn't matter which class is the most derived.

Figure 69-2 depicts the new class diagram, using virtual inheritance.

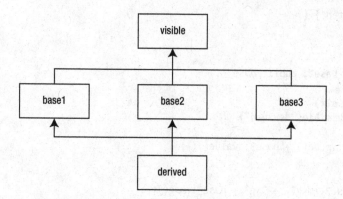

Figure 69-2. *Class diagram with virtual inheritance*

Java-Like Interfaces

Programming with interfaces has some important advantages. Being able to separate interfaces from implementations makes it easy to change implementations without affecting other code. If you have to use interfaces, you can easily do so in C++.

C++ has no formal notion of interfaces, but it supports interface-based programming. The essence of an interface in Java and similar languages is that an interface has no data members, and the member functions have no implementations. Recall from Exploration 38 that such a function is called a *pure virtual function*. Thus, an interface is merely an ordinary class in which you do not define any data members, and you declare all member functions as pure virtual.

For example, Java has the Hashable interface, which defines the hash and equalTo functions. Listing 69-3 shows the equivalent C++ class.

Listing 69-3. The Hashable Interface in C++

```
class Hashable
{
public:
   virtual ~Hashable();
   virtual unsigned long hash() const = 0;
   virtual bool equalTo(Hashable const&) const = 0;
};
```

Any class that implements the Hashable interface must override all the member functions. For example, HashableString implements Hashable for a string, as shown in Listing 69-4.

Listing 69-4. The HashableString Class

```
class HashableString : public Hashable
{
public:
   HashableString() : string_{} {}
   ~HashableString() override;
```

```
    unsigned long hash() const override;
    bool equalTo(Hashable const&) const override;

    // Implement the entire interface of std::string ...
private:
    std::string string_;
};
```

Note that HashableString does *not* derive from std::string. Instead, it encapsulates a string and delegates all string functions to the string_ object it holds.

The reason you must not derive from std::string is the same reason Hashable contains a virtual destructor. Recall from Exploration 39 that any class with at least one virtual function should make its destructor virtual. But std::string does not have a virtual destructor. This is a problem in programs that manipulate raw pointers. If HashableString were to derive from std::string and one part of a program allocates a new HashableString object and another deletes the same pointer as type std::string, the HashableString destructor is never called. This may seem like a problem that is easy to avoid, and it is, but in large, complex programs, it becomes easy for a small change to one part of the program to have surprising effects in an unrelated part of the program.

If HashableString does not derive from std::string, how can the program manage these hashable strings? The short answer is that it cannot. The long answer is that thinking in terms of Java solutions does not work well in C++, because C++ offers a better solution to this kind of problem: templates.

Interfaces vs. Templates

As you can see, C++ supports Java-style interfaces, but that style of programming can lead to difficulties. There are times when Java-like interfaces are the correct C++ solution. There are other situations, however, when C++ offers superior solutions, such as templates.

Instead of writing a HashableString class, write a hash<> class template and specialize the template for any type that has to be stored in a hash table. The primary template provides the default behavior; specialize hash<> for the std::string type. In this way, the string pool can easily store std::string pointers and destroy the string objects properly, and a hash table can compute hash values for strings (and anything else you have to store in the hash table). Listing 69-5 shows one way to write the hash<> class template and a specialization for std::string.

Listing 69-5. The hash<> Class Template

```
export module hash;

import <string>;

export template<class T>
class hash
{
public:
    std::size_t operator()(T const& x) const
    {
        return reinterpret_cast<std::size_t>(&x);
    }
};
```

```
export template<>
class hash<std::string>
{
public:
    std::size_t operator()(std::string const& str) const
    {
        std::size_t h(0);
        for (auto c : str)
            h = h << 1 | c;
        return h;
    }
};
```

(By the way, the standard library offers std::hash and specializes it for std::string. Trust your library's implementation to be vastly superior to the toy implementation in this Exploration.)

This approach gives all the functionality of the Hashable interface, but in a manner that allows any type to be hashable without giving up any well-defined behavior. In addition, the hash() function is no longer virtual and can even be an inline function. The speed-up can be considerable if the hash table is accessed in a critical performance path.

Mix-Ins

Another approach to multiple inheritance that you find in languages such as Ruby is the *mix-in*. A mix-in is a class that typically has no data members, although this is not a requirement in C++ (as it is in some languages). Usually, a C++ mix-in is a class template that defines some member functions that call upon the template arguments to provide input values for those functions.

A common idiom is for the mix-in template to take the derived class as a template argument. The mix-in can define operators that return derived class references to ensure that the API of the derived class is exactly what the user expects.

Confused yet? You aren't alone. This is a common idiom in C++, but one that takes time before it becomes familiar and natural. Listing 69-6 helps to clarify how this kind of mix-in works. This mix-in defines an assignment operator that takes its argument by value (later the caller decides whether to copy or move the source of the assignment) and swaps the argument with the current value. This is one of several common idioms for defining assignment operators.

Listing 69-6. The assignment_mixin Class Template

```
export module mixin;

export template<class T>
class assignment_mixin {
public:
    T& operator=(T rhs)
    {
        rhs.swap(static_cast<T&>(*this));
        return static_cast<T&>(*this);
    }
};
```

The trick is that instead of swapping *this, the mix-in class casts itself to a reference to the template argument, T. In this way, the mix-in never has to know anything about the derived class. The only requirement is that the class, T, must be copyable (so it can be an argument to the assignment function) and have a swap member function.

In order to use the assignment_mixin class, derive your class from the assignment_mixin (as well as any other mix-ins you wish to use), using the derived class name as the template argument. Listing 69-7 shows an example of how a class uses mix-ins.

Listing 69-7. Using mix-in Class Template

```
import <iostream>;
import <string>;
import <utility>;

import mixin; // Listing 69-6

class thing: public assignment_mixin<thing> {
public:
    thing() : value_{} {}
    thing(std::string s) : value_{std::move(s)} {}
    void swap(thing& other) { value_.swap(other.value_); }
    constexpr std::string const& str() const noexcept { return value_; }
private:
    std::string value_;
};

int main()
{
    thing one{};
    thing two{"two"};
    one = two;
    std::cout << one.str() << '\n';
}
```

This C++ idiom is hard to comprehend at first, so let's break it down. First, consider the assignment_mixin class template. Like many other templates, it takes a single template parameter. It defines a single member function, which happens to be an overloaded assignment operator. There's nothing particularly special about assignment_mixin.

But assignment_mixin has one important property: the compiler can compile the template even if the template argument is an incomplete class. The compiler doesn't have to expand the assignment operator until it is used, and at that point, T must be complete. But for the class itself, T can be incomplete. If the mix-in class were to declare a data member of type T, then the compiler would require that T be a complete type when the mix-in is instantiated, because it would have to know the size of the mix-in.

In other words, you can use assignment_mixin as a base class, even if the template argument is an incomplete class.

When the compiler processes a class definition, immediately upon seeing the class name, it records that name in the current scope as an incomplete type. Thus, when assignment_mixin<thing> appears in the base class list, the compiler is able to instantiate the base class template using the incomplete type, thing, as the template argument.

By the time the compiler gets to the end of the class definition, thing becomes a complete type. After that, you will be able to use the assignment operator, because when the compiler instantiates that template, it needs a complete type, and it has one.

Protected Access Level

In addition to the private and public access levels, C++ offers the protected access level. A protected member is accessible only to the class itself and to derived classes. To all other would-be users, a protected member is off-limits, just like private members.

Most members are private or public. Use protected members only when you are designing a class hierarchy and you deliberately want derived classes to call a certain member function but don't want anyone else to call it.

Mix-in classes sometimes have a protected constructor. This ensures that no one tries to construct a stand-alone instance of the class. Listing 69-8 shows assignment_mixin with a protected constructor.

Listing 69-8. Adding a Protected Constructor to the assignment_mixin Class Template

```
export module mixin;

export template<class T>
class assignment_mixin {
public:
  T& operator=(T rhs)
  {
    rhs.swap(static_cast<T&>(*this));
    return static_cast<T&>(*this);
  }
protected:
  assignment_mixin() {}
};
```

Multiple inheritance also appears in the C++ standard library. You know about istream for input and ostream for output. The library also has iostream, so a single stream can perform input and output. As you might expect, iostream derives from istream and ostream. The only quirk has nothing to do with multiple inheritance: iostream is defined in the <istream> header. The <iostream> header defines the names std::cin, std::cout, and so on. The header name is an accident of history.

The next Exploration continues your advanced study of types, by looking at policies and traits.

Concepts, Traits, and Policies

Although you may still be growing accustomed to templates, it's time to explore some common tools used to write templates: concepts, traits, and policies. Programming with concepts relates closely to traits, which relate closely to policies. Together and separately, they probably introduce a new programming style for you, but this style forms the foundation for the C++ standard library. As you will discover in this Exploration, these techniques are extremely flexible and powerful. This Exploration looks at these techniques and how to take advantage of them.

Case Study: Iterators

Consider the humble iterator. Consider the `std::advance` function (Exploration 46). The advance function changes the position to which an iterator points. The advance function knows nothing about container types; it knows only about iterators. Yet somehow, it knows that if you try to advance a `vector`'s iterator, it can do so simply by adding an integer to the iterator. But if you advance a `list`'s iterator, the advance function must step the iterator one position at a time until it arrives at the desired destination. In other words, the advance function implements the optimal algorithm for changing the iterator's position. The only information available to the advance function must come from the iterators themselves, and the key piece of information is the iterator kind. In particular, only random access and contiguous iterators permit rapid advancement via addition. All other iterators must follow the step-by-step approach. Bidirectional, random access, and contiguous iterators can go backward, but forward and input iterators cannot. (Output iterators require an assignment to produce an output value, so you cannot use advance on an output iterator.) So how does advance know what kind of iterator it has and how to choose the correct implementation?

In most OOP languages, an iterator would derive from a common base class, which would implement a virtual advance function. The advance algorithm would call that virtual function and let normal object-oriented dispatching take care of the details. Or maybe overloading would let you define multiple advance functions that differ in the use of the base class as a parameter type. C++ certainly could take either approach, but it doesn't.

A simple solution is to use constraints for overloaded advance functions. The three functions needed are as follows:

- *Random access and contiguous iterators*: Use addition
- *Bidirectional iterators*: Step-by-step forward or backward
- *Forward and input iterators*: Step-by-step forward only

The `<iterator>` module defines several concepts that you can use as constraints to ensure that each advance function definition applies only to the appropriate iterator kind. **Try defining the advance functions** before looking at my solution in Listing 70-1.

© Ray Lischner 2020
R. Lischner, *Exploring C++20*, https://doi.org/10.1007/978-1-4842-5961-0_70

Listing 70-1. One Possible Implementation of std::advance

```
import <deque>;
import <iostream>;
import <iterator>;
import <list>;
import <string_view>;
import <vector>;

void trace(std::string_view msg)
{
    std::cout << msg << '\n';
}

template<class Iterator, class Distance>
requires std::random_access_iterator<Iterator> and std::integral<Distance>
void advance(Iterator& iterator, Distance distance)
{
    trace("random access or contiguous advance");
    iterator += distance;
}

template<class Iterator, class Distance>
requires std::bidirectional_iterator<Iterator> and std::integral<Distance>
void advance(Iterator& iterator, Distance distance)
{
    trace("bidirectional iterator");
    for ( ; distance < 0; ++distance)
        --iterator;
    for ( ; distance > 0; --distance)
        ++iterator;
}

template<class Iterator, class Distance>
requires std::input_iterator<Iterator> and std::unsigned_integral<Distance>
void advance(Iterator& iterator, Distance distance)
{
    trace("forward or input iterator");
    for ( ; distance > 0; --distance)
        ++iterator;
}

template<class Iterator, class Distance>
void test(std::string_view label, Iterator iterator, Distance distance)
{
    advance(iterator, distance);
    std::cout << label << *iterator << '\n';
}
```

```
int main()
{
    std::deque<int> deque{ 1, 2, 3 };
    test("deque: ", deque.end(), -2);

    std::list<int> list{ 1, 2, 3 };
    test("list: ", list.end(), -2);

    std::vector<int> vector{ 1, 2, 3};
    test("vector: ", vector.end(), -2);

    test("istream: ", std::istream_iterator<int>{}, 2);
}
```

Another technique uses a single function, but relies on type traits to distinguish the different iterator categories. The <iterator> module defines various template classes that describe common traits or attributes of iterator types. The most important is std::iterator_traits<T>, which defines a member type, iterator_category. The advance function can test that type and compare it with std::random_access_ iterator_tag and other iterator tag types to determine the iterator's kind. Other traits are more focused, such as incrementable_traits, which defines the member difference_type for any iterator that either defines its own difference_type memory or allows subtraction of iterators, in which case difference_type is the type of the subtraction result.

Combine the iterator traits with other traits class templates that are defined in <type_traits>, such as std::is_same<T,U>, which determines whether T and U are the same type. More useful in this case is the template is_base_of<B, D> to test whether B is a base class of D. This helps you because the iterator tag types form a class hierarchy of capability; thus, std::is_base_of<std::input_iterator_tag, T> is true if T is any iterator tag type except std::output_iterator_tag. A trait is "true" when it has a compile-time data member value that is true. The type std::true_type is the most common way to express this.

The easiest way to use the traits for the advance function is to use the if constexpr statement. This is a special kind of conditional that is evaluated at compile time. The code in the body of the if constexpr statement is compiled only when the condition is true. Listing 70-2 shows this traits-oriented style of writing advance.

Listing 70-2. Implementing std::advance with Type Traits

```
import <deque>;
import <iostream>;
import <iterator>;
import <list>;
import <string_view>;
import <type_traits>;
import <vector>;

void trace(std::string_view msg)
{
    std::cout << msg << '\n';
}

template<class Iterator, class Distance>
requires std::input_iterator<Iterator> and std::integral<Distance>
void advance(Iterator& iterator, Distance distance)
{
```

```
    using tag = std::iterator_traits<Iterator>::iterator_category;
    if constexpr(std::is_base_of<std::random_access_iterator_tag, tag>::value)
    {
      trace("random access+ iterator");
      iterator += distance;
    }
    else {
      trace("input+ iterator");
      if constexpr(std::is_base_of<std::bidirectional_iterator_tag,tag>::value)
      {
        while (distance++ < 0)
          --iterator;
      }
      while (distance-- > 0)
          ++iterator;
    }
}

template<class Iterator, class Distance>
void test(std::string_view label, Iterator iterator, Distance distance)
{
    advance(iterator, distance);
    std::cout << label << *iterator << '\n';
}

int main()
{
    std::deque<int> deque{ 1, 2, 3 };
    test("deque: ", deque.end(), -2);

    std::list<int> list{ 1, 2, 3 };
    test("list: ", list.end(), -2);

    std::vector<int> vector{ 1, 2, 3};
    test("vector: ", vector.end(), -2);

    test("istream: ", std::istream_iterator<int>{}, 2);
}
```

Type Traits

The <type_traits> header (first introduced in Exploration 53) defines a suite of traits templates that describe the characteristics of a type. They range from simple queries, such as std::is_integral<>, which tells you whether a type is one of the built-in integral types, to more sophisticated queries, such as std::is_nothrow_move_constructible<>, which tells you whether a class has a noexcept move constructor. Some traits modify types, such as std::remove_reference<>, which transforms int& to int, for example.

The std::move() function uses type traits, just to name one use of type traits in the standard library. Remember that all it does is change an lvalue to an rvalue. It uses remove_reference to strip the reference from its argument and then adds && to turn the result into an rvalue reference, as follows:

```
template<class T>
typename std::remove_reference<T>::type&& move(T&& t) noexcept
{
    return static_cast<typename std::remove_reference<T>::type&&>(t);
}
```

Notice the use of the type member typedef. That is how the type traits expose the result of their transformation. The query traits declare type to be a typedef for std::true_type or std::false_type; these classes declare a value member to be true or false at compile time. Although you can create an instance of true_type or false_type and evaluate them at runtime, the typical use is to use them to specialize a template.

Type traits often form the basis for defining concepts. Defining concepts is an advanced topic, so I do not cover it in depth, but it helps to get a sense of how a concept is defined. Knowing that the type traits std::is_integral<T> determines whether a type is one of the built-in integral types, you can define a concept integral<T> as follows:

```
template<class T>
concept integral = std::is_integral<T>::value;
```

A concept is a way of assigning a name to a constraint. The value after the equal sign is a Boolean expression, treating other concepts as Boolean values. For example, knowing that integral is a concept and is_signed is a type trait, define the concept signed_integral as follows:

```
template<class T>
concept signed_integral = integral<T> and std::is_signed<T>::value;
```

Concepts can get very complicated very quickly. For now, let's tackle a more mundane traits class, std::char_traits.

Case Study: char_traits

Among the difficulties in working with characters in C++ is that the char type may be signed or unsigned. The size of a char relative to the size of an int varies from compiler to compiler. The range of valid character values also varies from one implementation to another and can even change while a program is running. A time-honored convention is to use int to store a value that may be a char or a special value that marks end-of-file, but nothing in the standard supports this convention. You may need to use unsigned int or long.

In order to write portable code, you need a traits class to provide a typedef for the integer type to use, the value of the end-of-file marker, and so on. That's exactly what char_traits is for. When you use std::char_traits<char>::int_type, you know you can safely store any char value or the end-of-file marker (which is std::char_traits<char>::eof()).

The standard istream class has a get() function that returns an input character or the special end-of-file marker when there is no more input. The standard ostream class offers put(c) to write a character. **Use these functions with char_traits to write a function that copies its standard input to its standard output, one character at a time.** Call eof() to obtain the special end-of-file value and eq_int_type(a,b) to compare two integer representations of characters for equality. Both functions are static member functions of the char_traits template, which you must instantiate with the desired character type. Call to_char_type to convert the integer representation back to a char. Compare your solution with Listing 70-3.

Listing 70-3. Using Character Traits when Copying Input to Output

```
import <iostream>;
import <string>;        // for char_traits

int main()
{
  using char_traits = std::char_traits<char>; // for brevity and clarity
  char_traits::int_type c{};
  while (c = std::cin.get(), not char_traits::eq_int_type(c, char_traits::eof()))
    std::cout.put(char_traits::to_char_type(c));
}
```

First, notice the loop condition. A comma serves many purposes in C++, separating parameters in function and template declarations, separating values in function calls and initializers, separating declarators in a declaration, and so on. A comma can also separate two expressions where only one is expected; the first sub-expression is evaluated, the result is discarded, and then the second is evaluated. The result of the entire expression is the result of the second sub-expression. In this case, the first sub-expression assigns get() to c, and the second sub-expression calls eq_int_type, so the result of the loop condition is the return value from eq_int_type, testing whether the result of get, as stored in c, is equal to the end-of-file marker. Another way to write the loop condition is as follows:

```
not char_traits::eq_int_type(c = std::cin.get(), char_traits::eof())
```

I don't like to bury assignments in the middle of an expression, so I prefer to use the comma operator in this case. Other developers have a strong aversion to the comma operator. They prefer the embedded assignment style. Another solution is to use a for loop instead of a while loop, as follows:

```
for (char_traits::int_type c = std::cin.get();
     not char_traits::eq_int_type(c, char_traits::eof());
     c = std::cin.get())
```

The for loop solution has the advantage of limiting the scope of the variable, c. But it has the disadvantage of repeating the call to std::cin.get(). Any of these solutions is acceptable; pick a style and stick with it.

In this case, char_traits seems to make everything more complicated. After all, comparing two integers for equality is easier and clearer when using the == operator. On the other hand, using a member function gives the library writer the opportunity for added logic, such as checking for invalid character values.

In theory, you could write a char_traits specialization that, for instance, implements case-insensitive comparison. In that case, the eq() (which compares two characters for equality) and eq_int_type() functions would certainly require extra logic. On the other hand, you learned in Exploration 59 that such a traits class cannot be written for many international character sets, at least not without knowing the locale.

In the real world, specializations of char_traits are rare.

The char_traits class template is interesting nonetheless. A pure traits class template would implement only typedef members, static data members, and sometimes a member function that returns a constant, such as char_traits::eof(). Another good example of such a traits class is std::numeric_limits. Functions such as eq_int_type() are not traits, which describe a type. Instead, they are policy functions. A policy class template contains member functions that specify behavior, or policies. The next section looks at policies.

Policy-Based Programming

A *policy* is a class or class template that another class template can use to customize its behavior. The line between traits and policy is fuzzy, but to me, traits are static characteristics and policies are dynamic behavior. In the standard library, the string and stream classes use the char_traits policy class template to obtain type-specific behavior for comparing characters, copying character arrays, and more. The standard library provides policy implementations for the char and wchar_t types.

Suppose you are trying to write a high-performance server. After careful design, implementation, and testing, you discover that the performance of std::string introduces significant overhead. In your particular application, memory is abundant, but processor time is at a premium. Wouldn't it be nice to be able to flip a switch and change your std::string implementation from one that is optimized for space into one that is optimized for speed? Instead, you must write your own string replacement that meets your needs. In writing your own class, you end up rewriting the many member functions, such as find_first_of, that have nothing to do with your particular implementation but are essentially the same for most string implementations. What a waste of time.

Imagine how simple your job would be if you had a string class template that took an extra template argument with which you could select a storage mechanism for the string, substituting memory-optimized or processor-optimized implementations according to your needs. That, in a nutshell, is what policy-based programming is all about.

In a way, the std::string class offers this flexibility because std::string is actually a specialization of std::basic_string for the char type and for a particular memory allocation policy. In fact, all of the standard container templates (except array) take an allocator template parameter. Writing a new allocator is beyond the scope of this book, so instead, we will write a simpler, hypothetical policy class that can guide the implementation of a mystring class.

For the sake of simplicity, this book implements only a few of the member functions of std::string. Completing the interface of std::string is left as an exercise for the reader. Listing 70-4 shows the new string class template and a few of its member functions. Take a look, and you can see how it takes advantage of the Storage policy.

Listing 70-4. The mystring Class Template

```
import <algorithm>;
import <string>;

template<class Char, class Storage, class Traits = std::char_traits<Char>>
class mystring {
public:
    using value_type = Char;
    using size_type = std::size_t;
    using iterator = typename Storage::iterator;
    using const_iterator = Storage::const_iterator;

    mystring() : storage_{} {}
    mystring(mystring&&) = default;
    mystring(mystring const&) = default;
    mystring(Storage const& storage) : storage_{storage} {}
    mystring(Char const* ptr, size_type size) : storage_{} {
        resize(size);
        std::copy(ptr, ptr + size, begin());
    }

    static constexpr size_type npos = static_cast<size_type>(-1);
```

```cpp
  mystring& operator=(mystring const&) = default;
  mystring& operator=(mystring&&) = default;

  void swap(mystring& str) { storage_.swap(str.storage_); }

  Char operator[](size_type i) const { return *(storage_.begin() + i); }
  Char& operator[](size_type i)       { return *(storage_.begin() + i); }

  void resize(size_type size, Char value = Char()) {
    storage_.resize(size, value);
  }
  void reserve(size_type size)    { storage_.reserve(size); }
  size_type size() const noexcept { return storage_.end() - storage_.begin(); }
  size_type max_size() const noexcept { return storage_.max_size(); }
  bool empty() const noexcept     { return size() == 0; }
  void clear()                    { resize(0); }
  void push_back(Char c)          { resize(size() + 1, c); }

  Char const* data() const        { return storage_.c_str(); }
  Char const* c_str() const       { return storage_.c_str(); }

  iterator begin()                { return storage_.begin(); }
  const_iterator begin() const    { return storage_.begin(); }
  const_iterator cbegin() const   { return storage_.begin(); }
  iterator end()                  { return storage_.end(); }
  const_iterator end() const      { return storage_.end(); }
  const_iterator cend() const     { return storage_.end(); }

  size_type find(mystring const& s, size_type pos = 0) const {
    pos = std::min(pos, size());
    auto result{ std::search(begin() + pos, end(),
                             s.begin(), s.end(), Traits::eq) };
    if (result == end())
      return npos;
    else
      return static_cast<size_type>(result - begin());
  }

private:
  Storage storage_;
};

template<class Char, class Storage1, class Storage2, class Traits>
bool operator <(mystring<Char, Storage1, Traits> const& a,
                mystring<Char, Storage2, Traits> const& b)
{
  return std::lexicographical_compare(
    a.begin(), a.end(), b.begin(), b.end(), Traits::lt
  );

}
```

```
template<class Char, class Storage1, class Storage2, class Traits>
bool operator ==(mystring<Char, Storage1, Traits> const& a,
                 mystring<Char, Storage2, Traits> const& b)
{
    return std::equal(a.begin(), a.end(), b.begin(), b.end(), Traits::eq);
}
```

The mystring class relies on Traits for comparing characters and Storage for storing them. The Storage policy must provide iterators for accessing the characters themselves and a few basic member functions (data, max_size, reserve, resize, swap), and the mystring class provides the public interface, such as the assignment operator and search member functions.

Public comparison functions use standard algorithms and Traits for comparisons. Notice how the comparison functions require their two operands to have the same Traits (otherwise, how could the strings be compared in a meaningful way?) but allow different Storage. It doesn't matter how the strings store their contents if you want to know only whether two strings contain the same characters.

The next step is to write some storage policy templates. The storage policy is parameterized on the character type. The simplest Storage is vector_storage, which stores the string contents in a vector. Recall from Exploration 21 that a C character string ends with a null character. The c_str() member function returns a pointer to a C-style character array. In order to simplify the implementation of c_str, the vector stores a trailing null character after the string contents. Listing 70-5 shows part of an implementation of vector_storage. You can complete the implementation on your own.

Listing 70-5. The vector_storage Class Template

```
import <vector>;

template<class Char>
class vector_storage {
public:
    using size_type = std::size_t;
    using value_type = Char;
    using iterator = std::vector<Char>::iterator;
    using const_iterator = std::vector<Char>::const_iterator;

    vector_storage() : string_{1, Char{}} {}

    void swap(vector_storage& storage) { string_.swap(storage.string_); }
    size_type max_size() const { return string_.max_size() - 1; }
    void reserve(size_type size) { string_.reserve(size + 1); }
    void resize(size_type newsize, value_type value) {
        // if the string grows, overwrite the null character, then resize
        if (newsize >= string_.size()) {
            string_[string_.size() - 1] = value;
            string_.resize(newsize + 1, value);
        }
        else
            string_.resize(newsize + 1);
        string_[string_.size() - 1] = Char{};
    }
    Char const* c_str() const { return &string_[0]; }
```

```
iterator begin()              { return string_.begin(); }
const_iterator begin() const { return string_.begin(); }
// Skip over the trailing null character at the end of the vector
iterator end()               { return string_.end() - 1; }
const_iterator end() const   { return string_.end() - 1; }

private:
    std::vector<Char> string_;
};
```

The only difficulty in writing vector_storage is that the vector stores a trailing null character, so the c_str function can return a valid C-style character array. Therefore, the end function has to adjust the iterator that it returns.

Another possibility for a storage policy is array_storage, which is just like vector_storage, except it uses an array. By using an array, all storage is local. The array size is the maximum capacity of the string, but the string size can vary up to that maximum. **Write array_storage**. Compare your result with mine in Listing 70-6.

Listing 70-6. The array_storage Class Template

```
import <algorithm>;
import <stdexcept>;
import <array>;

template<class Char, std::size_t MaxSize>
class array_storage {
public:
    using array_type = std::array<Char, MaxSize>;
    using size_type = std::size_t;
    using value_type = Char;
    using iterator = array_type::iterator;
    using const_iterator = array_type::const_iterator;

    array_storage() : size_(0), string_() { string_[0] = Char(); }

    void swap(array_storage& storage) {
        string_.swap(storage.string_);
        std::swap(size_, storage.size_);
    }
    size_type max_size() const { return string_.max_size() - 1; }
    void reserve(size_type size) {
        if (size > max_size()) throw std::length_error("reserve");
    }
    void resize(size_type newsize, value_type value) {
        if (newsize > max_size())
            throw std::length_error("resize");
        if (newsize > size_)
            std::fill(begin() + size_, begin() + newsize, value);
        size_ = newsize;
        string_[size_] = Char{};
    }
    Char const* c_str() const { return &string_[0]; }
```

```
iterator begin()               { return string_.begin(); }
const_iterator begin() const  { return string_.begin(); }
iterator end()                 { return begin() + size_; }
const_iterator end() const    { return begin() + size_; }
private:
  size_type size_;
  array_type string_;
};
```

One difficulty when writing new string classes is that you must write new I/O functions too. Unfortunately, this takes a fair bit of work and a solid understanding of the stream class templates and stream buffers. Handling padding and field adjustment is easy, but there are subtleties to the I/O streams that I have not covered, such as integration with C stdio, tying input and output streams so that prompts appear before the user is asked for input, and so on. So just copy my solution in Listing 70-7 into the mystring module.

Listing 70-7. Output Function for mystring

```
template<class Char, class Storage, class Traits>
std::basic_ostream<Char, Traits>&
  operator<<(std::basic_ostream<Char, Traits>& stream,
             mystring<Char, Storage, Traits> const& string)
{
  typename std::basic_ostream<Char, Traits>::sentry sentry{stream};
  if (sentry)
  {
    bool needs_fill{stream.width() != 0 and string.size() > std::size_t(stream.width())};
    bool is_left_adjust{
      (stream.flags() & std::ios_base::adjustfield) == std::ios_base::left };
    if (needs_fill and not is_left_adjust)
    {
      for (std::size_t i{stream.width() - string.size()}; i != 0; --i)
        stream.rdbuf()->sputc(stream.fill());
    }
    stream.rdbuf()->sputn(string.data(), string.size());
    if (needs_fill and is_left_adjust)
    {
      for (std::size_t i{stream.width() - string.size()}; i != 0; --i)
        stream.rdbuf()->sputc(stream.fill());
    }
  }
  stream.width(0);
  return stream;
}
```

The sentry class manages some bookkeeping on behalf of the stream. The output function handles padding and adjustment. If you are curious about the details, consult a good reference.

The input function also has a sentry class, which skips leading white space on your behalf. The input function has to read characters until it gets to another white space character or the string fills or the width limit is reached. See Listing 70-8 for my version.

Listing 70-8. Input Function for mystring

```cpp
template<class Char, class Storage, class Traits>
std::basic_istream<Char, Traits>&
  operator>>(std::basic_istream<Char, Traits>& stream,
             mystring<Char, Storage, Traits>& string)
{
  typename std::basic_istream<Char, Traits>::sentry sentry{stream};
  if (sentry)
  {
    std::ctype<Char> const& ctype(
      std::use_facet<std::ctype<Char>>(stream.getloc()) );
    std::ios_base::iostate state{ std::ios_base::goodbit };
    std::size_t max_chars{ string.max_size() };
    if (stream.width() != 0 and std::size_t(stream.width()) < max_chars)
      max_chars = stream.width();
    string.clear();
    while (max_chars-- != 0) {
      typename Traits::int_type c{ stream.rdbuf()->sgetc() };
      if (Traits::eq_int_type(Traits::eof(), c)) {
        state |= std::ios_base::eofbit;
        break; // is_eof
      }
      else if (ctype.is(ctype.space, Traits::to_char_type(c)))
        break;
      else {
        string.push_back(Traits::to_char_type(c));
        stream.rdbuf()->sbumpc();
      }
    }
    if (string.empty())
      state |= std::ios_base::failbit;
    stream.setstate(state);
    stream.width(0);
  }
  return stream;
}
```

The break statement exits a loop immediately. You are probably familiar with this statement or something similar. Experienced programmers may be surprised that no example has required this statement until now. One reason is that I gloss over error-handling, which would otherwise be a common reason to break out of a loop. In this case, when the input reaches end-of-file or white space, it is time to exit the loop. The partner to break is continue, which immediately reiterates the loop. In a for loop, continue evaluates the iterate part of the loop header and then the condition. I have rarely needed to use continue in real life and could not think of any reasonable example that uses continue, but I mention it only for the sake of completeness.

As you know, the compiler finds your I/O operators by matching the type of the right-hand operand, mystring, with the type of the function parameter. In this simple case, you can easily see how the compiler performs the matching and finds the right function. Throw some namespaces into the mix, and add some type conversions, and everything gets a little bit more muddled. The next Exploration delves more closely into namespaces and the rules that the C++ compiler applies in order to find your overloaded function names (or not find them and, therefore, how to fix that problem).

■ ■ ■

Names, Namespaces, and Templates

The basics of using namespaces and templates are straightforward and easy to learn. Taking advantage of argument-dependent lookup (ADL) is also simple: declare free functions and operators in the same namespace as your classes. But sometimes life isn't so simple. Especially when using templates, you can get stuck in strange corners, and the compiler issues bizarre and useless messages, and you realize you should have spent more time studying names, namespaces, and templates beyond the basics.

The detailed rules can be excruciatingly complicated, because they must cover all the pathological cases, for example, to explain why the following is legal (albeit resulting in some compiler warnings) and what it means

```
enum X { X };
void XX(enum X X=::X) { if (enum X X=X) X; }
```

and why the following is illegal:

```
enum X { X } X;
void XX(X X=X) { if (X X=X) X; }
```

But rational programmers don't write code in that manner, and some commonsense guidelines go a long way toward simplifying the complicated rules. Thus, this Exploration provides more details than earlier in the book but omits many picky details that matter only to entrants in obfuscated C++ contests.

Common Rules

Certain rules apply to all types of name lookup. (Subsequent sections will examine the rules particular to various contexts.) The basic rule is that the compiler must know what a name means when it sees the name in source code.

Most names must be declared earlier in the file (or in a module or included header) than where the name is used. The only exception is in the definition of a member function: a name can be another member of the same class, even if the member is declared later in the class definition than the use of that name. Names must be unique within a scope, except for overloaded functions and operators. The compiler issues an error if you attempt to declare two names that would conflict, such as two variables with the same name in the same scope or a data member and member function with the same name in a single class.

Functions can have multiple declarations with the same name, following the rules for overloading, that is, argument number or types must be different, const qualification must be different for member functions, or constraints must enable the compiler to distinguish among overloaded functions.

© Ray Lischner 2020

R. Lischner, *Exploring C++20*, https://doi.org/10.1007/978-1-4842-5961-0_71

Access rules (public, private, or protected) have no effect on name lookup rules for members of a class (nested types and typedefs, data members, and member functions). The usual name lookup rules identify the proper declaration, and only then does the compiler check whether access to the name is permitted.

Whether a name is that of a virtual function has no effect on name lookup. The name is looked up normally, and once the name is found, then the compiler checks whether the name is that of a virtual function. If so, and if the object is accessed via a reference or pointer, the compiler generates the necessary code to perform a runtime lookup of the actual function.

Template specializations do not impact name lookup. The compiler looks for the declaration of the primary template. Once that is found, then the compiler uses the template arguments to determine which specialization, if any, to use.

Name Lookup in Templates

Templates complicate name lookup. In particular, a name can depend on a template parameter. Such a dependent name has different lookup rules than nondependent names. Dependent names can change meaning according to the template arguments used in a template specialization. One specialization may declare a name as a type, and another may declare it as a function. (Of course, such a programming style is highly discouraged, but the rules of C++ must allow for such possibilities.)

Lookup of nondependent names follows the usual name lookup rules where the template is defined. Lookup of dependent names may include lookup in namespaces associated with the template instantiation in addition to the normal rules that apply where the template is defined. Later sections provide additional details, according to the kind of name lookup being performed.

Three Kinds of Name Lookup

C++ defines three kinds of name lookup: member access operators; names prefaced by class, enumeration, or namespace names; and bare names.

- A class member access operator is . or ->. The left-hand side is an expression that yields an object of class type, reference to an object, or pointer to an object. The dot (.) requires an object or reference, and -> requires a pointer or an object that defines the -> operator. The right-hand side is a member name (data member or member function). For example, in the expression cout.width(3), cout is the object and width is the member name.

- A class, enumeration, or namespace name may be followed by the scope operator (::) and a name, such as std::string or std::string::npos. The name is said to be *qualified* by the class, enumeration, or namespace name. No other kind of name may appear to the left of the scope operator. The compiler looks up the name in the scope of the class, enumeration, or namespace. The name itself may be another class, enumerator, or namespace name, or it may be a function, variable, or typedef name. For example, in std::filesystem::path::value_type, std and filesystem are namespace names, path is a class, and value_type is a member typedef.

- A plain identifier or operator is called an *unqualified* name. The name can be a namespace name, type name, function name, or object name, depending on context. Different contexts have slightly different lookup rules.

The next three sections describe each style of name lookup in more detail.

Member Access Operators

The simplest rules are for member access operators. The left-hand side of the member access operator (. or ->) determines the context for the lookup. The object must have class type (or pointer or reference to a class type), and the name on the right-hand side must be a data member or member function of that class or of an ancestor class. The search begins with the declared type of the object and continues with its base class (or classes, searching multiple classes from left to right, in order of declaration), and their base classes, and so on, stopping at the first class with a matching name.

If the name is a function, the compiler collects all declarations of the same name in the same class and chooses one function according to the rules of function and operator overloading. Note that the compiler does not consider any functions in ancestor classes. The name lookup stops as soon as the name is found. If you want a base class's names to participate in operator overloading, employ a using declaration in the derived class to bring the base class names into the derived class context.

In the body of a member function, the left-hand object can be the this keyword, which is a pointer to the object on the left-hand side of the member access operator. If the member function is declared with the const qualifier, this is a pointer to const. If a base class is a template parameter or depends on a template parameter, the compiler does not know which members may be inherited from the base class until the template is instantiated. You should use this-> to access an inherited member, to tell the compiler that the name is a member name, and the compiler will look up the name when it instantiates the template.

Listing 71-1 demonstrates several uses for member access operators.

Listing 71-1. Member Access Operators

```
import <cmath>;
import <iostream>;

template<class T>
class point2d {
public:
   point2d(T x, T y) : x_{x}, y_{y} {}
   virtual ~point2d() {}
   T x() const { return x_; }
   T y() const { return y_; }
   T abs() const { return std::sqrt(x() * x() + y() * y()); }
   virtual void print(std::ostream& stream) const {
      stream << '(' << x() << ", " << y() << ')';
   }
private:
   T x_, y_;
};

template<class T>
class point3d : public point2d<T> {
public:
   point3d(T x, T y, T z) : point2d<T>{x, y}, z_{z} {}
   T z() const { return z_; }
   T abs() const {
      return static_cast<T>(std::sqrt(this->x() * this->x() +
               this->y() * this->y() +
               this->z() * this->z()));
   }
```

```
        virtual void print(std::ostream& stream) const {
            stream << '(' << this->x() << ", " << this->y() << ", " << z() << ')';
        }
private:
    T z_;
};

template<class T>
std::ostream& operator<<(std::ostream& stream, point2d<T> const& pt)
{
    pt.print(stream);
    return stream;
}

int main()
{
    point3d<int> origin{0, 0, 0};
    std::cout << "abs(origin) = " << origin.abs() << '\n';

    point3d<int> unit{1, 1, 1};
    point2d<int>* ptr{ &unit };
    std::cout << "abs(unit) = " << ptr->abs() << '\n';
    std::cout << "*ptr = " << *ptr << '\n';
}
```

The main() function uses member name lookup the way you are used to seeing it. This usage is simple to understand, and you have been using it throughout this book. The use of member name lookup in point3d::abs(), however, is more interesting. The use of this-> is required, because the base class point2d<T> depends on the template parameter, T, which means the compiler does not know the base class until the template is instantiated. Only then can it know whether x() and y() are inherited from the base class or from some other context. When it compiles abs(), it needs to know what to do with x() and y(), so using this->x() and this->y() tells the compiler to expect to find these member functions in a base class when the template is instantiated. If it cannot find them, it will issue an error message.

The operator<< function takes a reference to a point2d instance and calls its print function. The virtual function is dispatched to the real function, which in this case is point3d::print. You know how this works, so this is just a reminder of how the compiler looks up the name print in the point2d class template, because that is the type of the pt function parameter.

Qualified Name Lookup

A *qualified* name uses the scope (::) operator. You have been using qualified names from the very first program. The name std::string is qualified, which means the name string is looked up in a context specified by the std:: qualifier. In this simple case, std names a namespace, so string is looked up in that namespace.

The qualifier can also be a class name or the name of a scoped enumeration. Class names can nest, so the left- and right-hand side of the scope operator may be a class name. If the left-hand name is that of an enumerated type, the right-hand name must be an enumerator in that type.

The compiler starts its search with the left-most name. If the left-most name starts with a scope operator (e.g., ::std::string), the compiler looks up that name in the global scope. Otherwise, it uses the usual name lookup rules for unqualified names (as described in the next section) to determine the scope that it will use for the right-hand side of the scope operator. If the right-hand name is followed by another scope operator, the identified name must be that of a namespace, class, or scoped enumeration, and the compiler looks up the right-hand name in that scope. The process repeats until the compiler has looked up the right-most name.

Within a namespace, a using **directive** tells the compiler to search in the target namespace as well as the namespace that contains the using directive. In the following example, the qualified name ns2::Integer tells the compiler to search in namespace ns2 for name Integer. Because ns2 contains a using directive, the compiler also searches in namespace ns1 and so finds the Integer typedef.

```
namespace ns1 { typedef int Integer; }
namespace ns2 { using namespace ns1; }
namespace ns3 { ns2::Integer x; }
```

A using **declaration** is slightly different. A using directive affects which namespaces the compiler searches to find a name. A using declaration doesn't change the set of namespaces to search but merely adds one name to the containing namespace. In the following example, the using declaration brings the name Integer into namespace ns2, just as though the typedef were written in ns2.

```
namespace ns1 { typedef int Integer; }
namespace ns2 { using ns1::Integer; }
namespace ns3 { ns2::Integer x; }
```

When a name depends on a template parameter, the compiler must know whether the name is that of a type or something else (function or object), because it affects how the compiler parses the template body. Because the name is dependent, it could be a type in one specialization and a function in another. So you have to tell the compiler what to expect. If the name should be a type, preface the qualified name with the keyword typename. Without the typename keyword, the compiler assumes the name is that of a function or object. You need the typename keyword with a dependent type, but it doesn't hurt if you provide it before a nondependent type.

Listing 71-2 shows several examples of qualified names.

Listing 71-2. Qualified Name Lookup

```
import <chrono>;
import <iostream>;

namespace outer {
   namespace inner {
      class base {
      public:
         int value() const { return 1; }
         static int value(long x) { return static_cast<int>(x); }
      };
   }

   template<class T>
   class derived : public inner::base {
   public:
      typedef T value_type;
      using inner::base::value;
      static value_type example;
      value_type value(value_type i) const { return i * example; }
   };
```

```
    template<class T>
    typename derived<T>::value_type derived<T>::example = 2;
}

template<class T>
class more_derived : public outer::derived<T>{
public:
    typedef outer::derived<T> base_type;
    typedef typename base_type::value_type value_type;
    more_derived(value_type v) : value_{this->value(v)} {}
    value_type get_value() const { return value_; }
private:
    value_type value_;
};

int main()
{
    std::chrono::system_clock::time_point now{std::chrono::system_clock::now()};
    std::cout << now.time_since_epoch().count() << '\n';

    outer::derived<int> d;
    std::cout << d.value() << '\n';
    std::cout << d.value(42L) << '\n';
    std::cout << outer::inner::base::value(2) << '\n';

    more_derived<int> md(2);
    std::cout << md.get_value() << '\n';
}
```

The standard chrono library uses a nested namespace, `std::chrono`. Within that namespace, the system_clock class has a member typedef, `time_point`, and a function, `now()`.

The `now()` function is static, so it is called as a qualified name, not by using a member access operator. Although it operates on an object, it behaves as a free function. The only difference between `now()` and a completely free function is that its name is qualified by a class name instead of a namespace name. Exploration 41 briefly touched on static functions. They are not used often, but this is one of those instances when such a function is useful. The `now()` function is declared with the `static` qualifier, which means the function does not need an object, the function body has no `this` pointer, and the usual way to call the function is with a qualified name.

A data member may be `static` too. A member function (ordinary or static) can refer to a static data member normally, or you can use a qualified name to access the member from outside the class. One additional difference between a static member function and a free function is that a static member function can access private static members of the class. If you declare a static data member, you must also provide a definition for that member, typically in the same source file where member functions are defined. Recall that a non-static data member does not have a definition, because the instance of the data member is created when the containing object is created. Static data members are independent of any objects, so they must be defined independently too.

In Listing 71-2, the first call to `d.value()` calls `base::value()`. Without the `using` declaration in derived, the only signature for `value()` is `value(value_type i)`, which doesn't match `value()`, and so would result in a compile error. But the using `inner::base::value` declaration injects the value name from `inner::base`, adding the functions `value()` and `value(long)` as additional functions overloading the name value. Thus, when the compiler looks up `d.value()`, it searches all three signatures to find the `value()` that the using declaration injected into derived. The second call, d.value(42L), invokes value(long). Even though the function is static, it can be called using a member access operator. The compiler ignores the object but uses the object's type as the context for looking up the name. The final call to value(2) is qualified by the class name, so it searches only the value functions in class base, finds value(long), and converts the int 2 to long.

In the most_derived class template, the base class depends on the template parameter, T. Thus, the base_type typedef is dependent. The compiler needs to know what base_type::value_type is, so the typename keyword informs the compiler that value_type is a type.

Unqualified Name Lookup

A name without a member access operator or a qualifier is *unqualified*. The precise rules for looking up an unqualified name depend on the context. For example, inside a member function, the compiler searches other members of the class and then inherited members, before searching in the class's namespace and then outer namespaces.

The rules are commonsense but complicated, and the details apply primarily to compiler writers who must get all the details correct. For most programmers, you can get by with commonsense and a few guidelines:

- Names are looked up first in the local scope, then in outer scopes.

- In a class, names are looked up among the class members, then in ancestor classes.

- In a template, the compiler must resolve every unqualified object and type name when the template is defined, without regard to the instantiation context. Thus, it does *not* search a base class for names, if the base class depends on a template parameter.

- If a name cannot be found in the class or ancestors, or if the name is called outside of any class context, the compiler searches the immediate namespace, then outer namespaces.

- If a name is a function or operator, the compiler also searches the namespaces of the function arguments and their outer namespaces, according to the rules of argument-dependent lookup (ADL). In a template, namespaces for the template declaration and instantiation are searched.

Listing 71-3 contains several examples of unqualified name lookup.

Listing 71-3. Unqualified Name Lookup

```
import <iostream>;

namespace outer {
   namespace inner {
      struct point { int x, y; };
      inline std::ostream& operator<<(std::ostream& stream, point const& p)
      {
         stream << '(' << p.x << ", " << p.y << ')';
         return stream;
      }
   }
}
```

```
typedef int Integer;

int main()
{
   const int multiplier{2};
   for (Integer i : { 1, 2, 3}) {
      outer::inner::point p{ i, i * multiplier };
      std::cout << p << '\n';
   }
}
```

Argument-Dependent Lookup

The most interesting form of unqualified name lookup is argument-dependent lookup. As the name implies, the compiler looks up a function name in the namespaces determined by the function arguments. As a guideline, the compiler assembles the broadest, most inclusive set of classes and namespaces that it reasonably can, to maximize the search space for a name.

More precisely, if a search finds a member function, the compiler does not apply ADL, and the search stops there. Otherwise, the compiler assembles an additional set of classes and namespaces to search and combines them with the namespaces it searches for normal lookup. The compiler builds this additional set by checking the types of the function arguments. For each function argument, the class or namespace in which the argument's type is declared is added to the set. In addition, if the argument's type is a class, the ancestor classes and their namespaces are also added. If the argument is a pointer, the additional classes and namespaces are those of the base type. If you pass a function as an argument, that function's parameter types are added to the search space. When the compiler searches the additional ADL-only namespaces, it searches only for matching function names, ignoring types and variables.

If the function is a template, the additional classes and namespaces include those where the template is defined and where the template is instantiated.

Listing 71-4 shows several examples of argument-dependent lookup. The listing uses the definition of rational from Exploration 53, in the numeric namespace.

Listing 71-4. Argument-Dependent Name Lookup

```
import <cmath>;
import <iostream>;
import rational;

namespace data {
  template<class T>
  struct point {
    T x, y;
  };
  template<class Ch, class Tr, class T>
  std::basic_ostream<Ch, Tr>& operator<<(std::basic_ostream<Ch, Tr>& stream, point<T>
  const& pt)
  {
    stream << '(' << pt.x << ", " << pt.y << ')';
    return stream;
  }
```

```
  template<class T>
  T abs(point<T> const& pt) {
    using namespace std;
    return sqrt(pt.x * pt.x + pt.y * pt.y);
  }
}

namespace numeric {
    template<class T>
    rational<T> sqrt(rational<T> r)
    {
      using std::sqrt;
      return rational<T>{sqrt(static_cast<double>(r))};
    }
}

int main()
{
    using namespace std;
    data::point<numeric::rational<int>> a{ numeric::rational<int>{1, 2},
numeric::rational<int>{2, 4} };
    std::cout << "abs(" << a << ") = " << abs(a) << '\n';
}
```

Start with main() and follow the name lookups.

The first name is data, which is looked up as an unqualified name. The compiler finds the namespace data, declared in the global namespace. The compiler then knows to look up point in the data namespace, and it finds the class template. Similarly, the compiler looks up numeric and then rational.

The compiler constructs a and adds the name to the local scope.

The compiler looks up std and then cout, which it finds, because cout was declared in the <iostream> header. Next, the compiler looks up the unqualified name, a, which it finds in the local scope. But then it has to look up abs.

The compiler searches first in the local scope and then in the global scope. The using directive tells the compiler to search namespace std too. That exhausts the possibilities for normal lookup, so the compiler must turn to argument-dependent lookup.

The compiler assembles its set of scopes to search. First, it adds data to the namespaces to search. Because point is a template, the compiler also searches the namespace where the template is instantiated, which is the global namespace. It already searched there, but that's okay. Once the set is complete, the compiler searches for and finds abs in namespace data.

In order to instantiate the template abs, with the template argument numeric::rational<int>, the compiler must lookup operator*. It cannot find a declaration in the local scope, namespace data, namespace std, or the global namespace. Using argument-dependent lookup, it finds operator* in the numeric namespace, where rational is declared. It performs the same lookup for operator+.

In order to find sqrt, the compiler again uses argument-dependent lookup. When we last visited the rational class, it lacked a sqrt function, so Listing 71-4 provides a crude one. It converts the rational to a double, calls sqrt, and then converts back to rational. The compiler finds sqrt in namespace std.

Finally, the compiler must again apply argument-dependent lookup for operator<<. When the compiler compiles operator<< in point, it doesn't know about operator<< for rational, but it doesn't have to until the template is instantiated. As you can see, writing code that takes advantage of argument-dependent lookup is straightforward, if you follow simple guidelines. The next Exploration takes a closer look at the rules for resolving overloaded functions and operators. Again, you will find complicated rules that can be made simple by following some basic guidelines.

EXPLORATION 72

■ ■ ■

Overloaded Functions and Operators

Exploration 25 introduced the notion of overloaded functions. Exploration 31 continued the journey with overloaded operators. Since then, we've managed to get by with a commonsense understanding of overloading. I would be remiss if I did not delve deeper into this subject, so let's finish the story of overloading by examining the rules of overloaded functions and operators in greater depth. (Operators and functions follow the same rules, so in this Exploration, understand that *function* applies equally to functions and user-defined operators.)

Type Conversion

Before jumping into the deep end of the overloading pool, I need to fill in some missing pieces with respect to type conversion. Recall from Exploration 26 that the compiler promotes certain types to other types, such as short to int. It can also convert a type, such as int, to another type, such as long.

Another way to convert one type to another is with a one-argument constructor. You can think of rational{1} as a way to convert the int literal 1 to the rational type. When you declare a one-argument constructor, you can tell the compiler whether you want it to perform such type conversion implicitly or require an explicit type conversion. That is, if the constructor is implicit (the default), a function that declares its parameter type to be rational can take an integer argument, and the compiler automatically constructs a rational object from the int, as in the following:

```
rational reciprocal(rational const& r)
{
  return rational{r.denominator(), r.numerator()};
}
rational half{ reciprocal(2) };
```

To prohibit such implicit construction, use the explicit specifier on the constructor. That forces the user to explicitly name the type in order to invoke the constructor. For example, std::vector has a constructor that takes an integer as its sole argument, which initializes the vector with that many default-initialized elements. The constructor is explicit to avoid statements such as the following:

```
std::vector<int> v;
v = 42;
```

© Ray Lischner 2020
R. Lischner, *Exploring C++20*, https://doi.org/10.1007/978-1-4842-5961-0_72

If the constructor were not explicit, the compiler would automatically construct a vector from the integer 42 and assign that vector to v. Because the constructor is explicit, the compiler balks and reports an error.

Another way to convert one type to another is with a type-conversion operator. Write such an operator with the operator keyword, followed by the destination type. Like a one-argument constructor, you can declare the type-conversion operator to be explicit. Instead of the convert or as_float functions in rational, you could also write type-conversion operators, as follows:

```
explicit operator float() const {
  return float(numerator()) / float(denominator());
}
```

One context in which the compiler automatically invokes a type-conversion operator is a loop or if-statement condition. Because you are using the expression in a condition, and the condition must be Boolean, the compiler considers such a use to be an explicit conversion to type bool. If you implement a type-conversion operator for type bool, always use the explicit specifier. You will be able to test objects of your type in a condition, and you will avoid a nasty problem in which the compiler converts your type to bool and then promotes the bool to int. You don't really want to be able to write, for example:

```
int i;
i = std::cin; // if conversion to bool were not explicit, i would get 0 or 1
```

In the following discussion of overload resolution, type conversion plays a major role. The compiler doesn't care how it converts one type to another, only whether it must perform a conversion, and whether the conversion is built into the language or user-defined. Constructors are equivalent to type-conversion operators.

Review of Overloaded Functions

Let's refresh the memory a bit. A function name is *overloaded* when two or more function declarations declare the same name in the same scope. C++ imposes some restrictions on when you are allowed to overload a function name.

The primary restriction is that overloaded functions must have different argument lists. This means the number of arguments must be different, or the type of at least one argument must be different.

```
void print(int value);
void print(double value);       // valid overload: different argument type
void print(int value, int width); // valid overload: different number of arguments
```

You are not allowed to define two functions in the same scope when the functions differ only in the return type.

```
void print(int);
int print(int);  // illegal
```

Member functions can also differ by the presence or absence of the const qualifier.

```
class demo {
   void print();
   void print() const; // valid: const qualifier is different
};
```

A member function cannot be overloaded with a static member function in the same class.

```
class demo {
   void print();
   static void print(); // illegal
};
```

A key point is that overloading occurs within a single scope. Names in one scope have no influence or impact on names in another scope. Remember that a code block is a scope (Exploration 13), a class is a scope (Exploration 41), and a namespace is a scope (Exploration 56).

Thus, member functions in a base class are in that class's scope and do not impact overloading of names in a derived class, which has its own scope, separate and distinct from the base class's scope.

When you define a function in a derived class, it hides all functions with the same name in a base class or in an outer scope, even if those functions take different arguments. This rule is a specific example of the general rule that a name in an inner scope hides names in outer scopes. Thus, any name in a derived class hides names in base classes and at namespace scope. Any name in a block hides names in outer blocks and so on. The only way to call a hidden function from a derived class is to qualify the function name, as shown in Listing 72-1.

Listing 72-1. Qualifying a Member Function with the Base Class Name

```
import <iostream>;

class base {
public:
   void print(int x) { std::cout << "int: " << x << '\n'; }
};
class derived : public base {
public:
   void print(double x) { std::cout << "double: " << x << '\n'; }
};
int main()
{
   derived d{};
   d.print(3);            // prints double: 3
   d.print(3.0);          // prints double: 3
   d.base::print(3);      // prints int: 3
   d.base::print(3.0);    // prints int: 3
}
```

Sometimes, however, you want overloading to take into account functions in the derived class and the functions from the base class too. The solution is to inject the base class name into the derived class scope. You do this with a *using* declaration (Exploration 52). **Modify Listing 72-1 so derived sees both print functions.** Change main so it calls d.print with an int argument and with a double argument, with no qualifying names. **What output do you expect?**

_____

_____

Try it and compare your result with that in Listing 72-2.

631

Listing 72-2. Overloading Named with a using Declaration

```
import <iostream>;

class base {
public:
   void print(int x) { std::cout << "int: " << x << '\n'; }
};
class derived : public base {
public:
   void print(double x) { std::cout << "double: " << x << '\n'; }
   using base::print;
};
int main()
{
   derived d{};
   d.print(3);            // prints int: 3
   d.print(3.0);          // prints double: 3
}
```

A using declaration imports all the overloaded functions with that name. To see this, **add print(long)** **to the base class and a corresponding function call to main.** Now your example should look something like Listing 72-3.

Listing 72-3. Adding a Base Class Overload

```
import <iostream>;

class base {
public:
   void print(int x) { std::cout << "int: " << x << '\n'; }
   void print(long x) { std::cout << "long: " << x << '\n'; }
};
class derived : public base {
public:
   void print(double x) { std::cout << "double: " << x << '\n'; }
   using base::print;
};
int main()
{
   derived d{};
   d.print(3);         // prints int: 3
   d.print(3.0);       // prints double: 3
   d.print(3L);        // prints long: 3
}
```

The overload rules usually work well. You can clearly see which print function the compiler selects for each function call in main. Sometimes, however, the rules get murkier.

For example, suppose you were to add the line d.print(3.0f); to main. **What do you expect the program to print?**

_____

The compiler promotes the float 3.0f to type double and calls print(double), so the output is as follows:

```
double: 3
```

That was too easy. What about a short? Try **d.print(short(3))**. **What happens?**

_____

The compiler promotes the short to type int and produces the following output:

```
int: 3
```

That was still too easy. Now try unsigned. Add **d.print(3u)**. **What happens?**

_____

That doesn't work at all, does it? The error message probably says something about an ambiguous overload or function call. To understand what went wrong, you need a better understanding of how overloading works in C++, and that's what the rest of this Exploration is all about.

Overload Resolution

The compiler applies its normal lookup rules (Exploration 71) to find the declaration for a function name. The compiler stops searching when it finds the first occurrence of the desired name, but that scope may have multiple declarations with the same name. For a type or variable, that would be an error, but functions may have multiple, or overloaded, declarations with the same name.

After the compiler finds a declaration for the function name it is looking up, it finds all the function declarations of that name in the same scope and applies its overloading rules to choose the one declaration that it deems to match the function arguments the best. This process is called *resolving* the overloaded name.

To resolve an overload, the compiler considers the arguments and their types, the types of the function parameters in the function declarations, and type conversions and promotions that are necessary to convert the argument types to match the parameter types. Like name lookup, the detailed rules are complicated, subtle, and sometimes surprising. But if you avoid writing pathological overloads, you can usually get by with some commonsense guidelines.

Overload resolution starts after the compiler finds a declaration of the function name. The compiler collects all declarations of the same name in the same scope. This means that the compiler does not include functions of the same name from any base or ancestor classes. A using declaration can bring such names into the derived class scope and, thus, have them participate in overload resolution. If the function name is unqualified, the compiler looks for member and nonmember functions. A using directive, on the other hand, has no effect on overload resolution, because it does not alter any names in a namespace.

If the function is a constructor, and there is one argument, the compiler also considers type-conversion operators that return the desired class or a derived class.

The compiler then discards any functions with the wrong number of parameters or those for which the function arguments cannot be converted to the corresponding parameter type. It checks constraints and drops from consideration any function that fails its constraint checks. When matching member functions, the compiler adds an implicit parameter, which is a pointer to the object, as though this were a function parameter.

Finally, the compiler ranks all the remaining functions by measuring what it needs to do to convert each argument to the corresponding parameter type, as explained in the next section. If there is a unique winner with the best rank, that compiler has successfully resolved the overload. If not, the compiler applies a few tie-breaker rules to try to select the best-ranked function. If the compiler cannot pick a single winner, it reports an ambiguity error. If it has a winner, it continues with the next compilation step, which is to check access levels for member functions. The best-ranked overload might not be accessible, but that doesn't impact how the compiler resolves the overload.

Ranking Functions

In order to rank functions, the compiler determines how it would convert each argument to the corresponding parameter type. The executive summary is that the best-ranked function is the one that requires the least work to convert all the arguments to the desired parameter types.

The compiler has several tools at its disposal to convert one type to another. Many of these you've seen earlier in the book, such as promoting arithmetic types (Exploration 26), converting a derived class reference to a base class reference (Exploration 37), or calling a type-conversion operator. The compiler assembles a series of conversions into an *implicit conversion sequence* (ICS). An ICS is a sequence of small conversion steps that the compiler can apply to a function call argument with the end result of converting the argument to the type of the corresponding function parameter.

The compiler has ranking rules to determine whether one ICS is better than another. The compiler tries to find one function for which the ICS of every argument is the best (or tied for best) ICS among all overloaded names, and at least one ICS is unambiguously the best. If so, it picks that function as the best-ranked. Otherwise, if it has a set of functions that are all tied for best set of ICSes, it goes to a tie-breaker, as described in the next section. The remainder of this section discusses how the compiler ranks ICSes.

First, some terminology. An ICS may involve standard conversions or user-defined conversions. A *standard* conversion is inherent in the C++ language, such as arithmetic conversions. A *user-defined* conversion involves constructors and type-conversion operators on class and enumerated types. A *standard ICS* is an ICS that contains only standard conversions. A *user-defined ICS* consists of a series of standard conversions with one user-defined conversion anywhere in the sequence. (Thus, any overload that requires two user-derived conversions in order to convert the argument to the parameter type never even gets this far, because the compiler cannot convert the argument to the parameter type and so drops that function signature from consideration.)

For example, converting short to const int is a standard ICS with two steps: promoting short to int and adding the const qualifier. Converting a character string literal to std::string is a user-defined ICS that contains a standard conversion (array of const char converted to pointer to const char), followed by a user-defined conversion (the std::string constructor).

One exception is that invoking a copy constructor to copy identical source and destination type or derived class source to a base class type is a standard conversion, not a user-defined conversion, even though the conversions invoke user-defined copy constructors.

The compiler has to pick the best ICS of the functions that remain under consideration. As part of this determination, it must be able to compare standard conversions within an ICS. A standard conversion falls into one of three categories. In order from best to worst, the categories are exact match, promotion, and other conversion.

An *exact match* is when the argument type is the same as the parameter type. Examples of exact match conversions are as follows:

- Changing only the qualification, for example, the argument is type int and the parameter is const int (but not pointer to const or reference to const)

- Converting an array to a pointer (Exploration 59), for example, char[10] to char*

- Converting an lvalue to an rvalue, for example, int& to int

A *promotion* (Exploration 26) is an implicit conversion from a smaller arithmetic type (such as short) to a larger type (such as int). The compiler considers promotion better than conversion, because a promotion does not lose any information, but a conversion might.

All other implicit type conversions—for example, arithmetic conversions that discard information (such as long to int) and derived class pointers to base class pointers—fall into the final category of miscellaneous conversions.

The category of a sequence is the category of the worst conversion step in the sequence. For example, converting short to const int involves an *exact match* (const) and a *promotion* (short to int), so the category for the ICS as a whole is *promotion*.

If one argument is an implicit object argument (for member function calls), the compiler compares any conversions needed for it too.

Now that you know how the compiler orders standard conversions by category, you can see how it uses this information to compare ICSes. The compiler applies the following rules to determine which of two ICSes is better:

- A standard ICS is better than a user-defined ICS.

- An ICS with a better category is better than an ICS with a worse category.

- An ICS that is a proper subset of another ICS is better.

- A user-defined ICS, ICS1, is better than another user-defined ICS, ICS2, if they have the same user conversion and the second standard conversion in ICS1 is better than the second standard conversion of ICS2.

- Less restrictive types are better than more restrictive ones. This means an ICS with target type T1 is better than an ICS with target type T2, if T1 and T2 have the same base type, but T2 is const and T1 is not.

- A standard conversion sequence ICS1 is better than ICS2, if they have the same rank, but

  - ICS1 converts a pointer to bool.

  - ICS1 and ICS2 convert pointers to classes related by inheritance, and ICS1 is a "smaller" conversion. A smaller conversion is one that hops over fewer intermediate base classes. For example, if A derives from B and B from C, then converting B* to C* is better than converting A* to C*, and converting C* to void* is better than A* to void*.

List Initialization

One complication is the possibility of a function argument that has no type because it is not an expression. Instead, the argument is a curly-brace-enclosed list of values, such as the brace-enclosed list that is used for universal initialization. The compiler has some special rules for determining the conversion sequence of a list.

If the parameter type is a class with a constructor that takes a single argument of type std::initializer_list<T>, and every member of the brace-enclosed list can be converted to T, the compiler treats the argument as a user-defined conversion to std::initializer_list<T>. All the container classes, for example, have such a constructor.

Otherwise, the compiler tries to find a constructor for the parameter type such that each element of the brace-enclosed list is an argument to the constructor. If it succeeds, the compiler considers the list a user-defined conversion to the parameter type. Note that another user-defined conversion sequence is allowed for each constructor argument.

The compiler considers `std::initializer_list` initialization better than the other constructor list initialization. That's why `std::string{42, 'x'}` does not invoke the `std::string(42, 'x')` constructor: the compiler prefers treating `{42, 'x'}` as `std::initializer_list`, which results in a string with two characters, one with code point 42 and the letter x, and not the constructor that creates a string with 42 repetitions of the letter x.

If the parameter type is not a class, and the brace-enclosed list contains a single element, the compiler unwraps the value from the curly braces and applies the normal ICS that results from the enclosed value.

Tie-Breakers

If the compiler cannot find one function that unambiguously ranks higher than the others, it applies a few final rules to try to pick a winner. The compiler checks the following rules in order. If one rule yields a winner, the compiler stops at that point and uses the winning function. Otherwise, it continues with the next tie-breaker:

- Although return type is not considered part of overload resolution, if the overloaded function call is used in a user-defined initialization, the function's return type that invokes a better standard conversion sequence wins.

- A non-template function beats a function template.

- A more-specialized function template beats a less-specialized function template. (A reference or pointer template parameter is more specialized than a non-reference or non-pointer parameter. A `const` parameter is more specialized than non-`const`.)

- Otherwise, the compiler reports an ambiguity error.

Listing 72-4 shows some examples of overloading and how C++ ranks functions.

Listing 72-4. Ranking Functions for Overload Resolution

```
import <iostream>;
import <string>;

void print(std::string_view str) { std::cout << str; }
void print(int x)                 { std::cout << "int: " << x; }
void print(double x)              { std::cout << "double: " << x; }

class base {
public:
  void print(std::string_view str) const { ::print(str); ::print("\n"); }
  void print(std::string_view s1, std::string_view s2)
  {
    print(s1); print(s2);
  }
};

class convert : public base {
public:
  convert()                  { print("convert()"); }
  convert(double)            { print("convert(double)"); }
  operator int() const    { print("convert::operator int()"); return 42; }
  operator float() const { print("convert::operator float()"); return 3.14159f; }
};
```

```cpp
class demo : public base {
public:
  demo(int)      { print("demo(int)"); }
  demo(long)     { print("demo(long)"); }
  demo(convert)  { print("demo(convert)"); }
  demo(int, int) { print("demo(int, int)"); }
};

class other {
public:
  other()        { std::cout << "other::other()\n"; }
  other(int,int) { std::cout << "other::other(int, int)\n"; }
  operator convert() const
  {
    std::cout << "other::operator convert()\n"; return convert();
  }
};

int operator+(demo const&, demo const&)
{
  print("operator+(demo,demo)\n"); return 42;
}

int operator+(int, demo const&) { print("operator+(int,demo)\n"); return 42; }

int main()
{
  other x{};
  demo d{x};
  3L + d;
  short s{2};
  d + s;
}
```

What output do you expect from the program in Listing 69-4?

_____

_____

_____

_____

_____

Most of the time, commonsense rules help you understand how C++ resolves overloading. Sometimes, however, you find the compiler reporting an ambiguity when you did not expect any. Other times, the compiler cannot resolve an overload when you expected it to succeed. The really bad cases are when you make a mistake and the compiler is able to find a unique function, but one that is different from the one you expect. Your tests fail, but when reading the code, you look in the wrong place, because you expect the compiler to complain about bad code.

Sometimes, your compiler helps you by identifying the functions that are tied for best rank. Sometimes, however, you might have to sit down with the rules and go over them carefully to figure out why the compiler isn't happy. To help you prepare for that day, Listing 72-5 presents some overloading errors. **See if you can find and fix the problems.**

Listing 72-5. Fix the Overloading Errors

```
import <iostream>;
import <string>;

void easy(long) {}
void easy(double) {}
void call_easy() {
    easy(42);
}

void pointer(double*) {}
void pointer(void*) {}
const int zero = 0;
void call_pointer() {
    pointer(&zero);
}

int add(int a) { return a; }
int add(int a, int b) { return a + b; }
int add(int a, int b, int c) { return a + b + c; }
int add(int a, int b, int c, int d) { return a + b + c + d; }
int add(int a, int b, int c, int d, int e) { return a + b + c + d + e; }
void call_add() {
    add(1, 2, 3L, 4.0);
}

void ref(int const&) {}
void ref(int) {}
void call_ref() {
    int x;
    ref(x);
}

class base {};
class derived : public base {};
class sibling : public base {};
class most_derived : public derived {};

void tree(derived&, sibling&) {}
void tree(most_derived&, base&) {}
void call_tree() {
    sibling s;
    most_derived md;
    tree(md, s);
}
```

The argument to easy() is an int, but the overloads are for long and double. Both conversions have conversion rank, and neither one is better than the other, so the compiler issues an ambiguity error.

The problem with pointer() is that neither overload is viable. If zero were not const, the conversion to void* would be the sole viable candidate.

The add() function has all int parameters, but one argument is long and another is double. No problem, the compiler can convert long to int and double to int. You may not like the results, but it is able to do it, so it does. In other words, the problem here is that the compiler does not have a problem with this function. This isn't really an overloading problem, but you may not see it that way if you run into this problem at work.

Do you see the missing & in the second ref() function? The compiler considers both ref() functions to be equally good. If you declare the second to be ref(int&), it becomes the best viable candidate. The exact reason is that the type of x is int&, not int, that is, x is an int lvalue, an object that the program can modify. The subtle distinction has not been important before now, but with respect to overloading, the difference is crucial. The conversion from an lvalue to an rvalue has rank exact match, but it is a conversion step. The conversion from int& to int const& also has exact match. Faced with two candidates with one exact match conversion each, the compiler cannot decide which one is better. Changing int to int& removes the conversion step, and that function becomes the unambiguous best.

Both tree() functions require one conversion from derived class reference to base class reference, so the compiler cannot decide which one is better. The first call to tree requires a conversion of the first argument from most_derived& to derived&. The second call requires a conversion of the second argument from sibling& to base&.

Remember that the purpose of overloading is to allow a single logical operation across a variety of types, or to allow a single logical operation (such as constructing a string) to be invoked in a variety of ways. These rules will help guide you to make good choices when you decide to overload a function.

Tip When you write overloaded functions, you should make sure that every implementation of a particular function name has the same logical behavior. For example, when you use an output operator, cout << x, you just let the compiler pick the correct overload for operator<<, and you don't have to concern yourself with the detailed rules as laid out in this Exploration. All the rules apply, but the standard declares a reasonable set of overloads that work with the built-in types and key library types, such as std::string.

Default Arguments

Now that you think overloading is so frightfully complicated that you never want to overload a function, I will add yet another complexity. C++ lets you define a default argument for a parameter, which lets a function call omit the corresponding argument. You can define default arguments for any number of parameters, provided you omit the right-most arguments and don't skip any. You can provide default arguments for every parameter if you wish. Default arguments are often easy to understand. Read Listing 72-6 for an example.

Listing 72-6. Default Arguments

```cpp
import <iostream>;

int add(int x = 0, int y = 0)
{
  return x + y;
}
```

```
int main()
{
  std::cout << add() << '\n';
  std::cout << add(5) << '\n';
  std::cout << add(32, add(4, add(6))) << '\n';
}
```

What does the program in Listing 72-6 print?

_____

_____

_____

It's not hard to predict the results, which are shown in the following output:

```
0
5
42
```

Default arguments offer a shortcut, in lieu of overloading. For example, instead of writing several constructors for the rational type, you can get by with one constructor and default arguments, as follows:

```
template<class T> class rational {
public:
  rational(T const& num = T{0}, T const& den = T{1})
  : numerator_{num}, denominator_{den}
  {
    reduce();
  }
  ...omitted for brevity...
};
```

Our definition of a default constructor must change somewhat. Instead of being a constructor that declares no parameters, a default constructor is one that you can call with no arguments. This rational constructor meets that requirement.

As you may have guessed, default arguments complicate overload resolution. When the compiler searches for overloaded functions, it checks every argument that explicitly appears in the function call but does not check default argument types against their corresponding parameter types. As a result, you can run into ambiguous situations more easily with default arguments. For example, suppose you added the example rational constructor to the existing class template without deleting the old constructors. The following definitions would both result in ambiguity errors:

```
rational<int> zero{};
rational<int> one{1};
```

Default arguments have their uses, but overloading usually gives you more control. For example, by overloading the rational constructors, we avoid calling reduce() when we know the denominator is 1. Using inline functions, one overloaded function can call another, which often eliminates the need for default arguments completely. If you are unsure whether to use default arguments or overloading, I recommend overloading.

Although you may not believe me, my intention was not to scare you away from overloading functions. Rarely will you have to delve into the subtleties of overloading. Most of the time, you can rely on common sense. But sometimes, the compiler disagrees with your common sense. Knowing the compiler's rules can help you escape from a jam when the compiler complains about an ambiguous overload or other problems.

The next Exploration visits another aspect of C++ programming for which the rules can be complicated and scary: metaprogramming, or writing programs that run at compile time.

■ ■ ■

Programming at Compile Time

C++ offers many opportunities to write code that runs at compile time instead of at runtime. Templates, for example, provide a unique, functional programming environment, albeit one with a tortuous syntax. In C++ 20, some new keywords offer more precise ways for you to control what takes place at compile time instead of runtime. Some compile-time programming techniques are called metaprogramming, but this term is loosely defined and some may use it exclusively for programming with types instead of values. However you name it, compile-time programming is a valuable aspect of overall C++ programming.

Compile-Time Functions

Tell the compiler that you want it to be able to evaluate a function at compile time with the constexpr or consteval keyword. Use either keyword (but not both) among the type specifiers for the function's return type, as you have seen often in this book:

```
consteval double square(double x) { return x * x; }
constexpr double cube(double x) { return x * x * x; }
```

For consteval functions, the function arguments must be compile-time constants, and the compiler always calls the function at compile time to produce a constant result.

For constexpr functions, if you call the function with compile-time constant arguments, the compiler calls the function at compile time and produces a constant result. But you can also call the function without constant arguments, and the compiler treats the function as an ordinary inline function and generates appropriate runtime code to produce a non-constant result.

Assuming a variable named value, square(3.0) becomes 9.0 at compile time, and square(value) is not allowed. Calling cube(3.0) becomes 27.0 at compile time, and cube(value) is computed at runtime with the value variable. A constexpr function is implicitly inline when it is evaluated at runtime.

A constexpr or consteval function has some restrictions. Most restrictions apply to both kinds of functions. The return type, parameter types, and types of variables in the function must be what are called *literal* types. A literal type is one that can be constructed and destroyed at compile time. Built-in fundamental types, enumerations, and pointers obviously fit in this class. For a class to be literal, it must have a constexpr destructor and literal data members. The constructor being invoked must be constexpr, although the class can have other constructors that are not constexpr.

A constexpr constructor can call only other constexpr constructors, which means all base class constructors must be constexpr. If a class has a constexpr destructor, all of its base classes must have constexpr destructors (or no destructor at all using =delete).

One difference of note is that a destructor cannot be declared with consteval.

Of course, when you declare a function to be constexpr, the compiler needs the function definition, so you cannot put a constexpr declaration in a module interface and try to hide its definition in a separate module implementation. The definition must go into the module interface.

© Ray Lischner 2020
R. Lischner, *Exploring C++20*, https://doi.org/10.1007/978-1-4842-5961-0_73

There is one challenge when writing constexpr functions. It is not possible to report an error to the user, such as throwing an exception. For example, it seems reasonable to declare all of the rational constructors to be constexpr, but that means calling reduce(), which throws an exception if the denominator is zero. This means constructing a constexpr rational object with a zero denominator is illegal, but the compiler is not required to issue an error message. The burden is on the programmer who uses rational to ensure that 0 is never used as a denominator of a constexpr rational object. With that caveat, **copy the declaration for the rational class template and ensure that every function that can be constexpr is constexpr.** See Listing 73-1 for my take.

Listing 73-1. Adding constexpr Throughout the rational Class Template

```
export module numeric;

import <concepts>;
import <iostream>;
import <numeric>;
import <sstream>;
import <stdexcept>;

export template<class T>
requires std::integral<T>
class rational
{
public:
    using value_type = T;
    constexpr rational() : rational{0} {}
    constexpr rational(value_type num) : numerator_{num}, denominator_{1} {}
    constexpr rational(value_type num, value_type den)
    : numerator_{num}, denominator_{den}
    {
        reduce();
    }

    constexpr value_type numerator() const { return numerator_; }
    constexpr value_type denominator() const { return denominator_; }

    constexpr rational& operator*=(rational const& rhs) {
        numerator_ *= rhs.numerator_;
        denominator_ *= rhs.denominator_;
        reduce();
        return *this;
    }
    constexpr rational& operator/=(rational const& rhs) {
        numerator_ *= rhs.denominator_;
        denominator_ *= rhs.numerator_;
        reduce();
        return *this;
    }

    ... every member function can be constexpr
```

```
private:
    constexpr void reduce() {
        if (denominator_ == 0)
            throw std::invalid_argument{"denominator is zero"};
        if (denominator_ < 0)
        {
            denominator_ = -denominator_;
            numerator_ = -numerator_;
        }
        auto div{std::gcd(numerator_, denominator_)};
        numerator_ = numerator_ / div;
        denominator_ = denominator_ / div;
    }

    value_type numerator_;
    value_type denominator_;
};

export template<class T>
constexpr bool operator==(rational<T> const& lhs, rational<T> const& rhs)
{
    return lhs.numerator() == rhs.numerator() and
           lhs.denominator() == rhs.denominator();
}

// Every free function except I/O can be constexpr
export template<class T, class Ch, class Tr>
std::basic_ostream<Ch,Tr>& operator<<(std::basic_ostream<Ch, Tr>& stream, rational<T>
const& r)
{
    std::basic_ostringstream<Ch,Tr> tmp;
    tmp << r.numerator() << '/' << r.denominator();
    return stream << tmp.str();
}
```

Compile-Time Variables

The constexpr specifier also works with named objects. A constexpr object is implicitly const. It must have an initializer that calls only constexpr functions or a constexpr constructor.

You can also initialize a compile-time static variable with the constinit keyword. The variable must have static lifetime, that is, be declared at namespace scope or with the static keyword. The compiler always ensures that such variables are initialized before main() begins execution. (Or, for a static variable that is defined inside a function, before the function is called for the first time.) But if a static variable's initial value depends on the value of another variable, it is undefined which variable is initialized first. By declaring a static variable with constinit, the compiler determines the value at compile time and uses that fixed value to initialize the variable, and all variables that depend on it see that constant value. The key difference between constinit and the other const-related keywords is that constinit applies only to initialization. The object is not necessarily const. Listing 73-2 demonstrates some uses for constexpr and constinit objects.

645

Listing 73-2. Adding `constexpr` Throughout the rational Class Template

```
import <iostream>;
import rational;

constinit rational<long> r{355, 113};
constinit rational<long> const q{31416, 10000};

int main()
{
    constexpr rational<long> p{2};
    r /= q;
    r *= p;
    std::cout << r << '\n';
}
```

Variable-Length Template Argument Lists

You can define a template that takes any number of template arguments (called a *variadic template*). This ability is not specifically related to compile-time programming, but it is advanced and belongs near the end of the book. A number of compile-time programming idioms involve variable-length templates, so it seems appropriate to include this topic here.

Many of the uses for variable-length templates are for library authors, but that doesn't mean others can't join in. To declare a template parameter that can accept any number of arguments, use an ellipsis after the class or typename keyword for a type template parameter or after the type in a value template parameter. Such a parameter is called a *parameter pack*. The following are some simple examples:

```
template<class... Ts> struct List {};
template<int... Ns> struct Numbers {};
```

Instantiate the template with any number of template arguments:

```
using int_type = List<int>;
using Char_types = List<char, unsigned char, signed char>;
using One_two_three = Numbers<1, 2, 3>;
```

You can also declare a function parameter pack, so the function can take any number of arguments of any type, such as the following:

```
template<class... Types>
void list(Types... args);
```

When you call the function, the parameter pack contains the type of each function argument. In the following example, the compiler implicitly determines that the Types template argument is <int, char, std::string>.

```
list(1, 'x', std::string{"yz"});
```

The sizeof... operator returns the number of elements in the parameter pack. You can, for example, define a Size template to compute the number of arguments in a parameter pack, as shown here:

```
template<class... Ts>
struct Size { constexpr static std::size_t value = sizeof...(Ts); };
static_assert(Size<int, char, long>::value == 3);
```

The static_assert declaration checks a compile-time Boolean expression and causes a compiler error if the condition is false. You can add a second argument to static_assert() to give a helpful message. Often simply seeing the expression is adequate. The more problems you can detect at compile time, the better.

To use a parameter pack, you typically expand it with a pattern followed by an ellipsis. The pattern can be the parameter name, a type that uses the parameter, an expression that uses the function parameter pack, and so on.

Listing 73-3 shows a print() function that takes a stream followed by any number of arguments of any type. It prints each value by expanding the parameter pack. The std::forward() function forwards a value to a function without altering or copying it (called "perfect forwarding"). The compiler expands the pack expression std::forward<Types>(rest)... into std::forward(r) for each argument r in rest. By passing rvalue references everywhere and using std::forward(), the print() function can pass references to its arguments with a minimum of overhead. Notice that nowhere is there a test for the size of the parameter pack. The pack is expanded at compile time, and an overloaded function ends the expansion when the pack is empty.

Listing 73-3. Using a Function Parameter Pack to Print Arbitrary Values

```
import <iostream>;
import <utility>;

// Forward declaration.
template<class... Args>
void print(std::ostream& stream, Args&&...);

// Print the first value in the list, then recursively
// call print() to print the rest of the list.
template<class T, class... Args>
void print_split(std::ostream& stream, T&& head, Args&& ... rest)
{
   stream << head << ' ';
   print(stream, std::forward<Args>(rest)...);
}

// End recursion when there are no more values to print.
void print_split(std::ostream&)
{}

// Print an arbitrary list of values to a stream.
template<class... Args>
void print(std::ostream& stream, Args&&... args)
{
   print_split(stream, std::forward<Args>(args)...);
}

int main()
{
   print(std::cout, 42, 'x', "hello", 3.14159, 0, '\n');
}
```

User-Defined Literals

A common use for compile-time programming is to define your own literals. The standard library defines literals such as "view"sv to be a shortcut for std::string_view{"view"}. User-defined literals always begin with an underscore to avoid conflict with existing or future literals in the standard library.

Define a literal as operator"" followed by the literal name. You can define character, numeric, or string literals. The compiler looks for functions that take the value as an argument or the characters that make up the value as a template parameter pack. Listing 73-4 shows the _rev literal, which operates on integers to reverse the bits.

Listing 73-4. Defining a Literal Operator to Reverse Bits in an Integer

```cpp
consteval unsigned long long operator"" _rev(unsigned long long value)
{
    unsigned long long reversed{0};
    for (std::size_t i{std::numeric_limits<unsigned long long>::digits}; i > 0; --i)
    {
        auto bit{ value & 1 };
        value >>= 1;
        reversed = (reversed << 1) | bit;
    }
    return reversed;
}
static_assert(0_rev == 0);
static_assert(0x1234567890abcdef_rev == 0xf7b3d5091e6a2c48ULL);
```

The template form of user-defined literals is especially challenging to write because the compiler passes the exact form that the user writes, which means your operator must interpret binary, octal, decimal, and hexadecimal numbers with interspersed apostrophes (0b1011'0010_rev, 0373_rev, 179_rev, and 0xb3_rev are all the same value). Letting the compiler parse the number is much easier.

Types As Values

Metaprogramming with values is made easier with constexpr functions, but much metaprogramming involves types, which requires an entirely different viewpoint. When metaprogramming with types, a type takes on the role of a value. There is no way to define a variable, only template arguments, so you devise templates that declare the template parameters you need to store type information. A "function" in a metaprogram (sometimes called a *metafunction*) is just another template, so its arguments are template arguments.

For example, the standard library contains the metafunction is_same (defined in <type_traits>). This template takes two template arguments and yields a type as its result. The metafunctions in the standard library return a result with class members. If the result is a type, the member typedef is called type. The type member for a predicate such as is_same is a metaprogramming Boolean value. If the two argument types are the same type, the result is std::true_type (also defined in <type_traits>). If the argument types are different, the result is std::false_type.

Because true_type and false_type are themselves metaprogramming types, they also have type member typedefs. The value of true_type::type is true_type; ditto for false_type. Sometimes a metaprogram has to treat a metaprogramming value as an actual value. Thus, metaprogramming types that represent values have a static data member named value. As you may expect, true_type::value is true and false_type::value is false.

How would you write **is_same**? You have to declare the member typedef type to std::true_type or std::false_type, depending on the template arguments. An easy way to do this, and to obtain the convenience value static data member at the same time, is to derive is_same from true_type or false_type, depending on the template arguments. This is a straightforward implementation of partial specialization, as you can see in Listing 73-5.

Listing 73-5. Implementing the is_same Metafunction

```
template<class T, class U>
struct is_same : std::false_type {};

template<class T>
struct is_same<T, T> : std::true_type {};
```

Let's write another metafunction, one that is not in the standard library. This one is called promote. It takes a single template argument and yields int if the template argument is bool, short, char, or variations and yields the argument itself otherwise. In other words, it implements a simplified subset of the C++ rules for integer promotion. How would you write **promote**? This time, the result is pure type, so there is no value member. The simplest way is the most direct. Listing 73-6 shows one possibility.

Listing 73-6. One Implementation of the promote Metafunction

```
template<class T> struct promote          { typedef T type; };
template<> struct promote<bool>           { typedef int type; };
template<> struct promote<char>           { typedef int type; };
template<> struct promote<signed char>    { typedef int type; };
template<> struct promote<unsigned char>  { typedef int type; };
template<> struct promote<short>          { typedef int type; };
template<> struct promote<unsigned short> { typedef int type; };
```

Another way to implement promote is to use template parameter packs. Suppose you have a metafunction, is_member, which tests its first argument to determine whether it appears in the parameter pack formed by its remaining arguments. That is, is_member<int, char> is false_type, and is_member<int, short, int, long> yields true_type. Given is_member, how would you implement promote? Listing 73-7 shows one way, using partial specialization on the result of is_member.

Listing 73-7. Another Implementation of the promote Metafunction

```
// Primary template when IsMember=std::true_type, that is, T is in the
// list of types to promote to int.
template<class IsMember, class T>
struct get_member {
   using type = int;
};

// false means T is not in the list, so leave the type alone.
template<class T>
struct get_member<std::false_type, T>
{
   using type = T;
};
```

```
template<class T>
struct promote {
    using type = get_member<typename is_member<T,
        bool, unsigned char, signed char, char, unsigned short, short>::type, T>::type;
};
```

Remember that typename is required when naming a type that depends on a template parameter. The type member of a metafunction certainly qualifies as a dependent type name. This implementation uses partial specialization to determine the result from is_member. Using is_member to implement promote might seem to be more complicated, but if the list of types is long, or is likely to grow as an application evolves, the is_member approach seems more inviting. Although using is_member is easy, writing it is not so easy. Remember how Listing 73-4 splits off the head of the function pack? Use the same technique to split the parameter pack, that is, write a helper class that has a Head template parameter and a Rest template parameter pack. Listing 73-8 shows one way to implement is_member.

Listing 73-8. Implementing the is_member Metafunction

```
template<class Check, class... Args> struct is_member;

// Helper metafunction to separate Args into Head, Rest
template<class Check, class Head, class... Rest>
struct is_member_helper :
    std::conditional<std::is_same<Check, Head>::value,
        std::true_type,
        is_member<Check, Rest...>>::type
{};

// Partial specialization for empty Args
template<class Check, class Head>
struct is_member_helper<Check, Head> : std::is_same<Check, Head>::type {};

/// Test whether Check is the same type as a type in Args.
template<class Check, class... Args>
struct is_member : is_member_helper<Check, Args...> {};
```

Instead of writing a custom metafunction that specializes on std::false_type, Listing 73-8 uses a standard metafunction, std::conditional. It is usually better to use the standard library whenever possible, and you can rewrite Listing 73-7 to use std::conditional. To help you understand this important metafunction, the next section discusses std::conditional in depth.

Conditional Types

One key aspect of metaprogramming is making decisions at compile time. To do that, you need a conditional operator. C++ offers a few different ways to do this in different contexts. For example, inside a function, you can use if constexpr. In a template definition, you might be able to use constraints. And the standard library offers two styles of conditionals in the <type_traits> header.

To test a condition, use std::conditional<Condition, IfTrue, IfFalse>::type. The Condition is a bool value, and IfType and IfFalse are types. The type member is a typedef for IfTrue if Condition is true and is a typedef for IfFalse if Condition is false.

Try writing your own implementation of **std::conditional**. Your standard library may be different but won't be too terribly different from my solution in Listing 73-9.

Listing 73-9. One Way to Implement std::conditional

```
template<bool Condition, class IfTrue, class IfFalse>
struct conditional
{
    using type = IfFalse;
};

template<class IfTrue, class IfFalse>
struct conditional<true, IfTrue, IfFalse>
{
    using type = IfTrue;
};
```

Another way to look at std::conditional is to consider it an array of two types, indexed by a bool value. What about an array of types indexed by an integer? The standard library doesn't have such a template, but you can write one. Use a template parameter pack and an integer selector. If the selector is invalid, do not define the type member typedef. For example, choice<2, int, long, char, float, double>::type would be char, and choice<2, int, long> would not declare a type member. Try writing **choice**. Again, you will probably want two mutually recursive classes. One class strips the first template parameter from the parameter pack and decrements the index. Template specialization terminates the recursion. Compare your solution with mine in Listing 73-10.

Listing 73-10. Implementing an Integer-Keyed Type Choice

```
import <type_traits>;

// forward declaration
template<std::size_t, class...>
struct choice;

// Default: subtract one, drop the head of the list, and recurse.
template<std::size_t N, class T, class... Types>
struct choice_split {
    using type = choice<N-1, Types...>::type;
};

// Index 0: pick the first type in the list.
template<class T, class... Ts>
struct choice_split<0, T, Ts...> {
    using type = T;
};

// Define type member as the N-th type in Types.
template<std::size_t N, class... Types>
struct choice {
    using type = choice_split<N, Types...>::type;
};

// N is out of bounds
template<std::size_t N>
struct choice<N> {};
```

```
// Tests

static_assert(std::is_same<int,
    typename choice<0, int, long, char>::type>::value, "error in choice<0>");
static_assert(std::is_same<long,
    typename choice<1, int, long, char>::type>::value, "error in choice<1>");
static_assert(std::is_same<char,
    typename choice<2, int, long, char>::type>::value, "error in choice<2>");
```

Use the new choice template to choose one option from among many. On one project, I defined three styles of iterators for different trade-offs of safety and performance. The fast iterator worked as fast as possible, with no safety checks. The safe iterator would check just enough to avoid undefined behavior. The pedantic iterator was used for debugging and checked everything possible, with no regard for speed. I could pick which iterator style I wanted by defining ITERATOR_TYPE as 0, 1, or 2, for example:

```
using iterator = choice<ITERATOR_TYPE,
    pedantic_iterator, safe_iterator, fast_iterator>::type;
```

Substitution Failure Is Not An Error (SFINAE)

A programming technique introduced by Daveed Vandevoorde goes by the unwieldy name of SFINAE (pronounced ess-finn-ee), for *Substitution Failure Is Not An Error*. Briefly, if the compiler attempts to instantiate an invalid template function, the compiler does not consider it an error but merely discards that instantiation from consideration when resolving overloads. This concept was widespread prior to the introduction of constraints in C++ 20, so you need to at least be able to read code that uses SFINAE. New code that uses constraints is much easier to read and maintain.

For example, suppose you are writing data in some data encoding, such as ASN.1 BER, XDR, JSON, and so on. The details of the encoding are unimportant for this exercise. What matters is that we want to treat all integers the same and all floating-point numbers the same, but treat integers differently from floating-point numbers. That is, we want to use templates to reduce the amount of repetitive coding, but we want distinct implementations for certain types. We cannot partially specialize functions, so we must use overloading.

The problem is how to declare three template functions, all with the name encode, such that one is a template function for any integer, another for any floating-point type, and another for strings.

One approach is to declare overloads for the largest integer type and largest floating-point type. The compiler will convert the actual types to the larger types. This is simple to implement but incurs a runtime cost, which can be significant in some environments. We need a better solution.

Similar to std::conditional, std::enable_if takes a Boolean value and an if-true type. Unlike std::conditional, it has no if-false branch. Instead, the type member is not defined. This can trigger SFINAE when the compiler looks for the type member, cannot find it for a certain template argument, and so discards that function signature for that argument.

Using enable_if, you can declare overloaded encode functions but enable one function only when is_integral is true, another for floating-point types, and so on. The goal is not to disable the encode() function but to guide the compiler's resolution of overloading.

The <type_traits> header has several introspection traits. Every type is categorized as class, enumeration, integer, floating-point, and so on. This book is not about binary data encoding, so the guts of this example will write text to a stream, but it will serve to illustrate how to use enable_if.

The normal rules of overloading still apply. That is, different functions must have different arguments. So using enable_if for the return type doesn't help. This time, enable_if will be used as another argument to encode, but with a default value that hides it from the caller. (Note that using enable_if for the primary argument to the function doesn't work, because it breaks the compiler's ability to deduce the template type from the function's argument type.) Specifically, the enable_if argument is made into a pointer type, with nullptr as the default value, to ensure that there is no extra code constructing or passing this additional argument. With inlining, the compiler can even optimize away the extra argument, so there is no runtime penalty. Listing 73-11 shows one way to solve this problem.

Listing 73-11 Using enable_if to Direct Overload Resolution

```
import <iostream>;
import <type_traits>;

template<class T>
void encode(std::ostream& stream, T const& int_value,
   typename std::enable_if<std::is_integral<T>::value, T>::type* = nullptr)
{
   // All integer types end up here.
   stream << "int: " << int_value << '\n';
}

template<class T>
void encode(std::ostream& stream, T const& enum_value,
   typename std::enable_if<std::is_enum<T>::value>::type* = nullptr)
{
   // All enumerated types end up here.
   // Record the underlying integer value.
   stream << "enum: " <<
     _static_cast<typename std::underlying_type<T>::type>(enum_value) << '\n';
}

template<class T>
void encode(std::ostream& stream, T const& float_value,
   typename std::enable_if<std::is_floating_point<T>::value>::type* = nullptr)
{
   // All floating-point types end up here.
   stream << "float: " << float_value << '\n';
}

// enable_if forms cooperate with normal overloading
void encode(std::ostream& stream, std::string const& string_value)
{
   stream << "str: " << string_value << '\n';
}

int main()
{
   encode(std::cout, 1);
   enum class color { red, green, blue };
   encode(std::cout, color::blue);
   encode(std::cout, 3.0);
   encode(std::cout, std::string("string"));
}
```

That concludes your exploration of C++ 20. The next and final Exploration is a capstone project to incorporate everything you have learned. I hope that you have enjoyed your journey and that you will plan many more excursions to complete your understanding and mastery of this language.

EXPLORATION 74

Project 4: Calculator

Now is the time to apply everything you have learned in this book, by writing a simple textual calculator. If you type 1 + 2, for example, the calculator prints 3. This project can be as complicated as you wish or dare to make it. I recommend starting small and adding capability slowly and incrementally:

1. Start with a simple parser to read numbers and operators. If you are familiar with a parser generator, such as Bison or ANTLR, go ahead and use it. If you are feeling adventurous, try learning about Spirit, which is part of the Boost project. Spirit makes use of C++ operator overloading to implement a BNF-like syntax for writing a parser in C++ without requiring additional tools. If you don't want to involve other tools or libraries, I recommend a simple LISP-like syntax, so you don't spend all your time on the parser. The code on this book's website implements a simple, recursive-descent parser. Implement the basic arithmetic operators first: +, -, *, and /. Use double for all numbers. Do something helpful when dividing by zero.

2. Add variables and the = operator. Initialize the calculator with some useful constants, such as pi.

3. The big leap forward is not to evaluate every expression when it is typed but to create a parse tree. This requires some work on the parser, not to mention the addition of the parse-tree classes, that is, classes to represent expressions, variables, and values.

4. Given variables and parse trees, it is a smaller step to define functions and call user-defined functions.

5. Finally, add the ability to save functions to a file, and load them from a file. Now you can create libraries of useful functions.

6. If you are truly ambitious, try supporting multiple types. Use the pimpl idiom (Exploration 65) to define a number class and a number_impl class. Let the calculator use the number class, which frees it from the number_impl class. Implement derived classes for the types you want to support: integer, double, rational, and so on.

As you can see, this kind of project can continue as long as you want it to. There will always be another feature to add. Just be sure to add features in small increments.

Similarly, your journey toward C++ expertise never ends. There will always be new surprises—waiting just around the corner, in the middle of your next project, with the next compiler upgrade. As I write this, the standardization committee has finished work on C++ 20 and is already working on C++ 23. After that will come the next language-revision cycle, and the next, and the next.

I wish you luck on your voyage, and I hope you enjoy the Explorations to come.

© Ray Lischner 2020
R. Lischner, *Exploring C++20*, https://doi.org/10.1007/978-1-4842-5961-0_74

Index

A

Absolute value (absval) function
        template, 393
absval function, 412
Access levels
        class keyword, 272
        inheritance, 272
        privacy setting, 249
        public keyword, 272, 273
        rational class, 253–257
acehigh_less function, 465
advance function, 344
advance() member function, 352
Algorithms
        getline function, 149
        Palindromes, 150, 151
Argument-dependent lookup (ADL), 444, 619
        compiler, 627
        function arguments, 626
        numeric namespace, 626
        operator<<, 627
Arithmetic operators, 215–218, 378, 379
Arrays and vectors, 62
        problem, 61
artifact_impl class, 552
artifact Pimpl Wrapper Class, 553, 554
Assignment operators, 225, 226, 378, 379
Associative containers
        acehigh_less, 465
        card module, 466, 467
        high-card program, 464
        ordered containers, 449
        unordered containers, 449, 466

B

back_inserter, 349
bad() member function, 223
base() member function, 349
begin() member function, 73
Bidirectional iterator, 342

Big and little numbers
        byte-sized integers, 177
        conversion, 180
        discovering number of bits, 173
        integer arithmetic, 180
        integer literals, 175, 176
        long integers, 174
        overload resolution, 180–182
        promotion, 180
        short integers, 174
        type casting, 177, 178
        user-defined literal, 179
Big-endian platform, 487
Binary search algorithms, 332, 334
Bits
        bitmasks, 573, 574
        integer
                bitwise operators, 572
                Flags Functions, 573
                formatting flags, 571
                manipulators, 571
                setf Member Function, 572
                unsetf Member Function, 573
        safe shifting
                bitfields, 582, 583
                overflow, 581
                portability, 583
                rotating integers, 582
                signed types, 576
                std, 584–586
                type conversions, 577–580
                unsigned types, 575–577
        shifting, 574, 575
bmi() function, 247
Body mass index (BMI), 199, 200, 242
Bogus Metabolic Index (BMI), 285
Books and magazines
        actions, 260
        attributes, 260
        behaviors, 260
        categorizations, 260
        differences, 259

© Ray Lischner 2020
R. Lischner, *Exploring C++20*, https://doi.org/10.1007/978-1-4842-5961-0

■ V

■ W, X, Y, Z

Printed in the United States
By Bookmasters